1,300

Critical Evaluations

of

Selected Novels and Plays

1,300
Critical Evaluations
of
Selected Novels and Plays

OFFPRINTS OF ALL THE NEW MATERIAL FROM THE
12-VOLUME REVISED EDITION OF *MASTERPLOTS*

Edited by
FRANK N. MAGILL

Volume Three
McT - Rob
1309 - 1934

SALEM PRESS

Englewood Cliffs

LIBRARY OF CONGRESS CATALOG CARD NUMBER: 78-55387

Complete Set: ISBN 0-89356-043-X
Volume 3:   ISBN 0-89356-046-4

Some of the material in this work also appears in *Masterplots*, Revised Edition (1976).

PRINTED IN THE UNITED STATES OF AMERICA

LIST OF TITLES IN VOLUME THREE

LIST OF TITLES

McTEAGUE

Type of work: Novel
Author: Frank Norris (1870-1902)
Type of plot: Naturalism
Time of plot: 1890's
Locale: San Francisco and Death Valley
First published: 1899

Generally considered Norris' best novel, McTeague *follows the lives of three people drawn inevitably to catastrophe through their own inherited qualities acted upon by environmental forces. The novel is powerful and terrifying in its evocation of a naturalistic world in which people are victims of forces beyond their control.*

McTeague presents a unique challenge to the critic. It is a gripping story of human emotions and the relentless pressures of heredity and environment that distort the soul; it is also a melodrama with stereotyped characters, lurid action, and a creaking machinery of symbols that includes everything from dental equipment to snarling dogs. Nevertheless, despite its obvious weaknesses, *McTeague* is exactly what Alfred Kazin has said it is: "The first great tragic portrait in America of an acquisitive society." Norris' novel initiates the literary treatment of a theme that eventually informed significant American literary works such as Theodore Dreiser's "An American Tragedy" and Arthur Miller's "Death of a Salesman."

McTeague himself is a crude but well-meaning hulk of a man whose gentle temper suggests "the draft horse, immensely strong, stupid, docile, obedient." His brutishness is under control as long as he can putter with his dentistry and sleep off his steam beer in the dental chair. Once he is eroticized by Trina, however, McTeague is sucked into a world of feelings that undermine the self-control his undisturbed life has made possible. Once he and Trina marry, McTeague becomes vulnerable to her avarice and Marcus' jealousy and envy. These destructive emotions, not characteristic of McTeague himself, release the underlying primitiveness of his character. When Marcus bites McTeague's earlobe during the wrestling match at the family picnic, the gentle "draft horse" rises with "the hideous yelling of a hurt beast, the squealing of a wounded elephant . . . . It was something no longer human; it was rather an echo from the jungle." For Norris, man is fundamentally an animal, his world ruled by harsh laws of survival.

McTeague's brutalization is tragic because the humanity he had achieved was so touching in its vulnerability. Also he is strikingly innocent of avarice. Although the release of McTeague's brutish animal quality results in two slayings, Norris suggests greater dehumanization in the mad greed of Trina counting her gold coins and Zerkov dreaming of Maria's gold plate. McTeague becomes an animal, but they defy nature itself in the hideousness of their moral and psychological deformity.

It is here that the melodramatic elements of the novel threaten its power. Nevertheless, Norris succeeds in conveying the irony that the nonbrutes in an acquisitive society are more lethal than the brutes, or innocents, who are not conceived in its bowels. McTeague comes from a nonurban world, and it is a testimony to his instincts for self-preservation that he flees back to the mountains after killing Trina. She, Marcus, and Zerkov are all shaped by the city and its acquisitive and artificial environment, and they are all annihilated violently to dramatize the hopelessness of their origins.

Perhaps Norris overdoes the pettiness and petit-bourgeois traits of Trina's Swiss family Sieppe. And his portrait of the psychotic Zerkov hovers close to anti-Semitism. But the shallowness of the characterizations serves a larger symbolic purpose. All these people are what they are because their environment is a kind of hell, a swarming, competitive world. If Norris indulges in harsh stereotypes, it is because society produces them. "I never truckled . . . . I told them the truth. They liked it or they didn't like it. What had that to do with me?" This was Norris' literary creed, and he adhered to it relentlessly in other Naturalist works of social criticism such as *The Octopus* (1901) and *The Pit* (1903). Even in situations that unobservant readers might dismiss as sentimentalism, Norris preserves his sardonic and tough-minded view of the world. The budding love affair between old Mister Grannis and Miss Baker, which reads like a contrast to the deteriorating marriage of McTeague and Trina, is, in reality, a bitter comment on the frustrations of isolation in the congested city. These two old people have conducted their romance through the wall that separates their rooms for so long that their final coming together is a cruelly ironic comment on the life they have never lived.

The central symbol in *McTeague* is gold. Everyone craves it: Maria, the servant girl, is full of stories about the ancestral gold plate of her family. She captivates Zerkov with descriptions of it and steals gold fillings from McTeague's dental parlor. Trina counts her gold coins into the night, deriving a fiercer erotic joy from this than from the bear hugs of her husband. Marcus covets Trina's lottery winnings and finally brings about his own death in struggling over the gold with McTeague in the middle of Death Valley. Only McTeague is indifferent to the glitter of gold. For him it is merely a tool of his trade. When he runs off with Trina's money, he is motivated not by greed, as all critics of the novel agree, but by revenge.

Erich von Stroheim made a famous film of *McTeague* and called it *Greed*. He is said to have followed *McTeague* page by page, "never missing a paragraph." Any reader of *McTeague* will agree that Norris moves through his story with what Kenneth Rexroth has called "a relentless photographic veracity." Scene after scene unfolds with a visual precision and crispness that leaves an indelible impression on the mind and does much to dispel the reservations that the melodramatic action arouses. There is a relentless and powerful movement in these pictures. From the opening scenes describing McTeague on a Sunday in his cozy dental office slumbering or lazily playing his concertina, to the violent closing scene of the novel in which McTeague and Marcus are locked in a violent death struggle in the middle of the greatest wasteland in America, the reader is swept steadily along to increasingly arresting visual involvements. The eye wins over the mind. The environment is rendered with a concreteness that reveals its central power in the novel.

Peter A. Brier

MADAME BOVARY

Type of work: Novel
Author: Gustave Flaubert (1821-1880)
Type of plot: Psychological realism
Time of plot: Mid-nineteenth century
Locale: France
First published: 1857

This masterpiece of realism is an in-depth psychological study of a beautiful but bored and restless woman whose romantic fantasies and yearnings lead her to seek diversion from the monotony of her married life. Madame Bovary *was one of the first novels of its kind to come out of France, and caused a great deal of controversy among contemporary readers and critics; some were shocked at the presentation of the spoiled, romantic adulteress, while others saw the novel as moral and applauded Flaubert's skill and honesty of treatment.*

From the time of Baudelaire to the present, many critics have noted, either approvingly or disapprovingly, Flaubert's application of an accomplished and beautifully sustained style to a banal subject matter in *Madame Bovary*. Of course, in Flaubert's own time, many readers objected to vulgarity as well as banality in the use of an adultress as heroine. Baudelaire, however, offered the telling defense against this criticism in his acknowledgment that the logic of the work as a whole provides an indictment of the immoral behavior.

Flaubert himself viewed his book as "all cunning and stylistic ruse." His intention was to write "a book about nothing, a book with no exterior attachment . . . a book which would have almost no subject." However, Flaubert's goals were not as purely aesthetic as they might initially seem in that he did not mean to eschew significance entirely. Rather, he meant that any subject matter, no matter how trivial, could be raised to art by language and pattern. Like Stendahl and Balzac, he believed that quotidian matters could be treated seriously, but Flaubert goes further than his predecessors in refusing to provide narrative guidance and interpretation.

Erich Auerbach has observed that Flaubert seems simply to pick scenes which are significant and to endow them with language that allows them to be interpreted. As a result, many commentators have seen Flaubert as the first modern novelist, even a precursor of the antinovelist, because of his unwillingness to deal with subject matter in the traditional manner. Certainly he represents a break with the past to the extent that the novel had been essentially narration. Although he does retain the story, he makes the novel over, in his own words, into "a coloration, a nuance."

At the heart of the novel is a provincial dreamer, a romantic who distorts her environment and ultimately destroys herself with wish fulfillments born of the desperate boredom of her circumscribed situation. Her romantic illusions, however, are not the theme of the novel so much as they are the prime example of the human stupidity which dominates all of the characters. Charles is trapped by his subhuman complacency as much as Emma is by her vain imaginings. The surrounding figures, more types than fully developed characters, represent contemporary failures—the irresponsible seducer, the usurer, the inadequate priest, the town rationalist. Each is isolated from the others by his own obsession or deficiency and all contribute to the overwhelming stagnation which smothers Emma.

Martin Furnell has divided the novel into three parts, each of which is controlled by an action and a dominant image. In the first part, Emma marries Charles and the dominant image is in her visit to Le Vaubyessard. The marriage is the central fact of her discontent, while the visit ostensibly provides her with a view of the opulent life she so desperately and nonspecifically craves. In the second part of the novel, she is seduced by the conscienceless landowner Rodolphe, and the dominant image is the Comices Agricoles, the elaborate fair with its rustic and vulgar trappings. To Emma, as she is succumbing to Rodolphe, the Comices Agricoles is the very symbol of the limitations of her life. Naturally she is not capable of consciously making such an interpretation. If she were, her perception might save her. Moreover, what she does not realize is that her affair is as banal as the fair. The third part of the novel describes her seduction by Léon and the dominant image is the meeting in Rouen Cathedral. The cathedral becomes both church and boudoir, populated not only by images of saints but also by a statue of Diane de Poitiers, a notable adultress. Once again, Emma reaches out to the grand but is compromised by her own limitations and those of her situation.

The dominant images, which reveal the ambiguity as well as the frustration of her predicament, are reinforced and refined by a series of recurrent, minor images. A striking example is the plaster statue of a curé which deteriorates as Emma is progressively debased. The image is extended by a contract of the curé's statue with a statue of Cupid: love and sexuality rise as the holy man disintegrates.Later, the damage to the curé's foot reminds us of Charles's peasant boots, which resemble a clubfoot, and of the amputation of Hippolyte's leg as a result of Charles's desperate desire to please Emma.As these complex images recur, they bind together the varieties of stupidity and vanity.

Even more revolutionary than the use of imagery is the point of view, the series of perspectives from which Flaubert narrates the story. He does not assume the stance of the distanced observer, but repeatedly shifts the point of view to avail himself of multiple angles of vision. The narrative begins and ends with Charles. Although Flaubert never allows Charles a first person presentation, we see the beginning of the novel and, indeed, are introduced to Emma from Charles's perspective.We finally return to view the debris of the conclusion from the vantage point of this uncomprehending victim.

For most of the novel we see from Emma's perspective, but there is such a deft playing off of Emma's perceptions against the narrator's control that we are able to analyze her perceptions in a broader context rather than simply accept them as fact. The details of Charles's eating habits, for example, become both a sign of his bovinity, to Emma and us, and a sign of Emma's discontent, to us. As we look out from Emma's or Charles's eyes, interpretations emerge which are beyond the mental capacity of either character. Flaubert presents what they perceive as a means of representing what they fail to perceive. An advantage of this method is that, while we become aware of Emma's shortcomings, a sympathy develops. We recognize the oppressiveness of her circumstances, the triviality of her evil, and the relative sensitivity of her kind of stupidity.

Apparently subjective presentations, controlled and ordered by Flaubert's selection of image and detail, reveal what the characters themselves do not understand. Emma's romantic idealism is the prime example. If Flaubert cannot make tragedy out of these ingredients, he can quite powerfully describe, in his miniscule characters, personal and social frustration on a grand scale.

Edward E. Foster

MADEMOISELLE DE MAUPIN

Type of work: Novel
Author: Théophile Gautier (1811-1872)
Type of plot: Sentimental romance
Time of plot: Early nineteenth century
Locale: France
First published: 1835

Written as a challenge to the hypocrisy of his time, Gautier's novel was intended to celebrate moral freedom in art. The plot of this occasionally sensual novel was partly drawn from Shakespeare's As You Like It.

Gautier's preface to *Mademoiselle de Maupin* castigates utilitarian critics (among several other varieties), and it indicates the author's intention to give the public a novel which will illustrate his belief that "there is nothing truly beautiful but that which can never be of any use whatever." The book does not inculcate virtue; its protagonist is an aesthete who denigrates Christianity for having feminized the ancient pagan representation of nude male beauty. The leading characters are all motivated by sexual desire—there is nothing *useful* from beginning to end. Yet, though *Mademoiselle de Maupin* was daring and defiant in its day, it will strike a reader familiar with *Ulysses, Lady Chatterley's Lover,* or the fiction of Henry Miller as titillating in only a few scenes. What shocked the bourgeois in other days seems rather mild now.

Almost entirely an epistolary novel, *Mademoiselle de Maupin* represents a type that has been out of fashion for more than a hundred years. The early part, especially, requires patience from readers accustomed to novels narrated by an author. The first five chapters, covering more than a hundred pages, are a series of wordy, rambling letters from d'Albert to his friend Silvio revealing the writer increasingly as a bored (and often boring) young man who dreams of an ideal mistress while he secures and makes do with a real one whom he does not deserve. Having wearied of Rosette, he peevishly remarks at one point, "I had what I had desired so long, a mistress of my own like my horse and my sword." Pampered as a child, he now classes as mere property the woman he sleeps with when the urge comes upon him. On another occasion he writes, "I consider woman, after the manner of the ancients, as a beautiful slave designed for pleasure."

At the end of the novel, when Madelaine finally grants d'Albert a single perfect night, one feels that he was lucky to get this much. Madelaine, independent-minded and gifted with common sense which the poetic d'Albert lacks, understands her own bisexual nature, and she has learned enough about men to know that d'Albert could weary of her as he has already grown tired of Rosette. It is better for him to be left with the beautiful memory of a dream fulfilled. Madelaine's parting request is that d'Albert comfort Rosette, but one cannot imagine him succeeding well with a woman whose heart's desire has disappeared. For Rosette, d'Albert would always be a poor substitute for her lost Théodore, just as for d'Albert his forlorn mistress would be a sad exchange for the lovely chimera that briefly came to life and then departed.

THE MADRAS HOUSE

Type of work: Drama
Author: Harley Granville-Barker (1877-1946)
Type of plot: Social criticism
Time of plot: Early twentieth century
Locale: London
First presented: 1910

A problem play of the type popularized by Ibsen and Shaw, The Madras House *attempts to deal realistically with several related themes: the contrast between sexual honesty and sexual hypocrisy, the contrast between bourgeois respectability and honesty in human dealings, the inevitability of social change, and the contrast in personal relations between expressed motives and real motives.*

Near the beginning of Harley Granville-Barker's *The Madras House,* the protagonist, Philip Madras, says "what are the two most important things in a man's character? His attitude towards money and his attitude toward women." That states the subject matter of this lively, provocative drama— money, women, and the relationship between them in Edwardian England. Although the play is loosely structured around the pending sale of Madras House, the real action of the play centers on two dynamic characters who challenge the social and moral assumptions of upper-class English society: Miss Yates, an employee of the firm and a soon-to-be unwed mother, and Constantine Madras, the returning black sheep of the Madras family.

Marion Yates's assault on Edwardian propriety comes from the fact that she refuses to accept either of the roles assigned a girl in her situation; she is neither a "bad girl" nor a "victimized" one. She asks no favors, declines to name the prospective father, and, finally, refuses all offers of financial aid.

Constantine presents a different kind of moral challenge. An incorrigible philanderer, he left his wife in England and went to a country, Southern Arabia, where he could indulge his sensual instincts free from social restraints. He found a religion, Muhammedanism, which allowed him to do so without hesitation or guilt. His casual sexuality shocks his proper English relatives, but his rational defenses of his conduct pose severe tests to their moral assumptions. He makes an especially telling point when he compares his "honest" harem to the unnatural "industrial seraglio" maintained at Madras House where the economic system makes "slaves" out of the women. Although it is clear that Constantine's lechery is actually based on a disdain for women, his blatant doctrine of male superiority is refreshing when contrasted with the hypocritical double standard practiced by conventional English gentlemen.

But the focal point of the drama lies in the "education" of Philip Madras. When Marion Yates confronts him with her problem, he is most impressed by her courage, energy, and innate moral sense; he sees the injustice of her situation and feels extremely frustrated because, trapped in his role as an owner of Madras House, he can do nothing to help her. As he confesses: "I have unconventional opinions, but I don't do unconventional things." Philip is also annoyed by his father's refusal to see women as other than objects of pleasure, but he comes to realize that his own disinterested "understanding" is little better. He accepts the justice of his wife's comment that he is an intellectual edition of his father.

Thus, Philip comes to terms with his own attitudes and feelings, especially as they relate to his career and marriage. He at last accepts his wife Jessica as a separate person and includes her in his plans. But, as for her, they both have to admit that, in Edwardian England at least, there is no meaningful social role for her to play.

Jessica's speech merely trails off and *Madras House* ends on a problematical note. Granville-Barker has dramatically explored the problem of sexual inequality as thoroughly as any playwright of his era and the result is amusing and provocative. But he arrives at no solid conclusions because the answers were not to be found in the society of his time. Nor, perhaps, are they to be found even in our own time.

MAGGIE: A GIRL OF THE STREETS

Type of work: Novel
Author: Stephen Crane (1871-1900)
Type of plot: Social criticism
Time of plot: Late nineteenth century
Locale: New York
First published: 1893

Maggie: A Girl of the Streets *was the first novel to deal realistically and straightforwardly with the sordid life of the slums. It gave rise to the school of naturalistic fiction of Norris, Dreiser, and others. Despite its faults of style and structure, it remains of historical and literary importance.*

Published in 1893 when Crane was only twenty-two years old, *Maggie: A Girl of the Streets* heralded a major new talent in American literature. Little in Crane's early background would seem to have anticipated a work such as *Maggie: A Girl of the Streets,* or the deeply pessimistic attitude toward life reflected there. Son of a small-town Methodist minister, Crane had never really experienced the sort of life and community environment indigenous to the novel except for his observations during some months in New York. But, as he was to prove so brilliantly in *The Red Badge of Courage,* Crane's imagination and genius could extrapolate with uncanny accuracy the patterns of lives he had seen remotely if at all. This may be accounted for at least in part by the fact that Crane, even at the youthful age of twenty-two, already was developing the style and technique of a literary naturalism which essentially saw the novel as a kind of theoretical scientifically-controlled experiment into which characters were placed for observation. As Émile Zola, the acknowledged father of naturalism, had written, "a novelist must be only a scientist, an analyst, an anatomist, and his work must have the certainty, the solidity, and the practical application of a work of science."

Many of Crane's contemporaries, here and abroad, arrived at their naturalistic philosophy through reading in the biological sciences, particularly in the works of Charles Darwin and Herbert Spencer, both of whom contributed immeasurably to the development of the movement. Crane, however, does not appear to have reached his position so much through reading science as from his study of the French and Russian authors who were the earliest pioneers of naturalism in literature. The literary sources of his philosophy of the novel, though, in no way weaken Crane's theoretical framework, and he stands among Hamlin Garland, Frank Norris, Jack London, and Theodore Dreiser as a major figure of American Naturalism. As an artist, Crane is, in his best work, superior to any of these writers. Since *Maggie: A Girl of the Streets* is not of that caliber artistically, however, it is best treated as representational of the naturalistic novel.

An extreme form of the realism which had characterized the previous generation of writers—especially Henry James and Mark Twain in the United States—naturalism resulted from the adaption of the principles of pessimistic scientific determinism to literature. According to these principles, man is a helpless and weak animal caught up in internal or external forces over which he can assert no control, and which ultimately threaten to destroy him. The universe, as perceived from this point of view, operates entirely on Newtonian mechanical principles and has neither intelligent guidance nor moral purpose. From Darwin the naturalists adopted the concept of biological determinism which characterizes his *On the Origin of Species,* while Herbert Spencer gave them a theory of society reflecting the law of tooth and claw and the survival of the fittest. In general, these writers fall into one of two camps: those who emphasize the biological nature of man and show him attempting to utilize his animal instincts to survive in a hostile world, and those who are more concerned with man in the social environment and present him as a product of socio-economic forces against which he can hardly hope to prevail. Crane, who wrote in Hamlin Garland's copy of *Maggie: A Girl of the Streets* that the novel illustrated the way in which environment was a shaping force in man's life, was at this stage of his career clearly in the latter camp.

In one sense, *Maggie: A Girl of the Streets* is as much about environment as about Maggie and the other characters in any specific sense. Crane, after all, did not even name his characters in his early drafts, preferring to treat them as generalized and representative types rather than as individualized characters. Also, he shows no interest in getting into the mental or psychic lives of his characters to discover for us their private selves. All this suggests the extent to which environment, rather than character, is at the heart of the work. Later Crane would develop more interest in the psychological dimension than he shows here, though he would never entirely abandon the view of man caught up in external forces beyond his control. On these grounds, most readers are likely to quarrel with William Dean Howells, who professed to see an approximation of the Fate characteristic of Greek tragedy in Crane's determinism. Stephen Crane's sense of the environment both as shaping force and destructive power is so strong that Maggie can only dramatize man's pathetic weakness in the face of cosmic power—lacking even the illusion of freedom, she cannot illustrate the powerful sense of human potential even in adversity found in true tragedy.

But the faults—and they are many—of this novel should not be allowed to detract from its important place in the development of the American novel. It has been variously called the first truly modern American novel, and the novel which first clearly differentiated the American from the English novel tradition, and persuasive arguments can be made for both insights. Crane was able in this early novel to open up for consideration by his successors an entire level of social life not heretofore seriously treated by American authors, though many writers had sentimentalized the slums. Even more revolutionary was his challenge, well before Dreiser's *Sister Carrie,* to the Victorian taboos against any real treatment of sex in the novel by writing honestly and frankly and sympathetically about a "fallen woman." Further, Crane's treatment of the hypocritical religious values his characters frequently mouth to justify their most inhumane acts anticipates that loss of traditional values which looms so large in the writing of this century. Though he published his greatest work, *The Red Badge of Courage,* in 1895, Crane was essentially a twentieth century writer, and his *Maggie: A Girl of the Streets* was America's first novel which could truly be called modern. Without Crane's short and brilliant career, modern literature might not have developed as it did in this country.

William E. Grant

THE MAGIC MOUNTAIN

Type of work: Novel
Author: Thomas Mann (1875–1955)
Type of plot: Philosophical chronicle
Time of plot: 1907-1914
Locale: Davos, Switzerland
First published: 1924

A huge novel concerned with perspectives of history and philosophy in our time, this book is considered one of the great intellectual achievements of the twentieth century. Modern ideologies and beliefs are represented by characters such as the Italian humanist, the absolutist Jewish Jesuit, a German doctor, a Polish scientist, and the hedonistic Mynheer Peeperkorn.

The Magic Mountain, begun in 1912 but written largely after World War I, was actually planned as a novella, inspired by Mann's own brief stay at the sanatorium at Davos, Switzerland. In fact, his early novella "Tristan" lays much of the groundwork for the later novel. *The Magic Mountain,* however, grew in bulk and complexity to become a veritable mirror of European society in the period leading up to World War I. It lies directly in the tradition of the German *Bildüngsroman,* or novel of development, which goes back to Goethe's *Wilhelm Meister.* In this genre, a relatively unformed character is exposed to manifold aspects of life and various influences, often quite conscious attempts to educate or mold his attitude. In a gradual process, his character achieves form, erroneous goals are cast aside, and the true calling and, more important, the right relationship to life are found. Hans Castorp is just such a character when he arrives from the flatlands for a brief visit at Berghof. Mann emphasizes his bourgeois background, and the lack of firm convictions and direction in his life. For Mann, the North German type—Hans is from Hamburg—had always represented the solid, respectable middle-class life. Yet Hans is also something of a quester, curious and adventuresome in the spiritual and intellectual realm. He observes the new world of the sanatorium avidly, and becomes involved with the personalities there, inquiring and holding long conversations. The narrative voice of the novel, as in most of Mann's works, has a certain degree of ironic distance, but the pace of the work is very much tied to Castorp's own experience of events and temporal rhythms. The three weeks of his planned visit stretch out to seven years and the work becomes the record of the growth of his character in a microcosm of European society.

Mann's style had developed out of the nineteenth century Realist school, and he observes and describes reality lovingly and with minute care. Yet his work becomes increasingly symbolic in his major novels, and the structure of these novels becomes increasingly expressive of symbolic values. Thus the individual character development of Castorp reflects the problems of European thought as a whole, and the various ideas to which he is exposed represent various intellectual and spiritual currents of the epoch. Castorp initially falls prey to a fascination with death, a dangerous attraction to the irresponsible freedom of the mountain world, the temptation to turn inward and to fall in love with sickness. He studies the illness whose symptoms he himself soon exhibits. He visits the "moribundi," and has long talks with Behrens and Krokowski, two of the doctors. Here life is seen as a process of decay, and even the intellect and the emotions are reduced to unconscious urges in the new psychology of Freud. Castorp crystallizes these ideas in his feverish love for Clavdia Chauchat, who represents the Russian temperament—the urge to lose oneself, to give in to the emotions, to live life for the sake of life. She is contrasted to Settembrini, the Italian intellectual, educator, and humanist. He is an optimist, believing in the perfectability of man by reason, and he opposes the fascination with death that Castorp manifests. Settembrini is again contrasted to Naphta, his intellectual opponent, an irrationalist, a Jew turned Jesuit, with a highly Nietzschean viewpoint. He is a pessimist, deriding Settembrini's optimism and ridiculing his arguments as inconsistent. In actuality, neither figure is meant to convert Castorp; their arguments cancel each other, as does so much else in the novel. Castorp finds his own position midway between the various opposing forces. This occurs primarily in the chapter "Snow." If the magic mountain is a timeless realm above the immediate concerns of the world, "Snow" is a hermetic world within that realm. Castorp loses his way in a snow storm, and exhausted, in danger of death, he has a dream, a vision in which he sees juxtaposed an idyllic world of tropical paradise, peopled by gentle and happy folk, while in a temple there is performed a terrible ritual of human sacrifice. Here the two poles of human life are symbolized, and Castorp's response is clear and decisive: life is inseparably bound up with death, the horrible is real and cannot be denied. But for the sake of goodness and love, man must not grant death dominion over his thoughts.

It is following this chapter that the figure of Mynheer Peeperkorn dominates the novel for a time, a figure of great vitality, simple in his thoughts, but of powerful personality, in love with his life-force, terrified of losing it, committing suicide finally rather than face decay. He, like the other figures, represents an aspect of contemporary European thought and attitudes. Indeed, his traits, like those of Settembrini and Naphta were drawn from life, from figures known to Mann. Thus, the novel has something of the autobiographical, and represents a stage in Mann's own thought. In the realm he has constructed, all these aspects—fictional *Bildüngsroman,* intellectual autobiography and symbolic portrait of the prewar era—merge. This is made possible in part by the very foundation of the novel, the mountain. The small community is elevated above the flatlands, in the rarefied Alpine air, remote from the problems of the world and the demands of everyday life. Time is dissolved, the rhythm of the novel moves from sequences of hours to days, weeks, months, and finally years, all rendered indistinguishable by the precise daily routine. In this world outside of time, Hans can grow, can hover between conflicting opinions. Here he has freedom, most essentially in the "Snow" chapter, where even space is obliterated. Yet in contrast to the earlier Romantic outlook, this elevated position of freedom in isolation is not seen as a good thing, for though it provides an aesthetic space in which ideal development can occur, it is divorced from life, and life is the value which Hans's development leads him to affirm—life, with all of its horror as well as its beauty. The European world saw itself plunged into World War I, Thomas Mann saw himself jolted out of his apolitical aesthetic stance, and thus it is only fitting that Hans Castorp, too, must come down from the mountain to the world of time and action, even if only to be lost among the havoc of a world at war.

Steven C. Schaber

THE MAGNIFICENT OBSESSION

Type of work: Novel
Author: Lloyd C. Douglas (1877-1951)
Type of plot: Quasi-mysticism
Time of plot: Early twentieth century
Locale: Detroit and Europe
First published: 1929

This novel was written to expound an idea, and as such it was a successful piece of work. The author makes an excellent case for the theory of extending personality and gaining moral power by doing good for other individuals.

Immensely popular from the time of its publication, this novel belongs in the tradition of Charles Monroe Sheldon's *In His Steps* (1896)—the most widely sold novel in the history of this country. Sheldon's book is a sort of magazine version of *The Imitation of Christ*: a small town's citizenry resolves to precede every action with the question "What would Jesus do?" The idea catches fire and spreads to Chicago and beyond. Lloyd C. Douglas' romantic and religious novel is just as much an example of magazine fiction, but its tone is restrained and its flirtation with a kind of folksy mysticism has undeniable charm. But the implications are similar: the implementation of Dr. Hudson's selfless generosity in secret charity becomes a "magnificent obsession," a means of changing lives and awakening deeply spiritual and moral instincts.

Robert Merrick, the protagonist, is an enigma in the beginning of the story. First we see him as a careless playboy whose reputation is far from admirable. Soon we are plunged into Merrick's life and are aware of the internal struggle he faces in trying to make up for the unfortunate accidental death of Dr. Hudson. Merrick becomes obsessed with Hudson's philosophy of life which is only brought to the surface after his death. Hudson's unending kindnesses to many people leave Merrick dumbfounded and curious. He at first dismisses Hudson's ideas as foolish, crazy, and inappropriate. But with the support of Hudson's co-worker, confidante and friend, Nancy Ashford, Merrick is able to discover the beauty of Hudson's philosophy of life and adopt it as his own.

Nancy Ashford, the superintendent at the Hudson Clinic, and Helen Hudson, the young widow, interact most believably with Merrick and the other characters. Douglas has drawn these characters carefully and made them integral to the expansion of the theme and plot. Even though Nancy Ashford is a relatively minor character, she provides the encouragement and support Merrick needs thoughout the novel. Helen Hudson supplies the romantic element and acts as the seemingly unattainable love. She becomes Merrick's one great reward.

THE MAHABHARATA

Type of work: Poem
Author: Unknown
Type of plot: Heroic epic
Time of plot: Remote antiquity
Locale: Ancient India
First transcribed: Fifth century B.C.(?)

*This tremendous poetic effort is one of two national epics of the Hindu peoples,
the second being the* Ramayana. *It is both a history of prehistoric times and a
compendium of materials that throws light on the religious, social, political,
ethical, and moral ideals and practices of an old and memorable people.*

There are six facets of the *Mahabharata* which require closer examination.
First is the problem of language. Second is the question of literary form. Third
is the matter of structure. Fourth is the debate about interpretation. Fifth is
the analysis of the contents. And last is a partial list of analogs.

In regard to the language problem, modern readers usually rely on translations and should know about variations between one English translation and
another. These variations are not inaccuracies; rather, they are the result of
translators' differing points of view, all of which may lend insight into the
work. The serious student may thus consult more than one translation before
evaluating the poem.

Second is the question of literary form. The *Mahabharata* is classified as a
heroic (or "folk") epic to distinguish it from the literary epic and the mock
epic. But in some formal respects, it does not follow the pattern of the Western
epic. Whereas the Greek heroic epic contains twenty-four books and the
English literary epic has twelve, the *Mahabharata* consists of eighteen books.
The number eighteen does not appear to be arbitrary. The *Bhagavad-Gita*
(bk. 6, chs. 25-42) is a microcosm, divided into eighteen chapters; and the
war in which Duryodhana and his forces were defeated lasted eighteen days.
Also while most Western heroic epics are nationalistic in tone, the *Mahabharata* is concerned with a story of conflict primarily for high moral purpose, a
struggle between Good and Evil. In most other formal respects, it follows
traditional epic formulae.

Third is the matter of structure. The *Mahabharata* is not a unified epic poem
but a collection of poetry: myths, legends, secular as well as religious tales
and advice, folk wisdom, and religious poetry, among other things. And there
is an appendix, the *Harivamsa*, a genealogy of the god Hari (Vishnu), of
whom Krishna was the eighth avatar. As an anthology, this Hindu poem is
structurally comparable to the Judeo-Christian Bible. Although there is no
Bible, as such, in Hinduism, there is still a great quantity of sacred literature,
including the *Mahabharata* as well as the *Vedas,* the *Brahmanas,* the *Upanishads,* the *Puranas,* and the *Ramayana.* To the pious Hindu, the most familiar

is the *Gita*.

Fourth, as regards interpretation, a distinction must be made between literal and figurative readings of the text. The main story is very likely based upon a historical event: a war between two neighboring peoples, the Kurus and the Panchalas, who inhabited the west and east points of the Madhyadesa (the "middle land" between the Ganges and the Jumna) respectively, with the war ending in the overthrow of the Kuru dynasty. But later recensions transformed history into legend and theology. Hence, the *Mahabharata* may be construed both literally and figuratively. For instance, the *Gita* is literally a dialog between Arjuna and Krishna. Yet the circumstances and setting—the impending battle, Arjuna's ethical reservations, and the question-answer format—are merely devices to dramatize Krishna's ethical and metaphysical sermon (cf. The Sermon on the Mount). So the figurative or allegorical interpretation, which develops the idea of Good striving for supremacy over Evil, sees Arjuna as the individual soul and Krishna as the eternal Supreme Spirit which resides in each heart. Arjuna's chariot stands for the mortal Body. King Dhritarashtra's blindness represents ignorance, and his hundred sons are the evil tendencies of mankind. The battle, then, becomes a perennial one between the power of Good and the power of Evil. And the warrior who heeds the advice of the Supreme Spirit speaking from within will succeed physically in battle and spiritually in attaining the Highest Good.

Fifth is the analysis of the contents. While the *Mahabharata* is cast in the framework of an epic feud between the Kauravas (Evil) and the Pandavas (Good), this feud occupies only twenty to twenty-five percent of the work. Also included are the theosophic *Gita* and the *Harivamsa*. Consequently, approximately seventy percent of the poem is composed of philosophy, poems, and stories, primarily of a legendary or mythological nature. Among the best known of the legends is the tale of Sakuntala (bk. 1), whose son Bharata founded the Great Bharata dynasty of Indian kings. Sakuntala's story also appears in a separate poetic drama, *Sakuntala*, by Kalidasa (c. fifth century A.D.). Another popular tale is that of Savitri whose love for her husband and devotion to her father-in-law triumphed over Yama, the god of death. In both of these legends, women have prominent roles as heroines. They are evidence of the high place women held in ancient Indian culture. The *Mahabharata* also provided ethical guidance and in time became an authoritative treatise on dharma (truth, duty, righteousness), inculcating the divine origin of Brahman institutions, the caste system, and the superiority of the priestly caste not only over people but also over kings.

Finally, the Western reader may find it helpful to note analogs between the *Mahabharata* and Western literature in order to compare cultural concepts and assumptions. The *Mahabharata* and the Bible share a similar format. The story of Savitri and the story of Ruth have much in common. The polyandry of Princess Draupadi with the Pandavas is reflected in the levirate marriages

of the Old Testament. Likewise, the game of dice between Duryodhana and
Yudhishthira also occurs in both the Bible (cf. the "casting of lots") and
Western folklore and literature. Equally common is the identity change or
the disguise as manifested in, among other incidents, the discovery that
Yudhishthira's faithful dog was in reality the god of justice. Such changes are
also seen in Ovid's *Metamorphoses,* in *The Second Shepherd's Play,* in
Shakespeare's *As You Like It* and *Twelfth Night,* and in many folktales. And
the parallel between King Dhritarashtra and King Lear is quite clear. The
richest source of analogs to the *Mahabharata* is found in Greek mythology.
The bow-and-arrow feat of strength for the hand of Princess Draupadi is
mirrored in the test of Penelope's suitors. The twelve-year exile and wandering of the Pandavas has its parallel in the *Odyssey,* just as the battle between
the Pandavas and the Kauravas is echoed in the *Iliad.* And where Mount Meru
was the dwelling place of the Hindu gods, Mount Olympus was the Greek
counterpart. So as Yudhishthira descended into the lower regions, the Greek
Orpheus descended into the underworld. These and other analogs suggest
that the Hindu epic has much in common with familiar aspects of Western
literature. For these reasons, the *Mahabharata* has been uniquely compatible
with Western culture.

Joanne G. Kashdan

THE MAID OF HONOUR

Type of work: Drama
Author: Philip Massinger (1583-1640)
Type of plot: Tragi-comedy
Time of plot: The Renaissance
Locale: Palermo and Siena, Italy
First presented: c. 1623

One of the foremost Jacobean playwrights, Massinger created in The Maid of Honour *two memorable characters and several scenes of great skill, despite the improbabilities which tend to weaken the play as a whole.*

Philip Massinger was a dramatist who enjoyed fame in his own time and was one of the cornerstones of the King's Men. Although the democratic ideas he often proposed in his plays were unpopular with Charles I, he enjoyed Court favor—so much so that Charles's wife broke established precedent in order to see one of Massinger's plays. In 1634, rather than have the players come to Court, which was the usual pattern of behavior when Royalty wished to see a performance, she went to Blackfriars. That she chose this action speaks highly for Massinger's talents as a playwright. Indeed, some scholars have given him credit for the portions of *The Two Noble Kinsmen* and *Henry VIII* that were not written by John Fletcher, because technically his verse so closely resembles that of William Shakespeare.

The Maid of Honour, classified as a tragi-comedy, was published in 1632 in quarto. Sometime between 1623 and 1632 the play was performed at the Phoenix by the Queen's Men. Contrary to the practice of most English playwrights of the time, Massinger elected to have as his central character a woman—Camiola. The basis of the plot for *The Maid of Honour* was probably a story from William Painter's *Palace of Pleasure,* which had also provided John Webster with the central female character of the Duchess in *The Duchess of Malfi* (c. 1613). Unlike most of his contemporaries who wrote tragi-comedy, Massinger also spent more time in the development of his characters, in moralizing, and in careful plot development.

The character of Camiola, the maid, is developed by Massinger to heights that make her distinguished among her counterparts through her bravery, virtuosity, self-respect, and gift for love. For his moralizing in *The Maid of Honour,* Massinger adopted a technique which, aside from providing an avenue for moralizing, aided in character development. The technique—so apparent in the drama of the Middle Ages and Renaissance, particularly in the morality play—was testing. This process of testing allowed Massinger to set at odds various forces within his characters; and, in the struggle to resolve the conflict, the fully-developed character was born. Shakespeare had used the technique in *Hamlet*; Christopher Marlowe used it in *Doctor Faustus*; and Massinger used it with Camiola and Bertoldo. In testing their love for each other and fealty to spiritual oaths, Massinger is able to bring about a masterful climax which allows King Roberto to exclaim that Camioia "is a fair example/For noble maids to imitate." Massinger's skillful hand at the somewhat surprising climax gives support to the critical opinion that in his collaborations with John Fletcher, it was Massinger who was responsible for the exposition and denouement.

THE MAID'S TRAGEDY

Type of work: Drama
Authors: Francis Beaumont (1584?-1616) and John Fletcher (1579-1625)
Type of plot: Revenge tragedy
Time of plot: The legendary past
Locale: Rhodes
First published: c. 1610

Although The Maid's Tragedy *is marred by sentimentality and by improbabilities, it is a tightly constructed play that never falters in its development from beginning to end. The plot was original with Beaumont and Fletcher, but the play does contain scenes which echo Shakespeare.*

Mainly the work of Beaumont, *The Maid's Tragedy* nonetheless reflects the characters of both collaborators. Amintor's emphasis on the divinity of the King is true to Beaumont's sensibility, while Melantius' insistence on the right of the wronged subject to revenge against his ruler marks the influence of Fletcher. Just as the two characters are complimentary in their views, so were the private and artistic personalities and talents of these famous collaborators. With its pathetic, romantic revenge theme, its unity of action and time, its variety of vivid characters, and its highly skillful manipulation and concentration of a complex plot, *The Maid's Tragedy* attests to the theatrical success of this double authorship. Perhaps the death of Aspatia takes too long, and perhaps her death makes the play teeter precariously on the line between tragedy and comedy; but Melantius' inability to kill himself restores a practical, salutary perspective.

Aside from the intricacy of its plot, the play is most notable for the diversity and conviction of its characters. Evadne is a fine portrait of shameless womanhood, as she tells the King, "I love with my ambition/Not with my eyes" (3.1). Her self-revelation to Amintor on their wedding night is an unforgettable scene of mocking cruelty (2.1) that seems almost to justify Amintor's anti-feminism. That anti-female strain in his personality is counterbalanced by Aspatia's anti-male attitude that culminates, ironically, in her assumption of a male disguise that causes her death. Amintor, however, is a puzzling character, whose long-suffering is frankly incredible; similarly, Aspatia's insistence on a duel with him seems excessive. Yet Amintor is convincing, in all his ambivalence, when he seeks unsuccessfully to hide his grief from Melantius. Melantius is quixotic, his emotions, loyalties, and words changing as quickly as he can express them. So, in the scene with Amintor (3.2), he moves from preferring family to friendship to the very opposite position, by means of a dramatic experience—the aborted duel with his friend. At the end, he restores order to the state by declaring that he was not moved by ambition (5.3), and his survival marks the victory of practicality over romanticism. Nor should the portrait of a confused, worried, and cowardly old man whose one virtue is honesty—in Calianax—be overlooked. When he says, "Put in my name too" (5.3) we are happy that Melantius complies.

MAIN STREET

Type of work: Novel
Author: Sinclair Lewis (1885-1951)
Type of plot: Social satire
Time of plot: c. 1910-1920
Locale: Small Midwestern town
First published: 1920

In this portrait of a typical small Midwestern town called Gopher Prairie, Lewis satirizes the smug complacency, narrow-mindedness, hypocrisy, and resistance to change of the small-town mentality. Despite its social criticism, however, Main Street *reflects Lewis' affection for his home town of Sauk Center, Minnesota, upon which Gopher Prairie was based.*

Sinclair Lewis frequently had difficulty in determining in his own mind whether his works were meant as bitterly comic satires of American life and values or whether they were planned as complex novels centering around the lives of the series of characters he made famous. One of the difficulties of reading Lewis is that these two conflicting sorts of writing are both present in many of his works, and frequently at odds with each other. This is demonstrably true of *Main Street* which cannot simply be called a satire of life in small-town America. For all the satire of small-town attitudes and values, Lewis is not unequivocal in his attack as a satirist might be expected to be. Actually, he finds quite a lot of value in the best *Main Street* has to offer, and he seems to see Carol Kennicott's reconciliation with the town at the end of the novel as a triumph more than a failure on her part. Thus, though *Main Street* is, as it has been frequently called, a revolt against the village, it is a revolt marked by the complexity of Lewis' attitude toward Gopher Prairie and toward its real-life counterpart, Sauk Center, Minnesota, where Lewis spent his early years.

Lewis' characters, particularly Will and Carol Kennicott, are another complicating factor in this novel which prevents its being simply a satire. Unlike the one-dimensional figures typical of satire, the Kennicotts develop into somewhat rounded characters who demand attention and sympathy in their own rights. Carol in particular, as the central figure of the novel, is developed more novelistically than satirically as Lewis traces her development from a very naïve and foolishly idealistic young woman into a more tolerant and understanding human being. Ironically, for the reader to adopt only the critical and satiric portrait of the small town which lies at the surface of *Main Street* would be for him to embrace the same overly-simplistic attitudes which characterized Carol at the beginning of the novel, and which she must escape as evidence of her maturity.

During the early part of the century, Americans tended to accept on faith the premise that all that was best in life was epitomized by the small-town environment. Though by no means the first author to attack this premise, Lewis with *Main Street* achieved the widespread popularity which gave new prominence to this revolt against the small town. Lewis, himself a small-town boy, knew at first hand the discrepancy between the vision of the village as a Utopia and the actuality of its bleak cultural and moral atmosphere. As Lewis makes clear in his prologue, *Main Street* is an analogue for all such towns, and by his treatment of Gopher Prairie, Lewis sought to strike a satiric blow at the very heartland of America. Rather than a Utopia, Lewis discovers in the provincial mentality of the small town a surfiet of hypocrisy, bigotry, ignorance, cruelty, and, perhaps most damning of all, a crippling dullness and conformity which is essentially hostile to any possibility of intellectual or emotional life. Ironically, though, even while ruthlessly exposing these negative qualities of the small town, Lewis finds, particularly in the matter-of-fact courage and determination of Will Kennicott, some of the very qualities which have given the small town its reputation as the strength of America. The fact is, Lewis was himself ambivalent in his attitude toward the village, and this indecisiveness creeps into the novel to mitigate his castigation of middle America.

The action of the novel centers around Carol Kennicott's discovery of the nature of life and society in Gopher Prairie, and culminates with her eventual compromise with the town. For Lewis' purposes, Carol is an excellent device to enable him to expose the bleak heart of the midwestern town by contrasting its qualities and values with her own. Young, educated, intelligent, and idealistic, Carol can bring the vision to Gopher Prairie to see what it lacks, and so far as that is her purpose, she performs well. It is when she performs as a character in her own right that we begin to see Lewis' attitude toward her as being more complicated than simply approving her values in contrast to those of the town. Carol's idealism is accompanied by a naïveté and intolerance which but poorly qualify her to accomplish the reforms she advocates because she can only hope to change Gopher Prairie by becoming part of it. The polarization she brings about by trying too much too soon makes it improbable that she should ever be able to realize her ambitions for the town unless she learns to accommodate to—though not necessarily to approve of—its values. After running away to Washington only to discover that the values of the city are not too different from those of the village, Carol is in a better position to adopt a more tolerant attitude toward the villagers. As we see her at the end of the novel, she has made an effort to come to terms with her environment by working to evolve realistic reforms rather than seeking a radical overthrow of entrenched values and institutions. In losing her naïveté, Carol gains in terms of her ability to confront reality, and even to change it over a period of time.

Actually, most of Carol's reforms are too superficial really to cure what Lewis called the village virus. Her concern is more with manners than values, and she would only substitute the slick sophistication of the city for the provincial dullness she finds so intolerable. The perfect foil to her is Will Kennicott who, while epitomizing all the worst of the town's boorishness, goes about his daily medical practice with quiet efficiency, determination, and even courage that Lewis clearly admires. Will's presence makes it impossible simply to accept Carol's assessment of the vulgarity of the town as Lewis' final word. It is Gopher Prairie that finally triumps as Carol reconciles herself to its full reality.

William E. Grant

THE MALCONTENT

Type of work: Drama
Author: John Marston (1576-1634)
Type of plot: Romantic comedy
Time of plot: Thirteenth century
Locale: Genoa, Italy
First presented: 1604

This uneven tragicomedy explores both serious issues, such as the restoration of the rightful state leadership, and supposedly comic issues, such as pandering, cuckoldry, and Court toadies. Marston tended to overwrite, extending his descriptive phrases and figures of speech to the point of monotony, but some scenes do contain the spark of life and give the drama interest.

The Malcontent belongs to that large group of English Renaissance dramas called tragicomedies. That is, it is a play which contains serious situations, situations full of tragic possibilities, but averts these possibilities because of various controls within the play. As in *Measure for Measure,* we have in *The Malcontent* a figure in disguise who keeps watch over the situation, never letting the forces of evil finally get the upper hand. At the ideal time to bring the plot to a comic conclusion, he reveals his true identity. Further, Altofronto, in his disguise as Malevole, is not seeking blood revenge as the wronged man in a tragedy might be. Though Altofronto finally asserts control, the plot of political intrigue slips perilously close to disaster before justice is done.

Marston dedicated this play to Ben Jonson, and, particularly in its satiric parts, Jonson's influence can be seen. Though the satire is more bitter than in Jonson's satiric comedies, it is, like his, designed to be corrective. By holding vices of the court up to ridicule, Marston further shows how much dramatic satire in his day owed to the morality play tradition. Though the satire is bitter, Marston does not allow it to reach the corrosive level we find in the tragedies of Webster, and so keeps the play true to its happy ending.

Perhaps the strongest aspect of the play is its rich character portraits. Mendoza, for example, serves as a marvelous figure of the Machiavellian villain. In the characters of Pietro and Altofronto we see contrasting types; the first is weak and ineffectual, but the latter, though a skeptic, is forceful enough to alter society for the better. In fact, the pessimistic spirit embodied in Altofronto seems an incarnation of the time—almost a forerunner of the darker visions to come on the Jacobean stage. Additionally, the telling satire on the lust and greed of court life lifts the play beyond the ordinary into an effective commentary on the political corruption of the day.

THE MALTESE FALCON

Type of work: Novel
Author: Dashiell Hammett (1894-1961)
Type of plot: Mystery romance
Time of plot: Twentieth century
Locale: San Francisco
First published: 1930

A detective novel of the hardboiled school, The Maltese Falcon's *distinction lies in the fact that the detective himself becomes involved in crime. Written in racy, colloquial language, the book pretends to be no more than entertainment, but it is a classic example of its type and has influenced many subsequent writers, both in and out of the detective genre.*

The Maltese Falcon introduces the detective Sam Spade, a rough, crude, unassuming, and peculiarly unattractive private eye. His appearance is anything but that of a hero's: he lacks wavy hair, a charming smile, or an athletic physique. An antihero, a negative character cast in a positive role, his success, however, is directly related to his nonheroic qualities. Since his world is the underside of respectability, the seedy areas of San Francisco in which he is usually employed in some sort of marital espionage, Spade must adopt his methods to the environment in order to survive. Indeed what finally comes clear is that the detective is the only truly sane and perhaps just man in the novel. He deals with the evil and treacherous, those like the satanic Gutman, as well as the police, who are for the most part stupid or only intent upon making an arrest, the matter of justice being of no large consequence.

Spade's role as the isolated antihero who brings justice to a corrupt world is a familiar figure in American folklore and literature. *The Maltese Falcon* is in some sense a modern, urban staging of the traditional Western story with Spade as the lone gunman, without credentials, combating the greed of the adventurers in their pursuit of wealth (in the Western, it was gold, here it is the falcon). Notably different, however, is the fact that the heroine in Hammett's novel, Brigid O'Shaughnessy, unlike the Western heroine, is herself treacherous and guilty; and Spade, for all his virtue, is not above dishonest gain. For all the similarities, then, we are in a radically different world in *The Maltese Falcon,* one of lost innocence, where heroism is impossible and trust and affection have disappeared. The whole is unsavory and decayed.

THE MAN OF FEELING

Type of work: Novel
Author: Henry Mackenzie (1745-1831)
Type of plot: Sentimental romance
Time of plot: Mid-eighteenth century
Locale: England
First published: 1771

The unhappy life and pathetic death of Mr. Harley, the "man of feeling," is told in a deliberately formless fashion that allows Mackenzie to speak directly to the reader, to describe realistically eighteenth century English life, and to indulge in the favorite themes of his age: the loneliness of the delicate mind, the unhappiness of love beyond one's station, the vainglory of riches, the hardships of the poor, and the glorification of benevolence.

Mr. Harley may strike modern readers as a poor excuse for a hero, especially when compared to the witty Restoration rakes, the resourceful Robinson Crusoe, the robust and good-hearted Tom Jones, or even the whimsically sentimental Tristram Shandy. But Mackenzie is less interested in creating a convincing or engaging hero than in stimulating certain responses from his readers. If compassion and disinterested benevolence were the most admirable qualities of humanity, then Mackenzie would generate such impulses in his readers by showing them at work in his hero. Harley is a sensitive soul motivated almost exclusively by natural generosity of heart and by the conviction that the greatest satisfaction in life is derived from bestowing charity upon others. At the same time, he is thoroughly indifferent to his own self-interest. In a form reminiscent of the picaresque tale, he moves through a series of episodes in which piteous and touching misfortunes are recounted. By relieving the suffering of unfortunates, Harley not only creates gratitude and love in his beneficiaries, but also enriches his own soul—and by a kind of narrative sympathy, the souls of his readers.

In contrast to Harley, who "was not formed for the bustle of the busy, nor the dissipation of the gay," the world is "selfish, interested, and unthinking." The unreal aura of benevolence and good nature is offset by Mackenzie's numerous pictures of widespread deceit and cruelty. But in presenting these scenes, Mackenzie is not interested in being witty or cynical: humor is a quality conspicuously absent from this work. The author aims primarily to bring tears to the eyes of his readers; for tears are the chief signs of a refined and delicate feeling, and the capacity for such feeling is the chief requisite of nobility of character.

THE MAN OF MODE

Type of work: Drama
Author: Sir George Etherege (1634?-1691)
Type of plot: Comedy of manners
Time of plot: The 1670's
Locale: London
First presented: 1676

As the first important Restoration comic dramatist, George Etherege's influence was crucial in the development of that epoch. In The Man of Mode *he created three characters who were to endure, both as stereotypes and as individualized characterizations: Dorimant, the ideal courtier-rake; Harriet, the vibrant, witty lady who lures him into matrimony; and Sir Fopling Flutter, the Frenchified dandy, who spawned a host of successors.*

The Man of Mode is, along with Wycherley's *The Country Wife* and Congreve's *The Way of the World,* one of the finest comedies of Restoration theater. It owes its critical acclaim to its etched-in-acid portrait of love rituals in contemporary London high society, the brilliance of its dialogue, and—surprisingly enough—the humanity of its characters.

All of the character types in Etherege's last play are the stock-in-trade of Restoration comedy. Dorimant is fashionably witty rake who enjoys juggling two or three mistresses at the same time. In one of the running metaphors of the play, he holds passion in love to be merely a disease, and fortunately only a temporary one. "Constancy at my years?" he asks Mrs. Loveit, " . . . you might as well expect the fruit of autumn ripens i' the spring." The heroine is, of course, beautiful, but more important, fully a match in wit for Dorimant. Her ability to discomfit him in their verbal battles is the main reason for his conceding to her the war over his bachelorhood. Harriet has no intention of becoming one more in the long line of Dorimant's mistresses. Other conventional types include the Frenchified Sir Fopling Flutter, the standard by which all later stage fops were to be judged; the cast-off mistress, the hero's confidant, a couple of foolish older people, and a pair of lovers in the "high" plot, who set off, through their idealized love, the more earthbound love of Dorimant and Harriet. Basing their relationship on a compromise between passion and social forms, Harriet tells Dorimant: "Though I wish you devout, I would not have you turn fanatic."

Earlier critics of Restoration comedy lamented the pernicious morality of such plays as *The Man of Mode,* which appeared to sanction, or at least accept, libertinism. More recent critics have seen dramatists like Etherege striving to present an acceptable mean of behavior in matters of love. Dorimant, for instance, is neither as boorishly crude as country gentlemen like Old Bellair, nor as excessively fastidious about his dress and grooming as Sir Fopling, who likes to entertain himself in front of a mirror. Harriet, who maintains that "women ought to be no more fond of dressing than fools should be of talking," is similar to Dorimant in this respect. Both hero and heroine prefer to make do with a minimum of affectation and pretense, though, of course, complete honesty in love is seen to be either unrealistic in the case of Young Bellair and Emilia, or unwise, in the case of Mrs. Loveit, who wears her anguished heart on her passionate sleeve. We may be apprehensive that Dorimant's love for Harriet may be no more permanent than any of his previous *inamorata*—and indeed, it may not be. What gives their future relationship at least a reasonable chance is the similarity of the two in temperament and wit. Only with Harriet, a woman whose insight into his true nature is penetrating, does Dorimant speak with utter sincerity and feeling.

We like the characters not because we recognize them as types, but because we recognize them as human. Dorimant, by all accounts, should be an unsympathetic character: he is callous and cynical in his treatment of people, and his wit may seem inadequate compensation for his larger defects of character. As Bellinda realizes, there is a point beyond which his brutal treatment of women stops being amusing, and becomes ugly, even to those who profit by it. Dorimant, however, like his victims, is vulnerable: his humiliations in the Mall and later, before his former and present mistresses, as well as his awkwardness before the incisive Harriet, show us a vain man almost pathetically in need of "reputation"; that is, the reputation of being a dispassionate and consummate rake. Etherege's treatment of Mrs. Loveit is also multifaceted. On the one hand, the extravagance and violence of her passion make her a figure to be ridiculed. On the other, she is a figure of pathos. Her only crime, after all, is loving Dorimant too much. A careful reading of the play will reveal her not as a caricature, but as a woman treated by the playwright with understanding, sympathy, and even dignity: "I would die to satisfy [your love]" she tells Dorimant, "I will not, to save you from a thousand racks, do a shameless thing to please your vanity." Such probing treatment of personal and social behavior, in a genre almost rigidly standardized in its conventions, is a major reason for the continued fascination the play exerts even in our own time.

THE MAN WHO WAS THURSDAY

Type of work: Novel
Author: Gilbert Keith Chesterton (1874-1936)
Type of plot: Symbolic allegory
Time of plot: Early twentieth century
Locale: London
First published: 1908

What begins as a humorous parody of the intrigue-adventure tale, turns gradually into a vigorous, delightful, ambiguous allegorical fantasy that explores the relationship between man, society, nature, and god.

Many of the difficulties in reading *The Man Who Was Thursday* can be resolved by keeping the novel's subtitle, "A Nightmare," firmly in mind. After debating poetry and anarchy with his friend Lucian Gregory, Gabriel Syme is stimulated into a reverie in which symbolic events occur and, the adventure completed, he returns to reality. As long as one is aware of this dream structure, the apparently illogical and progressively symbolic actions should create no special difficulties—although it is unlikely that any two readers will arrive at precisely the same interpretation of the meaning behind Syme's encounter with the enigmatic Sunday.

Chesterton states in his *Autobiography* that *The Man Who Was Thursday* was the product of his intellectually and spiritually unsettled youth: "The whole story is a nightmare of things, not as they are, but as they seemed to the young half-pessimist of the 1890's." Initially, the major targets of the satire are the negative philosophies that seemed to him to dominate the intellectual atmosphere of the late Victorian period. As Chesterton suggested in the poetic dedication to E. C. Bentley, "Science announced nonentity and art admired decay."

Each of the "anarchists" embodies one possible perversion of intellect: Gogol (Tuesday) is the stereotypical anarchist; Professor de Worms (Friday), the perverted scholarly intelligence; Dr. Bull (Saturday), cold, scientific rationalism; Marquis de St. Eustache (Wednesday), decadent aristocracy and death worship; and the Secretary (Monday), political fanaticism and power madness. But this political satire changes into something else as each of the supposed anarchists is in turn exposed as an upholder of the moral order. "I thought it would be fun," Chesterton commented in an interview, "to make the tearing away of menacing masks reveal benevolence."

Syme, however, prefers the old world of clearly defined good and evil. However disruptive evil may be, it is preferable to moral and spiritual ambiguity. As he runs from a mob he believes to be in the service of Sunday (they turn out to be good citizens who think him to be an anarchist), Syme speculates on his new view of reality: "Was not everything, after all, like this bewildering woodland, this dance of dark and light? Everything only a glimpse, the glimpse always unforeseen, and always forgotten. . . . He had found the thing which the modern people call Impressionism, which is another name for that final skepticism which can find no floor to the universe." Thus, Syme's nightmare turns from a crusade against tangible evil to a search for reality itself and that reality—or absence of it—seems to be embodied in Sunday.

This search for reality ends, following a wildly comic chase after Sunday, in the fantastic, symbolic final scene of the book where Sunday "reveals" his identity—only to leave the meaning of the novel more ambiguous than ever. With all of the detectives dressed in elaborate costumes that suggest their days in "Genesis," Sunday identifies himself. "I am the Sabbath. I am the peace of God." The detectives, however, are not satisfied; they challenge him to explain and justify his behavior. But the skepticism of the believers is submerged by the negations of the true denier, Lucian Gregory, who presents himself as the authentic anarchist: "I am the destroyer. I would destroy the world if I could."

Gregory issues two challenges that bring the book to its ideological climax. He demands that the five detectives—representatives of human moral order —justify themselves in light of the fact that they have never suffered. Syme, speaking for Chesterton and humanity denies the anarchist's charge: "We have been broken upon the wheel," he retorts, "we have descended into Hell!" Then the challenge is put directly to Sunday: "Have you ever suffered?" Sunday answers with another question and brings the dream-fantasy to an end: "Can ye drink of the cup that I drink of?"

Once questioned about Sunday's identity, Chesterton said: "I think you can take him to stand for Nature as distinguished from God. Huge, boisterous, full of vitality, dancing with a hundred legs, bright with the glare of the sun, and at first sight, somewhat regardless of us and our desires." But when asked about Sunday's final question, Chesterton admitted that it "seems to mean that Sunday is God. That is the only serious note in the book. The face of Sunday changes, you tear off the mask of Nature and you find God."

Thus, the story that Chesterton began as a comic parody of the intrigue-adventure novel ends as a speculation on Divine Ambiguity. Chesterton suggests that the pessimism of the Anarchist is simply wrong, but the optimism of the Pantheist is inadequate. What remains is the God behind Nature, who embraces both limited views, and demands a faith and commitment beyond rationalization and speculation.

THE MAN WITHOUT A COUNTRY

Type of work: Short story
Author: Edward Everett Hale (1822-1909)
Type of plot: Historical romance
Time of plot: Nineteenth century
Locale: United States and the high seas
First published: 1863

Written originally as propaganda for the bitterly fought Ohio governor's campaign of 1863, The Man Without a Country *has become recognized as the classic expression of American nationalism. Cut off from his native land by a rash youthful statement and deed, Philip Nolan learns the true meaning of patriotism through a long and pathetic exile.*

Although Edward Everett Hale lived a long, vigorous, colorful life as a journalist, novelist, editor, historian, reformer, and Christian minister (including a stint as Senate chaplain), his present-day fame rests almost entirely on his first well-known publication, the short story called *The Man Without a Country.*

Hale was a young man when he first determined to write a fiction about an "exile" who longs for home, but it took the national trauma of the Civil War and, in particular, the 1863 Ohio gubernatorial campaign to crystallize his idea into *The Man Without a Country.* When one candidate proclaimed that he did not want to live in a country led by Abraham Lincoln, Hale became enraged and wrote his short, patriotic fiction as a political polemic. Ironically, Hale's effort had no effect whatsoever on the specific election, since its first publication in the *Atlantic* magazine was delayed until well after the event (the pro-Southern candidate was trounced anyway). Instead, it caught the public fancy and quickly became the great and popular artistic embodiment of American patriotic sentiment.

The factors behind its immediate impact are not hard to understand—the trauma of the Civil War, a roused and committed public opinion, the atmosphere of fervent nationalism and jingoism—but the reasons for its continued popularity are somewhat more difficult to pinpoint. It is easy enough to fault the story for thin characterization, vague scenes, sentimentality, and blatant didacticism, but such a judgment misses the nature and intention of the work. *The Man Without a Country* is a secular parable. It is not a realistic story that is spoiled by too much rhetoric; it is a didactic story—even a sermon— that is given color and vigor through the use of "realistic" narrative devices. In the final analysis, the greatness of *The Man Without a Country* lies in its perfect blending of rhetoric and storytelling.

Once the reader accepts Philip Nolan's unlikely sentence as fact, the rest of the story follows believably. The realism of the tale is enhanced by Hale's quasi-documentary approach. In the best nineteenth century tradition, the "reality" of the tale is certified by the manner of its telling. The narrator of the story claims to be an old naval officer recounting his experiences with Nolan. These experiences are given plausibility through the use of specific details: ships, places, historical events and Naval procedures. Hale is especially skillful in fitting Nolan's story into the real events surrounding the downfall of Aaron Burr. The narrator's reasonable explanation for the "suppression" of Nolan's story, coupled with the fact that Hale originally published the story anonymously, convinced nineteenth century readers that Philip Nolan was a real person; for years, even after Hale acknowledged the piece as his own fiction, the Navy Department received protests and inquiries on the matter. The device may have long ago been exposed as fictional, but it still gives the story a strong sense of reality and immediacy.

The action of the tale moves swiftly and easily. In each scene Nolan emerges from his mysterious cabin to confront another reminder of his exile —the reading of Walter Scott's poem on patriotism, a shipboard dance with an old female acquaintance, combat with a British ship, contact with a slave ship. The climax of the tale occurs when, as Nolan lies dying, the reader is finally admitted to his cabin and encounters a miniature America made out of bits and pieces. Admittedly the emotions evoked are sentimental and pathetic, rather than tragic, but as a distillation of nationalistic attitudes and evocation of patriotic emotions, *The Man Without a Country* unquestionably realizes the author's stated intention to create a "sensation story with a national moral" directed "towards the formation of a sentiment of love for the nation."

MANETTE SALOMON

Type of work: Novel
Authors: Edmond (1822-1896) and Jules (1830-1870) de Goncourt
Type of plot: Naturalism
Time of plot: Nineteenth century
Locale: Paris
First published: 1867

In Manette Salomon, *one of the best examples of the Goncourt brothers' mature fiction, the destructive potential of romantic love and bourgeois materialism on artistic creativity is explored through a minutely detailed examination of the Parisian art world and the careers of several painters.*

The idea of a novel about painters and their milieu first occurred to the Goncourt brothers fifteen years before they actually began work on the book which was to become *Manette Salomon.* Ever since their youth they had known painters and studied the art of painting. It was inevitable that they should devote a novel to the subject. The result was one of their finest and most controversial books.

Much of the novel is based on firsthand experience. The studio described is one which the brothers frequently visited; many of the characters are drawn from life. When it was published, the novel received mixed notices, although Flaubert wrote to the authors praising the skill of the work. Many critics then did not know how to interpret the realistic and rather gray tone of the picture of the bohemian life of the artists; but today, it is this very realism which fascinates the reader and which is the book's principal merit.

Two aspects of the novel seem curious to the reader a century later: the obvious anti-Semitism which runs through the book, and the extreme misogyny. Women are portrayed almost exclusively as grasping, predatory creatures, capable of exerting only negative influences on men in general and on artists in particular. Coriolis, Manette's victim, eventually sinks to the condition of a brute; he later states that celibacy is the only state that leaves an artist his freedom and power. Both casual love affairs and the "foolish happiness" of marriage are to be avoided. The melancholy and disgust which so dominated the personalities of the authors strongly color both the characters of this novel and the general tone of the narrative.

Manette Salomon presents an authentic, if prejudiced, picture of the artistic trends of the time, of the new vogue for Japanese art, the exhibitions, the rivalries, and the great salons. Although the character of Manette is not completely believable, the sketches of the artists and the portrayal of the historical moment in the Parisian art world guarantee the novel's continued importance.

MANFRED

Type of work: Poem
Author: George Gordon, Lord Byron (1788-1824)
Type of plot: Romantic tragedy
Time of plot: No set time
Locale: The Alps
First published: 1817

Manfred is Byron's first presentation of the revolt theme that became so central to his poetry. Stimulated by his own experiences and feelings—social ostracism, the outraged virtue of English society, separation from Augusta Leigh—Byron shaped them into a passionate, brooding study of the individual who cannot seek deliverance from any social institution, but must work out his own destiny in isolation.

Lame, handsome, and with a personality magnetic to both men and women, Byron lived three lives: adventurer, lover, and poet. His adventures included a shipwreck, a bout with fever, the swimming of the Hellespont and the rescue of a girl about to be drowned. His first speech in the House of Lords was in defense of the working man—a radical position at the time.

Byron the lover was dubbed "mad, bad and dangerous to know" by Lady Caroline Lamb, darling of London society. His presumed incestuous relationship with his half-sister Augusta Leigh caused society to turn against him. Later the sight of him could cause a riot.

Byron the poet is a major figure. *Childe Harold's Pilgrimage* and *Don Juan* are classics. *Manfred*, a shorter work, is important as a transition piece because it was written in Venice following *Childe Harold* and just prior to *Don Juan*.

Manfred is Byron's first great poem of revolt, spurred by an autobiographical urge. It is a rationalization of social ostracism, an explanation of the failure to cope with the outraged virtues of English society. Byron was perhaps also disturbed by separation from Augusta Leigh at the time.

The dramatic poem parallels Goethe's *Faust* with its wild mountain scenery and its theme of man learning to summon spirits. Manfred's adventures are symbolic ones, and the play is full of philosophical references. Unlike Faust, Manfred makes no contact with the devil. Therefore he dies free of hell's powers.

Manfred is a study of an isolated individual who cannot seek deliverance from any external social machinery, but who must work out his own destiny.

MANHATTAN TRANSFER

Type of work: Novel
Author: John Dos Passos (1896-1970)
Type of plot: Impressionistic realism
Time of plot: World War I
Locale: New York City
First published: 1925

It was in Manhattan Transfer *that John Dos Passos first developed the deliberately episodic, fragmentary, almost cinematic techniques that were to characterize his masterpiece, the* USA *trilogy. In this novel he interlaces the stories of several different individuals, representing all social and economic levels, to dramatize both particular fates and the disjointed, frenzied nature of modern urban life.*

Dos Passos is commonly regarded as one of the most interesting and accurate commentators on American life in the mid-twentieth century. Like many of his writer friends he went to Europe during World War I and was deeply influenced by modernist experimentalism in the arts, in the Paris of the 1920's. His first novel to attract notice, *Three Soldiers* (1921), treated the wartime experience. In his next novel to gain recognition, *Manhattan Transfer* (1925), he turned his attention entirely to American life as it is centered in New York City. *Manhattan Transfer* is an experimental novel and not an entirely successful one. It points the way toward Dos Passos' greatest achievement, the 1937 trilogy *USA (The 42nd Parallel, 1919, The Big Money)*.

In *Manhattan Transfer* Dos Passos tried to capture the spirit of America as reflected in a multitude of characters living and working in Manhattan. Under the influence of cubist painting, imagist poetry, and Joyce's *Ulysses,* Dos Passos decided to present a series of sharply rendered fragments from the experiences of his characters. The novel really has no central character and no plot. It is an attempt to describe *the whole of society* in a fragmented documentary fashion. Some readers will be frustrated by this approach but when the enormity of Dos Passos' objective is seen, perhaps an appreciation of his attempt will be felt.

Three characters stand out: Ellen Thatcher becomes a successful actress and entertainer. She is a golden girl who lures men but who remains ultimately unsatisfied. In George Baldwin, we have a conventional portrait of a young lawyer who rises through sharp practices to political power. The newspaperman Jimmy Herf is perhaps the only character in the novel who escapes the destructive vortex of the city. The fragmented nature of Dos Passos' narrative suggests a raw, ugly, vigorous, and highly-charged urban life in which wholeness and continuity are almost impossible to achieve.

MANON LESCAUT

Type of work: Novel
Author: Abbé Prévost (Antoine François Prévost d'Exiles, 1697-1763)
Type of plot: Sentimental romance
Time of plot: 1700
Locale: France and New Orleans
First published: 1731

Manon Lescaut *is an early example of the sentimental romance and as such it has had a considerable influence on romantic fiction in different literatures. Despite its dubious morality, sentimental excesses, and illogical plottings, the novel remains quite readable due to the stark simplicity of the writing and the complexity and variety of the characterizations.*

L'Abbé Antoine François Prévost d'Exiles led nearly as adventurous a life as the Chevalier des Grieux. Some critics have pointed to parallels in the lives of author and character, suggesting that *Manon Lescaut* is at least partially an autobiographical novel. Whatever the case, Prévost was by turns a Jesuit novice, a soldier, and a priest of the Benedictine order; however, he frequently took unauthorized secular leaves from his religious duties, which resulted in the civil penalty of exile (thus explaining his addition of "d'Exiles" to his surname). These periods of absence and exile were Prévost's most productive literary periods in an immensely prolific writing career. Prévost is credited with forty-seven translations—among them, Samuel Richardson's novels *Pamela, Clarissa,* and *Sir Richard Grandison* (all significant for their treatment of virtue and vice, a crucial theme in *Manon Lescaut*)—and sixty-six original works of his own, including a twenty-volume periodical, a seventeen-volume travelogue, memoirs, and novels.

The series *Mémoires d'un homme de qualité* (1728-1731) is variously calculated to contain six or seven novels, depending upon whether or not *Manon Lescaut* is included. One school of thought includes *Manon Lescaut* because it is, like the other six novels, a romance, while another school excludes it on the grounds that it far surpasses the other six novels in literary quality. The novel is certainly exceptional; within the short span of forty years, it inspired three operas—Auber's *Manon Lescaut* (1858), Massenet's *Manon* (1884), and Puccini's *Manon Lescaut* (1893). In addition, Prévost issued the novel in a revised edition—testimony to its popularity and the author's conviction of its importance. The first edition (1731) was substantially emended and much improved in the 1753 second edition, which eliminated a great deal of superfluous language.

Manon Lescaut is an important novel because it shaped a substantial portion of subsequent romantic fiction; however, it does have intrinsic qualities of its own which recommend it beyond historical precedent as literature in its own right. Structurally, it has elements of the "frame story." The narration begins in the first person by an unidentified lawyer—a device to lend credibility—of apparently mature years who recounts a meeting with the Chevalier de Grieux and Manon Lescaut as they are en route to America. The lawyer befriends the pair but hears nothing about them until two years later, when he chances to meet de Grieux, who then recounts in minute detail (first-person narrative) the entire tale of his and Manon's misadventures. This "frame story" device is at least as old as medieval literature, taking its cue from Boccaccio's *Decameron* and Chaucer's *Canterbury Tales* but perhaps even traceable to Ovid. Yet in the hands of Prévost, the tale is stark and spare, containing no wasted words, no didacticism, and no moral over-simplification. Characterizations are quite complex; characters display good and bad, strong and weak in equal measure. Such economical style is unique for Prévost, who was otherwise given to rococo exaggerations and helps to account for the novel's superiority over the *Mémoires d'un homme de qualité*.

MAN'S FATE

Type of work: Novel
Author: André Malraux (1895-1967)
Type of plot: Social criticism
Time of plot: 1927
Locale: Shanghai, China
First published: 1933

Based in part on Malraux's firsthand experience as an agitator during the Chinese Communists' failed revolution of 1927, Man's Fate *is a powerful, if consciously fragmentary, vision of modern political and social upheaval. In it the author explores the nature, meaning, and morality of individual commitment and action in times of revolutionary change.*

In this novel, depicting the aborted Communist Revolution in China in 1927, André Malraux presents three types of revolutionaries. Each is attracted to the revolution for different reasons and reacts to the events in a distinctive manner.

Ch'en, the terrorist, is shown in the opening scene of the novel in the process of committing his first murder. This experience is so intense that he feels himself separated from those who have been killed. His sense of isolation leads him to believe that individual acts of terrorism are superior to any other form of revolutionary action. He ultimately comes to the conclusion that the only way to have the revolution is to kill Chiang. He initially attempts to perform this act with the aid of two comrades, but the attempt fails. He then decides to perform the deed alone. Ironically, he is killed while throwing himself with a grenade on a car he believes to be occupied by Chiang. Although Chiang is not in the car, Ch'en has died a death consistent with his beliefs, a death that has given his life meaning.

Kyo is the theorist who finds it difficult to reconcile his belief in Marxist theory with the realities of the revolution. For example, although he theoretically believes that no person can be the property of another and that love is free, he is obviously jealous when his wife, May, tells him that she has slept with another man. Kyo is drawn to the revolution because of his belief in the need for human dignity. He loses faith in Communist theory when he finds out (during a trip to Hankow) that the leaders of the Party are willing to betray the people on orders from Moscow. Kyo believes that Communist theory is only of value if it helps the masses to live a more dignified life; he cannot reconcile his beliefs with the political machinations that confront him. During a brief stay in jail, he sees human beings submitted to the most degrading humiliation. When offered a choice of life or death, he chooses death with dignity rather than life with humiliation. His death, although very different from Ch'en's, is consistent with his life. He chooses his death, committing suicide by taking cyanide.

Katov is the most experienced of the three for he had fought in the Russian Revolution. Unlike Ch'en who cherished his solitude, Katov cherishes his solidarity with his comrades. Like the others, his death is consistent with his life. Although he, like Kyo, has a cyanide pill, Katov chooses to share his pill with two young, frightened comrades. Since there is only enough cyanide to kill two men, his gift of the capsule is the supreme sacrifice, for Katov must now face death by being thrown alive into the boiler of a train engine. But he believes his sacrifice gives his life meaning, for through his sacrifice he has achieved the fraternity for which he had fought in the revolution.

Although these three men are very different, they are similar in joining the revolution in order to give meaning to their lives. Each acts as a revolutionary and dies as a revolutionary in a manner consistent with his beliefs.

MANSFIELD PARK

Type of work: Novel
Author: Jane Austen (1775-1817)
Type of plot: Social criticism
Time of plot: Early nineteenth century
Locale: Northamptonshire, England
First published: 1814

Mansfield Park is essentially a "Cinderella story" in which the heroine, Fanny Price, wins happiness after a long and demeaning series of experiences as the "poor relation" at Mansfield Park. Fanny wins the love of Edmund Bertram and the approbation of his family because she embodies those virtues which Jane Austen thought most valuable: charity, loyalty, honesty, self-knowledge, and plain goodness.

Despite the centrality of the theme of courtship in Austen's work, *Mansfield Park* is not primarily about a man and woman discovering their compatibility; this is not a novel constructed solely on the premise that "a single man in possession of a good fortune must be in want of a wife," the "universal truth" that launches *Pride and Prejudice.* Rather, *Mansfield Park* is a book about a place (as its title implies), and that place proves to be a touchstone for social and personal values, a haven of comfort and permanence, what Lionel Trilling, one of Austen's most distinguished critics, has called the "Great Good Place."

Fanny is drawn with little charm, but this is done primarily to underscore her outstanding characteristic, which is character itself. Although charm temporarily rules at Mansfield Park, in the wit and grace of the Crawfords and in the mode and spirit of the "theatrical," its beguiling attractions are put in a sober perspective with Sir Thomas' return. Eventually, Fanny's essential honesty and plainness, which initially relegates her to the background at Mansfield Park, become the very traits that identify her with Mansfield Park's values.

Henry Crawford first simply pursues Fanny as a sport, but he eventually is enamored of her plain goodness. Sir Thomas misjudges her and orders indefinite exile, but after his return Fanny seems to him the truest "daughter" Mansfield Park has produced. Edmund is finally cured of his superficiality by the example of Mary Crawford's indifference to his sister's fate, and it is only then that he proves worthy of Fanny. Jane Austen has so constructed the novel that her seemingly passive heroine reverses social fate, produces a change of heart in a Lothario, and indirectly restores intelligence to a weak-minded lover. Evidently, Austen did not believe that the stability of a home had everything to do with charm.

THE MARBLE FAUN

Type of work: Novel
Author: Nathaniel Hawthorne (1804-1864)
Type of plot: Allegorical romance
Time of plot: Mid-nineteenth century
Locale: Rome
First published: 1860

In his last completed novel, The Marble Faun, *Hawthorne transported his lifelong preoccupations with sin, alienation, and moral responsibility from Puritan New England to Rome, the center of culture, art, and Catholicism. The book is a study of the birth of the human conscience, the consequences of a crime committed by a simple, pagan spirit who, through his impulsive deed, experiences guilt, suffering, and finally, regeneration. Although the novel is too ambiguous and chaotic to rank with Hawthorne's best, the ambitiousness of its insights, complexity of its characterizations, and power of several separate scenes give a lasting impact.*

Throughout his writing career, Nathaniel Hawthorne was preoccupied with the theme of man's fall into sin and mortality. Symbolic representations of Adam and Eden underlie much of his most exciting work, so it should be appropriate that he should turn to this theme again in his last major romance. Unfortunately, the reality of the work does not come up to its promise, and Hawthorne's use of the theme of the fall of man is far less skillful here than in some of the earlier stories. His usually subtle symbolic method turns into a somewhat heavy-handed allegory, and the rather slight and simple story is too often padded with descriptions of Rome and its art (frequently lifted with little alteration from his notebooks) which have almost no organic relationship to the theme of the novel. But, even though the weakest of Hawthorne's major romances, *The Marble Faun* is not without redeeming features, and its faults as well as its virtues teach us about Hawthorne's view of the world. Most accessible through its major characters, the work illustrates several of Hawthorne's most typical character types, and through their interactions dramatizes some of the themes which most preoccupied him.

The story and its theme most particularly center around Donatello, the contemporary counterpart of the Faun of Praxiteles. For Hawthorne, Donatello's faun-like qualities are associated with the innocence and animalistic nature of man before his fall brought him to the knowledge of sin and death. Donatello's country estate is a counterpart to Eden and suggests a pagan and pre-Christian paradise, bypassed by time, in which primordial innocence has been kept alive. But, though touching in its childlike qualities, Donatello's innocence is not one of which Hawthorne can approve. Because it lacks the knowledge of sin which is part of man's humanity, it is sub-human and cannot comprehend the real nature of the world. Even more importantly, salva-

tion is a direct result of sin, so Donatello, existing outside the world of sin
and death, is not a candidate for God's greatest gift to man. Thus, when
Miriam, acting the part of an Eve figure, tempts Donatello to murder, she is
the instrument bringing about his fall into humanity. The irony of Hawthorne's
scheme is obvious, as the "fall" is in fact a rise from the sub-human condition.
This story is a classic example of the idea of the "fortunate fall" which
argues that the fall was necessary so man could achieve salvation from his
sins. Thus, the price Donatello will be called upon to pay in guilt, suffering,
and shame is no more than the price of his initiation into the human race
with its blessing of salvation as well as its cost in pain.

The two women in *The Marble Faun* are typical of the extremes of Hawthorne's fictional women. Miriam, one of the dark ladies who frequently
appear in his works, represents one moral extreme, while Hilda, whose innocence and religious faith are everywhere manifest, represents the other. Ironically, though, each of them serves as a salvation figure by becoming the
instrument of humanizing the man with whom she is associated. Miriam's
temptation of Donatello and her own ambiguous past with its suggestions of
sin and guilt define her as an Eve figure tempting Donatello to the sin which
will humanize him. Hilda, presented in terms of such innocence and virtue
as to be almost unreal, is a different sort of salvation figure. In her case, she
brings Kenyon from his cold isolation into the human race by awakening his
ability to love. Ironically, Miriam is the more appealing of the two women
for most readers because of her interesting complexities of character, but it is
clearly Hilda who represents for Hawthorne the moral standard the novel is
meant to affirm. But, by making her too incorruptible a symbol of Christian
goodness, Hawthorne has also made her so one-dimensional as to strain our
credibility.

The character in the novel closest to Hawthorne himself is the sculptor,
Kenyon. Hawthorne refers to him at one point as "a man of marble," and
implies that such a description fits his moral nature as well as his profession.
Like the light and dark ladies, and the pre-lapsarian Adamic figure represented
by Donatello, Kenyon is a recurrent type in Hawthorne's work. For Hawthorne, the artist—as well as the scientist who frequently appears in his works
—by his very nature tends to isolate himself from humanity and become a
cold observer who, without emotion of his own, exploits others' lives for his
own ends. In his isolation, the artist suppresses what is human in himself for
his art until he, in effect, loses his soul to it. Though his moral condition does
not exactly parallel Donatello's, Kenyon is equally outside the human community, and he too is a candidate for salvation. It is Hilda who saves Kenyon,
not through a dramatic temptation to sin, but through awakening that which
is most human in his own heart—the ability to love. Though it may strain
credibility to imagine Hilda as functioning within a love relationship—she
seems too ethereal for so mundane a situation—Hawthorne's message of the

redeeming power of love and sympathy is clear enough.

While the flaws of *The Marble Faun* are obvious faults in the total effect the novel achieves, the individual components of the work nevertheless save it from obscurity. The character types here presented are among the most important of Hawthorne's figures, while the dual themes of the "fortunate fall" and crime and punishment place the work within the great western tradition which deals with those topics, and it does bear comparison to them. Further, the setting of the novel in Rome anticipates the European novels of Henry James and the international novel which has remained a part of our literary tradition since James popularized it. Thus, though not a great novel, *The Marble Faun* is a significant work, and as such continues to hold a solid place in the American literary tradition.

William E. Grant

MARCHING ON

Type of work: Novel
Author: James Boyd (1888-1944)
Type of plot: Historical romance
Time of plot: The Civil War period
Locale: North Carolina
First published: 1927

Marching On *combines the romantic story of a poor boy's persistent love for a rich girl with a naturalistic treatment of infantry combat during the Civil War. Although the mixture is unsuccessful—the love affair is too implausible for a realistic novel and the war detail undercuts the romance—Boyd does succeed in depicting the spirit of the soldiers who fought heroically for a lost cause.*

Published two years after *Drums,* his first novel, *Marching On* continues to explore the emerging identity of America's common man. The heroes of both works have the same last name, Fraser, although Boyd never suggests a family connection. Whereas the hero of his first novel, John, comes from a simpler background than the aristocratic types with whom he consorts, the social gap between James in *Marching On* and the Prevost family is much wider. The second novel, despite the fact that its plot reads like a conventional romance (poor boy yearns for rich girl; goes off to battle and wins her love), is actually sharper in its social criticism than the first.

Drums pulls social classes together to face a common enemy, the British during the American Revolution. *Marching On* underscores the social injustice of the Plantation system during the Civil War period. As a result, James Fraser's dedicated support of the Confederate cause is tragic and ironic in contrast to John Fraser's personal fulfillment in the cause of the Revolution some eighty-five years earlier. James suffers imprisonment and endless agonies as a foot soldier in defense of a social system that cuts him off from Stewart, the woman he loves. To compare the naturalistic description of James and his fellow soldiers caught up in their endless marching with the heroic description of the marching men of the Revolutionary army at the close of *Drums* is to focus very clearly on the major difference between the two works.

The romance between James and Stewart has been dismissed as socially impossible during Civil War days. In fairness to Boyd, it must be acknowledged that in this instance he attempted a form of historical symbolism rather than historical realism. The Civil War *did* result in a social leveling of the South that freed both landowners and white yeomen from the dehumanizing effect of insurmountable social barriers.

MARDI

Type of work: Novel
Author: Herman Melville (1819-1891)
Type of plot: Symbolic allegory
Time of plot: Mid-nineteenth century
Locale: The islands of the Western Pacific
First published: 1849

Mardi *represented a double turning point in Herman Melville's career. On the one hand, it was his first attempt to deal with serious social, philosophical, and moral issues in a quasi-symbolic narrative form, and, as such, it prefigures* Moby Dick. *On the other, it was this book that lost him the audience he had entertained with his earlier sea adventures,* Typee *and* Omoo. *From this point on Melville's popularity rapidly declined as the profundity of his work increased.*

So ambitiously widespread and uncharted was Herman Melville's own quest for ideas and knowledge during the writing of this book, that it is impossible to extract from *Mardi* any consistent attitude toward religion, government, art, or the nature of man generally. Filled with recondite allusions to historical as well as topical events, and exhibiting a mixture of philosophies ranging from Stoicism to Transcendentalism, *Mardi* reflects the multitude of concerns Melville had as an artist and as a man. Most conspicuous, perhaps, is his mixed, unresolved feelings in *Mardi* toward popular ideas of his times regarding the success of democracy and the primacy of the free individual.

Melville is cautious in *Mardi,* for example, about too easily taking for granted the achievements of democracy in the United States, or in too readily accepting its confident assumptions about the basic nature of man. During the late 1840's most Americans were loudly jingoistic; they took pride in congratulating themselves on the apparent successes of the democratic experiment in America and in glorifying, under the influence of Emersonian individualism, the nature of the free, independent man. But in the chapters in *Mardi* on Vivenza (the United States) and Dominora (England), Melville satirically challenges these popular assumptions. He points out the continuance of the institution of slavery in the United States, cautioning his fellow countrymen that a democracy may actually be less free than a monarchy, especially when what is called freedom is only a disguise for man's misuse of individual authority and responsibility.

Melville insists in the chapter on Vivenza that freedom is not just political, and that true freedom implies also some adherence to outside authority as well. As Babbalanja tells Media, "None need a king; but many need a ruler."

Hence, Taji's futile quest after the symbolic Yillah is a further example of Melville's mixed attitude toward the integrity of the wholly free individual. Taji's independent pursuit of the Absolute Truth represented by Yillah is presented ambiguously by Melville as being both foolhardy and heroic. It is

better, Taji insists, "to sink in boundless deeps, than float over vulgar shoals."
On the other hand, his fate at the end of *Mardi,* as pursuer and as pursued
"over an endless sea," casts doubt upon the value as well as the validity of
his self-reliance.

This fact, taken together with the chronological position of *Mardi* in
Melville's works, suggests his growing awareness at the time of writing *Mardi*
of the moral and metaphysical complexities of man's universe. Hence, while
he saw the necessity for man's complete freedom in seeking truth, he nevertheless also recognized his limitations and need for outside authority as well.

MARIA CHAPDELAINE

Type of work: Novel
Author: Louis Hémon (1880-1913)
Type of plot: Regional romance
Time of plot: Early twentieth century
Locale: Northern Quebec
First published: 1916

This realistic, unsentimental, yet deeply moving account of a young girl's growing up in the arduous environment of Lake St. John in northern Quebec had astounding success in the early 1920's and has been acknowledged as a classic of French Canadian literature.

Reading *Maria Chapdelaine,* one would assume that Louis Hémon was a native of northern Quebec; surely only long familiarity with the weather, the land, the people, and their speech and customs could have prepared him for the moving descriptions in the novel and for his realistic portrayal of pioneer characters. Actually, however, he lived in the northern wilderness for only a few months, and his earlier articles and sports stories for French newspapers, written while he lived in England, scarcely seem predecessors of the novel that was to become a classic of French Canadian literature. Perhaps it was because he *was* a foreigner with an observant eye, an ear for dialect, and a deep admiration for the simple folk of the Lake St. John country that he could write so convincingly.

As a longtime urban dweller, Hémon could well picture the sad disillusionment of the educated, city-bred Frenchman and his two sons who had fled the city with romantic anticipation of breathing the fresh air and enjoying the beauty of the great forests of the north. Hémon had learned that nature in this country could be harsh and deadly as well as kind and lovely. He had felt the bitter cold of the Canadian winter, he had suffered the bites of black-flies and mosquitoes in warm weather, and he had seen what drought can do to a farmer's fields. He had learned also that to survive in the wilderness one need not be literate (many of the French Canadians at that time could neither read nor write), but that one must be strong and tough.

Hémon's knowledge of the people he was writing about and his sense of proportion kept him from descending into sentimentality in emotional scenes. He pictures the burden of grief that Maria bears after the death of François Paradis, but then shows how she bravely puts this grief behind her and determines to accept the challenge of wilderness life with Eutrope Gagnon. When Mrs. Chapdelaine begins to suffer from her undiagnosed agony, the reader shudders inwardly, but Hémon makes no Dickensian effort to draw tears; he portrays briefly and simply the relief of the family as the wife and mother is finally released from her torture to attain the heavenly home that they are devoutly assured she has earned.

MARIA MAGDALENA

Type of work: Drama
Author: Friedrich Hebbel (1813-1863)
Type of plot: Domestic realism
Time of plot: Nineteenth century
Locale: Germany
First presented: 1844

Freidrich Hebbel was the first important dramatist to attempt to grant heroic stature to middle-class characters in a realistic domestic context. In Maria Magdalena, *his finest example of this new bourgeois tragedy, we find the tragedy of the individual fused with a type of realism that was new to all literature of the time and especially the drama.*

Maria Magdalena marks a turning point in German literature, as the first "bourgeois tragedy." Not until Hebbel had there been a play which confined itself to this social stratum, and which developed the tragedy out of conditions and attitudes peculiar to it. Hebbel, who was a disciple of Hegel, developed an elaborate theory of tragedy, embracing all of creation, which he saw as engaged in a gigantic process as individuals clash against one another, each an element in the development of the whole. His dramas represent clashes between an individual and the prevailing mores of an age, which have become institutionalized and rigid. The dramas stand thus at turning points in the development of mankind, when an old system is about to give way to a new, yet still possesses the power to destroy those who represent the new.

In *Maria Magdalena* traditional Christian morality, represented by Anthony, has petrified into an unbending code of honor. Master Anthony is not an evil man—he forgives his debtors—but in dealing with Karl and Clara, he is rigid and fanatical in his demands for unwavering virtue. The mother, too, though gentler, dies of shock when her son is arrested. In this framework, Clara, who has sinned, but who needs compassion and understanding, is caught between the evil of Leonard and the unyielding virtue of her father. Even the secretary, who loves her, feels obligated to challenge Leonard to a duel before he can marry her. Thus, a many-sided conflict arises, which destroys everyone. Had anyone had such compassion as Christ showed to Mary Magdalene, the tragedy would have been averted: this is where Anthony's Christianity is revealed as sterile, loveless, and inadequate to the needs of his family. He is left alone and uncomprehending, while the dead Clara represents the hope for a coming age of that compassion and love which is true Christianity.

MARIANNE

Type of work: Novel
Author: Pierre Carlet de Chamblain de Marivaux (1688-1763)
Type of plot: Novel of manners
Time of plot: Late seventeenth century
Locale: France
First published: 1731-1741

Although episodic, fragmentary, and incomplete, Marianne *must be ranked as one of the most important precursors of the modern novel. In this narrative Marivaux presents the everyday situations and lives of ordinary people in careful, realistic detail with a style that is remarkable for its subtleties, its precise but unusual and mannered diction, and its refinement of phrase.*

The renewal of French interest in *Marianne* is slowly bringing this long-neglected novel to the attention of scholars in the English-speaking world. *Marianne* was one of the most important influences on the English novel of the eighteenth century. It was an immediate popular success, appearing in mid-year of 1736, only five years after its first publication in France. The first translation was done by Mrs. Collyer, about whom little is known. Her translation was a very good one, when one views those parts of her novel which are in fact translations from the French. Unfortunately she felt compelled to finish the incomplete manuscript, resulting in the readers of *Marianne, or The Virtuous Orphan* being exposed to more than Marivaux had written. Mrs. Collyer's translation remains the standard one, primarily because of her exceptional gift of translating in a style and vocabulary which closely approximates the French of Marivaux. She understood his style and method so well, in fact, that for decades the English audience read *The Virtuous Orphan* without the least suspicion that it was not entirely the work of Marivaux.

One reason for her success may be the episodic and erratic nature of Marivaux's work in the original. The novel was thirteen years in the writing which accounts for some inconsistencies in the body of the narrative. Also, the epistolary structure is weak as Marivaux sees it. He was aware of the form and its limitations, and his novels reflect all the difficulties which the genre developed. Yet he produced a novel of great importance, flawed and incomplete as it is.

Marivaux defies classification. While portions of the novel do indicate some influence from the picaresque, primarily from Le Sage's works, *Marianne* is not a picaresque novel. Nor is it Romanesque, though it does bear superficial resemblance to many other works of that form. What can be said of *Marianne* is that the main character is a remarkable breakthrough for the cause of characterization in the novel, and that Marivaux managed to create Marianne through a highly realistic novel, though most of the characteristics of the realistic novel as we know it in the twentieth century are missing from this early example. The student interested in reading Marivaux's novel in translation is advised to use an annotated copy of Mrs. Collyer's translation, which still provides the most accurate facsimile of Marivaux's original.

MARIUS THE EPICUREAN

Type of work: Novel
Author: Walter Pater (1839-1894)
Type of plot: Philosophical romance
Time of plot: Second century
Locale: The Roman Empire
First published: 1885

Marius the Epicurean *was Pater's answer to those who had misunderstood his views on art and philosophy. It is, in great part, a fictional rendering of Pater's own struggle for a philosophical position, and the personality of Marius is a reflection of the author himself. The volume is also an appreciation of the culture of the second century of the Christian era in Roman Italy.*

In his portrayal of Marius the Epicurean, Pater shows what might have happened during Marcus Aurelius' reign to a young man of Marius' sort. Unconsciously, with precision and accuracy, he also delineates the nature of a middle-aged, middle-class, bachelor-scholar about the year 1880. And, because Pater thought that the purpose of higher education was to teach art and poetry, he incorporates this philosophy into Marius' development. Perhaps this is the reason that *Marius the Epicurean* contains more poetry—not from books and pictures, but from life as Pater saw it—than any of his works.

The setting of Marius' spiritual journey is chiefly in Rome. It is in this, "the most religious city of the world," that we are given glimpses of many various religions: the religion of Numa, the religion of Isis, the medical cult of Aesculapius, and the new Christianity. It is by mentioning these various religions and having Marius influenced by them that Pater is, from the beginning, able to present a deeply serious tone to the work.

Having chosen the appropriate setting, Pater selects from history, philosophy, art, and literature of the age, characters which best suited his purpose. Such characters as Lucius, Apuleius, Cornelius, Fronto, Marcus Aurelius, and Lucien are leading figures in the Latin literature of Marius' day. The Greek physician Galen is also introduced, and the future patron saint of Christian music, Cecilia, is presented. Ideas of Pliny, Tibullus, Lucretius, Horace, and Vergil are sprinkled throughout the book, and add to the overall philosophical and literary atmosphere. With the imaginary life of Marius as his framework, Pater is able to present what is to him the most important and impressive ideas of the period.

Like Carlyle's *Sartor Resartus, Marius the Epicurean* is one of those not-easily classified books. From its opening pages one is aware of an unusual reading experience. Void of the kind of intricate complexities of Carlyle, Pater's writing is often obscure, but in a more leisurely and poetic manner. (For Pater's lengthy views on style, one should consult his *Appreciation with an Essay on Style.*) Whereas many great Victorian literary artists tended to scream loudly their various doctrines, Pater, usually in a calm, almost somber tone, whispers and murmurs to his audience. It is because each phrase is intricately fashioned that *Marius the Epicurean* is often referred to not only as a philosophical romance (rather than a novel), but also as a prose-poem. The many details of the story are easily forgotten, but the overall tonal effect of the work remains. It is not the figures, lingering in misty shadows, that capture the attention; the philosophy, aesthetics, and religious doctrines are not easily associated with any concrete individual or personality. The characters serve mainly as a vehicle through which Pater can fulfill his major purpose—exposing his listener to the intellectual and philosophical timbre of ancient Rome.

MARKET HARBOROUGH

Type of work: Novel
Author: George J. Whyte-Melville (1821-1878)
Type of plot: Sporting romance
Time of plot: Nineteenth century
Locale: England
First published: 1861

Although a thin narrative thread is provided by John Standish Sawyer's leisurely courtship of Cecilia Dove and his efforts to win the steeplechase race, Market Harborough *is basically a series of realistic hunting episodes fastened together by the presence of the same character.*

As a forerunner of Siegfried Sassoon's *Memoirs of a Fox-Hunting Man* and Caroline Gordon's *Aleck Maury, Sportsman, Market Harborough* stands at the front of a distinguished, if minor, literary tradition. Like both later novels, the book's interest lies in the skill with which the author portrays the hunting scenes and the enthusiasm of the principal characters. The milieu of the novel is limited, but within its confines the book provides a vivid picture of a particular world and range of interests. John Standish Sawyer presents a unique picture of a kind of individual seldom seen any more; after two world wars, the world does not seem able to afford men who devote their entire lives to fox hunting. Yet, Sawyer is a likable man, for all his narrowness, and one is not sorry when, at the end of the book, it is apparent that he is to continue his life devoted to hunting.

Market Harborough is a particularly English novel, its tone suggesting an approach to life that would be difficult to find elsewhere. There is a gentleness and stately grace to the life portrayed in the narrative, a stylized approach to existence that at times seems almost unreal. The horses, the hounds, and the fashionable hunters have nothing whatever to do with the real problems of the world. Children may be working twelve hours a day in London factories, but one finds no sign of that fact within the pages of *Market Harborough*. This novel of 1861 (the year of *Great Expectations*) is far removed from the world of Charles Dickens' novels, yet its picture of its limited scene is authentic and interesting. The heroine, Cecilia Dove, begins as a picture-post-card figure, but develops into a girl filled with life. The strange courtship of John Sawyer and Cecilia Dove is described with a great deal of charm. Perhaps the book is not to everyone's taste, but it possesses a distinct, if specialized, place in English literature, and will always find its devoted readers.

MARMION

Type of work: Poem
Author: Sir Walter Scott (1771-1832)
Type of plot: Semihistorical romance
Time of plot: Early sixteenth century
Locale: The Scottish Border
First published: 1808

Even though one of Scott's best-known dramatic poems, Marmion *lacks the perfection of detail that marks his best work. Hurriedly written, largely unrevised and unpolished, and burdened with a series of irrelevant introductions to each canto,* Marmion *frequently seems forced and melodramatic—although it does possess much of the lyrical beauty and brisk action which we associate with Scott's metrical romances.*

Well known for his ability to depict the action and glory of battle and human turmoil in historical novels such as *Old Mortality* and *The Heart of Midlothian,* Sir Walter Scott was able to do the same thing even better in narrative poetry. Oliver Elton *(Survey of English Literature from 1780-1830,* Vol. I, 1912) writes that "for actual fighting, for duels to the death, for downright taunting and 'flyting,' Scott's verse is a better vehicle than his prose."

The passionate thrust of his octosyllabic rhymes carries the action forward at an exciting pace. Ears accustomed to the rhymed heroic couplets of Alexander Pope were startled by the tonal versatility of Scott's verse. Not only did it capture the color and speed of battle, as in the famous description of the fighting on Flodden Field in Canto IV of *Marmion,* but it also managed panoramic and stately effects such as the scene painting in the introductory letter to Canto I and the view to Edinburg as seen by Marmion over Blackford Hill.

Unfortunately, the descriptive passages in *Marmion* often appear merely decorative—ostentatious victories in verse technique. The plot is disjointed and characterization is very weak. Roughly similar to *Ivanhoe* (both works include an unscrupulous knight, a pilgrim guide who is no pilgrim, chivalric combat between the rivals), the plot of *Marmion* turns on the stock device of a forged letter; the introductory epistles give us, as David Daiches (*Sir Walter Scott and His World,* London, 1971) says "an account of the development of his [Scott's] sensibility," but they do not exactly propel the cumbersome parts of the story forward. Marmion himself is a pasteboard villain; he scowls to order like the melodramatic antagonist of a cheap Gothic tale. He affects but has none of the genuine Satanism of the dark heroes in Byron's verse tales that followed in the years shortly after the publication of *Marmion.* Nevertheless, the sheer vigor, ease, and drive of the verse is impressive. It drove Thomas Hardy to describe *Marmion* as the most Homeric poem in the language.

MARRIAGE À LA MODE

Type of work: Drama
Author: John Dryden (1631-1700)
Type of plot: Comedy of manners
Time of plot: Seventeenth century
Locale: Sicily
First presented: 1673

Marriage á la Mode *is a curious mixture of heroic tragedy and comedy of manners. One plot concerns the seventeenth century playful attitude toward married love; another, court intrigue and romance. Since the two plots are only superficially connected, the play lacks artistic unity. Skillful characterization, however, especially in the comic plot, has saved the work from oblivion.*

In his comedy *Marriage à la Mode,* John Dryden illustrates that view of life prevalent in Restoration drama which sees man as a creature of appetite constantly searching for new sensations and always battling to steal or conquer other men's property. In both of the play's dual plots, one concerned with romantic conquest and the other with court intrigue, the characters play out this view of life through their actions; but in the end, Dryden leads them to a very different conclusion from the one no doubt expected by a Restoration audience.

All the partners in the romantic plot share the belief that a desired love conquest loses its attractiveness the moment it is possessed. In their pursuit of women, Rhodophil and Palamede are like sated, jaded gourmets in frantic search of new delicacies to please their palates. They are caught in a dilemma which seems to have no solution: if love depends on desire, how can one love one's partner when desire for them has been satisfied? Unable to solve this riddle, the characters have accepted the proposition that extra-marital affairs are a must; the opening song in the play states this premise—no one should feel bound to a silly marriage vow once passion has cooled off in the relationship. Operating on this assumption, the characters hopelessly entangle themselves in a confusion of affairs: Palamede, engaged to Melantha, tries to seduce Rhodophil's wife Doralice, while Rhodophil is busily securing Melantha as his mistress. Their exploits are described in a series of images relating sex to appetite, sport, war, and stolen property, as each fights to conquer other people's partners while safeguarding his own from like treatment.

Similarly, the plot dealing with court politics is pervaded with the same belief in the attraction of the forbidden and in man's need to dominate. Melantha understands the social hierarchy within which she is battling to ascend, and she knows that manners and dress are the signs by which different classes or castes are identified. Thus she constantly assimiliates the ever-changing modes of dress and behavior currently in vogue; she wears the latest fashion as faithfully as she parrots the newest gossip or adheres to the most recent opinion of Leonidas. And when she feels discouraged in the daily battle for popularity at court, she can always comfort herself with her vast moral superiority to those lowly creatures not connected with the palace —the women who live in the city, or worse, in the country.

By the end of *Marriage à la Mode,* however, Dryden has come full circle from the proposal stated in the opening song, by showing that a life of indulged appetites can only lead to satiety and discomfort. Miserable and at the point of fighting, Palamede and Rhodophil agree to halt competition and abide by rules of mutual respect for each other's property. The message of the play is that marital love and peace are possible if man can curb his greed for greener pastures and enjoy the estate at home.

THE MARRIAGE OF FIGARO

Type of work: Drama
Author: Pierre Augustin Caron de Beaumarchais (1732-1799)
Type of plot: Romantic comedy
Time of plot: Eighteenth century
Locale: Spain
First presented: 1784

Continuing the merry tale of the clever barber of Seville, Beaumarchais takes
Figaro through more intrigues and adventures in The Marriage of Figaro. *Again*
the shrewd and clever barber's high good humor and adroit wit are a match for all.

The basis of the rollicking humor that pervades this comic masterpiece is sensual gaiety. Each character is bent on his or her own pleasure, with frivolity forever triumphant. Figaro certainly dominates the action, though he does not always direct it. Quite the contrary, he is constantly learning something new and unexpected. He did not know, at first, that the count coveted Suzanne, any more than he knew that Marceline was his mother, or Dr. Bártholo was his father. There is something about him of the nineteenth century romantic hero, whom he prefigures. He perceives himself as an outsider to society, almost to life itself. At heart, he is a revolutionary who dreams of taking his master's place. He demands the right to think and speak freely, and he ridicules everything that the *ancien régime* is based on: nobility, justice, authority. He claims his right to pleasure, most notably in his famous soliloquy: "Because you are a great lord [the count], you think you are a great genius; you simply took the trouble to be born, that's all. . . ."

Among the feminine portraits, that of Suzanne stands out for its piquancy. She knows her place, though she is bold enough in her remarks to the count. She will brook no flirting before marriage; her ideas on marital fidelity are altogether firm. She bestows a resounding slap on Figaro, believing herself deceived by him. But even with her, as is the case with everyone in the play, there is a suspicion of frivolity. Chérubin has grasped that with Suzanne it is possible to hope, even to dare. It delights her to be pursued amorously by an adolescent, barely past puberty, who in a few short years will surely have a great career as a lover.

The role of the countess is the subtlest of all. Still young and attractive, her situation as neglected wife obliges her to appear sad and serious. Disappointed in love, she discovers her maternal instincts being awakened by Chérubin. Nevertheless, she cannot fail to perceive that the young scamp is pursuing her as he pursues all women, in the hope of making a conquest. Thus, in the final analysis, it is Beaumarchais' view that love conquers all.

MARSE CHAN

Type of work: Short story
Author: Thomas Nelson Page (1853-1922)
Type of plot: Regional romance
Time of plot: Civil War period
Locale: Virginia
First published: 1887

"Marse Chan," from In Ole Virginia, *combines realistic regional setting and dialect with a romanticized vision of Old Virginia. The character of Marse Chan, as Page's version of the southern hero, is the main character in that myth of the old South that Page devoted his literary efforts to celebrating.*

The origins of *Marse Chan* are important for they prepare the reader for the tone of the story and the mood the author wishes to create. The world of this short story is a mythical and sentimental one which is structured around the life of Southerners in ante-bellum Virginia. It happened that Page was shown a letter which had been taken from the pocket of a dead private on one of the battlefields near Richmond. Basically, the letter contained the words of a young girl in Georgia to her sweetheart in the Confederate army. She told him how much she loved him, and that she was sorry she had been so cruel to him before he went away. She professed that her love had been constant and had grown since they were small children. The writer also implored her beloved to come home during his first furlough so that they could be married. The soldier died in battle, and never made it home. Page remarked that "he [the soldier] got his furlough through a bullet," and it was only a few days later that *Marse Chan* was written. Thomas Page was moved by the true story of the letter, and made it the basis for this successful and well-received short story.

Marse Chan contains all of the ingredients for a Southern local color story. The ideas of honor, loyalty, battle, love, death, and an ideal hero and heroine are contained within the incident upon which *Marse Chan* is based, so they fit naturally into the structure of Page's version of the story. Page was extremely interested in Southern literature and life. He sought to convert this story into life through the use of the black narrator, Sam, whose retelling of the story created a sentimentalized past which was not bound by complete accuracy and attention to detail.

Sam relates the story as only a loyal and faithful manservant could. Sam's romantic, superstitious, and nostalgic viewpoint provides a wealth of background material for the listener, a white man who questions Sam about the area and its inhabitants. The reader also becomes an attentive listener who hears Sam's story. Even though Page adapted *Marse Chan* from a true story, he added a new dimension which could be seen in much of his later writing—the full characterization of the Southern hero. To Page, and definitely to Sam,

Marse Chan represented a young boy who grew up to defend a civilization while adhering to a code of Southern heroism. From the beginning of the tale, we are aware of Marse Chan's "sacredness," his "special" place in the household. Throughout his youth he remains loyal to the black servant, and devoted to the wishes and ideas of his father. Anne Chamberlin, the young woman in his life, is respected totally, and her every wish is met. The overpowering chivalry of the South in those times is matter of fact to Marse Chan. Anne's initial rebuff after his profession of love to her is not in any way contested by Marse Chan, whose only desire is to please the woman he loves. Page incorporates the realistic with the romantic and ideal. Anne remains the ideal until the end, never really offering a believable relationship to the hero, yet providing an essential element to the tragedy of the story.

Perhaps the most believable character is Sam, the narrator. He tells the story as he sees it, and the characters he remembers belong to a mythical past filled with Southern heroes and heroines. Page was enamored with this picture of Southern history and in this re-creation of an event through a short story, he sought to preserve it as though it were a record of historical fact.

MARTIN CHUZZLEWIT

Type of work: Novel
Author: Charles Dickens (1812-1870)
Type of plot: Sentimental-mystery romance
Time of plot: Nineteenth century
Locale: England and America
First published: 1843-1844

Despite serious flaws in plotting, tonality, and emphasis, Martin Chuzzlewit *is rich in characterization, Dickensian humor, and dramatic impact. In addition, in the grotesque and unflattering scenes of American life, the writer offers his most outrageous caricatures. The pictures of rude frontier life fade, however, beside his portraits of Mr. Pecksniff, the arch-hypocrite, and the cockney vitality of Mrs. Gamp, perhaps the author's best humorous character.*

Martin Chuzzlewit was written in serial form soon after Dickens returned from his first American tour. The first few numbers not being well-received, he injected the American material in hopes of warming up his readership. He achieved the desired effect, but at the expense of tonal unity; the American descriptions are farcical at best, and detract from the seriousness of young Martin's interior struggle and enlightenment. Old Martin's simple-minded scheme to test the young lovers mars the work further, as does the *opera buffa* dénouement. Nor does the ideal of womanhood depicted in Ruth Pinch as cheerful companion and competent housewife add much to the general design.

But in other aspects the novel deserves to rank among Dickens' best; the representation of fraud as a social, rather than a merely legal quantity, is an example. The Anglo-Bengalee Disinterested Loan and Life Insurance Company represents that sort of fraud which can be prosecuted; but the kind of fraud practiced by Sairah Gamp upon her employers, by old Martin upon the lovers, by young Martin on his grandfather, by old Martin on Pecksniff, and by Pecksniff on everybody, is more pervasive and less palpable, so finally more damaging to society.

In addition to its thematic unity, the novel deserves recognition as the vehicle for its two paramount characterizations: Mr. Pecksniff and Sairey Gamp. Pecksniff is a paragon of that freedom from scruple which, by a fine command of moralistic rhetoric, cows and cozens people of real conscience like Tom Pinch; by trumpeting his own virtue, he steals a march on more modest natures who seem to onlookers (even to themselves) to acknowledge blame by their silence. As for Mrs. Gamp, that vile, vivid, old carrion-crow— for all the humor arising from her free-associated speech, her gluttony, and her pietism—she stands in the novel, according to Angus Wilson, as "the repository of female learning, of the secret knowledge shared together by which Victorian women . . . claimed some sacred position in a society made by men to their abasement."

THE MASTER BUILDER

Type of work: Drama
Author: Henrik Ibsen (1828-1906)
Type of plot: Psychological realism
Time of plot: Nineteenth century
Locale: Norway
First presented: 1892

The Master Builder is the first play in the last phase of Ibsen's long and extraordinary career. Ibsen turns, in these late plays, from a realistic presentation of modern society to a subjective, symbolic, almost lyrical dramatization of man's inner psychological and spiritual struggles. It is also clear that Ibsen closely identifies himself with the protagonists in these late works, especially The Master Builder.

Ibsen completed *The Master Builder* in 1892, two years after the stormy but mostly favorable reception of *Hedda Gabler*. Whereas he had labored slowly and revised with care the earlier play, his work on *The Master Builder* proceeded smoothly, requiring few major changes from the first draft to the finished manuscript. One year before, Ibsen had left Munich to return to Norway, where he resided in Oslo until his death in 1906. His return to his native land, an event marked by great professional success and personal satisfaction, corresponded with a significant change in his dramatic style. His early romantic plays in verse—*The Vikings at Helgoland* (1858), *Brand* (1866), *Peer Gynt* (1867)—are generally lofty, treating historical or epical subjects. The second period of his creative work, including *The Pillars of Society* (1877), *A Doll's House* (1879), *Ghosts* (1881), *An Enemy of the People* (1882), *The Wild Duck* (1884), consists of social dramas, written in conversational, realistic prose. The last period, beginning with *The Master Builder* and including *Little Eyolf* (1894), *John Gabriel Borkman* (1896), and *When We Dead Awaken* (1900), is noted for qualities often described as metaphysical or spiritual. Confessional plays with a clear autobiographical impulse and written in a style that moves easily from prose to prose-poetry, they break new ground in the history of the late nineteenth century European theater.

Although Ibsen never denied the subjective character of *The Master Builder,* the play should not be studied merely as a symbolic summary of the writer's life. Instead, it is a great work of dramatic art and, judged solely on the basis of its structural values, one of Ibsen's most finely crafted pieces. Nevertheless, as a confessional drama, *The Master Builder* certainly presents some of Ibsen's important ideas and obsessions. For example, like Halvard Solness, Ibsen was impressed with (although not neurotically dismayed by) the success of younger writers. Ibsen himself wrote of Camilla Collett: "A new generation is now ready to welcome and understand you." Also like

Solness, Ibsen was attracted to youthful girls. Critics generally believe that Hilda Wangel is modeled upon Emilie Bardach, who was also a part-proto-type for Hedda Gabler. At any rate, shortly after the production of *The Master Builder,* Emilie sent the author a photograph signed "Princess of Orangia," which apparently annoyed him. If Emilie was not the single inspira-tion for Hilda, then surely another of Ibsen's young friends might have been part of the composite picture, beginning with Engelcke Friis and continuing with Helene Raff, Hilda Andersen, or, the youngest, Edith Brandes.

In many other ways, the career of the Master Builder parallels Ibsen's own. Solness began by building churches. Later he decided to design "only houses for people to live in." Finally, to please himself and reassert his will to achieve the impossible, he designed a splendid house with a tower, fanciful as a "castle-in-the-air." Ibsen's experience with the theater similarly consisted of three stages: Romantic poetic drama; social drama intended to reform outworn traditions; and at last, personal drama with a special concern for a philosophy of life and death. There are other parallels as well. The high point of Solness' art as a Master Builder was the time he climbed a church tower and, as was the custom among Norwegian builders at that time (much like the christening of a ship), hung a garland at the topmost spire. Hilda had seen the triumph of her hero and remembered the precise date. "It was ten years ago," she said; "on the nineteenth of September." It was on September 20, 1889, that Ibsen wrote on the visitor's ledger at Gossensass: "The great, pain-ful joy of striving for the unattainable." Also, like Solness, Ibsen was troubled by great heights. When he was a youth, he attempted to scale a mountain in Italy but discontinued his ascent in fear, lying flat to the ground clutching a boulder. Finally, like the Master Builder, he was deeply interested in the power of thought-transference. In fact, Ibsen was an avid follower of studies on hypnotism and spiritualism.

However interesting are the similarities between the author's life and parallel themes of the play, *The Master Builder* is best enjoyed as theater rather than autobiography. The sharply defined conflicts of the play are resolved only at the conclusion. For this reason, the play "performs" especially well, although within recent decades it has never been quite so popular as *Hedda Gabler, A Doll's House, Ghosts,* or *The Wild Duck.* The central conflict is that between high aspiration—romantic dreams to attain the impossible—and the limitations of reality. As Master Builder, Solness has achieved a measure of financial success and even fame, but, as he discloses to Dr. Herdal and later, more completely, to Hilda, he considers himself a mere shell, a failure. Having defied God at the church tower, he has since feared that he will be cursed for his presumptuousness. At first he believes that the younger generation will be the agent of his destruction. Later, as he allies himself with the idealism of Hilda, he fears that his downfall will come not so much from rivals like Ragnar Brovik, but from the failure of his own will.

All his life he has depended upon "Helpers and Servers" to advance his career. Although a genius in his own right, he has nevertheless had to fight the world. And his powerful will, like the nearly hypnotic force that controls the affections of Kaia Fosli, has directed the Helpers and Servers to perform his wishes. Without assistance, though, he loses confidence in his art.

Finally, however, Solness understands that the enemy to his peace lies not outside himself but within. He really has no need to fear the young, and he does not require the blind obedience of servitors. His failings are those of conscience. He believes that he is going insane. So terrible is his sense of guilt—guilt because of his conduct toward his wife; guilt because he has abandoned the dreams of creating great edifices, churches; guilt because he has defied God—that he becomes increasingly isolated, almost paranoid. When Hilda encourages him to perform the impossible, to prove to the world that only he should be allowed to build, his inner conflict breaks. He determines to hazard everything, even his life, to satisfy his princess and provide her with her promised kingdom—to top a wreath at the tower of the new house.

At this point in the drama, the center of conflict shifts from Solness—now that he has made his idealistic decision—to Hilda. Will she allow the Master Builder to risk his life simply to satisfy her own iron will (or from another viewpoint, the passions of a spoiled child)? She knows that Solness experiences giddiness when he is climbing. Ragnar tells her that the Master Builder has always been afraid to place the wreath on the topmost place, that other workmen perform the task. Yet she steadfastly demands her "castle-in-the-air." In a romantic bond with the artist, she has identified her passion with his. Like the Viking women of old, with whom she has declared her kinship, she disdains a bourgeois conscience. For in her sprightly way she too is a warrior, and with a "robust" conscience she demands of her hero a sacrifice to prove his manhood.

A modern audience may perhaps judge Hilda more harshly than would Ibsen. As a character of social realism, she is idealistic to the point of folly. Careless (in Act I she carries her belongings, including dirty underwear, in a knapsack rather than a trunk), selfish, and willful, she contrasts with the sober, self-sacrificing, dutiful Aline Solness, the Master Builder's wife. Yet when the viewer comes to understand Mrs. Solness better, he sees that she has lived too narrow a life, devoid of romantic risks and heroism. She has never dared to confide to her husband the secret of her own guilt—that after the fire which had destroyed her ancestral house, she had lamented the loss of her nine dolls more grievously than that of her twin sons, who died shortly afterward. While the viewer sympathizes with her human frailty (for she is not to be condemned for grasping firmly to such petty symbols of the past), he also sees in a contrasted light the heroic striving of Hilda. Her Viking conscience is robust. The trolls (hobgoblins that are symbols both of destructive and creative forces) that guide her life are still strong, not diminished by civilization. At the end of the play—when she shrieks with wild intensity, "My—my Master Builder!"—she identifies his romantic achievement with her own. She has willed his triumph. To Ibsen, the death of a mere man, even a genius, is an insignificant price for such a triumph. In his visionary play, the Master Builder lives on in his work and in Hilda.

Leslie B. Mittleman

THE MASTER OF BALLANTRAE

Type of work: Novel
Author: Robert Louis Stevenson (1850-1894)
Type of plot: Adventure romance
Time of plot: Mid-eighteenth century
Locale: Scotland, India, France, America
First published: 1889

This novel is provocative and stimulating, both as an exciting narrative of familial intrigue and as a quasi-philosophical study of man's innate capacity for evil and self-destruction. Although less famous than, and artistically inferior to, Treasure Island *or* Kidnapped, *the seriousness and complexity of* The Master of Ballantrae *have led many critics to rate it as Stevenson's best work.*

Marred by weak setting and an uneven plot, *The Master of Ballantrae* is nonetheless a remarkable study in human insufficiency. Stevenson structures his moral fable around a tragic view of man's proclivity for evil, evidenced first and most powerfully in the person of James Durie, and, later, in his once-virtuous brother, Henry.

It would be incorrect to term the novel an allegory; it is nothing so firm in either its moral or narrative patterns. Rather, it is an intricate ethical *exemplum* which borrows richly, even indiscriminately, from Biblical legend and from *Paradise Lost.* Cain and Abel, Esau and Jacob, the Prodigal Son (here unrepentant) are all obvious references, as is the splendor of Milton's Satan, made radiant in the character of James. (Throughout the tale he is almost an archetypal Satan.)

The first part of the book locates its ethical absolutes in the two brothers —one good (Henry), one bad (James). Directed by Ephraim Mackellar's irresolute judgments, the reader has little difficulty establishing the moral natures of the two men, but beginning with Henry's presumed slaying of James, the novel takes on an imposing moral obliquity. In a gradual, then more sudden fashion, Henry becomes something of a villain in his own right, and possibly a madman if the narrator can be believed. For the reader familiar with *Dr. Jekyll and Mr. Hyde* (1886), this turnabout, of course, is no novelty, for Stevenson repeats the notion of a man destroying what is (by implication) part of himself. The human tragedy depicted in the book, then, is clear: Satan tempts and man falls, made insufficient not so much by weak virtue as by newfound strength in evil.

The tale is ostensibly a "history" of the kind so common in the eighteenth century (the temporal setting of the work). Thus the narrator, Mackellar, documents his facts, sorts out truth from rumor, and calls attention to his own conjectures. But Stevenson does much more than imitate a century-old *genre.* The reporter-narrator becomes himself a figure of interest, a firm believer in Providence and a moral prism, as it were, through which judgments of several kinds are refracted. Thus, point of view is made to call into question the very nature of truth itself (the most common word in the novel is "know") to the point where *The Master of Ballantrae* becomes a study in epistemological doubt. If one cannot know human nature, the book seems to argue, neither can one know the greater mystery of evil and of the Providence which permits it to flourish.

MASTRO-DON GESUALDO

Type of work: Novel
Author: Giovanni Verga (1840-1922)
Type of plot: Social chronicle
Time of plot: First half of the nineteenth century
Locale: San Giovanni, Sicily
First published: 1889

Mastro-don Gesualdo, the second in an unfinished trilogy titled I Vinti *(The Defeated), is a naturalistic study of the rise and fall of an ambitious Sicilian peasant. His efforts to elevate himself place Mastro-don (workman-gentleman) Gesualdo between two worlds—the peasantry and the gentry—and his marriage to one of the Trao family, who are of the gentry, only widens the gap between him and the others on either side.*

Although solidly in the late nineteenth century tradition of realism, *Mastro-don Gesualdo* is a unique book in many respects. Gesualdo Motta, despite his peasant background, assumes, by the end of the novel, the stature of a tragic figure. Like Emma Bovary and Willy Loman, he never understands his own tragedy or the flaws of his own character which propel him to his fate, but his force of personality and drive, his vision and intense purpose, lift him beyond the essentially petty world in which he struggles, and, more importantly, raise him to the status of a symbol. He is clever and strong and soon amasses a fortune and acquires the power that usually accompanies riches, but he does not comprehend the inner drive which pushes him relentlessly to seek ever more money, more power, although to the people around him he can never be more than a rich peasant.

The title "Mastro-don" literally means "Sir-Workman," with all of the ironic implications that the name suggests. Here are the seeds of his tragedy. His very lack of inner life, the flatness of his perceptions, must inevitably turn against him and destroy his victory. He is a sympathetic figure, despite his limitations, for his vitality and ambition and uninhibited emotions give him a humanity all too rarely encountered in literature.

Verga was a highly sophisticated craftsman who deliberately attempted to transform his Italian prose into the rough, dynamic style of the Sicilian vernacular. The result in this novel is a marvelous vitality in the writing and lively, realistic dialogue. The scenes are presented with effective dramatic force and are rich in an irreverent peasant humor. From the spectacular, perfectly realized opening scene of the fire in the villa, the novel moves swiftly and dramatically to its conclusion, the pathetic death of Gesualdo after his money and lands are stripped from him. The other characters are as vividly presented as the protagonist, particularly the impulsive Bianca and the rest of the ruthless Trao clan. *Mastro-don Gesualdo* deserves recognition and a high position in the history of realism in fiction for its attempt to portray the tragedy of a man without inner vision.

MAX HAVELAAR

Type of work: Novel
Author: Multatuli (Eduard Douwes Dekker, 1820-1887)
Type of plot: Political satire
Time of plot: 1857
Locale: Java
First published: 1860

Written from the author's personal experience, Max Havelaar *is a potent satire on colonial maladministration, governmental blundering, and the smugness and hypocrisy of middle-class Europeans. The primary artistic strategy, the placing of a decent man of good will in a situation that demands moral action, is supported by a wide variety of narrative devices, all presented with a biting and pervasive irony.*

As with so much of Dekker's literary work, *Max Havelaar* is a complex and unconventional novel, utilizing many forms in one, including the essay, poetry, short story, and other narrative devices within the framework of Batavus Drystubble's first-person story. Part of the book is devoted to descriptions of Javanese society and the impact of Europeans and European ideas and practices on Java and its people. This is often related in an apparently objective manner, although it is all structured so as to produce the maximum ironic effect. Dekker was a skilled literary craftsman, and he used his unorthodox methods to manipulate reader interest and sympathy. The deliberate shattering at the end of the book of the carefully constructed framework, destroying the fictional characters who had been "writing" the book, adds another dimension to the novel, and startles the reader into objectivity; the contrivance works much as Brecht's later device of interrupting the action of his plays in order to put across his message separately from the emotional appeal of the drama. Dekker wrote with the daring and flare of a true genius, and *Max Havelaar* is a unique and important novel.

Dekker's use of a narrator opposed to the point of view that he himself espouses results in a sophisticated, humorous narrative, despite the fervor and sincerity of the author's intent to reveal the horrors of the Javanese plantations. Drystubble, the narrator, is a Dutch Babbitt of 1857; his recounting of the story is heavily laced with an unintentional irony. His platitudes and narrowminded remarks are never intended to be accepted at face value by the reader. Dekker's technique is one used often by much later satirists and novelists. Dekker's atheistic views and opposition to the influence of the Church (particularly on freedom of thought and on economic development) are worked into the novel. Even more than seeking to expose the life of the plantation workers, Dekker wanted to startle his readers into thinking for themselves. His famous aphorism, "Man's calling is to be a human being," would be ridiculed by his narrator Drystubble, in *Max Havelaar,* but nevertheless, it underlies the structure and intent of the entire work.

Above all, Max Havelaar is portrayed as a decent, honorable human being. He is not intended to be Christlike in his virtue, but rather to be the example of what every conscientious and decent man should naturally be, in the ordinary course of existence. A human being with a conscience could not react other than Max Havelaar does to the conditions that he confronts. As a man of integrity and feeling, Max Havelaar accepts the responsibility of the lives placed within his sphere of influence, and his wife agrees with and co-operates with his efforts. He acts no differently in Java than he did in Europe, except that the conditions are so much worse in Java. Fundamentally, *Max Havelaar,* although satirical in large part, is a moral book, and like all great satires and all great works of literature, it takes a moral stand and deals with basic human issues.

THE MAYOR OF CASTERBRIDGE

Type of work: Novel
Author: Thomas Hardy (1840-1928)
Type of plot: Psychological realism
Time of plot: Nineteenth century
Locale: "Wessex," England
First published: 1886

Many critics consider Michael Henchard, the mayor of Casterbridge, to be Hardy's finest tragic hero. As in all Hardy novels, the forces of nature dwarf and manipulate human beings. But Henchard is a man who contains the violence of nature within himself, and it is this fact that both guarantees his defeat and gives that defeat the force of classical tragedy.

This is the first novel in which Thomas Hardy focuses his primary attention upon one individual; all other characters are drawn without depth so that in contrast Michael Henchard stands out in great animal strength and weakness. The story is *his* tragedy, although the two women with whom he is intimately involved die: his wife Susan, whom he sold with their child when a young man in a state of drunken recklessness; and Lucetta, with whom he has a secret affair, and who subsequently marries his rival, Farfrae. But death is not the main disaster of this narrative; rather, it is the slow downfall and disintegration of a "man of character."

The Mayor of Casterbridge marks a great development in Hardy as artist. He masterfully delineates Henchard's character and the complex social and economic life of Casterbridge. Both Michael Henchard and his town are governed by the grain market; the mayor's rise and fall are dependent not so much on his personal relations with Susan, Farfrae, Lucetta, and Elizabeth-Jane, as upon fluctuations of the harvest. The power struggle between Henchard and Farfrae is engendered and governed not by their abilities and popularity with the townsfolk, but more basically by the supply and demand of grain. Even sexual interests, which figure largely in the story, are dominated by the shifting economics of Casterbridge fortunes.

Also notable are the new dimensions Hardy has given both individuals and events; these have greater symbolism than those in his earlier works. For example, primitive ritual is suggested by the marriage transaction that begins Henchard's tragedy, and some critics suggest that the mayor himself has attributes or implicit qualities of a vegetation god or corn king.

Henchard also has affinities with Melville's Ahab in a relentless pursuit of revenge in the face of adverse circumstances and nature's power, though both men recognize that such pursuit must lead to their destruction. The story's course also demonstrates supernatural revenge for the hero's violation of moral order—a revenge which relentlessly demands the violator's atonement and death. This is crime and punishment beyond human control, though ironically Henchard's own character is the instrument for the retribution.

The past, whose sinister force Hardy constantly invokes, is best symbolized by the Roman earthworks of Casterbridge, particularly the amphitheater where gladiatorial combats were once held. For Casterbridge citizens it is a place of furtive assignations, even murders because of its obscure location and "dismal privacy." This spot Henchard chooses for a meeting with his long-lost wife, Susan. He also selects another area surrounded by an ancient Roman earthwork for his ill-advised Casterbridge entertainment, which, in contrast to Farfrae's dance in town, turns out to be a failure.

Henchard seems a pawn of the goddess Fortune, who throws him from a position of assured success down to the bottom of her wheel; in this respect *The Mayor of Casterbridge* is a tragedy in a long *de casibus* tradition, one which shows, because of Fortune's fickle nature, the downfall of a man with incipient greatness and strength. Henchard also resembles the Greek tragic hero who through destructive acts arising from his own character destroys himself. But it attests to Hardy's artistry that in his ruin, Henchard is to the reader stronger and elicits more admiration than does the clever Farfrae, who, in turn, has risen to the position of fortune and happiness Henchard once had.

THE MAYOR OF ZALAMEA

Type of work: Drama
Author: Pedro Calderón de la Barca (1600-1681)
Type of plot: Romantic tragedy
Time of plot: Sixteenth century
Locale: Zalamea, Spain
First presented: 1636

The Mayor of Zalamea *is generally acknowledged to be Calderón de la Barca's greatest work. In this play the theme of honor, central to all of the playwright's work, is placed on a broad folk basis that gives it a sweep and humanity lacking in most of his other dramas.*

The Mayor of Zalamea has achieved a place in the first rank of dramatic masterpieces through the author's sensitive blending of lofty themes with skillful artistry. The result is a perfect harmony and unity of thought and style. The play, generally assigned to the category of *costumbristic* drama, that is, drama based partly on history or popular tradition, is a recast of a work originally written by Lope de Vega. It has become, however, one of Calderón de la Barca's most popular plays.

The predominant theme of *The Mayor of Zalamea* centers on the concept of honor, particularly in the first two acts where it is sharply contrasted with dishonor as personified in the deeds of Captain Alvaro. The tightly knit plot which delineates this theme is an action of cause and effect which finds its roots in conflict. The principal causes of the conflict are the lodging of troops in a house where there is an unmarried female, Isabel, and the captain's curiosity concerning a beauty he is forbidden to see. The effects of these situations are predictable and the resultant action is fast moving, bristling with an abduction, a sexual assault, a garroting, and a jurisdictional battle which can only be resolved by the king. The incidents are structured on a ladder arrangement in that each one develops from the preceding one both logically and psychologically, which, incidentally, escalates into a tide of mounting tension by the end of each act.

The major conflict is depicted on two levels, exterior and interior. Each level involves a question of jurisdiction. The exterior conflict revolves around the clash between Crespo and Lope over the question of whether the king's justice is to be administered by the military or the civilian authorities. The external conflicts are set forth as debates or arguments and encompass the theme of honor. It is difficult for the modern reader to comprehend the concept of honor, the overestimation of a single virtue that often does not even seem like a virtue to us. Honor as a theme in Calderón de la Barca's work was manifold faces—it ranges from a matter of religion to a parody of social convention.

The interior conflict also evolves from the concept of honor, although not as obviously as the exterior conflict. The internal problem centers on the decision Crespo must make as to whether he should act in his capacity as a father or as the newly elected Mayor of Zalamea. He finally chooses the latter because it embraces a broader sphere of justice than does the personal. The author's style, like the action, is simple and direct. The argumentative aspects of the style are obvious in the aforementioned debates over the concept of honor, but the quaint patter of the lower characters reveals an aspect of Calderón de la Barca's style that adds a high degree of realism and naturalness to the dialogue. If the debates on honor seem artificial to today's reader, the oaths of Rebolledo, a raw recruit, who curses the officer who forces the troops to march without rest, are timeless bits of dialogue.

Like the style, the characterizations are significant for their attention to variety and detail. A case in point is Pedro Crespo who represents justice and prudence, but, at the same time, while being symbolic of virtue, is very much a flesh and blood character with human defects. The soldiers think of him as vain, pompous, and presumptuous. He is proud of his lineage but he also has a sense of honor and personal dignity. Calderón's technique of revealing aspects of one character through the eyes of another is a strong factor in making the person more human and balanced in the eyes of the reader.

The Mayor of Zalamea is an allegory: the Spanish king, as representative of God, finally recalls all of the players to their fixed and rightful positions within specific boundaries. Thus, while Crespo, for example, has an identity as a human being, on another level he is representative of the abstract virtue of justice, while Captain Alvaro comprises the embodiment of several dishonorable traits. Calderón's characters have many faces in order to communicate the many variations on the author's themes.

The Mayor of Zalamea is today considered to be Calderón's most popular drama. In critical discussions of this work, it is common to read time and time again that it is unlike any of the author's other works. Some critics call it a revolutionary play while others refer to it as a social drama, or Calderón's only drama of character. And yet this play does not necessarily occupy an exceptional place in the playwright's canon. It is Calderón's usual kind of play—unusual only in that the protagonist is a common man. Calderón did not choose this story because of its social themes but because the plot was perfectly suited to the stage. Calderón was primarily a man of the theater, and the most significant argument in his selection of material was that of its applicability to the stage.

The premiere of *The Mayor of Zalamea* took place in 1643. The play has been staged in Paris ever since 1772 under the title *The Peasant Magistrate* in an adaption by Jean Marie Collot d'Herbois. The first known German performance of this play, entitled *Magistrate Graumann* or *Incidents on a March,* was offered in 1778 in Hamburg by Friedrich Ludwig Schröder. Throughout the nineteenth century, this work was one of the most frequently performed plays in European theater. The role of Crespo, the mayor, became one of those parts sought after by actors. The drama is still being staged frequently in our own century.

Stephen Hanson

MEASURE FOR MEASURE

Type of work: Drama
Author: William Shakespeare (1564-1616)
Type of plot: Tragi-comedy
Time of plot: Sixteenth century
Locale: Vienna
First presented: c. 1603

Written when Shakespeare was also creating his major tragedies, Measure for Measure *has been called the darkest of his dark comedies. The shape of the play is comic, but its substance veers very close to tragedy. Before they are allowed a happy ending, the characters must all face the truth of their own morality and the fact of their personal mortality.*

Measure for Measure is one of those troubled plays, like *All's Well That Ends Well* and *Troilus and Cressida,* composed during the same years that Shakespeare was writing his greatest tragedies. Neither tragedies, nor comedies, nor histories, these dark and often bitter dramas have frequently been described as problem plays. Not the least of the problems, of course, is the one of literary classification, but the term generally refers to plays which examine a thesis. The main concern in this play is a rather grim consideration of the nature of justice and morality in both civic and psychological contexts.

The tone of this and the other problem plays is so gloomy and pessimistic that critics have tended to try to find biographical or historical causes for their bleakness. Some have argued that they reflect a period of personal disillusionment for the playwright, but there is no external evidence to corroborate this supposition. Others have laid the blame on the ghastly decadence of the Jacobean period. However, although other dramatists, such as Marston and Dekker, did write comparable plays around the same time, the historical evidence suggests that the period was, on the contrary, rather optimistic. What is clear is that Shakespeare has created a world as rotten as Denmark but without a tragic figure sufficient to purge and redeem it. The result is a threatened world, supported by comic remedies rather than purified by tragic suffering. Consequently, *Measure for Measure* remains a shadowy, ambiguous, and disquieting world even though it ends with political and personal resolutions.

The immediate source of the play seems to be George Whetstone's *History of Promos and Cassandra* or Whetstone's narrative version of the same story in his *Heptameron of Civil Discourses.* Behind Whetstone are a narrative and a dramatic version by Cinthio, from whom Shakespeare derived the plot of *Othello.* However, *Measure for Measure* is such an eclectic amalgamation of items from a wide variety of literary and historical *loci* that a precise identification of sources is impossible. Indeed, the plot is essentially a conflation of three ancient folk tales, which J. W. Lever calls the Corrupt Magistrate, the

Disguised Ruler, and the Substituted Bedmate. Shakespeare integrates these with disparate other materials into a disturbing, indeterminate analysis of justice, morality, and integrity.

The title of the play comes from the Scriptural text: "With what measure ye mete, it shall be measured to you again." As the play develops and expands on this quotation, we find that we cannot be satisfied with a simple but generous resolution "to do unto others what you would have them do unto you," because the play pursues its text so relentlessly that any easy confidence in poetic justice is undermined. We cannot be sure that good intentions and a clean heart will preserve us. In the final analysis, the action tends to support an admonition to "Judge not that ye be not judged," which of course can be either Christian charity or cynical irresponsibility.

Yet, we are in a world in which the civil authorities must judge others. Indeed, that is where the play begins. Vienna, as the Duke himself realizes, is in a moral shambles. Bawdry and licentiousness of all sorts are rampant in the city and the Duke accepts responsibility for laxity in enforcing the law. Corruption seethes through the whole society down to the base characters, who are engaged less in a comic subplot than in a series of vulgar exemplifications of the pervasive moral decay. The Duke intends to let Angelo, renowned for probity and puritanical stringency, act as vice-regent and, through stern measures, set the state right.

The chilling paradox is that Angelo almost immediately falls victim to the sexual licence he is supposed to eliminate. To compound the paradox, Claudio, whom Angelo condemns for impregnating Juliet, had at least acted out of love with a full intention to marry. Things do not turn out to be as they seemed. Not only is justice not done, it is itself threatened and mocked. Perfect justice yields to temptation while apparent vice is extenuated by circumstances.

Isabella also does not behave as we would expect. Called upon to intercede for her brother, she is faced with Angelo's harsh proposition. The dilemma is especially nasty since the choice is between *her* honor and *Claudio's* life. For her, neither is a noble alternative and, of course, Claudio is not strong enough to offer himself up for her and turn the play into a tragedy. Unfortunately, when Claudio is reluctant, she behaves petulantly rather than graciously. True, her position is intolerable, but she does spend more time speaking in defense of her virtue than in acting virtuously. For all her religious aspirations, which are eventually abandoned, she is not large enough to ennoble her moral context.

The Duke is always lurking in the background, watching developments, capable of intervening so as to avoid disaster. Indeed, we are tempted to blame him for being so slow to step in. Of course, if the Duke had intervened earlier, or had never withdrawn, we would have had "business as usual" rather than a play which examines the ambiguities of guilt and extenuation, justice and mercy. He allows the characters to act out the complex patterns of moral responsibility, which are the heart of the play. For example, when Angelo, thinking that he is with Isabella, is in fact with Mariana, his act is objectively less evil than he thinks because he is really with the woman to whom he had earlier plighted troth. Yet, in intention, he is more culpable than Claudio, whom he had imprisoned. Such are the intricate complications of behavior in the flawed world of *Measure for Measure.*

The justice that the Duke finally administers brings about a comic resolution. Pardons and marriages unravel the complications which varying degrees of evil have occasioned, but no one in the play escapes untainted. The Duke, after a period of moral spectatorship which borders on irresponsibility, restores order. Angelo loses his virtue and reputation, but gains a wife. Isabella abandons her extreme religious commitment, but finds herself more human and is rewarded with a marriage proposal. Everything works out: justice prevails, tempered with mercy. But we are left with an unsettled feeling that tendencies towards corruption and excess may be inextricably blended with what is best and most noble in us.

Edward E. Foster

MEDEA

Type of work: Drama
Author: Euripides (480-406 B.C.)
Type of plot: Classical tragedy
Time of plot: Remote antiquity
Locale: Corinth
First presented: 431 B.C.

Medea is one of the most fascinating, complex, and dynamic heroine-villainesses in dramatic literature. Few characters have been able to provoke such a range of emotional reactions: sympathy for her pain; wonder at the intensity of her emotions; admiration for her purpose, intellect, and style as a manipulator; fear, when her plan is understood; and horror as it is mercilessly carried out.

Commonly regarded as Euripides' greatest work, *Medea* is a powerful study of an impassioned love turned into furious hatred. As a tragedy this play is completely un-Aristotelian in concept and technique, but it has a nerve-jarring impact. It also reveals the extent to which Euripides diverges from his fellow tragedians, Aeschylus and Sophocles, in his depiction of human pain. With *Medea* there is no comforting philosophy to put the tragic agony at a safe psychological distance. Instead, Euripides tries to make Medea as close to an actual woman as possible, and to show her fiery lust for vengeance in naked action with nothing to mitigate its effect. We are witnesses to a hideous passion, and we cannot be certain whether Euripides approves of it or condemns it. He simply presents it objectively so that we understand Medea, but he leaves it to us to determine his meaning.

Euripides was probably in his fifties when this play was first produced in 431 B.C., an age when a sensitive man is fully aware of the agony that life can inflict on a person. What struck him most was the universality of suffering. Confronted with pain, every other human reality seemed to dissolve. In the face of Medea's consuming hatred, kingship, laws, culture, self-esteem, and even motherly love have become meaningless. In *Medea* Euripides portrays a very important aspect of terrible suffering; namely, the desire of the sufferer to create the identical agony in the person who caused it. The dramatist recognized the crucial link between anguish and hate. Reports of Euripides say that he was a bookish recluse, but it is understandable that a man as vulnerable to human misery as he was should shut himself off from people.

He turned to the old legend of Jason and the Golden Fleece to illustrate his preoccupation. Euripides takes up the story after all of Jason's successes have been accomplished with Medea's help. Jason has deserted Medea to marry the Greek princess, Glauce, leaving Medea with two small sons. As the nurse remarks in her opening monologue, Medea is not one to take such a betrayal lightly. Although Medea is prostrate with bitter grief and hoping to die as the play begins, the nurse knows how murderous her mistress really is, and she fears for the safety of Medea's sons. A common technique of Euripides is to use the opening speech or section to explain the background of the action and to suggest the climactic development.

Medea is a barbarian princess and sorceress who is accustomed to having her own way in everything. Furthermore, as a barbarian she has none of the restraints that civilization imposes. However, Jason is a Greek, subject to law, rationality, and practical calculation. As a result, he seems cold and indifferent, set beside Medea, who is a creature of passion. But this is merely a surface appearance. Euripides exposes the inner layers of their psyches with unflinching honesty in the course of the play.

As a woman of passion, Medea is wholly committed to Jason as the object of her emotional life, whether in love or hate. When she loved Jason she did not hesitate to kill her brother, betray her father and country, or instigate Pelias' murder for Jason's sake. And she is equally amoral in her hatred. The drama consists of the unfolding of her plans for revenge and their ultimate execution. When Medea first appears on stage before a chorus of sympathetic women, she is the image of the wronged woman, and we feel pity for her. At the end of the play, after a bloodbath of four persons that includes her sons, and which leaves Jason's life a total desolation, we feel only horror.

These murders are as coldly calculated as any in *Macbeth,* and Medea feels no penitence whatever. It is precisely the icy manner in which she goes about the killings that inspires dread. She caters to Creon in order to gain time to kill him and his daughter, Glauce. Medea plans to kill Jason too, but when she sees Aegeus heartsick at being childless, she determines to render Jason childless, wifeless, and friendless. Medea pretends a reconciliation with Jason to slay Creon and Glauce in a loathsome fashion. And then, after hesitating to kill her sons because of temporary softness, she butchers them without mercy. Medea is a practitioner of black magic, a cold-blooded murderess, and a total monster; but under Euripides' spell we understand her.

The passion by which she lives makes her both subhuman and superhuman. When Euripides finally has her escape in a dragon-drawn chariot through the air, we come to realize that Medea is a piece of raw nature—female, barbaric, violent, destructive, inhumanly powerful, and beyond all moral standards. Jason becomes entangled with a force that crushes his dignity and detachment, that tears his successes to tatters. At the end he is in exactly the same position as Medea. Both are bereaved of mate, children, and friends. Both are free to grow old without comfort. And both are utterly empty inside, except that Jason is now filled with the same burning hatred that possessed Medea.

This play operates on several levels. The antagonism between Jason and Medea can be read as the enmity between man and woman, between intelligence and passion, between civilization and barbarism, or between man and nature. In each instance the woman, the passions, the barbarian, the forces of nature—all embodied in Medea—have the power to turn and reduce the masculine elements to nothing. *Medea* is a strong, depressing, fearsome drama in which Euripides presents his vision of life as starkly as possible.

James Weigel, Jr.

MEEK HERITAGE

Type of work: Novel
Author: Frans Eemil Sillanpää (1888-1964)
Type of plot: Impressionistic realism
Time of plot: 1857-1917
Locale: Finland
First published: 1919

Jussi, the protagonist of Meek Heritage, *symbolizes the lower-class Finn who accepts the harsh climate, grubbing toil, and cruel class cleavages as his natural lot. He lives, rebels, and even dies with little awareness of himself or the world he lives in. Only the vague stirrings of nationalistic feeling that enter near the end slightly mitigate the book's pervading melancholy.*

Meek Heritage begins and ends with the death of the protagonist, Jussi Toivola. His death is caused by men to whom he means nothing more than another body. Jussi Toivola's insignificance is underlined through the novel by the way his name keeps changing. When he is young, he is called Jussi; as an adult making his own way in the world, he becomes Juha. When he begins to rise a little, the people around him take to calling him Janne, but when his status again declines he once more becomes Juha. He is nothing more than the social status he possesses, and that is usually lowly enough.

Jussi grows up feeling that he has no control over his own life. The events in his existence are like acts of God: they happen without reason, and he must endure them. It never occurs to him that he might be able to shape his own destiny. Fatalistic, absentminded, Jussi accepts what comes, as do most of the peasants in the novel. Passively, they wait for life to decide what it will do with them. The primitive world of Jussi's childhood marks him for life. The peasants he is raised among might be living in the Middle Ages, rather than during the end of the nineteenth century. To the child Jussi, grown-ups are a mysterious problem of nature, to be feared and avoided. His father, old Benjamin, possesses nothing but contempt for either women or children. All a boy can do is wait for the time when he will be a man and can torment women and children as his father did. Meanwhile, everyone struggles on, from week to week, month to month, aware of nothing beyond their tight little world. They do not even think of the country they live in; the term "Finnish nation" means nothing to them. In the depths of their souls, these rough, ignorant beings nurse a bitter mysterious melancholy.

The author points out that from the distance of time, this primitive world might seem interesting or even attractive in its simplicity, but it was nothing but drab misery to those who had to live in it. Particularly to the women, the dominant color of life was a permanent gray. But, if one survived, there would be a turning point, some place in the beginning of adulthood, when life might almost seem desirable. For a brief moment, a spark of hope might burn in one's breast. A few individuals did manage to go up in the world, to find a bit of happiness. But, usually, a new grayness settled over the remainder of one's life. In the last report, one found oneself alone: this was the chief lesson that life taught Jussi. Dreams were futile. Survival was all.

If Jussi could have been said to possess any philosophy, it was a kind of fatalism. His parents died while he was young, and other events tossed him here and there, eventually returning him to the place of his birth. Coincidences piled on top of one another until they resembled fate. He did not protest. He accepted everything. Jussi did not understand his own emotions, his attitudes, fears, hopes. He occasionally wondered how his emotions came to possess him, and what they had to do with the events in his life. But he was happiest when he did not have time or energy to think.

Jussi's relations with Rina and their subsequent marriage temporarily seem to transform the bleakness of his life, but the illusion is only fleeting. Soon he is overwhelmed by a greater emptiness than ever before. All that happens in his life is a series of jerks, little jolts along the path from birth to death. After each jerk, he submits to wherever he finds himself. What good would it do him to dwell on what has happened? Life is life, whatever form it takes, and the only absolute is that life must be lived. There is no religion in this primitive existence, except a few meaningless rituals undertaken with no understanding.

An unusual evenness of tone pervades the book. Whatever happens, the prose flows on, even and steady, like life itself. The narrative is constructed in such a way to suggest the tree-filled spaces, the wildness and oppression of this land to the far north, and the relentless unyielding nature of life a century ago in Finland. Sillanpää found a precise and fluid prose to describe the world of his principal character, Jussi, and to convey the hopelessness of his existence. There is a beauty to Sillanpää's art, but little to Jussi's existence.

In the background, throughout the novel, hovers the theme of the growing Finnish national movement, meaningless to Jussi and the people around him, but soon to catch the population's attention. The burden of responsibilities (children and wife) give life what meaning it has for Jussi. When he loses his burden, he discovers that he has nothing. His untrained mind is left in a vacuum, prey for thoughts which he cannot control. Changes happen in the world beyond, but he is only vaguely aware of them. Almost accidentally, now old, he is drawn into the turmoil of the times. No one would have suspected that Jussi would turn into a rebel; he always had been so docile and meek, so accepting of his fate. It is as if history determines that it will have its way, regardless of the desires or interest of the individual.

Once Jussi begins to think, to question his lot and the lot of the peasant laborers like himself, there is no stopping him. Without responsibilities, he becomes more outspoken, joins the movement, even assumes some responsibility. But he does not hate the farmers, he insists; he only wants them to stop living on another man's sweat. He does not understand the meaning of what is happening, but he knows that it is Revolution, and he rather likes the idea. Yet, when everything collapses around him, he longs for the past, an idealized vision of a past that never was.

The author attempts to end on an optimistic note, but the prevailing sensation at the end of the book is gloom. Jussi was shot, hardly knowing why. Was he condemned because he suffered all of his life? Must he pay for the decades of misery?

Frans Eemil Sillanpää was the son, himself, of a Finnish farmer. Most of his work deals with the lives of the peasants in western Finland. At first, his novels were known only in Scandinavia, where they very very popular, but later they were translated into other languages and were admired for their unsparing, if poetic, realism. In 1939, when Sillanpää went to Sweden to accept the Nobel Prize, Russia was already invading Finland; he took his family with him across the border to escape the invading Russian forces. Later, he returned to Finland, and died in Helsinki in June, 1964. His work has a special meaning to the Scandinavian reader, but people everywhere can appreciate the richness of his prose and the ultimate meanings of his books and their vision of the hard realities of life.

Bruce D. Reeves

MELMOTH THE WANDERER

Type of work: Novel
Author: Charles Robert Maturin (1782-1824)
Type of plot: Gothic romance
Time of plot: Early nineteenth century
Locale: Ireland
First published: 1820

Many literary scholars have called this book the greatest of the novels of terror so popular in early nineteenth century English fiction. Maturin elevates Melmoth the Wanderer *above the excesses that characterize the genre by complex plotting, intense individual scenes, vivid characterization, and, above all, by his powerful Faustlike theme as embodied in the fate of his hero-villain, John Melmoth.*

Although Maturin lamented that he was forced to write *Melmoth the Wanderer* out of economic necessity (he was out of favor with the Church hierarchy, deeply in debt, and the sole support of eleven people), it would be a mistake to regard *Melmoth the Wanderer* simply as a "potboiler" written only for money. Even in the "unseemly character as a writer of romances," Maturin remained the preacher, and this novel is a profound social, moral, and religious statement—perhaps even a fictionalized sermon.

Structurally, it is the most complex of the important Gothic novels. It is actually a series of stories set one into another like a nest of Chinese boxes. In the frame story, young John Melmoth visits his dying uncle and inherits, among other things, a vague story about a daemonic ancestor, also named John Melmoth, a picture of the man, and a manuscript, "The Tale of Stanton," which is the first of the novel's stories. Then he takes in a shipwrecked Spaniard, Alonzo Moncada, who tells his story, "The Tale of the Spaniard," in the center of which "The Tale of the Parricide" occurs. After recounting his own story, Moncada then retells "The Tale of the Indians," a story given to him for translation by an old Jew. Two additional narratives, "Tale of Guzman's Family" and "The Lover's Tale" are inserted within the "Indians" story. These finished, Melmoth himself then returns to conclude the novel by paying his debt to the power of darkness.

Although different in substance, each narrative contains similar thematic elements and, excepting the "Parricide's Tale," each tale climaxes at the point where Melmoth intrudes upon the suffering victim and makes his diabolical offer. Thus Maturin gives us an elaborate theme and variation structure which continually develops and reinforces his ideas as well as tantalizing us with new and different shocks, torments, and sensations. And always in the background, moving in and out of the narratives, is the brooding presence of Melmoth, whose own story and fate are revealed in bits and pieces as the novel progresses.

The overriding thematic motif of the novel concerns the ways in which man's greatest natural inclinations—to worship God and to love one another

—are perverted and distorted by individual weaknesses and institutional corruption. Several other notions reinforce those major ideas: the effects of an unchecked thirst for knowledge, the nature of madness and its relationship to fanaticism, the saving power of love, the family as a moral unit, the line between love and hate, human isolation and alienation, and the relationship between money and happiness.

In the "Stanton" story, Maturin introduces a number of these themes. Stanton is made vulnerable to Melmoth's appeal because he, too, has an insatiable curiosity about the forbidden. Fortunately for his soul, he rejects this side of himself when put to the ultimate test. Because of his erratic behavior, Stanton is also made the victim of a familial betrayal when an unscrupulous relative has him committed to Bedlam—the first in a series of such betrayals. All of the stories, in one way or another, involve either the destructive cruelties present in a "bad" family or the positive strengths of a "good" one.

In the madhouse scenes, Maturin begins his exploration of the moral and psychological nature of insanity which continues throughout the book. Although some are pure victims, most of the inmates of the asylum are fanatics who have simply pushed their religious or political proclivities to their "logical" conclusions. Maturin shows little sympathy for such madmen, although he recognizes that they differ from the "normal" only in being socially inconvenient; when madness is brought into socially acceptable institutions, Maturin suggests, it becomes not only tolerable, but even dominant.

Maturin's analysis of the perversion of the religious impulse and the corruption of institutionalized religion—especially Spanish Catholicism—is treated most fully in "The Tale of the Spaniard." Although anti-Catholicism, especially anti-monasticism, had been a staple element of the Gothic novel since Matthew Lewis' *The Monk* (1796), Maturin's treatment of the subject is probably the most intense and convincing, because he concentrates on the psychological damage of such institutional confinement rather than the more lurid and sensational accounts rendered by his contemporaries.

Under the rigid, arbitrary, artificial authority of such a life all natural human capacities are stifled; the firmest faith is dissipated; the kindliest nature is thwarted; and the keenest intellect is stultified. The endlessly repetitious and absurd routine creates an ennui that is poisonous. Petty spite, gossip, and cruelty become the way of life. The smallest infractions of the silliest rules are treated as major crimes and any person who exhibits the slightest trace of individualism becomes the monastery scapegoat.

The most blatant example of this institutional corruption can be seen in the "parricide" who is taken into the monastery in spite of, or *because of,* his criminal nature, and who works out his salvation by instigating the damnation of others. As a parricide he represents the ultimate betrayal of the familial relationship; because, unlike Melmoth, he enjoys his deeds, he is the most extreme example of human evil—but his sadism is the inevitable end product of the social system he represents.

The extent of his diabolism, and the most "Gothic" scene in the novel, is seen in the climax to his story. As he and Moncada wait huddled in the underground tunnel, he gleefully tells how he lured an errant couple into the same subterranean vault, nailed them in, and listened as, without food or water, their love turned to hate: "It was on the fourth night that I heard the shriek of the wretched female—her lover, in the agony of hunger, had fastened his teeth in her shoulder—that bosom on which he had so often luxuriated, became a meal to him now." Nowhere is Maturin's theme of the perversion of the natural into the destructive presented with more gruesome clarity.

But, however impressive some of the individual scenes may be, it is the central character of Melmoth that makes the novel memorable. He is, in many ways, the supreme Gothic "hero-villain." Melmoth is damned, but, like Faustus, his damnation is the product, not of an evil nature, but of a questing spirit that simply cannot accept human limitations.

In "The Tale of the Indians" Melmoth's character is most clearly presented. The last two stories in the novel, "The Tale of Guzman's Family" and "Tale of the Lover" add little to Melmoth's saga and are the least Gothic, most sentimental, and dramatically weakest in the book. But in the "Indians" tale, Melmoth himself assumes an active role and reveals truly human emotions. It is in this love affair between Melmoth and the native girl, Immalee, which resembles Goethe's "Faust-Margaret" story, that Melmoth's fate is actually decided: only the power of innocent love can save him from his chosen damnation—if he has the strength to accept it.

Since Immalee has grown up in an idyllic state of nature, she is ignorant of society's corrupting influences. It is Melmoth who introduces her to human decadence, although, even from the beginning, he is ambivalent in his feelings toward her. He is reluctant to tempt her consciously, and his teachings are more of a response to her eagerness than an attempt to ensnare her. For her part, Immalee's spontaneous love for him causes her to desire further information about his world, even though this new knowledge proves painful.

Thus, Melmoth becomes the tormented lover as well as the Satanic tempter. He would love her, but he fears that such love will damn her also. So he alternately woos and thrusts her away; he entices her and warns her against himself. In the end he succumbs to his role as tempter, but not before he has struggled desperately with a soul that he no longer believed he possessed. Because Melmoth makes his awful proposal to her, he is damned; because Immalee refuses, she is saved.

The central irony is, of course, that her love could have saved them both. There is no bargain with the devil that cannot be abrogated by love. Melmoth's damnation comes, finally, not from his formal contract with Satan, but from his lack of belief in the power of the human spirit. Accepting the corruption he describes as the whole truth, Melmoth does not see the evidences of human worth around him: the love exhibited by the Walbergs ("Guzman's Family"), by Elinor Mortimer ("Lover's Tale"), and, most of all, by Immalee.

Because he embraces evil, Melmoth's condemnation is inevitable; but, because of his lost potential, it is tragic. Thus, for all of the sensationalism and crudity characteristic of the Gothic novel, it contains the elements of classical tragedy. And no writer of Gothic romances came closer to realizing that possibility than Charles Robert Maturin in *Melmoth the Wanderer*.

Keith Neilson

THE MEMBER OF THE WEDDING

Type of work: Novel
Author: Carson McCullers (1917-1967)
Type of plot: Impressionistic realism
Time of plot: 1945
Locale: Georgia
First published: 1946

This sensitive, poignant novel, as well as the successful dramatization of it, utilizes the coming-of-age situation to explore the themes of human isolation, dissatisfaction, and the search to belong. When McCullers' adolescent heroine, Frankie Adams, is rejected by her brother and his bride, she learns to fend for herself. In so doing she not only grows up but also demonstrates that her feelings and needs do not simply indicate stages in life but are fundamental, permanent conditions of it.

Throughout her kinetic career as a novelist, short story writer, and playwright, Carson McCullers explored the human condition from several perspectives, but all with the common focus of loneliness and dissatisfaction. *The Heart Is a Lonely Hunter* (1940) reveals a deaf-mute's isolation in a Southern town, and it also draws parallels to the phenomenon of fascism. *Reflections in a Golden Eye* (1941) also takes place in the South, but with *The Member of the Wedding* anxieties are explored in finer detail. Then followed *The Ballad of the Sad Café* in 1951, a collection of short stories including the famous title piece, a novelette dramatized by Edward Albee in 1963. Her last two works were *The Square Root of Wonderful* (1958), a play; and a novel, *Clock Without Hands* (1961). McCuller's unpublished works, including some early poetry, appeared posthumously in 1971 under the title *The Mortgaged Heart*.

Although *The Member of the Wedding* certainly deals with themes of loneliness and dissatisfaction, the story is quite interesting as a discussion of the means through which a particular individual attempts to escape these isolating emotions. This psychological novel is enhanced by McCullers' masterful handling of language and point of view. Although the narrative is not in the first person, the language makes it clear that Frankie Addams' viewpoint is of primary concern. The result is that one is able both to observe Frankie objectively and at the same time to appreciate her emotions immediately. Frankie's feelings are, in addition, juxtaposed with the intrusion of adult observation (most often from Berenice and Mr. Addams) so that the reader has a realistic synthesis of information. The structural result is triangular: while there is exchange between adults and adolescent, the adult view cannot comprehend the adolescent because it has grown beyond that stage; the adolescent view cannot encompass the adult since it is not yet equipped; the reader completes the triangle, gaining the adolescent view through Frankie, and adding the adult view through appreciating the irony of Frankie's observations of adults.

Frankie, Berenice, and John Henry, despite apparent enmities, form a tribunal, sharing experiences and opinions and evaluating them both literally and symbolically, and each is essential in his role in the tribunal. Frankie, literally, is the causing factor of the group's existence: Berenice is hired to care for her, and John Henry is present because Frankie wants juvenile companionship to counter that of Berenice. Yet, although she realizes that she is not yet capable of understanding the functionings of the adult world, Frankie, aided by John Henry, symbolizes the almost divine nature often assigned to the child. Frankie *knows* certain truths, as Berenice occasionally confirms in bewilderment, because the girl's mind has not yet been spoiled by realities that obscure those truths. Her almost innate, although selective, knowledge is part of a literary and philosophical ideology most clearly typified by the Wordsworthian view of children. But Frankie's strongest understanding is also the most ironic: she realizes that she is incomplete and is terrified by reminders of that fact. However, in her earnest efforts to belong, to be completed, she is driving herself toward adulthood in which one loses this sort of innate knowledge.

Berenice, one of McCullers' most interesting characters, serves multiple functions. Just as she is employed to care for Frankie in many ways, she is also the pivotal character upon whom the novel depends on several levels of development. In simple terms, she is a counter-example of Frankie's search to belong and to love. Although McCullers' familiar theme of such unending search persists in Berenice, she illustrates that love, even when directed toward a vague objective, has the eventual effect of grace. In addition, she is a surrogate mother upon whom Frankie depends, made more credible by being representative of the black parent figure of many Southern novels. Frankie is locked into dependence upon Berenice, but it is dependence from a distance; although she longs to be independent of Berenice and all other authority figures, Frankie knows intuitively that she is not old enough to ignore Berenice. She knows the woman has function in her life, has necessary information to which she has not yet been exposed. She does not want to block Berenice out entirely (while the servant speaks to her, Frankie puts her fingers in her ears—but not far enough to prevent Berenice's voice from reaching her), since she would have to confront life later as an adult without sufficient data. Frankie knows instinctively that ignoring Berenice is only self-defeating. Berenice is, therefore, like an oracle; and she comes from the ancient literary tradition of the blind or one-eyed person who speaks the truth clearly because of his missing vision. Berenice has a glass eye ("glass" and "truth" are related etymologically in Latin); so Berenice sees truth through her glass eye, not through her physically functioning one. McCullers is thus able to elevate the group in the kitchen to mythic dimensions: Berenice is the oracle; John Henry is her acolyte; and Frankie is the pilgrim-initiate.

By emphasizing Frankie's progressive learning and by concentrating primarily on the emotions and experiences of only three days in Frankie's life, Carson McCullers achieves the effect of gradually increasing our expectations. By the end of *The Member of the Wedding* the reader has been led to believe that the day before the wedding is Frankie's "last afternoon" in town—if not literally, then at least figuratively. However, this increasing momentum is not followed by a fulfillment of expectation; Frankie is essentially unchanged by the trauma of disappointment. It is suddenly apparent that the initiation of youth into adulthood through artificial specific rites is a myth. The search for belonging is an unending one; it is simply one's orientation toward that search that can change by the natural process of maturing. In fact, as Berenice's life illustrates, the childlike element of selectively believing in salvation can be concomitantly protective, making both life and the search for social identity not only possible but also bearable.

Bonnie Fraser

THE MEMOIRS OF A CAVALIER

Type of work: Novel
Author: Daniel Defoe (1660-1731)
Type of plot: Adventure romance
Time of plot: 1630-1648
Locale: England and the Continent
First published: 1720

Although a work of fiction, The Memoirs of a Cavalier *was, like many of Defoe's other narratives, presented as a factual account. Defoe's rendering of war and social upheaval in early seventeenth century England and Europe from an upper-class perspective (unusual for this author) is impressive and believable and helps to validate Defoe's status as one of the progenitors of modern realistic fiction.*

Daniel Defoe has been called the first social historian, and certainly in his many prose fictions he explored the varied levels of the tempestuous society which he knew so well. *The Memoirs of a Cavalier* dealt with a somewhat higher level of society than he usually portrayed in novels such as *Moll Flanders* (1722) and *Roxana* (1724), but here, too, every detail is accurate and true. Defoe's plain, direct style and accumulation of detail hold the reader's interest through all of these pseudo-autobiographies. Defoe always wrote in the first person, and, through this device, could enter into the minds of his heroes and heroines, analyzing their motives for their actions. The men and women he wrote about are all placed in extraordinary circumstances, few more so than the Cavalier, and all struggle through a life which is a constant battle.

The Cavalier engages in actual warfare, is a participant in the making of history, and is caught in the turmoil of the larger world. Yet, like Defoe's other protagonists, he is essentially a loner. The unnamed Cavalier must stand alone amid the vastness of the concrete realities of the world, so meticulously and exhaustively detailed by the author. This approach to the hero provides the reader with a unique perspective; one feels that the ultimately tragic human condition is represented by the Cavalier, and that Defoe's vision of life as reflected in these pages is essentially bleak.

Defoe's active life is reflected in *The Memoirs of a Cavalier.* As a writer of government pamphlets and a spy, Defoe traveled and came in contact with many different aspects of society in many different parts of Europe. The restlessness which was apparently a vital part of Defoe's makeup as a man is present everywhere in this "memoir." The Cavalier, born with status and money, could have settled down to the life of a country squire, but he chose to enter into the violent and ever-changing world of the seventeenth century. Ultimately, he found a kind of peace, but not until he had passed through political and moral trials.

MEMOIRS OF A FOX-HUNTING MAN

Type of work: Novel
Author: Siegfried Sassoon (1886-1967)
Type of plot: Social chronicle
Time of plot: 1895-1916
Locale: England and France
First published: 1929

Memoirs of a Fox-Hunting Man, *the first of a three-volume series, is the barely concealed autobiography of the author, although we learn little about the inner workings of the real man. The book is essentially a mood piece that evokes a feeling of nostalgic reverie about a time, place, and social class that ended with World War I.*

The novel is a detailed picture of a faraway place and time, of a leisurely and safe world in which neighborhood cricket matches and fox-hunting afternoons provide the only excitement. Two world wars have since put an end to the trivial way of life described so lovingly by the author, but perhaps the class structure (he seems to imply) on which that world so precariously balanced was bound to perish. Reading Sassoon's meticulous descriptions gives the reader somewhat the sensation of peering into an old stereopticon at a frozen and dusty scene from long ago. George Sherston's values are certain, but are rooted in a previous century. Neither Sherston nor any of the other characters develop or grow; like stuffed animals in a museum, they simply continue being what they are, propped up in front of their occasionally changing backgrounds.

However, the descriptions are detailed and interesting, and an atmosphere of civilized charm spreads over the pages. There is little excitement—even in the section dealing with the war—not much character analysis, and no plot to speak of, yet *Memoirs of a Fox-Hunting Man* is a small classic of mood; a gentle irony that stops short of real satire adds an occasional tartness to the narrative without disrupting the even tone. Siegfried Sassoon's understated prose is clean and graceful and a pleasure to read.

Sherston deliberately limits his memoirs to certain aspects of his life; the reader learns almost nothing about his emotional life and little about his intellectual existence. Even many of his nonsporting activities are omitted from the narrative. At times, Sherston probably seems more shallow than he actually is. He is a sensitive man, sharply aware of the beauty around him, and dedicated to decency and honor. He says that he is tempted to write the mental history of his life in the war, but one ends the book still wondering what lies beneath the smooth surface of this man.

MEMOIRS OF A MIDGET

Type of work: Novel
Author: Walter de la Mare (1873-1956)
Type of plot: Fantasy
Time of plot: Late nineteenth century
Locale: England
First published: 1921

In Memoirs of a Midget, *Walter de la Mare uses the perspective of a naïve midget from which to satirize social behavior and attitudes. The life and career of tiny Miss M. provides a delightful mixture of fantasy, poetry, and realism that makes this book both stimulating and poignant.*

Two gardens in *Memoirs of a Midget* are of interest because in them Miss M. has her most memorable experiences. One garden is the forested, flowered area at Wanderlore, her family home in Kent. The other is the wooded park near Mrs. Bowater's home.

During her childhood, Miss M. enjoys the company of small animals and insects in the family garden. Here, too, she searches the treetops looking for Paradise, the first indication of her awareness of something beyond her small world. She also learns about death for the first time when she sees a dead mole.

Later, when she is living at Mrs. Bowater's house, Miss M. finds the woods nearby are an excellent place for viewing stars. The dark sky spangled with stars gives her a feeling that a great Being is in charge of the universe. She is surprised to learn that the sense of peace and order she gains there is not shared by Fanny, who dislikes the spot when she visits it with Miss M.

In these woods Miss M. becomes acquainted with Mr. Anon. She finds him unattractive in appearance, but pleasant to talk with. However, because she has led a sheltered life, she disbelieves him when he tries to explain to her that the world includes evil as well as good. At a later date, Mr. Anon tells her of a happy land in which people are so small that they are almost invisible. He also declares his love for Miss M.

After Mr. Anon's death, the grief-stricken Miss M. recognizes serious flaws in herself. The remote area of the woods where this self-discovery occurs seems ugly to her, as she seems to herself. She tries to commit suicide by eating the poisonous berries of the nightshade plant. Changing her mind, she prays to God for help.

Miss M. survives to find peace again and to complete her memoirs. Then she disappears. De la Mare does not tell us where she goes, but perhaps she travels to a land where people are small enough to be almost invisible and large enough to be happy.

MEMOIRS OF A PHYSICIAN

Type of work: Novel
Author: Alexandre Dumas, *père* (1802-1870)
Type of plot: Historical romance
Time of plot: Eighteenth century
Locale: Paris and environs
First published: 1846-1848

This novel, first in a five-volume sequence (the Marie Antoinette romances) describes the court life of France at the time of Louis XV and XVI. Memoirs of a Physician *is the intricate story of court intrigue in the closing days of the reign of Louis XV, with* dramatis personae *as diverse as the scheming Duc de Richelieu, the philosopher Rousseau, and the favorite-dominated king—all manipulated by the central character, the mysterious, magical Joseph Balsamo.*

Without doubt the most fascinating character in the *Memoirs of a Physician* is that remarkable impostor, the "arch-quack," Joseph Balsamo. From his first introduction, he is seen as a powerful and contradictory figure, a man of great resources and unscrupulous ambitions. And his passion for the unnatural and unexplainable adds to the fascination his personality holds for the reader. The phenomena of occultism had long fascinated Dumas, and it was inevitable that he should work it into one of his novels. However, the manner in which he used his interest in the *Memoirs of a Physician* is a spectacular success, one of the most remarkable examples of his genius. Dumas dabbled, at different times, in palmistry, phrenology, clairvoyance, and spiritualism. He was especially attracted to what later came to be called hypnotism. To test the reality of this power he made several experiments at the very time when he was writing the Joseph Balsamo sequences of the novel, and, apparently, with considerable success. In this novel, the possibilities of this and other unusual or unexplainable phenomena were stretched to the furthest demands of his fiction. But Dumas' skill was such that the reader willingly suspends disbelief and is drawn into the spell cast by the writer and his sorcerer character.

Joseph Balsamo, the "arch-quack," is presented with all of his quackeries, his schemes and ploys, his ruthless use of his "supernatural" powers to exploit the innocent and further his own ends. However, he believes in himself and in his mission to recreate humanity by destroying the existing order; as the head of a society of nihilists, whose motto is L. P. D. (*lilia pedibus destrus*), he directs the undermining of society's foundations. He loves nothing so much as pulling the strings by which the puppets are made to dance. Balsamo, or the Count of Fénix, as he is also known, is a unique and remarkable character, and he holds the reader's interest even after the virtuous characters are forgotten.

Many famous people appear in the pages of this long novel, some more successfully than others. Jean Jacques Rousseau is probably the most illustrious member of the cast, but his portrait does not quite come off; one suspects that Dumas held Rousseau in such high esteem that he could not entirely relax while drawing his portrait. Marat, that young surgeon who continually urges prompt and violent methods to cleanse society of its corruption, while less admirable, is realized more successfully than the old philosopher. He pulsates with a vitality and drive almost equal to that which infuses Balsamo with such remarkable life. In some respects, Madame du Barry, with her pet Negro Zamore and all of her intrigues to keep her position, is a triumph of characterization. Whatever the real du Barry was like, the reader feels that she *ought* to have been as Dumas describes her. And then there is the eminent churchman, the Cardinal de Rohan, and that wonderful scene in which he is dazzled by the sight of the alchemist Balsamo "making gold."

With great skill, Dumas weaves into his story the social conditions prevalent in Paris and the country at the time, the conditions that must inevitably lead to revolution. The brilliant opening scene of the families searching for the dead and injured after a great riot, quickly sets the tone of the entire novel. The division of the citizens of France into the revolutionaries and reactionaries is seen to be developing, and the tragic consequences are vividly foreshadowed. While the book is far from a social tract, Dumas seems to take delight in presenting the corruption of the court and the vices of the rich, and, above all, the exploitation of the poor by the powerful. Always, Dumas was fascinated by power and its various permutations. He explored in novel after novel the schemes and actions of the lovers of power, and their ruthless natures. In this novel of intrigue and insipient revolution, Dumas allows himself plenty of room to analyze his favorite subject.

The plot is as complicated and convoluted as most of the plots of Dumas' other novels, but the action moves swiftly and Dumas' narrative skill keeps the threads visible; the story is seldom incomprehensible. Even when the plot seems most tangled, the vivid characterizations hold the reader's interest. Perhaps more than many of Dumas' novels, *Memoirs of a Physician* presents some acute character analysis. The principal characters reveal themselves through their actions, as well as through their self-evaluations. However, the minor characters in the book and the young and idealistic lovers are much less successfully realized. They are inclined to be pawns of the plot.

The style of the writing, while vigorous, is not subtle. The dialogue is often completely unrealistic, the characters speaking to inform the reader, rather than one another, of their intentions. The melodrama of the plot carries over into the prose, and many chapters end with cliff-hanging episodes which are lushly overwritten. These scenes are frequently implausible, and the violence of the emotions and the posturing of the characters is sometimes laughable. Yet, despite, these flaws, which are, after all, as much the fault of the era of the author as they are of the author's craft, the novel remains a masterpiece. Dumas never tried to write like Flaubert and was not interested in realism, yet he managed to create a "real" world with his pen. The Paris and France of *Memoirs of a Physician* is as vivid to the reader as the provincial towns of Flaubert's masterpieces. And the breathless narrative drive, for which Dumas was so justly famous, continually holds the reader's attenion. If, as is likely, Dumas wrote this novel with the help of several assistants, no seams are visible. The style is consistent throughout, and the prose retains the vigor which characterized the author's earlier books.

Bruce D. Reeves

MEMOIRS OF AN INFANTRY OFFICER

Type of work: Novel
Author: Siegfried Sassoon (1886-1967)
Type of plot: Social chronicle
Time of plot: 1916-1917
Locale: France and England
First published: 1930

This book, the second of a trilogy that includes Memoirs of a Fox-Hunting Man *and* Sherston's Progress, *caricatures upper-class English behavior. The main character, George Sherston, encounters a detachment and casualness toward the war in his officers which finally prods him to rebel in a letter to his colonel protesting the needless prolongation of the war. The authorities, however, are too well-bred to take the letter seriously, and Sherston falls back into nonchalance.*

The irony occasionally employed by the author in his previous volume, *Memoirs of a Fox-Hunting Man,* gains in both frequency and power in this second book about the fortunes of George Sherston, sportsman and unwilling infantry officer. An unmistakable authenticity gives Sassoon's understated descriptions of the front lines during World War I an added power and poignancy. His simple yet detailed narrative of what actually happened in the trenches is accomplished with a mastery that recalls the descriptive prose of early Hemingway. George Sherston is no more impressed by the tunes of glory than Frederic Henry. Both of them soon believe that the war is little more than a bad, not very funny, joke; the difference is that Sherston, because of upper-class British conditioning, feels that he has no choice but to carry on, to the unknown end. He would not consider deserting.

Sherston feels safer, somehow, carrying Thomas Hardy's Wessex novels in his haversack, as he prepares for the Big Push. Hardy's England symbolizes to Sherston everything that he is fighting for—even as he becomes aware of the incompetence among those running the war. At times, the narrative seems almost to be a series of snapshots, quick impressions randomly collected and hastily sketched; but the book's sequences fall into a pattern calculated to lead the reader to certain implied but never forced conclusions, about war and society and life. The wirecutters that Sherston bought while on leave in London become a symbol of the army's incompetence, but Sassoon never underlines his point. He lets the events speak for themselves.

The plotless narrative becomes exhausting in its detailed piling up of incident after incident, but this seems to be part of the author's design: to convey the boredom as well as the horror of war. To the soldier, the trivia of life in the trenches looms as importantly as the grand moments, which come few and far between, and are seldom as grand as the newspaper accounts make them sound. The important consideration for Sherston seems to be that he never fall for the lie, never let that part of himself which he always holds aloof be touched by the foulness of the war. Only by maintaining his control in this way can he carry on and perform as expected of him—and as he expects of himself. After all, he concludes, since his peacetime existence has been idle and purposeless, the "big thing" was to "have been in the thick of a European War."

THE MENAECHMI

Type of work: Drama
Author: Titus Maccius Plautus (c. 255-184 B.C.)
Type of plot: Farce
Time of plot: Third century B.C.
Locale: Epidamnum, a city of Macedonia
First presented: Late third or early second century B.C.

The Menaechmi *is one of the best known of Plautus' comedies (Shakespeare used it for* The Comedy of Errors*). Exploiting the old comic device of confusion between identical twins, and confining the action to a single time and setting, Plautus pushes his farcical intrigues at a fast and furious pace that obscures the improbable coincidences and obtuseness of the characters.*

Well-constructed, witty, quick in pace, full of entertaining song and dance, *The Menaechmi* shows its author's ability to turn a dull idea into lively theater. The plot hinges on the mistaken identities created by a set of twins, one of whom is searching for the other. Undoubtedly Plautus borrowed the plot from an unknown Greek original, as he did with so many of his plays. But the effervescence of this comedy—its rapid, risqué ebullience—is peculiar to Plautus alone.

Although the story is not very complex, the dramatist handles the action with great dexterity, carefully signaling in advance which Menaechmus is which, so that the audience is in a position to relish the misunderstandings and confusions of the characters. Binding itself to a very narrow unity of time and place, the action occurs before the house of Erotium in little more than the time actually taken by a stage performance. This limitation creates a number of problems in verisimilitude, but the play moves so swiftly that the audience has no opportunity to grow uneasy at the improbable coincidences or the obtuseness of Menaechmus Sosicles.

A major irony in the play is that Menaechmus of Epidamnum is already leading a double life when his twin turns up to quadruple the confusion, slipping into his brother's two lives and creating havoc unintentionally. By the time the play ends, Menaechmus of Epidamnum is ready to throw everything up and make a new start. The intervening trouble seems to have shown him how unsatisfactory that double life really was. Around this bland pair revolve the stock types of farce—the fat cook, the courtesan, the shrewish wife, the parasite, the pompous doctor, the angry father-in-law. These characters have peopled the comic theater almost from its beginning. Shakespeare himself drew on *The Menaechmi* in writing *The Comedy of Errors,* which George Abbott in turn used as the basis for his musical comedy, *The Boys from Syracuse.* Amusingly, *The Menaechmi* itself was a musical comedy in its original state, and the cycle of borrowing may not be finished yet.

LE MENTEUR

Type of work: Drama
Author: Pierre Corneille (1606-1684)
Type of plot: Farce
Time of plot: Seventeenth century
Locale: Paris
First presented: 1643

Although Corneille's fame rests largely on his heroic dramas, it was as a writer of comedies that he first made his reputation. His best comedy, Le Menteur, was, however, written later in his career when he was at the peak of his abilities. Therefore, it demonstrates a skill in social observation and a complexity in characterization that is lacking in his earlier comedic efforts.

Le Menteur is often considered to be the best French comedy before the days of Molière. A comedy of intrigue, a type at which the Spaniards were particularly proficient, *Le Menteur* was derived from a comedy by Alarcón. The plot consists of a series of embarrassing situations in which the leading character is involved. After he has lied his way out of one predicament, his very lie entangles him in one still worse. The plot is complicated and many of the situations are highly improbable; however, these shortcomings are forgotten by the spectator because of the clever dialogue, quick repartee, and the quickness of wit of the leading character. One cannot help but admire the way the hero extricates himself from his plights.

This play was a landmark in French comedy because it refrained from farcical horseplay and obscenity. Its effectiveness largely depended upon the portrayal of life and manners in Paris. The characterization, in addition, was a marked step forward, and in Dorante and his father Geronte, Corneille created two characters whose personalities stand out with marked individuality. The hero is a type not unfamiliar to the modern stage, a mixture of boldness and insipidity, with something in him of young Marlow of *She Stoops to Conquer,* who finds it easier to lie than to tell the truth.

Perhaps the play does not contain the penetrating psychological observation that can be found in the later character studies of Molière, but it is an effective and often delightful piece of comedic stagecraft. The liar escapes with but slight punishment, marrying a girl other than the one he was courting, but the occasionally raised questions about the play's "immorality" are really groundless. The language of the comedy is much more natural than that of Corneille's earlier dramas and comedies. Instead of long stilted speeches, the characters converse in a dialogue that often sparkles. *Le Menteur* is important historically, but also entertaining in its own right.

THE MERCHANT OF VENICE

Type of work: Drama
Author: William Shakespeare (1564-1616)
Type of plot: Tragi-comedy
Time of plot: Sixteenth century
Locale: Venice
First presented: c. 1596

In The Merchant of Venice *Shakespeare fuses a number of diverse, even contradictory, dramatic styles, ranging from folktale to romantic comedy to borderline tragedy, to create one of his most popular and moving plays. The encounter between the greedy Jew, Shylock, and the wise, fine Portia gives the play a grave beauty.*

Through the years *The Merchant of Venice* has been one of Shakespeare's most popular and most frequently acted plays. Not only has it an interesting and fast-moving plot, but it also evokes an idyllic, uncorrupted world reminiscent of folktale and romance. From the beginning with Antonio's nameless sadness, the world is bathed in light and music. The insistently improbable plot is complicated only by the evil influence of Shylock and he is disposed of by the end of Act IV. Yet Shakespeare uses this fragile vehicle to make some significant points about justice, mercy, and friendship, three typical Renaissance conversation pieces. Although some critics have suggested that the play contains all of the elements of tragedy only to be rescued by a comic resolution, the tone of the whole play creates a benevolent world in which, despite some opposition, we are always sure that things will work out for the best.

The story is based on ancient tales, which could have been drawn from many sources. It is actually two stories—the casket-plot, involving the choice by the suitor and his reward with Portia, and the bond-plot, involving the loan and the attempt to exact a pound of flesh. Shakespeare's genius here lies in the combination of the two. Although they intersect from the start in the character of Bassanio, who occasions Antonio's debt and is a suitor, they fully coalesce when Portia comes to Venice in disguise to make her plea and judgment for Antonio. At that point the bond-plot is unravelled by the casket-heroine and we have only the celebratory conclusion of the fifth act still to enjoy.

The most fascinating character both to audiences and critics has always been Shylock, the outsider, the anomaly in this felicitous world. Controversy rages over just what kind of villain Shylock is and just how villainous Shakespeare intended him to be. The matter has been complicated by a contemporary desire to try to absolve Shakespeare of the common medieval and Renaissance malady of anti-Semitism. Consequently, some commentators on the play have argued that in Shylock Shakespeare takes the stock character of the Jew, like Marlowe's Barabas in *The Jew of Malta,* and fleshes him out with complicating human characteristics. Some have gone so far as to argue that even in his villainy he is represented as a victim of the Christian society, the grotesque product of hatred and ostracism. Regardless of Shakespeare's personal views, the fact remains that in his hands Shylock becomes much more than a stock character.

The more significant dramatic question is: just what sort of character is Shylock and what sort of role is he called upon to play? Certainly he is an outsider both in appearance and action, a stranger to the light and gracious world of Venice and Belmont. His language is full of stridency and materialism which isolate him from the rest of the characters. He has no part in the network of beautiful friendships which unite the rest of the characters in the play. He is not wholly a comic character; despite his often appearing ridiculous, he poses too much of a potential threat to be dismissed lightly. Nor is he the cold and terrifying villain like Iago or Edmund, or even an engaging villain like Richard III; he is too ineffectual and too grotesque. He is a malevolent force, but he is finally overcome by the more generous world he lives in. That he is treated so badly by the Christians is the kind of irony that ultimately protects Shakespeare from charges of mindless anti-Semitism. Still, on the level of the romantic plot, he is also the serpent in the garden, deserving summary expulsion and the forced conversion which is, ironically, both a punishment and a charity.

The rest of the major characters have much more in common with each other as sharers in the common civilization of Venice. As they come into conflict with Shylock and form relationships with one another, they act out the ideals and commonplaces of high Renaissance culture. Antonio, in his small but pivotal role, is afflicted with a fashionable melancholy and a gift for friendship. It is a casually generous act of friendship which sets the bond-plot in motion. Bassanio frequently comments on friendship and knows how to accept generosity gracefully. But Bassanio is also a Renaissance lover as well as a model Renaissance friend. He is quite frankly as interested in Portia's money as in her wit and beauty; he unself-consciously represents a cultural integration of love and gain quite different from Shylock's materialism. And when he chooses the leaden casket, he does so for precisely the right traditional reason—a distrust of appearances, a recognition that the reality does not always correspond. Of course, his success as suitor is never really in doubt, but is rather danced out like a ballet. Everyone knows, or ought to know, that lead should be preferred to gaudy gold and silver and indeed the greatest treasure of all, a portrait of Portia, is inside. In addition, the third suitor is always the successful one in folktale. What the ballet provides is another opportunity for the expression of the culturally correct sentiments.

Portia too is a culture heroine. She is not merely an object of love, but a witty and intelligent woman whose ingenuity resolves the central dilemma.

That she too is not what she seems to be in the trial scene is another reminder of the familiar appearance/reality theme. More importantly she has the opportunity to discourse on the nature of mercy as opposed to strict justice and to give an object lesson that he who lives by the letter of the law will perish by it.

With Shylock safely, if a bit harshly, out of the way, the last act is an amusing festival of vindication of the cultural values. The characters have had their opportunity to comment on the proper issues—love, friendship, justice, and the disparity between appearances and reality. Now each receives his appropriate reward in marriages, reunions, and even the pleasantly gratuitous recovery of Antonio's fortune. There is no more trouble in paradise among the people of grace.

Edward E. Foster

THE MERRY WIVES OF WINDSOR

Type of work: Drama
Author: William Shakespeare (1564-1616)
Type of plot: Farce
Time of plot: Sixteenth century
Locale: England
First presented: c. 1597

Responding to popular pressure—especially that of Queen Elizabeth—Shakespeare resurrected his greatest comic figure, Sir John Falstaff, once more in The Merry Wives of Windsor. *If the "Fat Jack" of this play lacks the force and dimension he had in* Henry IV, Parts I and II, *he is still the central figure in a romp that demonstrates Shakespeare's facility as a master of farce.*

Under public pressure to bring back Sir John Falstaff after Prince Hal's arrogant dismissal of his boyhood friend in *Henry the Fourth, Part Two* and *Henry the Fifth,* Shakespeare reintroduces the fat knight in a slapstick romp, *The Merry Wives of Windsor.* On the one hand, the farce can be viewed as a ridiculous satire of the London Burghers, the Fords and the Pages, who, however, successfully outwit the not-so-sly fox of an aristocrat, Falstaff, who is trying in his usual way to disrupt the pleasures and the comforts of the conventional. In this vein, one might see the story in the line begun by Boccaccio's *Decameron.*

Another way of approaching the play is by viewing it as a comic resolve of a story similar in some incidents to Shakespeare's earlier play, *Romeo and Juliet.* Unwittingly, Falstaff in his buffoonery performs the role of diverting the Pages from the elopement of their daughter, Anne, and Fenton, the comic Romeo. A potential tragedy thus averted, young and free love is allowed to flourish. Even though without his direct intervention, Falstaff plays the same role which Shakespeare had assigned to him in the histories. As opposed to the deliberate Hal, who orders everything in his life, even his leisure with his cronies, Falstaff devotes his whole life to play, the gratification of the instincts and the preservation of the self. His dalliance with the Mistresses Page and Ford may be a mockery of good Burgher virtue, but he also pursues it with a good deal of pleasure, and pleasure for its own sake. Everyone wins in the process. Anne is married to the boy she loves; the Pages, the Fords, and Sir John all have a thoroughly fine time in the romp. The only loser is respectability, which takes a back seat to the loud, vulgar guffaws of "Fat Jack" Falstaff.

MESSER MARCO POLO

Type of work: Novelette
Author: Donn Byrne (Brian Oswald Donn-Byrne, 1889-1928)
Type of plot: Exotic romance
Time of plot: Thirteenth century
Locale: Venice and China
First published: 1921

A mixture of three elements gives this simple tale a unique flavor: a modern Irishman tells the adventures of a Christian Italian in pagan China. Thus, Irish mysticism mingles with the mystery of the East to produce a romantic and tragic love story based upon the visit of Marco Polo to the Court of Kubla Khan.

Donn Byrne called himself "the last of the Irish storytellers." His adversaries, of whom he had many, called him a synthetic "professional Irishman." There is truth in both views. Byrne was indeed Irish by parentage, upbringing, and sentiment, though he was born during a parental visit to Brooklyn. Well-educated, in Dublin and abroad, he first sought adventure in South America, dreaming of fame as a cowboy poet; but soon he moved to New York.

His first works, though critically praised, sold poorly, and for some years he scraped for a living, first in a garage, then on a series of newspapers, finally putting his considerable erudition to work as a lexicographer. Fiercely combative for the Orange cause, he was in constant conflict with the Sinn Fein sympathizers in New York, and he was involved with equal passion in the many literary disputes of the time.

Messer Marco Polo brought the author fame and some fortune in 1920, but his reckless generosity and extravagance soon forced him to flee his creditors. He traveled widely during his last years, continuing to write prolifically. On one night in 1928 he won enough money at a casino in Cannes to buy a castle in Cork, but he was killed in an automobile accident shortly after his return to Ireland.

There may well have been elements of the synthetic in Byrne's lifelong performance as a wild Irish "boyo," but in regard to his writing, there is no problem: art *is* synthetic by definition, and the only relevant question is whether it works. *Messer Marco Polo* works extremely well. The narrator's Irish allusions, locutions and—most poignantly—his rhythms transform a thin tale into a romantic fantasy that evokes the glamor of virtually every exotic name or place from Venice to Peking with remarkable wit and economy. Byrne unerringly strikes the appropriate tones of humor and pathos throughout his novel. Its stylistic beauty, its exquisite folk descriptions of setting and character make this one of the best modern romances.

MICAH CLARKE

Type of work: Novel
Author: Arthur Conan Doyle (1859-1930)
Type of plot: Historical romance
Time of plot: Late seventeenth century
Locale: England
First published: 1888

Micah Clarke, a stirring, authentic adventure story, is, unfortunately, despite Doyle's skill in the presentation, too unfamiliar, lengthy, and complex to interest most modern readers. Posterity has proven Doyle wrong in his belief that his literary reputation would ultimately rest on his historical fictions rather than on the relatively "trivial" Sherlock Holmes tales.

Sir Arthur Conan Doyle is best known for his most lasting and loved creation, Sherlock Holmes. The cycles of stories involving Holmes were written between 1891 and World War I. Less well-known are his historical novels, which include *Micah Clarke, The Exploits of Brigadier Gerard* (1896), and *Rodney Stone* (1896). Quite successful in their time, these novels have received little or no attention since the Boer War, and none is currently in print. Doyle, by profession a doctor of medicine, graduated from Edinburgh University and took up practice until 1890, when, encouraged by the popular reception of his first literary efforts, closed his practice and began to devote himself to writing full time.

Historical novels being then much in fashion, he undertook *Micah Clarke* from what is obviously a more than adequate knowledge of history. Narrated in the first person, it is a retrospective view of the speaker's adventures as a young man in the uprising associated with the Rye House Plot which sought to support the cause of James Scott, Duke of Monmouth, the natural son of Charles II, as successor. The anti-Church faction, composed for the most part of laborers and lower middle-class nonconformists, provided Doyle with the perfect vehicle for an accurate and interesting view of the Whig armed uprising. Doyle devoted much time and care to his characterization of Clarke and companions, and went so far as to include an appendix of relevant material on such various subjects as the speed with which couriers were able to deliver messages over long distances, the current law code concerning the borrowing and lending of horses, seventeenth century pronunciation, and the documentation of Monmouth's claim to legitimacy.

In spite of Doyle's reasonably readable style of narration, the novel is one which lacks interest for the modern audience, few of whom can be expected to know the historical background of the novel, and even fewer whose interest would be so abiding as to struggle through the complexities of plot and dialogue. Doyle's adherence to historical fact, while admirable, does not include enough general information to explain his references. His extreme attention to detail, his less than sophisticated ability to handle his plot line (an ability which he later developed superbly, as the Sherlock Holmes stories testify), and his essentially heavy-handed narrative approach make this novel a period piece rather than a work of general interest.

MICHAEL AND HIS LOST ANGEL

Type of work: Drama
Author: Henry Arthur Jones (1851-1929)
Type of plot: Social tragedy
Time of plot: Nineteenth century
Locale: England and Italy
First presented: 1896

In Michael and His Lost Angel, *Henry Arthur Jones modernizes the traditional theme of a ligious, morally rigid man's inner conflict between the claims of the spirit and the newly awakened needs of the flesh. Despite a contrived resolution, Jones presents the torments of his hero, Michael Feversham, and the complicated emotions of his sympathetic temptress, Audrie Lesden, with poignancy and seriousness.*

Henry Arthur Jones was the first of the British dramatists who were to revitalize the English theater at the end of the nineteenth and beginning of the twentieth centuries. The new realism and seriousness of the Continental drama, stimulated primarily by the impact of Henrik Ibsen's plays, prepared the theatrical atmosphere in England for a similar thrust into modernity. Although denying any direct Ibsen influence, Jones felt that the same seriousness could be brought to the English stage and that he was the playwright to do so. He made his position clear in a letter to *The Daily News* in 1883:

> The truth is that audiences want literature, they want poetry, but they do not want unactable, intractable imitations of Shakespeare's form without his vitality. They want life, they want reality; they demand that the characters they see on stage shall be, not the ghostly abstractions of the study, but living, breathing human beings, with good warm red blood in their veins.

During his most popular and successful years, Jones ably translated his polemic into such plays as *Saints and Sinners* (1884), *The Middleman* (1889), *The Liars* (1897), and *Mrs. Dane's Defence* (1900). The important exception in Jones's sequence of popular successes was *Michael and His Lost Angel.*

Since that time critics have taken a closer look at the play and some— including the playwright—have believed it to be his best. It is certainly one of his most ambitious and there are moments of considerable dramatic intensity and powerful character revelation. But, in the final analysis, the play lacks the necessary focus, and Michael's character remains a little too vague for tragedy.

Michael's change from the rigidly moralistic minister of Act I to the tormented, contrite Catholic convert of Act V is understandable, but not completely convincing. The moments in which he attempts to come to terms with his guilt and confusion are intense and agonized, and the scene where Michael confesses his sin directly to his congregation has a tragic feeling worthy of Hawthorne. But the overall characterization is somewhat dissipated by Jones' failure to dramatize Michael's feelings toward Audrie Lesden with precision. Is it a mature love that he accepts in spite of its effect on him, or is it only a periodic sexual infatuation?

Although Audrie's character is not as thoroughly developed as Michael's, her feelings toward him are easier to comprehend. At the beginning of the play she is torn between a cynical desire to manipulate a "good man" and a genuine romantic attraction. But, by the end of the play, her feelings have clarified: she loves the man, but hates his "pieties." "I think," she says at one point, "a little love on this earth is worth a good many paradises hereafter."

The dramatic climax of their relationship comes at the end of Act II, just prior to their "fatal" night together, when they *almost* crystalize and state their feelings to each other. But the act ends too soon and the issue is never raised as directly again. Thus, the affair is never completely in focus and the resolution of it, in Audrie's death and Michael's conversion to Catholicism, gives the impression of being a somewhat contrived "Victorian" ending that offends —and provokes—no one.

MIDDLEMARCH

Type of work: Novel
Author: George Eliot (Mary Ann Evans, 1819-1880)
Type of plot: Psychological realism
Time of plot: Nineteenth century
Locale: England
First published: 1871-1872

Middlemarch is the most comprehensive and sweeping of George Eliot's novels and is usually considered her masterpiece. Structuring the book around four major plotlines—the story of Dorothea Brooke, the story of Lydgate's marriage, the history of Mary Garth, and the fall ofe banker Bulstrode—the author creates a dynamic pattern that encompasses an entire spectrum of life, attitudes, and events in early nineteenth century England.

Modestly subtitled "A Study in Provincial Life," George Eliot's *Middlemarch* has long been recognized as a work of great psychological and moral penetration. Indeed, the novel has been compared with Tolstoy's *War and Peace* and Thackeray's *Vanity Fair* for its nearly epic sweep and its perspective of early nineteenth century history. Yet these comparisons are partly faulty. Unlike *War and Peace, Middlemarch* lacks a philosophical bias, a grand *Weltanschauung* that oversees the destinies of nations and generations. And unlike *Vanity Fair,* Eliot's novel is not neatly moralistic. In fact, much of *Middlemarch* is morally ambiguous, in the modern sense of the term. Eliot's concept of plot and character derives from psychological rather than philosophical or social necessity. This is another way of saying that *Middlemarch,* despite its Victorian trappings of complicated plot and subplot, its slow development of character, accumulated detail concerning time and place, its social density is—in many other respects—a "modern" novel that disturbs as well as comforts the reader.

At the height of her powers, George Eliot published *Middlemarch* in eight books, from December 1871 to December 1872, eight years before her death. She had already achieved a major reputation with *Adam Bede* (1859), *The Mill on the Floss* (1860), and *Silas Marner* (1861). But her most recent fiction, *Felix Holt, Radical* (1866), and *The Spanish Gypsy* (1868), both inferior to her best writing, had disappointed her public. *Middlemarch,* however, was received with considerable excitement and critical acclaim. Eliot's publisher, Blackwood, was so caught up with the action, as he received chapters of her novel by mail, that he wrote back to her asking questions about the fates of the characters, as though they were real people with real histories. As a matter of fact, Eliot researched the material for her novel scrupulously. Her discussion of the social climate in rural England directly before the passage of the Reform Bill of 1832 is convincingly detailed; she accurately describes the state of medical knowledge during Lydgate's time; and she treats the dress, habits, and speech of Middlemarch impeccably, creating the metaphor of a complete world, a piece of provincial England that is a microcosm of the greater world beyond.

Yet the theme of the novel itself revolves around the slenderest of threads: the mating of "unimportant" people. This theme, which engages the talents of other great writers as well—Jane Austen, Thomas Hardy, Henry James, D. H. Lawrence—allows George Eliot scope to examine the whole range of human nature. She is concerned with the mating of lovers, because they are most vulnerable in love, most nearly the victims of their romantic illusions. Each of the three sets of lovers in *Middlemarch*—Dorothea Brooke/Edward Casaubon/Will Ladislaw; Rosamond Vincy/Tertius Lydgate; and Mary Garth/Fred Vincy—mistake illusion for reality. Eventually all come to understand themselves better, whether or not they are completely reconciled with their mates. Each undergoes a sentimental education, a discipline of the spirit that teaches the heart its limitations.

Paradoxically, the greater capacity Eliot's characters have for romantic self-deception, the greater is their suffering and subsequent tempering of spirit. Mary Garth, plain, witty, honest, is too sensible to arouse our psychological curiosity to the same degree that we are interested in the proud Dorothea, rash Ladislaw, pathetic Casaubon, ambitious Lydgate, or pampered Rosamond. Mary loves simply, directly. Fred, her childhood sweetheart, is basically a good lad who must learn from his own misfortunes the lessons of thrift and perseverance. He "falls" in class, from that of an idle landowner to one of a decent but socially inferior manager of property. In truth, what he seems to lose in social prominence he more than recovers in the development of his moral character. Moreover, he wins as a mate the industrious Mary, who will strengthen his resolve and make of him an admirable provider like her father Caleb.

Dorothea, on the other hand, more idealistic and noble-hearted than Mary, chooses the worst possible mate as her first husband. Edward Casaubon, thirty years her senior, is a dull pedant, cold, hopelessly ineffectual as a scholar, absurd as a lover. Despite his intellectual pretensions, he is too timid, fussy, and dispirited ever to complete his masterwork, "A Key to All Mythologies." Even the title of his project is an absurdity. He conceals as long as possible his "key" from Dorothea, fearing that she will expose him as a sham. Yet it is possible that she might have endured the disgrace of her misplaced affection were Casaubon only more tender, reciprocating her own tenderness and self-sacrifice. But Casaubon, despotic to the last, tries to blight her spirit when he is alive and, through his will, to restrict her freedom when he is dead.

Dorothea's second choice of a mate, Will Ladislaw is very nearly the opposite of Casaubon. A rash, sometimes hypersensitive lover, he is capable of intense affection, above all of self-sacrifice. He is a worthy suitor for

Dorothea, who finds greatness in his ardor, if not his accomplishments. Yet Will, allowing for his greater vitality, is after all a logical successor to Casaubon. Dorothea had favored the elderly scholar because he was unworldly, despised by the common herd. In her imagination he seemed a saint of intellect. In time she comes to favor Will because he is also despised by most of the petty-minded bigots of Middlemarch, because he has suffered from injustice; and because he seems to her a saint of integrity. A Victorian St. Theresa, Dorothea is passive, great in aspiration rather than deed. Psychologically she requires a great object for her own self-sacrifice, and therefore chooses a destiny that will allow her the fullest measure of heroism.

Tertius Lydgate, quite the opposite, is a calculating, vigorous, ambitious young physician who attempts to move others to his own iron will. His aggressive energy contrasts with Dorothea's passiveness. However, like her, he is a victim of romantic illusion. He believes that he can master, through his intelligence and determination, those who possess power. Nevertheless, his choice of a mate, Rosamond Vincy, is a disastrous miscalculation. Rosamond's fragile beauty conceals a petulant, selfish will equal to his own. She dominates him through her own weakness rather than strength of character. Insensitive except to her own needs, she offers no scope for Lydgate's sensitive intelligence. In his frustration, he can only battle with himself. He comes to realize that he is defeated not only in his dreams of domestic happiness but in his essential judgment of the uses of power.

For George Eliot, moral choice does not exist in a sanctified vacuum; it requires an encounter with power. To even the least sophisticated dwellers in Middlemarch, power is represented by wealth and status. As the widow Mrs. Casaubon, Dorothea's social prestige rests upon her personal and inherited fortune. When she casts aside her estate under Casaubon's will to marry Ladislaw, she loses also a great measure of status. At the same time, she acquires moral integrity, a superior virtue for Eliot. Similarly, when Mary Garth rejects Mr. Featherstone's dying proposition to seize his wealth before his relatives make a shambles of his will, she chooses morally, justly, and comes to deserve the happiness that she eventually wins. As for Lydgate, whose moral choices are most nearly ambiguous, he returns Bulstrode's bribe to save himself from a social embarrassment, but his guilt runs deeper than mere miscalculation. He has associated himself, first through his choice of Tyke instead of the worthier Farebrother as vicar, with Bulstrode's manipulation of power. Lydgate's moral defeat is partial, for at least he understands the extent of his compromise with integrity. Bulstrode's defeat is total, for he loses both wealth and social standing. As for Middlemarch, that community of souls is a small world, populated with people of good will and bad, mean spirits and fine, and is the collective agent of moral will. After all, it is the town that endures, the final arbiter of moral judgment in a less than perfect world.

Leslie B. Mittleman

A MIDSUMMER NIGHT'S DREAM

Type of work: Drama
Author: William Shakespeare (1564-1616)
Type of plot: Romantic comedy
Time of plot: Remote antiquity
Locale: Athens
First presented: 1595

A Midsummer Night's Dream *is probably the most purely romantic of Shakespeare's comedies. Although the magic of Puck explains the lovers' erratic behavior, they are really responding to the essential capriciousness of young love in this pastoral romp that spoofs not only the vagaries of romance, but the nature of reality itself.*

In general, modern theater has been dominated by the techniques and presuppositions of literary realism. So, also, has it been with motion picture and television drama. In theater, with its proscenium stage, this has produced a phenomenon known as "three wall" drama. The effect described by this term is the impression, more or less successfully achieved in any given play, that it is as if there were a room and the audience feels itself watching, through the fourth wall, actors who are interacting without being aware of an audience before them. The Elizabethan conception of theater was quite different, and this sense of illusion was not given such priority.

In *A Midsummer Night's Dream* there is, as in many plays of the time, a lively mixture of realism and a more formal, more open, communication with the audience. Partly this derives from the stage itself, which in Shakespeare's time jutted out and was surrounded by the audience. Partly, it was so because there was, apparently, scarcely any scenery. Costumes and dialogue supplied, as Quince's prologue says, "all that you are like to know."

The more important aspects of this tradition were the morality plays and a general tradition of formal staging. This included not only the morality, but masques, tableaux, and processions. The essence of these traditions, for our purpose, is that the former, especially, relied on allegory and dumb shows. That is to say, there would be a dumb show at the beginning of each act showing in brief the action, and emblematically the moral of the principal drama. The drama itself was highly stylized. Sometimes the characters would be fully allegorical, with a name carried upon the breast of each actor denoting his role, such as "Good Will," "Avarice," and so on. They would engage in a moral conflict for a man's soul. An extreme form of these stylized productions were the tableaux: simple groupings of actors, with perhaps a symbolic backboard, showing a spiritual or philosophical moral.

A third traditional element important in this play is the pastoral. In brief, this pattern had it that the characters would leave city society to enter a forest or country setting, where they would undergo changes, to return to a more harmonious society.

A Midsummer Night's Dream exploits these elements to a great extent as support even for its particular themes: chiefly, that of Reason and Imagination. There is an obvious parallel between this theme with its *imaginary* quality of deep "engagement" by the audience in psychic realism (whatever its form), and the *reason* and intellect required by the more formal elements; that is, formal elements such as the self-commentary of the play, and the more imposing structural elements which derive from, or were added to, the traditions described above.

In this play we are "engaged" by the problems of the lovers and see these, as is suggested by this term, more or less as they do. We hope the two couples will end up properly matched and safe. Also, we hope all will be reconciled between Oberon and Titania, and so on. These naïve expectations are soon subjected to doubts, though, as Puck starts to switch the partners with his magic. An inevitable intellectualization begins as we notice how similar the absurd changes are to the fickle, yet fervently professed, loves of theatrical convention and reality. Only Demetrius comes back from the experience changed (back to his former love for Helena). But we are able to see the test of their loves, showing their enduring simplicity. Such guilelessness, as normal speech would have it, is "engaging," because it is a virtue even if the couple is Antony and Cleopatra; but it is inadequate by itself, in a world more complex than these lovers know.

In any case the theme of Reason and Imagination in this play goes beyond its importance for lovers, although they are the primary manifestations of the intoxicating effects of imagination here. The real focus of the play, however, is on the playwright's art itself. There are the subtler self-conscious notes of authorial presence in the structure and in the use of such devices as "mirroring." And there is the more explicit "metacommentary" centered in the play within the play.

"Mirroring" comes about in this play through the symmetry of relationships and events. In reflecting each other they give rise to a reciprocal commentary. The young lovers are so like each other that their speeches are almost interchangeable. Their supposed superiors in wisdom, Theseus and Hippolyta, as well as Oberon and Titania, have all had series of loves, and have more or less disastrously fallen out, including with each other's partners. The mirroring effect of Quince's play should be clear. As a travesty of the Romeo and Juliet story, it reflects the exaggerated passions of every character's romantic fancy.

This play within the play points to the notion of "metacommentary": Shakespeare commenting upon himself, and on the theater, actors, and audience alike. The play is known to have been first produced, like Quince's, for a noble marriage. But more importantly, the meanings of imagination, whether naïve, or structured by the author's intelligence, are forced upon the audience. Puck says that if the play offends, think it but a dream, of no consequence. His irony leaves us little room to avoid thinking of the play thus: we must not take the thing for something it is not (become lost in imagination), nor ignore it at the risk of admitting we have been dozing for two hours (have no imagination at all).

James Marc Hovde

THE MIKADO

Type of work: Comic opera
Author: W. S. Gilbert (1836-1911)
Type of plot: Social satire
Time of plot: Middle Ages
Locale: Titipu, Japan
First presented: 1885

The Mikado, or The Town of Titipu, is one of the best-known collaborations of librettist Sir William Gilbert and composer Sir Arthur Sullivan. The authors show off their talent for sparkling lyrics and dialogue, pointed satire, and high-spirited humor to best advantage in this two-act comic opera about an emperor's son, traveling in disguise, who falls in love with the ward of the Lord High Executioner.

Gilbert and Sullivan's *The Mikado* is an outstanding example of the comic effect of familiar characters and familiar behavior patterns being made humorous by an exotic setting. The setting is medieval Japan. One of the strands of the complex plot—that of a prince disguised as a minstrel to escape an undesirable marriage—resembles legend. This strand is solved in a legendary way by the marriage of the unwanted bride to the villain of the story.

Yet, this seeming legend of a far-off land is peopled by characters who are Victorian English to the core—Ko-Ko, a slightly nastier Sir Joseph Porter; Yum-Yum, a younger and more naïve Patience; Katisha, a typical Gilbert and Sullivan old maid; and Pooh-Bah, an entire modern bureaucracy in a single person. The final incongruity is Ko-Ko's song of the dying sparrow—a parody of a traditional song, but of a distinctly English one.

The minstrel's story is intertwined with the purely comic plot of Ko-Ko, the executioner guilty of a capital offense who must find somebody else to execute in order to justify his job. The job itself makes possible one of the most comprehensive hate songs ever written—the list of individuals who would not be missed if executed. Ko-Ko's agreement with the minstrel, allowing the latter to marry Yum-Yum, only to be beheaded thirty days later, is the *reductio ad absurdum* of the romantic theme in which the man dies rather than live without his beloved. Ultimately, of course, the couple are allowed to live happily ever after, but only because of the clever working out of the complex plot. Gilbert's use of mistaken identity and of the discovery of the living person presumed dead are excellent touches to this fine comic play.

THE MILL ON THE FLOSS

Type of work: Novel
Author: George Eliot (Mary Ann Evans, 1819-1880)
Type of plot: Domestic realism
Time of plot: Nineteenth century
Locale: England
First published: 1860

George Eliot probably identified with Maggie Tulliver, the heroine of The Mill on the Floss, *and that gives the novel much of its immediacy and charm, especially in the early chapters. Like Eliot, Maggie is a girl of deep sensitivity, intellectual capacity, and spiritual longings. But, unlike her creator, Maggie can never realize those inclinations and talents in the provincial, male-dominated environment that surrounds and finally destroys her.*

Shortly after George Eliot published *Adam Bede* in 1858, she began to work on a new novel under the tentative title "Sister Maggie." As the book was taking shape, she considered other possible titles—"The House of Tulliver," "The Tulliver Family," "The Tullivers"—before her editor, Blackwood, suggested *The Mill on the Floss,* a title she approved with some reservations. She objected at first that the "mill is not strictly on the Floss, being on its small tributary" and that the title "is of rather laborious utterance." Having voiced her usual nice concern for precise details and delicacy of style, she allowed that Blackwood's title was "the only alternate so far as we can see." On March 21, 1860, she completed the book, vacationed in Rome with her husband George Henry Lewes, and awaited the news of the critics' reception, which proved to be almost wholly favorable. With satisfaction Eliot wrote: "From all we can gather, the votes are rather on the side of 'The Mill' as a better book than 'Adam.'"

It is certainly the more poignant novel. Although both fictions have as their setting the Warwickshire background that George Eliot remembered from her youth, *The Mill on the Floss* is less genially picturesque, more concerned with psychological truth. *Adam Bede* concludes, probably contrary to the author's best artistic judgment, with a happy marriage for Adam and Dinah. But Tom and Maggie Tulliver die in the flood, their fate unmitigated by sentimentality. Indeed, much of the novel's power derives from the consistent play of tragic forces that appear early and unify the whole work.

As a boy, Tom entrusts his pet rabbits to his sister Maggie's care. Pre-occupied, she allows the creatures to die. Tom upbraids her bitterly, in spite of her tearful protestations, but finally forgives her. This childhood pattern of close sibling affection, followed by deep hurt and estrangement, then by reconciliation, becomes the structural pattern of the novel. Although Henry James admired the design of *The Mill on the Floss,* he criticized the conclusion for its melodrama. As a matter of fact, the conclusion is implicit in the story from the beginning. The flood that carries to their doom the beloved brother and sister is not so much an accidental catastrophe. Rather, it is symbolic of the tide that sweeps away two passionate souls divided in conflict yet united by the closest bonds of affection.

Tom Tulliver, like his father, has a tenacious will that is not always under control of his reason. Even as a child, he is fiercely although honorably competitive. He is slow to forgive injury. Robust and vigorous, he despises weakness in others. As a youth, he insults Philip Wakem by drawing attention to the hunchback's physical deformity. And when Maggie demeans, as Tom mistakenly believes, the good name of the Tulliver family through her foreshortened "elopement" with Stephen Guest, he scorns her as a pariah. Yet Tom's tempestuous nature is also capable of generosity. To redeem his father's good name and restore Dorlcote Mill to the family, he disciplines himself to work purposefully. To this end, he sacrifices his high spirits, his love of strenuous excitement, indeed any opportunities for courtship and marriage. He dies as he had lived and labored, the provider of the Tulliver family.

His sister Maggie, many of whose sprightly qualities are drawn from George Eliot's memories of her own childhood, is psychologically the more complex character. Whereas Tom is sturdily masculine, Maggie is sensitive, introspective, tenderly feminine. Quick to tears—to the modern reader perhaps too effusive in her emotions—she cannot control her sensibilities, just as her brother cannot hold his temper. As a youngster, she has much of the tomboy in her. She is energetic and, unlike the typical Victorian girl, fights for her place in the world. Intelligent, diligent, earnest, she would make better use of Mr. Stelling's classical schooling than her brother; but girls of her time rarely had the opportunity to advance in education. So she must content herself, although secretively restive, with the narrow place Victorian society allows for girls of her class. Like Dorothea Brooke in *Middlemarch,* she is attracted to a scholarly but fragile lover, Philip. Her sympathetic nature completes what is lacking in the young man's disposition—courage and self-esteem. And in turn he offers her a sense of artistic dedication for which she yearns.

Some astute critics of *The Mill on the Floss* have objected to Maggie's other suitor, Stephen Guest, who is Lucy Deane's fiancé. For Lucy, a more typical Victorian heroine, sweet but passive, the impetuous Stephen would be a satisfactory mate. According to Sir Leslie Stephen, Maggie, in her passion for Lucy's betrothed, throws herself away upon a "low creature." His daughter, Virginia Woolf, repeated Sir Leslie's judgment in describing Stephen's "courseness." But a modern view of the character does not support such hostile interpretations. Stephen is neither low nor coarse. Instead he is an ardent lover who rouses in Maggie a sexual response that she does not feel, in spite of her tender empathy, for Philip. Maggie's torment is to be torn between her promises to Philip (who certainly loves and needs her) and her deeper feelings for Stephen. On one hand, she senses the call of duty and propriety; on the other, she feels the sweep of wild emotion. She masters her feelings, betrays her needs as a woman, and returns to Philip.

For the same reason that some critics refuse to accept Maggie as a mature woman with normal sexual responses, some readers are troubled by the apparent change in her character as she grows from child to adult. So vital, charming, and convincing is the portrait of Maggie the girl, that readers may wish to cherish her youthful image. But Maggie the woman does not really change. Within the prudish conventions of the Victorian novel, George Eliot can only suggest her heroine's psychological and moral development. Nevertheless, she conveys a sense of Maggie's greater sexual vulnerability because of her "highly strung, hungry nature." When she renounces Stephen, she renounces her own happiness. From that point, her tragedy is inevitable. The provincial gossips of St. Ogg's cast her off. Her beloved brother rejects her. To be sure, her mother, Lucy, and Philip have faith in her to the last. But Maggie, characteristically, determines: "I must not, cannot seek my own happiness by sacrificing others." Thus, the flood waters that carry Maggie and her brother downstream cleanse their guilts, unite them as when they were children, innocent with hope. Finally in their death as in their life, Eliot tells us, they are "not divided."

Leslie B. Mittleman

THE MILL ON THE PO

Type of work: Novel
Author: Riccardo Bacchelli (1891-   )
Type of plot: Historical romance
Time of plot: 1812-1872
Locale: The region of the Po River near Ferrara
First published: 1938-1940

The epic sweep and poetic fervor of The Mill on the Po *give Bacchelli's novel a significant place in twentieth century Italian fiction. The stormy period of Italian unification forms the backdrop for an extended chronicle of the Scacerni clan as they strive to obtain peace and security without being submerged by the forces of history and nature.*

The Mill on the Po encompasses two parts of Bacchelli's Italian trilogy dealing with the lives and fortunes of the mythical Scacerni family. The device of the trilogy was quite popular in early twentieth century Italian fiction. It was utilized successfully by Verga and Fogazzaro as well as Bacchelli as a means to express a grandiose idea without the confines of a single novel. But, as is commonly the case, the trilogy itself is lost in literary history, whereas one particular part of the trilogy will stand apart as a great work. This is true of *The Mill on the Po,* which was not only the best of this trilogy, but also the masterpiece of Bacchelli's literary career.

This novel was written almost at the culmination of Bacchelli's personal victory over his own life. As a youth he was fraught with inner struggles which left marks on all of his earlier works. By the late 1930's when he wrote *The Mill on the Po,* however, he no longer was compelled to rely on semi-autobiographical themes, and from this point on his literary output was more prolific and of a higher quality than before.

The novel is set against the background of Italian unification in the late nineteenth century. This was one of the most important settings for Italian literature in the early part of this century. Bacchelli's work does not depend upon the unification theme for a large part of its thrust, however. It is merely the stage upon which the drama is set. The major emphasis or theme of the novel is the struggle of the common man against life.

Another important aspect of *The Mill on the Po* is the literary device of tracing one family's history from generation to generation. This has been used successfully by Giuseppe di Lampedusa in Italian and Edna Ferber in American literature. It is a plot scheme which has been particularly popular in the twentieth century and Bacchelli used it well. The backdrop of the Italian unification is the canvas upon which the family portrait is painted. Italian history moved at a different rate than the lives of the characters, and therefore is an effective background for a multi-generational novel such as this.

The Mill on the Po is actually a two-volume story which has episodes held together by history and the Scacerni family line. Though the portions of the novel are different, and indeed even the writing style and mood of the story changes from section to section, the historical setting on the one hand and the unchanging river Po on the other provide pivotal points on which the novel can progress.

Bacchelli was highly influenced by Alessandro Manzoni, the great nineteenth century Italian author of *The Betrothed*. *The Mill on the Po* and several of Bacchelli's other works show large traces of Manzonian influence in the narrative. Bacchelli, like Manzoni, was best as a historical novelist. Both wrote monumentally large works about day to day characters whose lives took place in a period of historical turmoil. And one of the reasons that Bacchelli was so successful was that, like Manzoni, he wrote readable works, not merely symbolic pieces of tragedy. In the period of the 1920's Italy was not known for her great literary output. Aside from the works of Grazia Deledda, Italo Svevo, and Bacchelli, Italian literature was at its lowest point of the century. The greats of the early part of the century, such as Verga and D'Annunzio, were either dead or no longer producing, and the budding authors of the thirties and forties had yet to come into the limelight. Perhaps because of this dry literary period, *The Mill on the Po* was very popular and well received critically. Its popularity has declined somewhat since then, however, especially outside of Italy, but it is still recommended reading for those who enjoy historical fiction, romance, and adventure.

In retrospect, the weakest point of the novel is the characterization. Though well drawn, the characters are stereotypes rather than individuals. Lazzaro and Cecilia represent the strong, pliable personalities who are able to deal with adversities and yet remain true to their ideals and themselves. Dosolina and Giuseppe, on the other hand, personify the weak and the frightened who would make the best out of life only if it were easy and on their own terms. Rather than accept changes Dosolina gives up, and Giuseppe tries to cheat his way out of bad situations. The problems which face the characters are so severe that the average reader can remember the adventures of the story far more easily than he can recall the details of an individual character's development.

Setting aside the meaning of "stock" characters and stereotypes, however, the reader can admire and love Lazzaro, just as he can hate Giuseppe. And when a novel portrays such an empathetic central character in such a good story, it is likely to be a popular work of fiction for a long time. The historical background and universal theme of man's struggle against the vicissitudes of life, added to its appealing main character put *The Mill on the Po* on a par with many of the great works of literature for enjoyment, if not for artistic merit.

Patricia Ann King

THE MINISTRY OF FEAR

Type of work: Novel
Author: Graham Greene (1904-   )
Type of plot: Psychological melodrama
Time of plot: World War II
Locale: London and environs
First published: 1943

The Ministry of Fear *is a "thriller" in the John Buchan tradition, where an ordinary man is thrust precipitously into a situation fraught with mystery, danger, and intrigue and left on his own to survive, solve the mystery, and bring the malefactors to justice. Nazi machinations during World War II provide the context for this exciting suspense novel, certainly one of Greene's best "entertainments."*

Graham Greene has often referred to his early novels as "entertainments." As entertaining as *This Gun for Hire, The Confidential Agent,* and *The Ministry of Fear* may be, in many ways they resemble finger exercises for his later mature novels. The same themes of guilt, sin, and the over-powering sense of evil that permeate such mature works as *The Heart of the Matter, The End of the Affair,* and *The Power and the Glory* have their analogues in *The Ministry of Fear* and the other "entertainments."

Arthur Rowe, driven by the guilt he continues to suffer as a result of the mercy-killing of his wife, is an essential innocent, like Scobie in *The Heart of the Matter,* or the nameless whiskey priest in *The Power and the Glory.* His actions, bumbling, ineffectual, and halting, are always undertaken without guile or malice. But in his mind, his act of mercy, indeed an excess of pity, haunts him throughout the pages of the novel. He is a pitiable, pitiful creature, snatched up by the horrors of an insane world, used as a tool by palpable evil, fascism. Subconsciously, Rowe, whose inner dedication seems to be to the statues of "Justice and Retribution," identifies his own act of pity or mercy with sin, and thus with the evil he hates. He is caught between two worlds—the realms of God and the Devil—a comic, futile person whose rules Rowe himself cannot comprehend.

Evil, and hence sin, is quite real to Greene, whether the evil be fascism, adultery, or a breach of faith to one's self. Evil is not a mere abstraction; rather, it looms almost as a creative force. Right actions, or the Good, seems spongy or ineffective by comparison. Yet, Rowe muddles through, and Greene seems to be saying that, despite the power of evil, and while the candle of goodness may not light up the entire world, personal integrity can be a protest against the dark. That is all that counts, for Rowe, in the end, is redeemed by love, however tentative and guarded the love may be.

MINNA VON BARNHELM

Type of work: Drama
Author: Gotthold Ephraim Lessing (1729-1781)
Type of plot: Romantic comedy
Time of plot: Eighteenth century
Locale: Germany
First presented: 1767

Minna von Barnhelm *is important both historically, as the first realistic comedy native to Germany, and for its stature in Lessing's canon as his finest nontragic play. The drama had much appeal for its original audience: the historical background touched their patriotism, its treatment of German soldiers and German women aroused their sympathy, and its amusing blend of comedy and pathos touched their hearts.*

Lessing's Minna von Barnhelm is his greatest comedy, and one of the great comedies of the German stage; it was also a landmark in the development of theatrical style, introducing in German literature the new realistic, contemporary comedy that had become fashionable in England and France. As Lessing's Miss Sara Sampson and Emilia Galotti introduced the bourgeois tragedy to the German stage, so Minna von Barnhelm represents the first comedy that departs from the baroque tradition of Molière which Lessing himself had followed in his early years. The play is set in a specific time and place, almost contemporary with the first production; in 1763 the Peace of Hubertusburg ended the Seven Years' War between Prussia and Austria, and in that same year the king of Prussia, Frederick II the Great, placed a large number of officers in the same situation Major Tellheim faced by releasing them from service without compensation for damages and losses. In the play, the plot is developed out of this situation, and the reminiscence of the conflict is underscored by the fact that the two protagonists, Tellheim and Minna, represent opposite sides in the war, as well as opposite aspects of the German character. Tellheim embodies the strict code of military honor, state-centered and unresponsive to personal motivations of the heart, that was coming to be regarded as typical of the fast-rising state of Prussia. In the peace treaty Prussia had retained the rich province of Silesia, which it had earlier seized from Austria, and thus secured its role as a major European power. Minna, a radiant portrait combining decisiveness, fortitude, wit, grace, and guile, is from Saxony, one of the allied states which had opposed Prussia, and which had been invaded at the beginning of the war. She is the feminine nature opposed to Tellheim's masculine military character, and she is linked to the other pole of German temperament, one that is associated with the South, Austria, and those old sections where culture had flourished in the centuries while Prussia was still barbarian. She is less idealistic and more pragmatic, more given to laughter than to tragedy, and not above playing tricks on the man she loves—for his own good.

The combination of elements puts the play in a very special situation, and determines to a certain extent its form. The basic conflict, that of an impoverished, wounded, and unjustly accused officer, whose code of honor will not let him accept help, is closer to tragedy than to comedy and the fact that Minna loves him, that he must remain noble in the eyes of the audience, prevents Lessing from making a mockery of his exaggerated adherence to what he regards as his duty. In fact, Tellheim's conscience, his idealism, is precisely what Minna loves about him, and Lessing does not want us to see it as a fault, except insofar as it prevents him from acknowledging the humanity that underlies his officership. Thus, in contrast to the comedy of Molière, in which a human fault, such as avarice or social climbing, is mocked, and the representative of the fault humiliated, Lessing presents us with a character whom his associates respect, and whose situation, historically real, could well be the material for tragedy. In this, he was following the lead of the English, who turned away from pure comedy to a mixture of somber and light tones, a sentimental comedy, closer to life as it is; less funny, admittedly, but far more engaging.

The pure comedy is now restricted to the secondary figures—all individual portraits, and yet comic types in a tradition that goes back to Menander and Plautus—the pert maid, the coarse manservant, the opportunist innkeeper. Lessing has given each an individual style of speech, most hilariously in the thick French accent of Riccaut de la Marlinière, the fast talking card sharp, who defines cheating as "corriger la fortune." These characters, like the protagonists, underscore the contemporary setting of the play. Indeed, the inn, "King of Portugal," was an actual Berlin locale and became famous through the play. But unlike the classical comedy, in which the servants often play a leading role in developing the plot, being pictured as more clever than their masters, the stage here really belongs to Tellheim and Minna, and the plot becomes a kind of campaign between the two, a contest of wit and will in which the thin line between comedy and tragedy is crossed and recrossed as first Tellheim, with his tragic self-image, and then Minna, with humor and humanity, gains the ascendant. It is worth noting that it is, in fact, a sham battle, a diversion that keeps the audience involved during five acts, although clearly neither Minna's plots nor Tellheim's obduracy can provide a satisfying solution.

Tellheim's dilemma is real, and his behavior, though exaggerated, is what the state would expect of a man in his position. Minna's ruse is nothing more than that—her feigning helplessness does bring out Tellheim's underlying magnanimity of character, but it could hardly be the basis for a resolution of the conflict. This resolution can only come from the man who created the conflict, the king, whose letter does in fact begin the denouement, in which the characters have to unravel the complications which they themselves have created. Thus, all the action of the play becomes a kind of much ado about nothing, and this resolution suddenly elevates the stage conflict out of the realm of grim reality into that cheerful sphere where pain is illusory and only joy proves real. This resolution through a *deus ex machina* is kept entirely within the realistic framework, and it fully preserves both the honor of Tell-heim and the rightness of Minna. Yet, at the same time, it leaves us with a poignant awareness of the vulnerability of even the best of men, of the danger in all excess, even that of virtue, of the nearness of comic fault to tragic flaw, and of the need for the preservation of humanity against all the institutional demands which threaten it.

Steven C. Schaber

A MIRROR FOR WITCHES

Type of work: Novel
Author: Esther Forbes (1894-1967)
Type of plot: Psychological realism
Time of plot: Seventeenth century
Locale: Massachusetts
First published: 1928

Drawing upon her New England heritage that goes back to Puritan times and may have even included a persecuted "witch," Esther Forbes has attempted to convey the reality of witch-hunting in Puritan Massachusetts by telling the story through the distorted mind of a woman, Doll Bilby, who actually believes herself to be in league with the Devil.

This is primarily a novel about psychology. Doll Bilby is a tormented, lonely, undersized woman who is hated by her barren stepmother. Hannah Bilby is jealous of the attention lavished on Doll by her husband, Jared. Doll is feared by the people of her Massachusetts village because of her stepmother's malicious gossip and the eccentric behavior of her stepmother's hatred has brought out in her. But Doll is not a witch and Bloody Shad is not her "demon prince." He is simply a pirate who has escaped jail and fled to Doll's part of the country. He passes himself off to her as a demon since he had heard of her reputation and was playing up to it. She is eager to believe him as a way of soothing her loneliness.

The whole course of action in the novel is much like that involving Doll and Bloody Shad. Doll was driven mad by the tales told about her, for after her stepfather's death she herself came to believe those tales. She was lonely and without comfort. Forsaken by the godly people of Puritan New England, she in turn forsook God and sought comfort from the devil whose servant she had long been told she was. She begins to walk abroad at night in search of her new god, Satan, and the world looks to be a better place to her after she has become mad. She was at peace with herself after she accepted the townspeople's view of her and began to accommodate herself to that view.

At one point she dreams that she rises up out of her body and flies about her bedroom. She flies out the window and goes walking in spirit over the meadows. She knew when she awoke that this was not a dream because she was wearing her slippers; they were wet with dew and covered with grass stains. She, of course, had been walking in her sleep. Forbes knows this and the reader knows this, but Forbes chooses to portray Doll's dream as actual fact involving astral projection and witchcraft. It is upon such a point that the novel flounders, and what could have been an engrossing tale about magic and the discernment of neurotic behavior turns out to be fundamentally disappointing.

Forbes writes this novel in a quasi-Puritan style. It is as if it were an example of a moral tale, written by a true believer, describing the harmful effects of trafficking with the forces of evil. Such writings do exist, but they should not be imitated by those who cannot do it brilliantly. The fact that Forbes does imitate it is one mistake, and it makes the novel seem like a poorly planned piece of work. This error is compounded by her presentation of the story in the guise of the Omniscient Narrator. The resulting combination of these two errors is a novel that often does not seem to know where it is going nor how to get there. *A Mirror for Witches* sometimes shows very well the psychological underpinnings of actions that the community of the novel chooses to see as magical, supernatural, or maleficent. But more often the novel is confusing, and the reader remains unsure of the psychological underpinning Forbes is trying to show.

The theory that previous ages may have recognized the truths of what is today called psychoanalysis but hidden these truths under a cloak of magic and mystery, is a fascinating one. It is unfortunate that Forbes was not more skillful in her treatment of this theme.

THE MISANTHROPE

Type of work: Drama
Author: Molière (Jean Baptiste Poquelin, 1622-1673)
Type of plot: Comedy of manners
Time of plot: Seventeenth century
Locale: Paris
First presented: 1666

The basic question in The Misanthrope—*whether Alceste is an honest man behaving decently in a corrupt society, or a self-righteous, egocentric prig refusing to abide by the elementary rules of social discourse—has stimulated a long and continuing debate, a debate that may reveal more about the social attitudes and mores of the critics than about the play itself.*

In a letter to a friend, Jean Jacques Rousseau, the eighteenth century writer and philosopher, stated that "the character of Alceste in [*The Misanthrope*] is that of a fair, open and . . . truly honest man [and] the poet makes him a subject of ridicule." To what extent are these statements true?

If one examines the play closely, one finds that although Alceste is subject to ridicule, so is the society he ridicules. In other words, Molière validates Alceste's criticism of the follies of the age: the hypocrisy of court life, the absurd manners required by all who attempt to appear at court, the dishonest practice of bribing judges in order to win a law suit, the ludicrous poetry written by those with no talent simply because writing poetry was one of the acts required of a gentleman of the time, the delight in gossiping even if the gossip were to destroy the good name of an individual. Molière attacks all of these practices through Alceste.

And all of these attacks are seen to be valid because these practices are not observed in the behavior of those who represent the golden mean: Philinte (Alceste's best friend) and Éliante (who loves Alceste and is, in turn, loved by Philinte). They leave the gossiping, the poetry writing, the absurd activities to others. However, there is an important distinction between their behavior and Alceste's. They are willing to acknowledge certain social customs as essential to maintaining a stable society and accept those who practice these customs. Alceste, on the contrary, not only refuses to conform, but delights in condemning all those who do conform.

Thus, although Molière would agree with Alceste's view of society (as shown by the assent of Philinte and Éliante), he would disagree with his excessive manner in attacking the social fabric. This leads to the first part of Rousseau's statement (that is, Alceste is "fair, open and truly honest"). For Molière takes great pains to show us that Alceste is none of these.

The opening scene of the play shows him condemning his friend Philinte for having shown civility to a man he hardly knows. Alceste calls Philinte's action a crime and declares he would rather die than commit such an indignity.

Alceste insists that acts of friendship should be reserved for those who are one's true friends. He declares that friendship has no meaning if it must be shared. His extreme reaction to Philinte's harmless act would seem to indicate that what Alceste resents most about the actions is that it reduces his relationship with Philinte to the same level as all other relationships; he insists that he wants to be singled out, chosen for his virtues, valued for himself. His attitude is hardly fair to Philinte, who fails to view his action as a criminal offense and maintains that in order to survive in society, one must sometimes compromise.

Although Alceste appears to be "open and truly honest," we find that his actions belie Rousseau's statement. When asked by Oronte to comment on a sonnet he has written, Alceste attacks it mercilessly. The poem is, obviously, of little merit, but Alceste again overreacts. One cannot help but wonder if Alceste's reaction to the poem stems from his knowledge that it was written to Célimène, whom he loves, by a rival, whom he detests.

It is, above all, in his relationship with Célimène, that we must question Alceste's openness and honesty. If he truly despises the falseness of his society, how can one account for his love for Célimène, the epitome of the falseness of that society? It is Célimène who recites nasty gossip about people, behind their backs, in the famous medallion scene. It is Célimène who leads on a number of suitors by writing loving letters to all of them. It is Célimène who is the quintessence of the hypocrisy of the society Alceste condemns. Yet, he loves her with a passion that overcomes his reason—a situation that serves as a source for comedy as well as tragedy in seventeenth century French drama.

Alceste is aware of all of Célimène's faults yet can do nothing to control his passion. The modest, reasonable Éliante would seem to be a more likely choice for his affections, but Célimène is the recipient of all his love. And, as with his friend Philinte, he refuses to share her love with anyone else. When she acknowledges that she enjoys her way of life, he chastises her in the extreme manner he used to criticize Philinte in the opening scene of the play. And can one call a man "fair" who, when he believes he has found proof that Célimène is untrue to him, turns to Éliante asking her to help him revenge himself on Célimène by accepting his heart? Éliante, fortunately, is reasonable enough to realize that Alceste is speaking in a moment of unreasonable anger and suggests that he not use her to seek revenge on Célimène.

The supreme example of Alceste's succumbing to the hypocrisy he professes to detest is presented in Act IV, scene iii. He confronts Célimène with what he believes to be her treachery. Rather than give him the answer he desires (that is, that she loves only him), she agrees with his charges. He is brought to a point of ultimate despair and begs her to *pretend* that she loves him, that such pretense will suffice. At this point, the comedy closely approaches tragedy, for we find Alceste, the upholder of truth and honesty, begging for deception.

The seventeenth century belief in the overwhelming power of uncontrollable passion can account, in part, for Alceste's behavior. However, one can find examples throughout the play clearly demonstrating that although Alceste is correct in upbraiding society for its hypocritical behavior, much of his criticism is directed at those whose esteem he desires. It would thus seem that part of his protest rests in his fear that if all are treated with the same courtesy, how can one "set the worthy man apart"? He wishes to be loved and honored for himself and not merely because society deems such behavior correct. He wants to be set apart: to be Philinte's *best* friend (and not share the social niceties that Philinte bestows on others), to be Célimène's only lover (and not share her company with that of other men).

It would thus appear that not only is the first part of Rousseau's statement incorrect, but Molière's title as well. Alceste is no misanthrope (his fondness for Philinte and Éliante and his love for Célimène are obvious). He does, however, abhor the sham of society. But although Alceste's ridicule of society is shown to be valid, his behavior is shown to be ridiculous. Thus the second part of Rousseau's statement is correct.

Phyllis Mael

THE MISER

Type of work: Drama
Author: Molière (Jean Baptiste Poquelin, 1622-1673)
Type of plot: Romantic comedy
Time of plot: Seventeenth century
Locale: Paris, France
First presented: 1668

In The Miser *Molière combines two popular comic situations into a hilarious comedy: the gulling of the miser and the frustrating of the old man who chases after a young wife. The miser, Harpagon, is one of Molière's greatest comedic creations, a grotesque example of greed and avarice, whose only redeeming quality is his final helplessness in the face of young love, mature generosity, and his own self-deceptions.*

The young modern reader of this play will find *The Miser* and other works of Molière an intellectual challenge. The France of King Louis XIV is indeed far removed from the modern reader's experience, but the humor of this old theatrical comedy is readily apparent and can be appreciated on many levels.

Molière had a special genius in his wit and in his imaginative use of comic artifices; he is renowned as a master of verbal irony. His successful use of comic repetition is exemplified in the scene "Without a dowry!" But Molière's genius goes beyond his artful use of language to his excellent portrayal of characters.

Harpagon is probably one of Molière's strongest characterizations; his personality is disclosed in the way he relates to his children, his household, and the society. He is self-righteous, hypocritical, egotistical, and miserly to the extreme. He tells his maid, ". . . be especially careful not to rub the furniture too hard, or you'll wear it out." He wants his daughter to marry without a dowry, but expects his bride to bring him one. He wants his cook to provide the best food without spending any money. In short, he wants the best of both worlds.

The epitome of his character is portrayed in the soliloquy in which he raves about his money being stolen. He suspects everyone of the deed including himself. "I'll order them to torture everyone in my house for a confession . . . my son, my daughter—and myself too!" Molière uses comic coincidences—implausible turns of events—to thwart Harpagon at every turn. In this ingeniously constructed plot, the will of the miser is constantly at odds with his fate, and with the members of his household. In this way the character of Harpagon generates comic irony. Harpagon's will is constantly frustrated. He finds his son to be the borrower from whom he wants to collect twenty-five percent interest as lender. The young woman he wants to marry is in love with his son. His steward, who has flattered his way into Harpagon's trust, is only interested in his daughter. In the end, when all his plans fail, he finds his only consolation in the return of his moneybox. This ironical comedy is probably one of Molière's most humorous works.

LES MISÉRABLES

Type of work: Novel
Author: Victor Hugo (1802-1885)
Type of plot: Social chronicle
Time of plot: About 1815 to 1835
Locale: France
First published: 1862

In this ultimate "pursuit" novel, Jean Valjean, an essentially innocent man, is tracked relentlessly for most of his lifetime by an implacable, abstract "justice" in the person of the fanatical Inspector Javert. With this action as the spine, Hugo then ranges widely to describe early nineteenth century France with a sweep, power, and concreteness that give the novel epic stature.

Essentially a detective story in plot, *Les Misérables* is a unique combination of melodrama and morality. It is filled with unlikely coincidences, with larger than life emotions and giantlike human beings, yet it all manages to ring true and move the reader. An epic of the people of Paris, with a vital and fascinating re-creation of the swarming Parisian underworld, the novel suggests the crowded, absorbing novels of Dickens and Dostoevski. The main theme of man's ceaseless combat with evil clearly emerges from the suspenseful plot, while the book as a whole gives a dramatic picture of the ebb and flow of life.

Victor Hugo claimed that the huge book was a "religious" work, and certainly religion does play an important part in the story. From the very beginning, the struggle between good and evil is foremost in the tale. Another theme which is of equal importance is that of fate or "destiny." However we attempt to chisel the "mysterious block" of which our life is made, Hugo writes, the "black vein of destiny" reappears continually. One can never be certain what fate has in store for one, until the last breath of life disappears. Mortals never are safe from the tricks of destiny, from the seemingly endless struggle.

The breathless pace of the novel probably has accounted for its tremendous popularity. The story is filled with dramatic and surprising action, many of the scenes ending with suspenseful episodes in the tradition of the melodramatic nineteenth century stage for which Hugo also wrote. Despite its digressions, the story moves quickly and excitingly, as the characters race across the countryside and through the narrow streets and alleys of Paris.

The characterizations, while on a grand—even epic—scale, are lifelike and believable. Many of them seem possessed by strange obsessions or hatreds, but Hugo makes it clear that they have been warped by society and their earlier lives. Although a romantic novel, *Les Misérables* has much in common with the naturalistic school which was to come into being a few decades later.

Perhaps the most terrifying and fascinating of all the characters who flood through the book's pages is Inspector Javert. Javert is clever, but not intelligent. He is consumed by the malice that often dwells within the narrow, ignorant individual. He can conceive of no point of view other than his own. Sympathy, mercy, and understanding require an insight that he does not possess. For him there is no such thing as an extenuating circumstance. He clings with mindless, insane tenacity to his belief in "duty." At his hands justice is warped beyond recognition. Through him, Hugo shows the back side of virtue.

The casual reader can still be moved by the author's search for justice in *Les Misérables,* and the more sophisticated can admire the novel's complex structure. Like so many of the greatest literary works, *Les Misérables* can be enjoyed many times by different kinds of readers, and on many different levels.

An important, if implied, theme of *Les Misérables* is the attainment of salvation through good works. Many of the characters of the novel give charity to those less fortunate. The dramatic opening scenes in which the convict, Jean Valjean, learns of goodness through the charity of the priest, establishes the importance of this theme. Later, Jean Valjean and Cosette give anonymous charity to others. Marius, in his goodness, gives charity to the disreputable Thénardier family.

Other Biblical virtues are dramatized in the novel, but none so effectively as that of love. By love, Hugo means not only romantic love, but love of humanity, the love of a kindhearted human being for another human being, the love that must be connected with genuine charity. Jean Valjean learns what love is during the course of the novel. "The bishop had caused the dawn of virtue on Jean's horizon; Cosette worked the dawn of love." Hugo makes it clear that a man cannot exist without love, for if he tries, he becomes warped and less than a man. Jean Valjean grows as a person, becomes a good and honorable man after he has found the love of the helpless little girl. By devoting his life to her, he finds the necessity of a meaning outside of his own life. Jean Valjean comes to value his own existence more because the girl is dependent upon him and loves him.

Victor Hugo knew how to write effectively and with simplicity of the common joys and sorrows of the average man and woman. His poetry and novels have always been popular with the common people, although they have at times been out of critical favor. The public mind was much moved by the generosity of his ideas and the warmth of their expression; more than a century after its publication, *Les Misérables* is still a favorite book with many people around the world. Much of Hugo's poetry and drama is not read or produced nowadays, but *Les Misérables* and *Notre Dame de Paris* will endure as long as people read.

The novel covers a time span of more than twenty years, from the fall of the first Napoleon to the revolts of a generation later. The most exciting scenes, described with breathless precision and dramatic flair, are those at the barricades. The characters are swept up in an action bigger than they are. Skillfully, Hugo weaves Marius and Javert, Eponine and the others, into the battles along the streets of Paris. But always Hugo's eye catches the details of the passing spectacle, from the old woman who props up a mattress in front of her window to stop the stray bullets to the dynamic flood of humanity coursing down the boulevards. It is here that Hugo's skill as a master of narrative is fully displayed. But never does he lose sight of the pathos of the individuals' struggles; the reader never forgets the principal characters and their plight amid the chaotic scenes. Perfectly, Hugo balances between the two elements which compose his masterpiece. The final scenes of the novel move relentlessly and excitingly to their inevitable conclusion. Perhaps Dostoevski probed deeper or Dickens caught the humor of life more fully, but Hugo was their equal in his ability to portray the individual heartache and tenderness, the human struggle of those caught up in the forces of history.

Bruce D. Reeves

MISS JULIE

Type of work: Drama
Author: August Strindberg (1849-1912)
Type of plot: Naturalism
Time of plot: Nineteenth century
Locale: A country estate in Sweden
First presented: 1888

No author has portrayed the "battle of the sexes" with more intensity than August Strindberg, and Miss Julie *is one of his most forceful examples. The play strips the action down to an elemental struggle between the aristocratic, romantic, haughty Julie and the poor, realistic, grasping Jean with survival at stake. But, in the end, the irrational inner drives overwhelm and destroy* both *of them in what is surely one of the most brutal short plays in the literature.*

Miss Julie was written by August Strindberg to be produced in Paris by André Antoine's avant-garde Théâtre Libre. This "naturalistic tragedy" is recognized as one of the greatest works of the Swedish playwright. Strindberg's power, complexity, and originality of technique and vision have led modern playwrights, such as Eugene O'Neill, to see him as the most modern of all playwrights.

Strindberg's achievements are all the more remarkable in view of the squalor of his upbringing. Born in Stockholm into a bankrupt family, one of twelve children, Strindberg was neglected by even his own mother. After her death when he was thirteen, his new stepmother added harshness to neglect. This early experience developed in him a strong, lifelong quarrel with any conventional authority figure, evidenced in his rejection of traditional stage techniques and the rejection of traditional beliefs and conventions of society in his plays. His private life was equally unconventional. His three marriages were each characterized by intense love-hate relationships. In addition to private tensions, Strindberg was prosecuted for blasphemy upon the publication of his short stories, *Married* (1886-1888). The combination of these tensions produced an unstable psychological state with spells of insanity and delusions of persecution. Between the years 1894-1896 the increasing violence of his hallucinations led to the crisis known as the "Inferno period." The inner torment of this psychological crisis gave rise to a shift in technique from the psychological naturalism of *The Father* and *Miss Julie* to symbolistic and expressionistic departures from external reality in the imaginative brilliance of dramas such as *A Dream Play* and *Ghost Sonata*.

While in Paris in 1883, Strindberg became familiar with the doctrine of literary naturalism espoused by Émile Zola, and he successfully applied this approach to drama, even sending a copy of his first naturalistic play to Zola for comments. The long "Foreword" Strindberg wrote for *Miss Julie* explains his use of naturalistic doctrine in the play, but Strindberg's final formulation of dramatic naturalism is found in his essay, "On Modern Drama and Modern Theater" (1889). There he suggests that the true essence of naturalism is a presentation of the polarization of the basic conflicts of life—love and hate, life and death—through the Darwinian principle of survival of the fittest found both in personal relationships and class conflicts. Strindberg's knowledge of psychology contributes in creating his powerful authentic dramas, which remain as moving in our time as when they were created.

Strindberg utilized numerous important innovations in writing and production which were ahead of his time. His dialogue, like Chekhov's, is meant to reproduce the pauses, wanderings, and flatness of everyday speech. He wrote the play to be presented in only one act without intermission to capitalize on the emotional involvement of the audience. In addition, he calls for music, mime, ballet, and improvisation to utilize the full range of actors' talents. He calls for new lighting techniques to illuminate faces better, allowing them to use less makeup and to appear more natural. Finally, he asks for a return to a smaller, more intimate theater with closer audience relationship.

Julie's complex motivations are ample evidence of Strindberg's art. We see her as a product of heredity and environment. Her mother was a low-born woman, full of hatred for woman's conventional place in society. She brought Julie up as a boy, creating in her a fascination with animals and a loathing for the opposite sex which causes self-disgust when her natural instincts attract her sexually to men. In addition, her mother suffered from strange attacks of mental instability which seems to carry over into Julie. Added to these problems is the biological determinant of Julie's menstrual cycle, which makes her more emotionally unstable than usual. There is also the strong element of chance: her father's absence frees Julie and Jean from customary restraints, and it is chance that leads the couple into the locked room. The sensual excitement of the Midsummer's Eve celebration contributes to the seduction and to Julie's final tragedy.

Jean's motivation, although less complex than Julie's, is also conditioned by his environment, his biological drives, his psychological desires, and his social aspirations. At the same time that he can despise the weaknesses of the old aristocrats, he finds himself unable to break his social conditioning. Only in the count's absence could Jean have brought himself to seduce Julie.

An added complication is the class conflict in which the decaying aristocracy, which Julie represents, must, by law of nature, be destroyed to make way for a stronger lower class that is more fit for survival in the modern world. Some things of value such as sensitivity and honor are lost; these are the qualities that break Julie and her father while brutality and lack of scruples insure Jean's final triumph. He survives because of his animal virility, his keen physical senses, and his strength of purpose. Religion has been discarded by the aristocracy as meaningless, and it is used by the working class to insure their innocence. Love is seen as another romantic illusion created by the aristocracy to be used, as Julie uses it, to explain animal instincts in an acceptable manner. Jean, the pragmatic realist from the lower class, has no such need for excuses for sexual release.

To underline his themes and characterizations, Strindberg uses recurring animal imagery which links man with his animal nature, a technique which may be seen in the dreams of Julie and Jean, the foreshadowing effect of Julie's mother, Julie's attitude toward her dog, and the brutal death of Julie's beautiful, caged bird.

Miss Julie is a "naturalistic tragedy" following the Aristotelian concepts of pity, fear, and catharsis. Pity is aroused in the viewer by the characters' inherent weaknesses and the social class structure they inhabit; fear is aroused when we realize that the same fate could overcome any of us; catharsis is produced when we realize that the old, decaying order must give way to the newer and stronger order for life to continue.

Ann E. Reynolds

MISS LONELYHEARTS

Type of work: Novel
Author: Nathanael West (Nathan Weinstein, 1903?-1940)
Type of plot: Social satire
Time of plot: Late 1920's
Locale: New York City
First published: 1933

Miss Lonelyhearts *was one of the first, and remains one of the best, examples of black humor in contemporary American fiction. This highly charged, bitterly ironical vision of a man destroyed by his hypersensitivity to the contradictions and pains of the modern world remains, along with* The Day of the Locust *(1939), one of the two minor masterpieces that West completed in his tragically short life.*

Nathanael West, born Nathan Weinstein, graduated from Tufts in 1924 with a major in Philosophy. Immediately upon graduation he left for Paris where he remained for two years. On his return from abroad he took a job as a hotel night clerk, a job for which he was not particularly suited but which enabled him to write. In 1931 his first short novel *The Dream Life of Balso Snell* was privately printed; it was remarkably unsuccessful. His next work, *Miss Lonelyhearts,* appeared in 1933; if anything, its lack of success surpassed his first novel—the publisher was forced to declare bankruptcy. In the same year he went to Hollywood where he lived until his death. While there he was acquainted with such prominent authors as William Faulkner and F. Scott Fitzgerald, and there in 1940 he married Eileen McKenny, famous as *My Sister Eileen* (written by Ruth McKenny). He and his wife were killed on December 22, 1940, in an automobile accident.

West was obsessed with the daydreams people live. Though Jewish, he considered Christ and the Christ figure the ultimate dream, a concept more comprehensible when one considers that, for West as for many other authors (Cervantes is a notable example), the word dream is synonymous with ideal. In *Miss Lonelyhearts* West explores the modern answers to man's dilemma. Miss Lonelyhearts himself is the central figure of the novel, the observer through whose eyes the reader sees a modern wasteland. The wasteland motif is represented by the letters which Miss Lonelyhearts receives. In each of these letters sex and the failure of sex are the central conflicts: a woman destroyed by repeated pregnancy; a noseless girl for whom sex is impossible; a retarded child who has been raped.

Obsessed with the pain of others, Miss Lonelyhearts confuses compassion with identification. He becomes a Christ figure who embraces his suppliant children with erotic abandon. He renders unto Eros what is Christ's in a confused and tormented ministry. Shrike's taunting remarks all originate in his contempt for Miss Lonelyheart's original assumption that pure good is a true, human motivation. Determined to make Miss Lonelyhearts confront his own corruption, Shrike taunts him with gibes ridiculing his spiritual vanity. In the end Miss Lonelyhearts becomes an integral part of the very wasteland he thought he could redeem. The gospel of Shrike, the Mephistophelian nay-sayer, is confirmed by the totally ridiculous sacrifice of Miss Lonelyhearts in the arms of Peter Doyle. Miss Lonelyhearts' dream of Christ-like self-sacrifice is parodied in the farcical embrace of seducer and cuckold rolling down the stairs.

MISS RAVENEL'S CONVERSION

Type of work: Novel
Author: John William De Forest (1826-1906)
Type of plot: Historical romance
Time of plot: The Civil War period
Locale: New England and Louisiana
First published: 1866

With the possible exception of Stephen Crane's The Red Badge of Courage, Miss Ravenel's Conversion *is the best and most modern nineteenth century novel written about the American Civil War. De Forest's realistic, understated, mature treatment of men and women caught up in the pains and stresses of enormous historical and cultural changes is as relevant and convincing today as it was when first published.*

In the development of modern realistic American fiction, few nineteenth century novels are more significant than *Miss Ravenel's Conversion*. In this brilliant Civil War novel, William De Forest explores issues and problems—war, political corruption, marriage, sex—with a realism and candor that would hardly be seen again in American literature before the turn of the century.

Most immediately impressive is De Forest's presentation of the war. Writing in simple, direct, but restrained language, selecting his scenes and details carefully, he conveys the futility, horror, violence, and weariness of battle with a vividness rarely equalled in American literature at least until after World War II. Avoiding descriptions of mass combat, De Forest concentrates on those lulls in battle when the terrible effects of combat can be seen in the actions of a few sharply described individuals, such as soldiers pretending normalcy in the midst of sudden death, or medics performing assembly-line amputations.

But the novel is perhaps even more impressive as a study of individuals caught up in the sweep of historical events. As the title suggests, the book centers on the "conversion" or education of Miss Lillie Ravenel. Her father, Dr. Ravenel, a Southern gentleman and self-converted "loyalist," supplies the moral idealism requisite to her growth. But it is her involvement with two lovers, Colonel John Carter and Edward Colburne, that completes the education.

The charming, sophisticated Colonel Carter is one of the most virile and forceful characters in American fiction. But, although spectacular in battle, he cannot adjust to peace. He is a man of simple courage and combat morality who is able to deal neither with the emotional difficulties of marriage nor the complexities of modern society. He loves Lillie, but his casual sexual morality cannot withstand the seductions of Mrs. Larue; he commands men adroitly in combat, but cannot manage money under pressure. It is appropriate that he dies in battle, and in doing so, attains a bit of tragic stature.

On the other hand, De Forest's Colburne, probably an idealized self-portrait, is a citizen-soldier. His does not have the automatic animal courage of the natural soldier, but the found courage of an ordinary citizen fighting for a cause in which he believes. His trial by experience purges him of his youthful naïveté and priggishness, and makes him worthy to be Lillie's second husband. And Lillie, in her turn, by virtue of having endured the war, the love, infidelity, and death of a husband, and the birth of a son, is converted from a frivolous, shallow, "secessionist" girl to De Forest's ideal—a mature, "loyalist," Christian mother.

MR. BRITLING SEES IT THROUGH

Type of work: Novel
Author: H. G. Wells (1866-1946)
Type of plot: Social criticism
Time of plot: World War I
Locale: England
First published: 1916

Mr. Britling, a Wellsian alter-ego, can almost be seen as a human seismograph recording the shifts in attitudes and feelings characteristic of the British public during World War I. Mr. Britling passes from optimism to despair and back to optimism as he ponders questions of war, religion, morality, and social reform.

This intensely autobiographical novel may be read in three ways: as the portrait of an eccentric, upper-class English family coping with war; as a record of the shifts in English public opinion during the years 1914-1916; and, as a plea for world government and theistic faith.

With astonishing honesty, Wells detailed his own confused psyche, marital infidelities, family tensions, and the ways of his community. The hockey games, costume parties, and easy conversations give way to endless anxiety over food supplies, mobilization, quartering, and the safety of Hugh and Teddy. Only with the departure of Heinrich do the Britlings realize the extent of their affection for him. Hugh's remarkable letters from the trenches and the description of Mr. Britling's mourning constitute some of Wells's best writing. The novel, immensely popular, provoked many expressions of sympathy. Ironically, the account of Hugh's death was one of the few departures from autobiography in the book.

Wells' views, like those of his contemporaries, changed frequently and radically during this period. Mr. Britling complacently trusts in civilizing reason to forestall war; he then is aggressively anti-German; despondency and a "plague on both houses" attitude follows; and this mood is ultimately superseded by the vision of a League of Nations. Through Direck and Heinrich, Wells articulates American and German viewpoints, and Lady Frensham speaks for the aristocracy, preoccupied with Irish Home Rule and women's suffrage. The touching "Ortheris" presents working class attitudes.

Britling ultimately sees his suffering through by means of faith. His political hope—that a world federation of democratic republics will soon emerge—is sustained by his experience of "a Presence so close that it was behind his eyes and in his brain and hands." His God is not omnipotent; He is the suffering at the heart of all human sorrows. He is a being who is with and for men, subject to all the terrors which assail them. Wells conceived of his theology as non-Christian, but he was actually preaching a central message of the New Testament.

MR. FACEY ROMFORD'S HOUNDS

Type of work: Novel
Author: Robert Smith Surtees (1803-1864)
Type of plot: Picaresque satire
Time of plot: Nineteenth century
Locale: England
First published: 1865

Using the classical comic device of the mistaken identity, as manipulated by his genial con-artist hero, Facey Romford, Surtees offers a boisterous, aggressive satirical treatment of country sporting life in mid-nineteenth century England.

The last of Surtees' comic-satiric novels, *Mr. Facey Romford's Hounds* was published posthumously, twenty-seven years after the author had collected his earliest sketches from *The New Sporting Magazine* and reprinted them, with John Leech's droll illustrations, as *Jorrocks' Jaunts and Jollities*. His eighth book, not part of the more popular Jorrocks series, continues the adventures of several characters who first appeared in *Mr. Sponge's Sporting Tour* (1853). Facey Romford, a minor figure in that novel, is now fully developed as a clever rascal pushing his way forward into high society. In his genial impudence, Facey resembles the grocer-sportsman John Jorrocks. But Jorrocks is essentially a London Cockney who aspires to be accepted by the landed aristocrats as a foxhunter. The Cockney rises in class partly as a result of his hard work, partly from his good common sense that judges people for their true worth. Facey, on the other hand, a native to the countryside, plays the games of the sportsman simply to thrust himself forward as a gentleman. A calculating but likable opportunist, his real sport is not racing with the hounds but hurdling the class barriers.

The slender idea of the novel upon which Surtees elaborates a tale with his customary humorous skills, is that Facey, a rustic confidence man, assumes the identity of his aristocratic namesake, Francis Romford, Esquire, of Abbey-field Park. It is a plot device, ingenious in its absurdity, that might have exercised the greater talents of a Mark Twain, who was always amused by the complications following an incident of mistaken identity. But Twain, unlike Surtees, was interested above all in the psychological and moral displacements resulting from the mistake. For all his vitality as a jovial rogue-hero, Facey lacks both a psychological and moral dimension. And although Twain's "Pudd'nhead" Wilson, in the mistaken judgment of the small-town yokels, appears to be a fool, he is really a sensitive, clever man. Facey, despite his success among the peers, remains a "pudd'nhead."

By 1865, when *Mr. Facey Romford's Hounds* appeared, Surtees' remembered world of sport hunting was slowly but unmistakably passing into legend. The reading public, for the most part urban and middle class, could not fully appreciate the scenes of hounds baying, foxes running in terror, and the ritual of pursuit by brightly clad, graceful horsemen. It was an idle age, with more than its share of cruelty, vanity, and waste. But Surtees described also, with wit and sympathy, the antics of the sporting country gentlemen, the shrewd upstarts like Jorrocks and Romford, and the veneer of manners of a comfortable, still-privileged class. Although his plots were mere contrivances to display comic episodes, his characters flimsy, and his themes repetitious, his language always had a cutting edge. In his own fashion Surtees was a master of the well-turned phrase, the appropriate epithet. As a satirist with a sure sense of the borders of the sane and inane, his best work resembles the early novels of Aldous Huxley and Evelyn Waugh, whose derisive laughter is directed at the bored, vapid aristocrats of the 1920's, thin-blooded descendants of Surtees' sporting heroes.

MR. MIDSHIPMAN EASY

Type of work: Novel
Author: Frederick Marryat (1792-1848)
Type of plot: Adventure romance
Time of plot: Napoleonic wars
Locale: Mediterranean Sea and European coastal waters
First published: 1836

Based upon Marryat's own experience, Mr. Midshipman Easy *accurately describes life aboard a British war vessel, including vivid accounts of several sea battles. At the same time, the author utilizes the adventure romance to demonstrate the virtues of his conservative Victorian principles by presenting the naval vessel as a microcosm of English society with all class divisions and distinctions firmly and properly in place.*

Mr. Midshipman Easy is an action-filled tale of adventure on the high seas, abounding with beliefs and assumptions from the conservative and of the spectrum of Victorian values. Captain Marryat's most avid audience was the British schoolboy population, which imbibed certain notions of class, religion, and sexual roles along with the exciting fare of Jack Easy's adventures.

Mr. Midshipman Easy is in many ways an anti-democratic tract. Marryat dramatizes his conservative stance by making the Royal Navy a microcosm of English society, which serves as the school where Jack grows to be both a man and a gentleman. Jack, who is born into the landed gentry class, is nevertheless reared on the egalitarian principles of his father, Nicodemus Easy, whom the author makes into an absurd and imbecilic figure in order to ridicule his ideas. When the hero runs off to join the Navy, which he envisions as the haven of freedom and equality, his reeducation begins. He learns that in the Navy, as in society generally, men are ordained by birth as well as natural talent to occupy given positions within the social structure. Thus, Wilson was meant to be a leader of other men, while Gascoigne, although he is a worthy and likable fellow, will always be a midshipman; and Jack, who soon discovers and accepts the fact that his gentlemanly birth earns him certain privileges, inevitably distinguishes himself and rises to the top of the authority hierarchy, commanding his own ship.

Marryat generously allows some men of humble origins, such as Sawbridge, to rise in the system eventually by dint of their unflagging loyalty, perseverance, and competence; but he also provides object lessons against presumption and false expectations such as the case of the midshipman who dies bitterly lamenting the fate that kept him from promotion. For the hero, the Navy is a stage in the growth process, a sort of preview glimpse of life before he comes into his full birthright; at the end of the novel, Jack realizes that his true place is at the Forest Hill estate keeping hounds and a full larder, hosting balls and banquets, and standing for Parliament.

In addition to his social outlook, Marryat's religious biases are made manifestly clear as well. A strain of anti-Catholicism runs throughout. Jack is nominally an Anglican—the English gentleman's religion—but is independent, sensible, and free-thinking in spirit. Marryat's views on women are even more traditional. Women characters appear on less than a dozen pages out of the entire novel, and when they do, it is in the form of one-dimensional and rather ludicrous stereotypes. Agnes Rebiera's sole function in the plot, for example, is to provide romantic interest and a suitable mate for the hero. While the novel is interesting and lively, the author's conservative stance and strong convictions will no doubt alienate many present-day readers.

MISTER ROBERTS

Type of work: Novel
Author: Thomas Heggen (1919-1949)
Type of plot: Humorous satire
Time of plot: Last months of World War II
Locale: Southwest Pacific
First published: 1946

Mister Roberts, *one of the first and most popular novels about World War II, differs from most other military books in being funny, almost farcical, while at the same time accurately and realistically describing the behavior of American servicemen. Stuck far behind the lines, the men of* The Reluctant *adopt bizarre tactics to combat their ennui and purposelessness, and in so doing, give the novel both its hilarious situations and its underlying feeling of sadness.*

Mister Roberts, originally published in 1946 in the *Atlantic Monthly,* is the first novel to give a realistic portrayal of the behind-the-lines, out-of-action Navy in World War II. Apathetic seamen and deadly, dull routine are not the usual stuff of novels, but Thomas Heggen has taken this basic material and woven it into a minor classic. The narrative, though leisurely, is vivid with a frankness characteristic of life at sea, including the salty language. But beneath the free and easy style, there are the solid underpinnings of an extremely effective satire showing the corrosive effects of boredom on men who, had they been in battle, might have been heroes. The conspiracies against the captain as the only means of retaliation against authority form a platform for a debunking of war on the part of Heggen, stirring vivid memories in readers of other captains and other lieutenants. Probably no officers could be so indolent and no captain so outrageously incompetent as those in *Mister Roberts,* but allowing for some hyperbole and caricature for satirical purposes, the book still contains some of the truest writing ever made concerning the military mind. As such, the book offers a relief from the general run of war literature. Often, however, the novel's humor obscures some of the story's meaning. Most readers, it is true, accept the rowdy succession of escapades and pranks, and humor is so predominant that the symbolic significance of Roberts' death in action at the end is hidden, and the incident, seen in the light of comedy, seems inappropriate. Nevertheless, in spite of this shortcoming, *Mister Roberts* is important as one of the best novels to mirror the less glorious side of war. The success of this work led the author, with Joshua Logan, to dramatize it into an even more successful play which opened in New York in 1948 for a run of 1157 performances.

MR. SPONGE'S SPORTING TOUR

Type of work: Novel
Author: Robert Smith Surtees (1803-1864)
Type of plot: Picaresque satire
Time of plot: Nineteenth century
Locale: England
First published: 1853

This novel satirizes the sporting classes in mid-nineteenth century England by means of a series of deft, vivid sketches, loosely connected by the comic forays of Soapey Sponge, a social-climbing sharper, whose cleverness and pushiness enable him to manipulate his social and financial betters with relative ease.

Mr. Sponge's Sporting Tour does not aim to be either the definitive study of fox hunting and the natural history and habits of the animals of the chase or a coherent, romantic novel. It is a series of pictures of vivid scenes filled out with character sketches. Within the limits of the author's intention, the book is quite successful.

Surtees wrote of what he saw and knew, and he put it on paper with an unself-conscious honesty. His style is awkward, his grammar is faulty, and frequently he seems to lose his place, but his descriptions of locale and character are filled with an amazing authenticity and charm which completely overcome the faults of the book. The very haphazard quality of the work gives it an immediacy and vitality which are unique. When Surtees describes the costumes of the characters, one knows for a fact that these clothes are precisely what they ought to be, and when a character is pigeonholed in his place in society, he too is precisely and accurately captured by the author's pen. Surtees knew the tough young touts and bucks, had observed the snobs and climbers, and he spared none of them. Because of this candor, *Mr. Sponge's Sporting Tour* is probably Surtees' best novel, and is much more readable than his more famous tales of Jorrocks.

The dialogue in the book is as leisurely and accurate as the descriptions. The boredom, the stuffiness, the stupidity of the talk is perfectly and mercilessly captured. Surtees himself was a country squire and had the prejudices of his kind. He hated the fashionable places and smart society and was suspicious of cleverness. These traits give his novel a prickly quality that is refreshing to the modern reader. Never does he attempt to enlist the reader's sympathy. There is little of the sentimental in this tale of bounders and thieves, *nouveaux riches* and snobs. The book is especially merciless toward the mobs which are overrunning the country and changing everything, to the annoyance of both Mr. Sponge and his creator. The interest of the incidents and characters, and the rich humor, although somewhat dated, more than compensate for the lack of plot in the book.

MR. WESTON'S GOOD WINE

Type of work: Novel
Author: T. F. Powys (1875-1953)
Type of plot: Quasi-mysticism
Time of plot: November 20, 1923
Locale: Folly Down, a village in western England
First published: 1927

As an invalid with limited worldly experience, T. F. Powys found it necessary to turn inward for both the subjects of his fiction and the sustenance of his personal needs. The result was a series of novels which reflect the small part of the world he knew, the rural English village, and his preoccupation with man's relationship to God and to his own inner self. Mr. Weston's Good Wine *is a provocative, undogmatic, deeply felt religious novel of strong conviction and unorthodox thought.*

Concerned with both religious and social themes, T. F. Powys sought in *Mr. Weston's Good Wine* to dramatize the inter-relationship of the mystical and the real. Beginning on an ordinary evening, outside a familiar English village with two businessmen conferring about their sales prospects, the novel proceeds into a time gap where the usual gives way to the fantastic and miraculous. It soon becomes apparent that Mr. Weston possesses supernatural powers; indeed he is seen as the divine puppeteer, the arranger of man's fortunes, directing reward and retribution in the microcosm of Folly Down. Or as Mr. Weston describes himself: He is the sanctifier and nurturer of man.

The sanctification of Folly Down's inhabitants is accomplished through the "good wine"; it is the spiritual catalyst, the sacrament, which not only accomplishes the inner-regeneration of the citizens but also their social amelioration. When Mr. Weston and Michael arrive, Folly Down's harmony has been disrupted by the wholesale seduction of the village maidens, and their resulting pregnancies. Further, the rector, God's agent on earth, has been rendered ineffective by a deep melancholy over the death of his wife which has driven him to despair. Full of sympathy, Mr. Weston grants him a peaceful death, in which he believes he will be reunited with his wife. A God of love, Mr. Weston then permits the erotic desires of both Tamar Grobe and Jenny Bunce. Finally he brings the Mumby boys, the seducers, to the altar.

During his three hours in Folly Down, Mr. Weston has celebrated, in effect, a Mass of love. Through the agency of wine, he has transformed the ordinary events of life into significant moments, uniting some of the inhabitants with one another in a human communion and others like the Reverend Mr. Grobe and his wife in a supernatural union.

MRS. DALLOWAY

Type of work: Novel
Author: Virginia Woolf (1882-1941)
Type of plot: Psychological realism
Time of plot: 1920's
Locale: London
First published: 1925

Mrs. Dalloway *traces a single day in the life of two characters, Clarissa Dalloway and Septimus Smith, largely through their impressions, thoughts, and feelings. For Clarissa the day culminates with a successful party; for Septimus it ends in suicide. In the complex psychological relationship between the two, Virginia Woolf suggests provocative ideas about the nature and meaning of life, love, time, and death.*

Mrs. Dalloway comes midway in Virginia Woolf's fiction-writing career, and near the beginning of her experiments with form and technique (just after *Jacob's Room,* her first experimental novel). The book is really two stories— Clarissa Dalloway's and Septimus Smith's—and the techniques by which Woolf united these two narrative strands are unusual and skillful. While writing the novel, Woolf commented in her diary on her new method of delineating character. Instead of explaining the characters' pasts chronologically, she uses a "tunnelling process": "I dig out beautiful caves behind my characters." The various characters appear in the present without explanation; various sense impressions—a squeaky hinge, a repeated phrase, a particular tree—call to their minds a memory and past becomes present. Such an evocation of the past is reminiscent of Proust, but Woolf's method does not involve the ego of the narrator. Woolf's "caves" reveal the past and at the same time give characters' reactions to present events. Woolf is then able to connect the "caves" and also her themes by structural techniques, both spatial and temporal.

Unlike that of James Joyce, Woolf's handling of the stream-of-consciousness method is always filtered and indirect; the narrator is in command, telling the reader, "Clarissa thought" or "For so it had always seemed to her." This ever-present narrative voice generally helps the reader by clarifying the characters' inner thoughts and mediating the commentary of the novel although, at times, it blurs the identity of the speaker. Woolf's use of the "voice" becomes more prominent in *To the Lighthouse* (1927), but disappears in *The Waves* (1931).

The structure of the book seems at first to lack unity, with its disparate characters and various scenes of street life. But Woolf uses many devices, both technical and thematic, to unite those elements. The day (in mid-June, 1923), moving uninterruptedly from the early morning to the late evening, is a single whole. Although the book is not divided into chapters or sections headed by titles or numbers, Woolf notes *some* of the shifts in time or scene by a short blank space in the manuscript. More often, however, the transition from one group of characters to another is accomplished by the remarking of something public, something common to the experience of both, something seen or heard. The world of Clarissa and her friends alternates with the world of Septimus Smith; and the sight of the motor car, the sight and sound of the skywriting plane, the running child, the woman singing, the omnibus, the ambulance, and the clock striking are the transitions connecting those two worlds. Moreover, the striking of the clocks ("first a warning, musical; then the hour, irrevocable") is noted at various other times to mark a shift from one character's consciousness to another within Clarissa's group. The exact time is given periodically, signaling the day's progress (noon comes at almost the exact center of the book) and stressing the irrevocable movement towards death, one of the book's themes. Usually at least two clocks are described as striking—first Big Ben, a masculine symbol; then a few seconds later, St. Margaret's, a feminine symbol, suggesting again the two genders of all existence, united in the echoes of the bells, "the leaden circles."

The main thematic devices used to unify the book are the similarity between Clarissa and Septimus, and the repetition of key words and phrases in the minds of various characters. The likeness between Clarissa and Septimus is most important, as each helps to explain the other, although they never meet. Both are lonely and contemplate suicide. Both feel guilty for their past lives, Septimus because he "cannot feel" the death of Evans, Clarissa because of her rejection of Peter and her tendency to dominate others. Both have homo-sexual feelings, Septimus for Evans, Clarissa for Sally Seton. More importantly, both want desperately to bring order out of life's chaos. Septimus achieves this momentarily with the making of Mrs. Peters' hat, and Clarissa creates a harmonious unity with her successful party. Septimus understands that the chaos will return and so takes his own life uniting himself with Death, the final order. Septimus' suicide forces Clarissa to see herself in a new and honest way, understanding for the first time her schemings for success. Clarissa "felt somehow very like him"; she does not pity him but identifies with his defiant "embracing" of death.

Certain phrases become thematic because they are so often repeated, gaining richer overtones of meaning at each use, as different characters interpret the phrases differently. "Fear no more," "if it were now to die," the sun, the waves—these are some of the phrases and images appearing over and over, especially in the thoughts of Septimus and Clarissa.

All the disparate strands of the story are joined at Clarissa's party, over which she presides like an artist over his creation. Not inferior to the painter Lily Briscoe as a creator, Clarissa's great talent is "knowing people almost by instinct," and she is able triumphantly to combine the right group of people at her party. Not only Clarissa, but Richard and Peter also come to a new realization about themselves at the party. Richard, who has been unable to verbalize his love for Clarissa, is finally able to tell his daughter Elizabeth he is proud of her. Peter realizes at the end that the terror and excitement he feels in Clarissa's presence indicate his true feeling for her.

The two figures who are given unfavorable treatment—Sir William, the psychiatrist, and Miss Kilman, the religious fanatic—insist on modes of existence inimical to the passionate desire of Clarissa and Septimus for wholeness. Claiming that Septimus "lacks proportion," Sir William nevertheless uses his profession to gain power over others and, as Clarissa understands, makes life "intolerable" for Septimus. Miss Kilman's life is built on evangelical religion; she feels herself better than Clarissa, whom she wants to humiliate. She proudly asserts that she will have a "religious victory," which will be "God's will."

The real action of the story is all within the minds of the characters, but Woolf gives these inner lives a reality and harmony which reveals the excitement and oneness of human existence. Clarissa and Septimus are really two aspects of the same being—the feminine and the masculine—united in Clarissa's ultimate awareness. *Mrs. Dalloway* remains the best introduction to Woolf's characteristic style and themes.

Margaret McFadden-Gerber

MRS. DANE'S DEFENCE

Type of work: Drama
Author: Henry Arthur Jones (1851-1929)
Type of plot: Social criticism
Time of plot: Early twentieth century
Locale: Near London
First presented: 1900

In Mrs. Dane's Defense, *Henry Arthur Jones exploits the common Victorian theme of the "fallen woman" to make some relevant comments on the mores of upper-class British society. If his criticisms seem mild and conventional today, they signaled a shift in sentiment in 1900 and helped pave the way for the more trenchant, realistic drama that would shortly dominate the English stage.*

The realistic British "well-made play" provided the transition between the artificial, elaborate, pseudo-poetic dramatic spectacles of the early nineteenth century and the realistic, iconoclastic theater of George Bernard Shaw and his successors. On the one hand the genre brought realism to the English stage—recognizable domestic scenes with actual furniture, doors and windows that opened and closed, functional props, colloquial dialogue, and natural acting. But, on the other hand, for all its surface realism and apparent concern with serious social issues, the British well-made play typically reflected assumptions and attitudes that reinforced, rather than challenged, the middle-class Victorian society that supported it. However, if the best of them did not actually attack the prevalent social and moral values, they did posit interesting questions and, occasionally, suggested ambiguous difficulties beneath the smug, placid surface of Victorian society. There is no better example of the powers and limits of the British well-made play than Henry Arthur Jones's *Mrs. Dane's Defence.*

For the first three acts *Mrs. Dane's Defence* is a typical well-made play, although the action seems less contrived and the characters more natural than usual. Like most examples of the genre, the action turns on concealed information which is gradually revealed in the course of the play, in this case the "true identity" and "notorious" past of the heroine, Mrs. Dane. Although her efforts to clear her name seem to be going well, the audience receives several hints that the gossip regarding her is really true. With mechanical precision the play builds to the powerful "scène à faire" ("obligatory scene") where Judge Daniel Carteret cross-examines Mrs. Dane and painfully extracts the truth from her. Having had her true identity revealed and her shady past exposed, Mrs. Dane would normally fall victim to Victorian convention, which demanded punishment (frequently death, at least social ostracism) for a woman of Mrs. Dane's sort. However, in the ambiguous denouement of Act IV *Mrs. Dane's Defence* veers somewhat from the well-made play pattern and introduces complexities that give the play a modernity that most plays of the genre—including all of Jones's others—conspicuously lack.

Beneath the surface problems of false identity and thwarted romance is a very subtle and interesting battle of the sexes. Sir Daniel Carteret represents the conventional "masculine" view; he demands truth at all costs and insists that the "exposed" pay the price of the misdeeds without regard to extenuating circumstances. This attitude clashes with the "feminine" approach advocated by his intended, Lady Eastney, who considers only the "human" aspects of problem and weighs motive and essential character more heavily than technical fact. Even after she learns Mrs. Dane's actual identity, Lady Eastney says: "Mrs. Dane shall leave this place, if she does leave it, without a stain on her character. And I intend that Mrs. Bulsom-Porter shall stay in it, if she does stay in it, as a self-confessed scandal-monger."

Lady Eastney wins the "public" battle in that Mrs. Dane's name is cleared and Mrs. Bulsom-Porter is openly embarrassed. And, in a sense, she also wins in her conflict with Sir Daniel, since she coerces him into accepting her strategy, even though he knows it is based on false information. But on the more important question of Mrs. Dane's engagement to Lionel Carteret, it is the judge's view that prevails.

The central irony is that, in order to impress his view of things on Lionel and Mrs. Dane, Sir Daniel, the apostle of truth at all costs, tells lies. He tells his son that he once made a "like sacrifice," when the opposite was true, and he threatens Mrs. Dane with ultimate exposure, when he actually knows that the secret is safe. Mrs. Dane analyzes the problem correctly when she says "Only we mustn't get found out. I'm afraid I've broken that part of the law." Thus, the essential hypocrisy and moral self-righteousness of upper middle-class Victorian society is exposed, in the character of its "most respectable" advocate, to a degree that, perhaps, Jones himself did not fully intend or realize.

THE MISTRESS OF THE INN

Type of work: Drama
Author: Carlo Goldoni (1707-1793)
Type of plot: Romantic comedy
Time of plot: Mid-eighteenth century
Locale: Florence, Italy
First presented: 1752

If anything in Goldoni's canon can justify his title of "the Italian Molière," it is The Mistress of the Inn. *The vivaciousness and cleverness of Mirandolina, the title character, as she manipulates four men of different social stations, give the play a liveliness, naturalness, and humanity that make it a dramatic triumph.*

The humor of *The Mistress of the Inn* is based upon certain assumptions of class and social structure as well as upon the positions of man and woman relative to each other in society. The heroine's contacts in the play are made possible by virtue of the fact that she is an innkeeper. For, as a rule, by contrast, women of a nobler class did not encounter large numbers of men in eighteenth century Italy. Although Goldoni underscores Mirandolina's virtue often, her position suggested a certain moral looseness to audiences of the time. Indeed, a woman of mid-eighteenth century Italy would not consider conducting herself with Mirandolina's freedom; such behavior toward men would have been answered with claims that the woman was immoral and unfeminine. In addition, such a woman would have lost her social position altogether. Although we do not necessarily find independence in women humorous now, a woman who defied men was a subject for laughter two hundred years ago. Yet, just as we find Mirandolina's self-assurance and cleverness admirable, so were they admired by Goldoni's audience, but for different reasons. Goldoni's contemporaries must have delighted in seeing Mirandolina triumph over the foolish men in the play, not because her conquests were men, but because they were fools. In truth, Goldoni's audience would not have wanted women to be victorious over men in actuality, or even to challenge long-established male prerogatives. The humor of this battle between the sexes is safe and acceptable because it is not in any way realistic.

The second way in which social distinctions are used for humorous effect is through the opposition between the old gentry and the *nouveau riche*. The Count represents the newly moneyed class while the Marquis is of the old nobility, impoverished but clinging to his pride in his ancient rank. He scorns the bought title of the Count, insisting that lineage cannot be purchased. But in the practical world the man with money has the advantage, and the prestige of an old family is easily swept aside. The Marquis babbles about the refinements that come from breeding, about "taste" and "protection" and "honor." But when the Count flashes a diamond ring, Mirandolina cannot resist. Eighteenth century Italy was a country in transition, lagging behind the other European countries in economic and political developments, and the contest between these two absurd figures reflects the conditions that existed at the time. Many of the old families were being overwhelmed by the newly affluent commercial families; the power was changing hands, being yielded to the ruthless and shrewd. And soon the supreme upstart of them all, Napoleon Bonaparte, would appear on the scene.

In *The Mistress of the Inn,* Goldoni combines old dramatic traditions with his own innovations. For example, the convention of the insolent, shrewd servant (Fabricius) goes back to ancient Roman, and even Greek, comedy. Also, the character of Mirandolina suggests some of the independent courtesans of the old Roman comedies. But, on the other hand, the sense of the momentary scene in the Inn is new to Goldoni; the audience always is aware that life is going on around these characters on the stage, that the events of the comedy are not occurring in a vacuum. Part of the vitality of the play is due to this feeling of the everchanging quality of human life.

But the characters themselves are the primary reason for the play's long success. They are broadly sketched, but each possesses a goodnatured vitality. Mirandolina does not marry out of her class, which would have shocked the eighteenth century audiences, but the possibility that she will do so tantalizes the audience until the very end. Her gaiety and cleverness control the proceedings, playing on the self-centered males as on musical instruments. They, in turn, respond to her efforts according to their personalities, everjealous of one another, ridiculing one another, proud and arrogant, yet not matches for this earthy, witty female.

Carlo Goldoni was a prolific dramatist, his work completely reforming the comedy of his day. The son of a Venetian doctor, he ran away from school with a company of players. Although he eventually took a degree in law, the theater was always his first love. After making a false start with a lyric tragedy, he found his natural bent with a comedy in verse. He felt that a radical change was necessary in the Italian theater and followed Molière's example by attempting to depict the realities of social life in as natural a manner as possible. Today, his plays do not seem realistic, but they were a startling departure from what came before him. He freed his actors from the traditional practice of wearing masks on the stage and suppressed improvisation by writing out the parts in full. He eventually replaced the haphazard Italian farces of the day, the *commedia dell'arte,* with his own style of comedy of manners. His plays were both earthy and moral in tone, and attempted a faithful "mirror of life." He wrote for several companies during his career, during one season alone producing as many as sixteen original plays. Later, he went to Paris to direct the *Comedie Italienne* and wrote and directed for the French Court at Versailles. But, as a result of the Revolution, he died in poverty in Paris, in 1793. His best plays, however, which reflect the true life of the varied social classes in his native land, have endured and will continue to be enjoyed by audiences around the world. They possess a gaiety and shrewdness unsurpassed in modern drama, and present a tantalizing picture of a dynamic and rapidly changing moment in history.

Bruce D. Reeves

MITHRIDATE

Type of work: Drama
Author: Jean Baptiste Racine (1639-1699)
Type of plot: Historical tragedy
Time of plot: First century B.C.
Locale: Nymphée, on the Bosphorus
First presented: 1673

In Mithridate *Racine adds a love story to a historical pageant to create a drama about an old man in love with a young woman and jealous of his two sons. The two main characters are interesting in their complexity: Mithridate offers a contrast between the indomitable will power of the warrior and the blindness and confusion of the unhappy lover; Monime harmoniously combines all the gentleness and strength of Racine's heroines.*

Partly because of his bellicose nature and partly because of the envy inspired by his unusual talent, Racine was regularly involved in one imbroglio or another. In the case of *Mithridate,* however, from its first performance early in 1673, even his adversaries agreed that he had created a triumph. The play was greatly admired at the royal court. Since the seventeenth century, however, *Mithridate* has not maintained a degree of popularity equal to that of Racine's best-known tragedies. For example, from 1680 to 1965 *Phèdre* and *Andromache* were each produced slightly in excess of thirteen hundred times, whereas *Mithridate* was played only 644 times.

For Racine, particularly adept at portraying the subtleties of the feminine heart, *Mithridate* is an unusually masculine play. The choice of a male historical figure, in this case a despotic oriental king, as central character in his new play was no doubt influenced by his desire to compete with the allegedly more virile theater of the aging Corneille and to silence those critics prone to blame the softness, or femininity, of plays like *Bérénice* (1670) and *Bajazet* (1672), his two previous tragedies. The plot is more complex than that of Racine's earlier plays. Its basic element is the secret: new revelations serve to build the foundation on which the plot develops. Xiphares reveals his love to Monime in the first act. Not until late in the second act does Monime return the favor. In Act III Mithridate discloses his plan to attack Rome. Then, threatened with imprisonment, Pharnace informs Mithridate of Xiphares' love for Monime. Finally, Monime, tricked by Mithridate, admits that she loves Xiphares. In Act IV Monime discloses the truth to Xiphares: it was she who revealed their secret to Mithridate. Throughout the play, Pharnace nourishes his secret: the Roman legions are on the way to Nymphée.

The old king is the central figure whose presence links closely the otherwise disparate elements of the dramatic action. We see him in a double focus: as implacable enemy of Rome he is cast in the role of adversary to his son

Pharnace, who seeks conciliation with Rome; as passionate lover, he becomes a rival of Xiphares, also in love with the queen, though otherwise loyal. The entanglement is further complicated by the allusions to incidents that took place before the action of the play: Xiphares' mother had betrayed Mithridate to the Romans; Mithridate had sacrificed two of his sons, the result of his "cruel suspicions."

As tragic hero, Mithridate is a complex and ambiguous character. There is a strong element of fate, constantly evoked by the king's frequent references to his long series of past misfortunes. These misfortunes, of both a sentimental (love) and heroic (war) nature, assure our sympathy for the aging warrior. But, inasmuch as we feel a natural sympathy for Monime and Xiphares, as young lovers struggling to find a basis on which to approach each other, Mithridate appears hateful in his efforts to coerce the queen into granting him her affection. There is a curious and most delicate balance between, on the one hand, the grandeur of the old king, inspired for the most part by the narration of his past greatness as a warrior, and, on the other hand, the meanness of his present machinations, the duplicity of his dissimulations, and the violence of his outbursts of anger and jealousy.

Mithridate, though imperious and passionate, is really little more than a shell of his former self. His past power has evaporated; the effort to marry Monime represents a last opportunity to reestablish evidence of his manhood. Aside from his age—which, were there the slightest hint of anything grotesque in his character or actions, would instantly situate him with Molière's comic lovers, given to infatuations with women much younger than themselves— Mithridate is not unlike Othello. His destruction is brought about by a blind passion which easily, or perhaps inevitably, gives rise to a fatal jealousy. Therein lies the tragic flaw of this king, essentially noble, though at the same time cruel and violent.

The evolution of the dramatic action depends, in a large measure, on the undercurrent of intrigue and deception that informs the play. Mithridate relentlessly strives to determine the hidden motives of the other protagonists. For example, on his arrival in Nymphée he must know why his sons are not at their assigned posts. There is an unusual dependence on misunderstanding. Mithridate, particularly, is constantly manipulating people through ruse. He himself, we learn early in the play, launched the false report of his death. He has a decided proclivity for expressing himself in ambiguous terms, especially in talking about his sons; instead of naming them, he uses terms such as "treacherous son" and "audacious son." Other characters cannot be sure whom he is talking about. In just this manner, Monime is easily tricked by the duplicity of his language. The result is that Mithridate is a completely isolated figure, having no one in whom he can confide. He has three soliloquies, more than any other Racinian hero.

Unlike certain other tragedies, notably *Bajazet, Mithridate* does not end in general slaughter. At the end, the doomed king is torn between opposing sentiments: in his decision to unite Xiphares and Monime he triumphs over the baser emotions of jealousy and desire for revenge that, at least until then, had appeared to motivate him consistently. The "happy end" applies, of course, only to the young couple. In spite of it, the king's noble death assures a properly tragic denouement to the play.

Robert Eisner

MOBY DICK

Type of work: Novel
Author: Herman Melville (1819-1891)
Type of plot: Symbolic allegory
Time of plot: Early nineteenth century
Locale: The high seas
First published: 1851

Herman Melville brought many disparate elements together in Moby Dick: *a realistic picture of the whaling industry, an adventure-romance of the sea, an epic quest, a Faustian bargain, and metaphysical speculation. Although it is unlikely that any one interpretation of Ahab's obsessive pursuit of the white whale will ever be generally accepted, the depth, sweep, and power of the author's vision guarantees the novel's stature as one of the world's proven masterpieces.*

Although his early adventure novels—*Typee* (1846), *Omoo* (1847), *Redburn* (1849), and *White Jacket* (1850)—brought Melville a notable amount of popularity and financial success during his lifetime, it was not until nearly fifty years after his death—in the 1920's and 1930's—that he received universal critical recognition as one of the greatest American authors of the nineteenth century. Melville took part in the first great period of American literature—the period that included Poe, Emerson, Hawthorne, Whitman, and Thoreau. For complexity, originality, psychological penetration, breadth, and symbolic richness, Melville achieved his greatest artistic expression with the book he wrote when he was thirty, *Moby Dick*. Between the time of his birth in New York City and his return there to research and write his masterpiece, Melville had circled the globe of experience—working as a bank messenger, salesman, farmhand, schoolteacher (like his narrator, Ishmael), engineer and surveyor, bowling alley attendant, cabin boy, and whaleman in the Pacific on the *Acushnet*. His involvement in the mutinous Pacific voyage, combined with J. N. Reynold's accounts of a notorious whale called "Mocha Dick" (in *The Knickerbocker Magazine,* 1839) that wrought havoc in the 1840's and 1850's, certainly influenced the creation of *Moby Dick*.

The intertangled themes of this mighty novel express the artistic genius of a mind that, according to Hawthorne, "could neither believe nor be comfortable in unbelief." Many of those themes are characteristic of American romanticism: the "isolated self" and the pain of self-discovery, the insufficiency of conventional practical knowledge in the face of the "power of blackness," the demonic center to the world, the confrontation of evil and innocence, the fundamental imperfection of man, Faustian heroism, search for the ultimate truth, the inadequacy of human perception. The conflict between faith and doubt was one of the major issues of the century and *Moby Dick,* as Eric Mottram points out, is part of "a huge exploration of the historical and psychological origins and development of self, society and the desire to create and destroy gods and heroes."

Moby Dick is, moreover, a unique literary form, combining elements of the psychological and picaresque novel; sea story and allegory; the epic of "literal and metaphorical quest"; the satire of social and religious events; the emotional intensity of the lyric genre, both in diction and metaphor; Cervantian romance; Dantesque mysticism; Rabelaisian humor; Shakespearean drama (both tragedy and comedy), complete with stage directions; journalistic travel book; and scientific treatise on cetology. Melville was inspired by Hawthorne's example to give his story the unifying quality of a moral parable, although his own particular genius refused to allow that parable an unequivocal, single rendering. Both in style and theme, Melville was also influenced by Spenser, Shakespeare, Dante, Cervantes, Robert Burton, Sir Thomas Carlyle, Thomas Browne, and vastly miscellaneous reading in the New York Public Library (as witnessed by the two "Etymologies" and the marvelous "Extracts" that precede the text itself, items from the writer's notes and files that he could not bear to discard). It was because they did not know how to respond to its complexities of form and style that the book was "broiled in hell fire" by contemporary readers and critics. Even today the rich mixture of its verbal texture—an almost euphuistic flamboyance balanced by dry, analytical expository prose—requires a correspondingly unique sensitivity on the part of the reader. The most remarkable thing about the plot is that Moby Dick does not appear physically until after five hundred pages; and is not even mentioned by name until nearly two hundred pages have passed.

Whether it be the knowledge of reality, an embodiment of the primitive forces of nature, the deep subconscious energies of mankind, fate or destiny inevitably victorious over illusory free will, or simply the unknown in experience, it is what Moby Dick stands for that occupies the narrator's emphasis and the reader's attention through the greater part of the novel. In many ways, the great white whale may be compared to Spenser's "blatant beast" (who, in *The Faerie Queene,* also represents the indeterminable elusive quarry, and also escapes at the end to continue haunting the world). Nor is it surprising that *Moby Dick* is often considered to be "the American epic." The novel is replete with the elements characteristic of that genre: the piling up of classical, Biblical, historical allusions to provide innumerable parallels and tangents that have the effect of universalizing the scope of action; the narrator's strong sense of the fatefulness of the events he recounts, and his corresponding awareness of his own singular importance as the narrator of momentous, otherwise unrecorded, events; Queequeg as Ishmael's "heroic companion"; the "folk" flavor provided by countless proverbial statements; the leisurely pace of the narrative, with its frequent digressions and parentheses; the epic confrontation of life and death on a suitably grand stage (the sea), with its consequences for the human City (the *Pequod*); the employment of microcosms to explicate the whole (for example, the painting in the Spouter Inn, the Nantucket pulpit, the crow's nest); epithetical characterization; a cyclic notion of time and events; an epic race of heroes, the Nantucket whalers with their Biblical and exotic names; the mystical power of objects like Ahab's chair, the doubloon, or the *Pequod* itself; the alienated, sulking hero (Ahab); the use of lists to enhance the impression of an all-inclusive compass. Finally, *Moby Dick* shares the usually didactic purpose of folk epic; on one level, its purpose is to teach the reader about whales; on another level, it is to inspire the reader to become, himself, a heroic whaleman.

All this richness of purpose and presentation is somehow made enticing by Melville's masterly invention of his narrator. Ishmael immediately establishes a comfortable rapport with the reader in the unforgettable opening lines of the novel. He is both the objective observer and a participant in the events observed and recounted, both spectator and narrator. But he is much more than the conventional wanderer-witness. As a schoolmaster and sometime voyager, he combines his book learning with firsthand experience to make him an informed observer and a convincing, moving reporter. Simply by surviving he transcends the Byronic heroism of Ahab, as the wholesome overcoming the sinister.

Kenneth John Atchity

THE MOCK ASTROLOGER

Type of work: Drama
Author: Pedro Calderón de la Barca (1600-1681)
Type of plot: Farce
Time of plot: Seventeenth century
Locale: Madrid
First presented: c. 1624

The Mock Astrologer *is one of Calderón de la Barca's early comedies, reflecting the influences of his immediate predecessors, Tirso de Molina and Lope de Vega. Although a strident satire against grafters, impostors, and especially astrologers,* The Mock Astrologer *is basically a fast-moving farce intended more for entertainment than education.*

The Mock Astrologer satirizes astrology, which had adherents even in devout Catholic Spain of the Golden Age. Calderón, like other literary greats of the time in Spain and Portugal, did not take astrology seriously but sometimes felt compelled to bludgeon it as a pseudoscience that had an unfortunate hold on gullible people. The pretensions of Don Diego to extrasensory talent were typical of the astrological plague that had afflicted Europe sporadically for centuries, despite the opposition of Christianity. Thus, as a playwright steeped in Christian theology, Calderón was aware of the Biblical injunction against a misuse of astrology and sought to expose the folly of this practice to Spain's dramatic public. The crude machinations of Don Diego are consequently lampooned, along with the simplemindedness of anyone naïve enough to place faith in such deception. The play thus has a simple plot to which complications are added in a manner typical of Calderónian drama, especially the paralysis of action through a pretense.

The Mock Astrologer's evasion of reality, and Calderón's poetic handling of this flight, has a baroque tinge. The baroque law of contrast therefore attains maximum effect through the contrast of Don Diego's supposed magic prowess with the empty reality of his true incapacity. Deception governs Don Diego's behavior as he flutters between th two lives of truly being and only potentially being. Typical also of Calderón's dramatic craft is the largeness of Don Diego's role as an antagonist, which symbolizes negation and evil. As protagonist, Don Juan symbolizes the positive and good, and the Don Diego-Don Juan confrontation is somewhat reminiscent of that between Caesar and Brutus in Shakespeare. Continued contrast, movement, and flight are also used by Calderón in *The Mock Astrologer* to enhance the mocking of reality; the word *burla* (mockery) or its synonyms are used seventy times in the play.

Some critics feel that Calderón avoided a deep study of his play's personalities because he had an instinctive, baroque aversion to empty and undecorated space and inner emptiness. *The Mock Astrologer* does portray external shapes through its lyric poetry and erudition, which are apparently used deliberately to expose the appearance of learnedness in personalities such as Don Diego who hollowly crave knowledge without studying.

Even the play's apparently brisk action is more pretense than reality, since decisive action is paralyzed by the dreamy, fictional pretenses of both Don Diego and Don Juan, and the latter's suspended-action courting of Dona María from a distance for two years. Calderón thus emphasizes the clash between the world of reality and the world of fiction, and implies—in a manner so typically Calderónian—that all in this life is truth and that all is a lie.

MODERN CHIVALRY

Type of work: Novel
Author: Hugh Henry Brackenridge (1748-1816)
Type of plot: Picaresque satire
Time of plot: First years of the United States
Locale: Pennsylvania
First published: 1792-1815

Modern Chivalry *was the direct, immediate artistic expression of Hugh Henry Brackenridge's experiences as a political figure during America's formative years. Captain John Farrago is the sensible new American citizen; Teague O'Regan represents the potential excesses of the new political system.*

Hugh Henry Brackenridge was neither a writer who participated in politics nor a politician who wrote as an avocation; his writing and his politics were two sides of the same coin, a passionate involvement in the affairs of his time. Brackenridge sought nothing less than the creation of the new American democracy, and, along with it, the new American literature.

Loosely modeled after *Don Quixote, Modern Chivalry* provides a satirical record of Brackenridge's political and social attitudes. The almost haphazard plot sequences and general unevenness in quality reflect the casual, off-and-on method of its composition. The book had first been provoked by a political defeat and became a running commentary on Brackenridge's experiences in public affairs, as well as an expression of his irritation at the follies he found in American society. Therefore, it appeared irregularly and unevenly over a twenty-three-year period, corresponding to the vicissitudes of Brackenridge's political fortunes.

This is not to say, however, that the book is arbitrary or ambiguous. The central themes of the novel are perfectly clear, the intellectual viewpoint is constant, and, although the book lacks specific direction, sooner or later Brackenridge turns his attention to most important American institutions and customs.

To Brackenridge the problem of the United States, once it freed itself from British rule, was how to build a democracy based upon a qualified, knowledgeable electorate. Always the moderate, Brackenridge denied the Federalist notion that the common man was incapable of functioning in a democratic society. But he was too familiar with frontier excesses and mob emotionalism to believe in the innate wisdom of the ordinary person. So he dramatized the problem in *Modern Chivalry.*

Captain John Farrago's frustrating attempts to keep track of his servant Teague O'Regan and to keep O'Regan—and those he meets—out of trouble provides the thinnest of plot lines. O'Regan is the ignorant, "innocent," common man, whose greed and capacity for self-deception are fed by the freedom, fluidity, and crudity of the frontier. Once his ambitions are ignited, he believes himself capable of accomplishing any feat or holding any office. The selfishness, foolishness, and volatility of the crowd reinforce these delusions, and O'Regan's vigorous identification with the worst attitudes and emotions of the mob wins him instant adulation. Thus he becomes, in short order, a political candidate, a clergyman, a lover, a philosopher, a university professor, a revenue collector, and so on. Few institutions or public types are spared as Brackenridge exposes the pretensions of the rich as well as the poor, the educated as well as the ignorant, the Eastern sophisticate as well as the Western backwoodsman. However, the author makes it clear, as he does so, that *education* is the answer to the excesses he pictures. Democracy is workable only if the so-called common man can be educated to understand and carry out his role as a citizen. Failing that, Brackenridge suggests, the future belongs to the O'Regans.

A MODERN COMEDY

Type of work: Novel
Author: John Galsworthy (1867-1933)
Type of plot: Social chronicle
Time of plot: 1922-1926
Locale: England and America
First published: 1924, 1926, 1928

With the three novels that comprise A Modern Comedy (The White Monkey, The Silver Spoon, Swan Song), *John Galsworthy completes his saga of the Forsyte family by chronicling the final evolution and death of his main character, Soames Forsyte. These books also carefully register the changing attitudes and mores of upper-middle-class England in the aftermath of World War I.*

This trilogy, the second half of the six novels comprising Galsworthy's Forsyte chronicles, sees the final transformation of Soames Forsyte from the despised husband of Irene in *The Man of Property* (1906) to the wholly sympathetic character who, by the time of his death in the closing novel *Swan Song* (1928), had become a public figure in the minds of British readers. The character of Soames reflects Galsworthy's own changing attitude toward the society he depicts. When he wrote *The Man of Property* Galsworthy was an angry young man, in revolt against the stolidly Victorian values of his own Forsytean family. He was emerging as an artist instead of engaging in their world of finance. More important, he had fallen desperately in love with his cousin Arthur Galsworthy's wife Ada, whose loveless marriage could not be terminated without inevitable scandal and social ostracism. After the death of Galsworthy's father the divorce did take place; Ada and John were married, and like young Jolyon and Irene, remained devoted to each other throughout their lives. The picture of Soames Forsyte as the cold but possessive husband may not be an accurate portrayal of Arthur Galsworthy; in actual fact Ada may have been more bored than bullied. What matters, however, is that John Galsworthy believed her to be the victim of unnamed horrors and this conviction flamed out in much of his early work. With their marriage and the consequent resolution of their personal dilemma, this theme recedes from his work and is finally reversed. In the first novel of *A Modern Comedy* Fleur's flirtations are treated with mild disapproval. In the third volume, when she revives her passionate love affair with Jon, the lovers are not, like Irene and Bosinney, a heroic pair facing a hostile world; it is now marriage that properly triumphs, and the moral order is restored when Fleur and Jon remain with their spouses.

The shift in the character of Soames began at the end of the first trilogy in *To Let* (1921), in which his love for his daughter softens the earlier rigidity of his character. In *The White Monkey* (1924), the first novel of this trilogy, Soames is seen in an increasingly favorable light. He behaves with integrity in the crisis of the insurance company board, scornfully rejecting business practices which would conceal the facts from the shareholders. Those sterling moral principles of the Forsytes which once appeared so narrow and constricting are now, in the postwar world of the 1920's, beginning to seem like strongholds of security in a rapidly deteriorating society.Soames's relation with Irene is now seen also from his point of view. There is never any condemnation of Irene herself, who remains always the exalted symbol of Ada, but as Soames catches glimpses of her throughout the later years, the reader sees his inability to comprehend what went wrong. What seemed in the first novel to be merely the possessiveness of the "man of property" is shown now to be the tragic passion of a man who could neither express love nor receive it. Each time Soames sees Irene the old anguish is revived; she is forever beautiful, mysterious, unattainable. Only in his love for his daughter can he find emotional fulfillment.

Throughout his life Galsworthy felt deep concern for the poor and actively supported liberal measures to alleviate poverty, but he is not at his best in dealing with such characters in his novels. The episodes involving Bicket and his wife Victorine and their desperate measures to acquire the means to emigrate to Australia are accurate enough in denoting their economic plight, but the characters themselves are not altogether convincing. Their mutual sacrifices for the sake of the other reflect a tendency to idealize the poor as noble victims of society rather than to present them as individualized characters. Galsworthy's view here seems unintentionally patronizing because it lacks the satiric eye which he turns so shrewdly on his own upper middle class.

Galsworthy's skill is at its best when he shows what happens to the Forsytean middle class when it moves into socially higher circles. By marrying Michael Mont, the son and heir of a baronet, Fleur has moved upward in the social scale. The salon she works so hard to assemble consists of a literary and artistic smart set comfortably sprinkled with an occasional title. For all her charm, however, Fleur tries too hard and meets a temporary defeat. In the second novel, *The Silver Spoon* (1926), the complete reversal of moral values from the Victorian-Edwardian society of the first trilogy to the decadence of the 1920's is deftly shown in the episode of Marjorie Ferrar's lawsuit. In defending the suit, Fleur's lawyers must prove that Marjorie has pursued a life of sexual freedom. A revelation which would in the earlier period have condemned Marjorie to social ostracism now makes her the heroine of the modern sophisticates who surround her, and it is Fleur who is cut for seeming to represent an outmoded moral prudery. This commentary on shifting values, however, is only a part of Galsworthy's satire. Marjorie, the granddaughter of an earl, represents that aristocratic arrogance which has always taken it for granted that the "best" people can do as they like. It is the middle class that is either bound by convention or engaged in a daring revolt against it.

In calling this trilogy *A Modern Comedy* Galsworthy makes it clear that he finds in postwar society a loss of permanence which renders the modern world insubstantial. While Soames Forsyte reacts with bewilderment to the changes, Galsworthy's own vision, broader than that of his character, sees much that is attractive in the new freedom; but his view is still close enough to that of Soames to see that with the gains there are also losses. The death of Soames is the end of an era, and only the spirit of Comedy, in the sense of ironic detachment, is appropriate to the new social scene.

Galsworthy's literary reputation has passed through several stages. Before the 1920's he was more widely known as a playwright than as a novelist and some critics writing at that time predicted that his fame would rest upon his plays of social protest. His novel *The Man of Property* had been highly praised, but it was not until the completion of the *Modern Comedy* trilogy that the entire Forsyte chronicle emerged as a major work of fiction. Today the plays, like many topical works, seem dated whereas the social chronicle has a wider appeal. Like his contemporaries Arnold Bennett and H. G. Wells, Galsworthy has been eclipsed by the more dazzling techniques of writers such as James Joyce and Virginia Woolf. However, the period in which the Forsyte chronicles are set is now far enough in the past for nostalgic attraction. The popularity of the British television series based upon the Forsyte novels has revived interest in Galsworthy's work, and it is probable that his reputation will ultimately rest upon this fictional document of a changing society.

Audrey C. Peterson

A MODERN INSTANCE

Type of work: Novel
Author: William Dean Howells (1837-1920)
Type of plot: Domestic realism
Time of plot: Nineteenth century
Locale: New England
First published: 1882

The "modern instance" is that of divorce, a subject seldom treated in nineteenth century American fiction. Although the divorce never actually occurs, the issue permeates the book and serves as a moral catalyst. While Howells' treatment of the subject may seem archaic, even quaint, to the modern reader, his willingness to deal with it forthrightly was a step in the direction of a more candid treatment of intimate relations between the sexes.

A reader of American novels who cut his teeth on Steinbeck and Hemingway and was perhaps adventurous enough to move on to Thomas Wolfe, Norman Mailer, and perhaps even Hunter Thompson would be baffled to find that William Dean Howells was once considered to be a modern writer. In fact, Howells is a prime example of the post-Civil War "realist" school. At first glance there would be little that would make him seem modern to today's readers.

One of the most glaringly antiquated aspects of *A Modern Instance* is the attitude it shows towards divorce. Divorce was cause for grave alarm. If it became accepted in society or easy to obtain, civilization, held together by strong family bonds, would crumble disastrously, Howells seems to tell the reader. If Halleck were to ask Marcia to marry him, even after Bartley's death, the moral depravity of this act would doom Western culture to the fate of Nineveh and Tyre, because Halleck had fallen in love with Marcia before she was abandoned by Bartley. Thus, to marry her would put a retroactive seal of approval upon his love of a married woman. This is too close to divorce for comfort, even though Howells leaves the matter unresolved at the end of the book.

What could be modern about this attitude towards divorce? The answer is simply that Howells must be taken in terms of his own time. The period of American history between the Civil War and Spanish-American War was one that corresponded to the high point of the Victorian Age in England. The attitude towards divorce described above and shown in *A Modern Instance* was not an odd one for that time. It is in this fact that the justification for Howells' claim to realism and modernism lies.

Divorce was one of those things that happened in America in the 1880's but was never recognized. The fact that Howells treated that theme was itself innovative and startling to many. Even though Howells' realism was part of a larger literary movement, this novel was a marvelously modern publication.

America at that time was also a nation very proud of itself and of its new postwar vigor. Howells' Social Darwinism shows us the vitality of the American belief in pragmatism and rationality, and the desire to see things as they actually were without moral or stylistic frills. This movement was not unique to America, of course, but Howells' novels show to what extent it affected American literature of the period. In effect, *A Modern Instance* claims that it is a true picture of an aspect of life—divorce—and the way people act when confronted with it.

To what extent did Howells reach his goal? He was modern for his time, but was he realistic? The two questions cannot be separated fairly because realism, meaning here accurate description of persons and places together with credible characterization and dialogue, would have been considered innovative. A consideration of the points of crisis in the novel would contribute to an answer.

One such point is Marcia and Bartley's elopement. A nonrealistic treatment of this would be romantic in the extreme. The central motif might be a romantic haze through which the reader would glimpse two hearts beating at last as one, secure and happy in their conquest of all obstacles. Instead, Howells treats the reader to a scene in which the first consideration is the sale of the horse and sled.

The period of marriage is also treated realistically. The problem of finding decent housing at an affordable price, the struggle to secure a living, and the routine of domestic life are all presented matter-of-factly. One episode from this part of the book seems particularly to have been drawn from life, and given a life of its own by Howells' skill. This is the scene in which Bartley begins his career as a journalist by drinking with a group of newspapermen at their club. In a spirit of slightly drunken camaraderie he is nominated and chosen a member. Then he pays his dues. This inclusion, in passing, of the matter of an entrance fee into the club is one of those gem-like little touches by which Howells is able to freeze an instant in the mind of the reader and to show realistically more than was thought to be there. This episode is one of several such gems.

The divorce crisis is handled without false sentiment or melodramatic histrionics. After a quarrel Marcia flees the house. Bartley packs a bag and waits for her to return. He finally gives up his waiting and leaves, as he had wanted to do. Marcia returns a half hour later and refuses to believe he has abandoned her. Far longer than one might think possible she keeps up the pretense that he is merely away on a trip. She eventually knows that she is fooling only herself, but not even this recognition, hinted at by Howells, forces her to drop the game. Such naïveté could strain a reader's credulity except that Howells has drawn by this point in the novel such a deft portrait of her that she is clearly recognizable as a woman who is essentially still a sheltered girl.

As for characterization, one of the elements of Howells' realism, the characters are exceptionally well drawn until the last quarter of the book, at which point the novel seems to fall apart. It rushes to an inconclusive ending. It is true, however, that the novel was written when Howells was exhausted, ill, and under pressure of a deadline. (The work was originally published as a serial in *Scribner's Magazine* under the title of "The New Medea.") Even though the characterizations and the structure of *A Modern Instance* falter towards the end of the book, the first parts offer well-delineated characterizations that seem to have been taken from life. Perhaps no higher compliment can be paid an author with pretensions to realism.

The major exception to this rule is the characterization of Kinney. He is of such a stock line, the philosophical backwoodsman, that it is possible that Howells intended him as comic relief. If this is the case, then it is a tribute to Howells' craftsmanship that he can skillfully use this buffoon to further the exposition of Bartley's character. Kinney does not seem so much to be drawn from life as he seems a fugitive from *Roughing It* or from one of the better works of Petroleum V. Nasby.

A Modern Instance is one of those few books which even after a century can reach us and awaken a sense of what life must have been like in a time that is farther off and further removed from us than most people today realize. It is a novel that deserves to be better known.

Glenn M. Edwards

A MODERN MIDAS

Type of work: Novel
Author: Maurus Jókai (1825-1904)
Type of plot: Philosophical romance
Time of plot: Nineteenth century
Locale: Hungary
First published: 1872

Maurus Jókai combined a career in the service of Hungarian politics with that of a master storyteller. A Modern Midas, an excellent example of the imaginative romance, which depends for its effects upon a wealth of incident and character, an involved plot mingling the ideal and the fantastic, and an idyllic, pastoral atmosphere, is typical of Jókai at his best.

Maurus Jókai's *A Modern Midas* must be read within the context of Turkish-Hungarian political relations to make sense to the modern Western reader. Beginning with military campaigns in the late fourteenth century, the Turks established in the early fifteenth century a dictatorial occupation of Hungary which lasted until 1718. The cruel and barbarian Turkish rule so outraged Hungarians that, even in 1787, a retaliatory war against the Turks was launched. Given this animosity against the Turks, Hungarians in Jókai's time and to this day feel a hostility against the Turks which rivals that of Armenians who suffered similarly at ruthless Turkish hands. Consequently, no amount of generosity or tolerance could possibly surmount the barriers between the good, well-meaning Hungarian Michael Timar and the Turkish Ali Tschorbadschi and his daughter, Timéa. Michael and Timéa's marriage was doomed before its start because of differences in cultural as well as socio-political heritage.

Michael tried valiantly to maintain an ethical stance, in keeping with his proud heritage as a Hungarian. Timéa, despite her abuse by the Brasowitsch family, retained the airs of a superior person from a dominant ethnic group. Her capacity to manage and increase Michael's estate during his absence is ample testimony to her self-sufficient capabilities. Michael in the meanwhile still had to negotiate with both Hungarian and Turkish governments to secure property rights on No Man's Land for Thérèse and Naomi. Jókai's Hungarian patriotism is fully revealed in this unlikely juxtaposition of personal allegiances and political antagonisms. Not surprisingly, as a consequence Michael is ultimately drawn to his ethnic and ethical soul mate, Naomi, in a relationship mutually fulfilling, however extralegal.

This modern Midas thus displays an integrity lacking in his earlier namesake, since Michael does not foresake all for money, then regret his concessions. He has sufficient wealth—accumulated through his own wit and craft—to enable him and Naomi, as well as Thérèse, to live comfortably. But he is not so greedy as to maintain an unhappy marriage with Timéa in order to increase his riches. Michael, therefore, epitomizes Jókai's ideal of principled social, economic, and political behavior under the conditions which prevailed at the time. As such, Michael, hero of *A Modern Midas,* is Jókai's answer—no matter how romanticized—to what Hungarian loyalty is about.

MOLL FLANDERS

Type of work: Novel
Author: Daniel Defoe (1660-1731)
Type of plot: Picaresque romance
Time of plot: Seventeenth century
Locale: England and the American colonies
First published: 1722

The best introduction to Defoe's classic picaresque, an important forerunner of the modern novel, is to quote its full title: The Fortunes and Misfortunes of the famous Moll Flanders, who was born in Newgate, and during a life of continued variety, for threescore years, besides her childhood, was twelve years a Whore, five times a Wife (thereof once to her own brother), twelve years a Thief, eight years a transported Felon in Virginia, at last grew rich, lived honest, and died a penitent. Written from her own Memorandums.

Ever since it was first published in 1722, the reading public has enjoyed *Moll Flanders* as the lusty, energetic tale of a seventeenth century adventuress and manipulator. Many readers have assumed the story is true biography; Daniel Defoe himself rather coyly suggests as much, perhaps because he feared such a scandalous story could not be published or would not be popular if it were seen as the work of the imagination.

In this, as in his other great novels, such as *Robinson Crusoe* and *A Journal of the Plague Year,* Defoe achieves his realistic effect by incorporating a wealth of authentic detail. Having been a pamphleteer and journalist much of his life, Defoe knew how well the concrete fact, the specific example, build plausibility. He has Moll relate her remarkable story simply, thoroughly, and with candor. She is literal-minded and bothers little with description or metaphor. (In his preface, Defoe claims to have cleaned up the language and omitted some of the more "vicious part of her life"; thus Moll's sexual adventures are related in curious, sometimes amusing circumlocutions.) Moll sticks mainly to the stark realities of her life except for passages in which she moralizes about her misdeeds.

Despite the verisimilitude, however, there is a problem of tone which frequently puzzles the modern reader and has stirred a lively controversy among critics. The question may be stated thus: is the story full of conscious irony, or is it told in utter sincerity? If the former is the case, most scholars agree *Moll Flanders* is a masterwork both as social commentary and fictional art; if the latter, there are lapses in the author's moral scheme and his literal ability.

The problem centers more on Moll's attitudes than her actions. Given her situation, that of a woman of no status but with large ambitions, her behavior is entirely plausible. In her childhood, Moll is dependent for her very survival upon the whims and kindnesses of strangers. By the time she is eight years old, she is already determined to be a "gentlewoman"—an ambition very nearly impossible to fulfill in seventeenth century England when one has neither family nor, more importantly, money. She is quick to recognize the value of money in assuring not only one's physical security but one's place in the world—and she aims for a comfortable place indeed. Money thus becomes her goal and eventually her god. To attain it, she uses whatever means are at hand; as a beautiful woman, her sexuality is the handiest means available. When, after a number of marriages and other less legitimate alliances, sex is no longer a spendable coin, she turns to thieving, and rapidly becomes a master of the trade.

We know from other of Defoe's writings that the author sympathized with the plight of women in his society; education and most trades (except the oldest profession) were closed to them, and for the most part their welfare was entirely dependent upon that of their husbands or other men in their lives. As a hardheaded pragmatist who finds herself in straitened circumstances, Moll is much akin to Becky Sharp and Scarlett O'Hara; all three use their own ingenuity to survive in a hostile world, and although we do not entirely condone their behavior, we can understand it.

But after Moll has acted, she reflects; and it is this reflection that poses our problem. For convenience, she marries the younger brother of the man who first seduced her. After he dies, she remarks that "He had been really a very good husband to me, and we lived very agreeably together," but then she quickly complains that because he had not had time to acquire much wealth, she was "not much mended by the match." Another five-year marriage also ends in her widowhood; she wastes not a word in grieving the husband who has given her "an uninterrupted course of ease and content," but laments the loss of his money at excessive length. Soon afterwards, she steals a gold necklace from a child and admits that she was tempted to kill the child to prevent any outcry. She rationalizes that "I only thought I had given the parents a just reproof for their negligence in leaving the poor lamb to come home by itself, and it would teach them to take more care another time."

These recollections are told from the point of view of a woman seventy years old. She spends a good deal of time explaining that poverty and fear of poverty drove her to all her wickedness; yet she never admits that even when she is relatively secure, she keeps on scheming and thieving. Like many another entrepreneur, she has come to find excitement and fulfillment in the turning of the profit, the successful clinching of a "deal," the accumulation of wealth for its own sake. Although she repents her flagrant sins—deception, thieving, whoring—she apparently never recognizes the sin of her spirit in basing all human relationships upon their monetary worth. Furthermore, although she closes her account by declaring that she and her husband are "resolved to spend the remainder of our years in sincere penitence for the wicked lives we have lived," they are now free from want, partly because of an inheritance, but also because of the proceeds from her years as master

thief. We see no indication that penitence goes any deeper than a rather grati-
fied feeling that she has made peace with her Maker (a peace made, by the
way, in Newgate prison while Moll was under sentence of death). There is
no evidence that she intends to make restitution of stolen goods or apply
herself in positive good works to offset some of her wicked deeds.

The question, then, is whether Defoe expects us to see the irony in what
one critic has called Moll's moral "muddle"; or whether he is so outraged at
what poverty and the lack of opportunity can do that he himself fails to see
the lapses in her moral system. We get a few clues from Defoe's life, but they
are contradictory. Like Moll, he was frequently haunted by poverty, like her
he spent months in the "hell" of Newgate. His steadfast stand as a Dissenter
(which made him a lifelong outsider in English society); his humane views
of the treatment of the poor, of women, of the downtrodden; his dogged and
successful efforts to pay every penny of a £17,000 bankruptcy—all
give evidence of a man of high and stern principles. On the other hand, he
worked for the Tories, then for the Whigs, writing, as Robert C. Elliott has
pointed out, with passion and conviction on both sides of controversial issues;
and in his numerous business ventures he was not above swindling (even his
own mother-in-law). His own dreams of status are attested by his love for
trade—"the whore I doated on"—and his addition of "De" to his name (his
father was James Foe) to provide a touch of gentility.

Critics have not resolved the debate over morality and irony in the novel.
But few will dispute that it is a fascinating account likely to hold the attention of readers for further centuries. Virginia Woolf went further: she named
Moll Flanders as one of the "few English novels which we can call indisput-
ably great."

Sally Buckner

THE MONK

Type of work: Novel
Author: Matthew Gregory Lewis (1775-1818)
Type of plot: Gothic romance
Time of plot: The Spanish Inquisition
Locale: Madrid, Spain
First published: 1796

The Monk was one of the best-selling Gothic novels of its time. Relying heavily on a Faustian theme and a stridently anti-Catholic bias, "Monk" Lewis concocted an improbable, sensational, generally disorganized horror story that nevertheless contains scenes of real dramatic power, and two malefactors, Ambrosio and Matilda, who rank with the best of the Romantic hero-villains and villainesses.

There are two facts about *The Monk* every reader must keep in mind. First, its lurid picture of the Spanish Church is characteristic of an exaggerated, purposely sensational attack on Catholic culture to be found in popular English fiction from the time of the Renaissance; second, it is a brilliant innovation in a literary form prescribed by Mrs. Radcliffe in her famous Gothic Romances. (*The Mysteries of Udolpho* appeared just a year before *The Monk.*) The second fact is the significant one.

Mrs. Radcliffe always supplied a rational explanation for her startling Gothic effects of horror or simple surprise. She was still enough of a child of eighteenth century Rationalism to adhere to the demands of phenomenal verisimilitude. Lewis, however, created in *The Monk* a totally self-indulgent romp of horror, terror, and sexual sadism. He pulled out all stops, and freed the Gothic Romance from any remaining obligations to credibility. Thirty years earlier Horace Walpole's *The Castle of Otranto* had proven that the marvelous needed no apologies, and Lewis merely extended the marvelous to include the forbidden and the incredible. What he discovered was a kind of psychological symbolism for inordinate evil. Ambrosio's beatific façade and satanic true self anticipate the theme of the "beauty of evil," a concept central to writers later in the century as different as Emily Brontë and Baudelaire.

Lewis also exploited his generation's fascination with Goethe's *Faust.* Ambrosio's pact with the devil and his final betrayal by Satan seem a vulgarization or parody of the Faustian myth. As a convention, the "pact-with-the-devil" held its own in Gothic fiction throughout its entire vogue. The last great Gothic Romance, *Melmoth the Wanderer* (1820) by Charles Maturin, relies heavily on it.

The main purpose of the Gothic novel was entertainment by shock, a trait readily apparent in certain motion pictures of the 1970's.

MONKEY

Type of work: Novel
Author: Wu Ch'eng-en (c. 1505-c. 1580)
Type of plot: Fantasy
Time of plot: Seventh century
Locale: China, India, and various mythical regions
First published: Sixteenth century

Monkey *was inspired by the pilgrimage of the Chinese priest Hsüan Tsang to India in the seventh century. Except for the priest and a few other historical personages, however, the novel is fantastic, with the whole mythical universe as its background. It may be interpreted both as a satire, with the rebellious monkey against the bureaucratic heavenly government, and as an allegory, a Buddhist* Pilgrim's Progress.

Starting his hundred-chapter novel with Monkey's birth in the creation myth, Wu-Ch'eng-en has made him a divine hero on an unflinching quest for immortality to which the subsequent pilgrimage is but the final fulfillment. Arthur Waley has thus used *Monkey* as the title of his partial yet witty translation of the book. The novel represents the "dual modes of myth and comedy." Myth here refers to the representation of any reality suggestive of the "archetypal patterns" of primeval humanity. Most fully developed myths in the novel have some organic relations with the story of Monkey, and these include the creation, the quest for immortality, the journey to the underworld, the fall from grace, the divine mercy, the mission, the redeeming pilgrimage, and the apotheosis.

Still, Monkey is not the only hero in the pilgrimage. He and Pigsy are a pair of complementary characters. Ever since Pigsy joined the pilgrims, he has always followed Monkey to subdue monsters, like the Great King of Miracles. When Monkey is alone, his adventures are not so interesting as those in which Pigsy joins him. Besides, the five pilgrims have almost achieved a harmony of personalities among themselves since they reached the Crow-cock Kingdom. On their way they have been transformed from isolated victims under fate into united victors over faith. As in the Cart-slow Kingdom, they not only help themselves, but they become the destined saviors of the suffering people.

This harmony of personalities among the pilgrims is vitally related not only to character development but also to the union of the "dual modes of myth and comedy" in the novel. For instance, the characters of Monkey and Pigsy gradually balance each other, while in the plot, Pigsy often provides a comic relief to temper Monkey's mythic adventures. The pilgrims' quest in the physical world is at once a quest within their personalities. As the quest goes on, the relations among them become more and more harmonious. It is chiefly through the harmony of their personalities that they at last attain their goal.

In Monkey's fearless quest for immortality, his determination has almost become a kind of destiny. In his heroic striving upward, he has reached a height of spiritual awareness, where time stands still. In most journey themes in world literature, the end is the beginning. The quest of Monkey also goes in a cycle, in which the perpetual process can be identified with the final goal. Buddha himself tells the pilgrims that even Mahayana scriptures ought to be left behind in a quest for enlightenment. Therefore, the plot of the quest is like a circle which has no end but the center of a core.

Myth and comedy are further related by the author's lyrical vision of life, and the lyrical style of his narrative. In his vivid description, the scenery of nature is charged with human feeling, while human feeling has thus gained an "objective correlative" from the described landscape. The translator has re-created much of the author's lyrical and colloquial style. Both of them have tried to enhance the actions by using some of the lively conventions of the oral traditions, like the recurring exclamation, "Dear Monkey!" The pilgrims' last calamity of the river hazard indicates the author's organic use of an old Chinese folk-motif to make up the mythic number of eighty-one, which storytellers tend to miscount in their oral performance.

MONSIEUR BEAUCAIRE

Type of work: Novelette
Author: Booth Tarkington (1869-1946)
Type of plot: Period romance
Time of plot: Early eighteenth century
Locale: Bath, England
First published: 1900

Booth Tarkington achieved international fame with the appearance of this slight and romantic story of disguise and intrigue. The truism embodied in Monsieur Beaucaire—*that a man's name is unimportant, that it is the man himself who is important—is proved delightfully enough, not by a nobody but by a real prince, and at the expense of a snobbish English aristocracy.*

Monsieur Beaucaire, an elegant but sprightly novelette, is quite different from Booth Tarkington's realistic, morally earnest fiction such as *The Magnificent Ambersons* (1918) or *Alice Adams* (1921), just as it is unlike the robustly comic juvenile novels treating the misadventures of Penrod, Sam, or Willie Baxter. Rather, the short novel resembles the mannered romantic comedy of Max Beerbohm or Leonard Merrick. Style rather than content is important. On the one hand, Tarkington imitates the genteel romanticism of Clyde Fitch's *Beau Brummel* (1890); on the other, he satirizes romantic conventions popular in fiction and the theater. With self-parodying elegance, he writes that the duke's mouth "foamed over with chaotic revilement." The scoundrel Winterset reveals anger when his "white lip showed a row of scarlet dots upon it." And when Beaucaire is forced to remove his disguise, he regrets that he must "assassinate" his poor mustache. Because Tarkington's language strains after effects of romantic hyperbole, his descriptions are often comic, even farcical. For example, Beaucaire, challenged to a duel by a "ruffing buck," laughs in his face and at twilight of the same day "pinks" the man "carefully through the right shoulder." Beaucaire then hands his "wet" sword over to his lackey and, bending over his fallen adversary, caps his insult to the unfortunate by calling him a "naughty man." In another scene Mr. Molyneaux, brought low by the intrepid Beaucaire, confesses that he and his men have been rewarded their just desserts, "his mouth full of dust and philosophy."

Tarkington not only exaggerates the heroic exploits of Beaucaire; he also exaggerates his hero's courtesy. In the final recognition scene, when Beaucaire identifies himself as the Duke of Orleans, he expresses his contempt for Lady Mary's snobbery. Then, feeling that he may have injured her feelings, he walks her to the door, "her hand fluttering faintly in his." In a scene of culminating romantic silliness, suddenly a great "hum of voices" can be heard, fiddles weave a wandering air, "a sweet French song of the *voyageur,*" and the onetime barber takes his majestic leave of the gasping multitudes.

Although Tarkington's readers appreciated the satire and humor woven into the romance, they also took seriously the author's main idea; that a person should be judged by his own merit, not by his social station. For the audience of a democracy, this message was particularly ingratiating. *Monsieur Beaucaire* was enormously successful both as a short novel and as a play with the same title (1901). Although Tarkington's hero is a Frenchman of the noble class, he is egalitarian and unpretentious; above all, he makes fools of the English aristocracy. For Americans of 1900, who had often been the butt of ridicule in the English press for their supposed vulgarity, Beaucaire's— and Tarkington's—revenge was sweet.

MONSIEUR D'OLIVE

Type of work: Drama
Author: George Chapman (c. 1559-1634)
Type of plot: Romantic comedy
Time of plot: Seventeenth century
Locale: An imaginary dukedom near France
First presented: 1604

Although George Chapman's major achievements lie in his attempts at the tragic form, Monsieur d'Olive *is a character comedy of real merit. In this play Chapman cleverly satirizes the petty political intrigues of early seventeenth century court life and creates a memorable comic character in d'Olive, a fluent, self-assured, ultimately ridiculous fop.*

This Jacobean comedy is made up of the usual two plots, one involving Vandome's coercion of retreating people back into the mainstream of life, the other depicting the fluent but foolish d'Olive. The two plots are not firmly connected in action, but thematic unity does exist. "Opinion" is the central idea of the play. Desire for the good opinion of others leads Marcellina into seclusion when she loses her husband's approval, induces Count St. Anne to forbid the burial of his dead wife to show his love for her, and causes d'Olive to be vulnerable to Roderigue and Mugeron's gulling in his eagerness to leave the obscurity of his private life and become an admired and followed public man.

Vandome acts as psychological midwife to both Marcellina and St. Anne. Both wish to live apart from the real world. Marcellina's love relationship with Vandome was Platonic, free of the flesh, but the world's opinion has defamed that love; her reaction is to live without the world. St. Anne apparently loved his wife, but she succumbed to death, that other susceptibility of the flesh; his reaction is to deny the fact of death. In both cases, Chapman causes Vandome to persuade these moral cowards to take up again the normal activities of life. To lead life as these two are living it is no virtue.

D'Olive too is drawn out of seclusion, though he seems only too happy to be so drawn. His acceptance of the Duke's appointment to the post of ambassador, his presumption in kissing the Duchess, and his sprightly but asinine verbosity, mark him clearly as a "Lord of Misrule" figure. He rises from a lower social order to a position of mock power, indulging his every whim and thereby creating the chaos out of which his society will renew itself. Typical of such figures, d'Olive is brought to defeat; but unlike most, he is rescued finally by the Duke, an action which is in keeping with the comic nature of the play.

MONSIEUR LECOQ

Type of work: Novel
Author: Émile Gaboriau (1835-1873)
Type of plot: Mystery romance
Time of plot: Nineteenth century
Locale: Paris
First published: 1869

Even though the plot structures of Gaboriau's early detective novels are far too complex and cumbersome for modern taste, his police investigator, Monsieur Lecoq, must be ranked as a major forerunner of the modern detective hero.

In the development of the modern detective story, Émile Gaboriau's two fictional investigators, Père Tabaret and Monsieur Lecoq, remain, with the possible exception of Wilkie Collins' Sergeant Cuff, the most important transitional figures between Edgar Allan Poe's C. Auguste Dupin and Conan Doyle's Sherlock Holmes. And, between them, they represent the two types of detectives that have dominated the genre.

Père Tabaret, the hero of Gaboriau's first crime novel, *L'Affaire Lerouge* (1866), is the talented amateur who, like Sherlock Holmes, fights crime to escape boredom and exercises talents that go unused in the everyday world. He works outside of official channels, entering the proceedings either at the request of the injured party or after the authorities have confessed their bafflement. Monsieur Lecoq, protagonist of Gaboriau's four other detective novels, is the professional policeman who works efficiently within the system, but must struggle almost as much with the bureaucratic rigidities of the institution and the mediocrity and jealousy of his colleagues as he does with the criminals. This is especially evident in Gaboriau's most famous novel, *Monsieur Lecoq.*

Although *Monsieur Lecoq* was one of Gaboriau's last novels, it describes Lecoq's first case. He is, therefore, much more believable and human than the remote, mysterious figure who appears and disappears in the other works. *Monsieur Lecoq* is the only book in which he is physically described, minus any disguise, and given a personal history. As a young man from a rich background, Lecoq suddenly found himself penniless and was forced to take a variety of relatively menial jobs. To alleviate boredom, he amused himself by inventing theoretical crimes. After describing one to his last employer, a famous astronomer, he was promptly fired and advised that "When one has your disposition, and is poor, one will either become a famous thief or a great detective. Choose." Thus, Lecoq has that touch of criminality which many detective writers have found an essential ingredient in the make-up of their fictional heroes.

Lecoq is no armchair detective; he follows the evidence actively, sparing himself no discomfort or danger. Unlike many subsequent detective stories, the solution in Gaboriau's novels comes in bits and pieces. There are few moments of sudden revelation, only the dogged tracking down of clues. As one aspect of the case becomes clear to Lecoq, it raises new questions which must, in turn, be laboriously answered.

But Lecoq is not only a superlative detective, he is also a most interesting personality. Observing his reactions to his own investigation is almost as interesting as the investigation itself. Not only must Lecoq deal with the criminal, he must also deal with the police bureaucracy and especially his superior, M. Gevrol. Consequently, he evolves a strategy in dealing with his colleagues that is as subtle and ingenious as that which he uses on the criminals. Lecoq knows that his own ambitions must ultimately conflict with Gevrol's authority and that, as a recent recruit, his career can be stifled by Gevrol before it begins. Thus, he gets permission to investigate the case by manipulating Gevrol's patronizing attitude and lack of imagination; he calls no attention to himself in the early stages of the investigation, turning the report in anonymously to avoid embarrassing his superior; and he selects Father Absinthe, an old officer known more for his drinking than his efficiency, as his partner, because the aged policeman will have no conflicting loyalties or ambitions. Once Lecoq has proven his ability to the department, he is able to stand up to Gevrol's spiteful machinations. Lecoq's emotional fluctuations between elation and depression according to the vicissitudes of the investigation, his barely controlled anger when something goes wrong, especially if it is the result of his own mistakes, his sense of humor and irony—all combine to make him a colorful and engrossing figure.

Thus, when the detective dominates the action, *Monsieur Lecoq* is a lively, entertaining novel. Unfortunately, Lecoq is not always present. In fact, in all of Gaboriau's crime novels, the detective's investigation occupies only a third to a half of the narrative. For this reason, some historians of the genre have even questioned the validity of *Monsieur Lecoq* as a detective novel. Gaboriau incorporates two structural elements into his novels that obscure the description of the investigation: the interrogation and the family chronicle.

Gaboriau was fascinated by legal procedures and especially by the process of interrogation which is central to the French judicial system. In *Monsieur Lecoq* Judge Segmuller's extremely lengthy questioning of the convict May is skillful, ingenious, and frequently witty. Even to a contemporary reader much of it is realistic and interesting. But, because of his own interest, as well as the popularity of courtroom fiction, Gaboriau devotes excessive amounts of space to interrogations which reveal little or nothing and do not further the action appreciably.

However, from the standpoint of the modern reader, a much more serious defect in his work is Gaboriau's insistence on the family chronicle as a central element in his books. Following a premise that has endured from his novels through Conan Doyle to Ross MacDonald, Gaboriau believed that the

most interesting and compelling crimes must involve personal, usually familial, relationships, and these become even more engrossing if the family
concerned is rich, famous, and aristocratic. The crime committed at the outset of the novel, it ultimately develops, is simply the final effect of a family
scandal or crime committed many years previously. Investigating the current
crime, therefore, leads the detective back to the original malefaction and
threatens not only the present criminal, but the entire clan that he represents.

But, unlike later users of this assumption, Gaboriau fails to integrate the
investigating side of the novel with the family scandal. Rather, the books
divide into two separate parts, the "investigation" and the "exposition." The
first part traces the investigation up to the point where the criminal's identity
is revealed. Thereupon, Gaboriau shifts his narrative focus to describe all the
factors leading up to the crime from the participants' point of view. It is
not until this domestic history reaches the point where the crime is committed
that the two separate plot lines are joined and the mystery resolved.

This rather disjointed narrative method was popular in the nineteenth
century because it allowed Gaboriau to incorporate into his crime novel
many of the currently popular motifs and situations at great length. He could
include family intrigues, scandals, lengthy, tangled love affairs, victimized
aristocratic women, blackmail, long delayed vengeance, family betrayals,
ostentatious displays of wealth, profligacy, complex frauds and hoaxes—all
presented with theatrical emphasis and moralistic overtones. But, for the
modern reader, these family chronicles are much too long, ornate, melodramatic, and implausible; by the time they are finished, all of the momentum
and interest regarding the original investigation has been lost.

Thus, the end of the first volume of *Monsieur Lecoq,* subtitled "L'Enquête,"
leaves both the detective and the reader frustrated. The criminal May has
been identified as the Duke of Sairmeuse, but he seems inaccessible and many
questions remain unanswered. Gaboriau added a second volume, subtitled
"L'Honneur du Nom," which answers these questions and leads, finally, to
justice for May and vindication for Lecoq, but it is unlikely that this sequel
will satisfy many modern readers. When he reaches the end of the first volume
and learns that approximately four hundred pages of domestic scandal must
be endured in order to resolve the situation, he will most likely give up the
whole project. For this reason, the crime novels of Émile Gaboriau, in spite
of many provocative and exciting moments, will probably be remembered as
important works in the history of detective fiction rather than as enduring
and currently readable works of art.

Keith Neilson

MONT-ORIOL

Type of work: Novel
Author: Guy de Maupassant (1850-1893)
Type of plot: Social satire
Time of plot: Mid-nineteenth century
Locale: Auvergne, France
First published: 1887

Maupassant tells two stories in Mont-Oriol. *The first deals with the love intrigues of Christiane Andermatt, her brother, and her lover; the second describes the financial scheming of William Andermatt, Father Oriol, and the physicians at the health resort.*

A masterpiece of ironic fiction, *Mont-Oriol* is written in the clear, understated prose for which Maupassant was noted. The novel's method unites romantic passages with others of subtle irony and sharp satire, all skillfully blended together with the author's pure, dry style and eye for the telling detail. Although the novel is critical of the society it represents, Maupassant makes his point without commenting directly, letting the story speak for itself. His manner is objective, but like his master, Flaubert, he selects so carefully what he chooses to show that the reader's intellect and emotions are guided subtly in the direction he intends. Maupassant's craftsmanship is near perfect.

A richness of symbols, rising naturally from the story, fills the book. The hot springs itself, which is the central location of the action, comes to represent the foolishness of many human aspirations and the greed of apparently civilized men. The rugged mountains, canyons, and beautiful scenery surrounding the hot springs seem to suggest a more noble possibility standing just beyond mortal grasp. The dead donkey encountered on the road and the wretched peasant family dragging the heavy cart up the hill remind the heroine, Christiane, of both the tenuousness of life and the struggle that life is and must be. Christiane's baby, at the end of the book, is for her and the reader a symbol of new hope for the future.

The satire in the novel is pointed and often very funny; the scenes of the patients submitting to the grotesque exercise machines are among the finest and sharpest ever written by Maupassant. All of the intricate financial intrigue over pieces of land, doweries, hot spring resorts, clinics, and other investments is presented with an ironic touch that ruthlessly exposes the personalities involved and their petty ambitions. Old Oriol and the fake cripple, Clovis, are handled particularly well, their lusty greed a perfect counterpoint for the more subtle scheming of the doctors and the banker, Andermatt.

A MONTH IN THE COUNTRY

Type of work: Drama
Author: Ivan Turgenev (1818-1883)
Type of plot: Realistic comedy
Time of plot: The 1840's
Locale: Russia
First presented: 1850

In A Month in the Country, *Turgenev presents the dramatic situation that was later to be perfected by Anton Chekhov in his great plays. A group of widely disparate Russian characters are gathered at a rural country estate where their dissatisfactions, longings, obsessions, and frustrated loves are gradually revealed, not so much in direct conflict as through minor incidents and subtle interior revelations.*

Ivan Turgenev was one of the first Russian writers to win fame outside Russia. Although best known both inside and outside Russia as a novelist, Turgenev was also a poet, a journalist, and a dramatist. The plays—he wrote about a dozen, some short and some long—came relatively early in his writing career, between 1843 and 1852. Of them, *A Month in the Country* is generally considered the best, even though *The Lady from the Provinces* (1851) makes a better stage production. *A Month in the Country* was a great favorite of the Moscow Art Theater and its eminent director, Konstantin Stanislavsky. The enduring popularity of the play, however, is less important than its historical position in the evolution of the Russian theater, since Turgenev's contribution anticipated the psychological realism and rather actionless plots of Anton Chekhov's later dramas.

Two of Turgenev's strong points are especially related to what has come to be known as the Chekhovian ambience. One is style; the other is characterization. Because Turgenev was a poet, his residual poetic talents later manifested themselves in the lyrical style which marks both his prose and his drama. The delicate grace of his style in treating nature and love—the incident in the raspberry patch, for instance—anticipates such typically Chekhovian settings as are found in *Uncle Vanya* (1899) and *The Cherry Orchard* (1904). Likewise, in characterization, Turgenev was a trailblazer. He shaped his characters not by asking "How do they look?" or "What are they doing?" but by searching for "What do the characters think and feel?" As a consequence of this method of characterization, the action of the play becomes internalized as mental and emotional events. Physical action, as it is usually understood, is reduced to a minimum. These circumstances were ideal for depicting strong women characters for which Turgenev has rightly been acclaimed. In addition, this technique of characterization was adopted and polished by Chekhov until it became the hallmark of his dramas.

A Month in the Country is a complex play, although the plot merely revolves around a simple love triangle. The theme is also easily stated—frustration—but more difficult to explain. All of the major characters are frustrated. Their needs and desires are unmet; their attempts at gaining satisfaction are thwarted by the indifference or the insensitivity of second parties, while they, in turn, ignore similar entreaties of third parties. They do not work at cross-purposes; rather, they work along parallel lines that never meet. The interaction, the human relationships—for of such stuff is the plot made—constitute an emotional and intellectual pattern best described as undulating, after the manner of ocean waves: high crests are separated by wide troughs. Beneath those wide troughs, life seethes with repression, suppression, and unmet needs which occasionally boil up to the crest of a breaker only to subside again, thwarted by the immutable pattern of frustration, until the next cresting of a breaker signals another emotional crisis. The pattern repeats itself with unremitting regularity. By the end of the play, the reader is emotionally bludgeoned into a resigned submission not unlike that of Natalya or Vera. For a play whose action is psychological rather than physical, *A Month in the Country* has a remarkable impact—and a lasting one, as Belyayev learns from his brief month in the country.

THE MOON AND SIXPENCE

Type of work: Novel
Author: W. Somerset Maugham (1874-1965)
Type of plot: Fictional biography
Time of plot: Nineteenth century
Locale: England, France, Tahiti
First published: 1919

A fictionalized biography of the French artist Paul Gauguin, this novel attempts to portray the character of the pure artist, the man who renounces everything, including human feelings, in the name of personal artistic expression.

The central fact about this novel is not its biographical allusions. The book is more about escape than Gauguin; in many ways, it is more about escape than art itself, which is often heralded as the book's true theme: a man coldly sets all persons and obligations aside in order to serve exclusively his art.

Despite his careful references to "Strickland—Gauguin's" taste in painters, Maugham does not really succeed in bringing painting to life in this book. What is missing is the profound presence of art itself, as music figures, for example, in Thomas Mann's *Doctor Faustus.* Strickland's involvement with his art is never sufficiently realized in idea, form, or characterization. As a result his coldness is often inhuman, and the immolations of Blanche and Ata to his genius do not really seem convincing. Ironically, Mrs. Strickland's bourgeois insensitivity to her husband seems much more appropriate as a deserved comic punishment; this, of course, is not Maugham's intention.

What does capture the reader's mind is Strickland's ability to get away, to cut himself off from all ties and land safely in a literal paradise. In his famous study of literary and social trends in the 1920's, (*Exile's Return,* 1934, rev. 1951), Malcolm Cowley notes that Maugham's novel was devoured by everyone because of its dramatization of the theme of escape. In the 1920's, the desperately self-destructive search for a life-style free of all restrictions found a signpost in Maugham's story. What seems to have struck these readers as convincing was precisely Strickland's detachment. They overlooked the shallowness of Maugham's treatment of art in their fascination with Strickland's coldness, his ruthlessness; they sensed that only such indifference could effectively challenge the cant of a postwar world that still dared to presume to moral authority. The book still has something of that power for contemporary readers.

THE MOONSTONE

Type of work: Novel
Author: Wilkie Collins (1824-1889)
Type of plot: Mystery romance
Time of plot: 1799-1849
Locale: India and England
First published: 1868

If not a true detective novel, The Moonstone *is, at the least, a classic mystery story. The theft of the cursed jewel is told in bits and pieces by several narrators who not only deepen the mystery, but also characterize themselves vividly and portray upper-middle-class life in Victorian England with fidelity.*

T. S. Eliot's well-known statement that *"The Moonstone* is the first, longest, and best of English detective novels" is probably true in a general way, although it needs considerable qualification. Strictly speaking, *The Moonstone* is a novel with a detective, not a detective novel. A crime is committed and the detective, Sergeant Cuff, is brought in. While exhibiting impressive investigative skills, he does not solve the crime; in fact, he even falsely accuses the book's heroine of stealing her own jewel. Following this mistake, Cuff fades from the book and does not reappear until near the end, when he recoups somewhat by identifying the true villain. By this time, however, most of the questions have been answered and Cuff's final revelation is anticlimactic. The mystery is actually solved in bits and pieces over a considerable period of time by a large number of people, the most important of which, Franklin Blake, discovers himself to be the thief.

All of this is not to minimize the importance of *The Moonstone* to the development of the detective story, but only to point out that it is primarily a "sensation novel" in which the detective plays a prominent role. Actually, Collins does establish a number of conventions that are still requisite in the detective novel. Sergeant Cuff is the prototype for a host of fictional investigators. His physical appearance could be a description of Sherlock Holmes or a dozen other literary detectives. Cuff also possesses a humanizing "quirk" (he raises roses) which remains a must even for today's detective hero. His techniques, especially the scientific reconstruction of the crime and the summary explanation in front of the assembled suspects, are still integral to the genre. Other conventions that Collins either introduced or popularized include the incompetent local policeman versus the efficient big city detective, the withheld evidence, the skillful shifting of suspicion from character to character, the adroit amateur who catches clues the professionals miss, and the "fair play method." The reader in this novel is provided the same clues as the participants, and can, if perceptive enough, solve the puzzle for himself.

One difference between most "sensation novels" and "detective novels" is the setting, which is usually foreign or exotic in the former and contemporary in the latter. Collins was one of the first modern writers to combine the two elements in the same book and nowhere does he do it more expertly than in *The Moonstone*. The "myth" of the "Moonstone," with all of its super-natural overtones, the presence of three threatening Indian fakirs, and the general aura of Oriental intrigue which Collins introduces into the midst of everyday middle-class English domestic routine creates a powerful tension and infuses the book with sinister and mysterious overtones.

Another "exotic" touch that adds to the suspense and impact of the novel lies in the way the mystery is finally elucidated. After all the strictly logical procedures have failed, the crime is solved by a probing of the hero's sub-conscious mind. Thus, it could be said that *The Moonstone* not only estab-lished the model for that most rational of forms, the detective novel, but was also one of the first important fictional explorations of irrational behavior and psychological fragmentation—a subject that was to become central in twentieth century fiction.

LE MORTE D'ARTHUR

Type of work: Chronicle
Author: Sir Thomas Malory (1400?-1471)
Type of plot: Chivalric romance
Time of plot: Golden Age of chivalry
Locale: Britain
First transcribed: c.1469; printed 1485

Le Morte d'Arthur is a monumental work which made the Arthurian cycle available for the first time in English. Malory took a body of legends, which had gone from the folklore of Celtic Britain into French literature by way of Brittany, gave those tales a typically English point of view, and added, amended, and deleted for his own purposes, to produce a work which has had tremendous influence on literature ever since.

The author of *Le Morte d'Arthur* was the unusual Sir Thomas Malory of Newbold Revel. The strange circumstances of his life contributed significantly to the shape and meaning of his masterwork. Born about 1400, he served with Richard Beauchamp, Earl of Warwick, was knighted in 1442, and was elected a Member of Parliament in 1445. For whatever reasons of military adventure, Malory turned to a life of irresponsible violence and spent most of his last twenty years, until his death in 1471, in prison. It was during his imprisonment that Malory composed, translated, and adapted his great rendering of the Arthurian material. His active, fifteenth century life accounts for many of the differences between his vigorous narrative and its contemplative, ruminative antecedents in chivalric literature. Malory lived just a little past the age of chivalry at a time when its elegance and leisure had to be rationalized.

Malory is the most influential of all the Arthurian writers. He was the source and delight of Spenser and the main wellspring of Tennyson's *Idylls of the King*. First printed by Caxton in one volume in 1485, *Le Morte d'Arthur* has been consistently popular ever since except during the Augustan period of the early eighteenth century. Caxton's printing is the source of all extant versions except a manuscript discovered in 1934 in the Fellows' Library of Winchester College. The Winchester manuscript, which seems generally more reliable than Caxton, not only made the identity of the author more certain but also showed that Caxton had condensed the original.

Of course, Malory's *Le Morte d'Arthur* is itself a condensation, adaptation, and rearrangement of earlier materials. It is based primarily on the French Arthurian Prose Cycle (1225-1230) known as the Vulgate, a conglomeration of courtly stories of Lancelot, ostensibly historical accounts of the court of Arthur, and stories of the quest for the Holy Grail. As Eugène Vinaver, the foremost editor and critic of Malory, has explained, the differences between the Vulgate and Malory's narrative are good indicators of the nature of

Malory's achievement.

The primary structure of the Vulgate is episodic and its narrative move-ment is largely backwards. Episodes prepare for and elucidate other episodes which may be chronologically prior. It did not grow by accretion; its shape is a reflection of an alternative aesthetic. The result is a web of themes in which forward movement of the narrative is subordinated to the demonstration and clarification of the dominant ideals of the work. Malory took this source, added matter from the fourteenth century English *Alliterative Morte d'Arthur* and, to a lesser extent from the *Stanzaic Morte,* and fashioned a new kind of fictional structure. The result is not simply condensation, but a disentangle-ment of the elements of the narrative and a recombination of them into an order, an emphasis, and a significance entirely alien to the sources.

Vinaver has identified two major ways in which Malory transformed the structure of the narrative. First, some episodes are made into self-contained units, almost short stories, by detachment from their context and the excision of extraneous detail. For example, in the Vulgate the incidents grouped to-gether by Malory as the story of the Knight of the Cart appeared long before the Grail quest; Malory puts them long after and organizes them as an exemplum of Lancelot's noble ideals rather than as a prefigurement of his amatory commitment. Consequently, by omission and shortening, Malory gives the episode a different significance. Malory's second mode of transfor-mation is to fashion a coherent narrative from bits and pieces scattered throughout his sources. In the story of the Fair Maid of Astolat, for example, he organizes disparate details into a sequential form.

The most striking change in the sources is Malory's imposition of a con-sistently forward chronological movement. Gone are the courtly disgressions and the significant configurations of explanatory episodes. Instead there is a straightforward narrative which alters both the tone and meaning of the original. Malory had no comprehension of or sympathy for the tradition of courtly love which permeated his sources. Where its vestiges cannot be omitted Malory translates them into something more compatible with his genius. Thus, Lancelot is no longer the "knight of the cart" because of courtly self-debasement for the beloved but because of a dedication to chivalric ideals. The elegance and controlled artificiality of his antecedents are changed by Malory into directness and moral earnestness. Lancelot becomes a Chris-tianized, somewhat sentimentalized, figure who is a model of the moderation that leads to supernatural rewards. Similarly, in the story of Pelleas and Ettard, Malory makes Pelleas' behavior more practical than courtly. After Ettard's infidelity, Malory substitutes the poetic justice of her death and Pelleas' happiness for the courtly self-abnegation demonstrated by Pelleas in the Vulgate.

Sometimes Malory's fiction suffers from the tension between his sources and his rendering of them. As E. K. Chambers has noted, characters are not always sustained on the same level of the narrative. Moreover, not all of the courtly and mysterious elements are completely rationalized into the new intention. Some undecipherable oddities result. However, *Le Morte d'Arthur* remains a vigorous and compelling narrative, full of the spirit of adventurous knighthood. As Vinaver has shown in detail, Malory has substituted outdoor images for courtly affectation, the real English countryside for the conventional French, vigorous speech for conventional dialogues, and direct, human relationships for the elaborate rituals of courtly love. All of this is accomplished in a blunt and lively prose which is the antithesis of the intricacies of the French sources and perfectly suited to Malory's more direct structure and more forthright moral attitude.

Edward E. Foster

THE MOTHER

Type of work: Novel
Author: Grazia Deledda (1872-1936)
Type of plot: Psychological realism
Time of plot: Early twentieth century
Locale: Sardinia
First published: 1920

The Mother is a searching study of the age-old conflict between authority and inclination. It takes place on the island of Sardinia, with its poor peasants, its inbred superstitions, and its Church-directed religion. The novel is structurally compact with a dramatic action that covers only two days and drives relentlessly to the tragic finale. The character of the mother, Maria Maddalena, dominates the book, but Paul, her anguished son, and Agnes, his confused sweetheart, are believable, sympathetic creations.

Grazia Deledda was the second Italian author to win the Nobel Prize for literature and one of the few women to do so. Her approach to literature was similar to other Italian novelists of the early part of this century in that she combined realism with a regionalistic background, but her genius for prose and characterization raised her above the average writer of her time.

Strangely enough, Deledda, like a number of other Nobel Prize-winning authors, is barely read outside her own country. Even at the time of her award in 1926, many contemporary literary critics had not heard of her, let alone read any of her works. The surprise of her award, however, was dispelled when her works became more prominently publicized and read.

The Mother, written in 1920 and translated into English for the first time in 1923, is regarded as her greatest work. It has a number of elements which, when analyzed, are seen in works of great literature from the time of the Greeks to the present. The elements of *The Mother* which assure its greatness are simplicity, characterization, and universality. The work has much more than these three basic elements, however. Deledda was a gifted writer who could describe in beautiful, yet uncluttered, prose the lives of common people, while at the same time make their circumstances seem as real to the reader as his own life.

Though she lived and worked in Rome for most of her life, Deledda was born and reared in a small town on the island of Sardinia. This locality was the setting for *The Mother* as it was for many of her works. The world of this type of town had small boundaries, and decisions were usually simple ones. In this novel the seemingly uncomplicated characters, however, are faced with decisions which overwhelm them. Paul, whose life had been laid out for him at an early age, is faced with the great temptation to reject his life as a celibate priest and flee with the woman he loves. Maria Maddalena, his mother and the principal character of the novel, is pushed into a situation where she must face the consequences of her decision to rear Paul for the priesthood—something which she had never before doubted was right. The third major character, Agnes, must decide how far her feelings for Paul will allow her to be alienated from the Church and the local townspeople.

These decisions and the events surrounding them comprise the backbone of the action of the novel. Maria Maddalena, who is involved in the action because of her love for her son and her faith in the Church, takes on the role of observer as well as protagonist. Through her eyes and thoughts the reader is brought into the plot and is able vicariously to experience the pain of such difficult circumstances as they are brought into the lives of the main characters.

The principal problem of the drama, the love of Paul and Agnes, should not be interpreted as an attempt at anticlericalism by Grazia Deledda. Even in the speeches of the former parish priest, Deledda shows great sympathy for human love and is not attempting to point an accusing finger. Neither is she making a strong plea for church reform or a married priesthood. Rather, she is showing a situation as it exists and how ordinary people deal with extraordinary problems.

In *The Mother*, the younger characters of Paul and Agnes, though they are pained by their decisions, are able to survive. But Maria Maddalena, the epitome of the loving, long-suffering mother, is unable to survive the pressure of the crisis and dies, quite symbolically, in the Church. It is symbolic because she accepted the teachings of the Church totally, and because it was her decision to make Paul a priest which led to this crisis and her death. Only briefly does she question the wisdom of her decision and the Church's laws. She sympathetically aches for her son and wonders why it is wrong for him to marry. But her questioning is short-lived and at the end she again totally accepts the Church's position and worries lest her son go against it and become an outcast.

The situation of a young boy being reared by a family whose sole ambition for him was that he become a priest was not an uncommon one in Italy. If a family decided that their son was to become a cleric, the boy usually accepted his role the way he might accept any predetermined profession. But being a priest, as Deledda shows, is not a profession but a way of life, and as such must either be accepted or rejected by free will. At the end of this novel Paul does make that decision, but it is done too late to save his mother. The strain of trying to save Paul from a life of sin is too much for Maria Maddalena and she dies, more out of relief than pain.

The beauty of Grazia Deledda's prose is, as in any novel, best appreciated in the original language, but is still highly pleasing in English translation. Her writings are smooth and economical. They display a beautiful simplicity which many critics have compared with Greek drama. Because of her greatness as an author, it is unfortunate that her works are seldom read outside Italy.

Stephen Hanson

MOTHER

Type of work: Novel
Author: Maxim Gorky (Aleksei Maksimovich Peshkov, 1868-1936)
Type of plot: Naturalism
Time of plot: First decade of the twentieth century
Locale: Russia
First published: 1907

Mother is one of those rare works that merges political vision with human experience. Written in the decade preceding the Russian Revolution, Gorky's political passion and his artistic brilliance combine to produce a great character in Pelagueya Vlasova, whose growth from the mother of a single son to the "mother" of all the revolutionaries is convincing and powerful.

At the turn of the twentieth century, the writings of Maxim Gorky poured out of Russia, exciting an interest throughout the world for their dramatic presentation of the struggles in progress within that largely unknown country. His representations of the bitter lives of the masses of that huge land caused a sensation whenever they were published or produced on the stage. One of the most famous of these early works, and his only long work devoted entirely to the Russian revolutionary movement, is *Mother*. Most of Gorky's early novels fail to sustain a continuous powerful narrative and succumb to a tendency to irrelevant discussions about the meaning of life, but *Mother* rises above these flaws and stands as a vivid and moving portrayal of a bitter struggle. If *Mother* is propaganda, it is propaganda raised to the level of art.

The expanding consciousness of Pelagueya, the mother, forms the binding framework of the novel and serves as the catalyst which unites the parts of the story into a coherent, dynamic vision and makes the book the masterpiece that it is. The reader sees in the course of the narrative the gradual growth of a movement, as seen in the radicalization of first the young man Pavel and then his mother. The mother is only forty when the story opens, but already she is an old woman, brutalized by years of poverty and beatings. Yet, spiritually she is not dead, and she painfully rises, learns the truth about herself and her world, and then seeks to help spread this truth. The numb fatalism which bound her when her husband was alive, her belief that the lot of women must always be despair, is gradually replaced by a hope for the future.

The two aspects of love, its pain and its strength, are movingly depicted. The mother wants to protect her son, but she knows that she must let him be free to do what he must do. At the same time, her growing love for the members of the Movement gives her the strength to remake her life and to brave hardship to contribute her share to the struggle. In turn, her love helps the others in the movement, and their united love for the poor, for the masses of humanity as yet unawakened, helps to keep all of them going. The Party is called the "spiritual mother" of the workingmen, and many times it is referred to as helping the masses to be "reborn." The primary task of the mother and her compatriots is to educate the people, to distribute literature which will help them to be "reborn." Awareness must be the first step to revolution. The people are equated with Jesus Christ in several passages, most particularly when the mother washes the feet of the peasant leader Ignaty. The symbolism is unobtrusive, yet effective.

The long novel is filled with powerful scenes, from the opening in which the terrified woman is beaten by her husband to the ending when she is killed while carrying on the work of her son. The trial of Pavel, her son, and his close friend Andrey, is effectively handled while the several riots and crowd scenes in the book are particularly well-written. Gorky's ability to handle large groups of people is remarkable. Each individual stands out distinctly, yet the sense of the tide of humanity is ever present. The individuals are very human, with human eccentricities and irrationalities. In real life no man or woman is always consistent to character, and Gorky knew this; his people are, above all, realistic, and his characterizations are the principal strength of his mosaic of the early days of the Russian Revolution.

MOURNING BECOMES ELECTRA

Type of work: Drama
Author: Eugene O'Neill (1888-1953)
Type of plot: Romantic tragedy
Time of plot: Shortly after the Civil War
Locale: New England
First presented: 1931

In Mourning Becomes Electra, *a trilogy* (Homecoming, The Hunted, The Haunted) *loosely based on Aeschylus'* Oresteia, *O'Neill dramatizes his conviction that the Greek concept of fate could be replaced by the modern notion of psychological—especially Freudian—determination. The Mannons are driven to their self-destructive behavior by inner needs and compulsions they can neither understand nor control. Such, O'Neill believed, was the material of contemporary tragedy.*

Eugene O'Neill, America's first dramatist to win international recognition, was awarded the Nobel Prize for literature in 1936. One of the most ambitious playwrights since Aeschylus and Shakespeare, he introduced the European movements of realism, naturalism, and expressionism to the American stage as devices to express his comprehensive interest in all of life. His plays often make stringent demands on the actors and audience: the long monologues of *The Iceman Cometh* and *Strange Interlude*; the unrelenting despair of *Long Day's Journey into Night*; the five-hour production length of *Mourning Becomes Electra*.

O'Neill, of Irish Catholic stock, literally grew up in the theater. He was born in a New York hotel while his father, the famous actor, James O'Neill, was starring in *The Count of Monte Cristo*. His mother, suffering from the pains of Eugene's birth, began taking morphine and soon became an addict. Many of O'Neill's plays deal with the intense love-hate relationships and tensions of his mother, father, brother, and himself. The most intensive and explicit of these is the powerful *Long Day's Journey into Night,* published posthumously in 1956. Before becoming a playwright, he briefly attended Princeton, worked as a sailor, and had a bout with tuberculosis. While in the sanatorium, he decided to become a playwright.

O'Neill's plays are bound together by consistent concerns. Embedded in them the reader will find a rejection of Victorian gentility, of materialism and opportunism, and of Puritan beliefs. He shared the postwar disillusionment with others of his generation who discovered that the Great War to end all wars had been a death trap for young men. His plays exhibit a keen sense of loss of the individual's relationship with his family, his nation, his society's values, with nature, and with God. Science, materialism, religion all fail to give O'Neill's heroes a satisfying meaning for life, or comfort from the fear of death. Still, they engage in often heroic struggles against total alienation.

Many of O'Neill's strongest plays center around the question of whether illusions are, after all, the only thing that make reality bearable. He also consistently incorporated popular Freudian psychology in an attempt to project the subconscious levels of his characters. *Mourning Becomes Electra*, a trilogy consisting of *Homecoming, The Hunted,* and *The Haunted,* although set at the end of the American Civil War, is an adaptation of the greatest of Aeschylus' trilogies, the *Oresteia.*

Mourning Becomes Electra illustrates the struggle between the life-force and death, in which attempts to express natural sensual desires and love of others or even of life itself are overcome by the many forms of death: repression derived from the Puritan religion; death-in-life engendered by society's values; isolation; war; and actual physical death. This struggle is present not only in the plot structure where each play culminates in an actual death, but also in the setting, the actors' faces, stances, and costumes, and repetitive refrains. Darkness, associated with death, pervades the plays: *Homecoming,* for instance, begins with the sunset, moves into twilight, and ends in the dark of night; *The Hunted* takes place during night; *The Haunted* spans two evenings and a late afternoon, indicating the inevitable coming of night, darkness, and death as Lavinia retreats to rejoin the host of dead Mannons.

The Mannon house itself, seen by the audience at the beginning of each play, stands amid the beauty and abundance of nature. It has a white Greek temple portico which, O'Neill directs, should resemble "an incongruous white mask fixed on the house to hide its somber grey ugliness." That the house is an ironic inversion of the affirmation and love of this life associated with the Greeks is soon obvious. Christine thinks of the house as a tomb of cold gray stone, and even Ezra compares it to a "white meeting house" of the Puritan Church, a temple dedicated to duty, denial of the beauty of life and love—to death. The house itself is not only alienated from nature, but is isolated from the community, built on the foundations of pride and hatred and Puritan beliefs. Its cold façade and isolation symbolize the family which lives within it, whose name indicates their spiritual relationship to Satan's chief helper Mammon. The "curse" of this house stems from the effects of materialism, Puritanism, alienation, and repression of all that is natural—a death-in-life.

The stiff, unnatural military bearing of the Mannons and the mask-like look of their faces are further evidence that the family is dead in the midst of life. Even the townspeople comment on the Mannons' "secret look." Their dead, mask-like faces—in portraits on Orin and Ezra, on Christine's face when she is about to commit suicide, on Lavinia's face after Orin's death—all indicate the Mannons' denial of life, their repression of their sensual natures, and their refusal or inability to communicate with others. The dark costumes of all the family also indicate the hold that death has on them and accentuates the green satin worn first by Christine and later by Lavinia as they struggle to break out of their tomb and reach life.

The instinct of love and life survives strongest in the women, but even they are defeated. The search for pure love through a mother-son relationship is futile, for the Oedipal complex leads beyond the bounds of a pure relationship, as Orin finally realizes. Family love, too, fails, as is evident in the relationships between Christine and Lavinia and Ezra and Orin. Even love between men and women fails—as in the cases of Christine and Ezra and Lavinia and Peter—to be sufficient to triumph over the alienation and loneliness of the Mannon world.

The leitmotiv of the South Sea islands, symbols of escape from the death cycle of heredity and environment of New England society, is present throughout the three plays. The islands represent a return to mother earth, a hope of belonging in an environment far removed from Puritan guilt and materialism. Brant has been to these islands; Ezra wishes for one; Orin dreams of being on one with Christine; Christine wants to go to an island; Orin and Lavinia do finally travel to the islands. However, they come to realize that they cannot become a permanent part of the island culture, but must return to the society to which they belong by birth and upbringing. As symbols of escape, then, the islands, too, finally fail.

The Mannons try all avenues of escape from their deathly isolation. David Mannon attempted to escape with Marie Brantôme, but finally turned to drinking and suicide. Ezra "escaped" through concentrating on his business and then on the business of death—war—before he realized the trap of death. Christine focuses her attempts to escape first on her son and then on Brant. Orin tries to escape through his mother's love, then through Hazel's, and finally, in desperation, suggests an incestuous relationship with Lavinia. Lavinia does not see the dimensions of the death trap and does not desire escape until her trip to the islands, where she experiences the abundance of guilt-free life. After her return, she is willing to let Orin die, just as Christine let Ezra die, in order to be free to love and live. But then, too late, she feels the curse of the guilt associated with the Puritan beliefs and realizes that she cannot escape. Lavinia learns Orin was right: the killer kills part of himself each time he kills until finally nothing alive is left in him. She underscores this in her last conversation with Peter, remarking, "Always the dead between [us]. . . . The dead are too strong." Death itself is the only real escape for the alienated, guilt-ridden Mannons.

Compared to its source, Aeschylus' *Oresteia,* O'Neill's themes and characterization seem shallow. Christine, who goads Ezra into a heart attack because of her hatred of his attitude toward their sexual relationship and her love of Brant, is no match for Clytemnestra, who revenges the death of her daughter, her insulted pride, and hatred of Agamemnon with a bloody knife. The neurotic weak Orin is likewise a lesser character than Orestes, whose strong speech of triumphant justice over his mother's slain body breaks only with his horrified vision of the Furies. Yet Ezra is more human than Agamemnon and Lavinia's complexities far outstrip Electra's: her recognition and acceptance of her fate is in the noble tradition of the tragic hero.

The radical difference in the intentions of the two playwrights accounts for some of these differences. Aeschylus, whose major themes are concerned with the victory of man's and the gods' laws, concludes his trilogy with the establishment of justice on earth and the reconciliation of Orestes with society and the gods, affirming that good has come out of evil, order from chaos, and wisdom from suffering. In *Mourning Becomes Electra,* however, the curse is not lifted, but confirmed at the end, as Lavinia gives up her futile struggle against the psychological effects of Puritanical guilt. O'Neill's major concerns are with the detrimental effects of the materialism; the alienation of man from meaningful relationships with others, nature, and God; the death heritage of Puritanical beliefs; and the psychological "furies" that drive us all. Although the psychological analysis of these representative members of American society may be oversimplified occasionally, in the hands of a good director and cast *Mourning Becomes Electra* is one of the few American plays which can truly be said to evoke the tragic emotions of pity, fear, and perhaps even awe in a modern audience.

Ann E. Reynolds

MUCH ADO ABOUT NOTHING

Type of work: Drama
Author: William Shakespeare (1564-1616)
Type of plot: Romantic comedy
Time of plot: Thirteenth century
Locale: Italy
First presented: 1598

Much Ado About Nothing focuses on two love affairs, the rivalry between the reluctant Beatrice and the confirmed bachelor Benedick, and the more serious courtship between Hero and Claudio. The former is one of the wittiest romantic conflicts in dramatic literature; the latter narrowly avoids catastrophe by means of a necessary, if contrived, manipulation of the plot to achieve a happy ending.

Much Ado About Nothing has in fact very much to do with "noting" (an intended pun on "nothing") or with half-seeing, with perceiving dimly or not at all. Out of all the misperceptions arises the comedy of Shakespeare's drama. Indeed if it can be said that one theme preoccupies Shakespeare more than any other it is that of perception. It informs not only his great histories and tragedies but his comedies as well. For example, an early history such as *Richard II,* which also involves tragic elements, proceeds not only from the title character's inability to function as a king but also from his failure to apprehend the nature of the new politics. Both Othello and King Lear are perfect representatives of the tragic consequences of the inability to see. Hindered by their egos they act in their own small worlds, oblivious to the reality that demands recognition. When they fail to take the real into account, whether it is the nature of evil or their own limitation, they must pay the full cost—their lives.

Although in *Much Ado About Nothing* the blindness of Leonato, Don Pedro, Claudio, and Benedick very nearly results in tragedy, it is the comic implications that emerge from mere noting rather than clear seeing which Shakespeare is concerned with. Yet if his mode is comic, his intention is serious. Besides the characters' inability to perceive Don John's obvious villainy, their superficial grasp of love, their failure to understand the nature of courtship and marriage, reveal their moral stupidity. Going further we see that the whole society is shot through with a kind of civilized shallowness. The play begins as an unspecified war ends and immediately we are struck by Leonato's and the messenger's lack of response to the casualty report. To the governor of Messina's question, "How many gentlemen have you lost in this action?" the messenger replies, "But few of any sort, and none of name." Leonato comments: "A victory is twice itself, when the achiever brings home full numbers." The heroes of the war, Don Pedro, Claudio, and Benedick, return in a high good humor, seemingly untouched by their experiences, seeking comfort, games, and diversion.

Only Beatrice is unimpressed by the soldiers' grand entrance; for she knows what they are. Between their "noble" actions, they, like Benedick, are no more than seducers, "valiant trencher" men or gluttons and leeches. Or like Claudio, they are vain young boys ready to fall in love on a whim. Even the stately Don Pedro is a fool who proposes to Beatrice on impulse after he has wooed the childish Hero for the inarticulate Claudio. After witnessing their behavior we look back to Beatrice's initial cynicism—"I had rather hear my dog bark at a crow, than a man swear he loves me"—and applaud it as wisdom.

Yet at last, Beatrice is as susceptible to flattery as Benedick. Like her eventual lover and husband, she is seduced by Don Pedro's deception, the masque he arranges to lead both Beatrice and Benedick to the altar. Both of them, after hearing that they are adored by the other, pledge their love and devotion. To be sure the scenes in which they are duped are full of innocent humor; but the comedy must not lead us astray of Shakespeare's rather bitter observations on the foppery of human love—or at least courtship as it is pursued in Messina.

Nor is their foppery and foolishness the end of the matter. Don John realizes that a vain lover betrayed is a cruel and indeed inhuman tyrant. With little effort he convinces Claudio and Don Pedro that the innocent Hero is no more than a common jade. Yet rather than break off the engagement in private, they wait until all meet at the altar to accuse the girl of "savage sensuality." Without compunction they leave her in a swoon believing her dead. Even the father, Leonato, would have her dead rather than shamed. It is at this moment that the witty and sophisticated aristocrats of Messina are revealed as grossly hypocritical, for beneath their glittering and refined manners lies a moronic and vicious ethic.

In vivid contrast to the decorous soldiers and politicians are Dogberry and his watchmen who certainly function—we are well reminded—as more than a slapstick diversion. Hilarious clowns as they attempt to ape their social betters in manners and speech, they are yet possessed by a common sense or—as one critic has observed—by an instinctual morality that enables them immediately to uncover the villainy of Don John's henchmen, Conrade and Borachio. As the latter says to the nobleman, Don Pedro, "I have deceived even your very eyes: what your wisdoms could not discover, these shallow fools have brought to light." Like the outspoken and bawdy Margaret who knows after all that underlying the aristocrats' courtly manners in the game of love is an unacknowledged lust, Dogberry and his bumbling followers get immediately to the issue and recognize villainy—even if they use the wrong words to describe it.

Still, at the end Shakespeare does not force the point to any great conclusion. After all we are not dealing here with characters of monumental stature; certainly they cannot bear revelations of substantial moral consequence. If they show compunction for their errors, they exhibit no significant remorse and are quite ready to get on with the rituals of their class. It finally does not seem to matter to Claudio that he marries Hero or someone who looks very much like her. And even Beatrice has apparently, once and for all, lost her maverick edge, and joins the strutting Benedick in the marriage dance. At least all ends well for those involved, if through no very great fault of their own. For everyone, of course, except Don John; and one suspects he should be concerned, for Benedick promises "brave punishments." If our illustrious heroes can be cruel to a young virgin, what can a real villain hope for?

David L. Kubal

MURDER IN THE CATHEDRAL

Type of work: Drama
Author: T. S. Eliot (1888-1965)
Type of plot: Religious chronicle
Time of plot: 1170
Locale: Canterbury, England
First presented: 1935

This liturgical drama, based on the martyrdom of St. Thomas Becket on the Canterbury Cathedral altar, was Eliot's first complete verse play and, as such, his initial attempt at developing a poetic drama that could recapture the traditional power of stage poetry, while at the same time speaking directly to the contemporary theatergoer.

Unlike many lesser artists who never seem to change their view of the world or the development of their art, T. S. Eliot grew throughout his career. In his youth he was primarily a satirist, mocking the conventions of society in poems such as *The Love Song of J. Alfred Prufrock* or *Portrait of the Lady.* Later he became a mosaic artist of exquisite sensibility as, fragment by fragment, he pieced together his damning portrait of post-World War I civilization in *The Waste Land.* Still later, finding his ethical pessimism essentially sterile, he climaxed his long interest in philosophy, theology, literary history, and government by becoming a royalist in politics, a classicist in literature, and an Anglo-Catholic in religion. Born in America and educated at Harvard, Eliot early settled in England, soon becoming more English than the English.

Throughout his early career he had developed more than a casual interest in the drama, not merely as an art form in and of itself, but in the theater as a means of instruction. His early fragments such as *Sweeney Agonistes* tantalize by their incompleteness, but *Murder in the Cathedral* demonstrates Eliot's mastery of the classic tragic form.

In this remarkably effective play, Eliot links devices derived from the Greeks—the chorus, static action, and Aristotelian purgation—with his profound commitment to the Anglo-Catholic liturgy. Thus *Murder in the Cathedral* in many ways resembles a medieval morality play whose purpose is to enlighten as well as entertain.

Yet *Murder in the Cathedral* is never merely morally instructive. It rises above didacticism because Archbishop Thomas Becket's internal anguish is made extremely personal by its modernity and timeliness. Becket's assassination becomes more real by the contemporary events it inevitably recalls and by the political and temporal events it evokes.

Eliot firmly believed that contemporary drama to be most effective had to be written in poetry, a belief he shared with William Butler Yeats, his Irish contemporary. Eliot's poetry is moving without being ostentatiously poetic because it reaches the audience on a level that Eliot himself termed "the auditory imagination." Responding from the unconscious, the spectators are drawn deeply into the drama and begin to share Becket's internal agonies by participating in the almost primitive rhythmic manipulations of Eliot's deceptively simple verse.

What makes Eliot's play so timely is that the four allurements offered to Thomas by the tempters are precisely the same ones the modern audience itself has also faced, whether consciously or unconsciously: worldly pleasure; temporal power; spiritual power; and, finally and most subtly, eternal glory. Thomas refutes all of them, quite directly, but is entranced for a time by the fourth tempter who indicates that if Thomas proceeds on his present course, he may be deliberately courting martyrdom in order to achieve eternal happiness with God. Eventually Thomas counters the argument with one of the most effective lines in the play: "The last temptation and the greatest treason/Is to do the right deed for the wrong reason."

Thus Thomas' certainty of the spiritual correctness of his own actions mirrors that of members of the audience, who slowly become aware of their own culpability in acting correctly for insufficient reason in any matter, or even of acting selfishly for a good end. The involvement of the audience so profoundly is another tribute to Eliot's genius.

Eliot also works on still another level, that of the conflict of powers, each perhaps justified in its own way. Thomas recognizes that some things are Caesar's, and that the king and the temporal power he represents have some justification. The king, moreover, had once been Thomas' closest friend and had, in fact, created him Archbishop. What are the debts to the temporal realm, to friendship, to gratitude? Thomas ponders. But at the same time he continues to maintain the primacy of the spiritual order over the temporal. If some things are Caesar's, they are Caesar's only because God permitted them to be.

Murder in the Cathedral was first staged in Canterbury Cathedral, that magnificent Gothic antiquity providing a most striking setting. Still often produced in a church edifice, the play gains an immediacy through the verisimilitude achieved by the combination of setting, liturgy, verse, and chorus, as well as the tensions created by the opposing forces at work in the drama. Eliot, however, in spite of Thomas' brilliant Christmas sermon which opens the second act, does not preach. It is not simply a case of Good versus Evil. Rather, the conflict is one of mystiques, each with a well-developed rationale. The choice appears to be between alternatives, not opposites. Thomas, who fears that he may be a victim of the sin of pride, must nevertheless proceed, to his damnation or to his salvation.

History records, of course, that the Shrine of St. Thomas Becket at Canterbury was among the most famous of medieval objects of devotion and pilgrimage, and Eliot is always conscious of history. Thus even the justifications of the knights who slew Thomas deserve serious attention, particularly in the modern era. And while the last of the knights attempts to maintain that Thomas' assassination should be viewed as suicide while of unsound mind, more than one modern historical critic has wondered if Thomas were not, as it were, "hell-bent" on heaven, a question that Thomas himself ponders. If in the end, we reject, perhaps quite properly, the justifications of the knights, we must ask how much of their own conscious rationalizations may be found in our own unconscious motivations.

Murder in the Cathedral is certainly not closet drama, and the themes of faith, justification, power, and internal and external conflict which it celebrates are often themes which recur in our world today. Thus Eliot has created a timeless work that looks forward to his own profoundly religious and mystical poems known as the *Four Quartets* and to his later modern treatments of very similar themes in plays such as *The Cocktail Party* and *The Confidential Clerk*. All of Eliot's later poetry and plays, however, must be read with *Murder in the Cathedral* in mind, for it represents a pivotal achievement in his distinguished career.

Willis E. McNelly

MUTINY ON THE BOUNTY

Type of work: Novel
Authors: Charles Nordhoff (1887-1947) and James Norman Hall (1887-1951)
Type of plot: Adventure romance
Time of plot: Late eighteenth century
Locale: South Pacific and Tahiti
First published: 1932

Although written as a novel and completely romantic in temper, Mutiny on the Bounty *is a great adventure story based on fact. The voyage of the* Bounty, *the mutiny aboard her, the exploit of Captain Bligh in piloting a small boat across 3,600 miles of open sea, the trial of the mutineers, and the final refuge of others on Pitcairn Island, are all matters of record.*

The first volume of their most commercially successful South Seas trilogy— followed by *Men Against the Sea* (1933) and *Pitcairn's Island* (1934)— *Mutiny on the Bounty* marked the high point of a rare and singularly happy literary collaboration that had begun when Charles Nordhoff and James Norman Hall served in France together prior to the United States's entry in World War I. Their joint books, like their individually written ones, are characterized by straightforward, vividly descriptive narrative that combines journalistic immediacy with historical verisimilitude to produce suspenseful, adventurous, entertaining reading.

Mutiny on the Bounty is based on an event which occurred in 1789, retaining actual historical characters and detailed background. Like Melville's Ishmael, their narrator had been a midshipman on the *Bounty* and so combines the roles of participant with objective observer and recorder. Although Hall wrote the English chapters and Nordhoff the Polynesian, the book contains a remarkable consistency of style and characterization. The cruelty of Captain Bligh and the stalwart integrity of Fletcher Christian draw upon a long literary tradition but manage to avoid stereotyping through the author's realistic portrayals of the two men.

The fascination of a bygone era of seamanship, a wealth of carefully researched detail, and a meticulously constructed true-life plot all work together from the first page of this novel to capture the reader's interest. The authors suggest early the basic personality traits of the main characters, dropping hints to foreshadow their development. Perhaps the characters are too cleanly cut to rank with the greatest of literature, too consistent to type to rise above figures in a romance, but they are successful within the framework of this novel. Nordhoff and Hall allow their story to speak for itself; by choosing an inexperienced young man as their narrator, they deliberately limit the depth of insight into the situation and characters involved that is possible. At the same time, the first-person narration increases the sense of immediacy of the tale, and renders it more plausible. The author of *Billy Budd* (1924) and *Moby Dick* (1851) undoubtedly would have penetrated far deeper into the minds and hearts of the tormented men trapped on the *Bounty,* particularly into the twisted personality of Bligh; the materials existed for a book of more intense vision and subtle characterization. Thus, *Mutiny on the Bounty,* while not great literature, is a superbly crafted piece of workmanship, a romance that will never cease to please readers.

MY ÁNTONIA

Type of work: Novel
Author: Willa Cather (1873-1947)
Type of plot: Regional chronicle
Time of plot: Late nineteenth and early twentieth centuries
Locale: Nebraska prairie land
First published: 1918

My Ántonia *is the story of a Bohemian girl whose family came from the Old Country to settle on the open prairies of Nebraska. While she lives on her farm and tills the soil, she is a child of the prairie, but when Ántonia goes to the city, she meets heartbreak, disillusionment, and social ostracism. Only after her return to the land which is her heritage does she find peace and meaning in life.*

The figure of the pioneer woman Ántonia Shimerda concentrates in itself a complex of values, an axis about which *My Ántonia* revolves. The novel in its turn illustrates two classical themes of American literature. Written in 1918, it reaches backward into the nineteenth century and beyond for its artistic and moral direction.

Willa Cather, the product of a genteel Virginia upbringing, found herself early in life transplanted to the frontier and forced to confront those vast blank spaces over which men had not yet succeeded in establishing the dominion of custom and convention. She saw a few brave settlers bearding the wilderness, meeting the physical challenge as well as the moral one of having to act straight out of their instincts without benefit of civilized constraints; for her these people, particularly the women, were a race apart. Antonia, with her noble simplicity, is among other things a monument to that vigorous race.

She is also an embodiment of a long tradition of fictional heroes of British and American romance. At the time the novel was written, literature and criticism in America were undergoing a change of direction. The thrust of literature in the new century owed much to the developing sciences; Lewis and Dreiser appeared on the scene with their sociological novels, signaling the rise of naturalism. Fictional characters would henceforth be viewed as interpreting in their acts the flaws and beauties of laws, institutions, and social structures. *My Ántonia* fits an older mold, a form in which the effects of colonial Puritanism can be detected. Specifically, the mode demands that the hero overcome or fail to overcome the strictures and hazards of his situation by his own wit, strength, or courage. This convention draws from the very wellspring of American life, the democratic belief in the wholeness and self-sufficiency of the individual, that is, in personal culpability, and in the absolute value of the personal conscience. Cather makes no real indictment of the society that scorns and undervalues Ántonia and the other hired girls; the social conventions are, with the land, simply the medium through which she fulfills her destiny. It is the peculiarly American sense of starting out brand-new in a new land, that sense of moral isolation, that adds poignance to the struggles of the individual against the vagaries of fortune. This theme of American newness and innocence, which R. B. Lewis calls "The Theme of the American Adam," has as a natural concomitant elements of temptation and fortunate fall. The serpent in Ántonia's story is the town of Black Hawk, where she quarrels with her benefactors and runs afoul of Larry Donovan. Seduced and abandoned, she returns to the land; but her experience has made her better able, as she tells Jim Burden, to prepare her children to face the world.

But if the town is Ántonia's downfall in terms of one theme, it is the grey backdrop against which she shines in terms of another; in the same way the prairie is her antagonist in one sense, and the natural force of which she is the flower in another. Jim Burden first finds her, significantly, actually living in the earth. Early on she begins to take on characteristics of the land: "Her neck came up strongly out of her shoulders, like the bole of a tree out of the turf"; " 'But she has such splendid color in her cheeks—like those big dark red plums.' " She works the land; she makes gardens; she nourishes the Harling children with food and stories. Her connection with the fertile earth is insisted upon. And the earth, the virgin land, is in this novel the source of physical vigor and the best resource of the soul. Jim Burden describes his first experience of the land as a feeling of cosmic unity: "Perhaps we feel like that when we die and become part of something entire, whether it is sun and air, or goodness and knowledge. At any rate, that is happiness; to be dissolved into something complete and great." The people who live on the prairie seem to him open and giving like the land; for instance, he says of Ántonia that "everything she said seemed to come right out of her heart." By contrast, the life of the town is pinched and ungenerous: "People's speech, their voices, their very glances, became furtive and repressed. Every individual taste, every natural appetite, was bridled by caution." Ántonia, in all her acts, shows the naturalness and boundless generosity of the plains; gives unstintingly of her strength and loyalty to her surly brother, to Jim and the Harling children, to Larry Donovan, and to her husband Cuzak; and pours out a flood of love and nurture upon her children. She alludes several times to her dislike of towns and cities and to her feeling of familiar friendship with the country. Toward the end of the book the figure of Ántonia and the infinite fertility of the land come together symbolically in an extremely vivid and moving image. Ántonia and her children have been showing Jim Burden the contents of their fruit cellar, and as they step outside, "[the children] all came running up the steps together, big and little, tow heads and gold heads and brown, and flashing little naked legs; a veritable explosion of life out of the dark cave into the sunlight." The cave might be the apotheosis of Ántonia's first home on the prairie, the latter redeeming the former by its fruitfulness.

Above all, the novel celebrates the early life on the plains of which Jim

Burden and Ántonia were a part. The long digressions about Peter and Pavel, Blind D'Arnault, the Cutters and others, the profoundly elegiac descriptions of Jake Marpole and Otto Fuchs, the sharply caught details of farm life, town life, landscape—these things are bent to the recreation of a simpler and better time, a hard life now gone beyond recall, but lovingly remembered.

Jan Kennedy Foster

THE MYSTERIES OF PARIS

Type of work: Novel
Author: Eugène Sue (1804-1857)
Type of plot: Mystery romance
Time of plot: Mid-nineteenth century
Locale: France and Germany
First published: 1842-1843

This unwieldy, complicated, six-volume novel may be seriously flawed from an artistic standpoint, but its wealth of characters, its vivid, realistic scenes of Parisian life in the mid-nineteenth century, and its sequence of melodramatic situations made the book a popular success in its own time and a historically interesting precursor of the naturalistic novel in our own.

Eugène Sue's *The Mysteries of Paris* is a long, complicated six-volume novel; originally serialized, it contains scores of main characters and countless minor ones. The main character is the aristocrat Rodolph, Grand Duke of Gerolstein, who at thirty-six, is a physically powerful, yet graceful man of astonishing vigor. He is a man of meditation as well as action "whose physical strength and presence of mind would always command an ascendancy over the multitude." Rodolph, equally at home among the poor and the aristocratic, uses his extraordinary physical and mental attributes to overcome problems and solve the mysteries of those with whom he comes in contact. Rodolph is not without problems himself, however, suffering from an ill-fated and annulled marriage to an evil woman; their union results in a daughter, Fleur-de-Marie, whom he searches for and saves from the slums of Paris. True to the romantic nature of the novel, Fleur-de-Marie becomes a nun to atone for her past, but is overcome when given the honor of being an abbess at the order, and dies: a strange death for someone who had the strength to survive the slums of Paris.

Sue was unable to resolve the problem that his narrator is fundamentally at odds with Rodolph. While the hero helps innumerable criminal types and other unfortunates to overcome their problems (often caused by disreputable aristocrats), primarily through his individual perseverance and strength, he does not call upon his "multitude" of friends to effect any of the social and political reforms that the narrator so frequently advocates. Thus, when Rodolph succeeds in solving intricately woven mysteries, the reader is not left with the urgent sense of social commitment which Sue wished to communicate.

Style in *The Mysteries of Paris* is subservient to content; the manner of writing is straightforward, with little attention paid to subtleties of expression or nuances. The author is most concerned with spreading before the reader a dramatic tale against a vivid, realistic background, without embellishments or sophisticated techniques. In this regard, he is a forerunner of Zola, Dreiser, and others of the naturalist school of fiction. The vigorous, melodramatic approach of the author to storytelling captures the reader's imagination and through its rough-and-ready method keeps this interest through the long, rambling volumes and complicated subplots. The coincidences of plot and improbabilities of the story are accepted and forgiven by the reader, as they are in Dickens' novels. Sue creates his own rules for writing a novel and, for him, they work admirably, so that he succeeds in the fundamental goal of any work of fiction: he gives the illusion of real life.

THE MYSTERIES OF UDOLPHO

Type of work: Novel
Author: Mrs. Ann Radcliffe (1764-1823)
Type of plot: Gothic romance
Time of plot: Late sixteenth century
Locale: France and Italy
First published: 1794

In her own age Ann Radcliffe was justly annointed "Queen of the Gothic Novel," a title that still remains valid. Emily St. Aubert, the main character in The Mysteries of Udolpho, *is the prototype of the threatened heroine of the gothic romance, and her adventures assume the pattern that is characteristic of the genre, a formula that is still popular today.*

Christmas Eve of 1764 saw the issuance of Horace Walpole's *The Castle of Otranto,* a story of supernatural terror set in a vaguely medieval past, complete with a gloomy castle, knights both chivalrous and wicked, and virtuous fair maidens in distress—the first English Gothic novel. During the previous summer, while Walpole at Strawberry Hill was transforming a nightmarish dream into a Gothic novel, Ann Ward was born in London. Twenty-three years later when she married law student William Radcliffe, the era of the Gothic novel was finally under way, having begun to flourish with Clara Reeve's professed imitation of *The Castle of Otranto* in *The Old English Baron* (1777). And Ann Radcliffe, born in the same year as the genre itself, was to be supreme among the Gothic novelists whose works were so popular in the last decades of the eighteenth century.

Her total output as a novelist, except for one posthumously published novel, comprises five Gothic novels, all immensely successful, published between 1789 and 1797. *The Mysteries of Udolpho* was her fourth and most popular. Mrs. Anna Laetitia Barbauld in her Preface to this novel for *British Novelists* (1810), noting that a "greater distinction is due to those which stand at the head of a class," asserts that "such are undoubtedly the novels of Mrs. Radcliffe." This estimate is still valid.

Nevertheless, Ann Radcliffe might have been relegated entirely to the pages of literary history had it not been for Jane Austen's delightful burlesque of Gothic novels, *Northanger Abbey,* in which a sentimental heroine under the inspiration of *The Mysteries of Udolpho* fancies herself involved in Gothic adventures. Through the exaggerated sentiment of her heroine, Jane Austen ridicules a major element in Gothic novels in general—in *The Mysteries of Udolpho* specifically—sensibility. A reliance upon feeling, in contradiction of the dominant rationalism of the eighteenth century, the cult of sensibility was nonetheless a vital part of the age. The man of sensibility was peculiarly receptive to the simple joys of country life, to the "sublime" as well as to the "beautiful" aspects of nature, and, above all, inclined to benevolence, his own depth of feeling compelling sympathy. And it was considered proper to manifest sensibility through such traits as a readiness to weep or faint and a taste of melancholia.

In *The Mysteries of Udolpho,* the "good" characters are endowed with sensibility; the "bad" are not. Emily St. Aubert, her father, and her lover Valancourt are exemplars of this highly refined capacity for feeling. St. Aubert, scorning worldly ambition, is retired from the world, represented by the city of Paris, to his rural estate, La Vallée, where his days are spent in literary, musical, and botanical pursuits, his pleasures heightened by his pensive melancholy. The villainous Montoni loves power and the wielding of it, responding to the idea of any daring exploit with eyes that appeared to gleam instantaneously with fire. At home in cities with their atmosphere of fashionable dissipation and political intrigue, he thrives in the solitary Castle of Udolpho only when he has made it a bustling military fortress. Cold, haughty, and brooding, he is—unlike the ingenuous St. Aubert—adept at dissimulation.

Much of Emily's anguish is caused by the lack of sensibility in Montoni's world, her own ingenuousness and benevolence misinterpreted as mere policy, spurring her enemies to further mischief. However, Emily's sensibility functions sometimes as an effective defense, her profuse tears and spells of fainting postponing immediate confrontations. Sometimes, too, sensibility assisted discovery, as Emily, shutting herself away to read, play her lute and sing, sketch, or simply meditate and gaze rapturously upon the landscape at hand, became vulnerable to mystery.

The conventionally spurious medieval setting, in this novel set in the year 1584, serves well the solitude of sensibility and gives scope for a range of feelings as the heroine is forced to travel about France and Italy, inhabiting gloomy, ruined castles from the Alps and the Apennines to the Adriatic and the Mediterranean, encountering chevaliers, noble ladies, courtesans, mercenary soldiers, bandits, peasants, monks, nuns, war, and murder—deaths by poisoning, by stiletto, by sword, by torture, by pistol, and by cannon fire. Emily's wide-ranging adventures in a remote, dark age are the fit trials of her sensibility, foreshadowed in her dying father's lecture on the danger of uncontrolled sensibility. And if the modern reader is overwhelmed by evidence of her frequent trembling, weeping, and fainting, Emily herself is more conscious of her constant endeavor to be resolute, her ultimate survival with honor unscathed sufficient proof of her strength of sensibility.

Although Jane Austen ridicules this excessive sensibility, she also allows Henry Tilney, her spokesman for reason, to praise Mrs. Radcliffe's novel, however facetiously, by claiming that he could hardly put down *The Mysteries of Udolpho* once he had begun reading it and, in fact, had finished the novel, hair standing on end, in two days. Henry's count of two entire days accurately indicates average reading time, but, more importantly, his appreciation of the suspense maintained throughout does justice to Mrs. Radcliffe's novelistic powers.

The essential quality which sustains Gothic suspense is a pervasive sense of the irrational elements in life. Emily herself provides the appropriate image in the description about her life appearing like the dream of a distempered imagination. Although basically a straightforward, chronological narrative, *The Mysteries of Udolpho* seems timeless and dreamlike, the sweeping length of the story suggesting the cinematic technique of slow-motion. The novel accomplishes shifts in scenery with the rapidity peculiar to dreams: now Emily is in Leghorn; now she is in a ship tossed amid white foam in a dark and stormy sea, incredibly, upon the very shores where lies the mysterious Château-le-Blanc. The vast amount of scenic description, written in the generalizing poetic diction of the eighteenth century, contributes to the unreal atmosphere suggestive of a dream world where forms are vague, where time and space ignore ordinary delimitations. Thus the Castle of Udolpho seems limitless in size; its actual shape and substance, typically viewed in the solemn evening dusk, seems indefinite, gloomy and sublime with clustered towers. Other scenes call up boundless space, for example, in recurrent images of blue-tinged views of distant mountain tops.

The repetitive pattern of Emily's adventures is also dreamlike: she is repeatedly trapped in a room with no light; again and again she flees down dark, labyrinthine passages or seemingly endless staircases. People who are rationally assumed to be far away suddenly materialize, often in shadowy forms, their features obscure, known to Emily only intuitively. Disembodied voices, music from unseen instruments, are commonplace. Continually beset with a dread of undefined evil, she experiences recurrently a paralysis of body and will before a danger imminent, yet concealed.

In these post-Freudian days, readers detect the realm of the subconscious emerging in Emily's nightmare world, not only in the repetitious, dreamlike patterns, but also in the very nature of her predicament—that of the pure, innocent "orphan child" whose physical attractions precipitate sword fights, subject her to would-be rapists who pursue her down the dark corridors, and render her helpless before the cold, cruel Montoni, whose so-called preposterous depravity holds for her the fascination of the abomination.

However, Mrs. Radcliffe is too much a part of the Age of Reason to permit irrationality to rule. Emily is preserved by her innate strength of sensibility from assaults on her person and her mind. In all her melancholy meditations, once her ordeal has ended, she is never required to wonder why Montoni appealed to her as he did when he was triumphant, bold, spirited, and commanding. Instead, her mind dismissing him as one who was insignificant, she settles down to a secure life with Valancourt, a candid and open-handed man. In her retirement to La Vallée, Emily may never be able to avoid counterparts of Madame Montoni, whose fashionable repartee recalls the comedy of manners in which Jane Austen was to excel, but she will be safe from such men as Montoni.

In the spirit of reason, the author also banishes the mystery of the supernatural happenings which provide so much suspense. Every inexplicable occurrence finally has its rational explanation. Mrs. Barbauld, herself a rationalist, complains with some justice about the protracted suspense and the high expectations which defuse Radcliffe's increment of horrors and nebulous challenges to the imagination. Nonetheless, when one has, like Henry Tilney, kept pace with this lengthy novel, the impression of Emily St. Aubert's nightmare world is more vivid than the skepticism of reason which explains away all the dark secrets. Ultimately, the vague shapings of the imagination triumph.

Catherine E. Moore

THE MYSTERIOUS ISLAND

Type of work: Novel
Author: Jules Verne (1828-1905)
Type of plot: Adventure romance
Time of plot: 1865-1869
Locale: An island in the South Pacific
First published: 1870

In a sense The Mysterious Island *is a sequel to* Twenty Thousand Leagues Under the Sea, *for in it Verne describes the death of Captain Nemo; but the novel is basically a story of survival and a celebration of the adaptability and ingenuity of intelligent, hardworking, God-fearing men. The wealth of scientific description and detail integrated into the narrative gives it credibility and justifies its claim as one of the first science fiction novels.*

The Mysterious Island can be placed in the tradition of *The Swiss Family Robinson* (1812-1813). That novel, appealing to a notion of romantic individualism popular in the mid-nineteenth century, spawned a number of adventure books in which ingenious heroes land in isolated places and make unique homes for themselves. *The Mysterious Island,* however, is superior to the mass of these imitations, and even to the original version of *The Swiss Family Robinson.* At the urging of his publisher, Hetzel, Verne turned an early, rather unpromising manuscript into *The Mysterious Island* by adding scientific data, mystery, dramatic complications, and a startling, original conclusion.

Apart from its interest as a story, *The Mysterious Island* is significant for the technological detail Verne included. Unlike many tales of *The Swiss Family Robinson* variety, unlike even many science fiction stories of the twentieth century, there are not merely the trappings of science; there is much scientific substance as well. Verne goes into the most detailed accounts of the ways in which tools, chemicals, and communications equipment can be manufactured from elementary materials. All this description, which may appear to be unrelated to the plot, is significant because it reflects the optimism of nineteenth century European society and especially the widespread confidence placed in technology. Although in some stories Verne suggests the danger of this new power, for the most part he is the celebrator of industrialism and especially the revolutionary technology which gives birth to it. But industrialization and technology were also massively abused during this period, largely for reasons of profit; so Verne's celebration was generally placed either in the future or in some imaginary place, as in *The Mysterious Island.* The technological descriptions in *The Mysterious Island* show, in effect, technical history from the most primitive beginnings to a reasonably advanced state; these descriptions may be said to recapitulate, in capsule form, the progress of mankind. Thus it is significant that the heroes are American, since the United States was seen at the time as a rising, dynamic industrial power, leading mankind to a new age.

Though Verne's ideas, and his enthusiasm for his ideas, are communicated well in the novel, there are serious literary flaws in the work. The most damaging of these is probably Verne's shallow characterizations; though his characters are generally adequate, they are never wholly successful or convincing. Nebuchadnezzar, for example, is little more than a stereotype. Verne is simply not interested in exploring depths of people's characters, though he is vitally interested in their achievements.

THE MYSTERY OF EDWIN DROOD

Type of work: Novel
Author: Charles Dickens (1812-1870)
Type of plot: Mystery romance
Time of plot: Mid-nineteenth century
Locale: England
First published: 1870

Even though Dickens died before he could offer the solution to the mystery of Edwin Drood, the novel is a fascinating character study and an incisive view of Victorian society even in its unfinished state. So intriguing is the plot that a host of subsequent authors have supplied their own versions of how the story should end.

The Mystery of Edwin Drood, left unfinished at Dickens' death, continues to fascinate the critics who have made several attempts to conclude it in accord with what they surmise to have been Dickens's intention. The consensus seems to be that Jack Jasper indeed was the murderer, although one critic argues that Edwin Drood was not even killed and sailed for India. Such literary detective work is entertaining but it should not distract us from the genuine interest of the remnant itself. In the fragment Dickens returns again to the scene of *David Copperfield*; but this time he fails to discover that peace he once found there and which had eluded him during the last decade of his life.

Indeed, Jack Jasper might be interpreted as representing the suffering Dickens who after his separation from his wife, some fifteen years before his death, found only occasional solace in the companionship of Ellen Ternan, a young actress. Jasper himself is haunted by the unattainable and youthful Rosa Bud, Edwin Drood's fiancée. Such is Jasper's obsession that he is driven to drugs and the foul opium dens of London's slums, the scenes of which are some of the most piteous in all of Dickens' fiction. Alienated from all life— Jasper at one point tells his young nephew, "The cramped monotony of my existence grinds me away by the grain"—he attempts to find in his "art" as a choirmaster of the cathedral a link to mankind. When this fails, out of despair he murders Drood—or so the speculation runs—to gain a surer access to Rosa's affections. But even if we cannot be sure of the actual course of events, the vividness of Jasper's character remains, an image of the suffering man, cut off from the sources of life, a portrait rendered with immediacy and deep compassion.

THE NAKED YEAR

Type of work: Novel
Author: Boris Pilnyak (Boris Andreyevich Vogau, 1894-1937?)
Type of plot: Regional chronicle
Time of plot: Early twentieth century
Locale: Russia
First published: 1922

Despite a plot that is fragmentary, disjointed, and impressionistic and characters that tend to be vague, unpredictable, or shallow, The Naked Year *is a powerful evocation of the mood, atmosphere, and historical reality of the brief, chaotic period between the collapse of the Old Regime and the Bolshevik consolidation of power.*

The "naked year" is, of course, 1917, the year of the Bolshevik revolution, and Boris Pilnyak's attempt to capture its essence in his narrative established him as Russia's first important post-revolutionary novelist. Ironically, however, it can be strongly argued that *The Naked Year* is neither a "novel" in form nor a Communistic document in substance. The fragmentary, lyrical, relatively plotless and characterless series of vignettes that make up the book are more like a sequence of random impressions and rhetorical digressions, thinly tied together in time and place, than a controlled, directed prose narrative. The origins and essence of the revolution, as Pilnyak presents them, do not conform to the tenants of Soviet political dogma.

In spite of its narrative difficulties and ideological impurity, *The Naked Year* was generally hailed as a masterpiece upon its publication in 1922. The main character of the book is the Russian people and the substance of it is their diverse reactions to the civil turmoil that swept across Russia from 1914 to the early 1920's. While Pilnyak uses a hodge-podge of prose styles and jumps from character to character and event to event with few formal transitions, he does focus most of the action in the town of Ordynin and on characters who represent all levels of Russian society—the Ratchin family is middle class, the Ordynins are aristocratic, Arkhip represents the rising peasantry—in a fairly complete, if unsystematic fashion. Thus, the reader comes away from *The Naked Year* with a coherent impression of life in revolutionary Russia, even if all of the parts do not fit into a neat whole.

The historical vision Pilnyak presents in the novel is that of a spontaneous peasant revolt overthrowing the old order. He sees the conflict not so much in terms of the bourgeoisie versus the proletariat, as the "natural" Eastern side of Russian culture, represented by the peasantry, in conflict with the "artificial" European urbanized Russia. Thus, the revolution was, to him, the cleansing force necessary and the Bolsheviks merely the agents of historical change—not the inevitable culmination of it.

Such unorthodox views did not please the revolutionary hierarchy, but the power and popularity of the novel, coupled with the relative instability of Soviet politics at the time, kept Pilnyak in the ranks of "accepted" writers. However, in later works, such as *A Tale of the Unextinguished Moon* (1927) —a direct attack on Stalin—and *Mahogany* (1929), he provoked the dictator's wrath and so, in spite of abject disavowals of his own works, pitiable recantations, and other "orthodox" writings, Boris Pilnyak was imprisoned during the Stalinist purges of the mid-1930's and presumably perished in neglect and disgrace.

NANA

Type of work: Novel
Author: Émile Zola (1840-1902)
Type of plot: Naturalism
Time of plot: 1860's
Locale: Paris and rural France
First published: 1880

Émile Zola was the major theoretician of the Naturalistic Movement, as well as one of its most able literary practitioners. Nana, one of his Rougon-Macquart series of novels picturing French life and society from 1852 to 1870, is an unsentimental, realistic portrayal of a courtesan. Nana is moronic, vulgar, greedy, and cruel, but her abject fate is the result of neither her faulty character nor her immorality; she is the victim of biological, hereditary, and environmental pressures.

Émile Zola's *Rougon-Macquart* series (1871-1893), including *Nana,* ran to an aggregate of twenty novels, exploring the naturalistic philosophy of literature. This philosophy was strongly influenced by the scientific method outlined in Claude Bernard's *Introduction to the Study of Experimental Medicine* (1865). Zola himself explained the relationship between science and literature in his theoretical works: *Le Roman Expérimental* (1880; a direct application of Bernard's principle to literature), *Les Romanciers naturalistes* (1881), and *Le Naturalisme au Théâtre* (1881). According to Zola, naturalism combined scientific determinism, pessimistic and mechanistic views of human behavior, pathological assumptions about human motivation, and a predilection for examining the life of the lower socio-economic classes. Thus, Zola's *Rougon-Macquart* series, designed after the model of Honoré de Balzac's *Comédie Humaine,* sought to portray the society of the Second Empire by "scientifically" describing conditions of life. However, Zola did not recognize that hereditary (biological) determinants were actually indefensible assumptions which could not *ipso facto* rationalize behavior. His attempt to trace through twenty novels a family epic of neuroses and alcoholism was therefore less than successful. Yet it did produce some memorable character studies—among them, *Nana*—in the multi-faceted collection of one-thousand-odd characters who appear in the series, depicting various social classes, circumstances, and places which Zola himself had observed.

Indeed, so attentive is Zola to naturalism's scientific principles that he paints in words as vivid a portrait of Nana as could be painted by the most adept realists. Of course, attention to detail as well as to psychological motivation is paramount in the naturalistic canon. Just as scientific experiments require exacting attention to statistical data, so also do naturalistic novels demand strict factual accounting. Thus, *Nana* satisfies its philosophical imperatives by providing such meticulous details as would be necessary for a laboratory report. These details evolve not only from the physical description of Nana herself but also from the development of the plot. Each twist and turn in Nana's life and fortune, for example, is as carefully documented as a research paper would be. No phenomenon is left unexplained. For Zola's approach to *Nana*—novel and character—is that of a scientist who leaves no possibility unexplored. Hence, in *Nana,* the protagonist is fully explored, fully psychologized.

While Nana is thus being thoroughly explored, Zola also develops the theme of the novel. Despite charges of pornography—not to mention the fact that Nana was an out-and-out prostitute—Zola nonetheless presents in the novel an unrelenting account of quasi-fashionable but decadent society. In much the same manner as a twentieth century commentator on the jet-set phenomenon, Zola chronicles the debaucheries of mid-nineteenth century Paris. Money, power, and sex dominate French society, according to Zola: Money buys power, and power commands sex. Thus the central characters, obsessed with the power of money, buy and sell themselves and one another with kaleidoscopic turnover. M. Mignon pimps for his wife; Madame Hugon, wittingly or unwittingly, sets up her son George for seduction by Nana; Nana herself accumulates an incredible number of lovers from Daguenet to Steiner to George Hugon to Count Muffat to Fontan to Count Xavier de Vandeuvres to Philippe Hugon to Satin to the Marquis de Chouard. The moral rot endemic in all of these people reaches its culmination in Nana's literal and symbolic contracting of smallpox from her neglected son.

Zola thus laid bare the political, social, and ethical bankruptcy of the Second Empire demimonde. He did it through plot development and through characterization. Nana's sequential—and sometimes simultaneous—liaisons constitute the thread of plot development. Her fortunes depend not upon her theatrical talents but upon her contacts with monied men who can keep her in style. Her only errors are those which involve sentiment rather than cold analysis and rational evaluation of her prospects for survival. Plot development thus reveals the theme of the novel as a study in how the economically disadvantaged cope with an inherently inequitable system. Zola's answer is: tenuously and insecurely. For in his characterization of Nana, Zola depicts a woman who is utterly insecure. Nana has no solid resources of her own other than her gorgeous body. She is vulgar; she is cheap; she is sordid. She is all of these degraded things because she has no confidence in her own worth as a human being. Hence, in her view, and in society's view, once she has lost her attractiveness to the debilities of disease, she is worthless.

Still, for all of Zola's professed adherence to naturalistic principles, his work has been judged at its artistic best precisely where he lapses from his systematic method into the natural rhythms of a novelist. The kernel of truth in this judgment certainly applies to *Nana*. Although the protagonist is most often described in great detail, she appears in the mind's eye of the reader at her seductive best when she is limned in only a few bold strokes. Likewise, the inexorable logic of the sordid and predominantly deterministic plot is occasionally softened, and not a little enhanced, by such tender scenes as Nana's meeting with George in the rain-drenched strawberry patch.

Similarly, Zola's dispassionately analytical language is brightened from time to time with passages of near-poetic prose. Above all, the naturalistic dictum that all characters, including the protagonist, must represent types and not be extraordinary is belied by Nana herself, for Nana is nothing if not extraordinary—in her beauty, in her greed, in her vulgarity. Indeed, these very contradictions, the unlikely combination of qualities, render her character atypical. Of course, Zola was quite distressed over his romantic tendencies, seeing them as flaws in the naturalistic scheme of things; however, he seemed blind to the flaws of naturalism systematically applied, especially its morbidity, its monotony, and its fundamental mediocrity. Yet in the final analysis, Zola's genius as an artist stems from his inability to follow any one theory undeviatingly, and the best of *Nana* can be attributed to that characteristic.

Joanna G. Kashdan

THE NAPOLEON OF NOTTING HILL

Type of work: Novel
Author: Gilbert Keith Chesterton (1874-1936)
Type of plot: Fantasy
Time of plot: Late twentieth century
Locale: London
First published: 1904

The Napoleon of Notting Hill is a delightful comic fantasy that celebrates spontaneous imagination and individual eccentricity in the face of a universally regimented, conformist, rational world. Chesterton's special talent in this novel, as in his religious speculation The Man Who Was Thursday, *is to utilize whimsical, humorous fantasy in the presentation of serious, provocative ideas.*

The two major characters of G. K. Chesterton's *The Napoleon of Notting Hill* enliven a drab world with humor and tyranny. Quinn refuses to take seriously either his office (King of England) or himself. He discerns the comic dimension in everything, and cavorts ridiculously in order to point out life's folly. Only one person takes him seriously. He is Adam Wayne.

Adam Wayne was born and reared within the slum neighborhood of Notting Hill. His fantasies of its beauty are unaffected by experience, and vastly enhanced by a chance encounter. When Adam was a boy, defending his make-believe territory with his make-believe armour and wooden sword, he struck the trespassing king who happened by. The king easily slipped into Wayne's fantasy and admonished him to defend his kingdom forever.

Ten years later, when the king's foolishness has produced small medieval neighborhood kingdoms, Wayne again emerges. He is the only man in the kingdom to revel in the king's commands. He is in title and in essence the "Provost of Notting Hill." Drawn by his fervor, the people of Notting Hill join his crusade and remain undefeated in the battle of the road.

Twenty years pass before war again rages. The king and Wayne fight together in the final battle, knowing they will be defeated because it is time. After the battle the king confesses that the great idea for which Wayne has lived was mere folly. Wayne is undisturbed, however, and declares that they are two opposites who work together toward one end. The king's humor, devoid of gravity, and Wayne's humorless fanaticism have rescued the kingdom from the doldrums. Now the common man can suffice without them. Wayne and Quinn are content that their extremes are no longer needed and go together into an unknown world.

The Napoleon of Notting Hill is not merely an entertaining comic tale. In it Chesterton presented some of his key political views. Associated with the English Guild Socialists and "distributists," Chesterton asserted the need for small areas of private property to maintain people's vital personalities. He saw the intimate neighborhoods, guilds, and agrarian patterns of the Middle Ages as providing a worthwhile example for modern social reform.

THE NARRATIVE OF ARTHUR GORDON PYM

Type of work: Short story
Author: Edgar Allan Poe (1809-1849)
Type of plot: Adventure romance
Time of plot: Early nineteenth century
Locale: High seas
First published: 1838

This extended tale, Poe's longest narrative fiction, has been given many labels—horror story, gothic parody, sea-adventure-romance, literary hoax, even a Western of a kind—but it continues to defy categorization. Whatever its type, however, it is one of the most startling revelations of Poe's bleak vision of the cosmos and man's precarious place in it.

Though incomplete and uneven, *The Narrative of Arthur Gordon Pym* is nevertheless one of Poe's most important evocations of the irrational power which ultimately dominates his universe. In this novella, the appearance of reason and order always deceives—the apparently benign is nothing more than a mask over horrors almost too frightening to contemplate. Poe repeatedly demonstrates this as, in the course of the story, an idyllic moonlight cruise leads to near-disaster, Pym's adventurous dream of stowing away becomes the nightmare of being buried alive, faithful Tiger changes into a raging beast. Men are subject to the same forces. Pym, first horrified by Peters' proposal, joins his companions in cannibalizing Parker's body. The "friendly" natives of Tslal prove treacherous savages. Finally, Nature itself, as exemplified by the strangely ambiguous white sea (which some critics have seen as suggestive of life-giving milk) flows into the ultimate horror of the metaphysical void.

Arthur Gordon Pym is the archetypal voyager or quester after knowledge whose initiation into the secrets of the universe is the substance of the work. Beginning as the adventurous boy of the opening chapter, he becomes, by the end of the story, the tragic pilgrim who dies a "sudden and distressing death" before he can relate the full extent of his discoveries. Like many of Poe's narrators, Pym represents himself as the epitome of the reasonable man, and throughout his adventures he seeks assurances that the universe reflects similar principles. Self-deceived on both counts, Pym seems unaware that his description of the Tslalians as "the most wicked, hypocritical, vindictive, bloodthirsty, and altogether fiendish race of men upon the face of the globe" is equally applicable to himself. Perhaps it is this knowledge that Pym comes to by his look upon the void, and with which he is unable to live.

A NARRATIVE OF THE LIFE OF DAVID CROCKETT

Type of work: Autobiography
Author: David Crockett (1786-1836)
Type of plot: History and adventure
Time of plot: 1780-1834
Locale: Tennessee
First published: 1834

Davy Crockett was, even in his own time, a folk hero, although there is some question as to the authenticity of his image: was it real or was it manufactured by Crockett and anti-Jacksonian politicians? Regardless of its value as biography, however, Crockett's narrative is an entertaining, if longwinded, folktale of the rugged-individualist frontiersman and the cultural values he embodied.

A Narrative of the Life of David Crockett appeared in print in 1834 while the author was serving a term in Congress. By that time Crockett had become a folk hero of such consequence that there had already appeared an unauthorized book, *Sketches and Eccentricities of Col. David Crockett, of West Tennessee,* which Crockett resented and which prompted him to write his own book. Crockett published a sequel in 1835, *An Account of Col. Crockett's Tour to the North and Down East,* in which the author's political complaints and harangues unfortunately detract from his rambunctious personality in print.

What is likable about Crockett in his autobiography is that he is unique, proud, ignorant, and boastful, the prototype of the "Rugged Individual" spinning yarns of frontier life. At the same time, this backwoodsman serving in Congress, unschooled and barely literate, seems primitive and picturesque, even in his own day.

As a narrator, Crockett is uneven, at times monotonous, yet at other times so well in possession of common sense that he is nearly witty, or, as Hamlin Garland put it, "whimsical." Garland's opinion that Crockett "was in a crude sort the direct progenitor of Lincoln and Mark Twain" seems generous, but on occasion Crockett manages a fine episode. For instance, his account in Chapter XI of deer hunts and of replenishing his powder supply on Christmas, 1822 shows him at his best as a dramatic storyteller.

Crockett's autobiography occupies a unique place in the library of American letters. Part history and part tall-tale, perhaps part political apology—for Crockett never tires of stating his differences with Andrew Jackson or his independence from the Party—his narrative is nothing if not idiosyncratic. It is, in Crockett's own words, "the exact image of its Author."

NATHAN THE WISE

Type of work: Drama
Author: Gotthold Ephraim Lessing (1729-1781)
Type of plot: Philosophic humanism
Time of plot: Twelfth century
Locale: Jerusalem
First published: 1779

Nathan the Wise *is a fitting climax to a great career, a deeply humane verse play expressing Lessing's enlightened philosophy. The high point of the drama occurs when Nathan relates the famous folk parable of the three rings which represent the three major religious faiths. The true faith (or ring) is that one which best serves mankind, Lessing suggests, thereby writing an eloquent plea for religious tolerance and freedom.*

Although the 1770's in Germany were dominated by the emotional "Storm and Stress" writers, they also produced the last works of Lessing, the greatest writer of the rationalistic Enlightenment—a philosopher, critic, theoretician, and dramatist. His last play, *Nathan the Wise,* is a landmark in German drama, preparing the way for Goethe's and Schiller's great humanistic dramas.

Lessing sets his play in the Holy Land—sacred to three world religions—after the Third Crusade, a period of bitter religious conflict, but he was addressing the problem of religious intolerance in his own time, and his ideas have not lost their force even for us. He makes a Jew the wise man of the story, a Jew who has suffered greatly at the hands of his pious enemies, but has risen above his hatred to a humanitarian love that puts the Christians in the play to shame. The Christians, fanatical, dogmatic, and even cruel, rank even below Saladin and the Moslems in respect to enlightenment. In this world of hostility and enmity, Nathan's parable of the rings places the question of ultimate truth beyond the knowledge of man, and evaluates the truth of a religion for each man in terms of the good it produces in his actions. It is important that a man be religious, but his creed is largely a matter of his culture.

The image of the parable is embodied and developed in the action of the play, in which each character is seen working his way out of prejudice and self-centeredness towards a realization of man's brotherhood, in the face of which their external differences are insignificant. The humanistic religion which Nathan teaches Recha is the essence of this faith, and the final revelation of the unexpected family relationships that bind all the characters together becomes a physical symbol of the metaphysical unity of man.

NATIVE SON

Type of work: Novel
Author: Richard Wright (1908-1960)
Type of plot: Social criticism
Time of plot: 1930's
Locale: An American city
First published: 1940

Richard Wright was the first black novelist of stature to break into the mainstream of American fiction, and Native Son *is his most representative and powerful book. Wright presents in Bigger Thomas a young man who is driven by anger, frustration, and hatred—directed both at the white world and at himself— that can only explode violently in both directions.*

Native Son, when it appeared in 1940, was without precedent in American literature. Previous black writing, including Wright's *Uncle Tom's Children,* had treated blacks as passive and innocent victims of racism suffering their lot in dignified silence. As Wright said of his own earlier work, the reading audience could escape into the self-indulgence of pity on reading such work rather than truly face the hard facts of racism. In Bigger Thomas, Wright created a character who was neither passive sufferer nor innocent victim. Instead, Wright reminded Americans of the full cost of bigotry in social and human terms by dramatizing the deep anger and hate and fear many blacks felt. Years after *Native Son's* appearance, James Baldwin would assert that every black person carries some degree of Bigger Thomas within himself. Perhaps so, but it is to Richard Wright's credit that he was the first American writer to bring those feelings into the open. We are reminded throughout the work that Bigger is a "native son," and his experience is quintessentially a part of the American experience. On the psychological, the sociological, and the philosophical levels, Wright explores the most disturbing implications of what it means to be black in America.

The basic tone of Wright's psychological treatment of Bigger is set in the opening scene in which Bigger and Buddy battle the rat. Here is a symbolic paradigm for the entire novel in which Bigger, like the rat, will be hunted down and destroyed. The rat, it must be understood, operates entirely at the instinctual level, and its viciousness is in response to fear. Recalling that "Fear" is the title of the first section of the novel as "Flight" is of the second suggests that Bigger too is a creature motivated by fear and acting instinctively. This is demonstrably true of his killing Mary Dalton while avoiding detection, and it shows up even earlier in the fight with Gus. Fearful of outside forces, particularly whites, Bigger is equally fearful of the repressed anger within himself as his several comments referring to his concern that he is destined to commit some terrible act indicates. Thus, throughout at least the first two sections of the novel, Bigger, before and after the murder, is operating at the animal level of pure instinct, and it is against this background that his development takes place.

Bigger's psychological state is an obvious result of the sociological conditions prevailing in the novel. As Bigger dramatizes the anger and pain of his race, the Daltons effectively represent the ruling white power structure. It is to Wright's credit that he does not give way to the temptation to create villains, but makes these whites generous, liberal, and humanitarian. It is ironic, of course, that even while giving a "chance" to Bigger and helping in ghetto programs, the Daltons are reaping the proceeds of ghetto housing. Appropriately, Wright uses the metaphor of blindness to characterize the attitude of the Daltons here as he will later to account for Max's failure to comprehend Bigger. But Bigger too is described as blind, because, in this world of *Native Son,* there is no real possibility of people seeing one another in clear human perspective. All the characters respond to one another as symbols rather than as people.

But Wright's use of the polarities of black and white symbolism are not limited to the literal and racial levels of the novel. The entire world of *Native Son,* as the story unfolds, is increasingly polarized into a symbolic black-white dichotomy. Especially during Part II, the snow which buries the city under a cold and hostile blanket of white becomes a more complicated manifestation of the white symbolism than that limited to the sociological level. At the same time, Bigger escapes not only into the black ghetto in search of safety and security, he seeks out the black interiors of abandoned buildings to hide both from the freezing snow and the death-dealing white mob. Finally, Bigger's flight ends with his being spread out against the white snow as though crucified.

It is not probable that Wright had heard of European existentialism when he wrote *Native Son,* so it is all the more remarkable that this novel should so clearly demonstrate concepts which anticipate Wright's embracing of the existentialist philosophy when he went to Europe in the late 1940's. Though Bigger very obviously commits the murder without premeditation, he quickly comes to the realization that somehow that act is the sum of his entire life. Rather than repudiating responsibility for his crime, or seeing himself as a victim of circumstances, either of which would be understandable, Bigger consciously and deliberately affirms the killing as the most creative act of his life. Whereas before he was in the position of constantly reacting—like the rat— he now sees himself as having responsibility for his own fate. Further, the world which before had seemed frighteningly ambiguous is now clearly revealed to him. For the first time in his life, Bigger has a positive sense of his own identity, and a concrete knowledge of how he relates to the world around him. Ironically, Max's case that Bigger is a victim of society threatens to deprive Bigger of the identity he has purchased at such terrible cost to himself, but, facing death at the end of the novel, he reaffirms his belief that he killed for something, and he faces death with the courage born of his one creative moment.

Wright's novel is not without faults, particularly the tedious final section in which Max argues a doctrinaire Marxist interpretation of Bigger's crime. Apparently, however, Wright himself could not fully accept this view, since Bigger's reaffirmation of responsibility contradicts Max's determinstic justification. In the final analysis, Bigger's insistence upon responsibility for his act demonstrates the human potential for freedom of act and will, and asserts human possibility in contrast to the Marxist vision of man as an animal trapped in a world he cannot control.

William E. Grant

NAUSEA

Type of work: Novel
Author: Jean-Paul Sartre (1905-   )
Type of plot: Philosophical realism
Time of plot: The 1930's
Locale: France
First published: 1938

In Nausea, *Sartre's first novel, the philosopher-novelist-dramatist delineates his Existentialist philosophy through a minute analysis of the interior life of Antoine Roquentin, a mild-mannered French historian. Roquentin experiences nausea and feels existence to be oppressive when he learns that life has no intrinsic meaning. Finding or* making *meaning thus becomes the object of Roquentin's life.*

Jean-Paul Sartre's name has become synonymous with Existentialism because he is the foremost proponent of that school of philosophy. His brilliant, wide-ranging mind, however, extends beyond philosophy to psychology, just as it chooses a variety of forms through which to express itself—including drama, film, the essay, and the novel. In *Nausea (La Nausée),* his first novel, Sartre used a diary format, with each entry carefully dated, almost as a parody of the historian's method; the novel, however, is a documented account not of world-shaking political events, but of one relatively unknown man's coming to grips with his own existence. Still, the diary format is convincing since its roots are firmly planted in realistic fictional techniques. It creates an aura of verisimilitude through Roquentin's first-person narration of his psychological disorientation.

The title of the novel, *Nausea,* is the key to Roquentin's disquietudes. The human condition, according to Existential philosophy, is characterized by alienation and anguish. In his writings, Sartre describes this state of being variously as an impervious mass or as a pliable substance, the latter being the case in *Nausea,* where life appears as an engulfing putty which overtakes and threatens to swallow Roquentin. The toxic nature of this metaphorical putty produces in Roquentin the alienation and consequent anguish which leads to what Sartre calls "nausea": a feeling of not being in touch with what others refer to as the real world. Is the problem exclusively psychological? Is Roquentin merely schizophrenic? The answer here must be "no," because Sartre's philosophy impinges upon characterization to make a didactic point past the demands of the novel.

Roquentin must cope with the Existential problems of his own life as well as those of others with whom he is involved. He must, for instance, confront the inevitability of change, as his early memory of Anny is shattered by the present reality of her fat and fickleness and venality. He must further reconcile himself to the preoccupation of others with their own Existential problems —a preoccupation which precludes their solicitous attention to his immediate needs. When Roquentin wants to bid fond adieu to his only two friends in Bouville, he finds one (The Self-Taught Man) unmasked as a homosexual and too harassed to notice Roquentin's departure; the other (Françoise) is so busy taking care of her café business that she can spare no more than a few seconds. As a result, Roquentin is left to his own devices and his own consolations, just as every other human being, according to Existential philosophy, is left alone to deal with his own existence on his own terms.

Sartre's Existential world is not a kind or compassionate one, yet it is not cruel. It is simply indifferent; but indifference may be the greatest cruelty of all. The humanist's tortured cry against the injustice of such a state of affairs —the Existentialist anguish—is unheeded in Sartre's unblinking look at life from an Existential viewpoint in *Nausea*. The novel rings true, our contrary wishes notwithstanding; therein lies its impact.

THE NAZARENE

Type of work: Novel
Author: Sholem Asch (1880-1957)
Type of plot: Religious chronicle
Time of plot: First and twentieth centuries
Locale: Poland, Italy, Palestine
First published: 1939

In order to present the life of Christ as an eyewitness account, Asch structures The Nazarene *on a series of flashbacks: Part One is related by Pan Viadomsky, a scholar living in the 1930's, who believes himself to be the reincarnation of the Hegemon of Jerusalem, Pilate's military governor. Part Two purports to be the Gospel according to Judah Ish-Kiriot; and Part Three is narrated by a young Jewish scholar, who imagines himself a reincarnation of Jochanan, a student under Nicodemon.*

Sholem Asch wrote *The Nazarene, The Apostle* (1943), and *Mary* (1949) as a trilogy chronicling the growth of Christianity and tracing its antecedents in the heritage of Judaism. From 1939 to 1949, he dedicated himself to the task of brilliantly portraying his conviction that Western culture grew from the twin roots of the Jewish and Christian faiths. All three novels, written originally in Yiddish and later translated into English, demonstrate Asch's erudition and scholarship, and his profound grasp of the spiritual unity between Christian and Jewish beliefs is extraordinary.

Asch is masterful in his realistic portrayal of character. The characterization of Pan Viadomsky, for example, is powerfully drawn. Independent, arrogant, and cruel, he hates the Jews and tries to discredit them. The portrait of Judah Ish-Kiriot is a sympathetic one; Asch gives the story of the man who betrays Christ for thirty pieces of silver a new twist. He presents Judah as a complex and disturbed person, who loves his Messiah but cannot say so, who believes in him fiercely yet objects to his tactics, who has waited all his life for the Savior and then betrays him when he comes. He is both learned and objective, unreasonable and jealous.

But perhaps the most memorable characterization is that of the Nazarene himself, Yeshua ben Joseph. His is the portrait of a man who vacillates, who is unsure of himself and afraid of the pain he must undergo to complete his mission. Asch skillfully shows the basic conflict within him; inasmuch as he has taken on the nature of man, he dreads suffering, while because of his Godlike nature, he knows both how intense his pain will be and how unavoidable it is. One of the most powerful scenes in the novel is that in which Yeshua struggles in the Garden of Gethsemane to overcome the weakness of the flesh and submit himself to the will of God.

The lives of these Biblical figures are given further dimension and humanity through the vividness and reality of their surroundings. Asch is a master of evocative description, as witnessed in the scene of Cornelius' entry into Jerusalem. The temple shines like a mass of molten gold in the setting sun; with its marble courts encircled with curtains fluttering in the breeze, its gateways, towers, and columns, it is a testimony of the Jew's reverence to the God of Israel, and a symbol of the ancient heritage of Christianity which Asch memorializes.

A NEST OF SIMPLE FOLK

Type of work: Novel
Author: Seán O'Faoláin (1900-   )
Type of plot: Regional chronicle
Time of plot: 1854-1916
Locale: Ireland
First published: 1933

Seán O'Faoláin must be ranked along with Sean O'Casey as one of the great chroniclers of the civil wars that ravaged Ireland in the late nineteenth and early twentieth centuries. And, like O'Casey, O'Faoláin describes the chaos, pain, folly, and passionate idealism of the period by focusing on the ways in which ordinary, believable people were affected by, and responded to, these traumatic events.

Seán O'Faoláin himself was active in the cause of Irish independence; during the fighting of the Irish Civil War he made bombs and hid from the police. After traveling in the United States, he returned to Ireland and was determined to capture her spirit in fiction. What had inspired him most in the wars was the fiery idealism of the Fenian movement, especially the way it raised average and even dissolute men to heights of self-sacrifice and bravery. But he was highly critical of the middle class, which he felt had sacrificed the cause of Irish Nationalism to a gross materialism. With the wiping away of the old aristocracy, Ireland had lost its traditional leadership, and the shopkeeper mentality of the postwar period could not sustain the promise of the Revolutionary days. O'Faoláin and Yeats were of one mind in their satirical contempt for the middle class.

In *A Nest of Simple Folk,* Leo Foxe-Donnell represents the old aristocratic ideal. Although a dissolute landowner and a reckless seducer of women, he is possessed by the Fenian spirit and risks his property and position by espousing the Revolutionary cause. When Denis is encouraged by his parents to be a scholar and observe conventional middle-class manners, he demurs and finally joins "old Leo" and the Revolution. His choice does not merely represent a political position. O'Faoláin's intention is to dramatize the son's rejection of the hypocrisy and self-interest of his father. Denis rejects the natural middle-class father for the dissolute Revolutionary one. Ireland's hope becomes the willingness of her youth to discard the new materialism for the old idealism.

In many of his novels and short stories O'Faoláin uses unconventional behavior to symbolize revolutionary idealism. For him the revolutionary is finally a possessed human being who points ways and cannot be expected to follow set paths.

NEW ATLANTIS

Type of work: Essay
Author: Sir Francis Bacon (1561-1626)
Type of plot: Utopian voyage
Time of plot: Sixteenth century
Locale: New Atlantis, an island in the Pacific Ocean
First published: 1627

The English Renaissance produced two classic treatments of the ideal state concept, Thomas More's Utopia *and Francis Bacon's* New Atlantis. *Since Bacon was both a devout believer and a great scientist, it is not surprising that his perfect society is based on a harmonious collaboration between religion and science.*

New Atlantis reflects Sir Francis Bacon's commitment to experimental curiosity and his devotion to order in the world. It is interesting to read his utopia with the idea that these two elements may either clash or harmonize. Often science has disturbed traditional beliefs by introducing society to discoveries which suddenly demand attention, and the changes that follow have often been painful and chaotic. This does not occur on New Atlantis because the island society's bond to Christianity is in no way threatened by its constant scientific explorations. Instead, Salomon's House, the scientific community, operates as a partner to the religious order.

This partnership produces an ideal unity rarely seen in actual societies. What stabilizes New Atlantis is the fact that its faith precedes and directs its scientific enterprises. Science is the junior partner, the appendage of religion. Each discovery supports rather than threatens the community because here relationships in the world, shown in physics or chemistry or elsewhere, are seen as examples of the presence of God. In this way the scientist sparks no revolution; he may, however, unveil complexities that perpetuate the inhabitants' view of a miraculous world. And so the science of this utopia pumps energy into its faith.

Considering the unified society it displays, Bacon's utopia is interesting to modern readers who live in a scientific age where empiricism and faith are generally opposed. Perhaps this contrast between our time, when nations are interdependent yet not in firm control of science, and the isolationism and reassuring science of a New Atlantis is what makes the study of utopias both fascinating and imperative as we examine the order of our world.

THE NEW GRUB STREET

Type of work: Novel
Author: George Gissing (1857-1903)
Type of plot: Social criticism
Time of plot: Nineteenth century
Locale: England
First published: 1891

The New Grub Street *is a portrait of the writing life in late-nineteenth century England. Gissing eschews popular sentimental and romantic views of the artistic world, presenting it simply as a business in which inspiration and talent are less important than persistence, aggressiveness, and self-merchandising. It is a milieu in which the mercenary Jasper Milvain succeeds, while the more honest and sensitive Edwin Reardon must fail.*

In his introduction to *The New Grub Street,* G. W. Stonier (1957) remarks that "Failure may not be more interesting than success, but at least it discovers more of the human situation. . . . " Without sentimentality and with stoical acceptance, Gissing chronicles the lives of writers, hacks to be more exact, who grind out their lives meeting publishers' deadlines and desperately waiting, as does Reardon, for the necessary inspiration to do something truly worthwhile. It never comes, in his case, and the rest of his life slips through his fingers while he waits.

Gissing's greatest bitterness is reserved for writers like Jasper Milvain, whose superficiality as artists and men, protects them from the crushing defeat inevitable for those who hold out for talent and lose. Jasper's eventual marriage to Amy, after Reardon's death, is a bittersweet, almost sardonic, touch. Amy, who could not remain "the wife of a clerk who is paid so much a week," leaves Reardon only to wind up at last the wife of a hypocrite who is literally a "clerk" type with no talent for more than hack pieces. But of course through clever manipulations Jasper has become an editor, a high earner.

Despite Gissing's melancholy sense of the hopelessness of most would-be writers ever succeeding to support themselves with a pen, his belief in talent and the true writer's industry and will to survive is charmingly captured in the portrait of Biffen. Biffen supports himself with giving language lessons and dreams of writing a realistic novel entitled "Mr. Bailey, Grocer": "There'll be nothing bestial in it, you know. . . . I shall do it slowly, lovingly."

Gissing hated the writer's life, but he did not hate writing itself. Even so, considering the facts of his mostly sordid life, it is remarkable that he published as much as he did.

THE NEW HÉLOÏSE

Type of work: Novel
Author: Jean Jacques Rousseau (1712-1778)
Type of plot: Philosophical romance
Time of plot: Early eighteenth century
Locale: Switzerland
First published: 1760

Julie: Or, The New Héloïse, *Rousseau's epistolary "seduction novel," is his major fictional attempt to reconcile the intuitive needs of the individual with the demands of an ordered society. To the modern reader, Rousseau's intentions seem more rhetorical than artistic, and the long philosophical digressions on education, natural love, the simple life, and man's innate goodness obscure the moving, passionate love affair between Julie d'Étange and Saint-Preux.*

Rousseau's *The New Héloïse,* published in Amsterdam to avoid French censorship, proved both an immediate success and a highly controversial object of attack. The mélange of long moral sermons, passionate rhetoric, and a current of strong sensuality provoked attacks by religious and philosophical authorities, and Rousseau was accused of self-contradiction, moral duplicity, and simple bad taste.

The model for the story is the historical romance between Peter Abélard, famed medieval scholar, and his pupil, Héloïse, which ended in tragedy and disgrace. Their story became legendary as a tragedy of love in conflict with the demands of society. The essential problem of the novel, then, is the relationship between the strongly self-centered, sexual motivations of the individual and the restraints of the social order.

In the first portion of the work, Saint-Preux and Julie are separated by the differences in rank and station, which are underscored by her father, who has promised her to another. The romance succeeds, however, in spite of the obstacles, and Julie first succumbs, then actively seeks union with Saint-Preux, becoming pregnant, though finally suffering a miscarriage and yielding to her father's will.

In the second section of the story, Julie, now under the tutelage of her husband, Wolmar, lives in a different sort of world, the estate at Clarens, where Wolmar's philosophical and educational principles seek to retrain the individual to desire that which is in harmony with the social order, rather than to struggle against it. Julie now becomes the ideal wife and mother, a model of virtue, claiming to be happy in all respects. Saint-Preux is subjected to a series of tests to measure the progress of his reeducation. He, too, succeeds in redirecting his will. Yet each of them is still vulnerable to the upwelling of passion from their past, and Julie's last letter confesses that she still loves Saint-Preux. Wolmar's virtuous society has only masked her passion and the basic problem is left unresolved.

A NEW WAY TO PAY OLD DEBTS

Type of work: Drama
Author: Philip Massinger (1583-1640)
Type of plot: Comedy of manners
Time of plot: Early seventeenth century
Locale: England
First presented: c. 1625

A new way to pay old debts is to use credit, of course. It is credit, seen in the actions of Lady Allworth, which enables the prodigal Wellborn to establish himself once again in the respectable world after having been cozened by his uncle, Sir Giles Overreach.

Although a prolific and workmanlike playwright, Massinger never achieved an outstanding individual style strong enough to distinguish him among his contemporaries or in theatrical history. Most of his serious plays, in fact, are now considered stale and tedious. After studying at Oxford, Massinger wrote plays in collaboration with Cyril Tourneur, John Fletcher, and Thomas Dekker; later he served for fifteen years as the principal playwright for Shakespeare's old company, the King's Men. *A New Way to Pay Old Debts* is clearly his one claim to enduring fame, having remained a popular histrionic vehicle to the present day. Sir Thomas Jay called the play admirable for "the crafty mazes of the cuning plot; / The polish'd phrase; the sweet expression; got / Neither by theft nor violence; the conceit / Fresh and unsullied." The plot, though not particularly original, is lively; and Sir Giles Overreach, a favorite with lead actors, was probably based on Sir Giles Mompessen (1584-1651), who had commissions from James I for controlling licenses to innkeepers and who, along with his legal associate Francis Michel (Marrall in the play), was prosecuted in 1621 and convicted in a shameful footnote to British legal history.

At the opening of the play, the scene in which Wellborn's fair-weather friends spurn the spendthrift nobleman in his time of need is reminiscent of Shakespeare's *Timon of Athens,* though much more realistically convincing because of the everyday scale of events. The themes of this comedy of manners are no more complicated than the plot, though they are nonetheless valid and convincingly handled. Overreach represents the senseless desire of the *nouveau riche* bourgeoisie to attain nobility, a desire which is paradoxical when accompanied by his disdain of the nobility's philosophical inability to fend successfully for themselves in the new mercantile world of common law. Lovell, then, is pitted against Sir Giles; birth and inherited riches are set against wealth won by individual industry. Overreach's complete lack of principle and scruple contrasts him with Lovell, but also makes him a much more interesting character. The scene between father and daughter, reminiscent of Jonson's *Volpone,* is the clearest presentation of the bourgeois willingness to make any means practicable for a determined end: "End me no ends," her father will later tell Margaret (5.1), echoing his words in this scene, "Virgin me no virgins!" (3.2) Moreover, Massinger neatly emphasizes the way in which Overreach—through the complicity of Greedy—sets about corrupting the very law he professes, to suit his vicious purpose. The avarice at the heart of the action is a satirical reflection of the central motivation of contemporary society as Massinger views it.

Overreach is the main character, whose forceful personality dominates the stage even when he is not there; scenes without him pale in dramatic interest by comparison; we wait only for him to return, to outrage us again even more. His explanation to Margaret recalls Marlowe's Barabas (in *The Jew of Malta*): "Was 't not to make thee great / That I have now, and still pursue, those ways / That hale down curses on me, which I mind not?" (3.2) Margaret, however, is obviously nothing more to her father than an object, a pawn he can move to his own will. Nobility of blood means nothing to her, everything to him—who can never know it. He is so vulgar that he has no understanding even of the spiritual nobility Margaret strives to maintain in the face of his demands that she prostitute herself freely to Lovell: "Stand not on form," he tells her in an echo of Falstaff, "words are no substances" (3.2). Just as Greedy values only what he can taste, Overreach treasures only what he can touch—and reach, physically. His relationship with Marrall, as it unfolds, proves that there is not even honor among thieves in this world. His bombastic boorishness is reflected with perfect irony when, expecting Lovell, he asks of Marrall, "Is the loud music I gave order for / Ready to receive him?" (3.2) The louder, in his uncultured opinion, the more impressive. His brazen, pompous overtures to Lovell in Act IV shock even our experienced sensibilities; we see clearly that he and the nobleman are two entirely different kinds of animals, and we may be a little uneasy to wonder which species most resembles our own. The catharsis for our sensibilities occurs shortly thereafter when young Allworth manages to gull Sir Giles, with one of his own characteristic legal tricks: "Good Master Allworth, / This shall be the best's night work you ever made". (4.3) From this point on we happily enjoy the pathetic spectacle of Overreach's fiscal and mental dissolution, until he is carried away in the outward shambles that finally correspond to his immoral being.

Not nearly as interesting are the other characters, though Justice Greedy is unforgettably entertaining as perhaps the most "compleat glutton" in stage history. Self-styled "arch-president of the boil'd, the roast, the bak'd," he is epitomized by Furnace: "His stomach's as insatiate as the grave." It is one of the most delightful comic ironies of the play that Greedy cannot eat the dinner he prepares with such anxiety lest the fawn not be roasted with "a Norfolk dumpling in its belly." Centered around Greedy are the uniformly sympathetic low-life characters of the cooks, butlers, and household attendants of the Lady Allworth. By comparison with her servants, the Lady herself is flat and uninteresting. Her advice to Allworth, in fact an uncannily accurate memory of her husband's dying advice to his son, makes her sound like a latter-day Polonius: "Beware ill company, for often men / Are like to those with whom they do converse." She, like the nondescript Lovell, is as dramatically superficial as she is morally shallow; she is worried more about appearances than realities, the very opposite of Overreach. In her own subtle way she sells herself as surely to Lovell as Overreach would have Margaret do.

Her son, too, is almost tiresomely virtuous, at his worst when he vows to his mother that he will serve Lovell loyally (1.2). She is all too right in calling him "like virgin parchment, capable of any/Inscription" and we wish that he were inscribed with more vivid ink. One of the great laughs of the play is Lovell's reaction to Allworth's simpering reception of his commission: "Nay, do not melt (4.1). Wellborn has at least a streak of the devil in him to make him interesting, though he has not the dramatic force we would expect from the pivotal figure in the plot. His undisclosed whispering to Lady Allworth in Act I, sc. 3, sets the wheels in motion that lead to the downfall of Overreach by his own trickery. More successful is the character of Marrall, who has the virtue of being a thoroughly despicable parasite without the partially redeeming intelligent self-irony of Jonson's Mosca. Marrall is, bluntly speaking, a hick out of his own depth; this is portrayed riotously in Amble's report of his toasting the Lady "in white broth"—and humbly thanking "my worship" for serving him wine. Marrall, in the end, becomes an exaggerated caricature of his own meanness as he offers to let Wellborn ride upon his own back and says, over-elaborately, "an it like your worship, / I hope Jack Marrall shall not live so long / To prove himself such an unmannerly beast . . . / As to be cover'd / When your worship's present (2.3)." We have no more sympathy for him than Wellborn does. And we are delighted when Wellborn, having paid his own old debts with credit, cancels Marrall's credit rating as the knave deserves.

Kenneth John Atchity

THE NEWCOMES

Type of work: Novel
Author: William Makepeace Thackeray (1811-1863)
Type of plot: Social criticism
Time of plot: Early nineteenth century
Locale: England
First published: 1853-1855

The Newcomes *is a family chronicle in which Thackeray demonstrates the evil effects of such nineteenth century social conventions as parental marriage choices, the over-indulgence in the accumulation of wealth, and the worldliness of the upper classes. Many consider Colonel Newcome to be Thackeray's most perfect fictional gentlemen, and the notion of the true gentleman is central to the ideals of social behavior Thackeray is attempting to illustrate.*

"I am about a new story," Thackeray wrote an American friend shortly after his first visit to the United States (1852-1853), "but don't know as yet if it will be any good. It seems to me I am too old for story-telling. . . . " Although at forty-three Thackeray was certainly not in his dotage, he had already behind him the success of *Vanity Fair* (1847-1848), *Pendennis* (1849-1850), and *Henry Esmond* (1852), his strength seemed to ebb, and to his friends he had the physical appearance of an old man broken in health. Nevertheless, he needed money ($20,000 was his estimate) so he began writing *The Newcomes,* often in ill health, throughout various places in Italy, Germany, and Switzerland, and published the novel serially, the first number in October 1853, the last in August 1855. Extensive even by Victorian standards, *The Newcomes* is a typical mid-nineteenth century family chronicle, detailed with cogent observation of manners and morals. Above all, in spite of its gentle comedy, it satirizes human follies that Thackeray particularly scorned: snobbery, greed, and misguided romantic idealism.

The chronicle is narrated by Arthur Pendennis, an older friend of Clive Newcome, who purports to "edit" the memoirs of "a most respectable family." At first a mere spokesman for the author, Pendennis gradually becomes a character in his own right, participating in, as well as commenting upon, the action. Prudish, smug, and whimsical, Pendennis provides an ironical insight into the other characters. His admiration for Colonel Newcome ("so chivalrous, generous, good looking") is uncritical to the point that it becomes amusing. Moreover, his fulminations upon folly, especially in the famous parody of moral anecdotes in Chapter 1, ring hollow at last, in view of the narrator's own punctilious regard for class and status, his social snobbery, his moralizing.

Typical of Thackeray's fiction, the heroes and heroines of the novel (Colonel Thomas Newcome, his son Clive, and Ethel and Rosey) are true-blue, the villains (Barnes Newcome, Lady Kew, and Mrs. Mackenzie) quite dastardly.

Yet even some of the unpleasant characters are redeemed, not always convincingly, by the author's pity. Barnes Newcome, the Colonel's longtime nemesis, is humiliated in the family election, promises to mistreat his wife no longer, and finally comes to terms with Clive. The cold-hearted Lady Kew leaves the bulk of her estate to Ethel. And Ethel herself, psychologically the most interesting personality in the book, develops from a charming but calculating young lady to a woman capable of self-sacrifice and deepest love. Unlike Rosey—simple, innocent, but vacuous—Ethel is sophisticated and clever. Her virtue, tested in life, is consequently earned. She becomes a worthy mate for Clive, and the tender author promises his readers that the couple will be both happy and wealthy.

As for Clive, he must also earn the reader's approval. Spoiled by his doting father, he makes the most of his good looks, his modest talents as an artist, and the honorable reputation of his family. Yet his young manhood is wasted in prodigality. Thwarted in his desire to marry Ethel, he chooses as second best the sweet but dull Rosey Mackenzie, then chafes at the restraints of wedlock. Nevertheless, like Ethel, he is educated by life, learns his limitations, and grows in self-respect. In Chapter 68, the emotional climax of the novel, Clive and his father come to regard each other as equals, man to man, without recriminations but with mutual respect and affection. Clive comes into his own as a person of worth, a gentleman.

Indeed, *The Newcomes* is a social novel of manners that teaches the Victorian reader how to recognize and, if possible become, a true gentleman (or gentle-lady). Colonel Newcome, the epitome of English gentility, may be a triumph of Grundyism—provincial morality—but the character is probably a bore to most modern readers. Too nearly perfect—that is to say, too proper, innocent, and augustly virtuous—his very rectitude becomes a subject for unconscious satire. As a matter of fact, some of Thackeray's reviewers detected in the author's creation of the Colonel an element of cynicism; one reviewer for *The Times*, London, went so far as to attack the book on the grounds of "morality and religion." But Thackeray's avowed intention was certainly not to satirize the true gentleman and his outmoded virtues. Rather, it was to expose the parvenu, the snob, the ingrate. He ridicules the upstart middle class, especially Anglo-Indian, society: ill-bred, vulgarly assertive, graspingly materialistic.

Above all, the thrust of Thackeray's satire is toward women rather than men. Barnes Newcome is a rascal, to be sure, but not a fool. However, Thackeray's obnoxious women manipulate their men, lead them into folly, either through their aggressiveness or their simpering, smiling domestic tyranny. "Theirs is a life of hypocrisy," concludes Pendennis, speaking for his author; and their chief wile is flattery. Even Ethel, the virtuous and clever heroine, does not wholly escape Thackeray's censure. When he criticizes her for prolonging her romance with Clive, he lays her weakness to a fault of her sex, rather than to a personal folly, and thereby partly "excuses" her. As for Rosey, Clive's unfortunate wife, she never transgresses the social prohibitions but is, like Amelia of *Vanity Fair,* a foolish innocent, to be protected and cherished like a pet. Her opposite is her mother, Mrs. Mackenzie, a tigress when cornered, truly a mean and fearful specimen of womankind.

Nevertheless, the reader's final impression of *The Newcomes* is not one of abrasive social satire, no matter how archly Thackeray pursues the objects of his chastisement. Rather it is one of reconciliation. At the end of the novel, Ethel and Clive are reunited. The good Colonel Newcome dies nobly as he had lived, a scene that is touching in its restrained dignity. And the reader hopes that the Newcome family, in spite of human folly, will endure. To Thackeray that hope, "Fable-land," is the harmless anodyne to the pain of living.

Leslie B. Mittleman

THE NIBELUNGENLIED

Type of work: Saga
Author: Unknown
Type of plot: Heroic epic
Time of plot: The Germanic legend, with the Burgundian story added from historical events
of about 437
Locale: North Central Europe
First transcribed: c. 1200

Chief among the battle sagas of Germanic peoples, The Nibelungenlied *has merged and remerged with countless other legends and myths. In it are echoes of the ancient worship of the pagan gods along with elements of Christian ritual, as well as tales, like the battle of Siegfried and the dragon, that go back to prehistoric myths. Even in the modern era, the saga persists in poetry, music, and fiction.*

The material which forms the subject matter of the Germanic heroic epics is derived from historical events which became part of an oral tradition and were passed down, sometimes for centuries, in the form of sagas, before being established in written form. The historical events which lie behind the Nibelung saga are to be found in the fifth and sixth centuries, the period of the tribal wanderings at the end of the Roman Empire. The Burgundians, under King Gundahari, whose capital was at Worms, were in fact destroyed by the Huns in 437. The Siegfried figure is probably of Merovingian origin and may derive from an intermarriage between the Burgundian and Frankish royal houses. The record of these events mingled with purely legendary elements is preserved in a number of works: besides the *Nibelungenlied,* the Scandinavian *Older Edda* of the ninth century is the most important. It was upon this latter source rather than the Germanic version that Richard Wagner based his four-part music drama, *The Ring of the Nibelung.* There are four main themes in the·saga tradition: the adventures of the young Siegfried, Siegfried's death, the destruction of the Burgundians, and the death of Attila. These elements occurred as separate works in the early stages of composition. In the present version of the saga composed by an anonymous German author around the year 1200, the various elements are woven together into a unified plot, linking the death of Siegfried with the destruction of the Burgundians through the motive of revenge. Traces of the older separate versions are evident, however, in such inner inconsistencies as the transformation of the character of Kriemhild, who appears initially as a model courtly figure, but becomes the bloodthirsty avenger of her husband's death in the second part. It is a mark of the artistic talent of the anonymous author that he fuses the core episodes with such care, and achieves a plausible and aesthetically satisfying work.

The *Nibelungenlied* is the product of the brilliant period of the Hohenstaufen dynasty of the Holy Roman Empire, a time when the courtly culture of Germany was at its height. The poet was probably of Austrian origin: the importance of the splendid court at Vienna and the noble figure of Bishop Pilgrim of Passau indicate that the poet may have enjoyed the patronage of these courts. That the poet remains anonymous is a tradition of the heroic epic form, evolving from the anonymous court singer of the wandering Germanic tribes. Whereas the writers of Arthurian epics and religious epics name themselves and often discuss their work in a prologue, the composer of the heroic epic remains outside his work, presenting his material more as history and without the self-conscious comments and digressions found in works such as *Parzival* or *Tristan and Isolde,* both of whose poets name themselves and go into some detail regarding their intentions and artistic conceptions. The work, which was written in four-line stanzas, bears the signs of its history of oral presentation—frequent repetition of rhyme words, the use of formulaic descriptions and filler lines, and general looseness of composition. The poem was not conceived as a written work, but represents a written record of an oral performance tradition. Even after assuming written form, the work would be read aloud to an audience, books being a scarce and expensive commodity in this period.

The purpose of the work, like that of courtly poetry in general, was to mirror courtly society itself in its splendor, color, and activity, and to present within that framework images of an idealized world in which larger than life figures act out the social rituals of the time and provide for the audience models of courtly behavior, of honor, fortitude, and noble bearing under great stress. Repeatedly in the work one observes long passages devoted to description of the festivities of the court, banquets, tournaments, processions, all filled with details of clothing and jewelry, splendid utensils and weapons. Questions of etiquette and precedence provide some of the central conflicts of the work while the lyrical episodes of the love between Siegfried and Kriemhild may be seen as an embodiment of the idealized conception of love celebrated by the Minnesänger. Although the grim events of the old dramatic saga material at times conflict with the more cultivated ideal of the thirteenth century, the poet succeeds even here in transforming the traditional material. Elements related to fairy-tale tradition—the stories of Siegfried's youth, the battle with the dragon, the magic aura surrounding Brünhild on her island— are largely suppressed.

The idealizing elements are developed, both in the first part, where Siegfried and Kriemhild stand out brightly against the menacing forces of the Burgundian court, especially Hagen, and in the second part, where, in spite of the atmosphere of betrayal and carnage, the high points are moments of fortitude and courage and the preservation of ethical integrity. Rüdiger, who finds himself torn between feudal loyalty to King Etzel and his loyalty and friendship for the Burgundians, to one of whom his daughter is engaged, is one of the greatest of these figures. The episode in which he finds himself obliged to fight against the Burgundian Gernot, to whom he has given the sword which now will kill him, is one of the most poignant scenes in the work.

The chain of crime and revenge finds cessation and resolution only in the lament for the fallen warriors, and it is in this tragic sense of the inevitable suffering that follows joy that the work preserves its links to the ancient Germanic heroic outlook, establishing its individuality against the more generally optimistic outlook of the Arthurian sagas. Here the fatalistic confrontation with destructive forces is opposed to the affirmation of order and the delight of life typical of much literature of the Hohenstaufen period. It is the tension between these two attitudes that provides much of the power of the work and lifts it into the realm of universal validity.

Steven C. Schaber

NICHOLAS NICKLEBY

Type of work: Novel
Author: Charles Dickens (1812-1870)
Type of plot: Sentimental romance
Time of plot: Early nineteenth century
Locale: England
First published: 1838-1839

In spite of a general disorganization and confusion in the plotting and the relative simplicity of the characterizations, Nicholas Nickleby *remains one of Dickens' finest early triumphs by virtue of its energy, comedy, and social realism. His portrayal of Wackford Squeers's mismanaged private school, based upon firsthand research, stimulated much public discussion and indignation, and eventually led to important reforms.*

Although Prime Minister Gladstone and Thomas Arnold, headmaster of Rugby, objected to *Nicholas Nickleby* on the grounds that the novel was insufficiently edifying, most Victorian readers—including Dickens' rival, Thackeray—admired it; from its initial sale of 50,000 copies, the book was one of Dickens' triumphs. The first of his novels in which the love story is the main subject, *Nicholas Nickleby* still retains many picaresque elements that appeared in *The Pickwick Papers* (1836-1837) and *Oliver Twist* (1837-1838). The characters still tend to be eccentrics dominated by a single passion (almost in the manner of Ben Jonson's "humors" characters, although lacking Jonson's theory of the psychology of humors); the minor characters in particular seem to be grotesques. Yet there is a vitality in the farcical elements of the novel which is delightful, despite the excesses. The influence of Smollett, both in the comedy and the tendency to realistic detail, is still strong in this early novel; Dickens' greatest strength in *Nicholas Nickleby* lies in the marvelous descriptions of people and places. The influence of melodramas still colors the plot, but Dickens breathes new life into old stock situations.

Even if the melodramatic and episodic structure of *Nicholas Nickleby* is unoriginal, confusing, and improbable, the comedy and vitality of the book are the result of genius. One feels the tremendous force of life, of the changing times, of youth and growth, on every page. Tales within tales seem to blossom; countless life stories crowd the chapters. It is a young man's creation, indignant, farcical, and romantic in turn; and it is filled with vivid scenes. At this stage of his career, Dickens was still attempting to provide something for everybody.

Yet because of his complicated, melodramatic plot, Dickens was not wholly successful in working out the psychology of the novel. As critic Douglas Bush has observed, the characters of Dickens' early fiction are given over to self-dramatization. Mrs. Nickleby, in particular, evades the responsibilities of her troubled life by nearly withdrawing into her blissful vision of the past. As she sees herself, she is a romantic heroine, although her admirer is only a lunatic neighbor who throws cucumbers over the wall. Like many other characters of the book—among them Vincent Crummles, Smike, and Nicholas himself—she is isolated in her own imagination, locked in an often inimical world. Her eccentricity, like that of most of the minor characters, is an outward symbol of estrangement from the hostile social mechanisms of convention, order, and mysterious power. Nicholas succeeds in love and fortune, not so much by his own resources, but through chance—good luck with the Cheeryble brothers, for example—and through his own amiable disposition. At this point in his development as a novelist, Dickens was unable to create—as he eventually would in David Copperfield, Pip, and other protagonists—a hero who is fully aware of his isolation and confronts his sense of guilt. So the reader must accept Nicholas on the level of the author's uncomplicated psychology: as a genial, deserving fellow whose good luck, good friends, and honest nature reward him with happiness, affection, and prosperity.

NICK OF THE WOODS

Type of work: Novel
Author: Robert Montgomery Bird (1806-1854)
Type of plot: Adventure romance
Time of plot: 1782
Locale: Kentucky
First published: 1837

Robert Montgomery Bird combines an exciting chase-and-capture adventure-romance with a realistic presentation of frontier life in Kentucky during the 1780's. His hero, Nathan Slaughter, is both a fascinating, if extreme, psychological study and a vivid early example of the secret hero of popular literature—the man of unknown identity who simply appears to rescue the weak from danger.

For many years after its initial publication in 1837, *Nick of the Woods* was one of the most famous and popular nineteenth century historical romances, both as a novel and as a series of dramatic adaptations. This popularity was well deserved. *Nick of the Woods* is above all a superb adventure novel. Utilizing the chase-capture-escape pattern developed by James Fenimore Cooper and others, Bird tells an exciting story of Indian warfare, villainy, treachery, and violence in a series of vivid, suspenseful action scenes along with several moments of intense personal drama.

However, the novel also shows the characteristic flaws of the form: an insipid and improbable romance between banal lovers; an excess of melodramatic, artificial plot complexity; and an overabundance of exaggerated, sentimental language. But none of these seriously divert the force and excitement of the adventure narrative.

Nick of the Woods is, however, more than just escapist adventure fare. In the first third of the book Bird succeeds in painting a realistic picture of life on the Kentucky frontier in the late eighteenth century. And, if his aristocratic personages are stereotypes, his frontier characters are realistic and vivid.

The most fascinating and powerful character in the novel is Nathan Slaughter, a supposedly nonviolent Quaker who is revealed in the end to be the "Jibbenainosay." The idea of a pacifist who, unknown even to himself, is periodically transformed into a bloodthirsty and invincible avenger may strike modern readers as trite. But the author's skill in developing and presenting the character makes him understandable and impressive.

Bird, a medical doctor with a serious interest in abnormal psychology, bases the split in his hero's personality on Nathan's inability to reconcile his deeply rooted nonviolent convictions with the experience of seeing his entire family murdered by Indians. Thus, Bird provides both an organic (he was scalped in the attack) and a psychological explanation for the Quaker's double nature.

This split in Slaughter's personality was, to Bird, an extreme example of man's basic duality. To the nonromantic doctor, proximity to nature, far from bringing out any innate nobility, provokes man's worst qualities and excesses. Therefore, since the Indian was closest to nature, he was the most animal-like of humans, with a basic savagery that not only delighted in unprovoked attacks on innocent settlers, but even took pleasure in the killing of women and children.

It is this aspect of the novel that has been most criticized, and Bird, himself, conceded his view to be an extreme one. But he felt it a necessary corrective to the "noble savage" sentiments of Cooper and others, and one that was much closer to the real experience of the American frontier.

NIELS LYHNE

Type of work: Novel
Author: Jens Peter Jacobsen (1847-1885)
Type of plot: Psychological realism
Time of plot: Nineteenth century
Locale: Denmark
First published: 1880

Niels Lyhne *is a sober, poetic, intense chronicle of one man's unsuccessful lifelong search for a center and meaning to his life. Although the novel has a number of strong scenes and vivid confrontations, the primary action of the book happens within the carefully delineated characters, especially that of the disillusioned protagonist.*

Jacobsen's original plan for *Niels Lyhne* dealt with a novel titled *The Atheist,* incorporating the historical impact of atheism on European youth between 1830 and 1865. But as he worked on the book, his approach changed. He decided that the atheistic material would be included only insofar as it was necessary for the understanding of the people, which was for him the main aspect of a novel. *Niels Lyhne* came to be a study of the struggle of a man to unite two portions of his personality, that which embraced fantasy and that which craved the solidity of reality. Although little-known in America, it is considered one of the great novels in European literature.

The struggle began in Niels Lyhne's childhood, his mother telling him fairy stories, trying to protect him from reality in the person of his father, a wornout believer in the intellect, a man who once had seemed to be romantic, but soon settled down to a complacent existence. As the child grew older, the struggle became more intense. Mr. Bigum, Niels's tutor, a fascinating and brilliant character, wanders through life congratulating himself on his own brilliance, smirking because nobody else suspects the riches that must dwell within him. The foolish Bigum makes his contribution to the essential flabbiness of Niels's nature; the boy Niels observes, learns, and dreams, and is seemingly surrounded by dreamers, people who avoid staring at the nakedness of truth. *Niels Lyhne* is a naturalistic novel in that it takes great pains to show the hereditary and social forces which mold the protagonist. But the story of Niels Lhyne is much more complex than any naturalistic formula. Jacobsen's famous style is often dazzling, with its cool precision and rich ornamentation and intensity, but it is Jacobsen's insight into human feelings which gives the book its greatness, even more than its memorable prose.

Jacobsen possessed a gift for freezing a moment in time, like a frame from a movie. Symbols enrich the power and meaning of the novel, from the beginning to the end, but few are as significant as the plaster cast of the hand holding an egg which Fennimore finds on the garbage heap and then smashes.

This event seems to foreshadow the end of the relationship among the three: Erik, the artist, Fennimore, his wife, and Niels. The author's description of Fennimore's reaction when Erik is killed, and the depth of his insight into her mental state, is extraordinary. It is significant that it is on the ice where Fennimore tells Niels of Erik's death—and that they both burn with the cold reality of their guilt. If the entire book can be said to burn with emotion, it is with the fierceness of ice.

Throughout his life, Niels cannot face reality. He invents his relationships with his friends as a youth, and as he grows older, still seeks refuge in fantasies. Even his atheism is a kind of escape for him, and when put to the test, his son's deathbed, he fails. Erik Refstruf, the artist, is more of a realist than Niels, producing statues and pictures while Niels dreams of writing poetry. The women Niels encounters in his life are all different and all portrayed with amazing insight. But none of them can help Niels; he must save himself if he is to be saved, and, ultimately, he fails. He never learned that while you can deceive others, you never can successfully cheat yourself. The philosophical and psychological insights of *Niels Lyhne,* and the beauty of its composition, place it high in the ranks of Danish and European literature.

THE NIGGER OF THE NARCISSUS

Type of work: Novel
Author: Joseph Conrad (Józef Teodor Konrad Korzeniowski, 1857-1924)
Type of plot: Psychological romance
Time of plot: Nineteenth century
Locale: Bombay to London
First published: 1897

The crew of the Narcissus, *isolated at sea, becomes a microcosm of humanity, and the "Nigger," James Wait, is both a tormented individual and a symbolic presence. Wait's impending death forces the crew, as well as the victim, to face their own mortality in one of the most intense and profound short novels ever written.*

In his Preface to *The Nigger of the Narcissus* Conrad speaks of art as a descent within man to the complexity and vulnerability beneath the surface, and in the novel he relentlessly explores the ambiguities which are at the heart of human commitment and compassion. Conrad says that he wishes to make us hear, feel, and "before all" see that ineffable "part of our being which is not dependent on wisdom."

The novel is narrowly circumscribed and confined. Not only do we leave behind the land, but we further descend into the microcosmic life of the forecastle. In this pressurized world, Conrad presents an analysis that is so concentrated, from Wait's boarding until his burial, that it almost becomes a parable of human fear, courage, and fellowship.

The central premise of the novel is James Wait's overpowering fear of death. Unable to face his fatal illness, Wait paradoxically transforms himself into a malingerer, who imposes on all around him, as a way of hiding the truth from himself. His name is a pun both on his reluctance to die and the burden he is to his peers. Correspondingly, the sailors react alternately with deep compassion and indignant suspicion. They long to help, but fear being duped by the generosity of their response. The crew collectively is man, isolated and inarticulate, sharing in the fear of death and struggling for the courage both to live and die. In the storm, each shows the capacity to rise above his fears and brave out primal dangers, but, as soon as the storm has ended, they are thrust back into the perplexity and immobility of self-concern which Wait epitomizes.

Finally, as Wait's body is being slid overboard, there is a final hesitation when something catches. The novel's ambiguities converge as Belfast poignantly crystallizes the fundamental issues in his frantic plea: "Jimmy, be a man! Go!"

NIGHT FLIGHT

Type of work: Novel
Author: Antoine de Saint-Exupéry (1900-1944)
Type of plot: Psychological realism
Time of plot: Early 1930's
Locale: South America
First published: 1931

This slim novel concerning the early days on the mail routes of South America deals with the dangers and difficulties of flying at night. Written largely from personal experience, in a dense, evocative, lyrical style, Saint-Exupéry combines poetic, philosophical reflections with sympathetic, realistic portrayals of dedicated men of action under great and continual stress.

When *Night Flight* was first published in 1931, most reviewers agreed that it was the beautiful poetic prose which gripped the imagination of the reader. Still the favorable impact which the novel had upon its readers was certainly also the result of an intensely intimate relationship between Saint-Exupéry and his subject. The author was an aviator and writer who looked at challenge and adventure through the eyes of a poet. The diction of the work reflects his experience of the glamor and terror of night flying as well as the metaphysical implications of abandoning one's spirit to fate.

Yet even when the reader is caught up in the musings of Fabien, the pilot, he is aware of the reality of the situation and the concrete facts of the plane's journey through the stormy night. Saint-Exupéry uses the airplane as the instrument around which to fashion a brief story about man and his extraordinary efforts to accomplish difficult tasks. His greatest praise is reserved for those of individual courage and steadfastness in pursuit of a worthwhile goal. Certainly Saint-Exupéry sees the pilots like Fabien and Pellerin as heroic, but his principal attention and sympathy is directed to the man who must stay on the ground, Rivière. The director must not only deal with the elements, the treacherous hazards of night flying, but he must also be a master psychologist, demanding discipline from his pilots and comforting their wives without losing control. If the author recognizes one basic element in heroism it is discipline, the discipline of oneself and that which is at one's disposal, whether it be men or machines. Indeed it is the same kind of restraint applied to artistic matters, those of style, character, and plot, which is Saint-Exupéry's major achievement.

A NIGHT IN THE LUXEMBOURG

Type of work: Novelette
Author: Rémy de Gourmont (1858-1915)
Type of plot: Rationalized mysticism
Time of plot: Early twentieth century
Locale: Paris
First published: 1906

At the time of its publication, this novelette was considered by many to be shocking, indecent, and blasphemous. This reaction was primarily due to the character of "He," an ambiguously Christ-like figure, who offers an Epicurean religion that emphasizes personal pleasure and living for the moment as a substitute for Christianity, a religion which, "He" insists, has been disastrous for mankind.

A member of the nineteenth century Symbolist School in France, Rémy de Gourmont in *Le Livre de Masques (The Book of Masques)* was one of the earliest critics to call attention to such later famous symbolists as J.-K. Huysmans and Stéphane Mallarmé. Gourmont's own art and thought were influenced by the symbolists. His two best-known works in English translation are *A Night in the Luxembourg* and *A Virgin Heart* (1907).

Classed as a novelette or novella, *A Night in the Luxembourg* is little more than a series of conversations, principally between the mysterious "He" and the journalist Sandy Rose whose original French name was Louis Dela-colombe. Both names are symbolic since the rose and the dove (*colombe*) have long symbolized love. The two words *rose* and *dove* appear frequently throughout the book like *leitmotivs* in a Wagner opera.

Dressed like a contemporary French gentleman, "He" yet seems to Rose to resemble conventional artistic portrayals of Jesus. As revealed in his conversation, however, he appears in his thought to be a more generalized inspirer of men of varied faiths throughout the ages. "I am not God," he says. "I am only a god." His philosophy concerning human life, with its emphasis on the virtue of being happy and the importance of living each moment as if it were eternal, is Epicurean. His favorite moral philosophers, he tells Rose, were Epicurus, who found happiness in pleasure, and Spinoza, who found fulfillment in asceticism.

Perhaps it was in part the reader identification of the physically Christ-like "He" with Jesus himself that brought forth the condemnation of *A Night in the Luxembourg* as a wicked, profane, and blasphemous book. "He" enunciates a philosophy which stresses love, but it is not the generalized love of mankind traditionally associated with Jesus. Rather, the love "He" speaks of is erotic, and this aroused the anger of both Catholics and Protestants. Also, "He" regrets and even scorns the conventional Christian denial of the fleshly joys of love. This seemed unforgivable to conservative Christians of the early twentieth century. Even in the latter part of the century, with its more lenient view of worldly pleasures, many Christians would be offended by Sandy Rose's strange friend. As Arthur Ransome announces in his translator's preface, *A Night in the Luxembourg* was written for a special group of readers. The book was intended for those who, like Rose, are skeptical and inquisitive, willing to question beliefs that have long been accepted as "true." One might remember that Emerson, a very different moral philosopher from de Gourmont, advised in "Self-Reliance": "He who would gather immortal palms must not be hindered by the name of goodness, but must explore if it be goodness. Nothing is at last sacred but the integrity of your own mind."

NIGHTMARE ABBEY

Type of work: Novel
Author: Thomas Love Peacock (1785-1866)
Type of plot: Social satire
Time of plot: Early nineteenth century
Locale: England
First published: 1818

Thomas Love Peacock created the novel of talk, a formula for satirizing literary and social fads, that has been frequently copied (especially by Aldous Huxley) but never duplicated. A group of eccentrics, mostly thinly disguised caricatures of contemporary celebrities, is gathered at a house party where they talk brilliantly, behave farcically, and, by the novel's end, pair up romantically. In Nightmare Abbey *Peacock utilizes this formula to perfection.*

Like Jane Austen's *Sense and Sensibility,* Thomas Love Peacock's *Nightmare Abbey* satirizes Gothic fiction, the popular and often meretricious writing that was contemporary with the best of Romantic poetry. But his satire is richer than hers because he is not restricted by the conventions of the novel of manners. His book is actually a parody: it ridicules Gothic fiction by outgothicizing it. Few Gothic novels can approach Peacock's secret passages and mysterious maidens.

J. B. Priestley calls *Nightmare Abbey* "one of the best literary satires in the language," and so it is. Its power emanates from a very clever ruse. Although it is a parody of Gothic fiction, the brunt of its satire is directed against the ideas and poses of the major Romantic poets. Peacock murders by association. In Mr. Flosky, Gothic spiritualism is identified with metaphysical obscurity: He "unintentionally" finds himself "within the limits of common sense," and he "never (gives) a plain answer to a question." Mr. Flosky is a thinly disguised Samuel Taylor Coleridge. Peacock has him announce: "This distinction between fancy and imagination is one of the most abstruse and important points of metaphysics. I have written several hundred pages to elucidate it. . . ." The *Biographia Literaria,* where Coleridge's famous chapter on the distinction between imagination and fancy first appeared, was published a year before *Nightmare Abbey.*

Peacock is just as hard on Byron, who in the person of Mr. Cypress, is ridiculed for excesses of melancholy and iconoclasm: " . . . a man who has quarrelled with his wife is absolved from all duty to his country. I have written an ode to tell the people as much, and they may take it as they list." And finally Shelley's involvement with Harriet Westbrook, the innkeeper's daughter, and Mary Godwin, the philosopher's daughter, is the basis of Scythrop's dual infatuation with Marionetta and Stella.

NINETEEN EIGHTY-FOUR

Type of work: Novel
Author: George Orwell (Eric Blair, 1903-1950)
Type of plot: Political satire
Time of plot: 1984
Locale: London
First published: 1949

Nineteen Eighty-Four *along with Aldous Huxley's* Brave New World *and* Yevgeni Zamyatin's We, *must be considered one of the three great early anti-Utopian novels, a genre that has become disturbingly popular in contemporary literature. Orwell's vision is especially bleak because it is not simply a flight of fancy, but is, rather, the logical projection of the social, cultural, and historical environment that Orwell observed when writing the book in 1948.*

The prophetic nature of *Nineteen Eighty-Four* should not obscure the fact the George Orwell has written a vivid novel of passions and emotions. All too often mesmerized and even frightened by the politics of tyranny that Orwell imagines, the reader has a tendency to overlook the personal drama of Winston Smith and Julia. Although their love begins on the basis of mere sexual need, it ultimately grows to one of tender affection; indeed, their relationship assumes all the ordinary and rather mundane attributes of a middle-class marriage.

This is not to deny that Winston's and Julia's love is connected to the central theme of an absolute slave state. In fact one of the tragedies of life in Oceania is that no act can remain merely personal; every thought, feeling, and action of the citizen is political since the Inner Party insists that no person shall have the right to privacy. The hero's and the heroine's simple act of copulation which develops into love is itself an act of political rebellion since it defies Big Brother and his prohibition against intimacy and love.

Yet in its own way Winston's and Julia's pure instinctual lust is the perfect act of rebellion in Oceania, since the State represents its polar opposite: pure reason. If Big Brother has anything to fear, it is instinct. Since the control of the mind has been perfected, the Party need not concern itself with thought crime. But since the instincts are irrational and uncontrollable, they remain the principal foe of the State and the only hope of freedom. For this reason the Ministry of Love houses the main law enforcement agency in Oceania. Of course, isolated as they are, Winston and Julia have no such hope—if it is even appropriate to speak of such a matter as hope in *Nineteen Eighty-Four.*

NO NAME

Type of work: Novel
Author: Wilkie Collins (1824-1889)
Type of plot: Domestic romance
Time of plot: Mid-nineteenth century
Locale: England
First published: 1862

No Name *rivaled* The Woman in White *and* The Moonstone *in popularity among readers of Collins' own day, although the modern reader may find Collins' propagandistic rhetoric a bit heavy. However, the author's skill at developing an intricate plot, his accurate picture of Victorian customs, manners, and morals, and his vivid characterization, especially of the strong-minded Magdalen Vanstone and the amiable rogue, Captain Wragge, still excite admiration.*

In *No Name,* Wilkie Collins made a serious attempt to overcome the sentimental stereotypes which had reduced Victorian heroines to unbelievable cardboard figures. While Collins sometimes suggested that most females are delicate, easily shattered creatures, his heroines are made of sterner stuff. Although not the intellectual equal of George Eliot's female protagonists, Magdalen Vanstone is superior to most of Dickens' women and shows herself to be a young woman of exceptional resilience and tenacity.

Written after the great success of *The Woman in White, No Name* did not follow the formula of the previous novel; *No Name* is suspenseful, but is in no way a mystery tale. Collins dared to risk his popularity with a theme that was extremely controversial in the middle of the nineteenth century: the injustice of society's treatment of illegitimate children. Perhaps he was drawn to the subject because of his own three illegitimate children. In any case, the sincerity of the author's feelings emerges when his characters speak out against the unjust laws of the period.

Wilkie Collins observed the Victorian household very carefully, particularly those two female institutions so prominent in nineteenth century fiction: the housekeeper and the governess. There is no sentimentalizing in the portraits of either Mrs. Le Count or Miss Garth; and Mrs. Wragge, the enormous, slovenly, slow-witted wife of Captain Wragge, provides a portrait of quite a different type of woman. Also, it is interesting to note that, with the exception of Captain Wragge, most of the men in the novel are either weak or grasping types, and far less interesting than the women.

Wilkie Collins suggests in *No Name* that the society of a hundred years ago was based on hypocrisy and injustice, but his message is woven skillfully into one of the complicated plots which he was a master at spinning.

NO TRIFLING WITH LOVE

Type of work: Drama
Author: Alfred de Musset (1810-1857)
Type of plot: Tragi-comedy
Time of plot: Nineteenth century
Locale: France
First presented: 1864; first published: 1834

Alfred de Musset did not write his plays for the stage; he used the dramatic form rather as a vehicle for lyric expression. No Trifling with Love (On ne Badine pas Avec l'Amour), *reflecting the writer's love affair with George Sand, is effective as a romantic defense of love, but has serious weaknesses as a stage play.*

Alfred de Musset's play represents a new kind of tragicomedy. Earlier examples of the genre (such as Shakespeare's *The Merchant of Venice*) resolved a potentially tragic plot with a happy ending, or (like Dryden's *The Spanish Friar*) alternated a potentially tragic main plot with a comic subplot. Musset's characteristically modern approach is to dramatize the tragic overtones with apparently comic action: he develops a comedy and resolves it with tragedy. Still in the future are tragicomedies like Beckett's *Waiting for Godot* in which the same action can be taken as comic or tragic—or both.

Most of the action of this play is time-honored material for sentimental, romantic, or even cynical comedy. A charming hero and a beautiful heroine, both high-born, go through the dramatic motions of alternately reaching toward and then rejecting each other, while their pride, vanity, and wit entertain us through various intrigues and counter-intrigues. In the process of Musset's play, however, the pawn and plaything of their intrigues, a common and impressionable country girl, kills herself for shattered love. Perdican offers a pathetic justification to God: "We are two senseless children, but our hearts are pure." For Musset and for us, this is not sufficient: love is not to be so trifled with. Camille, at least, has the moral fortitude to accept her responsibility for the catastrophe and to renounce the glib Perdican.

What is most interesting about this play is Musset's subtly drawn examination of love. In the first act, his theme appears to be a commonplace one— love is a complex and unpredictable quality. It is not subject to the precise expectations and course of development calculated in advance by the baron, a man so orderly that he knows to the minute how old his son and niece are, and manages to stage their return, after ten years absence, at the exact same moment from opposite doors. When things subsequently do not go just as he expects, his whole world turns upside down, and he is utterly unable to account for the discrepancy between his well-laid engineering and human actuality.

In the second act, however, the theme deepens as Musset turns to an examination of the value of love itself. Camille, who will accept nothing less than an ideal and eternal love, wants desperately to love. But she does not want to suffer. Such real love causes so much suffering and misery, her nuns have assured her, that, since it involves so much deceit, capriciousness, and betrayal, is it not better to avoid the problem entirely by withdrawing from the world into a cloister where the maimed and disabled from the battlefields of love can minister to one another? Contrasted to this is Perdican's more realistic view that love—fickle, temporary, cruel, and imperfect as it is —is nevertheless a part of life, and as such, must be faced and experienced, not avoided.

One is reminded of Milton, who could not "praise a fugitive and cloistered virtue, unexercised and unbreathed that never sallies out and sees her adversary, but slinks out of the race. . . ." One must not slink out of the race by becoming a nun, Musset suggests, but having chosen to run it, one should run it honestly, without pride or intrigue, and, above all, not at the expense of other people.

NOCTURNE

Type of work: Novel
Author: Frank Swinnerton (1884-   )
Type of plot: Domestic romance
Time of plot: Twentieth century
Locale: London
First published: 1917

Nocturne *is almost a drama, for the entire novel is written in the form of dialogues, with a strict adherence to the classical unity of time and only a little less so to the unities of place and action. The author reveals a shrewd insight into the psychological kinship in frustration of two sisters, Jenny and Emmy Blanchard, who have nothing in common in the way of physical appearance, personality, or character.*

Nocturne is a simple story about a few individuals, but the author, by concentrating his attention, is able to probe deeply into the feelings and attitudes of his characters. The novel explores the complexities of emotional ties between people: between sisters, between father and daughter, between girl and gentleman friend. None of these relationships is as simple as it at first appears. The girls, in particular, have learned to hide their emotions from each other; an almost stoic façade has become their sole method of self-protection. Their loneliness has given their grievances the opportunity to grow within their minds, and they feel mentally bruised and battered in their isolation.

Swinnerton's goal was to create a "fresh reality" out of the commonplaces of ordinary life. Deliberately taking simple people in a far from exceptional setting, he tried to show that, paradoxically, even they are unique individuals with unique—if universal—feelings. They all talk and think about freedom, but each has a different conception of what freedom would be for him or her. The contrast between the life styles of the rich and poor is highlighted when Jenny visits Keith Redington's yacht. To her sensibility, the contrast is startling, but even stronger than her aching for luxury is her craving for love.

Pa Blanchard, with his almost desperate hunger for news, illustrates brilliantly how much bored, trapped individuals rely on outside sensations for a feeling of being alive. With no radio or other electronic media to bring the world's violence into his parlor, he must rely on his daughters to bring him reports of murders and disasters. The sisters, despite their brusqueness, really are fond of each other. Jenny's belief that if they could all be sensible for half an hour "everything could be arranged and happiness could be made real for each of them" is the core of the book. Hungrily, they continue searching for happiness.

NORTHANGER ABBEY

Type of work: Novel
Author: Jane Austen (1775-1817)
Type of plot: Comedy of manners
Time of plot: Early nineteenth century
Locale: England
First published: 1818

In Northanger Abbey, *Jane Austen parodies the then-popular gothic novel to underscore a favorite theme of her early novels: the confusion in an immature mind between literature and life. Thus, beyond the gothic parody,* Northanger Abbey *is a subtle, lively novel about the maturing of her heroine, Catherine Morland.*

In all the history of the novel, perhaps no genre can claim more popularity than that of the Gothic novel of the late eighteenth century. Unfortunately, when *Northanger Abbey,* Jane Austen's parody of the Gothic novel, was published in 1818, a year after her death, the Gothic fad was all but over. However, her delightful mockery was actually written when such works were all the rage, about 1797-1798, and sold to a publisher in 1803, but for reasons unknown published posthumously. In her early twenties at the time of the composition, the young author lived in the quiet rectory where she was born, in the Hampshire village of Steventon, her circumstances resembling those of the young heroine of her novel—even to such amusements as poring over Gothic novels. The reader who has never perused Ann Radcliffe's *The Mysteries of Udolpho* (1794), which occupies so much of Catherine Morland's time and thoughts, will find other reasons to enjoy *Northanger Abbey*; but a knowledge of *The Mysteries of Udolpho* or any other Gothic novel will bring special rewards.

At one level, then, *Northanger Abbey* is an amusing parody of Gothic novels, with particular reference to *The Mysteries of Udolpho.* Nevertheless, Jane Austen's satire is not pointed simply at such novels with their mysterious castles and abbeys, gloomy villains, incredibly accomplished heroines, sublime landscapes, and supernatural claptrap. The romantic sensibility of the Gothic enthusiast is also a target. Thus *Northanger Abbey* is a comic study of the ironic discrepancies between the prosaic world in which Catherine lives and the fantastic shapes which her imagination, fed by Gothic novels, gives to that world. Throughout, the author holds up the contrast between the heroine's real situation and the Gothic world she fantasizes.

The prevailing irony begins with the first sentence: "No one who had ever seen Catherine Morland in her infancy would have supposed her born to be a heroine." As she grows up she develops neither the prodigious artistic and intellectual accomplishments necessary for the role nor the requisite beauty, being merely pretty. However, once her adventures get under way, she begins to assign stereotyped Gothic roles to her new acquaintances. Detecting villainy in General Tilney's haughty demeanor merely because in *The Mysteries of Udolpho* the evil Montoni is haughty, she overlooks his real defects of snobbery and materialism, traits which prove far more threatening to her than his hauteur.

Since the central feature of the Gothic novel is the sinister, dilapidated castle or abbey, Catherine's most cherished daydreams center upon Northanger Abbey and its long, damp passages. In reality, nothing is damp except an ordinary drizzling rain, nor is anything narrow or ruined, the Abbey having been thoroughly renovated for modern living. Try as she will, she cannot manufacture genuine Gothic horrors. Instead of dark revelations of murder and madness in the Tilney family, she faces self-revelation, her recognition that she has suffered from a delusion, a desire to be frightened.

If the ridicule of Gothicism and the exposure of false sensibility comprise one major theme, another more inclusive theme, common to all of Jane Austen's novels, is the problem of limitation. Catherine at seventeen is "launched into all the difficulties and dangers of six weeks residence at Bath," the fashionable resort, leaving a sheltered life in her village of Fullerton. She immediately discerns, however, a state of artificial confinement as a way of life in Bath:

> Catherine began to feel something of disappointment—she was tired of being continually pressed against by people, the generality of whose faces possessed nothing to interest, and with all of whom she was so wholly unacquainted, that she could not relieve the irksomeness of imprisonment by the exchange of a syllable with any of her fellow captives . . . she felt yet more awkwardness of having no party to join, no acquaintance to claim, no gentleman to assist them.

Jane Austen, throughout, continues to develop this initial image of an empty, fashionable routine in which each day brought its regular duties. But Catherine romanticizes this reality, her delusions culminating with the invitation to visit the Tilneys at Northanger Abbey, an invitation that delights and excites her. Thus the Gothic parody functions also as a study of one common response to a society circumscribed by empty rituals and relationships—escapism. This theme is resolved when Catherine's visions of romance are shattered by the mundane discoveries at Northanger Abbey, compelling her to abandon her romantic notions and choose the alternative of always acting in the future with common sense.

Nonetheless, in her dismissal of fantasy, she has not yet come to terms with the limitations in reality, the pressures of society which can impose imprisonment. Such experience is melodramatically represented by her expulsion from the Abbey—an order delivered without explanation, the time and manner of departure determined by General Tilney, and Catherine denied either friendship or common courtesy. With no alternatives, in a situation which resists good sense, Catherine is reduced to a passive awareness of the reality and substance of life. When she is shut off in her room at the Abbey, her mind is so occupied in the contemplation of actual and natural evil that she is numb to the loneliness of her situation. Confined in a hired carriage for the long, unfamiliar journey to Fullerton, she is conscious only of the pressing anxieties of thought. At home, her thought processes are lost in the reflection of her own change of feelings and spirit. She is the opposite of what she had been, an innocent.

Catherine has survived the transition from innocence to experience, proving to her mother, at least, that she can shift very well for herself. However, Catherine's maturity is tested no further. The restoration of her happiness depends less upon herself and Henry than it does upon General Tilney. Nor is she finally received by the General on the basis of personal merit. Ultimately, in the General's world, life is defined by money. When the Morlands prove to be a family of good financial standing, Catherine is free to marry the man of her choice.

Concerning the rapid turn of events in her denouement, Jane Austen wryly observes: "To begin perfect happiness at the respective ages of twenty-six and eighteen, is to do pretty well." However, despite the happy ending which concludes the novel, the author leaves Catherine upon the threshold only of the reality of life that her experiences have revealed. The area of her testing has already been defined, for example, in the discrepancy between her image of Henry's parsonage and General Tilney's. To Catherine, it is "something like Fullerton, but better: Fullerton had its faults, but Woodston probably had none."

Thus *Northanger Abbey* is a novel of initiation, its heroine ironically discovering in the world not a new freedom, but a new set of restrictions. Once undeceived of her romantic illusions of escape, she is returned, with a vengeance, to the world as it is, small but decent. As an early novel, *Northanger Abbey* points the way to Jane Austen's mature novels, in which the focus will be upon heroines who are constrained to deal with life within defined limitations.

Catherine E. Moore

THE NORTHERN LASS

Type of work: Drama
Author: Richard Brome (?-1652 or 1653)
Type of plot: Comedy of manners
Time of plot: Early seventeenth century
Locale: London
First presented: 1632

Richard Brome, first the servant and later the friend of Ben Jonson, wrote fifteen plays, alternating between romantic comedies and comedies of manners. The Northern Lass, catalogued in the latter group, often borders on pure farce because of its ridiculous situations and practical jokes. The plot twists and winds until it appears impossibly complicated, but Brome manipulates its several threads with considerable skill.

John Addington Symonds, the Victorian critic, observed that "the cock in the fable scratched up a pearl from the dunghill, and it is possible that some ingenious student may discover pearls in what is certainly the rubbish heap of Brome's plays." That harsh judgment may be unfair when applied to Brome's entire dramatic canon, but it is difficult to find much in *The Northern Lass* in the way of refutation. Just about everything Brome does in this early play—his characterizations, his dramatizations of contemporary mores and manners, his satiric jabs at various human and social targets—has been done better by such contemporaries as Middleton, Dekker, and Jonson. Still, this was a popular work in its time, and the commendatory verses preceding the play (by such contemporaries as Jonson, Dekker, and Ford) testify to the esteem in which Brome was held by playwrights of very high repute indeed.

All critics agree that Brome is a skillful plotter; and it is primarily the frenetic pace of the action, as the misunderstandings multiply, that holds the reader's interest. At one point, for instance, we have the spectacle of a false Sir Philip (actually Widgine) wooing a false northern lass (actually Constance Holdup). In addition, the activities of scheming underlings, working at various cross purposes, including Pace (Sir Philip's man), Howdee (Mistress Fitchow's man), Beavis (Mistress Trainwell's man), and Anvile (Widgine's tutor), among others, fuel the confusion even further. The numerous zig-zaggings of the action, however, may obscure the fact that even by comic standards, the chief ends to which the plot is working are precariously flimsy. The domineering and manipulative Mrs. Fitchow is hardly the type of woman who could make a man like Tridewell happy. Certainly the proposed union between the starry-eyed lovers, Sir Philip and Constance, seems to stand on not much less shaky ground. But with such an unusually complicated plot on his hands, Brome has little time to attend to the niceties of dramatic or thematic logic.

Beyond such stock comic conventions as making fun of country ignoramuses and marrying off the fool to a common prostitute, we can glimpse some of the deeper realities of contemporary life. For instance, divorce is one of the key motifs in the play. It is possible to sense Brome's indignation with the fact that divorce (after consummation of the marriage) was all but impossible to obtain, and even if it were obtained, as Mrs. Fitchow points out, neither partner could remarry while both still lived. In the comic resolution, of course, this potentially lethal problem is solved by a convenient *deus ex machina* (the false priest), and peace and happiness are restored to all. But the patent improbability of this resolution is highlighted by Nonsense, who vows to make a stage play out of the events that have transpired when he gets back to Cornwall.

NOSTROMO

Type of work: Novel
Author: Joseph Conrad (Józef Teodor Konrad Korzeniowski, 1857-1924)
Type of plot: Psychological romance
Time of plot: Early twentieth century
Locale: "Costaguana," on the north coast of South America
First published: 1904

Using the San Tomé mine as his focal point, Conrad presents a group of fascinating characters, representing a cross section of attitudes, character types, and economic levels, who contend with one another and with themselves for the silver and all it implies economically, politically, and morally. The result is a powerful, panoramic vision of man, both as a solitary individual and as a social animal, caught up in forces, both external and internal, that he can neither understand nor contain.

Conrad has always been known among the mass of readers as a great teller of sea stories. He is also a pertinent, even prophetic, commentator on what he called "land entanglements"—particularly on the subject of political revolution. Conrad's father was an active revolutionary in the cause of Polish independence; he died as the result of prolonged imprisonment for revolutionary "crimes." Three of Conrad's best novels are studies in political behavior: *Nostromo, The Secret Agent,* and *Under Western Eyes. Nostromo* is by far the most ambitious and complex of these works. It has a very large international cast of characters of all shapes and sizes and it employs the typical Conradian device of an intentionally jumbled (and sometimes confusing) chronology. As usual with Conrad the physical setting is handled superbly; the reader is drawn into the book through the wonderfully tactile descriptions of the land and sea. The setting in South America is also particularly appropriate to Conrad's skeptical consideration of progress achieved either by capitalism or revolution.

Nostromo is a study in the politics of wealth in an underdeveloped country. The central force in the novel is the silver of the San Tomé mine—a potential of wealth so immense that a humane and cultured civilization can be built upon it. At least this is the view of the idealist Charles Gould, the owner and developer of the mine. There are other views. From the start Gould is ready to maintain his power by force if necessary. He remembers how the mine destroyed his father. The mine attracts politicians and armed revolutionaries from the interior, but Gould is willing to blow up his treasure and half of Sulaco, the central city, in order to defeat the revolution. He succeeds, but Conrad means us to regard his success as partial at best. His obsession with the mine separates him from his wife. As with Conrad's other heroes, the demands of public action distort and cancel out his capacity for private affection.

One of the magnificences of the first half of *Nostromo* is that Gould and his silver are seen from so many angles. We are given a truly panoramic spectrum of attitude. For old Giorgio Viola, who was once a member of Garibaldi's red shirts, Gould's idealization of material interests is dangerous and wrong because it has the potential of violating a pure and disinterested love of liberty for all humanity. But Viola is as ineffectual as the austere and cultured leader of Sulaco's aristocracy, Don José Avellanos, whose unpublished manuscript "Thirty Years of Misrule" is used as gun wadding at the height of the revolution. Ranged against Avellanos and Viola, at the other end of the spectrum, are those sanguinary petty tyrants, Bento, Montero, and Sotillo, who want to run the country entirely for their own personal advantage. Sotillo represents their rapacity and blind lust for Gould's treasure. But the most interesting characters are those who occupy a middling position in the spectrum. Of these, two are central to any understanding of the novel. Between them they represent Conrad's own point of view most fully.

The dilettante Parisian boulevardier, Martin Decoud, may be the object of some of Conrad's most scourging irony, but his skeptical pronouncements as in his letter to his sister accord well with the facts of Sulaco's politics as Conrad presents them in the early stages of the novel.

Decoud saves the mine by arranging for a new rifle to be used in defense of Gould's material interests, but he does not share Gould's enthusiasm that the mine can act as the chief force in the process of civilizing the new republic. He views the whole business of revolution and counter-revolution as an elaborate charade, a comic opera.

The most trenchant charge against Gould is made by that other deeply skeptical character, Dr. Monygham. His judgment upon material interests is one of the most famous passages in the book:

> There is no peace and rest in the development of material interests. They have their law and their justice. But it is founded on expediency, and is inhuman; it is without the continuity and the force that can be found only in a moral principle. . . . The time approaches when all that the Gould Concession stands for shall weigh as heavily upon the people as the barbarism, cruelty, and misrule of a few years back.

It is clear that Conrad means his readers to take Monygham's judgment at its face value. The trouble is that the facts of Costaguana's post-revolutionary state do not agree with it. The land is temporarily at peace and is being developed in an orderly fashion by the mine as well as other material interests, and the workers seem better off as a result. Monygham is of course hinting at the workers' revolt against the suppression of material interests, but this revolt seems so far in the future that his judgment is robbed of much of its power. This surely accounts for part of the "hollowness" some critics have found in the novel.

The last section of the novel is concerned with Gould's successful resistance to the attempts of both church and military to take over the mine, and the moral degradation of the "incorruptible" man of the people, Nostromo. In this latter case, Conrad abandons the richness and density of his panoramic view of South American society and gives us a semi-allegorical dramatization of the taint of the silver within the soul of a single character.

Nostromo's fate is clearly related to the legend of the two gringos which begins the book, for the silver which he has hidden has this same power to curse his soul as the "fatal spell" cast by the treasure on the gringos. ("Their souls cannot tear themselves away from their bodies mounting guard over the discovered treasure. They are now rich and hungry and thirsty. . . . ") The result of Conrad's absorption with Nostromo at the end of the novel is twofold. First, we are denied a dramatization of the changing social conditions which would support Monygham's judgment. Second, and more important, the novel loses its superb richness and variety and comes dangerously close to insisting on the thesis that wealth is a universal corruptor, even that "money is the root of all evil."

For roughly two-thirds of its length *Nostromo* gives us one of the finest social panoramas in all of fiction. The ending suggests, however, that underneath the complex texture of the whole novel lies a rather simplistic idea: that both "material interests" and revolution are doomed to failure. Though set in South America, *Nostromo* suggests a world in which systems and conditions change very little because men do not.

Benjamin Nyce

O PIONEERS!

Type of work: Novel
Author: Willa Cather (1873-1947)
Type of plot: Regional chronicle
Time of plot: 1880-1910
Locale: Nebraska
First published: 1913

Willa Cather began her illustrious career as a novelist with two powerful narratives of pioneer life on the Nebraska prairie, O Pioneers! *and* My Antonia *(1918). The heroine of* O Pioneers!, *Alexandra Bergson, is the first of the sturdy young immigrant women who tame the harsh prairie land through strength of character, tenacity, and an ability to become one with it.*

Born in Virginia, Willa Cather grew up on Hamlin Garland's Middle Border. In 1884, her parents moved to Nebraska. Later, in 1895, she was graduated from the University of Nebraska. The gift of writing flowed through her veins, and before she wrote *O Pioneers!* and her other more memorable novels, she was the editor of *McClure's Magazine.* Even with fame and a comfortable life style, Willa never wanted to lose her past; she did not condemn it.

In her hands, the vivid recollections of youth on the limitless prairie became one of her most effective techniques. Firsthand experiences lent an authenticity to her work that was surpassed by few others at the time. Through her eyes and her sense of feeling, just as Alexandra Bergson sensed the potential of her homestead, the reader is presented with the personal meaning of an America of vast, open lands, and will more fully appreciate the "why" behind the winning of a very fertile section of the country.

The Bergsons were not the only Scandinavian immigrants attempting to carve out a new life in the Midwest. Over one million Norwegians and Swedes emigrated to the United States between 1820 and 1900. Many others, like Marie Tovesky's family, came from Eastern Europe. Still others, with roots deep in American soil, gave up their farms and businesses east of the Mississippi for a chance at the opportunities out West. The Swedish Bergson family was the author's primary subject in *O Pioneers!,* and yet, the flavor of cultural pluralism enhances the theme of the interface between settler and hostile land.

With skill and sympathy, the author re-creates the realities of prairie life that were undeveloped in most other sagas of the West. The reader experiences the uncertainties of the planting seasons, the frenzied activity at harvest time, and the numerous droughts and blizzards. The climate, with all of its unpredictable changes, is not over played. Only one who had lived there could so persuasively describe the potent forces of weather. Cather wrote of a region that was just beginning to enter the scientific age. Long before the arrival of the Bergsons, the Morrill Act of 1862 established state agricultural schools, and the land-grant college system, of which Nebraska was a part, started to grow. Created in the same year, the U.S. Department of Agriculture would disseminate scientific knowledge to farmers through the colleges, animal husbandry journals, and the like. Unlike her brothers Lou and Oscar, and many other settlers, Alexandra was receptive to these new ideas; they offered assistance in the taming of the land. Imaginative integration of real developments into the story became a necessity, if not a desire for the author. Perhaps the most impressive element in the author's testimony on prairie living is the epic struggle of immigrant pioneer women. Here lies the greatness of Cather's creativity.

Emotions and personal responses to circumstances are often left un-recorded for future generations, but the author's poignant memory of her own pioneer experiences and of inhabitants of towns similar to Hanover pre-serves their bleak lot. Environment and character development are carefully blended. Monotonous rolling hills, severe winters, the routine tilling of the resisting soil, the piercing wind, and the frustration over meager results created a restlessness in many settlers. Alexandra's brothers Lou and Oscar were bored with farming. The cultural shock of Americanization had been too much for them. Yet, her youngest brother, Emil, represented the brighter side of American opportunities. Frank Shabata's possessiveness, especially his concern over Marie's fidelity, became a fatal disease. Marie, the free spirit, was not to be possessed by any one man. Alexandra's independence was born of her inner spirit and sense of purpose. The West was subdued by people with her strength of character and perseverance.

Alexandra's self-control and determination were traits developed early in her life in a small seaport in Sweden. The primitive environment of Nebraska and the additional family responsibilities following her father's premature death forced her youthful personality into a demanding maturity. As a woman, she did not have the idle moments to display her feminine attributes as did others of more secure status. Life to Alexandra meant more than spending time to make herself attractive to possible suitors. Women, as would-be wives with handsome dowries or as extramarital lovers, were in demand throughout the West. She possessed a motherly instinct for her brood, often referring to her youngest brother, Emil, as her boy. There was a more im-portant purpose to her life, making her land bountiful.

Alexandra regarded the potentiality of her land with a spiritual reverence and as an obligation to the future. The mysticism of Crazy Ivar, and his appreciation of nature's creatures and of the seasonal procession, were under-stood by Alexandra, but she was no ordinary settler. She could have sold the farm and moved to the city as thousands of others had done when faced with severe hardship. The farm, the open lands, and the challenge, however, rep-resented to her the essence of life. Alexandra believed in the supremacy of moral and spiritual values over material possessions. Owning her own piece of the earth and making it productive, with a modest income, were possessions enough.

Novels concerning the inner conflicts of women, or about the attitudes of social disapproval toward single women of the frontier, would not have appealed to the reading public of rustic Hanover. They would have viewed her standing in the community in a variety of ways, and men were her most harsh critics. To frontier men, women were to be married and to have children. They considered the gentle sex subservient creatures to the wills of men. Women did not possess the same faculties of reason the men allegedly held. They were not supposed to own land. A woman's ownership of property was considered the freak result of a hardworking husband's untimely death, a mere temporary state of affairs until she married and the new mate gained title to the land. These were some of the reasons why Alexandra's brothers were concerned about her plans to marry Carl. They feared that Alexandra lacked enough sense to prevent Carl from assuming ownership of some of the land that also belonged to them. Other men might have been jealous.

Near forty, Alexandra was not a young, irresponsible girl. Carl was five years her junior, but earlier they had gone their separate ways and then finally decided to marry. Even with the tragedies of Emil's murder and of his murderer, Frank Shabata, Carl and Alexandra would endow the prairie with life and hope.

Eric H. Christianson

OBLOMOV

Type of work: Novel
Author: Ivan Alexandrovich Goncharov (1812-1891)
Type of plot: Social criticism
Time of plot: Early nineteenth century
Locale: Russia
First published: 1858

Amiable, educated, rich, and pampered, Oblomov is both physically and philosophically incapable of action, despite the proddings of love and concerned friendship. Oblomov's unwillingness—or inability—to act can be seen as a symbolic representation of that physical and moral paralysis characteristic of the nineteenth century Russian aristocracy and central to its historical collapse.

Literature, particularly historical literature, remains one of the best mediums through which to glance at the values and aspirations extant in a given society at a given time. Ivan Goncharov's *Oblomov* is a most perceptive and incisive statement—written by a Russian for Russians—about mid-nineteenth century Russian society, particularly the landed aristocracy.

Goncharov's portrayal of Russian society is as articulate as those of his contemporary, Turgenev. Like Turgenev, Goncharov sculpted a bust of Russia ruled by a lassitudinous, opaque aristocracy which lacked the sinew either to reshape Russian society or defend its historical privileges from those who sought to alter the power base in Russia. Oblomov, the lazy absentee landlord, is a concise symbol of Russian aristocracy. Goncharov needs four chapters to move his main character from his bed to his dressing stand. Even after rising in the afternoon, Oblomov does not dress himself. He is attended by a valet who obeys in somnambulist fashion the wishes of his master, and dresses him in an outdated smoking jacket. Too spent to act, Oblomov functions only with the service of those surrounding him.

Goncharov's indictment of his Russian society is as clear today as it was a century ago: the Russian landed nobility had lost its will and mandate to serve society. Lacking both, the class was tumbling toward a social crisis from which it was incapable of escaping. The events of 1917 proved the accuracy of Goncharov's perceptions. The Russian aristocracy had spent its last historical epoch in bed.

Unlike Turgenev, Goncharov did not attract a wide public. However, the impact of *Oblomov* on his literary contemporaries was immediate and lasting. Leading social critics of his day, such as Belinski and Chernyashevski, recognized and hailed the importance of Goncharov's criticism. The word "oblomov," meaning excessive laziness, became an integral part of the Russian language and the argot of European writers.

THE ODYSSEY

Type of work: Poem
Author: Homer (c. Ninth century B. C.)
Type of plot: Heroic epic
Time of plot: Years immediately following Trojan War
Locale: Greece and Mediterranean lands
First transcribed: Sixth century B. C.

The Iliad, *an epic about an incident in the Trojan War, and* The Odyssey, *concerned with Odysseus' difficulties in getting home after the war had been won by the Greeks, are the great epic masterpieces of Western literature and a storehouse of Greek folklore and myth. The* Odyssey, *with its sagacious, magnificent hero, its romantic theme, and its frequent change of scene, has enjoyed greater popularity than the* Iliad.

The *Odyssey* is undoubtedly the most popular epic of Western culture. Its chief character, Odysseus (Ulysses), has inspired more literary works than any other legendary hero. From Homer to Joyce, Kazantzakis, and after, Odysseus has been a central figure in European literature, and one who has undergone many sea changes. The *Odyssey* has the ingredients of a perennial best seller: pathos, sexuality, violence; a strong, resourceful hero with a firm purpose braving many dangers and hardships to accomplish it; a romantic account of exploits in strange places; a more or less realistic approach to characterization; a soundly constructed plot; and an author with a beautiful gift for description. It is, in fact, one of the greatest adventure stories of all time.

Of the poet, or poets, who wrote the poem there is only conjecture. Tradition says that Homer lived in Chios or Smyrna in Ionia, a part of Asia Minor; and it is probable that he, or they, composed this epic late in the ninth century B.C. The *Odyssey* was originally sung or recited, as evidenced by its style and content, and it was based on legend, folktale, and free invention, forming part of a minstrel tradition similar to that of the Middle Ages.

The style of the poem is visual, explanatory, repetitive, and stately. Like the *Iliad,* it has extended similes and repeated epithets, phrases, and sentences. Homer, whoever he was, wanted his audience to visualize and understand everything that happened. He grasped the principles of rhetoric, and he composed in a plain, direct fashion that possesses great eloquence and dignity.

Homer also had mastered certain crucial problems of organization. When the audience knows the story one is going to tell, as Homer's did, it becomes necessary to introduce diversions from the main action, to delay the climax as long as the audience can bear. In this manner the leisurely development of the plot stirs one's anticipation and gives the climactic scene redoubled force. But the intervening action must have interest on its own and must have a bearing on the main action. The *Odyssey* shows remarkable ability on all of these counts.

If the subject of the *Illiad* was the wrath of Achilles during the Trojan War, the subject of the *Odyssey* is the homecoming of Odysseus ten years after the Trojan War ended. The immediate action of the poem takes place in no more than a few weeks, dramatizing the very end of Odysseus' wanderings and his restoration of order at home. Yet Homer allows Odysseus to narrate his earlier adventures, from the sack of Troy to his confinement on Calypso's island, which extends the magnitude of the poem. And Homer, through Nestor and Menelaus, places Odysseus' homecoming into the wider context of the returns of all the major heroes from Troy, most of which were disastrous. Thus, the epic has a sweeping scope condensed into a very brief span of time.

The Telemachy (those first four books dealing with the travels and education of Telemachus) sets the stage for Odysseus' return. The gods make the arrangements, and then we are shown the terrible situation in Odysseus' palace, where the suitors are devouring Odysseus' substance, bullying his son, and growing very impatient with Penelope. They intend to kill Odysseus if he should ever return, and they arrange an ambush to kill Telemachus. Their radical abuse of hospitality is contrasted with the excellent relations between guest and host when Telemachus goes to visit Nestor and then Menelaus. In an epic whose theme is travel the auxiliary theme must be the nature of hospitality. In Odysseus' journeyings his best host is Alcinoüs and his worst is the savage Cyclops. Between these two extremes there are all sorts of gradations, which depend on whether the host helps or hinders Odysseus on his long way home.

At first Telemachus is a disheartened young man trying to be hospitable in a house where it is impossible. Then Athena, as Mentes, puts pluck into him with the idea that his long-lost father is alive and detained. Telemachus calls an assembly to state his grievances and then undertakes a hazardous trip to learn of his father. He plainly has the makings of a hero, and he proves himself his father's true son when he helps slay the rapacious suitors, after displaying some tact and cunning of his own.

Odysseus is the model of the worldly, well-traveled, persevering man who overcomes obstacles. He has courage, stamina, and power, but his real strength lies in his brain, which is shrewd, quick-witted, diplomatic, and resourceful. He is also very eloquent and persuasive. But he needs all of these qualities to survive and make his way home. His mettle is tested at every turn, either by dangers or temptations to remain in a place. Calypso even offers him immortality, but he is steadfast in his desire to return home. Athena may intercede for him with Zeus and aid and advise him, yet the will to return and the valor in doing so are Odysseus' alone. The one thing Odysseus found truly unbearable in his travels was stasis, being stranded for seven years, even though he had an amorous nymph for company.

However, a good deal of the book is taken up with Odysseus' preparations, having arrived at Ithaca, for killing the suitors. The point is that the suitors are the most formidable enemy Odysseus has encountered, since they number well over a hundred and there are only he and Telemachus to face them. It is here that his true strategic and tactical cunning comes in handy—the previous wanderings being a long prologue to this climactic exploit. After nine chapters in which nothing much happens, the killing of the suitors, their henchmen, and maids is stunning in its exulting, deliberate violence. The house of Odysseus is at last purged of its predators, and our emotions are restored to an equilibrium. One final, weak chapter is used to tidy up the plot. But we have already seen Odysseus in his full glory.

James Weigel, Jr.

OEDIPUS AT COLONUS

Type of work: Drama
Author: Sophocles (495?-406 B.C.)
Type of plot: Classical tragedy
Time of plot: Remote antiquity
Locale: Colonus, near Athens
First presented: 401 B.C.

Although the second of the Theban Plays chronologically, Oedipus at Colonus *was the last one written and may be taken as the thematic climax of the trilogy. In the end Oedipus accepts the fact of his guilt and its consequences, but he insists on his essential innocence with passion and conviction, making a last powerful affirmation of human dignity in the face of an incomprehensible universe.*

Written when Sophocles was about ninety and approaching death, *Oedipus at Colonus* is the dramatist's valedictory to the stage, to Athens, and to life. In its transcendent spiritual power it is reminiscent of Shakespeare's last great play, *The Tempest.* It was probably inevitable that Sophocles, a great Athenian patriot, should have written this play, a story dealing with the legendary past of his birthplace. Indeed, two of the high points of this drama are magnificent odes in praise of Colonus and Attica. *Oedipus at Colonus* represents the culmination of Sophocles' handling of the Cadmean legend, which he had treated earlier in *Antigone* and *Oedipus Tyrannus.* At the same time it is his last, luminous affirmation of human dignity in the face of an incomprehensible universe.

The theme of the suppliants, or refugees pleading for protection, was common in Greek tragedy. Both Aeschylus and Euripides had written patriotic dramas on this subject earlier. The pattern was simple. People threatened with capture sue a powerful but democratic king for aid and receive it. *Oedipus at Colonus* is remarkably similar in its patriotic content to Euripides' *The Suppliants.* Each play treats the Theban myth and features an aspect of the war of Seven Against Thebes; each conforms to the formula stated above; and each presents Theseus and Athens in a heroic light, as the defenders of the weak from tyrannical force. When Sophocles wrote his play, Athens was in the final throes of the disastrous Peloponnesian War, which would result in Athens' defeat at the hands of Sparta. In its arrogance of power the city had become rapacious and had undergone moral degeneration. So Sophocles' purpose in writing this play, at least from a civic viewpoint, was to remind the Athenians of their legendary respect for the rights of the helpless, a respect that up to that point had kept them safe from invaders. With the Greek tragedians, civic welfare depended directly on moral rectitude. By defending Oedipus and his daughters, Theseus insures the safety of Athens for generations. Sophocles shows Theseus acting disinterestedly, out of concern for these suppliants, as a model ruler. The playwright wished to inspire his fellow citizens with virtues they had cast aside: piety, courage in a good cause, manliness.

Yet Sophocles' patriotism went beyond state morality. In his two beautiful choral odes on Colonus and Attica there is an intense, wistful passion for the land itself and for the life it supported and for man's activities on it. There was, for Sophocles, something holy about the entire place. It is not accidental that the entire action of this play takes place before a sacred grove. Sophocles wanted his audience to feel the presence of divinity. The specific goddesses were the hideous and awesome Furies, who judged and punished evildoers. As agents of divine justice they preside invisibly over all that occurs in *Oedipus at Colonus.*

The center of this play, however, is not Theseus or Athens but a frightful beggar who has suffered terribly in his long life—the blind Oedipus. Although Oedipus is reconciled to exile, beggary, and blindness he is still proud and hot-tempered; and he cannot forgive the two men who inflicted exile and penury on him, Creon and Polynices. Oedipus has paid in full for the infamous deeds he committed in ignorance. He rightly insists upon his innocence, not of killing his father, marrying his mother, and having children by her, but of knowingly doing these things. Fate led him into that trap and the Furies punished him for it. His nobility consists in bearing his suffering with dignity. Even if he is the weakest and most pitiful of men in his blindness, and though he must be led around by a young teenaged girl, there is true manliness in him.

By contrast Creon is a man who lives by expediency, using force when persuasion fails, and who tamely submits when Theseus gains the upper hand. In pursuing a reasonable goal, namely the defense of Thebes, he is willing to use any means, including kidnaping Oedipus' only supports, his two daughters. His ruthlessness is highly distasteful. But even more unpleasant is Polynices' whining plea for Oedipus' aid in attacking Thebes. It stems from selfish ambition rather than concern for his poor father. One feels that the curses Oedipus levels at Creon, Polynices, Eteocles, and Thebes are justified and apt. In dishonoring a helpless blind man they incur calamity.

In this play Oedipus is a man preparing for death, as Sophocles must have been as he wrote it. Despite his hard destiny, and despite his power to curse men who have shamed him, Oedipus carries in his breast a profound blessing. In the end the Furies who hounded him bestow upon him a tremendous potency in death, the power to protect Athens for a long time, just as Athens had protected him. We never learn the ultimate reason for his suffering, but the manhood with which he faced it was the sole blessing he himself received, and that was all he needed. His mysterious and fearsome apotheosis amid flashes of lightning and earth tremors is the tribute the gods pay to Oedipus' supreme courage. Sophocles here wrote his last and most sublime testament on man's ability to take unmerited pain and transform it into glory.

James Weigel, Jr.

OEDIPUS TYRANNUS

Type of work: Drama
Author: Sophocles (495?-406 B. C.)
Type of plot: Classical tragedy
Time of plot: Remote antiquity
Locale: Thebes
First presented: c. 429 B. C.

Oedipus Tyrannus *is the first (chronologically; the second in order of composition) of the Theban Plays, which dramatize the effects of Oedipus' crime upon himself and his house. In finally realizing his guilt, in assuming the personal responsibility for his acts of patricide and incest, and in accepting blindness and exile to expiate those acts, Oedipus achieves a tragic stature that is, perhaps, unequaled in dramatic literature.*

Oedipus Tyrannus is the most famous of the ancient Greek tragedies. Aristotle considered it the supreme example of tragic drama and largely modeled his theory of tragedy on it. He mentions the play no less than eleven times in his *Poetics.* Freud in this century used the story to name the "Oedipus complex," which denotes the rivalry of male children with their fathers for the affection of their mothers. And Jean Cocteau adapted the tale to the modern stage in *The Infernal Machine.* Yet no matter what changes the Oedipus myth has undergone in two and a half millennia, the finest expression of it is still this tragedy by Sophocles.

Brilliantly conceived and written, *Oedipus Tyrannus* is a drama of self-discovery. Sophocles achieves an amazing compression and force by limiting the dramatic action to the day on which Oedipus learns the true nature of his birth and destiny. The fact that we already know these dark secrets, that Oedipus has unwittingly slain his true father and married his actual mother, begetting children with her, does nothing to destroy our suspense. We are drawn into Oedipus' search for the truth with all the tautness of a mystery story, and because we already know the truth we are aware of all the ironies in which Oedipus is enmeshed. Our knowledge enables us to fear the final revelation, but also to pity this man as his past is gradually and relentlessly uncovered to him.

The excellence of the plot is thoroughly integrated with the characterization of Oedipus, for it is he who impels the action forward in his concern for Thebes, his personal rashness, and his ignorance until everything is brought to light and he must face the consequences of all that he has done. He is flawed by a hot temper and impulsiveness, but without those traits his heroic course of self-discovery would never have occurred.

Fate for Sophocles is not something essentially outside of man but something inherent in his character and yet transcendant as well. Oracles and prophets in this play may show the will of the gods and indicate future events, but it is the individual character of a man that gives substance to them. Moreover, there is an element of freedom in man, an ability to choose, where the compulsions of character and the compulsions of the gods are powerless. It is in how a man meets the necessities of his destiny that freedom lies. He can succumb to fate's blows like a victim, and plead extenuating circumstances, or he can shoulder the full responsibility for what he does. In the first case he is merely pitiful, while in the second he is tragic, possessed of a greatness of soul that nothing can conquer.

A crucial point is that Oedipus is entirely unaware that he has killed his father and wedded his mother. He himself is the cause of the plague on Thebes, and in vowing to find the murderer of Laius and exile him he unconsciously pronounces judgment on himself. As king and as the hero who saved Thebes from the Sphinx, Oedipus is public-spirited. Believing in his own innocence, he is angry and incredulous when the provoked Teiresias accuses him of the crime, so he naturally jumps to the conclusion that Teiresias and Creon are conspirators against him. As plausible as that explanation may be, Oedipus maintains it with irrational vehemence, not even bothering to investigate it before he decides to have Creon put to death. Every act of his is performed in rashness, from his hot-tempered killing of Laius, to his investigation of the murder, to his violent blinding of himself, to his insistence on being exiled. He is a man of great pride and passion intent on serving Thebes, but until the evidence of his guilt begins piling up, he does not have the least tragic stature. He is merely a blind man sitting on the powderkeg of his past.

Ironically, his past is revealed to him by people who wish him well and who want to reassure him. Each time a character tries to comfort him with information, the information serves to damn him more thoroughly. Jocasta, in proving how false oracles can be, suggests to Oedipus unknowingly that he really did kill Laius, thus corroborating the oracles. The messenger from Corinth in reassuring Oedipus about his parentage brings his true parentage into question, but he says enough to convince Jocasta that Oedipus is her son. It is at this point that Oedipus' true heroism starts to emerge, for he determines to complete the search for the truth, knowing that he killed Laius and knowing that the result of his investigation may be utterly damnatory. His rashness here is no longer a liability but part of his absolute integrity.

Having learned the full truth of his dark destiny, his last act as king is to blind himself furiously over the dead body of Jocasta, his wife and mother. It is a terrible, agonizing moment, even in description. But in his depths of pain Oedipus is magnificent. He does not submit passively to his woe or plead that he committed his foul acts in ignorance, although he could do so with justice. He blinds himself in a rage of penitence, accepting total responsibility for what he did and determined to take the punishment of exile as well. As piteous as he appears in the final scene with Creon, there is more public spirit and more manhood in his fierce grief and his resolution of exile than in any other tragic hero in the history of the theater. He has unraveled his life to its utmost limits of agony and found there an unsurpassed grandeur of soul.

James Weigel, Jr.

OF HUMAN BONDAGE

Type of work: Novel
Author: W. Somerset Maugham (1874-1965)
Type of plot: Naturalism
Time of plot: Early twentieth century
Locale: England
First published: 1915

In Of Human Bondage. *Somerset Maugham's most important novel, the author tells of a young man's search for a way of life. It traces the thoughts and actions of a bitter, confused, warped boy, told with the mature wisdom of an author who had endured similar experiences and suffered some of the same tangled emotions in his own youth.*

Almost all of Somerset Maugham's writings deal, in one way or another, with the individual's attempt to assert his freedom from "human bondage." Because it is the most direct, thorough, and personal of his works, *Of Human Bondage* is generally considered to be his masterpiece and its hero, Philip Carey, to be a thinly disguised portrait of the author.

Like Carey, Somerset Maugham lost his beautiful, affectionate mother when he was quite young, was raised in an austere, financially pinched, religiously narrow environment, suffered abuse because of a physical handicap (he stammered), and fled to the continent as soon as he was able. From that point on the novel does not follow Maugham's personal life so literally, but it is clear that Philip's education follows Maugham's and that many of the characters and situations had their real life counterparts. *Of Human Bondage* was, as Maugham himself admitted, an "autobiographical novel."

The first "bondage" that Philip Carey must transcend—outgrow, really— is the oppressive environment of the vicarage. Deprived of his mother's love and thrust into a cold, moralistic milieu, young Philip is starved for affection and approval, but finds little of it in his uncle's household. William Carey, a childless, middle-aged parson, is never able to understand or warm up to the boy, and his wife, Aunt Louisa, although well-meaning, lacks the emotional strength necessary to give the boy the needed support. These insecurities are acerbated by his clubfoot which makes him an object of ridicule at school. The only mitigating factor in these early years is his uncle's library. Books become his only pleasure and excitement and help to mature him, while also providing him with an escape from everyday reality and encouraging his natural tendency toward daydreaming and indulging in fantasies. Thus, his early experiences fix several important character traits: his thirst for love; his extreme self-consciousness and over-sensitivity, especially with regard to his clubfoot; his need to dominate, and his envy of those who can; his distaste for social pieties and arbitrary moralities; and his taste for literature and the life of the imagination.

As soon as he is physically capable of it, Philip flees to Germany. There, following closely upon his first experience of personal freedom, Philip has his initial taste of intellectual and spiritual emancipation. Two new friends, Hayward and Weeks, introduce him to the world of ideas. Hayward becomes his mentor and gives him a thorough grounding in the great books of the day, but it is Weeks who supplies him with the one volume, Renan's *Vie de Jésus,* that has the most profound effect. It liberates Philip from his unconscious acceptance of Christian dogma and gives him an exultant new sense of personal freedom.

Philip's first intellectual awakening is followed shortly by his first sexual involvement. Back in Blackstable, he seduces Miss Wilkinson, an aging friend of his aunt, and quickly learns the difference between his idealized conception of sexual love and the reality he experiences with this frustrated, demanding, physically unpleasant woman. She satisfies none of his emotional needs and leaves him feeling ridiculous and vulnerable.

Miss Wilkinson also introduces him to a second crucial book, Murger's *Scènes de la vie de Bohème.* This romanticization of the lives and loves of the bohemian set stimulates Philip to attempt a career as a painter in Paris. He is at first fascinated by the atmosphere, the activity, and the personalities, especially the degenerate poet Cronshaw, but he soon sees the reality beneath the glamorous surface. From careful observation and repeated exposures he comes to understand the fakery, pretentiousness, and self-deception that characterizes most of this "artistic" activity. And for the untalented, the life is brutal and destructive. He watches talentless friends like Fanny Price and Miguel Ajuria waste their lives in a futile, feverish quest of the impossible. It is Fanny's suicide that finally ends his Paris pilgrimage.

Philip does not regret his Paris sojourn. He knows that he has had important experiences and has learned some valuable lessons. Nor is he disappointed to discover that he is without real ability. Even the truly talented artist is in a "bondage" to his discipline and must commit himself completely if he is to realize that talent. Philip has no taste for such total dedication; he would rather live than create. Art study in Paris has taught him how to look at things in a new way and that is, for him, a sufficient reward.

If Philip's experience with Miss Wilkinson gave him a taste of the reality of sex and love, it did not stifle his need for them. Upon his return from Paris, Philip begins one of the strangest and most intense romantic involvements in modern literature. There is nothing about Mildred Rogers that should logically attract Philip. She is physically unattractive, crude, stupid, and abrasive. Indeed, it is her very insolence that seems initially to interest him and, once attracted, he becomes obsessed with her. The fact that he rationally knows what Mildred is and consciously rejects her, has no effect whatsoever on his passion—a fact that Philip himself clearly recognizes. Given this powerful, irrational need, her continuing arrogance and abuse only excite his desire, and the more unavailable she seems, the more intense it becomes.

Mildred is, finally, like a fever that must be endured until it runs its course. And such, Maugham suggests, is the nature of romantic love. Once the fever is dissipated, Philip is "cured" and Mildred becomes simply an object of charity to him—at least that is Philip's belief. But, with the situation reversed, his adamant rejections of her sexuality must have at least some elements of subconscious revenge, and it is hard to believe that Philip does not, at some level, enjoy her final rage. In any event, the affair with Mildred has two lasting effects: Philip gains control of his passions and, at the same time, comes to understand the limits of rationality in the face of ungovernable emotions.

The last third of the novel has disappointed many readers. Especially disconcerting is the apparent contradiction between the sophisticated bleakness of Philip's final philosophical conclusion and the domestic felicity he expects to attain as a result of his marriage to a simple country girl.

A number of events bring Philip to his final intellectual position. Following the end of his affair with Mildred, he meets Thorpe Athelney and his family, endures a short period of economic deprivation, and learns of the meaningless death of two old friends, Cronshaw and Hayward. These circumstances bring him face to face with the last "bondage." Having emancipated himself from environmental, physical, cultural, religious, aesthetic, and emotional restraints, one final bond remains: Philip's need to "understand" the "meaning" of life.

Out of his anguished rumination Philip gains a new and final insight: "suddenly the answer occurred to him. . . . Life had no meaning. . . . Life was insignificant and death without consequence." Instead of depressing Philip, this "revelation," reminiscent of his earlier conversion from Christianity, excites him: "for the first time he was utterly free. . . . he was almighty because he had wrenched from chaos the secret of its nothingness."

To many, such an insight looks dismal, but to Philip—and Maugham—this view is exhilarating because it frees man to make the most of himself and his talents in purely human terms without any need to measure himself against any impossible transcendental absolutes.

It is in this context that Philip's marriage to Sally must be examined. Her father, Thorpe Athelney, is the only truly independent person that Philip meets during his lifetime. Athelney is free of the religious, cultural, social, and economic pressures that so distorted Philip's early environment. On the other hand he has no need to play any of the false artistic or rebel roles that Philip encountered during his Paris sojourn. Athelney follows no false gods and pursues no impossible dreams. He is, in short, his own man who has lived his life completely in accordance with his own needs, instincts, and desires. And the result has been personal satisfaction and happiness.

Since Philip accepts life as it is, he decides to settle for the one kind of happiness and existential meaning that he has seen demonstrated in action, not theory. Sally Athelney may not excite his passion or intellect, but he feels a "loving kindness" toward her and, to him, that promises a more satisfying life than to continue his search for nonexistent absolutes.

Thus, the resolution of the novel is not inconsistent and can be justified on an intellectual level. But artistically these final scenes remain unsatisfying. Maugham, himself, in his book of reminiscences *The Summing Up* (1938), admitted that his final vision of domestic contentment was the one experience in the novel that he did not know personally. "Turning my wishes into fiction," he wrote, "I drew a picture of the marriage I should like to make. Readers on the whole have found it the least satisfactory part of my book."

But, if Maugham did not find personal felicity in marriage, he did remain true to the ideas articulated in *Of Human Bondage*. Thus, he stated, in talking about the importance of the novel to his life: "It was the kind of effort that one can make once in a lifetime. I put everything into it, everything I knew, everything I experienced."

Keith Neilson

OF MICE AND MEN

Type of work: Novel
Author: John Steinbeck (1902-1968)
Type of plot: Sentimental melodrama
Time of plot: Twentieth century
Locale: Salinas Valley, California
First published: 1937

John Steinbeck compresses the tragic story of Of Mice and Men *into three days with dramatic intensity (it was later turned into a successful play), stark realism, and deep sympathy. In that brief time Curley has his hand smashed, his wife is murdered, the old swamper's dog is killed, Lennie loses his life, and George shoots his best friend.*

Five years before *Of Mice and Men* appeared Steinbeck showed his interest in what he called "unfinished children of nature," in a collection of short stories entitled *Pastures of Heaven.* Lennie Small is perhaps the finest expression of the writer's lifelong sympathy for the abused common man. Like *Tortilla Flat,* which brought Steinbeck immediate fame in 1935, and *In Dubious Battle* (1936), *Of Mice and Men* is set in the Salinas Valley of California where the writer himself spent many years as a migrant worker like the characters he depicts. Although he would go on to win the Pulitzer Prize for *The Grapes of Wrath* in 1939, and the Nobel Prize in 1962, Steinbeck's artistic temperament remained wedded to his concern with working-class problems that developed from his experience in this valley.

Yet *Of Mice and Men* is in no way a political statement. Its simplicity and grace make it a universal metaphor for the inhumanity of the human condition. Lennie—with his "shapeless face," his bear-like movements, his brute gentleness, and his selective forgetfulness—is one of the most sympathetic melodramatic figures of modern fiction (akin to Faulkner's Benjy, but more immediately accessible). He is not only convincingly childlike but is also consciously so—because he knows what will reinforce his relationship with George, the one thing he values besides all small, soft creatures. But just as Lennie's uncontrollable strength destroys those creatures inevitably, Lennie himself must be destroyed. George destroys him, out of love, because George recognizes that, like Candy's dog, Lennie does not belong in a world that does not protect the innocent from the inhumanity of selfish men. George's tragic action is the last gesture in their extraordinary relationship—a relationship the others fail to understand because it is based on tenderness rather than greed.

OF TIME AND THE RIVER

Type of work: Novel
Author: Thomas Wolfe (1900-1938)
Type of plot: Impressionistic realism
Time of plot: 1920's
Locale: Harvard, New York, France
First published: 1935

Subtitled A Legend of Man's Hunger in His Youth, *this long novel is a sequel to* Look Homeward, Angel: *it enjoys the youthful freshness and enthusiasm of the earlier work, yet benefits from Wolfe's growing experience as a stylist. Modeled after the author, Eugene Gant has an insatiable appetite for experience; a lonely and frightened man of seemingly inexhaustible energy, he attends Harvard, teaches at New York University, and tours France in his search to find meaning through action.*

Thomas Wolfe was six feet five inches tall and enormously heavy. Born in 1900, and endowed with a Niagara of uncontrollable energy, he thirsted wildly for life. He felt that he must visit all lands, pace all streets, follow all rural trails, meet all people, scan all faces, eat all food, drink all liquors, read all literature, love all women, capture all beauty, and "write, write, write." Time was his most lethal foe, and he predicted that only death, disease, or madness could stop him. Unable to curb his own intensity, he lamented a compulsion to do "too much of everything." Even in writing, he was devoid of the ability to select. He had great writing skills and was considered a literary phenomenon after 1929, when he published his first novel *Look Homeward, Angel,* which was followed in 1935 by *Of Time and the River.* At one time, William Faulkner considered him the best American novelist.

A slow-moving but intense novel of more than nine hundred pages that has the theme of a silent river flowing through time and darkness, *Of Time and the River* has passage after passage of splendid prose. The river always flows, always changes, but is always the same as it drinks dark and silent tides that "flow strangely from inland America." At twilight the river joins the harbor, which flows into the sea, but always the river runs like life itself through the secret night, groping like the novel for life's meaning. At times the purpose of the fine but endless descriptions of kitchens, foods, fields, woods, people, and trees is as mysterious as life's purpose is to Eugene Gant. Seasons are likened to the passing of life. October and November are painted so beautifully that they are reminiscent of Catholic concepts of November, the month of the souls in purgatory, when leaves and plants are dying, awaiting winter.

Besides its haunting vision of nocturnal America, the novel gives an unflattering view of "the mongrel and anonymous compost" of America's population. Bitter loathing is aimed at mediocre people, but also at Eugene Gant-

Thomas Wolfe himself. There are also fine street scenes of America and Europe. America's culture is scrutinized, and its fierce energy recognized, but the horror of mediocrity, of the common man, and of human flesh with its pasty complexion and "sagging folds" is stressed. We see jaded and weary people with lackluster eyes traveling through tunnels, the same faces that Eugene has seen everywhere in a thousand places and on a thousand occasions. The novel's ponderous pace does not change, and satiric irony is ladled out at Jews, middle-class Americans, rural police, laborers, uneducated people, and blacks. Most Jews are described in less than effusive terms, although there finally appears one good Jew, Fried. Some critics feel that Wolfe hurled his ironic darts at Jews because even though they were beyond the pale of "high" society in the 1920's, as was Wolfe himself, they were, unlike Wolfe, able to laugh and not be hurt. Blacks in the novel seem to have microscopic intellects, but an even more ghastly picture is drawn of two ultra-libidinous priests gorging themselves hoggishly at a sidewalk cafe in Marseilles, France. The lechery of these two fictional libertines is supreme, but several unkind critics have seen Thomas Wolfe autobiographically reincarnated in the enormous, bulky ringleader of the astounding pair. Such characterizations induced Leslie A. Fiedler to allege that the novel should be placed "not in a children's library, but in a high school library, on the shelf of masturbatory dreams."

Intellectual snobbery is endemic throughout the book, along with repetition and pessimism. But war's folly is lampooned, as well as the apparent hypocrisy of the conflict between age and youth. The problems confronting college youth, in an age when moral values are starting to be held in abeyance, are well drawn. So are the scenes of freshmen life in a large university, when youths sometimes deny God at seventeen and then stumble on without fixed goals.

Eugene Gant, like Thomas Wolfe, is lonely and has groundless fears. He feels that he can never be happy, and his wanderlust leads him over two continents, experiencing, tasting, always seeing. But he is looking for a secret portal to real life, as he gazes hungrily at the street scenes of America and Europe, asking himself: "Where shall I go? What shall I do?" He seeks reality through satiation, or possibly the reverse, and is obsessed by the passing of time's river. When Eugene arrives in England he feels the same loneliness that Wolfe calls "time-far," but he finds English street crowds more mellow, warm, and open than crowds in New England. Eugene is still choking in his own spiritual darkness, so the mark of dark time is visible in England, and, while breathing the gray European air, he realizes that it lacks the sparkle of America's. He journeys from England to France; naked desolation smothers his life, and he eventually realizes that he is an exile in Europe. He yearns for the remembered beauty of American landscapes, the vast fields, and distant blue hills and decides to return. In some ways, however, he has grown only in blubbery flesh, not in nobility. And even though he meets Esther, as he is about to sail back, he is still lonely.

Thomas Wolfe died in 1938, leaving vast stacks of written pages that were published posthumously as *The Web and the Rock* (1939) and *You Can't Go Home Again* (1940). His terminal illness struck suddenly just after he had finished the two gigantic manuscripts. Like Eugene Gant, Wolfe's main problem in life was loneliness; it could never have been solved in any other way.

William Freitas

THE OLD AND THE YOUNG

Type of work: Novel
Author: Luigi Pirandello (1867-1936)
Type of plot: Historical chronicle
Time of plot: 1891-1892
Locale: Sicily and Rome
First published: 1913

In this novel about the hectic life and bitter politics of Italy in the 1890's, Pirandello shows a society whose family ties are still ruptured by the effects of the revolutions of 1848 and 1860. Passages such as the mob murder scene and the description of the visit of two socialists to a cemetery to disinter the bodies of riot victims are unforgettable in their descriptive power.

Although primarily a historical novel, *The Old and the Young* also presents Pirandello's philosophical dialectic of life versus form in its various aspects: self versus mask, what we desire to be versus what we become, nature versus society, past ideals versus present realities, and feelings versus reason. For according to Pirandello, life is flux, flow, becoming. But in order for life to exist—to "be"—it must enter some form. Form, however, stifles life. Thus, the Pirandello paradox: life in order to "exist" must become form; once it becomes form, it ceases to be life.

There are various ways of escaping this dilemma. One way to escape the imprisonment of form is death, for death causes one to return to the eternal flow of life. In this novel, many individuals seek death through suicide to overcome the tragic realization that comes with the awareness of the dilemma of "life in form." This dilemma is presented historically and socially as the disappointment that occurred after the heroic ideals of the Risorgimento had become formalized and corrupted by the necessities of political form and expediency.

Another method of escape is abstracting oneself from life. This type of escape into pure form or pure abstraction necessitates the character's separation from any involvement in life and feeling. This is the choice of Don Cosmo who lives a life of pure reason in philosophy.

His brother, Don Ippolito, escapes the dilemma of life by retreating into conscious illusion; he lives in the past, in his archeological studies of the site upon which his palace rests. He converts his estate into a replica of the Bourbon past and lives a life of conscious madness. Other characters in the novel (Dianella and Mortara) escape the dilemma of life through unconscious madness.

The novel not only presents the dualism of life and form thematically, but structurally as well. Book One deals with the past, with Sicily, with the hopes of the Risorgimento, with life as possibility. Book Two presents Rome, the corruption of the heroes following the formalization of their heroic ideals, and the subsequent destruction of all hope, the escape from "reality."

Thus the setting of the novel, the depiction of a historical moment in Italian history, is interwoven with the basic Pirandellian theme of the conflict of life and form, and the multiple ways in which individuals cope with the awareness of this conflict.

THE OLD BACHELOR

Type of work: Drama
Author: William Congreve (1670-1729)
Type of plot: Comedy of intrigue
Time of plot: Seventeenth century
Locale: London
First presented: 1693

This first of Congreve's plays, written when he was only twenty-three, was standard Restoration fare in terms of its light plot about cuckolding, its witty and often risque dialogue, and its ridicule of anything Puritan. It is Congreve's brilliant style and infectious high spirits that raise his play far above those of his contemporaries, most of whom are long forgotten.

When Dryden finished reading the manuscript of *The Old Bachelor,* the grand old man of Restoration theater declared that he never saw such a first play in his life. Together with some other experienced playwrights, Dryden helped Congreve get his play into shape for the stage, and, with the added enhancement of music by England's leading composer, Henry Purcell, this fledgling dramatic effort propelled the young playwright to fame and fortune. The reasons are not hard to find. *The Old Bachelor* is cast in the tried and tested mold of Restoration comedy; but if the bottle is old, the wine is new. Congreve's dramatic situations are varied and interesting. Not too complicated to follow, his dialogue is sparkling, his characters appealing, and the obligatory Restoration cynicism tempered with just a hint of pathos.

Congreve uses such stock characters as skeptical, witty rakes, reluctant heroines, the cast-off mistress, the braggart soldier, the elderly cuckold, and the old, supposedly woman-hating bachelor, along with assorted fools and pimps. The philosophical assumptions behind the drama are also common Restoration currency: pursuing women is like pursuing game, the pleasure being in the pursuit more than in the catch (and certainly the game is not expected to pursue the hunter); there is no more ridiculous a sight in nature than the old bachelor taking a young wife; the married state, though it is the goal to which all strive, is by its very nature, an unsatisfying one; the most reprehensible faults of character are dullness, age, and taking oneself seriously.

One of the qualities that distinguishes Congreve from such earlier Restoration masters as Wycherley and Etherege (in addition to his more consistently brilliant dialogue) is that he shows a trace of compassion, as well as scorn for his characters. The cuckold Fondlewife, for instance, and to a greater extent, the old bachelor Heartwell, are figures of pathos as well as fun. The latter is aware of his dangerously intense feelings for Silvia, knows that he should resist them because they will only serve to make him look foolish, and yet he is unable to overcome his passion with reason. "O dotage, dotage!" he moans, "that ever that noble passion, lust, should ebb to this degree." We cannot help but sympathize as he writhes in the toils of the old, familiar snake, especially when he is mocked by others (including Belinda) for his folly. Luckily, Bellmour, with a stroke of generosity unusual in a Restoration rake, has taken pity on the poor man: "Heartwell is my friend; and tho he is blind, I must not see him fall into the snare and unwittingly marry a whore." Neither Wycherley nor Etherege would have troubled their heads for a moment about this piece of cruelty; indeed they would have considered it as more fodder for their comic resolutions.

At the end of the play all of the characters, even the fools, seem reasonably content, though their hopes and expectations have in some cases been thwarted. Congreve means us to rise from our comic repast with a good taste in our mouths, though spiced and sauced, to be sure, with the relieved Heartwell's dour conclusions on the perils of aging: "All coursers the first heat with vigour run; But 'tis with whip and spur the race is won."

THE OLD CURIOSITY SHOP

Type of work: Novel
Author: Charles Dickens (1812-1870)
Type of plot: Sentimental romance
Time of plot: Early nineteenth century
Locale: England
First published: 1840-1841

In its time one of Dickens' most popular novels, The Old Curiosity Shop *follows the misfortunes of Little Nell, an orphan whose grandfather's compulsive gambling forces the pair first to roam the countryside as beggars, then to work in a wax works and later as grave tenders in a country churchyard. In an extremely melodramatic ending, Little Nell and her grandfather die just as help is on the way in the form of* The Single Gentleman *and Nell's friend Kit Nubbles. Of all Dickens' novels,* The Old Curiosity Shop *is the most excessively sentimental, frequently approaching the maudlin.*

The Old Curiosity Shop is indeed a curious tale. All the characters, with the exception of the first person narrator, are presented as unbelievable, bizzare people. For example, the heroine, Nell, is portrayed as a "fairy," a "little creature" with a "slight figure" who "tripped" rather than walked but responded to situations with "great tears" or "heaving sobs." Her grandfather is an odd mixture of devotion and gambling compulsion; and Quilp, the misshapen dwarf, a combination of power hunger and strangulated sexual desire, a common characteristic in Dickens' villains, is the most grotesque of all. Indeed, if the novel itself can be defined, it might be seen as a sentimental, comic grotesque, certainly a tribute to Dickens' fertile and unorthodox imagination.

Holding all the characters and incidents together is the plot of Little Nell's and her grandfather's disappearance and their pursuit by both the forces of evil, led by Quilp, and the forces of virtue, headed by the anonymous Single Gentleman. The latter is a rich relative of good will seeking to restore the victims' fortune, again a familiar figure to Dickens' readers. Nell, or more properly, the ideal of Nell, mesmerizes everyone in the novel; she has also haunted all her readers. She represents that vulnerable innocence which seemed to have an unusual effect on the Victorians, signifying a state they felt that they had somehow lost forever.

Dickens' decision to let Nell die before she was united with her benefactor, The Single Gentleman, and her ardent admirer, Kit Nubbles, brought cries of protest from both sides of the Atlantic and is perhaps the most curious aspect of the entire novel. By allowing her to die, however, Dickens underscored his final intention: that his grotesque fiction was after all based more on reality than it was on the fantastic.

OLD FORTUNATUS

Type of work: Drama
Author: Thomas Dekker (c.1572-1632?)
Type of plot: Allegorical comedy
Time of plot: Tenth century
Locale: Cyprus, Babylon, England
First presented: 1599

This story of a father and son who could not escape the lure of riches contains excellent passages of poetry, wit, and humor. The plot, plagued from the start by structural weaknesses, was further impaired by later revisions; the play is too moralistic to be simply humorous, but too farcical to be seriously moral.

Old Fortunatus, coming early (1599) in Thomas Dekker's long playwriting career, shows his ability to create vivid, humorous episodes, but it also shows his penchant for moral allegory lacking either causal or thematic coordination. Dekker has packed too many divergent plots and themes into the play, first adapting the story of Fortunatus from a Dutch folktale (1596?), then adding the confusing debate between Virtue and Vice for a Court performance (1599).

Dekker began by making the Fortunatus folktale of the man with the inexhaustible purse and flying hat an example of Fortune's fickleness, a common medieval theme. The goddess Fortune gives Fortunatus ("lucky") a choice of her richest gifts, only to bring him to a sudden death. Dekker combines this Fortune theme, inconsistently, with the moral example of Fortunatus' tragic choice of wealth rather than wisdom. After his death, Fortunatus' sons enact a further moral lesson on the misuse of riches. The prodigal Andelocia lavishes his wealth on the English court, losing both purse and hat to the cunning courtiers and Agripyne, while the righteous Ampedo would hoard Fortune's gifts without benefit to himself or others. Their family servant, Shadow, provides humorous commentary on their actions.

The Virtue-Vice debate, essentially an allegorical masque, adds little to the play other than spectacular effects. Vice's apples of gold, readily consumed by Andelocia and the courtiers, show the characters' moral deformity by the horns that spring devilishly on their foreheads and that can be cured only by Virtue's less appealing apples. But Virtue's conquest of Vice in the final scene has little relation to the downfall of Fortunatus and his sons by their own weakness, so Virtue's triumph must depend upon her allegorically and dramatically weak appeal to Queen Elizabeth's extra-dramatic arbitration.

THE OLD MAID

Type of work: Novel
Author: Edith Wharton (1862-1937)
Type of plot: Social criticism
Time of plot: The 1850's
Locale: New York
First published: 1924

In this short novel, Wharton tells the dual story of Charlotte Lovell, a seemingly stiff and conventional middle-aged woman, and her more outgoing cousin Delia Ralston, a typical representative of genteel upper-class New York society. The irony and interest of the story are generated by the final revelation that "old maid" Charlotte is actually the mother of Tina, and has suffered silently throughout the years that Delia reared the girl, who never suspected her true origin.

The second volume in her *Old New York* tetralogy, Edith Wharton's *The Old Maid* was written fairly late in her literary career, and is so short that it barely qualifies as a novel. Furthermore, only a small portion of it consists of speeches by protagonist Charlotte Lovell, and none of it tells her inner thoughts. The story is told from the viewpoint of Charlotte's cousin, Delia Ralston. But Charlotte is the character referred to in the title, and *The Old Maid* is about two decades of misery which she suffers as she watches her daughter Tina grow up.

How is so much told in so little space? The answer lies in Edith Wharton's ingenious use of two relatively short sequences to show Charlotte's inner feelings. In the first, Tina, who has been spared knowledge of her origin, impudently refers to Charlotte as an "old maid," and Charlotte accepts the label. In the second, on the eve of Tina's wedding, Charlotte demands that she finally be recognized as Tina's mother, and accuses Delia not only of usurpation, but of loving Tina for being Clement Spender's child. These two sequences, like two well-placed bright lights, illuminate Charlotte's silent suffering throughout the rest of the story. They tell how Charlotte feels about each of Delia's kindnesses and each stage of Tina's growing up.

Delia, who represents the society of her time, has little understanding of Charlotte's pain until the final argument. Delia wears a disguise over her true feelings, but forces Charlotte to wear an even more deceptive disguise, to play the stiff maiden aunt instead of the loving mother. And, in the end, the only reward she can offer Charlotte for all of this pain is the conventional gesture of the bride's final kiss.

The superficiality of upper-class society, the masks its members wear, and their concern for appearance instead of reality are always in the background. But one need not hold membership in such a class to appreciate this poignant drama of confused roles and of love that must remain silent for the sake of the loved one.

THE OLD MAN AND THE SEA

Type of work: Novelette
Author: Ernest Hemingway (1899-1961)
Type of plot: Symbolic romance
Time of plot: Mid-twentieth century
Locale: Cuba and the Gulf Stream
First published: 1952

On the surface an exciting but tragic adventure story, The Old Man and the Sea *enjoys near-perfection of structure, restraint of treatment, and evocative simplicity of style. On a deeper level, the book is a fable of the unconquerable spirit of man, a creature capable of snatching spiritual victory from circumstances of disaster and apparent defeat; on yet another level, it is a religious parable which unobtrusively utilizes Christian symbols and metaphors.*

Hemingway began his career as a journalist with the *Kansas City Star* in 1917, and later was a wartime foreign correspondent for the *Toronto Star.* His first important collection of short stories, *In Our Time,* appeared in 1925, to be followed, in 1926, by what many consider to be his finest novel, *The Sun Also Rises.* During his long stay among other American expatriates in Paris, Hemingway was influenced by Gertrude Stein, Ezra Pound, and James Joyce. From their models, from his own journalistic background, and from his admiration for Mark Twain, Hemingway developed his own characteristic style—a style so idiosyncratic that it precluded imitation and, eventually, strangled Hemingway's own artistic development. The Hemingway style, further expressed in *A Farewell to Arms* (1929), then gradually sinking toward stereotypical stylization in *Death in the Afternoon* (1932), *The Green Hills of Africa* (1935), and *For Whom the Bell Tolls* (where it reaches its lowest point of self-caricature, undermining his most ambitious novel), is marked by consistent elements: understatement created by tersely realistic dialogue; use of everyday speech and simple vocabulary; avoidance of the abstract; straightforward sentence structure and paragraph development; spare and specific imagery; objective, reportorial viewpoint; and emphasis on "the real thing, the sequence of emotion and fact to make the emotion." This last, Wordsworthian, technique accounts for Hemingway's position as the most gifted of the "Lost Generation" writers.

Accompanying these stylistic traits is a set of consistent thematic concerns that have become known as the Hemingway "code": obsession with all outdoor pursuits and sports; identification with the primitive; constant confrontation with death; fascination with violence, and with the skillful control of violence; what he calls "holding the purity line through the maximum of exposure." The typical Hemingway hero, existential in a peculiarly American way, faces the sterility and failure and death of his contemporary world with steady-handed courage and a stoical resistance to pain that allows him a fleeting, but essentially human, nobility and grace.

After a decade of silence, while Hemingway was preoccupied with the turmoil of World War II, he published *Across the River and into the Trees* (1950)—an inferior book that led many to believe his genius had dried up. But two years later, drawn from his experiences in Cuba, *The Old Man and the Sea* appeared—to be awarded the Pulitzer Prize, and to lead to a Nobel Prize for Literature (1954) for his "mastery of the art of modern narration." As a kind of ultimate condensation of the Hemingway code, this novelette attains an austere dignity from its extreme simplicity of imagery, symbolism, setting, and character. As such it is in stark contrast with Melville's sprawling epic masterpiece with which it has much in common: *Moby Dick.*

Hemingway displays his genius of perception by using, without apology, the most obvious symbolic imagery; in fact, he creates his desired impact by admitting the ordinary (in the way of Robert Frost, whose "An Old Man's Winter's Night" resembles this book). An example is the statement that the old man's furled sail each evening "looked like a flag of permanent defeat." Here the admission of the obvious becomes ironic, since the old man is not, as he himself declares, *defeated*—although he is "destroyed." Aside from the two overt image-symbols of the lions on the beach and of "the great Di Maggio" ("who does all things perfectly even with the pain of the bone spur in his heel"), the implicit image of Christ stalks through the work until the reader understands that it is not, after all, a religious symbol, but a secular one that affirms that each man has his own agonies and crucifixion. As for setting, three elements stand out: the sea itself, which the old man regards as feminine—not as an enemy but as the *locus* in which man plays his little part with security and serenity derived from acceptance of her inevitable capriciousness; the intrusions of the outside world, with the jet plane high overhead and the tourist woman's ignorant comment at the end that shows total insensitivity to the common man's capacity for tragedy; and the sharks, which make "everything wrong" and stand for the heroic absurdity of human endeavors.

The old man's character is revealed to us in two ways: by the observations of the narrator, and by his own monologue. The latter device might seem theatrical and out of place if Hemingway had not taken pains to set up its employment openly: "He did not remember when he had first started to talk aloud when he was by himself." But the words he says to no one but himself reveal the old man's mind as clearly as, and even more poignantly than, the narrator's knowledge of his thoughts. We see him as the unvanquished (whose eyes are as young as the sea); with sufficient pride to allow humility; with unsuspected, though simple, introspection ("I am a strange old man"); with unquestioning trust in his own skills and in the folklore of his trade; with almost superhuman endurance; and with a noble acceptance of the limitations forced upon him by age. Before the drama is over, the old man projects his own qualities into the fish—his strength, his wisdom—until his initial hunter's indifference turns to pity and the fish becomes "friend" and "brother." "But I must kill him," the old man says, stating Hemingway's consciousness of naturalistic realism: "I am glad we do not have to try to kill the stars. . . . It is enough to live on the sea and kill our true brothers." Killing with dignity, as it is done also in the bullring, is an accepted part of the human condition. Only the graceless, undignified sharks (like the hyenas in "The Snows of Kilimanjaro") are abhorrent and diminish the tragic grandeur of the human drama.

The Old Man and the Sea is a direct descendant of *Moby Dick*. The size, strength, and mystery of the great marlin recall the presence of the elusive white whale; similarly, the strength, determination (like Ahab, the old man does not bother with eating or sleeping), and strangeness of Hemingway's hero may be compared to the epic qualities of Melville's. But the differences are as important as the similarities. In Melville, both the whale and Ahab have sinister, allusive, and unknown connotations that they seem to share between them and that are not revealed clearly to the reader—in the fashion of romanticism. Hemingway's realism does not present the struggle as a pseudo-sacred cosmic one between forces of darkness but as an everyday confrontation between the strength of an ordinary man and the power of nature. Hemingway's fish is huge, but he is not solitary and unique; the old man is not the oldest, nor the greatest, fisherman. Finally, neither the old man, nor the fish, is completely victorious. The fish does not kill the old man, nor does it make him older or wiser; it only makes him very tired.

Kenneth John Atchity

OLD MORTALITY

Type of work: Novelette
Author: Katherine Anne Porter (1894–   )
Type of plot: Social chronicle
Time of plot: 1885-1912
Locale: Texas and New Orleans
First published: 1939

Using her own Southern background and her experience with convent schools as a point of departure, Porter challenges romantic family myths about life and the past by presenting Miranda's maturing vision of the realities around her. Specific social causes are also dealt with, such as Cousin Eva's absorption in the women's suffrage movement and her consequent imprisonment.

Although each novelette in *Pale Horse, Pale Rider* is independent of the others, a unity can be perceived in both chronology and characters. "Old Mortality," the first of the three, is the earliest, and Miranda appears again in the last novelette. Miranda is the protagonist in many of Porter's other stories. In "Old Mortality" she is shown at three stages of her girlhood: as a child of about eight years, as an adolescent at the Catholic convent, and as a recently-eloped young woman of eighteen. A student of Porter's work will recognize that Miranda is Porter's alter-ego.

Porter brilliantly analyzes the discrepancy between the acceptable roles offered to Miranda by her family and her growing awareness of her own nature. Rebelliously, she dreams of being a racehorse jockey, a profession then absolutely closed to women. But Aunt Amy is still held up as a model; the family celebrates her escapades, love-life, and death. Miranda—small, snub-nosed, and freckled—knew that for her to become willowy, dark-haired, and pale like the accepted Amy would take a miracle.

The foil for Aunt Amy is Cousin Eva, who was called an old maid the moment she was born. Her own mother began the ill-treatment of Eva, calling attention to her buck teeth and lack of chin. Eva took refuge in scholarship and the women's rights movement, but was always tormented by the family. Miranda generally follows the family's opinion of Eva and does not come to appreciate her until, in the last section, the two meet while traveling home to Uncle Gabriel's funeral.

It is in speaking with Cousin Eva that Miranda understands that her own elopement was in effect a flight from her family, and that her marriage is just a new kind of tyranny. She decides that she must abandon the marriage if she is to gain her own identity and be free of the conventions forced on her by her family and society. For 1912, a time when a woman's "place" in the world was generally founded on her husband's position, Miranda's decision was a radical one.

OLD MORTALITY

Type of work: Novel
Author: Sir Walter Scott (1771-1832)
Type of plot: Historical romance
Time of plot: 1679
Locale: Scotland
First published: 1816

This novel about the struggle between the Covenanters and the Cavaliers in 1679 takes its title from the name of an old itinerant who wanders about Scotland caring for the tombstones of fallen Covenanters. The story, supposedly told by Old Mortality to the narrator, Jedediah Cleishbotham, is filled with dramatic interest in the Scott style, and contains several memorable characterizations.

Scott's best novels are those with a Scottish setting. The characterizations are less stilted than in his English romances, and the dialogue has the crisp ring of colloquial speech. The history of Scotland lay closer to the novelist's heart than the reign of Elizabeth (*Kenilworth*) or the times of the crusades (*Ivanhoe*). *The Heart of Midlothian* and *Old Mortality* represent Scott's highest achievement in the Scottish Romance.

Scott is fascinated by the marginal hero, the man or woman who by birth and experience straddles two backgrounds. His first hero, Waverly, literally "wavers" between his loyalty to the English crown and the attraction of the Highlanders. In *Old Mortality*, Henry Morton is an accomplished peacemaker who does not deny his Covenanter background despite his obvious social and personal preference for the established aristocracy.

In his person are combined the best characteristics of the novel's warring factions: "He had inherited from his father an undaunted courage, and a firm and uncompromising detestation of oppression whether in politics or religion. But his enthusiasm was unsullied by fanatic zeal, and unleavened by the sourness of the puritanical spirit." His marriage, at story's end, to Edith Bellenden is not only a romantic reward but a ritual of social accommodation. When Edith's mortally wounded fiance, Lord Evendale, puts Edith's hand in Henry's, he fashions the symbol of a social hope: the melding of all the Britons.

The supporting characters, partially rooted in historical fact, are effective embodiments of the cultural and social tensions that inform the action. Balfour is a convincing religious fanatic, and Claverhouse is the perfect cavalier: cynical, detached, cruel, and always concerned "to rectify the derangement of his dress." The narrative often crackles with an excitement of a distinctly melodramatic kind. When Claverhouse rescues Henry from the fanatical Covenanters who are about to murder him for being a suspected traitor, the effect is very much like that of a last minute rescue in motion pictures.

OLD ST. PAUL'S

Type of work: Novel
Author: William Harrison Ainsworth (1805-1882)
Type of plot: Historical romance
Time of plot: Mid-seventeenth century
Locale: London
First published: 1841

Although a minor novelist by comparison to Dickens and other of his Victorian contemporaries, Ainsworth in Old St. Paul's *shows himself a master of weaving a story out of the details and atmosphere of his historical setting. Although his plot is overly sentimental and melodramatic, the author's picture of plague-ridden London and the effects of fear upon its citizens is excellent.*

Old St. Paul's: A Tale of the Plague and the Fire, was based primarily on Daniel Defoe's *Journal of the Plague Year* and another lesser known book about the plague by Defoe. But, while some characters and much description are the same, the tone and style of the books are vastly different. Defoe was the great realist, concerned more than anything else with accurate description, however grotesque it might seem, but Ainsworth was a romantic novelist, using the material as it suited him to develop the particular tale that he had in mind. Thus he takes, for example, the piper who was carted off by mistake as a dead man, blinds him, and gives him a beautiful daughter who turns out to be the child of a nobleman. Although the background of the novel is realistic, the actions of the characters are highly stylized according to the conventions of Victorian fiction. Ainsworth was not an innovator; he accepted contemporary notions of characterization and sentiment, and used them in his work. *Old St. Paul's* thus presents a double vision of both the seventeenth century in which it is set and the nineteenth, when it was written.

In the romantic tradition, the villains in the novel, such as the Earl of Rochester and Paul Parravicin, are thoroughly wicked, and the virtuous, such as Stephen and Leonard, entirely noble. By the same token, the foolish, such as Blaize, are complete simpletons, and the wise extraordinarily perceptive. The outlines of the novel are bold and sharp, with little shading, but within its limitations, the book is both interesting and entertaining. The melodramatic plot, ingenious and complicated, is well handled and moves swiftly. Ainsworth obviously knew his readership and understood how to write for it. At the time this novel appeared, his works were nearly as popular as the novels of Dickens. Ainsworth never allowed his historical data to overwhelm him, but used it with skill as he needed it. This story of murder, love, and treachery seems almost to achieve a symbolic power unimagined by its author, as it moves against the background of the plague and the great, cleansing fire which followed.

THE OLD WIVES' TALE

Type of work: Novel
Author: Arnold Bennett (1867-1931)
Type of plot: Naturalism
Time of plot: Nineteenth century
Locale: England and Paris
First published: 1908

In this novel about the effects of passing time on human lives, Bennett offers striking character portraits of two sisters whose lives and personalities are in sharp contrast to each other. Set in the transitional era of the industrial revolution, the author uses colorful detail and events such as the siege of Paris primarily as background for the development of character.

Late nineteenth century literary naturalism insists on the determining forces of heredity and environment; realism also concentrates objectively on the social and historical conditions of experience, but it allows for a greater independence in the principal characters. Frank Norris' McTeague is a typical naturalist phenomenon: everything he is, from gentle dentist to brutal drunk, is the result of his biological and social background. Flaubert is a realist. His Emma Bovary, although corrupted by sentimental fantasies and trapped by her provincial life, pits her misguided energy against her fate and achieves tragic significance. Arnold Bennett's fiction is marked by a blending of these two literary movements. He cultivated detachment and technique in his writing because he felt that the English novel had neglected what he called a "scientific" eye; satire and sentiment, from Fielding to Dickens, had colored the author's presentation of reality. Bennett turned to France for new models: by absorbing realism and naturalism he became a master of the "impressions of the moment," but he retained an English sense for the uniqueness of character.

The Old Wives' Tale is his masterpiece. The title is revealing. Instead of describing a superstitious tale, Bennett's title dramatizes his objectivity by forcing us to interpret the phrase literally. The novel is about two women who become old, and their story, despite its inevitability, is far more wondrous in its simple reality than any fantastic or "superstitious" tale. What is remarkable about them is that despite their having lived entirely different lives, they emerge, at the end, remarkably similar. And this is primarily because of the moral fiber woven into their characters from earliest childhood. Neither woman "has any imagination" (which was Bennett's intention), but each has the stability of a rock. Constance leads a conventional life and never leaves St. Luke's square; Sophia runs off with an attractive salesman, is deserted in Paris, and runs a successful boarding house during the siege of Paris and the Commune. But for all the difference of circumstance in their lives, they remain the self-reliant middle-class daughters of John Baines.

Critic John Wain calls the result "the effect Bennett was aiming at: a parallelism amid contrast." This pattern is illustrative of what Bennett meant by technique and craftsmanship; it also reveals the interweaving of naturalist and realist values.

The "judicial murder" of Daniel Povey in the prison at Stafford parallels the public execution of the murderer Rivain which Sophia and Gerald take in as an unusual "attraction." This and many other parallels in the plot— for example, young Cyril's theft from the till at the shop, and Sophia's prudent appropriation of Gerald's £200—are done so cleverly that they never seem forced or artificial. Life is simply like this, says Bennett, and the range and sureness of his story vindicate his method.

Bennett's respect for his ordinary characters is intense. He admires their capacity for survival and never underestimates their souls. In the midst of bourgeois contentment, Constance is never free from a strange sadness. She lacks the imaginative power of a Hamlet, but feels a similar anguish: "The vast inherent melancholy of the universe did not exempt her." Her simple and undistinguished husband, Samuel Povey, dies of toxemia contracted from pneumonia. His death is oddly heroic, because the illness that kills him is a cruelly ironic reward for his selfless dedication to his poor cousin Daniel. Bennett is unequivocal in his praise. He concedes that he thought Povey a "little" man easy to ridicule but that his honesty finally earns a great deal of respect. The last of his life displays a touch of greatness that all souls, insists Bennett, have in common.

It is important that we understand that Constance's melancholy, Samuel's humility, and Sophia's passionate nature are secondary to what Bennett felt was the main stream running through all their natures: the blind will to survive. Fossette, the aged poodle, is the emblem of that instinct at the close of the novel. The great enemy of man and beast is time, and it always wins in the end. Readers may object to assigning Bennett such a cold view of things. To end on a beastly comparison between Fossette and Sophia seems out of keeping with Bennett's fondness and respect for his characters. And yet we remember that what Bennett praises the most in Sophia is precisely her pluck, her ability to survive in a totally alien environment. Her emotional life is not a rich one and the last glimpse of Gerald Scales as an old man does not rekindle her feelings. On the contrary, it paves the way for the stroke that kills her. Unlike Povey's death, which was senseless but pathetic because of his selflessness, Sophia's death is the result of an unbearable knowledge; she confronts her own death in Gerald's. Gerald's death strikes her as overwhelming in its sheer physical meaning. Once a handsome and vital young man who had excited her passions and moved her to abandon respectability, he is now a withered and aged corpse. Sophia is not concerned with his moral weakness or the grief he caused her. All she can think of is that a young man, once "proud" and bold, has been reduced to a horribly decimated version of his former self. The cruelty of time itself, which has made a mockery of all the feelings of love and hatred they shared, shatters her self-confidence. She can no longer separate herself from the mortality around her. When the inevitability of death becomes apparent, even to someone without imagination like Sophia, the will to survive is gone. Suddenly the full weight of her life, the great struggle for survival in Paris, descends with crushing force. It is more than she can stand. Although she fears death, she begs for its deliverance. She can take no more.

Despite all of the pressures and forces that shape *The Old Wives' Tale,* it does not end until the hearts of its protagonists stop beating.

Peter A. Brier

THE OLD WIVES' TALE

Type of work: Drama
Author: George Peele (1558?-1597?)
Type of plot: Comic fantasy
Time of plot: Indeterminate
Locale: England
First presented: c. 1593

This charming play, replete with a sorcerer, a princess, a beautiful and an ugly daughter, a magic well, and dozens of enchantments, must be seen rather than read to be properly enjoyed. Peele employed tales from his childhood and various folklore motifs in his story, from which Milton drew for his Comus.

Boisterous, light-hearted, zanily complicated, *The Old Wives' Tale* must be seen, or at least envisioned dramatically, to be appreciated. Unlike Peele's first successful play, *The Arraignment of Paris* (1582), *The Old Wives' Tale* is not a literary play, although it draws upon the mythical and pastoral sources used in the first play. Yet its cryptic riddles, jolly puns and merry wordplay, magic formulas, lewd innuendoes, and colloquial prose judiciously alternated with comically rhetorical verse give the play a rich verbal texture that adds greatly to its heady ebullience. Peele's *tour de force,* moreover, is a musical comedy; its joyful songs, often completely unconnected with the progress of the storyline, contribute perfectly to the formlessness of theme and general confusion of events—and must be *heard.* Peele may have meant to reflect his own character in Huanebango and Corebus. A member of the University Wits, his notorious and legendary life is chronicled in *The Merry Conceited Jests of George Peele, Sometimes a Student of Oxford* (1607).

Structurally the play is a free-for-all with concealed rules. It appears to be chaotically plotless but, in fact, is neatly drawn together into a fast-moving, immensely complex, and quickly finished combination of fairy tale and dream fancy. Calypha and Thelea find their parallels in Zantippa and Celanta; Erestus' quest is balanced by Eumenides', the maddened wife of the first by the ghost-companion of the second; and Madge is somehow strangely associated with the magician Sacrapant. In the magician, moreover, as well as in the bear-man, the wandering knight, the two opposite daughters, Peele succeeds in creating folk stock characters who remain in the popular tradition to this day. Events succeed one another so quickly that the reader is happily dazzled and swept along by the sheer energy of this exuberant nonsense as when Huanebango, having just entered, is struck down by a flame of fire. The frame, set up by Madge and the three pages, dissolves the boundary between the audience on the stage and the audience in the theater—and the confusion heightens our comic feeling of release and enjoyment, so that we join Erestus, Eumenides, and Huanebango in declaring that we are in the "April of age" thanks to this "merry winter's tale."

OLDTOWN FOLKS

Type of work: Novel
Author: Harriet Beecher Stowe (1811-1896)
Type of plot: Social chronicle
Time of plot: Late eighteenth century
Locale: Massachusetts
First published: 1869

Drawing upon her husband's recollections of his Massachusetts village of Natick for her picture of Oldtown and its citizens, Stowe presents quiet reminiscences through her narrator Horace Holyoke. Rather than having a definite plot, the novel consists of vivid pictures of New England life shortly after the Revolutionary War with particular emphasis on changing social patterns and new religious movements which replaced the collapsed Puritan theocracy.

Harriet Beecher Stowe's popular reputation rests on *Uncle Tom's Cabin* but her other novels, especially *Oldtown Folks,* also deserve attention for their literary qualities as distinct from the propagandistic aspects of her abolitionist novel. Indeed, *Oldtown Folks* is a fine example of realistic literature with a regional flavor, in its way a herald of such later works as Edgar Lee Masters' *Spoon River Anthology* and the regional novels of Sarah Orne Jewett.

In *Oldtown Folks,* Stowe recreates the ambience of delicately balanced life in a small New England town through her narrator Horace Holyoke. Three quite distinct religious persuasions, for example, coexisted in Oldtown, if not always amicably at least civilly. Yet the differences between strict, pre-destination Calvinists and potential-salvation-for-all Arminians could hardly be more vivid, while the Church of England (later Episcopalian) affiliation of "Lady" Lothrop merely added leaven to an already fermenting mix—and this at a time when and in a place where religious views dominated politics and society. Still, the accommodation achieved among residents of Oldtown, however uneasy, could well be a model for modern times, an exemplar of tolerance from an age of intolerance to twentieth century intolerances much in need of modification. Stowe's reminiscence—heavily reliant on her husband's New England experiences—is thus a timely study despite its seemingly antique air.

The only flaw in an otherwise admirably realistic novel is Stowe's sentimentality: her irresistible urge to marry Horace and Tina at the end of the novel—a "lived happily ever after" type of ending for two much-beleaguered people, and an inconsistency in an otherwise stark portrayal of real life. Even then, such a weakness is not anomalous, given Stowe's background. Reared by a strict Calvinist father, she was also strongly influenced by the liberal beliefs of her uncle, Samuel Foote. Under these ambivalent circumstances, Stowe ultimately abandoned her father's Calvinism without embracing her uncle's liberalism. Consequently, her loyalties and allegiances were divided, and that division is reflected in her resolution of the novel.

OLIVER TWIST

Type of work: Novel
Author: Charles Dickens (1812-1870)
Type of plot: Sentimental romance
Time of plot: Early nineteenth century
Locale: English provinces and London
First published: 1837-1839

When the new 1834 Poor Law abolishing supplemental aid to the poor was passed, families were broken up and their members placed in separate workhouses; in protest of this situation, Dickens began publishing Oliver Twist *in serial form in 1837. The novel depicts the world of poverty and crime in London which forced men, women, and children into lives of theft and prostitution. Written when the author was in his twenties,* Oliver Twist *foreshadows his later works in its complicated plot, skillful change of pace, and control of dramatic tension and climax.*

When *Oliver Twist* was published in the late 1830's, it shocked quite a few people. Clergymen and magazine editors accused the young novelist (Dickens was then under thirty) of writing an immoral book. In later editions, Dickens defended his book, explaining that one of his purposes had been to take the romance out of crime, to show the underworld of London as the sordid, filthy place that he knew it to be. Few of his readers have ever doubted that he succeeded in this task.

When Dickens began writing, a popular form of fiction was the so-called "Newgate novel," or the novel dealing in part with prison life and the rogues and highwaymen who ended up in prison. These heroes were often cousins of Macheath of *The Beggar's Opera* fame. Dickens took this tradition and form and turned it around, making it serve the purposes of his new realism. The Bill Sikes-Nancy subplot still contains the melodramatic elements, but Sikes is no Macheath and Nancy no Polly Peachum.

From the beginning of the book, when the grim birth of the infant who was to become Oliver is revealed, the reader is in an uncomfortably unromantic world. If people are starving to death, if children are "accidentally" killed off by their charitable keepers, if the innocent suffer and the cruel and unscrupulous prosper, Dickens does not hesitate to lay the facts out for all to see. Nancy is a prostitute, Bill is a murderer, Fagin is a fence, and the boys are pickpockets; and the supporting cast includes all manner of Bumbles and Thingummys and Mrs. Manns, individuals who never hesitate to deprive someone else of anything that they, themselves, could use. Poverty is the great leveler, the universal corruptor, and in the pages of *Oliver Twist* the results of this widespread poverty are portrayed with a startling lack of sentimentality. Dickens becomes sentimental when dealing with virtue, but never when dealing with vice.

The petty villains, the small-time corrupt officials, such as Bumble, are treated humorously, but Bill Sikes is portrayed with complete realism. Although Dickens' contemporaries thought that Bill was too relentlessly evil, Dickens challenged them to deny that such men existed in London, products of the foul life forced upon them from infancy. He holds up Bill Sikes for the reader to see in all of his blackness, without making any attempt to find "redeeming characteristics." Nancy is a more complicated character, both immoral and kindhearted. She is sentimental because she is basically good, while Bill is entirely practical, a man who will step on anybody who gets in his way—and feel no regrets.

With *Oliver Twist,* Dickens attempted a deliberate contrast to his previous work. While there is much humor in the novel, it is seldom like the humor of *The Pickwick Papers,* and is woven into a realistic and melodramatic narrative of a particularly grim and dark kind. The readers of Mr. Pickwick's exploits must have been startled when they picked up the magazines containing this new novel by Charles Dickens and discovered old Fagin teaching the innocent Oliver how to pick pockets, and read of children swigging gin like old drunkards. But Dickens was a man of many talents, and he introduced some new ones with this book. In *Oliver Twist,* Dickens exploited for the first time his abilities to invoke both pathos and horror, to combine these qualities to grip absolutely a reader's interest. United with the vitality which always infused Dickens' prose, these powers guaranteed this book a wide and faithful following as it was serialized.

Oliver Twist was the first of the young novelist's nightmare stories and the first of his social tracts. A certain amount of social protest could be read into Mr. Pickwick's time in prison, but it is a long distance from the prison of Mr. Pickwick to the almshouse in *Oliver Twist.* The leap from farce to melodrama and social reform was dramatically successful, and Dickens was to continue in the same vein for many years. Some critics called his work vulgar, but the masses loved it. He was accused of exaggeration, but as he made clear repeatedly, his readers had only to walk the streets of London to discover the characters and conditions of which he wrote so vividly. If his characterizations of some individuals suggested the "humours" theory of Ben Jonson rather than fully-rounded psychological portraits, the total effect of the characters in the book was that of an entire society, pulsing with life and energy.

In this book, Dickens displayed for the first time his amazing gift of entering into the psychology of a pathological individual. He follows closely Sikes and Fagin to their respective ends, and never flinches from revealing to the reader their true natures. The death of the unrepentant Sikes remains one of the most truly horrible scenes in English fiction. (When Dickens performed this passage to audiences in his public readings, it was common for ladies in the audience to scream or faint.) And when Fagin is sitting in court, awaiting the verdict of his trial, his thoughts roam from one triviality to another, although the fact of his approaching death by hanging is never far away. The combination of the irrelevant and the grimly pertinent suggests a kind of psychological realism that was completely new in 1838.

Dickens entertained a life-long fondness for the theater. His interest in the drama had a profound influence on his fiction. Dickens himself was an actor, and his readings from his books toward the end of his life became famous. In his novels, the actor in Dickens is also discernible. At times, the reader seems to feel that the author is impersonating a living individual, and often that is precisely the case. At other times, the plots bear the imprint of the popular stage fare of the day, including the heavy dose of melodrama, romance, and coincidence. All of these aspects are seen in *Oliver Twist,* particularly the violence of the melodrama and the coincidences which shuffle Oliver in and out of Mr. Brownlow's house. But over all, and ultimately much more important, stands the realism which Dickens used to unite the different elements of his story. Perhaps the greatest achievement of the author in this early novel was the giant stride forward he made in the realm of realism. He had not yet perfected his skills, but he knew the direction in which he was moving, and he was taking the novel with him.

Bruce D. Reeves

OMOO

Type of work: Novel
Author: Herman Melville (1819-1891)
Type of plot: Adventure romance
Time of plot: Early 1840's
Locale: Tahiti and the South Seas
First published: 1847

This sequel to Typee *takes its title from a word in the native dialect of the Marquesas Islands which signifies a wanderer among islands. The wanderer in the novel is Melville himself, whose twofold purpose in the novel is to relate his adventures in the Society Islands, and to expose the ill effects of the missionaries' presence in Polynesia. The novel contrasts the hypocrisy of pseudo-Christians to the sincerity and naïveté of the pagan islanders.*

Following his pattern in *Typee,* Melville in *Omoo* combines his own experiences and observations during his brief stay on several islands with material gathered from several books. The reader is led to believe that this account contains the narrator's true adventures supplemented by stories and other information given him by various friends or acquaintances. Early British reviewers of *Omoo* questioned whether a book which appeared to have been written by a cultured gentleman could really be the work of an ordinary American sailor. Twentieth century scholars have shown the considerable extent of Melville's borrowings, yet they grant that he added much style and insight to what he borrowed from others. In fact, the episodic picaresque tale contains a kind of unity through the revealed personality and turn of mind of the narrator.

Typee depicted only a few touches of humor mixed with romance in an island semi-paradise, but in *Omoo* the tone is largely comic and satiric. The Tahitians and other islanders are presented with more verisimilitude than were the Typees. Melville appears to have enjoyed himself during his travels with his roguish friend, Dr. Long Ghost (in reality a dissolute ship's steward named John Troy). Throughout much of the book narrator Melville seems as lazy and irresponsible as Long Ghost.

Omoo continues an attack, begun in *Typee,* against missionaries, rebuking them for their venality and their foolish attempts to change the lives and ways of the South Sea natives. The people of Tahiti and the other islands visited by the two rovers had experienced far more contact with Western visitors than had the Typees, and Melville was apalled by many of the harmful effects he observed. It has been pointed out in the present century that Melville himself was misled, and he in turn misled his readers when he blamed the perhaps misguided and ineffectual missionaries for the sins which lustful sailors and greedy traders had visited upon the trusting, naïve islanders. For the modern reader, however, *Omoo* is far more a rollicking adventure tale of faraway places than a serious narrative of social commentary and angry condemnation.

THE ORDEAL OF RICHARD FEVEREL

Type of work: Novel
Author: George Meredith (1828-1909)
Type of plot: Tragi-comedy
Time of plot: Mid-nineteenth century
Locale: England
First published: 1859

In this story of an idyllic romance between two sincere and idealistic young people, Meredith examines the results of a disillusioned, misogynistic father's attempt to rear his son according to a scientific system of education that all but excludes women. The sometimes artificial dialogue and the intellectual styles are characteristic of Meredith's works, but the details of the love story itself are told with captivating simplicity.

The Ordeal of Richard Feverel was Meredith's first novel, although he had already published poetry, journalism, and two entertaining prose fantasies; and it was not well received critically. George Eliot praised it, but other critics found it unconvincing and excessively intellectualized. Later critics have generally agreed that it is somewhat thesis-ridden, but they find its flaws counterbalanced by wit and emotional force, and it has remained probably the most popular if not the most admired of Meredith's novels.

There is no denying that at times Meredith's concern for his thesis acts to the detriment of the novel; in this, the novel serves as a kind of unintentional exemplification of the thesis, that life is too various, too rich, too spontaneous to conform to even the most admirable system. Few readers can quite believe that Richard would remain separated from Lucy for as long as the plot requires, and the deaths of both Lucy and Clare seem less from natural than from authorial causes. These events are necessary to Meredith's design, but he is unable to give them the quality of inevitability that other elements of the plot have.

Even so, the novel works remarkably well. Meredith may have intended to keep Sir Austin Feverel in center stage, demonstrating the fatuity of high intelligence and lofty ideals without the precious leaven of humor and common sense. The message is effectively conveyed, and Meredith's comic purpose is served by our last sight of Sir Austin still blindly clinging to his theories in the shipwreck of his beloved son's life. Yet it is the romantic pathos of the love of Richard and Lucy which most fully engages the reader and is most vivid at the conclusion. Meredith's later revisions, for a new edition, suggest that he recognized what had happened to his original intention and concluded that the gain in emotional power was worth preserving. To value intense feeling about strict adherence to a preconceived system was thoroughly Meredithian.

THE OREGON TRAIL

Type of work: Record of travel
Author: Francis Parkman (1823-1893)
Type of plot: Travel and adventure sketches
Time of plot: 1846
Locale: The Oregon Trail
First published: 1849

Realizing as early as the 1840's on his journey to the Rocky Mountains that the Indian, the mountain man, the trading post, and the buffalo were all passing figures in history, Parkman recorded his experience of the West with sympathy, interest, and objectivity. Although he saw a certain glamor in the subject, his descriptions and observations are mostly realistic and valid.

When Francis Parkman made the journey to Oregon in 1846, he kept a series of diaries, and these journals were the basis for his first book, *The Oregon Trail.* Unfortunately the editor found Parkman's notes too crude and earthy for public taste and in the transformation the writings were watered down.

In the foreword to the first edition Parkman stated that he was taking the trail to Oregon with his friend Quincy Shaw to study the Indians, and in this role Parkman proved to be a pioneer literary observer. While he did omit much ethnological material by today's standards, the work is full of data on the Sioux and other Plains tribes. His compatriots included Henry Chatillon, who already knew much about the Indians; and Parkman acquired information from the mountain man Thomas Fitzpatrick, another "walking encyclopaedia" of information about the West. His treatment of the Indians, while it is most descriptive, reflects unquestionably Parkman's views that the Indians were less than "civilized."

What Parkman learned and accomplished during this adventure would provide the background for his later works on France and England and their role in the New World. Additionally he called attention to the miracles of this land with all of its environmental blessings: the minerals, soil, timber, and water. Logically, then, *The Oregon Trail* focuses on the relation of men to the land and weather.

The work first appeared serially in *The Knickerbocker Magazine* beginning with the issue of February, 1847, and running until 1849. The travel he had undertaken was for Parkman the one great physical test of his life, and he ran some real risks of death. He suffered a nervous breakdown on his return to Boston in October, 1846. But he had accomplished what many writers of the twentieth century fail to undertake. He had traveled to observe at firsthand the region about which he would write.

This first work of Parkman reflects the attempts of a literary apprentice, for he exhibits a tendency to stress too many facts and is too emphatic in conversations. One who reads his later writings recognizes such formal devices as stereotyping, a flaw which often dilutes the prose in *The Oregon Trail*. Parkman tended to be too melodramatic at times, but he wrote as the events took place and was likely stimulated by the great adventure on which he had embarked. The descriptions thus become functional rather than mere background. A reader can sense that Parkman tried to write a history, but strained to use his self-conscious college writing techniques, such as the out-of-place Byronesque epigraphs which appear in both the serial and in the later editions of the work. Such literary formalities did not appear in the original journals, however.

Parkman, nonetheless, saw the importance of the struggles in the wilderness which made America unique. Subsequent historians have recognized this accomplishment. Frederick Jackson Turner in his classic essay on the closing of the frontier stressed the validity of Parkman's acute perceptions.

ORFEO

Type of work: Poetic drama with music
Author: Politian (Angelo Ambrogini, 1454-1494)
Type of plot: Mythological tragedy
Time of plot: Remote antiquity
Locale: Sicily
First presented: 1480

The first writer to adapt the pastoral romance to the stage was a young Tuscan, Angelo Ambrogini, who was asked by Cardinal Gonzago of Mantua to contribute some entertainment to a gala celebration held for Duke Sforza. The play has problems—characters introduced in the first act disappear, and the final act has nothing to do with the original problem—but it is important for its classical, nonreligious themes and its use of music, which foreshadowed Italian opera.

Politian, or Poliziano in the Italian form of his name, was one of the foremost members of the circle of Humanist scholars assembled in Florence under the patronage of Lorenzo de' Medici. He was the tutor of Lorenzo's Son, Piero, as well as professor of Greek and Latin in Florence. He left volumes of work in Latin, and poetry in the vernacular that was to become a cornerstone of Italian literature. His *Orfeo* cannot really be judged by the standards of later drama, for it was an experiment, and a form specially created for a specific occasion. Politian drew upon the tradition of the medieval mystery play, or *sacra rappresentazione,* and offered a secular variation, in which the prologue is spoken by Mercury rather than an angel, and the central figure is not a saint, but an artist-hero who suffers for love. The action is weak, and the work is highly lyrical in its mood, stressing elegiac emotions rather than dramatic events. The work contains classical variations of many features from religious plays—the shepherds transferred from nativity plays, and prayers addressed, not to the Virgin, but to the Queen of Hades, Proserpina.

The theme of *Orfeo* was significant to writers of the Renaissance as a symbol of the role of art in bringing order to a barbarous world. Orfeo came to stand for the artist who by his song is able to move nature, even stones, and who can turn back the forces of death. The Orfeo theme was later used by Peri, founder of Italian opera, and by Monteverdi, whose opera, *Orfeo* (1607), is still performed. If Politian's simple rendering of the tale does not fully develop the possibilities of the theme, it is significant, not only as a forerunner of Guarini's *Pastor Fido* and Tasso's *Aminta,* but as a charming lyrical fable, unfortunately now deprived of the music with which it once graced the court of the Gonzagas.

ORLANDO

Type of work: Novel
Author: Virginia Woolf (1882-1941)
Type of plot: Biographical fantasy
Time of plot: 1588-1928
Locale: England
First published: 1928

In this work, Woolf presents a free-flowing, symbolic three centuries of English family history. Orlando *is the fantasy-biography of a hero/heroine who is a sixteen-year-old boy in 1588 and a thirty-six-year-old woman in 1928. Woolf's technique merges past with present and gives free release to the imagination, unhampered as it is by calendar time.*

Orlando's subtitle, "A Biography," gives the clue to the first of two important considerations of the book, for *Orlando* is Virginia Woolf's parody of biography, a genre she knew well. Her father, Sir Leslie Stephen, was editor of the monumental *Dictionary of National Biography,* and Lytton Strachey, who himself had revolutionized biography with his *Eminent Victorians* and *Elizabeth and Essex,* was part of Woolf's circle, the "Bloomsbury group." Additionally, Woolf often reviewed biographies for British periodicals.

So *Orlando* plays at being a traditional biography—with a pompous narrator describing Orlando's person and motives, not always quite sure of the exact nature of his subject; a pretentious preface giving effusive acknowledgments to many colleagues; a scholarly index listing, among others, "Mr. M.," "the railway," and "Pippin, the spaniel." Woolf also parodies various literary forms, from the Elizabethan sonnet and the masque, a typical seventeenth century dramatic form, to Victorian feminine verse, the sentimental letter, and Virginia Woolf's own style.

Woolf explores the thin line between fiction and biography, and by means of her parody shows her awareness of the biographer's problem: how can one be objective, giving only historical fact, when the very structure of those facts, the words chosen for description, shows bias and subjectivity? Fiction and biography are intimately connected, and *Orlando* is Woolf's "fiction-biography."

The second important consideration in *Orlando* is the theme of androgyny. Orlando's physical person changes from one sex to the other; his/her consciousness remains the same, although in the later parts of the book, Orlando is much more capable of understanding both sexes, having by then experienced both. The androgynous mind (a consciousness neither masculine nor feminine, but partaking of both) was always looked upon as the ideal by Woolf. The device of the actual sex-change is symbolic of Woolf's belief that the artist must create not from the narrow vision of his own sex, but with the double vision of all humanity; an artist must be "woman-manly" or "man-womanly," not simply masculine or feminine.

ORLANDO FURIOSO

Type of work: Poem
Author: Ludovico Ariosto (1474-1533)
Type of plot: Chivalric romance
Time of plot: Eighth century
Locale: France, Spain, Africa
First published: 1516; enlarged edition, 1532

Consisting as it does of a great number of stories and episodes, this masterpiece of early Italian literature contains too many shifts of scene and incident to enjoy a controlling interior unity. The world of chivalry and the world of fantasy mingle in the poem's three main stories: the account of the wars of Charlemagne, the tale of Orlando's hopeless love for Angelica and his later madness, and the love story of Rogero and Bradamant, the supposed heirs of the great house of Este.

Son of a minor Lombardian military official, Ludovico Ariosto was initially encouraged to study law but was finally allowed to pursue his preference for literature by studying the classics. However, as the eldest of ten children, he was obliged in his mid-twenties to undertake the management of family affairs upon the death of his father. Shortly thereafter, although it grated against his independent spirit, he accepted an appointment to serve Cardinal Ippolito d'Este, and some years later entered the service of the Cardinal's brother Alphonso, Duke of Ferrara, who assigned Ariosto, among other tasks, to a brief (1522-1525) governorship of a lawless mountain province in the central peninsula. These experiences, particularly the latter, did much to undermine Ariosto's health, yet he survived until his fifty-ninth year when he succumbed to tuberculosis.

As for literary output, early translations of Plautus and Terence—from Latin to Italian—were followed by Ariosto's own Italian comedies, modeled after his classical mentors: *La Cassaria* (1508), *I Suppositi* (1509), *Il Negromante* (1520), *La Lena* (1529), and the unfinished *Gli Studenti*. In addition to his letters and some rather undistinguished Latin poems—posthumously edited for publication by his illegitimate son Virginio—Ariosto also wrote a number of pungent satires which rank not far behind his monumental *Orlando Furioso (Mad Orlando)* for literary merit.

Orlando Furioso is, of course, Ariosto's complement to Boiardo's *Orlando Innamorato,* but Ariosto's version differs greatly from Boiardo's. In its first edition (1516), *Orlando Furioso* contained forty cantos; the final edition (1532) contained forty-six. In between those editions, much polishing, revising, and improving took place, for Ariosto's artistic instincts would not rest until he was satisfied with the nuance of each word, the sound of each rhyme, the beat of each metrical foot, and the synthesis of all into exactly the right action, character, or setting which he was striving to describe. Ariosto's dedication to artistic perfection was coupled with a certain independence of mind which enabled the poet to portray knightly adventures from a more realistic point of view than Boiardo's fabulary tale did. It is just these qualities which make *Orlando Furioso* superior to *Orlando Innamorato*.

One of Ariosto's motives in composing his epic was to glorify the noble house of Este, rulers of Ferrara and Modena, under whose patronage Ariosto served. Hence, the main plot line of *Orlando Furioso* deals with the troubled romance between the pagan Saracen Rogero and the Christian French Bradamant. When at last they marry—having overcome many obstacles, not the least of which were Rogero's several infidelities—they found, so the story goes, the ancestral line of the Este family. One intriguing aspect of the Rogero-Bradamant union is its implication of marriage between pagan and Christian, despite the merely ceremonial ritual of Rogero's baptism and his killing of the Saracen Rodomont. But even more interesting is Bradamant's skill, resourcefulness, and courage as a warrior. Here is no clichéd helpless maiden in distress but a strong-minded and strong-armed knight who takes the initiative in finding her beloved Rogero, who takes part in wars, who defeats men in single combat (for example, Rodomont), and who defiantly declares she will marry none but the man who can match her or best her in battle. Stereotypes crumble in the face of Rogero and Bradamant, singly or united. Stereotypes of epic behavior and stereotypes of real behavior alike cannot stand up under Ariosto's skillful characterization, for the poet—indeed, the artist—convinces us of the plausibility of Rogero's and Bradamant's actions. In doing so, Ariosto demonstrates his consummate facility for imaginatively transforming incredible magic into verisimilitude.

Orlando's story, although his name lends itself to the title of the poem, is secondary. To be sure, Orlando's quest for Angelica, launched by Boiardo, provides Ariosto's point of departure. But the thrust of Ariosto's title is that Orlando—under the dual stress of searching for Angelica and fulfilling his knightly obligations—has temporarily parted company with his rational faculties; Orlando is thus *Furioso*. In the pre-Freudian sixteenth century, Orlando's psychiatric problems are of far less import than the empirical and pragmatic problems of, say, Agramant and Charlemagne or Rogero and Bradamant. Thus, Orlando's anguish over Angelica's liaison with Medoro and his subsequent shedding of human appurtenances is merely a personal tragedy without cosmic or global significance. This epoch, the Renaissance, was a watershed in Western consciousness. For all of the emphasis which Renaissance thinkers placed on the individual, society was still paramount, as it was in the succeeding Age of Reason. Not until the Romantic Age did thoughtful people consider the plight of the individual seriously. Consequently, Orlando and his aberrations were simply not matters of overriding importance, and Ariosto quite properly played them down.

Moreover, since Ariosto was thoroughly a product of the Renaissance and reflected its values and priorities in his writings, this calculated demotion of Orlando's role in the epic signals another aspect of Renaissance attitudes. This aspect pertains to the Renaissance view of history, a view which differs considerably from the modern one. For Ariosto, like virtually all other Renaissance writers, felt no compelling obligation to strict historical accuracy as most modern readers understand that concept. Shakespeare thus wrote his Roman plays as Renaissance dramas, and Ariosto too signified his Renaissance bias in *Orlando Furioso*. Hence, Ariosto depicts the Saracen Rodomont as killing Isabella in a fit of drunkenness. But Saracens, as devout Moslems, were and are prohibited by the *Koran* from consuming any alcoholic beverage. And certainly a Saracen Moslem—like Rodomont—battling Christian crusaders would honor the sumptuary proscriptions of the religion which he was defending. Yet this proscription and its implications are disregarded by Ariosto as a Christian, Western European, Renaissance poet. Still Ariosto incorporates into his poem elements of his time, his place, and theology which have no precise precedents in eighth century Christianity or Islam. Thus Ariosto portrays, only half-skeptically, events influenced by Merlin, the seeress Melissa, a magic ring, a hippogryph, the giantess Eriphilia, the conjurer Atlantes, and various supernaturally endowed herdsmen and hermits, among others. Although an apparent contradiction to the modern reader, this combination— a naïveté about historical factuality with an acceptance of the era's traditional credulity about magic—marks both Ariosto and *Orlando Furioso* as genuine products of the Renaissance and, in turn, a key to the study of Renaissance culture.

Joanne G. Kashdan

ORLANDO INNAMORATO

Type of work: Poem
Author: Matteo Maria Boiardo (c. 1440-1494)
Type of plot: Chivalric romance
Time of plot: Eighth century
Locale: France, India, Africa
First transcribed: 1486-1495

This is the second of three Italian chivalric romances based on the legendary history of Charlemagne and his paladins. The poem consists of sixty-nine cantos in ottava rima *and was left incomplete at Boiardo's death; Ariosto's* Orlando Furioso *was begun as a continuation of Boiardo's work.* Orlando Innamorato *tells the love story of the hero Orlando's passion for the bewitching Angelica, and recounts the adventures and love of Bradamant and Rogero, who were the supposed ancestors of the medieval house of Este. This work served as a model for Ariosto's* Orlando Furioso.

As a nobleman, Boiardo did not have to rely upon patronage for his living. Independently wealthy, he availed himself of the best educational opportunities, had connections in the highest circles, and spent much of his time fulfilling the duties of government appointments. His writing, originally in Italian, was done in his limited spare time when he could withdraw from the bustle of the court to the tranquility of one of his estates. His literary output was consequently rather small. He produced a sonnet sequence, noted for its sincere tone, and is best known for his *Orlando Innamorato* (Orlando in Love).

Orlando Innamorato was written for the amusement of the court. When another poet added three more books to Boiardo's incomplete poem, about a half century later, it was revised and published, becoming popular as a slick, sophisticated satire hardly resembling the original. Nevertheless, it served to inspire Ludovico Ariosto's masterpiece, *Orlando Furioso.*

The plot of *Orlando Innamorato,* dealing for the most part with compelling action, is episodic, and it contains many digressions. Through the filter of Boiardo's imagination, the poem combines the heroic Matter of France—in which Charlemagne is the main hero—with the courtly-love-oriented Matter of Britain—featuring Arthur—to demonstrate Boiardo's explicit bias that both emphases are necessary because love is the inspiration for all noble deeds. The poem's major themes are thus love and war: magic and fantasy, battle and pursuit. For example, the magic ring, the magician Malagigi, and the magic fountains of hate and love are of equal importance to the initial tournament competition for Angelica's hand, the politico-religious wars, and the principle of single combat to resolve group conflicts in the development of the plot. In this way, Boiardo creatively integrates love and chivalry as he set out to do.

ORLEY FARM

Type of work: Novel
Author: Anthony Trollope (1815-1882)
Type of plot: Domestic romance
Time of plot: Mid-nineteenth century
Locale: England
First published: 1862

In this lively and complicated story, Trollope calls into play all those elements which Victorian readers so enjoyed: a forged will, a false heir, a woman with a guilty secret, a chivalrous gentleman, romantic young love, a long court trial, expiation, and the defeat of villainy.

The narrative of *Orley Farm* proceeds with a leisurely pace seldom, if ever, found in modern novels. One of the charms of Trollope's long and richly detailed book is this lack of bustle. There seems to be time for everything in the Trollopian world. No troubles exist which cannot be postponed for a fortnight or six months. The legal technicalities and convolutions of the story are the least important parts of the novel to a modern reader. They are merely the framework upon which Trollope hangs his lively and vivid picture of mid-Victorian England. The characters are well drawn and amusing, but the reader has only mild interest as to who will triumph in the end. This kind of novel can be brought to a conclusion at almost any point (with all of the plot ends neatly tied up) or allowed to stretch on almost indefinitely.

Although the plot is not as thrilling as that of a Dickens or Wilkie Collins novel, and the social perceptions are not as profound as in a Thackeray story, and the moral problems are not handled with the philosophical insight of George Eliot, Trollope created an entire world in *Orley Farm* and his other great novels, and it is this achievement that his readers continue to treasure. Ordinary life is viewed with a gentle and endearing humor. For example, the alternating views of the Christmas festivities at the homes of the principal characters of *Orley Farm* give a delightful and vivid picture of traditional Victorian holiday customs through several social strata. The scene in the commercial room of the King's Head in which Mr. Kantwise demonstrates enthusiastically the merits of his new line of "Louey catorse" iron furniture is as funny today as when it was written. And equally humorous is the scene in which the parsimonious Mrs. Mason presents a damaged "new" set of the iron furniture to the open-mouthed curate and his wife. In scenes such as these (which usually have nothing to do with the plot) Trollope is at his best; and few authors have equaled the good-natured but sharp humor which seems to have been so effortlessly put on paper.

Trollope became notorious after the publication of his *Autobiography* for the deliberate method in which he wrote his novels. He rose regularly at 5:30 A.M. and wrote steadily for two hours and a half at the rate of 250 words every quarter of an hour. After the failure of his first books, he was proud of his ability at last to make money from his writing. Eventually, he made as much as thirty-five hundred pounds from a single novel and averaged nearly five thousand pounds a year. The poverty of his childhood and his mother's frantic scribbling to make ends meet seems to have been responsible for this calculated approach to his art. Yet, from the Barchester series on, his novels maintain an amazingly high quality, not suffering from his tremendous output. He was a professional writer and wrote "not because he had to tell a story, but because he had a story to tell." His craftsmanship was such that when he sat down each morning (Sundays included) he could write his story smoothly and well.

And he wrote with a humor which has endured to our own day. It is seldom forced and rarely emphasized; it seems to have come so naturally to Trollope that he hardly realized that he was permeating his novels with it. Almost incidentally, the everyday doings of life are tinged with Trollope's gentle, tolerant humor. It is far removed from the "black humor" of the twentieth century, but perhaps will outlast most such sophisticated literary fashions.

Nathaniel Hawthorne in 1860 paid Trollope this tribute: "Have you ever read the novels of Anthony Trollope? They precisely suit my taste—solid and substantial, written on the strength of beef and through the inspiration of ale, and just as real as if some giant had hewn a great lump out of the earth and put it under a glass case, with all its inhabitants going about their daily business, and not suspecting that they were being made a show of." It is this vitality and sense of authentic life that we today find so rewarding in Trollope's books; and *Orley Farm,* without heights of passion or depths of tragedy of extremes of farce, represents precisely this vision of real human beings captured as if by photography.

Although they are well drawn, the hero and heroine, Felix Graham and Madeline Stavely, are not the most prepossessing characters of *Orley Farm.* Far more interesting are Samuel Dockwrath, as he grubs around to find money to support his sixteen children, Mrs. Joseph Mason, as she stoops to ever more ridiculous attempts to save money and food even from her own family, Lucius Mason and his blind but idealistic games with scientific farming, and the magnificent old gentleman Sir Peregrine Orme, whose gallantry even leads him to propose marriage to a woman in need when he is well past seventy.

Trollope reveled in man's idiosyncrasies, but he admired the solid virtues which built the Empire. His pen spent more time sketching these human idiosyncrasies than in moralizing. The characters develop little, if at all; their personalities are full-blown from their first entrances. Yet the book does not suffer from this. Trollope's technique makes the most of each character's individuality without requiring growth or deep changes. His brightly colored

scenes and clearly drawn characters moving through neat plots suggest the
cinema, and it is quite true that his novels were the popular entertainment
of their day.

Trollope's ability to keep a score of personal relationships aloft like balls
in the air suggests the juggler's art as much as that of the novelist. Even
minor characters in *Orley Farm,* such as the jealous Mrs. Furnival and the
industrious young Mr. Crabwitz or Mary Snow, the would-be "moulded wife"
of Felix Graham, are glimpsed in the midst of their own busy and (to them)
important lives. They never give the impression of having been dragged into
the scene to fill up space like so many film extras. It is this sense of the
simultaneity of life on many different levels that gives the book its powerful
feeling of reality. The chief difference between *Orley Farm* and real life is
that the novel is never dull.

Bruce D. Reeves

OROONOKO

Type of work: Novel
Author: Mrs. Aphra Behn (1640-1689)
Type of plot: Didactic romance
Time of plot: Seventeenth century
Locale: Africa and Surinam
First published: 1688

A forerunner of English novels written on the theme of the "noble savage," Oroonoko *was also an early protest against the institution of slavery based upon the notion that primitive man was more noble and in tune with primal truths than his civilized brothers. Mrs. Behn—England's first woman to become a professional writer—writes in a style which sounds stilted to the modern ear; but her plot is dramatic, her setting colorful, and her atmosphere convincing.*

Though in many ways a conventional romance of its period, *Oroonoko* stands out from its genre. Like other romances, it deals with an exotic setting; but it is written with a vividness that seems to come from first-hand observation. Like other romances, it deals with a pair of star-crossed lovers; but this story seems to have almost archetypal overtones. In it we find echoes of the youthful passion of Romeo and Juliet; of Antony and Cleopatra; of Othello and Desdemona; and even of the love-death of Tristan and Isolde.

In other ways, *Oroonoko* extends beyond the confines of the traditional romance. Included in the hero's catalogue of almost superhuman virtues and feats are such astounding exploits as his slaying of a deadly tiger with seven bullets in its heart, and his near-fatal battle with a giant electric eel. What clearly distinguishes this romance from other contemporary examples of fiction, and at the same time increases its appeal to modern readers, is Behn's anti-slavery theme. In the author's descriptions of the barbaric treatment against the slaves at the hands of the "Christian" Europeans, and especially in Oroonoko's impassioned speech to his fellow slaves, urging them to throw off their fetters, we encounter a voice that we are to hear with increasing frequency and volume in the next two centuries.

But *Oroonoko* is perhaps most interesting for its treatment of a related issue that was to become of great significance—the noble savage. Behn uses this theme for the same purpose later writers use it: ironically to undercut the assumption of the "superiority" of white civilization by contrasting it with a race of people who, if they lack the sophistications of civilizations, also lack its corruptions. "These people represented to me an absolute idea of the first state of innocence, before man knew how to sin," says Behn. Oroonoko, the almost impossibly noble hero, is strong, handsome, intelligent, resourceful, outrageous, and forthright, as well as gentle and modest. His very appearance is enough to strike awe into all who behold him. But Oroonoko has one fatal flaw. He trusts in the honor of white men, and tragically believes that "a man of wit could not be a knave or villain."

The Europeans, however, are knaves and villains with a vengeance. Through treachery, lies, and ingratitude, Oroonoko is tricked into becoming a slave. When the ignominy of his situation drives him to rebellion, further treachery persuades him to yield rather than die the noble and heroic death he yearns for. And when he is once more in the hands of his enemies, he is whipped and then executed with a calculated brutality hard indeed to reconcile with the religion of his oppressors.

Such is Aphra Behn's commentary on "civilization." With a bitterness and an irony sometimes verging on the Swiftian, she lashes out against the accepted practices of "advanced" nations. "Such ill morals" wrote Behn, "are only practiced in Christian countries, where they prefer the bare name of religion; and without virtue or morality, think that sufficient."

THE ORPHAN

Type of work: Drama
Author: Thomas Otway (1652-1685)
Type of plot: Domestic tragedy
Time of plot: Seventeenth century
Locale: Bohemia
First presented: 1680

Although not so highly regarded as his Venice Preserved *(1682), Otway's* The Orphan *was performed until the early nineteenth century. The plot, supposedly based upon an actual incident, turns on a highly improbable situation; events seem planned to eke the most suffering from the main characters. The language in* The Orphan *echoes Shakespeare, particularly in* Romeo and Juliet, *and the character of hotheaded Chamont is reminiscent of Laertes in* Hamlet.

"Tender Otway" he was called, and with good reason, for Thomas Otway's plays abound in a direct appeal to feeling. He has also been called the "Byron of the Restoration," and the comparison is particularly illuminating when we consider their sudden popularity to his audience. Just as Byron awoke to find himself famous after the publication of the early cantos of *Childe Harold's Pilgrimage,* Otway, after the first performances of *The Orphan,* was credited with having done something entirely new in drama. Byron's poem revealed the hidden feelings of an isolated and brooding spirit; Otway's drama dared to explore the hidden anxieties and desires of ordinary people. Just as Byron's intensely subjective poetry offered an alternative to eighteenth century decorum, Otway's domestic tragedy relinquished the strict standards of Restoration heroic drama and poetry in both form and characterization. His appeal is not to aristocratic concepts of defiant and absolute heroism, nor is he a champion of Aristotelian unities. Otway's appeal is to pity.

He has been accused of contriving the plot in *The Orphan* so as to subject his characters to more suffering than should be their fate. Edmund Gosse, in his book on Otway, called the "foolish pretense of Castalio, the want of perception by Monimia, and the ruffianly crime of Polydore . . . all radical faults which go near to destroy the probability of the story." Otway does stretch credibility in his attempt to burden his characters with not only unavoidable suffering, but suffering without any moral cause. Even the Hobbesian villain of the piece, Polydore, who reminds us of Shakespeare's Edmund in *King Lear* by the way he stresses "Nature over law," is not entirely culpable. After all, he did not know that Monimia had married his brother. No one, Otway makes sure, is exempt from at least some pity.

Otway, like Dryden in *All for Love,* relied heavily on Shakespeare to inject his plays with the power of feeling and bold characterization that could free drama from the stylization of Restoration conventions. Certainly *The Orphan* in plot, character, and tone recalls aspects of both *Romeo and*

Juliet and *Othello*. But if Otway learned from Shakespeare how to put strong feelings of compassion and pity into a play, he learned little from his master about true terror and sublimity.

ORPHEUS AND EURYDICE

Type of work: Classical myth
Source: Unknown
Type of plot: Allegory of grief
Time of plot: Remote antiquity
Locale: Thrace and the Underworld
First transcribed: Unknown

This story of immortal love and of the power and inexpressible beauty of music dates from antiquity and has continued to appear in literature and music throughout every age. Probably best known to modern readers are the famous operatic versions of the story, including those by Monteverdi, Haydn, and Gluck. As in many myths, scenes of lyrical beauty and spiritual insight are combined with scenes of savage cruelty in the story of Orpheus and Eurydice.

The longest and most familiar version of this myth is found in Ovid's *Metamorphoses* (10.8-85 and 11.1-66), and Ovid may well have been inspired by Vergil's less florid account, carefully placed at the dramatic end of his Georgics (4.453-527). In Vergil, Eurydice is bitten by a snake as she flees the lustful rustic deity, Aristaeus. There, the Orpheus-Eurydice theme was most appropriate to Vergil's subject of rebirth and fruitfulness through sacrifice and discipline; indeed, this myth, perhaps more than any other, illustrates that man can never achieve victory over death without divine aid, and that human immortality can be gained only through art.

Through extraordinary powers of music, Orpheus was able to perform unnatural feats, such as moving beasts, trees, even rocks, and ultimately to obtain a rare favor from the rulers of the Dead; yet his lack of discipline, that is, his inability to obey the command of Proserpine and Hades to the letter, resulted in his failure to achieve for Eurydice victory over death. (But even if he had won, we must assume that death would have come again for them both.) Nevertheless, there is a hopeful side to the myth: eventually the two lovers are permanently united in death. This may be satisfying romantically, but it is less important than Orpheus' legacy to us, symbolized by his severed head continuing to sing his beloved's name, harmoniously echoed by sympathetic nature. Orpheus, therefore, has achieved ultimate victory over death: his art has given him the life after death he sought for Eurydice. This is further symbolized in his burial by the Muses near Olympus, in Apollo's petrifying his head on Lesbos (an island renowned for its poets), and finally by the catasterism of Orpheus' lyre. Certainly Vergil, if not Ovid, had this victory in mind, since their versions broke with the tradition in which Orpheus succeeded in rescuing Eurydice from death.

Both parts of the original myth—the retrieval of Eurydice and the death of Orpheus—probably originated in pre-classical poetry, perhaps in cultic Orphism. Orpheus himself was believed to be the earliest of poets, along with

Musaeus (his son), Homer, and Hesiod. He is given a place among Jason's Argonauts. His remote Thracian origins lend mystery to his myth, and no doubt this had a bearing on the relatively restricted popularity of Orphism, which seems to have been more philosophy than religion. The aim of the Orphics was to lead a life of purity and purification, so that eventually the successively reincarnated soul, having purged itself of the Titanic (or earthly) element, would be pure spirit divinely born of Zeus through his son Dionysus, and thus would be released from the cycle, eternally to wander the Elysian fields.

Exactly how Orpheus is connected with this cult is unclear and indeed confusing. In Ovid's version Orpheus refuses to love any other woman; furthermore, he turns his attention to boys, which is why the Thracian women murder him. Yet, these women were Bacchants, that is, Dionysian orgiasts, and in other versions Dionysus himself directs them to kill Orpheus because the bard, in his devotion to Apollo the sun-god, has prevented the wine-god's acceptance in Thrace. On the other hand, the oracle established in Lesbos in honor of Orpheus was suppressed by Apollo. If Orpheus was the poet-priest-prophet of Apollo who refused the frenzy of Dionysus, it may well be that he became the cultic model whose sacrifice ironically inspired others to accept Dionysus. Orphic mysteries seem to have resembled the orgies of Dionysus, but whereas the Dionysiac is striving for that momentary ecstatic union with the god, the Orphic is striving for eternal peace.

The catabasis of Orpheus into the underworld obviously symbolizes an Orphic's death which will be followed by a new life, repeated until the cycle is complete. Other symbolic interpretations aside, the descent and return would be frightening were they not so entertaining. Having given us a whirlwind classic tour of the Underworld, including introductions to the King and Queen, Ovid slowly leads us back along the murky upward path until suddenly Orpheus' concern for Eurydice outstrips his easy promise. The pathos of this second separation is intensified by its swiftness, and by Orpheus' inability even to regain passage across the Styx, much less to see or hear his love again.

Few love stories from classical antiquity have made such an impression on succeeding ages. This myth became the subject of the first secular drama in vernacular, *Orfeo,* composed in the era of the Medici by Angelo Ambrogini (Politian). In 1600 the first Italian opera, *Euridice,* was composed. Gluck's *Orfeo ed Euridice* (1762) is considered the first "modern" opera for its balance of music and tragic drama, although a happy ending was supplied: Amore (Love) brings Euridice back to prevent Orfeo's suicide. Twentieth century playwrights have adapted the story to their own settings and purposes, among them, Jean Anouilh and Tennessee Williams. Composers such as Offenbach, Milhaud, and Stravinsky have borrowed the theme. In film, Vinicius de Moraes' Brazilian masterpiece, *Black Orpheus* (1957), takes place in Rio de Janeiro during Carnival and deftly uses the primitive color of the celebration to heighten the frenzy of Orpheus' search for his love who vainly tries to elude her stalking killer costumed as Death.

OTHELLO

Type of work: Drama
Author: William Shakespeare (1564-1616)
Type of plot: Romantic tragedy
Time of plot: Early sixteenth century
Locale: Venice and Cyprus
First presented: 1604

The Tragedy of Othello, The Moor of Venice *is concerned with the nature of good and evil and the struggle between the two forces in the human soul. Alone of the four great tragedies, this play is weakly motivated in the sense that the obsessive hatred of the villain Iago, perhaps the most sadistic and consummately evil character in any literature, is not sufficiently explained by his having been passed over for a promotion in Othello's army. Despite its tragic ending,* Othello *displays some optimism in its depiction of the triumph of love over hate, and of the love of one woman for another which is instrumental in bringing the villain to poetic justice.*

Although *Othello* has frequently been praised as Shakespeare's most unified tragedy, uncluttered with sub-plots, many critics have found the central character to be the most unheroic of Shakespeare's heroes. Some have found him stupid beyond redemption; others have described him as a passionate being overwhelmed by powerful emotion; still others have found him self-pitying and insensitive to the enormity of his actions. But all of these denigrations pale before the excitement and sympathy generated in the action of the play for the noble Moor.

Othello is an exotic. It is unlikely that Shakespeare would have cared whether or not Othello was black. More to the point is the fact that he was a foreigner from a fascinating and mysterious land. Certainly he is a passionate man, but he is not devoid of sensitivity. Rather, his problem is that he is thrust into the sophisticated and highly cultivated context of Renaissance Italy, a land which had a reputation in Shakespeare's England for connivance and intrigue. If anything, Othello is natural man confronted with the machinations and contrivances of a super-civilized society. His instincts are to be loving and trusting, but he is cast into a society where these natural virtues make one extremely vulnerable.

The prime source of that vulnerability is personified in the figure of Iago, perhaps Shakespeare's consummate villain. Iago is so evil, by nature, that he does not even need any motivation for his antagonism towards Othello. He has been passed over for promotion, but that is clearly a pretext for a malignant nature whose hatred for Othello needs no specific grounds. It is Othello, with his candor, his openness, his spontaneous and generous love, which Iago finds offensive. His suggestion that Othello has seduced his wife is an even flimsier fabrication to cover the essential corruption of his nature.

Iago sees other human beings only as victims or tools. He is the classical Renaissance atheist—an intelligent man, beyond moral scruple, who finds pleasure in the corruption of the virtuous and the abuse of the pliable. That he brings himself into danger is of no consequence, because, relying on wit, he believes that all can be duped and destroyed—and there is no further purpose to his life. For such a manipulator, Othello, a good man out of his cultural element, is the perfect target.

More so than in any other Shakespearean play, one character, Iago, is the stage manager of the whole action. Once he sets out to destroy Othello, he proceeds by plot and by innuendo to achieve his goal. He tells others just what he wishes them to know, sets one character against another, and develops an elaborate web of circumstantial evidence to dupe the vulnerable Moor. Edgar Stoll has argued that the extraordinary success of Iago in convincing other characters of his fabrications is simply a matter of the conventional ability of the Renaissance villain. Yet, there is more to the conflict than Iago's abilities, conventional or natural, for Othello is his perfect prey.

Othello bases his opinions and his human relationships on intuition rather than reason. His courtship with Desdemona is brief and his devotion absolute. His trust of his comrades, including Iago, is complete. It is not simply that Iago is universally believed. Ironically, he is able to fool everyone about everything except on the subject of Desdemona's chastity. On that subject it is only Othello that he is able to deceive. Roderigo, Cassio, and Emilia all reject Iago's allegations that Desdemona has been unfaithful. Only Othello is deceived, and he because Iago is able to make him play the game with unfamiliar rules.

Iago entices Othello to use Venetian criteria of truth rather than the intuition on which he should rely. Iago plants doubts in Othello's mind, but his decisive success comes when he gets Othello to demand "ocular proof." Although it seems that Othello is demanding conclusive evidence before jumping to the conclusion that his wife has been unfaithful, it is more important that he has accepted Iago's idea of concrete evidence. From that point on, it is easy for Iago to falsify evidence and create appearances that will lead to erroneous judgments. It is not that Othello behaves as an emotional primitive and easily allows his jealousy to overpower his better judgment. Certainly, he betrays hyper-emotional behavior in his rantings and his fits, but these are the result of his acceptance of what seems indisputable proof, documentary evidence. It takes a long time, and a lot of falsifications, before Othello finally abandons his intuitive perception of the truth of his domestic situation. As Othello himself recognizes, he is not quick to anger, but, once angered, his natural passion takes over. Iago's contrivances eventually loose that force.

The crime that Othello commits is made to appear all the more heinous because of the extreme loyalty of his wife. It is not that she is an innocent.

Her conversation reflects that she is a sophisticate, but there is no question of her total fidelity to her husband. The moral horror of the murder is intensified by the contrast between our perception of the extreme virtue of the victim with Othello's perception of himself as an instrument of justice. His chilling conviction reminds us of the essential probity of a man deranged by confrontation with an evil he cannot comprehend.

Some critics, such as T. S. Eliot, have argued that Othello never comes to an understanding of the gravity of his crime—that he realizes his error, but consoles himself in his final speech with cheering reminders of his own virtue. But that does not seem consistent with the valiant and honest military character who has thus far been depicted. Othello may have been grossly deceived, and he may be responsible for not clinging to the truth of his mutual love with Desdemona, but, in his final speech, he does seem to face up to his error with the same passion that had followed his earlier misconception. As he had believed that his murder of Desdemona was divine retribution, he believes that his suicide is a just act. His passionate nature believes it is meting out justice for the earlier transgression. We are promised that Iago will be tortured unto death, but Shakespeare dismisses Iago's punishment in order to focus on Othello's final act of expiation.

Edward E. Foster

THE OTHER ONE

Type of work: Novel
Author: Sidonie Gabrielle Claudine Colette (1873-1954)
Type of plot: Psychological realism
Time of plot: 1920's
Locale: Franche-Comté and Paris
First published: 1929

In The Other One, *one of Colette's last major novels, the author's sensibility has widened to an awareness of human motivation beyond the love relationship. The novel is an incisive and ironic analysis of a loving wife who prefers keeping the former mistress of her beloved but polygamous husband to facing loneliness without her. The portrait of Fanny is poignantly and sympathetically drawn, and reflects the author's artistry in portraying the complexities of human relationships.*

Colette's subtleness of tone and imagery in *The Other One* distinguishes this brief novel from the popular romance, for the plot and the characters who form an "eternal triangle," are so usual as to be clichéd. Like her renowned countrywomen Anaïs Nin and Marguerite Duras, Colette captures a mysterious tone suggestive of a lack of motivation. We often wonder why her characters act or speak as they do. A strange lassitude, a distaste for action, and a numbing languor reminiscent of Fanny's character combine to create the dominant mood.

This mood also helps to account for our perplexity about Jane's character. We are never allowed a look into Jane's mind; the point of view is most often Fanny's, and since Jane is the most arresting character, we are puzzled by this deprivation. Jane is, of course, "the other one." Neither Fanny nor Farou can manage without her and her irony, but for different reasons. For Fanny, Jane is both a buffer between her and Farou and, quite literally, a shoulder to cry on. For Farou, Jane is an essential part of his profession, as well as a convenient sexual object. The novel's French title, *La seconde,* gives added insight into Jane's role. *"La seconde"* suggests dueling and fencing, as well as the helper role; another meaning in French is "second class." Jane is *"la seconde"* in all these ways.

The repressed attraction between Fanny and Jane imparts a sensual quality to the tone. Their alliance is more than that of two women betrayed by the same man: Fanny's love for Jane has a definite sexual dimension, although this is never made explicit. That Colette was herself bisexual and forbidden by prevailing morality from treating this topic is an important consideration.

The imagery often creates a restrained horror, as bodies and parts of bodies are described as if they had autonomy. Colette thus associates herself with the great French philosophical tradition of mind-body dualism, a tradition stretching from Descartes to Sartre and Beckett. Jane's arm, always offered to Fanny, is "a flexible arm, tapering at the wrist like a serpent's neck and hollowed at the crook, soft, deft, officious." Farou's hand is described as having "the texture of a sage leaf," the wrist "green-veined." Such imagery adds to the feeling of repression, and one waits for the blow-up which never comes; for Fanny realizes that Jane is as necessary to her as is Farou.

OUR MUTUAL FRIEND

Type of work: Novel
Author: Charles Dickens (1812-1870)
Type of plot: Domestic romance
Time of plot. Mid-nineteenth century
Locale: London
First published: 1864-1866

This late novel, one of Dickens' longest, shows the author's creative powers on the wane; the plot is plagued by too-numerous subplots, excessive coincidences, labored humor, and trick turns of events. The sympathetic portrait of the Jew, Riah, is interesting and is seen by some critics as an atonement for prejudices aroused by the villainy of Fagin in Oliver Twist. *The novel contains many powerful descriptions of the Thames, which is painted as a mysterious and sinister background for scenes of murder and villainy.*

Critics generally view *Our Mutual Friend* as a work grand in conception but flawed in execution. It is Dickens' last finished work; he was ill during its writing, and its defects are of a kind that suggests a weakening of creative force. The main plot is over-buttressed with subplots, several of dubious relevance; some of the coincidences strain belief; a good deal of the humor falls flat; and a kind of ironical shorthand replaces the splendiferous verbiage of other works. Bella's "inexhaustible baby," for example, becomes abbreviated to "the Inexhaustible." But it is not, as some reviewers hold, merely old material reworked. Dickens' artistic purpose might have been weakened, but it was not dead; the chief symbol of the work is truly inspired, and the figure of the heroine's character attains a roundness and complexity unique in this author's vast canon.

The great symbol is Noddy Boffin's dustheaps. This equation of money with dirt, and the quest of money with the sifting of rubbish, pervades the work. The comical figure Wegg cuts in his lantern-lit scavenging on the dustheaps finds a sinister echo in Lizzie Hexam's father at his grisly occupation on the river, and a refined, though equally precise, reverberation in the economic maneuverings of the Lammles and the Veneerings. At every level of society, people of all ages are shown in the act of hunting for money. The heroine herself does so to a marked degree. That all this feverish activity for filthy lucre is just so much rummaging among rags and bones is the message of the work. The peculiar force of the dustheaps as a symbol resides in its absurdity, the high ironic comedy that clings to the activity of digging through refuse to find nonexistent gold, especially surreptitiously. It is as if the whole society were being not chastised, but made to appear mad.

The character of the heroine, Bella Wilfer, is a splendid creation, better even than her antecedent, Estella, of *Great Expectations.* Edith Dombey might be beautiful and yet bad; Estella might be cold, yet sorry for her coldness;

but never before had Dickens created a woman who could change her mind, evaluate, and redirect her own behavior. If there is any salvation for the society depicted in *Our Mutual Friend,* it lies in the courage and flexibility of mind that she shows in recognizing her folly and turning from it.

OUR TOWN

Type of work: Drama
Author: Thornton Wilder (1897-1975)
Type of plot: Domestic romance
Time of plot: 1901-1913
Locale: New Hampshire
First presented: 1938

In this Pulitzer Prize-winning play, Wilder portrays typical American small-town life, employing a bare minimum of scenery and utilizing a stage manager who remains onstage throughout the play, explaining the action and commenting philosophically on the characters and their lives. The love story of George Gibbs and Emily Webb is moving in its simplicity and tenderness.

Wilder once wrote that *Our Town* was an attempt to place a high value on even the small events of our life. Paradoxically, these events can only achieve their pricelessness when they are contrasted with the massive, unimaginable events of history—human, earth, and cosmic. For it is only against such a panoramic background that the full individuality and poignancy of our personal microcosms becomes evident. To measure minutiae against the vast infinities of creation need not result in despair so long as the entire continuum inspires wonder.

Both structure and dialogue in *Our Town* convey these awesome contrasts. Emily's youth, marriage, and death—the respective focal points of each act—transpire so swiftly that we wonder whether her life has any significance at all. Wilder reinforces this doubt by having various characters place the play's action in ever-widening contexts. Professor Willard fixes Grover's Corners in geological time; Mr. Webb defines the town in relation to the whole of American society; the Stage Manager speaks of the bank's time capsule which will be opened in a thousand years; Rebecca suggests that Emily's ultimate "address" is "the Solar System; the Universe; the Mind of God."

But while "belittling" Emily's life, Wilder also in effect magnifies it. By showing Emily in all her particularity, by emphasizing the numberless idiosyncracies which give her own world uniqueness, he creates a character who captures our attention and love. Grover's Corners, partly because it awakens deep nostalgia, also becomes distinctly loveable. Thus Wilder induces a special state of mind: one of fond attachment to utterly "insignificant" things. The fact, of course, that we cherish such things raises them to significance. That this marvelous paradox should be feelingly comprehended by his audience was Wilder's central aim.

Wilder's striking refusal to use traditional stage properties and his reliance on the pantomime techniques of Oriental theater was not only highly innovative, but served his thematic purpose as well. By having his audience imagine the paraphernalia of daily life, he required a concentration on and renewed appreciation of this background of minutiae.

OUR VILLAGE

Type of work: Tales and sketches
Author: Mary Russell Mitford (1787-1855)
Type of plot: Village chronicle
Time of plot: Early nineteenth century
Locale: Rural England
First published: 1824-1832

This pleasant collection of whimsical sketches of English rural life, first published individually over the course of eight years, contains no plot and little action. The joy of the work lies in the author's ability to show the importance of simple things, such as the laughter of children, the antics of dogs, and the beauty of wild flowers in the country.

It is noteworthy that these sketches, described by Miss Mitford as "half real and half imaginary, of a half imaginary and half real little spot on the sunny side of Berkshire," were concluded in 1832. That year saw the first of a series of political reform bills which finally put an end to an England dominated by the landed gentry and agriculture, an England celebrated by the author with sentiment and nostalgia. If her Victorian readers continued to make her happy rural village a myth of potent force, they came to realize—most of them grudgingly—that their fate was all bound up with the care and tending of the city and not the country. Yet they failed abjectly in that task.

One of the reasons the Victorians could not adequately handle the problems produced by the growth of urban industrialism was their emotional attachment to Miss Mitford's "Village"; or more precisely, that imaginary part of her village, that pastoral dream from which the social actualities were left out.

For the most part she suppresses or minimizes the severe depression of the 1820's, a trauma caused by the rapid and uncontrolled expansion of industrialism. She looks back to the last quarter of the eighteenth century, to her childhood, as a time which she considered stable and tranquil, and sentimentalizes the remnants of that age. But beyond that Miss Mitford propagates the myth of a past innocence and simplicity which finds its best expression for her in Shakespeare's Arcadian comedies.

All in all, then, *Our Village* is a delightful dream. It illuminates a constant in human experience: the feeling that at one time, sometime in the past, men were more virtuous and happier than they are in the present. But we must take care, as the Victorians did not always do, to guard our idea of the past by distinguishing between Miss Mitford's dream and the reality.

THE OVERCOAT

Type of work: Story
Author: Nikolai V. Gogol (1809-1852)
Type of plot: Social criticism
Time of plot: Early nineteenth century
Locale: St. Petersburg, Russia
First published: 1842

Having worked briefly as a civil servant, Gogol had no fondness for bureaucratic officialdom, and in this long tale he uses the wretched, ill-paid government clerk, Akakii Akakiievich Bashmachkin, to dramatize his view of the system and its effects on people. Gogol, often considered the father of nineteenth century Russian realism, achieves realistic description that avoids both bitterness and pathos.

Dostoevski's proclamation was correct: Gogol's *The Overcoat* was the source of modern Russian literature and the inspiration of many major nineteenth century Russian authors. No less than his fiction, Gogol's life, particularly in his social origins, his social orientation toward Russian society, and his literary aspirations, anticipated experiences common to many of his literary followers.

Gogol's life was aristocratic to the core, containing at the same time many of the most venerable and lackluster elements of this dominant Russian social class. He was the son of a Ukrainian noble who enjoyed some prestige and little wealth. Gogol early abandoned any thought of leading a bucolic life. Instead, he moved to St. Petersburg, the capital of tsarist Russia and attended a school designed to prepare him for a profession in the Department of Justice. A career in the Russian civil service was entirely in keeping with one of the most esteemed values of the nobility, service to society. Gogol hoped to achieve this goal as a bureaucrat rather than as an agronomist. However, after less than a year, he became intolerant of the tedium of the bureaucratic life and began to write. He led a dissident, cavalier life, wrote an epic poem and, after borrowing money from his mother that she could ill afford to lend, published his own work. The poem was unsuccessful. Distraught, Gogol purchased all the copies he could locate and burnt them. Ironically, Gogol framed his literary life with *autos-da-fé*. In fact, shortly before his death, Gogol spent an entire evening casually tossing a manuscript of the second part of *Dead Souls* into a stove. Disenchanted with St. Petersburg, with his literature, and with his career, Gogol again borrowed from his now nearly penniless mother and left Russia for Western Europe. Like other Russian writers who followed, such as Turgenev and Chekhov, Gogol spent most of his productive life in Western Europe. He died in Russia in 1852. At the time of his death he had become a religious fanatic and his death was the result of a grotesque religious fast. Even in his death, he was a model for future writers such as Dostoevski and Tolstoy, both of whom became religious zealots in their later lives.

Gogol's published works are relatively few in number. He is best remembered for *Dead Souls* (1842) and for the comedic drama *The Inspector General* (1836). The latter was Gogol's most successful work to appear during his lifetime. Spoofing the Russian bureaucracy, it brought cascades of laughter from the otherwise sober tsar Nicholas I. Of his shorter works, *The Overcoat* is the best known. Although Gogol rejected a formal career as a Russian bureaucrat, he never deviated from his commitment to the aristocratic ideal of service to society. In fact, age intensified his desire to better Russia, and he became convinced that he was chosen to deliver a great message to his countrymen.

In *The Overcoat,* Gogol tailored a trenchant and unmistakable, and often repeated, statement. The Russian bureaucracy, once the agent and symbol of enlightenment and change in Russia, had become in Gogol's time the instrument of oppression and sterility both for those whom it purported to serve and those who functioned within it. Akakii Akakiievich, possessing neither an inclination towards agriculture nor an ability therein, was a model bureaucrat; loyal and conscientious, faceless too, his days were spent as a copier of government documents, each day exactly like all the others. Underpaid and unpraised, Akakii was like all of his bureaucratic contemporaries, the foundation on which the nineteenth century Russian state stood. He rarely came in contact with the public. His vapid, tedious, and impersonal professional existence eradicated his personal life. Akakii was virtually isolated from society and from his own humanity. When his overcoat was stolen, he was forced into the role of Ivan Q. Public confronting an irritated and disinterested police magistrate who scolded him for his lack of respect and sent him unaided on his way. In the end, Akakii's death can be attributed as much to the newly acquired knowledge that the Russian bureaucracy is cold and unfeeling as to the loss of his coat.

It was precisely bureaucracy's icy inability to serve Russian society that forced Gogol to forsake a life as a civil servant. Yet, he could not divorce himself from his own however poorly practiced aristocratic ideal to serve society. Unable to serve from within the state, Gogol left Russia for Western Europe; unable to serve as a bureaucrat, Gogol left justice for literature. Service through literature: it was a difficult juxtaposition, and Gogol knew it. This perhaps irreconcilable problem accounts for an aspect of Gogol's literature which is unique; his humor. While Gogol fashioned in *The Overcoat* a literary pattern ideally suited to the needs of Russian writers, he wielded an unmistakably artistic needle. The unique Gogolian label is satire and humor, stitches conspicuously missing in the corpus of Russian *belles lettres.* While *Dead Souls* remains the author's humorous *magnum opus, The Overcoat* contains ample evidence of Gogol's gift of satire. The "important personage" is a title meant to deprecate the specialized jargon of Russian bureaucrats. While Dostoevski's dictum remains correct—Russian literature did come from Gogol's *The Overcoat*—no Russian writer ever duplicated Gogol's sense of humor. Maybe other Russian authors did not need to, but when Gogol lined his overcoat and all of his works with humor, he was shielding himself from what he considered to be the social insanities and the difficulty of his own literary mission.

The difficulty, or even the impossibility of service to Russia was the message contained in *The Overcoat*. Gogol, like all premier writers, identified a social problem the resolution of which became a mission for future Russian authors. After Gogol, writers did not hesitate to challenge the inadequacy of the Russian state and society even when, as was frequently the case, they were censored or incarcerated for doing so. While the mission was an arduous one, it did not deter Turgenev, Lermontov, Goncharov, Chekhov and others. And when the state censors turned a chilly and disapproving shoulder to their works, it is not surprising that Russian writers should find warmth and reassurance in Gogol's *The Overcoat*. It was the smartest literary fashion of the day and continued to fit the intellectual psyche of Russian writers for more than a hundred years.

John G. Tomlinson, Jr.

THE OX-BOW INCIDENT

Type of work: Novel
Author: Walter Van Tilburg Clark (1909-1971)
Type of plot: Regional realism
Time of plot: 1885
Locale: Nevada
First published: 1940

What seems in its beginning pages to be a typical Western with all the stage settings and characters of a cowboy thriller is actually a tense story of the cruel laws of survival. As the plot moves slowly but inexorably to its climax, the mob assumes the nature of a Greek chorus, now arguing on one side, now on the other, as Clark unfolds his saga of human misery.

Clark's *The Ox-Bow Incident* is set against a Nevada landscape in 1885, but its portrayal of mob justice is timeless. The tragedy in the novel involves not only the obvious one of innocent people who are wrongly punished. Clark illustrates how unjust and cruel acts can be carried out by intelligent and moral men who allow their sense of social duty to corrupt their greater, if less dominant, sense of human justice.

Bridger's Wells, Nevada, the initial setting for the novel's development, offered its citizens a limited variety of recreational diversions—eating, sleeping, drinking, cards, and fighting. Into that frontier setting stepped Gil Carter and Art Croft to learn that rustlers, who were at once murderers, had provided the place with an exciting alternative. Osgood, the Baptist minister from the only "working church" in town, realized early how tempers could sublimate one's reason and sense of justice. For the minister, however, the timing, if not also the place, was wrong. In times of despair, reason and justice become less attractive when immediate action seems convenient. Bartlett, a rancher who found rustling a particularly vile threat, argued that "justice" often proved ineffective and worked too slowly to guarantee that guilty men would pay the penalties for their crimes. "I say, stretch the bastards." Bartlett proved effective enough to persuade two score townspeople into forming an illegal posse even though none of the men he exhorted owned any cattle, and only two or three even knew the allegedly murdered man. Bartlett, the one rancher, physically weak and unsound though he appeared, had stigmatized any among his listeners who opposed his argument. Davies, the storekeeper, proved unsuccessful in his efforts to delay the manhunt by his words: "True law, the code of justice, the essence of our sensations of right and wrong, is the conscience of society. It has taken thousands of years to develop, and it is the greatest, the most distinguishing quality which has evolved with mankind." Notwithstanding the thoughtfulness of his argument, a new leader, Tetley, had by then emerged who, capitalizing on his own frustrations as well as on the gullibility of others, effected a peculiar reversal of the "conscience of society" so as to produce, in effect, a new concept of "justice."

Major Tetley's son Gerald, who was forced by his father to take part in the posse, painfully realized the weakness of individual men too afraid to challenge the mob, who convince themselves that to resist would be to admit weakness, to be the only hunter in a pack to quit. "How many of us do you think are really here because there have been cattle stolen, or because Kinkaid was shot?" he asks. In the absence of Sheriff Risley, who as the legally constituted police authority might have impeded the development toward lynch law, the formation of an illegal posse, the manhunt, and the lynchings all went ahead with the inevitability of a Shakespearean tragedy.

In the eleventh hour, no gesture which suggested innocence could spare the doomed men. Martin's emotional letter to his wife was to be shared among the posse by Davies in an effort to save the life of a man Davies believed was innocent. The effort was challenged by Martin himself, however, who used the incident to make another point, that even an initial promise to preserve the integrity of his letter would have proved futile among men in whom conscience had long since failed as a measure of just conduct. In a moment where bravery might understandably have failed among men about to be hanged, the Mexican removed a bullet from his own leg, washed the wound and dressed it with a fire-heated knife. He tossed the knife into the ground within an inch of where its owner's foot would have been had he not, in fear, drawn quickly away. The Mexican, who smiled often at the proceedings, did so again, seeing in the posse the absence of the very bravery they thought they all possessed. All sympathy that Martin's letter and the Mexican's courage might otherwise have created for the three doomed men never materialized, however, because most of the posse had simply made up their minds about the prisoners' fate already, or because they believed the rest had, and since they believed fledgling signs of sympathy were wrong and something which had to be concealed, Tetley had his day.

Davies, the one man who had had least to do with the hangings, and perhaps did most to prevent them, was himself riddled with guilt for the occasion of the crime. "Tetley couldn't help what he did," Davies believed. "Tetley's a beast. . . . But a beast is not to blame." The leader of the posse was successful only to the extent that he was allowed to achieve his goal. Davies, a peaceful man, even thought that he should have resorted to the gun, to violence if necessary, to prevent the illegal executions from taking place. He admitted too, however, that in not having a weapon he was glad his convictions did not have to be tested. Davies' sense of guilt and his sense of justice made him realize, as no one else could, how little he actually did to prevent the hangings from taking place. "I had everything, justice, pity, . . . and I let those three men hang because I was afraid. The . . . only thing Tetley had, guts, plain guts, and I didn't have it." The sensitive man, lacking the brute convictions of his opposite, is rendered impotent. His final confession is accompanied by laughter in the background.

The Ox-Bow Incident has no hero; yet it cries out for one in a world where the lessons of the Ox-Bow may not be remembered, much less learned. Inasmuch as the novel was written in 1937 and 1938, while Nazism bullied a world into submission, it is not a theme which was then out of step with world developments. Neither, according to Clark, does the story lack American application. "What I wanted to say was 'It can happen here. It has happened here, in minor but sufficiently indicative ways, a great many times.' "

Frank Joseph Mazzi

PAMELA

Type of work: Novel
Author: Samuel Richardson (1689-1761)
Type of plot: Sentimental romance
Time of plot: Early eighteenth century
Locale: England
First published: 1740-1741

Generally considered the first modern English novel, Pamela, or, Virtue Rewarded, *follows the adventures of a young servant girl, forced by poverty to work in a nobleman's house, through her letters to her parents. The epistolary form allows for much introspection on Pamela's part, and her letters read more like private diary entries. Intended by Richardson to be taken as models of behavior for virtuous lower-class girls, the letters are divided into two sections: the first set,* Aggressive Chastity, *relates Pamela's harrowing experiences in defending her chastity against Mr. B—'s advances; the second,* Provocative Prudence, *depicts Pamela's life as the new wife of reformed Mr. B—, which position she has attained as the reward for her virtue.*

Samuel Richardson has often been awarded the title "Father of the English Novel." Like most such titles, this one is an oversimplification of a complex issue, and one that has been particularly disputed by students of Richardson's contemporary Daniel Defoe, who is also justly noted for his important contributions to the genre. The importance of Richardson's position in the tradition of the novel, however, is undeniable, and is based on his redefinition of the form, through his success, in *Pamela,* in dealing with several of the major formal problems which Defoe and others had left unsolved.

The most significant of these problems was that of plot. Prior to the publication of *Pamela,* a novel was commonly defined as "a small tale, generally of love." Although this definition has more recently been applied to the novella, most of the sources in Richardson's era, notably Dr. Johnson's dictionary, construed it as referring to the novel. When *Pamela* appeared, it was considered a "dilated novel" because its subject matter was basically the single amorous episode which the short novels had previously emphasized. Yet its treatment was on a scale much closer to the romances of Defoe and Fielding, two authors who did not confront the definition problem in most of their works, which tended to deal with many episodes within a larger context. Such works, then, as *Moll Flanders* and *Tom Jones* fit more easily into the "romance" category under the eighteenth century definitions. It was Richardson who combined the scale of the romance and the scope of the traditional novel to form the basis of the form as we know it today. Richardson's use of the epistolary style—a style of which he was perhaps literature's foremost practitioner—facilitated the birth of the new form, although it causes some problems for modern readers.

Pamela's plot structure, based on a radically new concept in the novel form, is at once the work's major strength and weakness, as well as the subject of considerable controversy. Viewed in context with later novels, it appears awkward, contrived, and lacking in realism. Indeed, a major criticism of Richardson's novel concerns the question of how the major characters found the time in the midst of all of their adventures to be writing lengthy letters to one another. In a purely technical sense, perhaps the worst defect in the plot is that it is too long for its essential purpose, causing it to be static in movement and lacking in tension; it reaches a climax and resolution midway through the book, thus leaving hundreds of pages of dull and uneventful narrative. The account of Pamela's married life, serving as it does only to confirm her virtue in the eyes of the world, could have been trimmed considerably, thus enhancing the overall effect of the novel. As it is, the falling action of the novel, consisting of Mr. B's adultery and Pamela's forgiveness as well as the growing appreciation on the part of Mr. B. of his wife's virtue, is too unconvincing and sentimental.

The strength of the plot structure lies in Richardson's epistolary form which, its shortcomings notwithstanding, does convey a degree of realism. Letters are normally a means for the relation of one's common factual doings, and they presuppose an actual writer and an actual reader. Our preconceived notions concerning the normal functions of the mode make believable an actual maiden, an actual seducer, and an actual marriage. Richardson's manipulation of the machinery governing the epistles—the hidden pens and ink, the evasions and discoveries, and the secreting of letters in bosoms and underlinens—causes the effect to grow. The realism is further enhanced by the clustering and lingering effect which comes to surround each incident. An incident occurs and is reflected on, committed to paper, entrusted to a porter, and spied upon; it is either intercepted, or received, reflected upon, and responded to. The whole complex, repetitious effect, although it slows down the action, lends great credibility to the original incident.

Richardson's epistolary form, after establishing the necessary suspension of disbelief in readers regarding a servant girl who can read and write, also excuses logically much of Pamela's smooth and affected rhetoric; since a letter is an editing of life rather than life itself, the writer has an editorial option to tailor and refurbish experience. Thus Richardson, having posited a servant girl with a certain flair for writing, can justify a further suspension of disbelief, although sometimes not as much as the circumstances demand.

The weakest part of the plot structure in terms of realism is Richardson's handling of the sequence of incidents. The incidents in *Pamela,* while perhaps not disappointing our preconceived notions of drawing room and boudoir reality, are little more than interesting fits of manners and rarely reveal any depth of character or morals. These incidents are little more than stylistically balanced situations; outrages in the summer house are followed by contrition, and tearful farewells by triumphant reunions.

The same shallowness applies to some of Richardson's characters, who, being allegorical as demanded by the instructional premise of the novel, offer little depth of personality. Yet the heroine herself presents an interesting study; Pamela begins as the most fully allegorical figure and concludes by being the most fully human. Beginning in ignorance, she presents the prospect, particularly to readers steeped in Fielding, of becoming a satirical figure; yet she never does. Pamela is an incorruptibly good girl. What is interesting about her characterization is how the author converts us to accept the reality of his protagonist and her maidenly dilemma. He manages this by placing her in a crisis which is inherently genuine and appropriate to her way of life. He supplies her with neatly counterpoised groups of friends and enemies and fleshes out her vulnerability with an impressive strength and a striking ability to cope—a believable middle-class trait. The implied spectacle of her parents nervously hanging on from letter to letter adds further believability to the picture. Richardson also imbues Pamela with little vices which she realizes she has. Pamela, for example, knows that she is longwinded, prone to construe motives to her own advantage, and inclined to cling to praise and flattery. This realization of some of her own faults makes Pamela much more credible than a character who is merely symbolic and displays no insight into herself.

For all of Richardson's virtues and faults as a writer, it is his redefinition of the form of the novel that most makes him worth reading. *Pamela* was a radical departure from accepted concepts when it was first published, and in a sense it is a radical departure in our own day. While subsequent novelists learned from and modified Richardson's techniques, they for the most part drifted away from his epistolary form; while keeping his idea of treating a simple episode on a larger scale, they tended to follow the techniques developed by Fielding and Defoe. *Pamela* is thus as much of an anomaly today as it was in the eighteenth century. Yet it is a vital part of literary tradition and was instrumental in creating the novel as we know it now.

Patricia Ann King

PARADE'S END

Type of work: Novel
Author: Ford Madox Ford (Ford Madox Hueffer, 1873-1939)
Type of plot: Social chronicle
Time of plot: World War I and after
Locale: England and France
First published: 1924, 1925, 1926, 1928

Originally appearing as a tetralogy, Parade's End *was first published as a single unit in 1950. The novel tells the story of Christopher Tietjens, who calls himself "the last English Tory" because his type has been disappearing since the eighteenth century. He seeks truth, honor, and peace in the face of the hypocrisy and confusion of his own generation. Ford tells his story with a measure of subtlety and power, simplicity and restraint that has caused one critic to dub him England's most neglected novelist.*

Perhaps the most arresting character in *Parade's End* is Sylvia, Christopher Tietjens' beautiful but spiteful wife. As the account begins, she has run away with another man, merely to see how her husband will respond. Throughout the novel her sole aim is to break his gentlemanly "veneer"—or that quality which identifies Christopher as "the last English Tory." Sylvia's attacks on his honor are ruthless and constant; she employs any underhanded, dishonorable scheme to discredit him. She does not hesitate to brand him a socialist or to assert that he favors the murdering of babies. But Christopher's manners, which outrage his wife, are more than a veneer: they represent the simplicity and sincerity of not merely a lost generation but also a lost world. And it is not Sylvia alone who despises Tietjens' virtuous honesty. Indeed the whole civilization, seemingly in its final violent upheaval, seems bent upon its own destruction as well as the eradication of the last vestige of its honor, personified in Christopher.

Yet, ironically, that which appears so fragile, that which seems sure to give way under the stress of world war and the consequent revolution in manners and morals remains impervious—and indeed reinforced—at the conclusion. Despite all that can be brought to bear on Christopher's "veneer," it remains intact and strengthened in his love for Valentine and in Mark's dying perception. And to add to the irony, Sylvia herself is ultimately won over by Tietjens' constancy. With his major character, Ford has accomplished a rare feat in modern fiction: while convincing us of its authenticity, he has dramatized the virtue of innocence and, most surprising, shown us not merely its ability to survive but also its power, even in the worst of times, to prevail. That art can be consoling is no more evident than in *Parade's End.*

PARADISE LOST

Type of work: Poem
Author: John Milton (1608-1674)
Type of plot: Epic
Time of plot: The Beginning
Locale: Heaven, Hell, and Earth
First published: 1667

Considered the greatest epic in modern literature, Milton's poem in twelve books tells of man's happiness in the Garden of Eden and of his first disobedience; within this story, the angel Raphael tells Adam the history of Satan and his band of rebellious angels. The poem ends with the expulsion from Paradise and a vision of mankind's coming misery, but Michael also offers the future hope of the Redeemer who will one day bring salvation to mankind.

According to his biographers, Milton spent years preparing to write his great epic poem. When in 1660 he found himself an ever stronger defender of religious and moral faith of the Christian religion, he discarded his idea of a work dealing with the Arthurian legend and turned instead to the story of Adam and Eve in the Garden of Eden and called his poem *Paradise Lost.*

Contrary to the trend of his age towards writing poetry which reflected a sense of disorder—the Elizabethan Age was having to contend with the then-new theory of the Copernican universe, in which the earth is not the center—Milton reached for the grand, monumental epic form; and his own musical background lent him the proper ear for imbuing his epic with the sounds of organ chords. As though he were playing a multi-keyboard organ for a cathedral audience, Milton created sounds in his verse to correlate with his theme, a theme which covers all creation; the universe is his setting.

Paradise Lost echoes the *Iliad* in its epic structure; its twelve-book organization begins *in medias res,* or in the middle of things, as it recounts the creation of the universe with a picture of God, a mighty winged creature who, "dove-like sat'st brooding on the vast abyss/And mad'st it pregnant." Other epic conventions in the poem include the invocation of the muse and the epic question. *Paradise Lost* addresses the "Heavenly Muse," though of course Milton's invocation is not simply an imitation of Homer, but also a prayer:

> . . . what in me is dark
> Illumine, what is low raise and support;
> That to the highth of this great argument
> I may assert Eternal Providence,
> And justify the ways of God to men. (Book I, 22-26)

The epic question asks, in essence, why we live in a fallen world, what happened in the Garden of Eden, and what events made paradise lost to man.

> . . . say first what cause
> Moved our grand parents in that happy state,
> Favored of Heaven so highly, to fall off
> From their Creator, and transgress his will
> For one restraint, lords of the world besides?
> Who first seduced them to that foul revolt? (Book I, 28-33)

Satan is the guilty party. Swelled with excessive pride, he and his cohorts, all archangels and angels (the lowest ranks of divinity), had risen up against God in Heaven and had been banished forever. They landed in the darkness of Hell; through a bridge Satan later enters the world and the Garden of Eden to bring about the fall of man. It will become, as Milton shows us in *Paradise Lost,* the "fortunate fall," and will serve to prove that good can come out of evil, that good triumphs.

Satan is sometimes considered the hero, although in Miltonic terms he is wrong. The romantics, particularly Blake and Shelley, found in Satan's assertion of individuality and his rebellion against "tyranny" (in *Paradise Lost* Heaven is a monarchy, Hell a democracy) an admirable figure. They felt that the God of *Paradise Lost* was rather poorly characterized, as well as limited by his tyrannical nature.

But, in Milton's universe, all begins in God, and Satan's rebellion serves to illuminate the problematical question of free will in the Christian universe. How can it be argued that an omniscient God does not control the actions of man? Milton would say that God foresees, but does not predetermine. In other words, Adam and Eve must assume the responsibility for their own sin against God, even though God is omniscient. Thus, men still have freedom of choice.

What man must resist is pride, the result of too much faith in the human intellect. Like Satan, Adam too is guilty of believing in his own unconquerable mind; the assumption leads him into false logic and excessive pride, his greatest fault. Pride is traditionally the chief among the "seven deadly sins," followed by envy, wrath, sloth, avarice, gluttony, and lust. All the sins are perversions or excesses of love, except sloth, which is defective love. In a genealogical allegory of incest, Milton shows how Sin springs from the head of Satan to mate with him and produce Death; Death in turn mates with Sin to bear the Hell Hounds. This incestuous family group represents the effect of the sin of pride, with its inward-turning, self-perpetuating belief in the assertion of the individual.

By the time he wrote *Paradise Lost,* Milton was blind, a fact which creates yet another parallel between Milton and Homer. The fact of Milton's own blindness also lends poignancy to the symbolism of light and darkness in *Paradise Lost.* Much of Milton's meaning is carried in the poem by the imagery and symbolism of light and dark. As we see in Book III, there are two kinds of light: heavenly light, which comes from God, and worldly light, which comes from the sun. As a result, then, earthly light is not necessarily godly light; or, man's power of reasoning is not necessarily infallible. Man learns through logical processes, but the angels receive knowledge directly (through "inspiration"). Man maintains the possibility of receiving God's light, but such a reception is not automatic. According to the mythology of *Paradise Lost,* the stars shine at night to protect the world from chaos.

Milton enjoyed his early life in an ideal environment. His father, a banker, could afford the best possible education, and he tried to give it to his son, who displayed his literary and his other intellectual talents at an early age. Milton's father was a musician of some repute, and he taught his son to love music. In addition to having personal tutors at his home, Milton attended St. Paul's school in London. He often stayed up late reading, and it has been conjectured that his dedication to his studies led to his later blindness. He was a humanist and a believer in the scientific method; thus, he believed that man can better himself through conscious effort. Milton developed for himself a fine mind, but at the great cost of his eyesight. The third book of *Paradise Lost* ends on a personal note:

> Thus with the year
> Seasons return; but not to me returns
> Day, or the sweet approach of even or morn,
> Or sight of vernal bloom, or summer's rose,
> Or flocks, or herds, or human face divine;
> But cloud instead, and ever-during dark
> Surrounds me, from the cheerful ways of men
> Cut off, and for the book of knowledge fair
> Presented with a universal blank
> Of Nature's works to me expunged and rased,
> And wisdom at one entrance quite shut out.
> So much the rather thou, celestial Light,
> Shine inward, and the mind through all her powers
> Irradiate, there plant eyes, all mist from thence
> Purge and disperse, that I may see and tell
> Of things invisible to mortal sight.
> (Book III, 40-55)

Jean Marlowe

PARZIVAL

Type of work: Poem
Author: Wolfram von Eschenbach (c. 1170-1220)
Type of plot: Chivalric romance
Time of plot: The chivalric age
Locale: Western Europe
First published: Thirteenth century manuscript

Parzival, the masterpiece of Germany's greatest medieval poet, provided the basis of the great body of Wagner's operas written on knightly themes. Eschenbach was instrumental in raising the moral tone of the Arthurian legends by upholding in his poem such chivaliric virtues as fidelity to the plighted word, charity to one's fellowman, and reverence for God. In terms of plot, it is interesting to note the poet's use of a precious stone of supernatural powers as the Grail, rather than the chalice used at the last supper.

The life of Wolfram von Eschenbach, author of *Parzival,* spanned the end of the twelfth and the beginning of the thirteenth centuries. It was a time of political and religious turbulence—the Crusades reached their height in the twelfth century—but it was also a time of a flowering of the arts in general, and literature in particular. At a time when Richard the Lion-Hearted and John ruled England, some of the greatest names in German literature were already writing. Among Wolfram's contemporaries were Hartmann von Aue, Gottfried von Strassburg, and the lyric poet, Walter von der Vogelweide. The anonymous author of *The Song of the Nibelungs* also wrote at this time.

Wolfram was born about 1170, in Eschenbach, a small village on the border between Swabia and Bavaria. He was a knight, but of very limited means, and was therefore dependent on patronage for support during the composition of his works. He wrote *Parzival* somewhere between 1197 and 1215. His other works include a handful of lyrics, some fragments of a romance, and a poem, *Willehalm,* which was left unfinished. The date of Wolfram's death is not known, but it was probably before 1220.

The method of the composition of *Parzival* is in doubt, since Wolfram claimed not to be able to read or write. Since the poem comprises 24,810 lines, the oral composition of the work would have been a formidable task, but not one beyond possibility, or, for that matter, without precedent. In a time of near-universal illiteracy, what would today seem to be phenomenal feats of memory were taken for granted. The oldest works in many languages are poems of epic length composed orally and either learned by rote or recreated for recitation according to set formulas. It should be noted too that John Milton, prevented from writing by his blindness, composed *Paradise Lost* orally.

Wolfram's main source for his story was Chrétien de Troyes' *Li Contes del Gral.* This collection of Arthurian romances furnished Wolfram with the material for eleven of the sixteen books of his poem. The source of the initial two and final three books of *Parzival* remains a puzzle. Wolfram several times refers to a Provençal poet named Kyot, who supposedly gave him the correct version of the story. This Kyot is a mystery to scholars, though, for a variety of reasons. No Provençal poem on the Parzival theme has survived, if any ever existed. Kyot also bears a northern, not a southern French name, and most critics believe that Kyot is simply a joke of Wolfram's, as is, perhaps, his claim of illiteracy. Yet Wolfram's statements cannot be disposed of out of hand, since customarily, medieval poets worked from sources rather than the product of their own imagination.

Despite their cloudiness, Wolfram's sources are clear in comparison with the origin of the subject matter of which his poem is only one part—the Arthurian romances. Myth and legend shaped the origin of these tales of King Arthur and his court, and their beginnings are buried in now-lost Welsh and Irish stories. During the twelfth century, corresponding to a great rise in interest, written versions of the Arthurian material began to appear. About 1135, Geoffrey of Monmouth, a Welshman, composed in Latin a long compilation of fancy called *The History of the Kings of Britain,* the last third of which is devoted to Arthur. In 1155, an Anglo-Norman named Wace used Geoffrey's book as the basis for his French poem, *Brut* (the poem's title refers to a mythical Brutus, great-grandson of Aeneas, to whom Geoffrey had attributed the founding of the line of British kings). But neither Geoffrey nor Wace are used by Chrétien de Troyes; the French poet may have had other materials, now lost, from which he worked.

One other bit of Arthurian material should be mentioned: the *Mabinogion.* The *Mabinogion* is a Welsh collection of stories; it was put in writing after 1300, but probably composed at least a century earlier. The *Mabinogion* includes a version of the story that interested Wolfram, but the hero is named Peredur. (Chrétien de Troyes, either following his sources or for reasons of his own, did not use the Welsh form of the name; Parzival is Wolfram's rendition of the form used by Chrétien, Perceval.) Critics believe that *Peredur* is the existing version closest to the oral Welsh stories from which all the written versions are ultimately derived.

The object of Parzival's quest is, of course, the Grail in Wolfram's poem, but what the Grail is forms a story in itself. In the Welsh folklore from which so many of the romances derive, we hear of two miraculous objects—a horn of plenty, and a dish which increases the food placed in it. In Old French, the word for dish or platter was *graal,* and although Chrétien de Troyes used the word *graal,* the object of the quest, the Grail, is a jeweled relic. Nor is there a wonderful dish in *Parzival.* The Grail in Wolfram's work is apparently a magical gem—but the motif of plenty does appear: whatever food one wishes for appears at once in front of the gem; whatever drink one desires appears in his cup. Wherever Wolfram got this detail of his story, the source is definitely not Chrétien de Troyes. The conception of the Grail as the cup used by Christ at the Last Supper comes from a different tradition.

The poem itself is divided into sixteen books of rhyming couplets, grouped into sections of thirty lines. The poem is difficult to read in the original, since an involved syntax is characteristic of Wolfram's style, and the dialect in which he wrote is not a direct ancestor of modern German. Even readers of modern German find it convenient to use a translation.

When the Reformation came to Germany in the sixteenth century, Wolfram's poem was forgotten, and it did not again become popular until the nineteenth century. Wagner's opera *Parsifal* did much to recommend the poem to a wider audience. The careful structure of the poem, its wide-ranging action, its insightful handling of the growing character of Parzival himself, and its story—one that has fascinated readers of Western literature for almost a thousand years—place Wolfram's *Parzival* among the greatest works of our medieval heritage.

Walter Meyers

A PASSAGE TO INDIA

Type of work: Novel
Author: E. M. Forster (1879-1970)
Type of plot: Social criticism
Time of plot: About 1920
Locale: India
First published: 1924

A Passage to India can be read on two levels: political and mystic. Politically it deals with the tension between the British and the native Indians, as well as with the tension between Hindus and Moslems. Mystically it is concerned with the search for the infinite and eternal so characteristic of Oriental religion, and with the illogical and inexplicable in human life. The visit to the Marabar Caves illustrates the malignant side of mysticism, the Temple-Festival at the close, its benignity. Forster divides the novel into three sections which correspond to the three seasons of the Indian year: the Cold Weather, the Hot Weather, and the Rains.

E. M. Forster was a member of the intellectually select Bloomsbury group in London which flourished just before and after World War I. Educated at Cambridge, as were many of the group, Forster became one of England's leading novelists during the prewar Edwardian period. In the Bloomsbury group his friends included Lytton Strachey, the biographer; Virginia Woolf, the novelist; Clive Bell, the art critic; Roger Fry, a painter; John Maynard Keynes, the economist; and G. E. Moore, the philosopher. The group rejected convention and authority, placing great faith in its own intellect and good taste. Forster wrote several good novels between 1905-1910: *Where Angels Fear to Tread, The Longest Journey, A Room with a View,* and *Howards End.* After a hiatus of fourteen years, he published *A Passage to India* in 1924. No other novels were published during his lifetime. A posthumous novel, *Maurice,* was published after his death in 1970. He once confessed that he did not understand the post-World War I values and had nothing more to say. *A Passage to India,* however, belies this statement; it is a novel for all seasons.

Forster's title comes from the Whitman poem by the same name. This choice is ultimately ironic, for Whitman's vision is of the total unity of all people. In the novel the attempt to unite people fails at all levels.

The book is divided into three sections: Mosque, Cave, Temple. These divisions correspond to the three divisions of the Indian year: cool spring, hot summer, wet monsoon. Each section is dominated by its concomitant weather. Each section also focuses on one of the three ethnic groups involved: Moslem, Anglo-Indian, Hindu. The Cave could also be called "The Club." Just as the Mosque and the Temple are the Moslem and Hindu shrines, so is the Club the true Anglo-Indian shrine. Forster is not writing a religious novel, however. He realizes that religious-ethnic divisions control social modes of activity. The Moslems are emotional; the British rely on intellect. Only the Hindus, in the person of Godbole, have the capacity to love.

The novel is not merely a social or political commentary. Forster belittles social forms on all sides of the conflict. He favors, neither Indians nor British. The bridge party, Fielding's tea party, and Aziz's cave party are all failures. More important than social forms are the relationships among individuals. The novel's theme is the search for love and friendship. It is primarily the male-male relationships that have the capacity for mutual understanding, and it is the male characters that are most clearly defined. The females, Mrs. Moore and Adela Quested, have no real possibility of finding friendship across ethnic lines. Mrs. Moore is too old; Adela is too British. Both women want to see the "real" India, but they are unprepared for it when the experience comes. Mrs. Moore, at the mosque and the first cave, Adela, at the cave and the courtroom, discover the real India, and both suffer an almost catatonic withdrawal.

The male characters are more complex. Aziz with his Moslem sensitivity is determined to find humiliation no matter what the experience. He tries to be both physician and poet—healer of body and soul, but he is inept in both attempts. In the last section we see him abandoning both. More than a type, Aziz needs love and friendship. Ultimately he is incapable of establishing a satisfying relationship among his own people, with the Hindus, or, more importantly with Cecil Fielding. Moslem sensitivity prevents him from accepting friendship when it is offered.

Out of the multiple failures of the first two sections of the novel there is only the relationship between Aziz and Fielding that holds any promise of reconciliation. Moslem and Anglo-Indian, they meet in the final section in the Hindu province. Both men desire friendship and understanding, but it is too late. In the final scene the very land seems to separate them; they are not in tune with nature which is renewing itself in the monsoon downpour. Neither man has come to accept the irrational. They are not ready, in the Hindu sense of love, to accept things as they are. Only Godbole, a Hindu, can accept India and her people for what they are. The nothingness of the caves and the apparent chaos of the people do not disturb the Hindu.

The most crucial scene in *A Passage to India* is the visit to the Marabar Caves. They form the center of the novel. These caves puzzle and terrify both Moslems and Anglo-Indians. Only Godbole instinctively understands them. The Hindus possessed India before either Moslems or British. The caves are also elemental; they have been there from the beginnings of the earth. They are not Hindu holy places, but Godbole can respect them without fear. Cave worship is the cult of the female principle, the Sacred Womb, Mother Earth. The Marabar Caves, both womb and grave, demand total effacing of ego. The individual loses his identity; whatever is said returns to him as Ommm, the holy word.

To those who rely on the intellect the caves are terrifying and chaotic. The trip itself emphasizes the chaos that is India. Godbole can eat no meat; Aziz can eat no pork; the British must have their whisky and port. The confusion of the departure epitomizes the confusion that pervades the novel. Significantly it is Godbole, the one man who might have helped, who is left out. Once in the caves the party encounters the Nothingness that terrifies. Only Mrs. Moore seems to accept it on a limited scale, but the caves have reduced her will to live. She retreats from the world of experience; nothing matters any more. She came to India seeking peace; she finds it in death. Ironically, as her body is being lowered into the Indian Ocean, she is being mythified into the cult of Emiss Emoore.

The conclusion of the novel emphasizes the chaos of India, but it also hints at a pattern which the outsider, Moslem or British, cannot understand. Drenched in water and religion, the last chapters portray the rebirth of the God Shri Krishna. It is the recycling of the seasons, the rebirth and renewal of the earth, which signals the renewal of the Hindu religious cycle. Godbole shows that man may choose to accept and participate in the seeming chaos, or he can fight against it. But for true love and friendship, man must be in tune with the natural rhythms of the universe. One must accept. Neither Fielding nor Aziz, products of Western civilization, can accept the confusion without attempting to impose order. They still rely on the rational. Although they have moved toward the irrational in the course of the novel, they have not moved far enough.

Michael S. Reynolds

THE PASSION FLOWER

Type of work: Drama
Author: Jacinto Benavente y Martínez (1866-1954)
Type of plot: Tragedy
Time of plot: Early twentieth century
Locale: Castile, Spain
First presented: 1913

Bearing signs of Benevente's interest in Ibsen, Shakespeare, and Molière, The
Passion Flower *is in many ways more classic and universal than Spanish. The first
two acts of the play are violent melodrama, followed by a philosophical third act in
which the action is confined to the hearts of two women who love the same man, one
consciously, the other unconsciously.*

The Passion Flower is the rather cinematographic title given to the English
language version of Jacinto Benavente's *La malquerida,* the drama upon which
Benavente's British and American reputation largely rests. Its production by
Miss Nance O'Neil in 1920 met with huge success and was in part responsible
for the author's receiving the Nobel Prize in 1922.

Some critics have referred to the play as a classical drama, but scholars
attempting to analyze the play according to Aristotelian principles would find
it difficult to discover unity of action. At one juncture Raimunda, at another
Esteban, at another Acacia becomes the protagonist. It is not possible to say
that any one of the three is the hero or heroine of the tragedy. It would be
more realistic to state that the real protagonist of the play is the people and
that the chief theme of the drama lies in the gradual awakening of public
consciousness in this village of the Castilian uplands. The viewer sees, in
each successive act, the increasing upsurge of public opinion toward punish-
ing the guilty sinner. Initially, Norbert, the innocent one, is accused, but
gradually public opinion sifts the evidence, and as soon as he is proven
innocent, he is led home in triumph by large crowds. Though the people of
the village do not appear on the stage, and leave the principal actors to play
out the tragedy, the audience feels that, like an invisible chorus, the villagers
are commenting all the time on the tragic fatality of man.

This play, more than any other of the author's works, shows most clearly
how strong are the female characters of Benavente's plays. It is difficult for
male actors to play up to Benavente's heroines. It is also difficult to visualize
the proud Castilian type in Esteban who becomes the whimpering coward
who can hardly face the glance of his wife. In Esteban we are far from the
proud heroes of Spanish chivalry. No character could be less characteristic of
the man of Castile; he is not a man of flesh and blood, but a vague, unreal
character. In the early acts Esteban appears but little and never uttters any
but evasive words. After the murder has been committed, he becomes a
miserable coward and has not even the spirit to hold his head up and face

his servant Rubio. In the great scene with Raimunda, her strength and courage contrast with his cowardice. He is the most inglorious anti-hero ever
created by Benavente.

Acacia, from the beginning, is a rather strange character. Ever since her
mother's marriage to Esteban she has shown a reserve toward her stepfather in spite of his kindness and obvious affection. By subtle touches that
give an impression of gloomy sadness, Benavente instills increasing amounts
of mystery into Acacia's characterization. One of these touches is the use of
cleverly written dialogue that indicates either that a peculiar sexual hatred
exists between Acacia and Esteban, or that Acacia is an unbalanced neurotic.
This mystery continues throughout the drama. Raimunda, Acacia's mother,
is a character who is essentially submissive in temperament. Since she has
been under the sexual domination of her husband, it takes a rude awakening
to cause the scales to fall from her eyes and make her see him as he really is.
Until this point, Raimunda has lived on, blandly unconscious that tragedy was
near at hand. Consequently, when the crisis does come she is torn by conflicting emotions: she still loves her husband passionately, but she wants him
to suffer for his sin. This conflict is developed by Benavente in a brilliant
antithetic manner. He develops power by postponing the great scene of re-
crimination between husband and wife. If the confrontation had taken place
at the end of the second act, for example, there would have been no antithesis, as Raimunda was totally dominated by feelings of horror against
Esteban. But in the third act her feelings have softened and pity for him
has had time to weaken her resolve. No scene in Benavente's works provides
a greater example of antithesis. Being both an honorable and a religious
woman, Raimunda wishes Esteban to suffer to the fullest extent as an atonement to God for his sin—a spirit of justice characteristic of the Castilian
mind. But there is the soft, womanly side to her character, and seeing him
entrapped on all sides, like a wild beast, she feels compassion for him.

Benavente demonstrates great skill in dramatic technique and characterization to develop the antithesis that builds his play to a powerful climax. But
there is no doubt that the author, after working out brilliantly the first two
acts, was in a quandary regarding the denouement. All the events in the final
act are so arranged as to lead up willy-nilly to the theatrical climax where
Raimunda makes her daughter kiss Esteban and call him father. Raimunda,
in the final scenes, seems to lack a certain spontaneity, and at times goes
perilously close to the role of a stage-struck heroine of romantic drama.
After she learns at the end of the second act that Esteban loves Acacia and
has committed the murder on that account, it is hard to understand why she
does not keep him away from her. A woman who was passionately fond of
her husband and had heard the horrible news that was to ruin her life,
would have kept him out of the way until the trouble was past.

The production of this play raised many points of criticism. Some whose nerves were irritated by the roughness of this tragedy thought of the story only as a monstrous sin; others made many speculations as to whether the case of the love of Esteban for Acacia could be real. Yet in regard to these problems we can look back at Calderón and, more recently, at Ibsen and find that both of these authors have handled similar themes and differed little from Benavente in the nature of their treatment. Most criticism, however, has bowed before the public enthusiasm engendered by the play. *The Passion Flower* and the subsequent achievement of the Nobel Prize marked the summit of Benavente's literary career, and he has become a leading influence upon the modern generation of Spanish playwrights.

Stephen Hanson

THE PATHFINDER

Type of work: Novel
Author: James Fenimore Cooper (1789-1851)
Type of plot: Historical romance
Time of plot: 1756
Locale: Lake Ontario and surrounding territory
First published: 1840

The Pathfinder, *the third in the* Leatherstocking *series, portrays wilderness scout Natty Bumppo at the height of his powers; in this novel, Natty falls in love for the first and only time, but relinquishes his claim in deference to the man his beloved really loves. Typical of Cooper's novels,* The Pathfinder *freely blends fact and fiction; descriptions of places, such as the British fort at Oswego, are often historical, but the plotline is pure fiction.*

Of the five novels in James Fenimore Cooper's Leatherstocking series, *The Pathfinder* was the fourth to be written; but in the chronology of the hero Natty Bumppo's life it is the third tale, since it finds Natty resurrected and rejuvenated following his old age and death in *The Prairie,* written thirteen years earlier. *The Pathfinder* is distinguished by being the first and only Leatherstocking story in which the celibate and thoroughly independent frontier scout falls in love with a woman.

Cooper was an essentially romantic writer, and although as a thorough and competent historian he was easily able to back up his fictional narrative with factual information, his primary purpose was to stir the reader's imagination through idealized portraits of frontier life. Cooper's most lasting appeal lies in his gift for storytelling. Working with even the simplest and least original plot, he was able to capture and sustain reader interest by employing ambushes and chases, hairbreadth escapes, and harrowing violence, as well as sentiment, chivalry, and romance. Linked inextricably with such a colorful and adventure-filled storyline is the familiar Cooper setting; the primal beauty of forest and sea, the grandeur and rich abundance of unspoiled nature, provide an appropriate backdrop for courageous and manly deeds. The author was intimately familiar with the area around the mouth of the Oswego River, since he had spent the winter of 1808 there as a midshipman in the American Navy, and both his knowledge and love of the land are apparent in the descriptive passages of *The Pathfinder.*

Unfortunately, however, Cooper's talents as a storyteller and descriptive writer have obscured his merits as a serious artist whose works illustrate important social and religious concerns. One recurrent theme, for example, which comes through strongly in *The Pathfinder,* is the idea that to achieve happiness and self-fulfillment, a man must live according to his "gifts," or talents, be they great or limited. Cooper believed strongly in democracy, but in a conservative way. He felt that the American continent was the perfect environment in which men could develop fresh and individualistic forms of society, but he feared that people in the frontier were moving too close to anarchy. The key to success was every individual's recognition and willing acceptance of his place within the scheme of things—a place which was determined not by heredity but by natural talent, but which nevertheless still located each person in a "class." Thus, much of the interest in *The Pathfinder* stems from the question of Mabel Dunham's marriage, since it involves discoveries about talent and appropriate courses of action on the part not only of Mabel, but of Natty, Lieutenant Muir, Jasper Western, and Sergeant Dunham.

Besides his important awareness about his true talents and calling and proper relationship to society, Natty Bumppo in *The Pathfinder* has also reached a high level of consciousness in the religious area which reflects another crucial Cooper theme. Through his self-sufficient hero, the author conveys his conviction, which grew stronger as he grew older, that Divine Providence was involved in human destiny. Natty's is a natural piety, a faith taught him by nature, which he calls "the temple of the Lord;" as he explains simply, "It is not easy to dwell always in the presence of God, and not feel the power of his goodness."

PATIENCE

Type of work: Comic opera
Author: W. S. Gilbert (1836-1911)
Type of plot: Humorous satire
Time of plot: Nineteenth century
Locale: England
First presented: 1881

One of the favorites among the Gilbert and Sullivan operettas, Patience, Or, Bunthorne's Bride *was instantly popular and has continued to be frequently performed and enjoyed by diverse audiences. A gentle thrust at romantic love and unintelligible poetry, the story tells of a poet who pines away for the love of a simple milkmaid, who is trained by twenty lovesick maidens—themselves pining away after the poet Bunthorne—in the wiles of stylish love and courtship.*

In choosing "fleshly" and "idyllic" poets as his satirical targets, Gilbert was breaking no new ground. For five years, readers of *Punch* had laughed with caricaturist George Du Maurier at his "exquisites," Maudle and Postelthwaite. By 1881, Maudle had come to look and speak remarkably like Oscar Wilde. Wilde's reputation for wit, brilliance, and eccentric behavior had preceded him from Oxford, and he had become the willing exemplar of the "ultra-poetical, highly-aesthetical, out-of-the-way young man" of the aesthetic movement.

The movement, which began with the Pre-Raphaelites nearly thirty years earlier, included such gifted and disparate figures as the "fleshly" artist-poet Dante Rossetti, the quiet Oxford don Walter Pater, and the publicly outrageous A. C. Swinburne. It was to continue, as much helped as hindered by public ridicule, until Wilde's conviction for homosexuality in 1895 forced it underground for twenty-five years.

As his illustrations and various references in the libretto make clear, Gilbert visualized Bunthorne not as Wilde but as Swinburne. The producers, however, capitalized on Wilde's notoriety by making up the actor playing the role to resemble him as closely as possible. The audience so identified him, and Wilde's attendance at many performances added to the fun.

Neither the playful Swinburne, who wrote the best parodies of his own poetry, nor the self-mocking Wilde, who loved publicity of whatever kind, was likely to have been much offended by *Patience's* "harmless merriment." They were not even the sole objects of satire. The "rapturous maidens" and the very heavy Heavy Dragoons receive full share, and the vaporizings about true love and duty were more generally Victorian than "aesthetic." With the inestimable complement of Sullivan's witty and melodious score, *Patience* remains one of the most delightful and popular of Gilbert's works.

THE PATRICIAN

Type of work: Novel
Author: John Galsworthy (1867-1933)
Type of plot: Social criticism
Time of plot: Early twentieth century
Locale: England
First published: 1911

In this story about a member of the aristocracy and the Conservative Party who is temporarily influenced toward democratic ideals by a liberal leader in Parliament, Galsworthy seems at first to be making a plea for change, for a break with tradition, and for increased freedom for the majority. In the end, however, Eustace Carádoc returns to his former traditional beliefs, and much unhappiness comes to those who espouse doctrines of popular liberty.

The sense of loyalty between the members of a social class to the code to which they traditionally have been bound is impressively portrayed by Galsworthy in *The Patrician.* He also captures the narrowness of the viewpoint which cannot conceive of society as organized from within rather than held together by authority imposed from above. But Galsworthy drew back at some point, as if he did not dare to say as much about his characters and their caste as he might have. He seems to concern himself too much with maintaining a tone of dignity.

Although Galsworthy's vision of this civilization is sweeping and perceptive, he writes with a rather heavy-handed style. When he attempts a "poetic" description of a scene, his images seem forced and unnatural. Galsworthy's convention that women should be languid and elegant has dated his novel, as has his concept of the upright, upper-class male with the stiff upper lip. Lady Casterley is a sharply-etched, lively old lady, admirable in an unyielding manner, although not necessarily likable. The younger women tend to be romanticized to the point of vagueness.

Lord Valleys and the rest of his family feel sure that they are "decent" individuals, but actually they are smug in their complacency. He would think it only reasonable to put many of his tenants out of work to preserve the woodcock shooting on his estate. No one could ever convince him that he was immoral, yet it is because of him and the other senior members of his family that his son Eustace and his daughter Barbara both are prevented from matches in which they could be happy. One feels, at the end of the book, that life has been negated and the triumph has been that of a dead world. Perhaps, this is the real value of the novel, and of Galsworthy's vision.

THE PATRIOT

Type of work: Novel
Author: Antonio Fogazzaro (1842-1911)
Type of plot: Historical romance
Time of plot: Mid-nineteenth century
Locale: Italy
First published: 1896

The Patriot *is the first of three novels dealing with the nineteenth century Italian struggle for independence from Austria and for unification of the many small duchies and states into a single nation. On the personal level, the novel deals with individual searches for meaning and identity, and reflects Fogazzaro's deeply religious attitude.*

Antonio Fogazzaro had a relatively busy lifetime and produced a large body of excellent fiction which was of the realistic vein popular around the turn of the century. Being from Vicenza, he had a strong link with small town life and most of his works combine the backdrop of provincial life with a realism that is universal. Fogazzaro was also a deeply religious man; this too is reflected in his work. *The Patriot,* originally entitled *Piccolo mondo antico* (*Little World of Yesterday*), is part of a great trilogy of novels by Fogazzaro. Taken as a single work it has been regarded as the greatest Italian novel since Manzoni's *I Promessi Sposi,* written in the middle of the century.

This novel traces a popular theme of the late *Ottocento* (the nineteenth century): the quest for Italian unification which was attained in 1867 and its effects on the lives of ordinary people. The loves and misfortunes of Don Franco and his wife Luisa are constantly at odds with events taking place in the outside world.

The novel also combines a good plot with realistic characterizations and underlying themes of patriotism and religious belief. Fogazzaro's devotion and involvement in reforming the Italian Catholic Church is reflected in subtle ways in *The Patriot,* but came to full fruition in the last novel of the trilogy, *The Saint.* Although Fogazzaro may have felt that *The Saint* was his most representative work, however, it is *The Patriot* which has been read and praised the most because it does not subjugate plot and characterization to philosophical beliefs. This is an excellent novel which can be appreciated in any age; but although to understand it does not require a background knowledge of the real events surrounding its creation, such knowledge is always beneficial to the individual reader.

PAUL BUNYAN

Type of work: Short stories
Author: James Stevens (1892- 1971)
Type of plot: Folklore
Time of plot: From the Winter of the Blue Snow to the Spring That the Rain Came up from China
Locale: North America
First published: 1925

The Paul Bunyan tales, which originated in the storytelling tradition of logging camps along the Canadian border in the 1830's, are filled with wild exaggeration and hearty good humor in the best tall-tale style. In this modern collection of the stories of Paul, his loggers, and his blue ox, Babe, Stevens successfully captures the flavor of the north woods and the distinctive spirit and flair of American folklore.

It has been the usual pattern that folk heroes have evolved over the course of centuries, slowly developing their unique characters and accumulating their colorful histories through the oral traditions passed on by generations of storytellers. In a country as young as America, however, this pattern could not be played out, and folk figures scarcely had time to be conceived in the popular imagination before they were overtaken by a rapidly moving history. For this reason, out of a gallery of local heroes which included Mike Fink, Sam Patch, Pecos Bill, and Cap'n Stormalong, only Paul Bunyan has carried his fame into the twentieth century in a considerable body of popular fiction and in some serious literature as well.

Actually, mention of Paul Bunyan did not appear in print until as recently as 1910; over the course of the next decade, only a few scattered references were to be found, including a tale told in a lumber company's advertising brochure, and a 1916 article published by *Transactions of the Wisconsin Academy of Sciences, Arts, and Letters.* The latter, a study written by K. Bernice Stewart and Homer A. Watt, is one of the few remaining authentic sources of the Bunyan legends, since the rash of bestselling lumberjack stories which followed altered the original tales in many essentials to increase their appeal to a widespread reading audience. These popular adaptations, which flourished from the 1920's on, not only expunged the most vivid logging language and local-color detail in favor of a more business-oriented vocabulary, but also modified Paul's character to conform to modern standards of cleverness and success. But Paul Bunyan also found his way into literature of a more serious nature, including the poetry of Robert Frost, Carl Sandburg, and W. H. Auden.

The Paul Bunyan tales are products of the American frontier spirit. The numerous stories of lumberjack feats share many common themes and features, including a glorification of strength and endurance in the face of great odds; an admiration of shrewdness and cleverness; a love of hilarious, high-spirited fun; and an incorrigible tendency toward wild exaggeration. But above all the Paul Bunyan tales reflect man's primitive and universal impulse toward comic expression in the face of the grim realities of existence. Thus, the logger's exploits are based on very real dangers, be they log jams, forest fires, or mosquitoes; but Paul Bunyan's colossal strength and sharp Yankee wit and inventiveness surmount every obstacle. His foes are not only vanquished, but made to appear ridiculous, and the listeners' fears are purged in healthy, hearty laughter.

THE PEACE

Type of work: Drama
Author: Aristophanes (c. 448-c. 385 B.C.)
Type of plot: Satiric comedy
Time of plot: The Peloponnesian War
Locale: Athens
First presented: 421 B.C.

Written at a time when Sparta and Athens were ready to make peace after a decade of fighting, The Peace *reflects a spirit of optimism and gaiety. Although he foresees some of the difficulties which will need to be overcome within the various Greek states, Aristophanes is generally joyful in his attitude, and bawdy and ribald in his humor. Typically, the playwright sees the farming class as the stable force in society and the most hopeful means toward lasting peace.*

The Peace is an ebullient play, with ribald jokes, rapid-fire wit, and fantastic conceits. By 421 B.C. Athens and Sparta, after a decade of war, seemed ready to arrange a peace. No one would have welcomed this more than Aristophanes, who despised the Peloponnesian War and the shabby motives that impelled it. As a political comedy *The Peace* makes essentially the same points as his earlier drama, *The Acharnians:* war leads to starvation and misery, while peace offers plenitude, festivity, and cheer. Yet this play is more exuberant in its humor and more lyrical in extolling the virtues of an armistice.

Trygaeus is a comic version of Bellerophon, the hero who tried to enter Olympus on his winged horse, Pegasus, and who was hurled back to earth and lamed, while Zeus kept Pegasus. The parallel between the two is funny. Trygaeus riding to heaven on a fattened dung beetle, Zeus keeping the dung beetle to draw his chariot, and Trygaeus returning to earth with a limp shows that Aristophanes' mockery spared no one, not even the gods.

However, other comic ideas in the play bear directly on the theme of peace. The notion of War grinding the cities of Greece into a salad, or of Trygaeus finding farcical peacetime uses for the equipment of war, or of the starving seer wanting more bloodshed, are all very pointed devices for comically dramatizing the issues involved.

At one point the chorus launches into an unabashed song of praise for Aristophanes, claiming his plays to be superior artistically and morally to those of any other comic writer. It is a startling statement, but we have good reason to assume the truth of it. Aristophanes' plays are well constructed and fearless in their exposure of stupidity and vice, and in *The Peace,* if he was premature in celebrating the cessation of war, he did anticipate the cause of the war's continuance in the lack of cooperative effort between the Greek cities. He also spared himself nothing in trying to make the warmongers see the folly of their ways.

THE PEASANTS

Type of work: Novel
Author: Ladislas Reymont (1868-1925)
Type of plot: Social chronicle
Time of plot: Late nineteenth century
Locale: Poland
First published: 1902-1909

Structuring his plot around the seasons, Reymont's novel is divided into sections entitled Autumn, Winter, Spring, *and* Summer. *In addition to being a heartwarmingly human narrative,* The Peasants *is a sociological document; Reymont covers all the perennial problems of nineteenth century Europe, including overpopulation, poor and overworked soil, widespread ignorance, and imperialism.*

Although *The Peasants* was not translated into English until 1924, when its author won the Nobel Prize, the Germans had already recognized its worth. It has been rumored that during the German occupation of Poland in World War I, German officers were required to read and study the novel as a text to enable them to understand the Polish customs and mores, and thus, have more success in controlling the stubborn and proud peasants than did the previous occupants, the Russians.

As an intimate, detailed picture of the Polish peasant, the book is magnificent. Using a naturalistic approach, Reymont gives an unbiased account of both the sordidness and the beauty of the peasants' lives. Between these extremes, there seems to be no middle ground. Life is either filled with animal joy and lustiness (as is shown in the elaborate details of the three-day celebration of Matthias and Yagna's wedding) or with intimate details of poverty, despair, and illness. Yet the peasants never surrender; they all accept their fate.

The novel is more than a sociological analysis of Polish life, however, for Reymont creates characters who are individual and vital. He explores in detail the universal struggles of society: the poor who produce against the rich who exploit; the young who struggle for what is legally theirs against the old who desperately try to hold on to their hard-earned land. He examines the eternal conflicts—between the sexes—between man and nature, between religion and superstition—including the lonely struggle of the individual asserting and defending himself in a harsh, unyielding, threatening world.

Reymont never allows himself to abandon the basic standard of naturalism —objectivity. Although the reader becomes more involved with some characters than others, the involvement is never caused by Reymont's intervention.

Yagna is perhaps the most interesting character in the novel. She is one of the few villagers not motivated by greed; true, she delightedly accepts a scarf and ribbons Matthias buys for her at the fair, but she is completely uninterested in the marriage settlement, which is handled by her greedy mother Dominikova. The mother realizes the problems that may arise from the May-

December marriage, but she is eager to obtain the six acres Matthias offers. Yet, she does not force Yagna to marry; Yagna does not really care. Rather, Yagna is motivated solely by animal spirit. Married to an old man, her health and vitality drive her into the younger arms of Antek and Matthew, but it is this same animalism that initially attracts Matthias to her. Her attitude is to let her mother handle such things as marriage settlements; her own interests are more physical.

Yagna is driven by sexual passions she cannot begin to understand. She does not appear concerned about the quarrel she has caused between Antek and his father, nor does she worry about the rupture she has caused between Antek and Hanka. She sees only Antek's youth and that is sufficient for her. She has the same intensity of sexual attraction for Matthew and is unable to control her passion. When he creeps into her darkened cottage before the wedding, she defends herself before her mother by pleading that she could not keep him off.

Yet, Yagna cannot transfer her passionate feelings to old Matthias Boryna and this he, a deeply proud man, resents. Although he has heard rumors about Yagna with Antek and Matthew, he ignores them, until he sees her creeping into the warm protection of the strawstack with Antek. He then shows no mercy and blocks the entrance to the stack before he sets fire to the rick, hoping that both will be burned alive.

When Matthias takes Yagna back as a serving girl, the young woman accepts it stoically and does not beg for mercy. Like the true peasant she is, she accepts her lot with resignation and spends no time in self-recrimination. Her position is essentially tragic in the naturalistic sense. Young, attractive, and full of natural self-interest, she allows herself to be controlled by forces she cannot understand.

It is hard to visualize Antek as a sympathetic character because all his actions are motivated by jealousy or greed. He abuses Hanka, his wife, and defies both her and his father when he makes no secret of his affair with Yagna. After being expelled from his father's house, he finally gets a job at the mill, but spends all of his wages at the tavern so that Hanka and her children are completely dependent upon Hanka's destitute, sick old father. And when, during the harsh winter, Hanka is nearly frozen while gathering forest wood in a raging snowstorm, it is Old Boryna, not Antek, who comes to her aid. Yet, in spite of the hatred Antek bears his father, he instinctively kills the squire's woodcutter who attacks Matthias. Thus, through Antek, the author indicates that underneath the hardness and materialism of the villagers, a vestige of mutual concern remains. It is this element that keeps the book from depicting total despair. In spite of the bitter environment, all of the peasants retain a zest for life revealed in their delight in celebrations, and in their love for food, drink, dance, and brightly colored clothes and ribbons. The dignity of man is described as the peasants stop individual bickering to join forces against the squire and his men who attempt to overtake the ancestral forests of the peasants.

The book is an amazing portrait of common life in a Polish village. Reymont presents all details of daily life—sowing and harvesting the cabbage crops, house life, clothing, furniture, and food. The notes of the translator are invaluable, for without them, the reader might not understand the importance of certain ceremonies, traditions, and superstitions which are so much a part of the Polish culture.

When the four-volume work appeared, many reviewers criticized it for redundancy, but, in a work more prose epic than novel, each detail enhances the rest. It becomes more than just a narrative of Polish life; its universal aspect describes the emotions and impulses alive in the peasant everywhere. The work must be read as a whole, beginning with *Autumn* and ending with the harvest scenes of *Summer,* for then the reader may view a splendid picture of life in all aspects.

Vina Nickels Oldach

PEDER VICTORIOUS

Type of work: Novel
Author: O. E. Rölvaag (1876-1931)
Type of plot: Regional romance
Time of plot: Late nineteenth century
Locale: The Dakota Territory
First published: 1929

A sequel to Giants in the Earth, Peder Victorious *does not have the power of the former work, possibly because the struggle it describes is no longer for outright survival, but merely for adaptation to a new culture. Set twenty years after* Giants in the Earth, *this novel deals with the Holm family, and particularly with the conflict between the older generation, who fight to retain their old language and customs, and the younger generation, who are under constant pressure from the outside to Americanize themselves in every way.*

America has been called a "melting pot"; it combines a variety of ethnic entities which only peripherally merge with one another. This problem is at the heart of Ole Edvart Rölvaag's *Peder Victorious.* After the initial wave of English colonial immigrants to America in the seventeenth century, subsequent influxes of other European minority groups have had to adjust to the dominantly Anglo norm. Scandinavians thus found themselves alienated from the prevailing culture by language, food, and custom. The dilemma revolved around the degree of assimilation one was prepared to accept. The issue was crucial. It went without saying that command of English—the language of survival—was necessary; but whether or not to perpetuate native usage by teaching children Norwegian as well as English became a vital issue.

How valuable is one's cultural heritage? Only on an individual basis can the question be answered and even then not entirely accurately. Yet it is precisely that complex question which Rölvaag raises in *Peder Victorious.* There is no denying Rölvaag's ethnic ties; and there is no ignoring Rölvaag's national commitments to America. There is also no evasion of the fundamental conflict between the two. Must the Holm family give up its cherished practices in a new land? The answer lay not in absolutes but in the adjustments each generation made according to its needs. Thus, Beret Holm and the Reverend Mr. Gabrielsen adhered to the old ways, but Peder had to adjust to new ways. Only in that way could he be victorious.

The compromises notwithstanding, contemporary needs, generational differences, and ethnic identifications were ultimately resolved. But the final solution still lay in the future. Generations to come would still question the judgments of Beret and Peder and would still challenge the necessity for making a distinction between being "American" and maintaining a fidelity to a highly valued ethnic identification. Yet Rölvaag concluded his novel on the hopeful note that the demands of one's cultural heritage and the demands of assimilationist America could be reconciled.

PEDRO SÁNCHEZ

Type of work: Novel
Author: José María de Pereda (1833-1906)
Type of plot: Picaresque romance
Time of plot: 1852-1879
Locale: Santander and Madrid
First published: 1883

In this modern picaresque novel, Pereda offers an autobiographically based satire of all aspects of life and politics in Madrid as we follow his hero's varied career as office seeker, journalist, political agitator, revolutionary, social lion, and governor. In the manner typical of picaresque heroes, there is nothing noble about Pedro; he is an ordinary man with a weak moral sense, yet he arouses sympathy merely through the contrast of his basically decent nature with the snobbery and villainy surrounding him.

Essentially a realist, Pereda attempted to express his moral convictions through his novels, while portraying honestly the conditions of life in Spain as he saw them. *Pedro Sánchez* is one of his most successful explorations of the character of the Spanish people, despite its essentially pessimistic political message. He had come to feel by the time he wrote *Pedro Sánchez* that the revolution was not working, and to feel scorn for the newly rich who exploited liberalism for their personal ends. The novel shows the sincere disillusion of an enthusiast who left the provinces and plunged into the political life of the capital. Perhaps his didactic tendency injured his effects, and his grim satire did occasionally degenerate into caricature, but Pereda understood character, and it is for this reason that *Pedro Sánchez* endures.

Pereda's keen sense of the ridiculous is everywhere evident in *Pedro Sánchez;* the novel displays a broad range of humor, from gentle irony to biting satire. Pereda excelled in his ability to portray the common man and to reproduce the popular vernacular with all of its lusty humor. In this regard, although the novel is essentially a picaresque romance, *Pedro Sánchez* did carry forward realism in the Spanish novel. The characters in the book are real human beings, flawed and foolish, and intrinsically human. The author does not condescend to his lowly born characters; he understands them and portrays them with zest. Above all, he is never sentimental about his characters. Pedro is one of the great characters of Spanish literature, never idealized, but sympathetic and understandable. Women are relegated to secondary roles in the novel and in the author's view of society.

The narrative centers around the revolution of 1854, which Pereda witnessed as a student in Madrid; his hero's impressions very likely are his own. With great skill, the author moves Pedro through the stages of success, from journalist to revolutionary leader and official, always looking out for his own interests. But Pedro pays a price for his opportunism, the price of ultimate disillusionment. It is significant that he finally returns to his own native village, after his years of political intrigue. If the book has any message, it is that one should distrust the claims of would-be political saviors; a healthy skepticism should greet the birth of any new movement. Revolutions come and go, but the people endure.

PEER GYNT

Type of work: Drama
Author: Henrik Ibsen (1828-1906)
Type of plot: Satiric fantasy
Time of plot: Mid-nineteenth century
Locale: Norway
First presented: 1867

In this satire with its jaunty and boastful yet lovable hero, Ibsen treats symbolically the theme of individualism. The drama is an episodic fantasy, woven of folklore, satire, and symbolism, which is rich in dramatic intensity and emotional impact; and although Ibsen deals with the degeneration of the human soul, he ends on a triumphant note in upholding the redeeming power of love. Because of its unorthodoxy and untheatrical design, however, Peer Gynt *is difficult to present on the stage.*

Peer Gynt was Henrik Ibsen's last verse play; his later dramas were written in prose, in keeping with his shift to more realistic themes. *Peer Gynt,* however, remains a masterpiece of fantasy and surreal effects, but Ibsen's delicately graceful eloquence makes the play difficult to stage, especially in a realistically oriented theater. In effect, Ibsen's play resembles a picaresque novel. It is episodic, tied together by the protagonist, and involves a journey filled with disparate adventures. *Peer Gynt* has been faulted by some critics for being overloaded with "spectacle": too many rapid changes of exotic scene. It is just such qualities, however, which lend the play its greatest strength.

In fact, such inspiration prompted Ibsen himself in 1874 to request that his famous contemporary, the Norwegian composer Edvard Grieg, compose incidental music for *Peer Gynt.* Grieg undertook the project with reluctance, having personal and artistic reservations about its feasibility. But after two years of strenuous work, he completed the job, and in 1876, Ibsen's *Peer Gynt* was performed with Grieg's *Peer Gynt,* two orchestral suites of unsurpassing beauty including "Anitra's Dance," "In the Hall of the Mountain King," and "Solveig's Song," among others. To a large extent, this artistic collaboration proved fruitful because both Ibsen and Grieg intuitively agreed about the uniquely and distinctively Norwegian qualities of *Peer Gynt.* The protagonist, as drawn by the playwright, could have no other ethnic identity; the music, as composed by the musician, could have no other cultural origin, for Grieg was a master at absorbing and utilizing peasant and folkloric themes. Indeed, it has been somewhat acerbically observed that *Peer Gynt* will be remembered not as Ibsen's play but as Grieg's music. Although there is a certain truth to that observation, *Peer Gynt,* the play, is no less worthy of attention on its own merits.

The play describes the adventures of an egocentric but imaginative opportunist. To be sure, Peer is a lovable rogue, but a self-obsessed one nonetheless: his preoccupation with himself—his own gratification—is his egocentricity; his upwardly mobile changes of locality and women constitute his opportunism; his exotic tastes suggest his imaginative approach toward coping with life. Still, his final return to native hearth and native woman—as he buries his head in Solveig's waiting lap—indicates the limits of adventuring which Ibsen will tolerate.

Finally, it is this inevitable return to the home territory which makes *Peer Gynt* an irrevocably, unavoidably, categorically Norwegian play, whatever other features of the drama may appeal to a non-Norwegian audience. Such a concept of territoriality is concisely expressed in a line from Mikhail Bulgakov's Russian play, *The Days of the Turbins,* where one character flatly asserts, "Homeland is homeland," implying an influence of national identity which transcends egocentricity and opportunism as well as political affiliation and religious preference. Thus Peer returns to the land of *Peer Gynt* in a denouement which clearly shows his own as well as Ibsen's ultimate commitments, and those commitments, at last, lend the play its compelling force.

PEG WOFFINGTON

Type of work: Novel
Author: Charles Reade (1814-1884)
Type of plot: Sentimental romance
Time of plot: Eighteenth century
Locale: England
First published: 1853

Based on the life of a celebrated Irish actress, Peg Woffington *contains delightfully entertaining dialogues between critics and artists in which the critics inevitably come out on the bottom. Although too sentimental for many modern readers' tastes, Mrs. Woffington's story is nevertheless a witty look at what goes on behind the scenes in the theater.*

In an essay on Charles Reade written shortly after his death, A. C. Swinburne mentions a critical controversy as to whether Reade "was or was not a man of genius—whether his genius, if he had such a thing, was wide or narrow, deep or shallow, complete or incomplete." One cannot imagine such a controversy now about Reade. He is remembered primarily for *The Cloister and the Hearth,* one of the best of all English historical novels. His many "problem novels," written possibly under the influence of Dickens, have largely been forgotten, as have his numerous plays which he himself considered more important than his novels.

Reade's first novel, *Peg Woffington,* was adapted at the suggestion of an actress friend, Mrs. Laura Seymour, from a popular play, *Masks and Faces* (1852), which he had written with Tom Taylor, a well-known dramatist of the period. The dramatic source is evident throughout the novel in the story itself, in the theatrical locale of much of the book, in several of the characters (Clive, Quinn, and Cibber are barely disguised actual people), in most of the important scenes, and in the dialogue, some of which appears as in the printed edition of a play. At one point Reade makes the authorial observation that "the stage is a representation not of stage, but of life; and . . . an actor ought to speak and act in imitation of human beings." The modern reader might offer a similar criticism of *Peg Woffington.* It is stagy and melodramatic and much of it is incredible, particularly the "big" scene of the portrait hoax in which the poseurs are humiliated and sweet country innocence and truth triumph.

Reade himself was not aware of the overly-sentimental quality of his novel simply because such sentimentality was accepted—even demanded—by his Victorian reading audience. In fact, because of the wealth of factual data in the story, which inspired one critic to term the novel "more than half a memoir," Reade regarded his work as a truth rather than a lie, reporting instead of fiction. What he could not realize was the extent to which he altered Peg Woffington's character to make her a suitable heroine by Victorian standards. In contrast to the scandalous life led by her real-life model, Peg's improprieties are carefully presented as being not her fault; Reade painstakingly places the blame for her conduct on her immoral environment, implying that circumstances force her to lead a life she would never have freely chosen. This idea is ultimately proven by later events in the plot, as we discover that Peg is, in her heart, virtuous, generous, and pure. Her abandonment of the stage, friendship with Mabel Vane, and devotion to the poor prove her true worth in Victorian terms, just as they bog the modern reader down with their wild improbability and blatant sentimentalism.

Reade makes plenteous use of author intrusion and exclamation points, as in: "Reader, it was too true! . . . Mr. Vane was a married man!" so that one is often reminded of the words flashed on the screen of a silent film melodrama. There is some play of waspish wit in exchanges involving old actors and young actors and the two theater critics Snarl and Soaper, but these stings are less penetrating in print than one imagines they may have been on a London stage when this kind of satire was fashionable. The brief, pointed insult being a perennially popular form of stage humor, many of the "one-liners" in *Peg Woffington* might even be easily adapted for use in a modern television comedy skit.

PELLE THE CONQUEROR

Type of work: Novel
Author: Martin Andersen Nexö (1869-1954)
Type of plot: Social criticism
Time of plot: Late nineteenth century
Locale: Denmark
First published: 1906-1910

Although the background of Pelle the Conqueror *is the struggle between workers and employers during the rise of the labor movement in Denmark at the end of the nineteenth century, Nexö never allows social criticism to override the interest of the personal narrative. The story of a young man's successful climb from poverty is a perennially appealing one, and is enhanced by the author's warmly realistic descriptions of the common people, their customs, and their problems.*

Pelle the Conqueror, like much successful radical and socialist literature, is basically autobiographical; like Martin Andersen Nexö, who was born in one of the poorest slums of Copenhagen, the central character of *Pelle the Conqueror* is a working class individual. Pelle, while he follows his own particular destiny, also represents choices for the working-class movement as a whole; and there can be no doubt that, beyond telling an interesting story, Nexö intended through *Pelle the Conqueror* to help transform the life of working people. Lasse, Pelle, Kalle, and Erik are all meant to serve both as social types and as indicators of working-class responses.

Lasse, Pelle's father, is already an old widower when the first book begins; he is conservative, unwilling to rebel, and resigned to his fate. But Pelle dreams of being like Erik, a fighter and rebel. But Erik's problem is that he is subject to rages; he is meant to suggest a certain type of rural worker, angry but without plans or organization, who rebels blindly. One day, goaded beyond endurance, Erik assaults the bailiff and is smashed on the head and reduced to a state of passivity and near idiocy. Kalle, at the other extreme, is willing to accept everything in a "good natured" manner. Erik and Kalle thus signify conflicting aspects of the rural working poor who, as a group, vacillate between blind rebellion and passive acceptance.

Since it is the rural working class which at the onset of industrialization is attracted to the city and which becomes the urban proletariat, Pelle's youth is meant to parallel the youth of the working class. Likewise, the adolescence of the working class, corresponding to the stage of handicraft industry, is pictured in *Apprenticeship,* Nexö's second volume in *Pelle the Conqueror.* Pelle's maturity as a workingman is portrayed in *The Great Struggle* (the third volume), which takes place during a time of trade union activity on a mass scale. The final volume of *Pelle the Conqueror, Daybreak,* contains Nexö's ideas for the future: profit sharing, communal living near nature, and human solidarity. More radical solutions (revolutionary communism) are rejected, and Pelle is shown, finally, at rest.

Nexö's novel, which influenced socialist and communist writers around the world, including the proletarian writers of the United States, stands as a monumental vision of class history and struggle summarized and dramatized in the life of a single, interesting man. Nexö is a competent novelist who does an excellent job of dramatizing, individualizing, and organizing a vast subject.

PÉLLÉAS AND MÉLISANDE

Type of work: Drama
Author: Maurice Maeterlinck (1862-1949)
Type of plot: Symbolic tragedy
Time of plot: The Middle Ages
Locale: Allemonde
First presented: 1893; first published: 1892

Perhaps better known today for Debussy's operatic version, Pélléas *and* Mélisande *is a symbolic retelling of Dante's* Paolo *and* Francesca. *It is the most successful of Maeterlinck's dramas, in which he gave free play to his anti-naturalistic imagination; having been widely acclaimed for his crusade against realism in the theater for several years, however, the playwright was overtaken by changing times and his popularity, by 1910, had waned considerably.*

During the years between 1890 and 1911 when he received the Nobel Prize, the Belgian poet Maurice Maeterlinck was an important figure in European drama, a member of the Symbolist movement that revolted against the prevailing trend of naturalism represented by Ibsen, Zola, and Hauptmann. He was closely allied to the circles of French painters, poets, and musicians who comprised this Symbolist movement. *Pélléas and Mélisande* is his masterpiece, although it has survived primarily through Debussy's setting of the text. Given the intentions of the author, this is perhaps not inappropriate, for even in the first production, the aim was to remove the story from the real world and to create a dream world of elusive impressions, precisely such as occurs in Debussy's score. The settings for the first production used the techniques of the "Nabis" painters (Bonnard, Vuillard, Roussel), including sombre tones, delicate color nuances, dim lighting, strong shadow effects, and a gauze curtain stretched across the front of the stage to blur the outlines and underline the ambiguity and mystery of the play.

The story may be perceived on two levels: on the surface, it is a medieval setting of themes popular with the naturalists, such as social convention versus natural law, or the plight of the woman caught in a loveless marriage and destroyed when she follows the promptings of her heart. But for Maeterlinck this is not to be seen as a social problem. His drama cannot be localized in place or time; the entire play is shrouded in uncertainty, even as to the real identity of the characters. Mélisande seems linked to the mysterious fluid depths of wells and springs, while the hunter Golaud, who loves her, is basically a man of power. Mélisande represents beauty and love, but she is also elusive, and drawn to Golaud's brother, and opposite, the poetic Pélléas. Mélisande is both child and temptress, bringing both love and death. The characters seem to move in an elaborate pattern, creating symbolic relationships, but always leaving room for the reader to find the ultimate meaning, or the ultimate mystery, in his own world of visions and dreams.

PEÑAS ARRIBA

Type of work: Novel
Author: José María de Pereda (1833-1906)
Type of plot: Regional romance
Time of plot: Late nineteenth century
Locale: Santander, Spain
First published: 1895

Among Pereda's novels, Peñas Arriba *is equaled in craftsmanship only by his* Sotileza *(1884); while the earlier work is set on the seacoast and describes the lives of the Santander fishermen, this novel deals with the mountainous region of northern Spain. Pereda is a master at presenting moral scruples and the heroic self-sacrifice of individual human souls; in* Peñas Arriba *he also dramatically states his philosophical and ethical convictions and his doctrine of the value of a simple way of living.*

José María de Pereda never left his ancestral country home in mountainous northern Spain, except for one stint as a Carlist artillery officer; he loved his hilly native countryside and its old folkways, and like Marcelo at the end of his novel *Peñas Arriba,* could hardly bear to leave it even for short trips. He appreciated open air, honest toil, and healthy country people devoted to God, and was disgusted by large cities, with their corrupt politicians and their affectation of foreign manners. His writings reflect his respect for peasants and his admiration of patriarchal, rural society based on the contributions of individual talent and the code of *noblesse oblige.*

After 1876, Pereda became a champion of conservatism and the literary flag bearer of defeated Carlism; for a time he was considered Spain's best modern novelist of the Realist school. His works can be classified in two groups: those set in his beloved mountains and the coastal zone near Santander, which glorify regional beauty, and those set in Madrid, which attack city life, materialism, and alien-inspired radicalism. Pereda's masterpiece, *Peñas Arriba,* belongs to the first group; this novel of his native north sings the grandeur of the majestic mountains whose presence dominates the story. The snow episodes and descriptions are particularly memorable, as well as important symbolically; they are crucial to the theme of a novel which is in many ways a polemic on the superiority of country people over city people.

The plot shows how blasé young Marcelo has been debauched by city life and how he is gradually rescued from venality by contact with normal country living and with his wise old uncle Celso, the patriarch of his ancestral mountain village. *Peñas Arriba* is also a regionalist novel of characters, an art gallery of people and landscapes. The classic style reflects Pereda's sensitivity and literary zeal, as well as his mystic love of nature, which has been compared to Wordsworth's. His vast vocabulary and ability to paint scenes in vivid word pictures are impressive. The uncomplicated plot is developed through a steady chain of movingly written scenes and passages of great descriptive beauty.

When Pereda died in 1906, he was still convinced that Spain's taproot was in its north. There, he believed, family faith went back to the Reconquest against the Moors, and, in times of national danger, red-bereted Carlist Requetés still appeared everywhere "as thickly as cherries on the trees." Although not widely read outside Spain today, *Peñas Arriba* is still a lyrical celebration of the beauties of the little-known mountain regions of northern Spain.

PENDENNIS

Type of work: Novel
Author: William Makepeace Thackeray (1811-1863)
Type of plot: Social satire
Time of plot: Mid-nineteenth century
Locale: England
First published: 1848-1850

In this long, loosely organized novel, sprinkled with chatty philosophical discussions with the reader, Thackeray opposes selfish scheming for material wealth and social advancement. The most consistent theme, brought out with often piercing irony, is the self-conscious, rigid snobbery between classes in England, and the unceasing efforts of the middle class to become "gentlemen." This theme is illustrated particularly in the experiences of Pen, who is torn between his uncle's efforts to help him rise socially and his mother's efforts to keep him natural and unspoiled.

In his own preface, Thackeray refers to Fielding's depiction of the nature of man in *Tom Jones* and laments Victorian curbs on such revelations; nonetheless, he aims for truth and his episodic depiction of a callow youth's development into what some may find a callow young gentleman is satirically honest. As in *Vanity Fair,* Thackeray also provides revealing social coverage, from the conniving servant Morgan, through the eminently bread-and-butter actress—enchantress Fotheringay (Pen's first love), through the socially expedient Lord Clavering and his equally expedient stepdaughter, Blanche. Thackeray's range of social classes is broad, his judgments mellow, for he sees the symbiosis of society as complex. Though the reader may wince at the major's snobbism, he may also admit to the author's dexterity in extricating Pen from an infatuation, in aiding another of Pen's "unworthy" loves (the lower-class Fanny), and in outmaneuvering a blackmailer.

No critic can find *Pendennis* a perfect novel—it is too intellectually shallow for that. But readers can find plentiful delight in Pen's amours, in Thackeray's skillful portrayal of self-deception and social aspirations, and in the authorial commentary that is a hallmark of his style. Perhaps readers may also want to follow Pen's development as the narrator in Thackeray's *The Newcomes* and *The Adventures of Philip.*

The History of Pendennis, His Fortunes and Misfortunes, His Friends and His Greatest Enemy was published in monthly installments during the years 1848-1850. Thackeray attempted to provide a less melancholy, less cynical portrait of society than that in *Vanity Fair,* published shortly before. His protagonist, Arthur Pendennis, appears in the familiar *bildüngsroman* pattern —adolescence, love affairs, schooling, career aspirations, and marriage. But the novel also assumes aspects of the *künstlerroman* because Pen becomes a journalist and successful novelist and, in sections twentieth century readers may find a bit tedious, carries on extended dialogues about the nature of art and writing with a fellow journalist, George Warrington. Naturally, many readers can find abundant autobiographical material in Thackeray's attempt to expose "the real nature of a young man."

This "exposure" appeared serially at the same time as did Dickens' *David Copperfield*, another *bildüngsroman*, and readers may find comparisons of the two authors' realism revealing. Thackeray's own frank design is to set the focus on his hero's greatest enemy—himself. Pictured is an irresolute young man tempted by fauns and a sensuous mermaid on one side, counterbalanced by a respectable wife and children on the other. Further tensions are at play as well, for Pen, a pampered only son, is tempted by the worldly Regency social values espoused by his uncle, Major Pendennis. An apothecary's son, Pen is nurtured in his uncle's social snobbishness. But as an aspiring artist, he constantly explores his own feelings, albeit self-centeredly, and ultimately turns the problems of truth and transformation of experience into fiction.

PENGUIN ISLAND

Type of work: Novel
Author: Anatole France (Jacques Anatole Thibault, 1844-1924)
Type of plot: Fantasy
Time of plot: Ancient times to the present
Locale: Mythical Alca
First published: 1908

Penguin Island, *a satiric and ironic burlesque of history, is doubly amusing to those who are familiar with the history of France, although the universality of the themes presented also makes the satire recognizable to any reader. Using as his starting point the story of a blinded monk who mistakenly baptizes a group of penguins, whom God then changes to men, France satirizes politics, sexual mores, the Church, and other social institutions.*

With its mixture of satire, burlesque, and fantasy, *Penguin Island* resembles Voltaire's *Candide* (1759) and Thornton Wilder's play *The Skin of Our Teeth* (1942). Like *Candide,* Anatole France's episodic novel is a reasoned attack upon unreason. Unlike Voltaire's book, which ridicules philosophical error for the most part, *Penguin Island* attacks the absurdities that have fastened onto human customs and institutions. For its flights into fantasy and its ambitious attempt to explain the course of civilization in terms of a burlesque of history—past, present, and future—*Penguin Island* also may be compared to Wilder's *The Skin of Our Teeth.* Both works turn history into myth, comment with tolerance upon human follies, and suggest that a dim, ambiguous purpose ultimately controls man's destiny. But Wilder's comedy is essentially optimistic and melioristic; in spite of natural and social disasters, his message is that the man-animal will not only survive but actually improve his lot in the universe. France, on the other hand, is pessimistic. He believes that mankind's course is cyclical, not forward; by the conclusion of *Penguin Island* the human race has reached the apex of its scientific and technological advance, after which point it retreats into barbarism. The future of Penguinia is not much brighter than its past; every movement forward is succeeded by a step backward, until the cycle is repeated endlessly. Whatever divine force operates in the universe, France seems to believe, its machinery—just as its intelligence—is beyond the understanding of man.

Yet the author, always amiable, treats a doomed mankind with kindly tolerance instead of scorn. Although his satire occasionally has a cutting edge, he is more often the gentle ironist than the stern moralist. France exposes folly but does not bitterly castigate the foolish. The two great subjects for his satire are the follies of human customs and institutions. Throughout history—or mythologized French history, his special field of investigation—the author analyzes the conventions of woman's social role as opposed to the condition of her biological nature. Her real nature, France believes, is that of sexual temptress, concerned only, or mostly, with the satisfaction of her physical needs. For example, the blessed Maël, creator (so to speak) of the race of Alca, describes woman as a "cleverly constructed snare" by which a man is taken before he suspects the trap. Moreover, Maël opines that, for vulnerable man, the imagined sexual lure of a woman is more powerful than her real body. As proof of this idea, Orberosia is more attractive to the male pseudo-penguins when she is clothed than when she is nude. An Eve-figure, Orberosia is flagrantly promiscuous (among her many lovers is a hunch-backed neatherd), unfaithful to her husband Kraken, yet she maintains the necessary social fiction of chastity. She even pretends to be the sole virgin among the Alcas. Similarly, Queen Glamorgan tempts the pure monk Oddoul, who repulses her lascivious advances; for his chastity, he is disgraced; the "angel" Gudrune derides him as impotent; and a woman empties a chamber pot upon his head. So long as Glamorgan pretends to be chaste she is socially accepted, no matter what may be her true morality. Other licentious women are safe from censure so long as they perform a role of conventional virtue: Queen Crucha; the fickle Viscountess Olive; and the adulterous Eveline Cérès. The appearance, not the fact, of virtue is important for women to maintain.

Just as France contrasts the pretended with the actual condition of women's chastity, so he contrasts ideal with real social institutions. Ideally, the state is intended to protect the weak, but in fact it protects the powerful. To conceal abuses of power, social institutions employ fictions that make them appear benevolent. Even in heaven, among a council of the blessed, St. Augustine argues that it is form, not substance which matters. And St. Gal agrees that in the signs of religion and the laws of salvation, "form necessarily prevails over essence." Among men, the national state, created by brute force, employs laws to formularize its power. The monk Bullock interprets the actions of a madman who bites the nose of his adversary as a sign of the creation of law; the murderer of a farmer, similarly, he condones as one who establishes the rights of property. Taxes take money from the poor but never a proportionate share from the rich. And the modern national state, according to France, is nothing more than an institution to consolidate wealth and, through warfare, to extend its influence. Trinco (Napoleon) is the great hero of Penguinia because he creates an empire, no matter at what cost. "Glory never costs too much," says a patriotic guide to young Djambi. Yet patriotism itself becomes formularized. As Colonel Marchand observes, the armies of all nations are "the finest in the world"; so every nation must use its military force to test its strength. And the Prince des Boscénos cynically argues that just causes, in order to triumph, need force more than unjust. Thus the national powers mobilize, not to protect the weak but to support the mighty.

In the celebrated Book VI, "The Affair of the Eighty Thousand Trusses of Hay," France shows how the Dreyfus case demonstrates in microcosm the abuses of institutional power. All the institutions of the state and of society

—the government bureaucracy, the army, the Church—oppose Pyrot (Dreyfus). At first only his Jewish relatives, seven hundred strong, dare to support his just cause. Later, the courageous writer Colomban (Émile Zola), along with liberals of different persuasions, join the battle as Pyrotists. But they fight not only against falsehood (the Count de Maubec has never delivered the eighty thousand trusses of hay, so Pyrot could not have stolen the lot); they also fight prejudice and tradition. As Father Cornemuse puts the matter, Pyrot must be guilty, because he has been convicted; and the courts must be defended even if they are corrupt. Only after Justice Chaussepied examines the so-called evidence against the defendant—seven hundred and thirty-two square yards of debris containing not a shred of proof, not a single word about the accused—does he declare the case a farce. Yet Justice Chaussepied's correct ruling results not so much from a recognition of the truth as of expediency; if he had allowed the folly to continue, the Pyrot case would have destroyed the political institutions of the state. Thus the author once again drives home his point: that man is a slave to customs and conventions. In *Penguin Island,* France shows how little headway reason, honesty, and justice make against these ancient stumbling-blocks to progress.

Leslie B. Mittleman

THE PEOPLE OF JUVIK

Type of work: Novel
Author: Olav Duun (1876-1939)
Type of plot: Social chronicle
Time of plot: 1800-1918
Locale: Namdal district, Norway
First published: 1918-1923

A vast saga stretching over several hundred years but focusing on more than six generations of Norwegians between 1800 and 1918, The People of Juvik *is composed of six novels, any one of which may be read separately. The novels are reminiscent of the Norse tales in tone and narrative technique. Duun's methods are matter-of-fact, but lightened by his use of local color and by his device of setting superstitious and ancient customs against a realistic background. The author uses* landsmaal, *the language of the common people, rather than the* riksmaal, *or literary language, employed by Ibsen, Hamsun, and others.*

Olav Duun's *The People of Juvik,* though a work of the twentieth century, has been compared in style and prose to the sagas of the Middle Ages. Because of Duun's simple, straightforward prose, again reminiscent of the sagas, his epic was rather difficult to translate from the original Norwegian and was not rendered into foreign languages until it was well known in its own country as a work of monumental proportions. Duun was particularly suited to write an epic novel such as this since his background was that of a simple peasant, similar to the type of people portrayed in the six novelettes who lived in the twentieth century just as their ancestors had done one thousand years before.

The author claimed to have no particular literary or philosophical influence in his writings, but preferred to consider himself as a product of his entire environment and education. Unlike many modern authors who can be placed in one or another "school," Duun stands as a unique entity. Critically, *The People of Juvik,* as well as the rest of Duun's work, has been almost totally ignored for the last few decades. The author's works, like the man himself, do not lend themselves to discussion, but instead tend to be highly unique and individualistic pieces. The student of Norwegian literature who wishes to analyze and discuss might better approach the works of Ibsen—especially if he wishes to unravel and dissect. Though Duun is astute in his observations on his subjects, he does not try to force the reader to accept his point of view, but rather allows the narrative to reveal its meaning naturally.

PEPITA JIMÉNEZ

Type of work: Novel
Author: Juan Valera (Juan Valera y Alcalá Galiano, 1824-1905)
Type of plot: Psychological realism
Time of plot: c. 1870
Locale: Andalusia, Spain
First published: 1874

When at the age of forty-six diplomat Juan Valera decided to put on paper his thoughts about philosophy and religion, the effort grew into a story which began the renascence of the Spanish novel. Despite his unconvincing dialogue and his tendency to stop up the flow of narrative with extended philosophizing, Valera is proficient in description and character analysis. A psychologically oriented epistolary novel with a minimum of external action, Pepita Jiménez *is based on the thesis that a priest is born and not made.*

Although better known as a novelist, Valera was a distinguished essayist long before he started writing novels. He was never particularly interested in this genre and preferred to devote his energies to poetry, short stories, essays and other forms which he felt allowed a greater outlet for his preoccupation with structure, Valera is considered the best stylist of nineteenth century Spain.

Naturalism—or rather the peculiar brand of naturalism which the Spaniards adopted—and realism were the two literary currents in vogue when Valera decided to write his first novel. Valera felt a profound antipathy for naturalism with its emphasis on what he considered the gross and the vulgar, and he disliked realism for its lack of imagination. He believed that a good novel must be both inventive and amusing. Searching for an alternative to either naturalism or realism, he decided on a new form, the psychological novel. To be sure, his work remained within the general framework of realism, but unlike his contemporaries, he chose to describe an interior reality rather than the objective reality.

Many interpretations have been given to *Pepita Jiménez,* but the analysis most consistent with the work itself is that of Menendez Pelayo, who described the novel as a criticism of false mysticism. The work is not, as some have claimed, about the triumph of man's sinful nature over asceticism; rather, it shows the victory of love over pseudomysticism.

Indications of Don Luis' false piety and lack of vocation for the priesthood abound in the novel. That he believes himself to be one of the "chosen" merely illustrates his lack of self-awareness and his immense pride. He is so concerned with appearances that he is prepared to return to the seminary even after he realizes the true nature of his feelings for Pepita.

Through his letters to his uncle, we get an insight into Don Luis' mental processes and become gradually aware of his flaws of character and his self-deceit. The psychological conflict ensuing from the contradictions between

Don Luis' stated beliefs and his actual feelings is what interests Valera. When Don Luis finally overcomes his delusions of spiritual grandeur and accepts his humanity, he is able to receive and return Pepita's love. At last his flesh and his spirit are reconciled in a true and happy equilibrium.

PEREGRINE PICKLE

Type of work: Novel
Author: Tobias Smollett (1721-1771)
Type of plot: Picaresque romance
Time of plot: Early eighteenth century
Locale: England and the continent
First published: 1751

Following the misadventures of Peregrine, a rascally hero whose follies, extravagances, and practical jokes sometimes approach villainy, this picaresque novel reveals the chicaneries of Smollett's time. The author satirizes with wit and humor the manners and morals of early eighteenth century English life.

The second of Smollett's novels, *Peregrine Pickle,* appeared only three years after *Roderick Random.* It is twice the length of that first work, and, in the opinion of most modern critics, about half as interesting. Certainly there is plenty of sportive comedy and wry wit as Perry forays, picaro-fashion, across the Continent and then through England. But midway in the novel the adventures begin to pall, if only because of their repetitiveness and simple accretion.

This is a strangely uneven book—even for Smollet, who is often capable of marked fluctuations in his artistry. The tone is one of unnerving harshness, of a satire verging near insolence. In a similar vein, its action, as many readers have noted, is often gratuitously violent, despite Smollett's obvious concern with exposing the violence of eighteenth century London life. And its picaresque hero seems at times incredibly disparate as a moral agent. Admittedly, this—or a version of this—is characteristic of Roderick Random, Tom Jones, and a host of similar figures, but one cannot avoid feeling that Smollett too often rubs out the spot of nobility in his hero. The net effect is that of a book occasionally out of control and a hero gone with it.

But there is also much to recommend the novel; and although it was not received with the same success as *Roderick Random,* Smollett's audience clearly enjoyed reading it. Much of the satire takes up predictable subjects: French gallantry and customs, the popularized Grand Tour, politics—both national and international—female vanity, polite adultery, and especially Roman Catholicism. Much of it, too, is very topical, as in the case of the physician whom Perry meets—almost surely a caricature of the poet Mark Akenside—and the ignoramus Pallet, who is thought by some to represent William Hogarth. There is also the very long interpolation entitled "The Memoirs of a Lady of Quality," which recounts the amorous adventures of Frances Viscount Vane. However forbidding the length, then, *Peregrine Pickle* does contain a number of pointed and amusing episodes.

PERICLES, PRINCE OF TYRE

Type of work: Drama
Author: William Shakespeare (1564-1616)
Type of plot: Romantic comedy
Time of plot: Hellenistic period
Locale: Eastern Mediterranean Sea and its littorals
First presented: c. 1607

Scholars agree that only the last three acts of this play were written by Shakespeare. The plot, taken from Twine's Pattern of Painful Adventures *and Gower's* Confessio Amantis, *is made up of all the hairbreadth escapes, endless travels, and miraculous reunions so typical of Hellenistic romances. Patience and goodness are rewarded, villainy punished, and numerous vicissitudes forgotten as the principals are tearfully reunited at the end.*

Recent scholarship indicates that Shakespeare revised the entire play of *Pericles,* from an earlier version by another playwright, probably Thomas Heywood. The play was tremendously popular in its day and was the basis of a prose version by George Wilkins. *Pericles* is now considered to have been the first of the tragi-comedies, or dark romances, which became so popular on the Jacobean stage. The play disregards consideration of time and place, delights in romantic improbabilities, and employs the obscure, compact style of Shakespeare's late plays; probably it paved the way not only for *Cymbeline, The Winter's Tale* and *The Tempest,* but also for the plays of Beaumont and Fletcher.

Although seldom performed, *Pericles* does possess an interesting, romantic story and a certain sentimental beauty. It abounds in sensational situations and surprises, although parts of its theme might be considered unpleasant. The similarities between it and Shakespeare's late plays are striking. The likeness between Marina in *Pericles* and Perdita in *The Winter's Tale* is obvious; the meeting between father and daughter, long separated, is suggestive of *Cymbeline,* and the reunion of Pericles and Thaisa anticipates that of Leontes and Hermione. Pericles and Cerimon are wise and superior men in the manner of Prospero. The themes of reunion after long division, reconciliation, and forgiveness seem to recur in all of these late plays, beginning with *Pericles.* Storms appear twice in the play, as if they were a symbol of the storms of life. There are children lost and found again, parents divided and reunited, a wife rejected and ill-used and restored again. The recurring myth of lost royalty recovered apparently had some special significance for Shakespeare and his audience. The play is one of the most suggestive of Shakespeare's works, perhaps because it is difficult to know how much of it actually is from his hand. Certainly, it seems to be heavy with symbols, and to be particularly concerned with the concept of lost authority or control, without which life cannot properly be conducted. It is possible that some allusion to the late queen is intended, but the meaning may have been more personal to Shakespeare, and may reflect a change or confusion in his own life.

The atmosphere, like that of *The Tempest,* is all sea and music. The brothel scenes are recognizably Shakespearean, with their references to disease that were such jokes to the Jacobeans. There is a hint of the attitudes of *Timon of Athens,* a certain anger and disgust with humanity, in the midst of the poetry and music. Up to the third act, Shakespeare's revisions apparently were mostly confined to style, but comparison to the prose story based on the earlier version of the play suggests that with the fourth act he began to make extensive revisions in the plot, as well. Certainly, the later scenes are superior in quality to the earlier ones. There is a subtlety and delicacy in the handling of certain scenes—such as when Pericles strikes Marina when she reproves him for his stubborn grief—that marks them as clearly from the hand of Shakespeare. *Pericles,* because of its uncertain place in the canon, has probably long been underrated as a play. Its importance, however, as the beginning of a new style for Shakespeare and other Jacobean playwrights, cannot be overestimated.

THE PERSIANS

Type of work: Drama
Author: Aeschylus (525-456 B.C.)
Type of plot: Historical tragedy
Time of plot: 480 B.C.
Locale: Susa, capital of Persia
First presented: 472 B.C.

Glorification of Greece is achieved indirectly through a plot concerned wholly with the Persian reaction to Xerxes' defeat at Salamis, where, tradition has it, Aeschylus was a soldier. Although not a tragedy in the classical Greek sense, the play has its own kind of power and enjoys several magnificent descriptive passages.

The Persians is the one play we have by Aeschylus that is complete in itself and not part of a trilogy. It is also the only surviving Greek tragedy that used contemporary history as its subject. This drama celebrates the Greek victory over Xerxes and his Persian army in 480-479 B.C. Yet it does so in an oblique way by showing the stages in which the Persian court learns the magnitude of their defeat. Since the setting is Persia and all the characters are Persian, Aeschylus gains the remoteness and detachment necessary for tragedy. However, even though the theme of the play is the humbling of overbearing pride, which was standard in Greek tragedy, the drama is never truly tragic.

This is because the Greeks could feel little pity at the downfall of their enemies. The play was produced in 472 B.C. under the sponsorship of Pericles, seven years after the victory; and the Greeks could only rejoice in their god-given invincibility and their prowess in war. Aeschylus himself fought the Persians at Marathon in 490 B.C. and later at Salamis. His epitaph made the single boast that the Persians had not forgotten his valor in battle. In fact, Aeschylus reaches his poetic climax in the play when he describes the awesome Greek triumph at Salamis.

This is not to say that The Persians gloats over the miseries of the defeated Persians. A modern reader might find the play full of compassion, but this is not how the Greeks saw it. The drama reveals the folly of trying to conquer Greece, a land of free, strong men who were favored by the gods. The Persians are seen as a slavish nation, whipped into a massive war machine, and subject to the will of a presumptuous tyrant. Thus their debacle is well-deserved. An Athenian audience could watch the drama impassively, hearing their own praises voiced by the enemy, and see the Persian agony as the workings of an ineluctable justice. Essentially The Persians is an unalloyed tribute to Greek manhood.

PERSUASION

Type of work: Novel
Author: Jane Austen (1775-1817)
Type of plot: Comedy of manners
Time of plot: Early nineteenth century
Locale: Somersetshire and Bath, England
First published: 1818

In this last completed novel by Jane Austen, the tone is mellow, the atmosphere autumnal; even the satire is noticeably gentler than in her other works. The story of a love affair which is culminated only after a broken engagement and a separation of eight long and lonely years, Persuasion *has a certain melancholy quality despite its finally happy ending.*

If Jane Austen's last completed work, finished on July 18, 1816, exactly one year before her death, can be characterized as "Autumnal," it can also be regarded as a novel of new beginnings. Opening in the fall, the action of *Persuasion* concludes in the early spring of 1815 with the marriage of Anne Elliot and Captain Wentworth. Adding to this note of regeneration is the fact that the heroine, a repressed, timid spinster of the landed gentry at the outset, has achieved a new state of independence at the conclusion. This freedom she demonstrates by marrying a man who is outside her own class, a man who was once forbidden to her. Yet her liberty, as Anne realizes, is won at a price—for she must relinquish a certain security to take up the tenuous position of a naval officer's wife, never knowing when another war might begin. Indeed, at the time of her marriage, the peace in Europe was hardly secure and the Battle of Waterloo was still to be fought.

Read in this light, Anne's choice of Captain Wentworth over the future baronet of Kellynch Hall, William Elliot, dramatizes Jane Austen's conviction that the gentry had lost its moral force; that out of a fear of social change it had grown inbred and restrictive, denying its own members, especially the young, a vital existence. In *Persuasion* the upper reaches of the gentry, mean-spirited and socially irresponsible, no longer possesses the creative intelligence of Mr. Darcy of *Pride and Prejudice* or the moral integrity of Mr. Knightley of *Emma.*

Anne's escape from domination by her father and sister preserves her own self, threatened with suffocation by an effete class. Her victory and her happiness in marriage are rendered bittersweet, however, by the loss of long-established connections and an uncertain future. It is in just this alloy that we recognize the autumnal nature of *Persuasion.*

PETER IBBETSON

Type of work: Novel
Author: George du Maurier (1834-1896)
Type of plot: Historical romance
Time of plot: Mid-nineteenth century
Locale: France and England
First published: 1891

In this strange story which mingles fantasy with reality through the abnormal mind of its murderer-hero, du Maurier explores the dream world of Peter. By means of his extraordinary ability to "dream true," Peter leads a rich life of the mind in which he visits the past and his beloved friend Mimsy; in his dream world loneliness is replaced by love, void by meaning, and empty present by rich past.

An eminent British illustrator and caricaturist, George du Maurier in his later life wrote three successful novels, the most notable of which, *Peter Ibbetson,* drew upon his happy childhood in France. *Peter Ibbetson* was a novel far ahead of its time, a work of powerful imagination and perhaps of genius. The novel seems to suggest that one can overcome physical, temporal and even spatial limitations to find a spiritual transcendence, if one is not afraid to make the attempt and risk the consequences. The book analyzes the nature of memory and explores the mystery of dreams. The author suggests a simultaneity of past and present which is the basic premise of the novel.

In dreams, Peter Ibbetson lived his past and, at the same time, observed it from the present. He entered upon a life within a life, a more intense existence. His dreams were a guide for his waking life, if he would but follow them. Shared dreams brought Peter and the Duchess of Towers (Mimsy Seraskier from his childhood in Passey) together again; and thus began their strange communion, which is the heart of this unusual and powerful book.

Peter Ibbetson is an honest attempt to deal with basic issues, to explore the meaning of life, and, in fact, to question what life and death are. The author's answers are no more vague than those of many other authors more celebrated for their philosophical novels, and his manner of approaching these possible answers is both dramatic and moving. There is no other book in English literature like *Peter Ibbetson*; one would have took to Russian or German literature to find anything comparable. (The closest novels might be those of Hermann Hesse, written decades later.) Yet, the novel is, at the same time, very British.

"Happiness," Mary (Mimsy) tells Peter, "is like time and space—we make and measure it ourselves. . . ." Perhaps this is the basic message of this complicated and daring novel; but, aside from any message, it is a tender and memorable love story and an extraordinary literary achievement.

PETER PAN

Type of work: Drama
Author: James M. Barrie (1860-1937)
Type of plot: Romantic fantasy
Time of plot: Anytime
Locale: England
First presented: 1904; later version, 1928

This romantic fantasy portrays the joys of perpetual childhood. Because of its ability to convincingly evoke the mood of carefree days and joyous dreams, Barrie's charming, whimsical play marks the high point of pure fantasy in the modern theater. The drama has enjoyed perennial success on the stage; Barrie also wrote a novel version of the story entitled Peter and Wendy.

James Barrie insisted that he did not recall having written *Peter Pan,* his most famous work and probably the greatest of all children's plays. In fact, the final stage version grew over a number of years in a haphazard fashion. It began as a six-chapter segment in an adult novel, *The White Bird* (1902), then became, in turn, a three act stage play (1904), a novel based on the earlier prose version (1906), a longer novel, *Peter and Wendy* (1911), taken from the play with an extra chapter "When Wendy Grew Up," and finally emerged as the well-known drama in 1928. But in spite of all these versions and revisions, Barrie may have been right in saying that he was not the primary author of *Peter Pan.* As he explains in his delightful "dedication," the real genesis of *Peter Pan* came from a series of stories he made up and told to five young brothers, the sons of close friends, in the late 1890's and the summer of 1901: "I made Peter by rubbing the five of you violently together, as savages with two sticks produce a fire. That is all he is, the spark I got from you."

One of the primary reasons for the popularity of *Peter Pan* has been that Barrie, one of the shrewdest judges of public taste ever to write, takes the two most basic elements of popular children's literature—the fairy tale story and the adventure tale—and synthesizes them into a single work. Utilizing an extraordinary theatrical sense, he compresses an enormous amount of vivid detail into the temporal and spatial limitations of the stage. Nearly as much happens in the play as in *Peter and Wendy,* a full length novel. Almost every fantasy adventure imaginable is presented in *Peter Pan*—encounters with Indians and pirates, wild beasts (wolves, a crocodile)—and each scene climaxes with a "cliff-hanger." Wendy is accidentally shot by an arrow, Peter gets abandoned on a rock with the water rushing up, the children are captured by pirates, Tinker Bell is poisoned and near death (to be rescued by the audience), and Captain Hook threatens the boys with walking-the-plank.

At the same time, the play offers the safety of an ideal children's dream. The beasts look ferocious, but are easily tamed (the boys foiled the wild animals by looking between their legs at them). Benevolent magic pervades the atmosphere, and is always available when needed (to save Wendy from the arrow, Peter from the rock); and for all of his daemonic appearance, Captain Hook is obviously no match for Peter who, in fact, toys with the pirate leader in their final clash.

In addition to providing excitement on the plot level, *Peter Pan* also evokes basic emotional and psychological responses from both children and adults. The primary struggle in the play is over possession of Wendy—as a *Mother*. Thus, the play explores the ambivalent attitudes of children toward parents, and, by extension, the human conflict between a desire for "pure" freedom versus the need to be part of a family and a society. The authoritarian father-figure, Captain Hook, is villainous (traditionally the same actor plays Hook and Mr. Darling), but the "mother," Wendy, is idealized. While the children are having adventures, they play at being siblings in a family, and, when offered adoption into a real one, they gleefully desert Never Land to join the Darling household.

Only Peter refuses to grow up, and even his rejection is based on disappointment at having been abandoned. (Once, in his absence from home, his mother had forgotten about him and when he returned, there was another boy sleeping in his bed). So only Peter remains in Never Land. At the end of the play, he has forgotten most of the adventures he had had with Wendy and the others. For Peter there can be neither past nor future, only the joyous immediate moment. It is a state of being that all, children and adults alike, can enjoy for a few delightful hours in the theater—before returning to the real world where children grow up and parents grow older.

PETER SIMPLE

Type of work: Novel
Author: Frederick Marryat (1792-1848)
Type of plot: Adventure romance
Time of plot: Early nineteenth century
Locale: England, France, various ships at sea
First published: 1834

Captain Marryat's novels of the sea belong to a tradition stretching from Smollett in the eighteenth century to C. S. Forester in the twentieth. Based on the author's personal knowledge from his service in the British Navy during the Napoleonic wars, Peter Simple *is filled with colorful sea lore and lively accounts of naval traditions.*

Marryat is a spinner of yarns. Unafraid of coincidence, sentimental or wildly improbable actions, he wrote a "few million" words that still live despite the puerility of his stories or the contrivance of his plots. His secret is energy, the indefatigable energy of a man who had experienced most of the incredible adventures he recorded in his fiction.

Like Conrad (the writer of the sea who eventually eclipsed Marryat's reputation), Marryat spent twenty years at sea before he took to fiction, and largely because of the range of his actual naval experiences Marryat's work has an even greater ring of authenticity than Conrad's. For one thing, Conrad had never tasted the warfare and violence that Marryat had known intimately in the Napoleonic Wars. Marryat's realism established the robust, humorous and "steel-nerved" themes and tones associated with fiction about the sea from his time to ours. Conrad himself credited Marryat with the creation of the modern myth of the sea; for example, the sea as a test of man's courage, virtue, and endurance. Certainly the works of Kipling, and even Hemingway, attest the justice of Conrad's judgment.

One of the most engaging traits of Marryat's fiction is its readability. The limpid style keeps action alive from page to page despite the contrivance of the plotting. Without relying on arcane mariners' terminology, Marryat succeeds in depicting with unusual clarity the most intricate actions involving ships, the sea, and men in struggle. He is a master of verisimilitude: we see in detail, as well as with panoramic scope, all the things he wants us to see. The real measure of his achievement is the fact that illustrations to his works are superfluous. Even young readers, and they have always been his principle audience, will not complain of the lack of pictures. They are there in the words.

PETER WHIFFLE

Type of work: Novel
Author: Carl Van Vechten (1880-1964)
Type of plot: Simulated biography
Time of plot: 1907-1919
Locale: New York, Paris, Italy
First published: 1922

This odd fictitious biography follows the career of a young man who hates to work. On the night his mother's brother dies and leaves him a fortune, he decides to become a writer. Van Vechten's theme becomes apparent in Peter's final discovery that not everyone is born to create art, but, rather, that the majority of people are meant to enjoy the works of others.

Carl Van Vechten, music critic, essayist, novelist, and photographer, was one of the primary figures in the American literary renaissance of the 1920's, both as an artist and as a personality. Clever, gregarious, sophisticated, and a talented party-giver, Van Vechten numbered among his friends almost all of the important literary and cultural personages of his time. His apartments in Paris and New York became centers of cultural activity.

Out of this milieu, especially from his early years in Paris, Van Vechten wrote *Peter Whiffle,* a novel set in the first quarter of the twentieth century. The novel's unique appeal lies in its balance between the realistic descriptions and social observations of the artistic life in Paris, New York, and Florence, and the exotic, fantastic, humorously developed "biography" of Peter.

The realistic anchor comes from Van Vechten's decision to place himself, as a character, at the novel's center. As the narrator and confidant of Peter, he presents the cultural environment of the period with feeling and precision. Van Vechten conveys a sense of personal involvement as he accurately describes local customs and inhabitants, social mores and peculiarities, as well as real places and events with careful attention to concrete details and physical actuality. He chronicles the social gatherings and artistic happenings of the time, using actual names in some cases, thinly disguised and suggestive ones in others.

But Peter Whiffle is hardly a "real" character; his "biography" is an ironical, whimsical fantasy. Peter is charming and amusing, but lacks any solid identity. The book traces his attempts to find one through artistic creativity—and his failure to do so. In his ambition to become a writer, Peter systematically commits himself to every artistic fad that has excited the fancy of modern writers. Each time he devotes himself to a new set of experiments, he surrounds himself in the trappings of the new approach and absorbs himself in the life style appropriate to it. He even renames his cat accordingly. Peter begins imitating Henry James's emphasis on style and form to the exclusion of subject matter, moves on to a cataloging of phenomena à la

Whitman, to "bloody and dirty" revolutionary writing, to a flirtation with Africa that suggests Rimbaud, to pure subject matter without any style in the mode of Dreiser, to experiments with diabolism and black magic, and finally to a slow death from exhaustion and futility. In dying, Peter acknowledges his incapacity as a writer, his talent as a spectator, and, at last, turns to his cat for the *real* answer.

PHÈDRE

Type of work: Drama
Author: Jean Baptiste Racine (1639-1699)
Type of plot: Classical tragedy
Time of plot: Remote antiquity
Locale: Troezen, in Ancient Greece
First presented: 1677

Racine based this tragedy on Euripides' Hippolytus but shifted his focus to the character of Phaedra, who appears only briefly in the Greek play. The playwright explores once again in Phèdre the problem of the extent to which human beings are capable of free will and therefore responsible for their actions.

The issue of free will, predestination, and grace that interested Racine in the seventeenth century was a restatement, in theological terms, of a problem of universal concern. To what extent is one free to create his own existence and be responsible for his actions? Are the terms of human existence within the arena of human control or are they pre-established by some external force? Can human suffering be justified as the result of one's actions or is it the imposition of a capricious deity?

The specific manner in which these questions are answered depends upon one's view of human nature and human potential. When one chooses between predestination and free will, he is either asserting or denying his belief in one's ability to make wise and ethically sound decisions. Emphasis on the dignity of man and on his potential for choice often coincides with an optimism regarding human behavior. Conversely, a belief in man as a depraved and irresponsible creature will be found in conjunction with a distrust of man's ability to act in a positive and meaningful way. This view of the human condition is presented in *Phèdre* by Racine and shows man as predetermined or predestined.

Racine was reared by the Jansenists at Port-Royal, and he returned to Port-Royal after completing *Phèdre*. The Jansenists held ideas on the problem of free will and predestination in opposition to the dominant position of the Catholic Church as set forth by the Jesuits.

The Jesuits attempted to bring salvation within the grasp of all men, whereas the Jansenists emphasized a rigid determinism. They rejected the Jesuit doctrine that man could attain his salvation through good works and insisted that man was predestined to salvation or damnation. This denial of free will was based on the conviction that man was left completely corrupt and devoid of rational control after the fall. Man was incapable of participating in the process of regeneration because original sin had deprived him of his will. The passions had gained control of man, and they could only lead to evil. Human passion was seen as capable of leading to falsehood, crime, suicide, and general destruction. It is inevitable that the Jansenists would regard with alarm any doctrine that allowed for the activity of human free will. Only God's gift of mercy could save man, and that mercy was reserved for those who had been elected to salvation.

The basic ideas in *Phèdre* present a similar distrust of the passions, a similar curtailment of free will, and a consequent emphasis upon man's lack of control. Human passion is depicted as controlling reason. The area of human choice and responsibility is severely limited. Phèdre is pursued by an overwhelming sense of fatality.

In the Preface to *Phèdre,* however, Racine suggests the possibility of free will. He states that Phèdre is "neither completely guilty nor completely innocent. She is involved, by her destiny and by the anger of the gods, in an illicit passion of which she is the first to be horrified. She makes every effort to overcome it."

Does Phèdre actually make the effort Racine attributes to her? To what extent is she free to make a choice? To what extent is this merely the illusion of free will? For Racine continues to state in the Preface that "her crime is more a punishment of the gods than an act of her will."

Phèdre's genealogy would seem to support the argument of fatality. She is initially referred to, not by name, but as the "daughter of Minos and Pasiphae." Throughout the play, she gives the appearance of being overwhelmed by a cruel destiny that is linked to her past. She exhibits perfect lucidity regarding the full implications of her situation, yet she seems incapable of resolving her dilemma. All of her actions are performed "in spite of myself."

Phèdre's fall precedes the opening of the play and is the result of passion overwhelming reason. We learn that Phèdre made numerous but ineffective attempts to overcome her love for Hippolyte. She built a temple to Venus, sacrificed innumerable victims, and attempted to surmount her passion through prayer.

As the play opens, Phèdre resorts to her final effort—suicide. Ironically her attempted suicide will only serve to add physical weakness to her already weakened emotional condition and prevent her from overcoming the temptations with which she will be confronted.

The first temptation is offered by her nurse, Oenone. By implying that her suicide would constitute betrayal of the gods, her husband, and her children, Oenone attempts to persuade Phèdre to turn back on death and reveal her love for Hippolyte.

The news of Thésée's apparent death further tempts Phèdre by removing the crime of potential adultery. In addition, Phèdre is tempted to offer the crown to Hippolyte in order to protect her children and appeal to his political aspirations.

Her interview with Hippolyte, however, turns into a confession of love which unfolds without any semblance of rational control. Although she expresses shame at her declaration, her passion is presented as part of the destiny of her entire race. At the moment following the confession to Hippolyte, Phèdre prays to Venus, not as in the past to free her from passion, but to enflame Hippolyte with a comparable passion. Whereas Phèdre had previously implored Oenone to aid her in overcoming her love, she now beseeches her assistance in furthering it.

Thésée's return presents Phèdre with a choice of either revealing or denying her love for Hippolyte. She, however, allows Oenone to deceive Thésée by accusing Hippolyte of fostering the illicit passion. Yet is this actually a moment of choice, assuming that choice involves a rational action? On the contrary, Phèdre's statement to her nurse at the end of Act III, scene iii, implies complete lack of control.

The final temptation to which Phèdre succumbs is her refusal to reverse the course of events by confessing her lies to Thésée. Once again Phèdre is prevented from acting in a rational manner, for upon learning of Hippolyte's love for Aricie, she is overwhelmed by a blinding jealousy and even goes so far as to wish for the destruction of Aricie.

Despite Racine's enigmatic remarks in the Preface, the pattern of temptation and defeat developed in the play eliminates entirely the possibility of free will. Although Phèdre wishes to overcome her passion, all of her efforts are in vain. The series of temptations in Phèdre serves to emphasize her lack of control and conspires to bring about her ruin. From the possibility of an early death with honor. Phèdre is led, through a series of defeats, to a guilty and dishonorable death.

The play concludes on a note of pessimism. There is no possibility of salvation for those afflicted with passion. Racine presents man's fate as predestined and not subject to human control.

Phyllis Mael

PHILASTER

Type of work: Drama
Authors: Francis Beaumont (1584?-1616) and John Fletcher (1579-1625)
Type of plot: Tragi-comedy
Time of plot: The romantic past
Locale: Sicily
First presented: c. 1609

It is believed by scholars that Philaster, Or, Love Lies A-Bleeding *was written for the most part by Beaumont, although the rich imagery and the echoes of Shakespearean themes seem to substantiate the collaboration of Fletcher, who served his apprenticeship under the master. At first very popular, the play later lost favor with Restoration audiences, who did not respond well to the character of the hero; and modern readers often feel that Euphrasia deserved a better fate.*

When William Shakespeare was at the height of his powers, two men met who began the most famous dramatic collaboration in the history of the English theater. The names of John Fletcher and Francis Beaumont are so closely linked even today that most histories of drama discuss them together.

John Fletcher, the older of the two men, was born in 1579, the son of the Bishop of London. Very little is known of his early life, but his father's death, and his large family, probably made it necessary for John to find employment early. He became the most productive playwright for the acting company known as the King's Men, and continued to write until his death in 1625 of the plague.

Francis Beaumont was also born into an aristocratic family, in 1584. As a young man, he studied law at the Inner Temple in London. He may have begun writing during this time (he never practiced law), since in 1602 he had already published anonymously his erotic poem *Salmacis and Hermaphroditus.* Beaumont became a member of Ben Jonson's circle of writers at this time, and it was probably as one of this group that he met John Fletcher. They had formed their acquaintance by 1607, and Beaumont must have begun his writing for the stage shortly thereafter. Beaumont's most enduring work on his own is the comedy *The Knight of the Burning Pestle.* Apparently he stopped writing altogether after his marriage in 1613; he died only three years later, in the year of Shakespeare's death.

Together Beaumont and Fletcher wrote at least eight plays, and their knowledge of the language and habits of gentlemen served them well in turning out plays for the aristocratic audience which had become steadily more important since the death of Queen Elizabeth. This audience had a taste for escape in the drama they liked, and *Philaster,* the authors' first great success together, was a play eminently suited to fit it. The play is in fact almost the typical tragi-comedy.

When the play was first produced in 1609, the original audience would already have known the term tragi-comedy. As Fletcher himself said in his preface to *The Faithful Shepherdess,* "A tragi-comedy is not so called in respect of mirth and killing, but in respect it wants deaths, which is enough to make it no tragedy, yet brings some near it, which is enough to make it no comedy." The modern reader might more willingly call the play a melodrama. It contains all the characteristics of that variety of entertainment: disguises, sudden disclosures, unexpected reversals of fortune, characters whose emotions change with every scene, and a last act devoted to making sure that everything comes out right.

As a tragi-comedy, *Philaster* has nothing stand in the way of the action of the plot: the characters move obediently as necessary. If we were to judge this play by more exacting standards, we would have to agree with the villain's estimate of Philaster in the first scene: "He's mad; beyond cure, mad." For example, Philaster loves Arethusa passionately, yet in the third act his love turns immediately to hate at the unsubstantiated report of her unfaithfulness. He is ready to kill Arethusa's supposed lover Bellario, but the youth denies the charge so strongly that Philaster cannot bring himself to use his sword.

Although some scenes still seem very humorous, there is not a great deal of comedy in the play—Fletcher was right in denying that the genre was called tragi-comedy because of mirth. Rather, *Philaster* must have confirmed some of the most deeply held beliefs of the aristocrats in the audience: true nobility ennobles its possessor and, above all, the true heir to the throne cannot be cheated out of his inheritance.

It is too harsh, though, to judge the play by realistic standards. Its characters are not meant to be inhabitants of the real world. Beaumont and Fletcher have taken pains to remove the action from the realm of familiarity, thus making acceptance of the play as fantasy all the easier. To prevent a comparison of manners, they set the play in faraway Sicily (a location that must have seemed as remote to the average Englishman of the time as Patagonia does to us); to prevent a comparison of morals, they remove the action from the Christian world: God is never spoken of, though "the gods" are frequently invoked. No cleric appears in the play, and "destiny" substitutes for providence in the complaints of the characters. The aim is clearly to allow the audience to suspend its conviction that raging jealousy is a vice, that attacking the weak is cowardly, and that suicide is a sin.

If we accept the authors' initial evaluation of the characters, and take them for what they are intended to be, types rather than imitations of life, we can enjoy them as stock characters—the hero who loves honor better than life, the heroine who loves virtue better than life, the villain who loves life better than honor or virtue—and watch them go through their paces while they move the play forward, untangling one involvement after another until we reach the happy ending.

To keep the play moving without interruption, Beaumont and Fletcher employ a simple and straightforward verse line, with little of the inversions of syntax characteristic of, for example, Shakespearean dramatic speeches. As is customary in plays of the period, lower-class characters speak prose, as do some members of the court in comic scenes. Occasionally the speeches of emotionally charged characters break down into bombast, but this failure of control in language is not overly frequent.

Many of the lines are well written by the most demanding standards: the *double entendre* of the comic scenes has not lost its vigor, and relatively little of the play needs glossing for the modern reader. If we were to see the play, modernized for the occasion, we might consider it melodrama, but we would certainly agree that it was superior melodrama.

Walter E. Meyers

PHILOCTETES

Type of work: Drama
Author: Sophocles (c. 496-406 or 405 B.C.)
Type of plot: Classical tragedy
Time of plot: The Trojan War
Locale: The island of Lemnos
First presented: 409 B.C.

Philoctetes *is remarkably similar in theme to Sophocles' last play,* Oedipus at Colonus. *In both plays the hero has become hateful to his society and has been rejected by it, but eventually is again needed by that society, and is therefore restored by the gods and sent to resume his powers. Like Creon in the Oedipus plays, Odysseus is inhumanly insensitive to the sufferings of the hero; however, alone among Sophocles' works,* Philoctetes *has a happy ending.*

For a lesser playwright, relieving Philoctetes of his excruciating physical suffering might be the stuff of an adequate drama. Sophocles, however, uses the wound as a symbolic image of the injury done to Philoctetes' psyche, that is, to his own sense of integrity. By his hatred of all the Greeks, especially Odysseus, he has long fed a psychological ulcer, the ugliness of which is conveyed by the debilitating torment and pervasive stench of the snakebite. But the unseen wound is incomparably deeper and more loathesome since it has turned Philoctetes against humanity, while the snakebite has only kept him from personal glory. The bow to which he clings is more than his means of survival in the wilds; it represents his last touch with his own identity, despite his alienation. Much like Aeschylus' Prometheus, Philoctetes knows his worth, but stubbornly cannot see the sense in yielding to compromise. His foil is Odysseus, but basically, in terms of the action of the drama, they are alike: each is coldly willing to exact a sacrifice to achieve selfish ends.

If it were not for the noble Neoptolemus, it might be difficult to recognize the nobility of Philoctetes. Although well-instructed in deceit, the relatively innocent Neoptolemus is shocked at the injustice done Philoctetes. Our own identification comes through Neoptolemus: like him, we want the war to end; but can it be done at the expense of this pathetic but good man's life? Neoptolemus matures in this play by suffering along with Philoctetes; Odysseus, however, remains the same, and so would Philoctetes himself, were it not for Herakles, a third figure with whom Philoctetes may be compared. Herakles, too, had suffered terribly for no deliberate reason, but by dutifully performing the tasks allotted him, he achieved immortality.

PHINEAS FINN

Type of work: Novel
Author: Anthony Trollope (1815-1882)
Type of plot: Political romance
Time of plot: Mid-nineteenth century
Locale: The British Isles
First published: 1869

Phineas Finn, the Irish Member *is an objective account of the successful but brief parliamentary career of a guilelessly opportunistic young man who lacks the fortune which would give him independence from his party. The novel is also noteworthy for its dispassionate account of the passage of the Reform Bill.*

Two sources contributed to the creation of *Phineas Finn*. First, Anthony Trollope wanted above everything to be a Member of Parliament. He regarded such service as the highest calling for an Englishman and was bitterly disappointed when his one attempt at election failed. Meanwhile, however, he had begun to live vicariously the life of an MP in the great political novels now known as the "Palliser" series, of which *Phineas Finn* is the second of six. A second source for *Phineas Finn* was Trollope's residence in Ireland, where he served as a postal official during most of the period from 1841 to 1859. Unlike most British government officials, he liked the Irish and was in turn generally liked by them, and thus created Phineas, one of the most engaging Irishmen in fiction.

Phineas advances rapidly in the political world largely because he is so likeable. His reception in the drawing rooms of the great Whig families opens doors of patronage to him and draws him into the fringes of the world of political power. The novel gives some fine analysis of how the parliamentary system works, always with an eye to what is practical as well as to what is ideal. Should a man always vote with his party, even against his personal belief on a particular issue? If not, then can a party ever achieve effective action without the essential loyalty of its members? Such questions are as alive today as they were a century ago, and Trollope makes it clear that no easy answer exists. Phineas learns the value of conformity to his party in a series of episodes throughout the novel, finally asserting his independence on the Irish issue and consequently losing his office. He is, however, far from a political martyr; his influential friends find him a post in Ireland, a solution which Trollope sees as fitting because it is practical. A good public servant should be rewarded, and patronage, he implies, is as good a system as any for dealing with the realities of political life. Trollope directs the same broad tolerance toward Phineas' fickleness. As he falls in love successively with Mary Flood Jones, Lady Laura, and Violet Effingham, he is each time convinced of his own sincerity, and Trollope seems to suggest that anyone so engagingly good-humored as Phineas cannot really be condemned. The tone of high comedy prevails in this novel, but it is a tone which darkens in the later Palliser novels.

PHINEAS REDUX

Type of work: Novel
Author: Anthony Trollope (1815-1882)
Type of plot: Political romance
Time of plot: Mid-nineteenth century
Locale: England
First published: 1874

The second of Trollope's parliamentary novels and the sequel to Phineas Finn, Phineas Redux *enjoys an entertaining plot and excellent characterizations. In relating the story of accusations of adultery and a trial for murder, the author fully exploits his genius for detailing the exasperatingly logical thought process which lie behind false rumors and misinformation.*

The fourth novel in the Palliser series of novels, *Phineas Redux* is one of Trollope's most delightful and rich books. Trollope himself considered the Palliser series his best achievement. By portraying a larger segment of English society than he had done previously, he attempted to identify and comment on the basic qualities of the national character and way of life. The characters in this series grow and develop emotionally, in contrast to the Barset characters, who remain static. Although the principal protagonists of the Palliser series are politicians, cabinet ministers, members of Parliament, or people exercising behind-the-scenes influence, little is said of the political principles which presumably governed the actions of ministers and legislators. Trollope preferred to concentrate on interpreting human nature in all of its variety rather than attempt to propound dogmas and abstractions. In this, as in many of his novels, Trollope's instinctive understanding of the hearts of men and women is nearly unparalleled in English fiction.

The material for this novel came from Trollope's own unsuccessful bid for Parliament in 1868, which might account for its stinging, satirical approach to politics. A number of the principal characters were based on real individuals, notably Daubney, who led the effort to separate Church and state, and who was based on Disraeli. Phineas Finn was inspired by a young Irish politician who was a protegé of Disraeli. Trollope was particularly fascinated by the great influence of women over politicians, and their efforts to control policy from the background. The women in this book are superbly drawn, from the noble Lady Glencora and the glamorous Madame Goesler, who so modestly repudiates the vast legacy left for her by the Duke of Omnium, to the tormented Lady Kennedy and the amusing Lady Baldock. Laura Kennedy is particularly well done; in her, Trollope ruthlessly shows the price a girl will sometimes pay for making a marriage of convenience. The physical collapse and spiritual agony of Laura Kennedy are portrayed with great power.

The novel is crowded with brilliant characters, interacting within the complicated but skillfully interwoven plots. The book provides the reader with a leisurely and entertaining account of life among the aristocrats, the scandals, the romances, the financial difficulties, and the intrigues. Social differences are subtly observed, as when Adelaid Palliser is shocked by Mr. Spooner daring to propose marriage to her, or in the picture of the senior Mr. Maule, living a limited existence of a very genteel nature and still hoping, at fifty-five, to land an heiress. Among the perfectly rendered characters the slimy Quintus Slide of the disreputable *People's Banner* must be mentioned, as well as the mad old Kennedy and that perfect gentleman, Plantagenet Palliser. The novel can be enjoyed for its humor and wonderful characterizations and also appreciated for its perceptive picture of the Victorian world and the people who ranked high in its social structure.

THE PHOENICIAN WOMEN

Type of work: Drama
Author: Euripides (c. 485-c. 406 B.C.)
Type of plot: Classical tragedy
Time of plot: Time of the War of the Seven against Thebes
Locale: Thebes
First presented: c. 410 B.C.

Possibly because its text was expanded by later writers, The Phoenician Women *is more packed with incident than any other Greek play. Also, in presenting the entire history of the line of Cadmus, Euripides has created a drama that is* polyproposon, *in which none of the characters can be considered the tragic hero or the focus of attention.*

Seven generations before the actions of this play Cadmus came to Greece from Phoenicia. Near the place where the city of Thebes would rise he slew Ares' dragon and established his reign over the bellicose Sparti, men sprung from the planted teeth of the dragon. Laïus, born of descendants of Cadmus and of one of the Sparti, outraged the hospitality of King Pelops by abducting and raping his beautiful son Chrysippus. The ensuing curse led to Laïus' parricide, Oedipus' incest, Jocasta's and Antigone's suicides, and the mutual fratricides of Eteocles and Polynices (themselves cursed by Oedipus). Thus, by using the chorus of Phoenician maidens to relate the history of Thebes, Euripides illustrates the near completion of the wretched Theban cycle. Throughout the play these foreign kinswomen keep the audience aware of the forces that have doomed this city. They frequently and variously allude to Oedipus' victory over the Sphinx (which victory paradoxically brought worse evils on Thebes), to incestuous propagation (which ends in incestuous slaughter), and to the curse of Ares (the maidens are traveling to Delphi to serve Apollo, who also had to pay a debt for slaying the Python). And so, by presenting this host of characters and by recalling Phoenician origins and royal curses, Euripides leaves little doubt that this is a tragedy of a people, not of one person.

The *Phoenissae* begs comparison with the earlier Theban plays of Aeschylus and Sophocles. Among Euripides' more obvious innovations in plot are Jocasta's surviving the discovery of Oedipus' identity, Oedipus' presence at Thebes during the war, the sacrifice of Menoeceus, and the defiant departure of Antigone with her exiled father. There are also several significant differences in characterization, not the least being Eteocles, whose role as defender of the city in Aeschylus' *Seven Against Thebes* is reduced to that of a self-serving wretch. In contrast with both Eteocles and Polynices, Creon's one son Haemon stands ready to marry Antigone if it will benefit the city; moreover, his other son Menoeceus selflessly offers himself to expiate after so many years Cadmus' crime against Ares, thus securing victory for the Thebans.

PHORMIO

Type of work: Drama
Author: Terence (Publius Terentius Afer, c. 190-159 B.C.)
Type of plot: Comedy of intrigue
Time of plot: Second century B.C.
Locale: Athens
First presented: 161 B.C.

In this play about the schemes of Phormio, a clever parasite and fascinating rogue, in behalf of two young men, Terence displays his dexterity in handling the most complicated plots without confusion. Even through the double plot—involving Phormio's engineering of circumstances to gain each man the woman of his choice—and a case of mistaken identity besides, the reader is never lost. There are no digressions, and each part of the play is closely knit to the structure, simultaneously furthering the development of both storylines.

Unlike much of Terence's work, *Phormio* is highly amusing. In addition to having one of the most engaging rascals in the history of the theater, this play is fast paced, brilliantly constructed, suspenseful, and rich in irony. Although Terence's ability in characterization is evident, *Phormio* tends to be more farcical than his other comedies, but also more vigorous. This may be due to the fact that the playwright did not adapt it from Menander, as was usually the case in Terence, but from *The Claimant* by Apollodorus of Carystus, a contemporary of Menander. But because the original source has not survived, it is difficult to judge how much of *Phormio* is derived from *The Claimant*. Certain features are distinctly Terentian, such as the dual romance, the excellent use of plot, the smooth colloquial dialogue, and the polished maxims. Others are attributable to the Greek New Comedy, such as the stock character types, the concentration on domestic problems, and the prominence of romance. The most likely estimate is that Terence took his material from Apollodorus in this play and reworked it according to his own formula, in the same way that Molière borrowed from *Phormio* in writing *Les Fourberies de Scapin.*

When the play was first produced at the Roman games in 161 B.C., Terence was about twenty-six and had established a reputation as a successful dramatist. Of low birth and originally a slave, he had enjoyed a meteoric rise in his fortunes, becoming a member of the Scipionic coterie, a group of Roman aristocrats interested in the importation of Greek culture. His success as a dramatist can be indirectly gauged from his Prologues, in which he self-confidently answers the attacks of the elderly playwright, Luscius Lanuvinus. We can picture the envious Luscius dismayed and threatened by the rising Terence. Unfortunately, the year after *Phormio* was presented Terence took a trip to Greece, from which he never returned. It is thought that his ship sank as he was returning to Rome in 159 B.C.

In *Phormio* Terence shows an unusual detachment from the plight of the two adolescent young men, Antipho and Phaedria, presenting them as rather silly, impulsive, and feckless youths who are helpless before their fathers. Instead of differentiating them, which is his normal practice, Terence emphasizes their similarity. Moreover, he pokes fun at their superficiality and self-absorption. Clearly, Terence was growing beyond the stage of taking youthful romances seriously. In this play we do not even see the young women whom Antipho and Phaedria love: they are incidental to the plot except as prizes.

What does interest Terence is the character of Phormio: self-possessed where the two youths are cowardly, roguish where the two youths wish to appear respectable, clever where the two youths are witless, and determined where the two youths are fickle. Phormio is mature and confident of his powers, the ideal hero of many young men. It is he alone who outwits the two formidable fathers to award Phaedria his flute player; and it is he who enabled Antipho to marry in the first place through a ruse that, surprisingly enough, turns out to be true. Terence, having outgrown his interest in adolescent lovers, apparently needed a more vital character to command the stage, and he found one in the adventurer Phormio.

Instead of giving Antipho and Phaedria contrasting qualities, Terence gives them different problems. Antipho's difficulty is to keep the wife he already has in the face of his father's opposition. Phaedria's trouble is that he cannot raise the money to purchase the mistress he loves from her pimp, who is presented as a practical businessman. Phormio undertakes to solve both problems, not so much for his own gain but to demonstrate his gift for intrigue. He wants to show off his virtuosity before the admiring slave Geta and the two young men. We witness him thinking on his feet, as it were, outfacing Demipho and his three toady lawyers, discarding a useless alibi, obtaining a large sum from Chremes under false pretenses, and adapting quickly to a dangerous situation in which Demipho is intent on regaining the money. In all of this, through chance and his quick wit, he is the master of the situation.

After all, Demipho and Chremes deserve to be swindled, as tightfisted and authoritarian old men. And their sons deserve a hard time before their problems are settled, being the shallow, erotic boys they are. The complex but clearly developed plot provides opportunities to witness the chagrin of all four in an amusing light. But the most amusing scenes are the climactic ones in which Chremes tries his hardest to keep the secret of his bigamous marriage from his wife, while Demipho's concern over money forces Phormio to reveal it, thereby insuring that Chremes will be henpecked for the rest of his life.

In the end, once the plot has been unraveled and the characters have received their proper rewards and punishments, Terentian comedy seems rather trivial and commonplace, requiring no great effort of thought. If it is amiable and technically skilled, the assumptions behind it are those of middle-class audiences everywhere: that young love should be fulfilled, that the old should make allowances for the fancies of youth, that parental authority should be respected by youth. These premises make Terence, along with Plautus, the forerunner of bourgeois comedy from Shakespeare to Neil Simon.

James Weigel, Jr.

PICKWICK PAPERS

Type of work: Novel
Author: Charles Dickens (1812-1870)
Type of plot: Comic romance
Time of plot: 1827-1828
Locale: England
First published: 1836-1837

These sketches, originally published in serial form, were planned as prose accompaniments to caricatures by a popular artist. The title derives from the character of Mr. Pickwick, a naïve, generous, lovable old gentleman who reigns over the activities of the Pickwick Club. Many of the comic highlights in the work spring from the imperturbable presence of mind and ready wit of Sam Weller, whose cleverness and humor are indispensable to the Pickwickians.

When in 1836 a publisher proposed that Charles Dickens write the text for a series of pictures by the sporting artist Robert Seymour, Dickens was experiencing the first thrill of fame as the author of *Sketches by Boz.* He was twenty-four, and had been for some years a court reporter and free-lance journalist; *Sketches by Boz* was his first literary effort of any length. The work that the publisher proposed was of a similar kind: short, usually humorous descriptions of cosmopolitan life, sometimes illustrated, and published monthly. Dickens, with the plan of a novel already in mind, but in need of cash, accepted the offer as a stopgap. He made one stipulation: that he and not Seymour have the choice of scenes to be treated. He did this because he himself was no sportsman and as a cockney had little knowledge of the country beyond what his journalistic travels had shown him. That he viewed the enterprise as an expedient is evident from the digressive character of the first few chapters.

Dickens was able to disguise his ignorance of country life by a canny selection of scenes and topics. Actual sporting scenes are kept to a minimum, and treated with broad humour and slight detail. Country elections, magistrates, and newspapers, on the other hand, he knew well, and the chapters describing the Eatanswill election and dealing with Mr. Nupkins, the mayor of Ipswich, and Mr. Pott, the editor of the Eatanswill *Gazette,* abound in atmosphere and choice observation. Most useful of all was his intimate knowledge of stagecoach travel, of life upon the road, and of the inhabitants and manners of inns great and small. The device of a journey by coach unifies the first part of the novel, and a large portion of the action, including several key scenes, takes place in inns and public houses; for example, Mr. Pickwick meets Sam Weller at the White Hart Inn, Mrs. Bardell is apprehended at the Spaniards, Sam is reunited with his father at the Marquis of Granby, and the Wellers plot Stiggins' discomfiture at the Blue Boar.

A theme that Dickens developed in later works appears in embryo here:

the quicksand quality of litigation. We note that every figure connected with the law is portrayed as venal if not downright criminal, except Mr. Perker who is merely depicted as a remarkably cold fish. Another feature of later works is the awkward treatment of women. The author's attitude toward the fair sex is extremely ambiguous. Two of the women in the novel are unqualifiedly good. Sam's Mary is described perennially as "the pretty housemaid," and the fact that Sam loves her appear to complete the list of her virtues in Dickens' view. As a character she has neither depth nor ethical range; no more has Arabella Allen, the dark-eyed girl with the "very nice little pair of boots." She is distinguished at first by flirtatious archness and later by a rather servile docility. The daughters of old Wardle first come to our attention in the act of spiting their spinster aunt, and never redeem this impression. Other female characters are rather poorly developed. None has, as do some of the male figures such as Jingle and Trotter, a human dimension.

Curious too are the author's sentiments about the institution of marriage. Mr. Winkle makes a runaway match, Mr. Snodgrass is only forestalled from doing so by a lack of parental opposition, and Mr. Tupman escapes after a ludicrously close call. But Mr. Pickwick, the great advocate of heart over head, is not and never has been married, and in fact shows his greatest strength as a character in his struggle for justice in a breach-of-promise suit; while Mr. Weller, the other beneficent father-figure of the work, makes no bones about his aversion to the connubial state: " '. . . vether it's worth while goin' through so much, to learn so little . . . is a matter o' taste. *I* rayther think it isn't.' "

Angus Wilson, among others, contends that *Pickwick Papers* is, like most first novels, autobiographical, however well-disguised. There is evidence for this position in the fact that Dickens' estimation of the women in his life also tended to extremes of adulation and contempt. More pertinent to the main thrust of the novel, which is the development of Pickwick from buffoon to "angel in tights," and the concurrent development of Sam, is the author's relationship to his father, whom he adored. The elder Dickens' imprisonment for debt in 1824 was the great trauma of the author's childhood; it was made the more galling by the fact that he, the eldest son, was put out to work at a blacking factory and was able to join the family circle in the prison only on Sundays. Scarcely more than a child, he felt unable either to aid or to comfort his father in his distress; at the same time, he felt that his father had abandoned him to an ungentle world.

As a young man, Dickens wrote into his first novel an account of those times as he would have wished them to be. Mr. Pickwick is the epitome of those qualities of Dickens senior that so endeared him to his son, unsinkable good spirits and kindness that does not count the cost. To these, Pickwick adds financial sense, ethical size, and most important, a sensitivity to the best feelings of his spiritual son, Sam Weller. Sam, in turn, bends all his cockney keenness of eye and wit, all his courage and steadfastness, to the service not only of this ideal father unjustly imprisoned, but also of his immensely endearing shadow-father Tony Weller. Clearly, this material has its roots in Dickens' life. But it is just as clear that his genius tapped a universal longing of sons to see their fathers as heroes, and themselves as heroic helpers.

Jan Kennedy Foster

THE PICTURE OF DORIAN GRAY

Type of work: Novel
Author: Oscar Wilde (1856-1900)
Type of plot: Fantasy
Time of plot: Late nineteenth century
Locale: England
First published: 1891

Although Oscar Wilde wrote that there is no such thing as a moral or unmoral book, Dorian Gray *is definitely a moral fable. In a rich blend of incredibly sensuous description, allegory, and symbolism, Wilde tells the fantastic tale of a young man who abandons himself to a life of vice. As Dorian's spirit deteriorates into ugliness and corruption, his body shows no sign of decay, since all the outward effects of aging and hard living are assumed by a magic portrait of him, painted when he was still pure and virtuous.*

The Picture of Dorian Gray is a curious offspring of the traditional novel form. Wilde called the novel "all conversation and no action." Further, his habit of crossing richly sensual description with starkly realistic glimpses of London "low life" gives the novel aspects of both romance and realism, although there are good reasons why *The Picture of Dorian Gray* is almost always considered a Romantic product.

In spite of its hybrid characteristics, *The Picture of Dorian Gray* continues to be a favorite seller, and has been through more reprints than anything else Wilde wrote. Dorian's bisexual appetite was a subject still scandalously taboo in the 1890's, and the novel was used as evidence against Wilde when he was tried for his homosexual activities. Stuart Mason's *Art and Morality* gives a detailed summary of the heated controversy surrounding the original publication of the book.

The lasting appeal of *The Picture of Dorian Gray,* however, may rather be attributed to the number of successful levels, all well-constructed and interlocking, on which the story operates. The most literal reading the novel offers is that of a detective story. (Wilde admired Sir Arthur Conan Doyle's Sherlock Holmes stories.) Vane functions as the detective in pursuit of the guilty man, and as avenger for his sister's death. A second level of meaning focuses on the idea of spiritual struggle, since Dorian's story hinges, like Faust's, on the fulfillment of the wish that youth be eternal. When Dorian tries to rid himself of guilt, he violates the terms of the "contract," thus calling back into operation the normal laws of life, and the damned man is forced to shoulder his own guilt as he and his portrait exchange roles.

The emphasis on psychological awareness of the self which the novel's dialogue reflects, opens up a third level of interpretation. Intensely conscious of themselves, Wilde's characters take a Jamesian interest in analyzing their own psychological states, to the point of narcissism. This is accompanied by negation and the constant turning away from one another. Dorian's experience leads him to the final negation that "ugliness is the only reality," and so he annihilates himself.

PIERRE

Type of work: Novel
Author: Herman Melville (1819-1891)
Type of plot: Philosophical tragedy
Time of plot: Early nineteenth century
Locale: New York
First published: 1852

This novel is the story of Pierre Glendinning, whose defense of his illegitimate half-sister Isabel leads to incestuous desires which finally provoke Pierre's suicide and bring misery and ruin to his entire family. Probably the least read of Melville's works because of its obscure and sometimes confused symbolism, this novel is considered by scholars as an experiment on the author's part and an attempt to break away from the mold set by his previous novels of the sea and the Pacific islands.

Pierre is a Hamlet in reverse; he acts too soon, in everything that he does, and brings about catastrophes greater than anything brought on by Hamlet's delay. That ironic observation, made by F. O. Matthiessen in his classic study, *American Renaissance* (1941), is the key to understanding what Melville meant by his novel's subtitle, *The Ambiguities.* Pierre finds it impossible to hedge, to be anything but purely realistic in all his actions. The result is that despite his pure intentions, his conduct results in great suffering for all those around him.

If Pierre had mastered the gist of "Chronometricals and Horologicals," the pamphlet he read on his way to New York, he would have understood that the only way "God's truth and man's truth correspond is through their contradictions." But such ambiguity is unacceptable to his idealism, and he literally immolates himself to a totally unrealistic ethics. In order to save his half-sister's honor, he lives with her in what looks to the world like marital respectability; instead of providing for her security, the arrangement ultimately destroys both of them. Pierre can do no right, because he tries to live as if he could avoid doing any wrong at all.

These are strong suggestions that Pierre is driven by subconscious desires that actually force him into his self-destructive behavior. Perhaps the greatest ambiguity—and irony—of all is that his supposed idealism is merely a sublimation of his darkest instincts, that the incestuous attraction to "dark" Isabel is actually stronger than the claims of Lucy's innocent "whiteness." The Oedipal relationship to his mother is certainly an indication of psychological pressures. Again, the similarities to Hamlet are striking.

There are finally too many "ambiguities" for us to trust Melville's control of his own theme. *Pierre* seems an incoherent nightmare in comparison to *Moby Dick*, but the spiritual courage of its agonizing questions reminds us of the exploratory vision of his masterpiece.

THE PILGRIMAGE OF CHARLEMAGNE

Type of work: Poem
Author: Unknown
Type of plot: Heroic legend
Time of plot: c. 800
Locale: Paris, Jerusalem, Constantinople
First transcribed: c. 1100

This medieval legend, developed through countless retellings by jongleurs and preserved in a single extant manuscript, is written in 870 Alexandrine lines of verse. The most notable feature of the narrative is the bragging session engaged in by Charlemagne and his twelve peers while they are guests of Emperor Hugo of Constantinople; overheard by one of Hugo's spies, the men are called upon to make good their boasts. When they succeed in doing so, the Emperor becomes Charlemagne's vassal.

Some modern scholars have claimed that medieval writers were deficient in imagination and thus unable to create plots, that instead they depended upon historical events to provide their stories. Charlemagne's journey to Jerusalem, a complete fabrication, is a literary work which clearly demonstrates that heroic legends as embodied in medieval romances did not, and did not need to, rely on historical events. Charlemagne never went to Jerusalem. In fact, the closest he came to Jerusalem was when the Patriarch of Jerusalem sent him the keys to the city and to the Holy Sepulcher as a reward for his generous support of Christian churches in the Holy Land. But he never literally used the keys. Charlemagne's imaginary pilgrimage to Jerusalem thus indicates that medieval writers were able to combine real persons with fantasized events to create original literature of a kind which would now be likened to a historical novel.

The source of this tale is alleged to have been the Abbey of St. Denis, which claimed to possess a number of holy relics brought back by Charlemagne from the Holy Land. The best known of these putative relics was the Crown of Thorns. However, the skeptical eye of modern scholarship credits missionary zeal at least, and venality at most, for the well-spring of this tale of Charlemagne's pilgrimage.

As for the vanity, the arrogance, the braggadocio of Charlemagne's spurious exploits, such actions undoubtedly create a reasonable counter-balance for the more respectful histories and legends depicting Charlemagne as a pious, noble, and high-minded leader of men. When Charlemagne is portrayed as threatened by the possibility that Emperor Hugo was more handsome than he, for example, Charlemagne becomes less imperial and more human. And while such impertinent questions were certainly never raised in Charlemagne's authoritarian times, the freer atmosphere of the High Middle Ages—sometimes characterized as "The Renaissance of the Twelfth Century," during

which time this poem appears to have been written—would surely have toler-
ated such irreverence. Thus, the earthy tale of Charlemagne's imagined trip
to Jerusalem suggests but another facet of Charlemagne's undoubtedly multi-
faceted personality, however fanciful the depiction may be.

THE PILGRIM'S PROGRESS

Type of work: Novel
Author: John Bunyan (1628-1688)
Type of plot: Religious allegory
Time of plot: Any time since Christ
Locale: Anywhere
First published: 1678

One of the most widely read books in English literature, The Pilgrim's Progress *is a prose allegory relating the journey and adventures of Christian, who flees the City of Destruction and sets out for the Celestial City. Since Bunyan, a devout Puritan, wished his book to be accessible to the common people, he wrote in a straightforward, unadorned prose that has simple grandeur and nobility appropriate to its subject matter. Much of the success of* The Pilgrim's Progress *is also due to its vivid characterizations, which come alive as real people rather than merely one-dimensional symbols.*

The seventeenth century was an age of literary outpouring. Shakespeare reached his mature heights with *Hamlet* and *The Tempest* early in the century; it was the great age of Jacobean drama, the century of the flowering of the sonnet and of Renaissance lyric poetry. Squarely in the middle of the literary products of this humanistic age—the high-water-mark in some respects of humanistic philosophy, with its belief in the importance of man and of man's interests—appeared John Bunyan's *The Pilgrim's Progress.*

The Pilgrim's Progress reaches back to medieval literature for its dream-vision form; Bunyan's narrator goes to sleep and dreams his fable of the Christian religion. Bunyan's "novel" is a classic example of the multi-faceted literary face of the century, reflecting as it does the popularity of the conversion story during the time; but, more significantly, it shows with much skill one of the most attractive qualities of the age, for Bunyan draws on his humanist contemporaries and their techniques to make his tale of the salvation of a soul one of the unique masterpieces of English literature.

The Pilgrim's Progress is in fact unique. It is usually classified as a novel, but according to traditional definitions of the novel genre, *The Pilgrim's Progress* is decidedly too predestined in the outcome of its plot to make it engaging, as a novel should be.

In fact, it is Bunyan's literary genius which endowed the book with classic appeal. The success of *The Pilgrim's Progress,* as distinguished from the countless other stories of personal salvation which were written at about the same time, is its ability to show the Christian experience through Christian the character's eyes. By making all the pitfalls, the specters of doubt and fear, and the religious terror that Christian experiences real to this believable, impressionable narrator, Bunyan makes them just as real to his reader. Hence, the reader of the book is really not any more sure than Christian that his salvation is assured. Bunyan has struck a true and profound element of Christianity through his use of the humanistic technique of viewing events through the eyes of his narrator.

Christian is a gullible, hence believable, character. He understands, perhaps too well for his own soul's well-being, the doubts and terrors that plague the would-be good Christian. His comments on "Little-faith," for example, amply illustrate this characteristic. Christian, like a good humanist, understands "Little-faith's" loss of faith under dire and trying conditions:

> Grief! ay, a grief indeed. Would it not have been so to any of us, had we been used as he, to be robbed, and wounded too, and that in a strange place, as he was? It is a wonder he did not die with grief, poor heart! I was told that he scattered almost all the rest of the way with nothing but doleful and bitter complaints; telling also to all that overtook him, or that he overtook in the way as he went, where he was robbed, and how; who they were that did it, and what he lost; how he was wounded, and that he hardly escaped with his life.

Christian himself suffers through his commitment to his faith. His journey is a test of endurance; the "straight-and-narrow path" is not necessarily filled with rejoicing, as Bunyan shows us, for example, in the scene of the "river of God," also called the "river of the water of life":

> Now, I beheld in my dream, that they had not journeyed far, but the river and the way for a time parted; at which they were not a little sorry; yet they durst not go out of the way. Now the way from the river was rough, and their feet tender, by reason of their travels; *so the souls of the pilgrims were much discouraged because of the way.*

In this instance Christian and his companion traveler Hopeful find a meadow paralleling their way, and an inviting stile to help them cross the fence. So they choose the easier path. After awhile, it becomes pitch dark, and they lose their way. To make matters worse, a traveler ahead of them falls into a pit, and is "dashed in pieces with his fall." Christian and Hopeful, rushing to the pit, hear only groans. The two of them repent, and muster courage to return to the river. By now the waters have risen greatly, adding to their dangers. "Yet they adventured to go back, but it was so dark, and the flood was so high, that in their going back they had like to have been drowned nine or ten times." These are the perils and dangers of trying to be a Christian in the world. With a stroke of genius Bunyan turns what could be a dry, pessimistic sermon into high adventure.

Bunyan himself seemed most productive in his own life when under duress. *The Pilgrim's Progress* was begun and largely written during prison terms Bunyan served for preaching without a license. A Baptist minister, he was a religious outlaw after the Restoration restored the Church of England, but refused to stop preaching. Originally arrested in 1660 and sentenced to three months, he eventually served twelve years because he continued to preach. He wrote his autobiography, *Grace Abounding to the Chief of Sinners,* during these years.

In *Grace Abounding to the Chief of Sinners,* Bunyan reveals that he considers himself to be a chief sinner, and he relates the experiences of his dissolute youth and as a reckless member of the parliamentary army for three years beginning when he was sixteen. Thus, we assume that Christian's trials in *The Pilgrim's Progress* originated in real life with a man who knew temptation.

The Pilgrim's Progress has been translated into more than one hundred languages over the centuries, and the simple story seems to continue to have appeal. It combines Biblical language and the subject of simple folk in a combination that brings popularity. Bunyan's ability to draw pictures with words, too, has no doubt aided the novel's classic success. One critic has noted that Bunyan seems to have thought in pictures. In this way Bunyan heightens the dramatic effect of his story, for example, with the picture of Christian opening the book at the beginning of the dream, reading, weeping, and asking "What shall I do?" The effect is tableau.

Bunyan himself was apparently a simple man, or at any rate, had a keen sense of priorities about his life. In his autobiography, for example, he does not name his father or mother, and he hardly mentions such ordinary points in time as his birthplace or home. *Grace Abounding to the Chief of Sinners* tends to emphasize Bunyan's own personal conflicts, while playing down other people in his life. Bunyan understood well what was real to him, and it is this sense of realism which has made *The Pilgrim's Progress* a classic. *The Pilgrim's Progress* is thoroughly convincing in describing the momentousness of Christian's experiences. Bunyan's ability to convey with a sense of realism this significance endows the novel with the enduring quality of being able to strike a note of universality among the millions who read the book.

Jean G. Marlowe

THE PILLARS OF SOCIETY

Type of work: Drama
Author: Henrik Ibsen (1828-1906)
Type of plot: Psychological realism
Time of plot: Nineteenth century
Locale: Norwegian seaport
First presented: 1877

Important because this is the first of Ibsen's plays in which he set the pattern of realism and social-oriented thematic concerns, The Pillars of Society *tells the story of a town leader's fall into corruption and dishonesty. The plot, complicated and unwieldy at times and almost too mechanical in arrangement and solution, has a contrived happy ending in which Bernick repents, makes a public confession of his guilt, and begins a reformed life based on truth.*

Measured against such Ibsen masterpieces of social realism as *A Doll's House* (1879), *Ghosts* (1881), and *The Wild Duck* (1884), *The Pillars of Society* is obviously an inferior work. But it was the drama in which he first committed himself to the realistic form and is, therefore, crucial to an understanding and appreciation of Ibsen's theater.

The Pillars of Society contains in embryo most of the major subjects, themes, and character types that were to dominate Ibsen's plays over the succeeding dozen years. There are three obvious concerns in *The Pillars of Society* that became central to his realistic dramas: the nature and powers of "society," the relationship between exceptional individuals and that society, and the manner in which suppressed corruption in the past inevitably surfaces to destroy present success.

Nineteenth century middle-class Norwegian society was, to Ibsen, hypocritical, materialistic, stifling, and essentially corrupt. The alliance between narrow religious moralism, with its emphasis on sin, guilt, and rigidly controlled behavior, and selfish business interests, with their respectable façade that concealed the greedy exploitation of the many by the few, had resulted in a society that corrupts or stifles all evidences of creativity or imagination.

The exceptional individual has one of two choices: involvement or rejection. If he accepts the community's mores and practices, he will inevitably be corrupted; if he rejects them, social ostracism and condemnation are the necessary consequences. Karsten Bernick accepted the values and exploited them in his drive for money, power, and respectability.

For the nonconformist, social isolation is the only option—if the individual is strong enough to make the break. Lona Hessel has the requisite determination and imparts enough of it to Johan Tönnesen to enable them both to flee the country. But the price of such a divorce from their roots is great and the impulse to return and find some sort of "compromise," with all its dangers of contamination, is very strong.

In addition to presenting the pervasive atmosphere of inhibition and hypocrisy, Ibsen usually structures his realistic social plays on specific examples of concealed corruption. Karsten Bernick has based his public image, his business success, and his marriage on a lie when, as a young man, he enticed his fiancée's brother, Johan Tönnesen, into taking the blame for his illicit love affair, then later blamed him for the "theft" of the "Bernick family fortune." In Ibsen's view, however, nothing can be successfully founded on a lie. Bernick's affair with Mrs. Dorf and the subsequent voluntary disgrace of Johan necessarily tempt Bernick to expand the lie to cover his company's financial insolvency: to abandon the woman he really loves in favor of a financially advantageous match; to commit conscious fraud; and finally, to attempt murder. In *The Pillars of Society,* as in other plays, it is a figure out of the past, Lona Hessel, who crystalizes these pressures and forces the revelation.

In spite of the complexities and ambiguities that Ibsen explores in *The Pillars of Society,* he supplies a conventional "happy ending." This final victory of optimism over dramatic logic is one of the signs that this play stands at the beginning of Ibsen's mature career. But if the story is more contrived, the characters more manipulated, and the themes more boldly stated than in Ibsen's subsequent masterpieces, all of the ingredients are present in *The Pillars of Society* that make it the essential play in Ibsen's transition from an impressive, but traditional, nineteenth century playwright to his historical role as "the father of modern drama."

THE PILOT

Type of work: Novel
Author: James Fenimore Cooper (1789-1851)
Type of plot: Historical romance
Time of plot: Revolutionary War
Locale: Northeastern coast of England
First published: 1823

For the technical material of this story, the first genuine sea novel, Cooper drew upon his six years of experience in the United States Navy. While the pilot of the title is never named, he is generally understood to be John Paul Jones.

The Pilot is a novel that combines military adventure, a certain romantic interest, and a political analysis within the confines of a particular historical era. The mixture is not always successful, but aspects of *The Pilot* remain interesting both as literature and political argument.

Cooper said that *The Pilot* was originally conceived as a sea novel, one which would be accurate in its details of naval life and strategy. One way that Cooper demonstrated his expertise was in the multitude and variety of the technical terms he uses. This terminology is so pervasive in *The Pilot* that much of the action, especially during sea battles, is nearly incomprehensible. On the other hand, this mystification (resembling the "wood lore" of the *Leatherstocking* series) does work to make the pilot himself, the hero of the novel, appear superhuman. The reader, to whom much of the terminology remains inaccessible, can only marvel at the skill and knowledge of Cooper's hero who not only defeats the enemy in several battles but stands above the other officers (such as Griffith) in sea-faring skill.

In *The Pilot* Cooper claims to have drawn his characters according to "palpable nature," without reference to unknown or metaphysical qualities. This intention, though undoubtedly sincere (and a reaction against the excesses of romantic fiction), is not carried out in practice in regard to the pilot himself who, the reader is meant to understand, embodies the ideal qualities of a leader. For example, the pilot is calm even under the most severe stress. Cooper opens the novel with Mr. Gray extricating the ship from a severe storm. Everyone else is terrified, and with good reason it appears, but the pilot is completely steady, absolutely unafraid.

Furthermore, when the pilot gives an order the crew obeys as if he were the commander. Cooper describes this obedience in almost mystical terms. The pilot is able to impose discipline when no one else can. So Cooper's intention to describe his characters only according to "palpable nature" is subordinated to the need he felt for portraying an authentic leader, hero, and warrior. This need flows from the political intent of the work. *The Pilot* raises a political question that was important in Cooper's own life and, more significantly, was critical during the Revolutionary War. The issue was one of loyalty.

The Pilot is a novel centered on characters torn between conflicting loyalties. When the War for Independence began, men and women in the colonies were faced with a clear choice. Those Americans who remained loyal to England were disloyal to the emerging nation. Those who fought on the side of the revolution were accused of treason. This accusation is, for example, repeated frequently by Colonel Howard and his supporters against the rebels.

To answer this charge it was necessary for Cooper to show both that a noble conception of loyalty was maintained by the Americans and that there were leaders among the rebels, wise, cool-headed and selfless, who could inspire genuine loyalty. It was to fill this requierment that Gray is described by Cooper as an authentic leader and hero and, most of all, is defended against the charge of treason. (John Paul Jones, born in Scotland, served in the English merchant marine before emigrating to America.) Treason and loyalty, then, cease being absolute terms, as Colonel Howard argues, and become politically relative.

It is in the romantic threads of the novel that Cooper attempts to show the divisions of loyalty, and the relative nature of the term, in its sharpest and most dramatic form. Alice Dunscombe is an old friend and sweetheart of Gray. But she was born in England and, unlike Gray, has remained passionately loyal to the land of her birth.

The two are united in the friendship of the past and, indeed, in their current feelings for each other. At the same time, they are divided by conflicting political loyalties. Thus, the reader is asked to judge the political beliefs and feelings of characters not in absolute terms but in historical terms. Cooper wants these characters understood as they understand themselves; so, although we may tend to sympathize with the views of the one rather than the other, we are still able to feel sympathy for each as a person.

The villain in The Pilot is Christopher Dillon; and Dillon's villainy lies not in his loyalty to England and to Colonel Howard, but in his cowardice and opportunism. He is to be judged, then, in his own terms. How sincere is he in his own beliefs? How willing is he to die for them? How honest as a man and gentleman is he?

Thus Mr. Gray, or John Paul Jones, has not committed treason precisely because he is loyal to his own beliefs; and he is not dishonest or cowardly— because he openly defends what he believes. Of course the content of these beliefs is another matter. As characters like Alice and Colonel Howard debate with the Americans, two distinct political positions emerge. On the one hand, the Colonel supports a notion of loyalty based on birth and on the established social and political order. Disruption of that order, he argues, leads to nothing but misery and bloodshed. The Americans answer that loyalty can only be freely and consciously given. Theirs is a romantic view, derived from the theory of social contract, a theory which states that political society is based only upon the agreement of each of its members to participate. Hence the Americans argue that they are loyal only to liberty and, furthermore, that liberty is a necessary condition for genuine loyalty. Cooper does capture the political arguments raging during the Revolutionary War. He not only expresses these arguments in terms of conflicting loyalties but penetrates the political assumptions behind the labels.

However, *The Pilot* also suffers from a weakness common to many novels that attempt to explore the political reality within a historical conflict. This weakness is especially evident in Cooper's big scenes (those scenes, for example, between Alice Dunscombe and John Paul Jones) where there is a tendency for characters to make speeches to the reader rather than to talk with one another. In other words, the ideas are expressed verbally rather than through dramatic action.

In *The Pilot* Cooper faced the double necessity of creating a hero—which he could only accomplish through action at sea—and, at the same time, of exploring the historical and political motives of that hero. The shape of *The Pilot,* and its strengths and weaknesses as a novel, flow from Cooper's attempt to resolve this difficulty.

Howard Lee Hertz

THE PIONEERS

Type of work: Novel
Author: James Fenimore Cooper (1789-1851)
Type of plot: Historical romance
Time of plot: 1793
Locale: New York State
First published: 1823

The Pioneers, *the first of the Leatherstocking Tales, is a romantic story of life in Upstate New York ten years after the Revolutionary War. The novel is filled with scenes of hunting and trapping life, and the description of Templeton is based upon the author's memories of his boyhood home of Cooperstown. The portrayal of Natty Bumppo and Indian John point to the tragedy of frontiersmen and Indians in a rapidly disappearing West.*

When the whole Leatherstocking series was published together in 1850, *The Pioneers,* originally the first, became the fourth title. In writing *The Pioneers,* Cooper did not plan it as the first of a series with a continuing hero. Thus, Natty Bumppo—with his skinny face, scraggy neck, enormous mouth, and single yellowed tusk—contrasts sharply with the romantic character that Leatherstocking was to become in Cooper's later portrayals of him as Hawkeye, Pathfinder, and Deerslayer. Yet his skill with a rifle, his knowledge of and love for the wilderness, his loyalty to Indian John Mohegan, and his independence in speaking his mind and asserting what he believes to be his rights all foreshadow the heroic frontiersman who was to reappear in the later tales.

The Pioneers is only in part a romance of the forest. It is largely a novel of manners in which Cooper contrasts the wilderness life of Leatherstocking and old Indian John with the village life of Templeton. Cooper is sympathetic toward the aging Leatherstocking (he is over seventy), who resents having to submit to a law which prohibits his killing a deer whenever he needs one. But the natural law of survival has come into conflict with the village social law which is necessary as increasing numbers of settlers fill up the land. Leatherstocking represents a way of life that is passing. The frontiersman prepares the way for settlement of wilderness territory. He then must bow to social laws or move farther into the wilderness in order to keep the natural freedom he treasures. If he chooses this latter course, he is only continuing a process of which he has already been a part. That Cooper did not disapprove of the eventual settlement, moving ever westward, of the land, the final sentence of *The Pioneers* makes clear: "He had gone far towards the setting sun,—the foremost in that band of Pioneers, who are opening the way for the march of our nation across the continent."

THE PIRATES OF PENZANCE

Type of work: Comic opera
Author: W. S. Gilbert (1836-1911)
Type of plot: Humorous romance
Time of plot: Nineteenth century
Locale: England
First presented: 1879

This perennial Gilbert and Sullivan favorite follows the antics of a band of pirates, a bevy of beautiful maidens, and an unforgettable Major General. The plot is built upon a hard-of-hearing nursemaid's mistake when she was given charge of a newborn infant: she heard "pirate" when she was instructed to apprentice the boy to a "pilot."

The Pirates of Penzance is the fourth major collaboration between W. S. Gilbert and the composer Arthur Sullivan. While Sullivan composed a number of serious operas and oratorios, along with a number of favorite hymns ("Onward! Christian Soldiers"), he is best remembered for his work with Gilbert, who provided a series of plays combining romance with social satire and parody of the conventional forms of Victorian theater. The texts lend themselves as well to musical parody of the Italian romantic operas of Donizetti, Bellini, and Verdi which were then in fashion. On the basis of the extraordinary success of these works, the team's theater manager, Richard D'Oyly Carte, was able to build the Savoy Theatre, which became a permanent home for the Gilbert and Sullivan operas.

The majority of these comic operas treat English subjects—the Royal Navy in *H.M.S. Pinafore,* which immediately preceded *The Pirates of Penzance,* and both the army and the police in *The Pirates of Penzance.* Sullivan said that he was inspired by the police chorus he had once used as a church organist. The figure of Stanley, "The Very Model of a Modern Major-General," is one of the more memorable creations, as is the police chorus with its famous lament, "When constabulary duty's to be done . . . A policeman's lot is not a happy one." The story almost perfectly fits Gilbert's description of the ideal plot, as a picturesque story presented in a vein of mock heroic seriousness. It gives opportunity for sentimental love ballads, the famous Gilbert and Sullivan patter-songs, and light-hearted spoofs of Victorian social convention. The plot, which hangs on such whimsy as a confusion between "Pilot" and "Pirate," and a birth on leap year day, is typical of the form, which, while linked to European prototypes, is the first indigenous English musical theater of significance since the Restoration period.

THE PIT

Type of work: Novel
Author: Frank Norris (1870-1902)
Type of plot: Naturalism
Time of plot: 1890's
Locale: Chicago
First published: 1903

This second and last novel of a planned trilogy on the wheat trade tells how wheat is bought and sold on the Board of Trade in Chicago. The Pit has the dual interest of an exciting and realistic account of how one man for a time cornered the world's wheat market, and the moving love story of two strong but very human characters.

Scientific theories and economic realities have often influenced a writer's assumptions and style. As a case in point, the biological and economic determinism popular in the late nineteenth century shaped the literary theory of naturalism which Émile Zola popularized in Europe. Stephen Crane, the first native proponent of this genre, introduced American readers to the forms of naturalism during the early 1890's, and was soon followed by Jack London, Theodore Dreiser, Frank Norris, and others. Ideally, the author employing the techniques of naturalism would have to deal with four implicitly antagonistic elements—frankness, objectivity, determinism, and fatalism. As with a scientific theory in the hands and heads of subjective human observers, naturalism often succumbed to a not-so-subtle moralism.

One of the most promising American followers of Zola, Frank Norris died a young man. His fame as a novelist had been secured by the publication of *McTeague* in 1899, and the brilliance of his career grew more intense with the appearance of *The Octopus* in 1901. The latter title was the first volume of Norris' intended Epic of the Wheat trilogy. *The Octopus* dealt with the production of wheat, while *The Pit* described the marketing of the grain, and the final, unwritten volume, *The Wolf,* was to have covered the consumption of wheat.

Like his mentor Zola, Norris depicts large, dramatic scenes, such as the vast expanses of the San Joaquin Valley in California, or the tumult on the floor of the Chicago Grain Exchange. These vivid scenes testify to the nation's fertile soil, a hard-working populace, the technological imagination of inventors, and the organizational flair of entrepreneurs. Considering the menacing determinism in the titles of Norris' books, it becomes evident that the human and social potential of the growing nation is countered by the fatalism of the life-cycle analogy, and the realities of the victors and the vanquished syndrome.

James and Howells were abandoned; Norris and his colleagues became the literary spokesmen of the Populists, and the vanguard of the muckrakers.

Norris sensed the passing of the old America, the land of warmth, community, and lasting personal relationships. He was eager to humanize the new emerging America that had been altered by the impersonal forces of urbanization, and controlled by unsavory business tactics. To others, the decline of the genteel tradition signaled the passing of the great race, and the entrance of mass culture. To Norris, both the individual and the masses were at the mercy of society, and its fixed patterns. Norris' voice was the voice of a generation, like many before, bewildered and adrift. He opposed the basic premise of a society without a core, a society in which the acquisition of money became a sanctified goal. The ideal of objectivity would have been difficult to achieve.

Zola bequeathed objectivity to naturalism, and Norris wrestled with its thin edge. *The Pit,* like its predecessor *The Octopus,* was a propaganda novel, but not a cheap diatribe. As an ethical person, Norris could not detach himself from the unethical values and practices of his society, but he could condemn them. He was candid in his descriptions of the undesirable changes that had taken place. A deterministic universe worked out its inexorable process through the activities that took place on the floor of the Chicago Grain Exchange. As if the occupants of that great building were a nation-wide audience viewing a play in its bowels, the pit, the Jadwins of the world rise and fall, just as they had throughout recorded history. Norris' characters were the microcosm of the larger society.

To be sure, there was some destruction of character in the principal personages in *The Pit,* but their demise represents something much larger than the individual. The acquisition of fortunes had its shortcomings. The new leisure class, the Curtis and Laura Jadwins of America, often discovered too late that wealth did not always improve the quality of life.

Chicago was an ideal location for the story. There one could find almost everything that money could buy. Chicago had become the clearing house for Western America, a mecca for would-be financiers, meat-packing tycoons, and grain gamblers. This was the raw, yet dynamic city that would later inspire Sandburg. At one time Jadwin gave up his speculating, but the addiction was too strong; eventually it nearly killed him. Such was the charisma of the city, of its seemingly infinite potential for success. Many had perished before Jadwin; tragedy was timeless and inevitable.

With the opening pages, the reader is presented with the inside story about the "pit." Anxiously waiting for the opening act of an opera, and the prestigious patrons, Laura hears of a man's failure to dominate the corn market. So, even prior to her introduction to Curtis Jadwin, Laura is acquainted with disaster, with the cruelties of the market. Yet, she is drawn to the men who speculate. She admires their social position, and envies their luxury-filled lives. Laura looks to the future as if nothing inopportune could possibly happen. She would not always face life with such naïveté.

Jadwin's friend Cressler had been lured back into wheat speculation, and he lost everything. Cressler committed suicide, leaving a widow, and Jadwin felt responsible for his death since it was Jadwin's attempt to corner the wheat market that caused Cressler to lose all his money.

Jadwin's efforts to corner the market could have been successful, but fate stepped in and, through nature, destroyed his plans: at a critical time a bumper crop flooded the market with millions of extra bushels of wheat— far more than Jadwin could buy to hold his position. He had tested luck once too often and now, overnight, was ruined financially and broken in health and spirit. In nursing her husband back to health, Laura asserted her strength as an individual and demonstrated her love for Curtis.

While the conclusion was tragic, it was not without optimistic innuendo. The Jadwins lost everything they thought life had to offer, but they had a future. They had each other's love for the first time in years. In possession of one of life's most simple common denominators, marriage, Curtis and Laura left Chicago, and with new hope moved to the West, probably to California. It was in California that Norris resided, and there naturalism most productively took root, and where the endless struggle of the individual against economic forces, as *The Octopus* proclaimed, was well under way.

Eric H. Christianson

THE PLAGUE

Type of work: Novel
Author: Albert Camus (1913-1960)
Type of plot: Impressionistic realism
Time of plot: The 1940's
Locale: Oran, Algeria
First published: 1947

In The Plague, *Camus places his characters in a scene of widespread death and horror in order to follow their responses and record their answers to the age-old question, "Why are we here?" As the bubonic plague sweeps through an Algerian port town, Camus focuses on the mind of a doctor, Bernard Rieux, whose decision in the face of hopeless calamity is to at least do what he can to alleviate human suffering for a few moments, and to continue to hope for the possibility of future joy.*

In the decade and a half that followed the end of World War II, as the West strived to repair the physical, psychic, and spiritual damage wrought by that holocaust, the voice of Albert Camus, with its reasoned yet passionate affirmation of human dignity in the face of an "absurd" universe—an absurdity made palpable by the Nazi horror—was one of the major artistic, philosophical, and moral sources of strength and direction.

The Plague (La Peste) is the most thorough fictional presentation of Camus' mature thinking. In earlier works—notably the play *Caligula* (1938), the novel *The Stranger* (1942), and the essay *"The Myth of Sisyphus"* (1942)—Camus articulated his concept of the "absurd." Man is "absurd" because he has neither metaphysical justification nor essential connection to the universe. He is part of no divine scheme and, since he is mortal, all of his actions, individual and collective, eventually come to nothing. The only question, then, is how can man deal with his absurdity?

Camus' answer lies in his concept of "revolt." Man "revolts" against his condition first by understanding it and then, in the face of his cosmic meaninglessness, creating his own human meanings. In the previously mentioned works Camus explored the problem in terms of the individual; in *The Plague* Camus extends his moral and philosophical analysis to the question of man as a social creature. What, Camus asks, in the face of an absurd universe, is man's relationship to, and responsibility for, his fellow man?

The paradox that lies at the center of Camus' "revolt" concept is that of heroic futility. One struggles in spite of—even because of—the fact that, ultimately, one must lose. If the idea of the absurd denies man's cosmic meaning, it affirms his common bond. Since all men must die, all men are brothers. Mutual coöperation, not self-indulgence, is the logical ethic that Camus derives from his absurd perspective. To give an artistic shape to these convictions, Camus chooses a "plague" as an appropriate metaphor for the human condition, since it intensifies this awareness of man's mortality and makes the common bond especially clear.

Camus carefully divides the novel into five parts which correspond to the progression of the pestilence. Parts I and V show life before the plague's onslaught and after its subsidence. Parts II and IV concentrate on the details of communal and personal suffering and, in particular, on the activities and reactions of the main characters as they do battle with the disease. Part III, the climax of the book, shows the epidemic at its height and the community reduced to a single collective entity, where time has stopped, personal distinctions are lost, and suffering and despair have become routine.

The story is narrated by Dr. Bernard Rieux, who waits until almost the end of the novel to identify himself, in a factual, impersonal, almost documentary style. His account is occasionally supplemented by extracts from the journal of Jean Tarrou, but these intrusions, while more subjective and colorful, are characterized by a running irony that also keeps the reader at a distance. Both narratives, however, are juxtaposed against vivid, emotionally charged scenes. This continual movement back and forth between narrative austerity and dramatic immediacy, and from lucid analysis to emotional conflict, gives *The Plague* much of its depth and impact.

Three of the principal characters—Rieux, Tarrou, and the clerk Joseph Grand—accept their obligation to battle the epidemic as soon as it is identified. Rieux is probably the character who comes the closest to speaking for Camus. As a medical doctor he has devoted his life to the losing battle with disease and death and so the plague is simply an intensification of his "normal" life. From the outset he accepts the plague as a fact and fights against it with all the skill, endurance, and energy he can muster. He finds his only "certitude" in his daily round. There is no heroism involved; only the logic of the situation. And even after the plague has retreated, Rieux has no conviction that his actions had anything to do with its "defeat." Yet Rieux learns much from his experience and, as the narrator, his is Camus' final word on the "meaning" of the ordeal.

Unlike Rieux, whose ideas are the practical consequence of his professional experience, Jean Tarrou first had the philosophical revelation and then shaped his life to it. Seeing his father, a prosecuting attorney, condemn a man to death, Tarrou became enraged with the inhumanity of his society and turned to revolutionary politics. But that, too, he came to realize, inevitably involved him in "condemning" others to death. Thus, he felt infected with the "plague"—defined as whatever destroys human life—long before coming to Oran and it has reduced him to a purposeless life colored only by the ironical observations he jots down in his journal. When the plague arrives he quickly and eagerly organizes the "sanitation squads"; the crisis gives him the opportunity to "side" with the "victims" of life's absurdity without fearing that his actions will inadvertently add to their misery. But such obvious, total commitments are not available under "normal" conditions and so Tarrou appropriately dies as one of the plague's last victims.

But both Rieux and Tarrou are too personally inhuman—Rieux with his "abstract" view of man, Tarrou with his desire for secular "sainthood"—to qualify as "'heroic"; the most admirable person in the book is the clerk Joseph Grand, who accepts his role in the plague automatically, needing neither professional nor philosophical justifications, simply because "people must help each other." His greater humanity is further demonstrated by the fact that, while carrying out his commitment to the victims of the plague, he continues to show active grief over the loss of his wife and tenaciously "revolts" in his artistic attempt to write the perfect novel (even though he cannot manage the "perfect" first sentence).

Among the other principal characters, the journalist Raymond Rambert opts for "personal happiness"; Father Paneloux presents the "Christian" reaction to the pestilence; and Cottard acts out the role of the "criminal."

Caught in Oran by accident when the plague breaks out, Rambert turns his energies to escape, exhausting every means, legal and otherwise, to rejoin his wife. It is in him that the issue of "exile" or separation from loved ones is most vividly presented. For most of the novel he rejects the view that the plague imposes a social obligation on all; he insists that individual survival and personal happiness are primary. And, although Rieux is the book's principal advocate of collective responsibility, the doctor admits to Rambert that happiness is as valid an option as service. Even when Rambert finally decides to remain voluntarily and continue the fight, the issue remains ambiguous. At the end, as Rambert embraces his wife, he still wonders if he made the right moral choice.

But if Rieux accepts Rambert's "happiness" as a decent option, he does not extend that tolerance to Father Paneloux's "Christian" view of the epidemic. *The Plague* has been called the most "anti-Christian" of Camus' books and that is probably correct, although it could be argued that the ethical values advocated are essentially "Christian" ones. As a system of beliefs, however, it is clear that Christianity—at least as understood by Paneloux—is tested by the pestilence and found wanting. However, if the priest's beliefs are inadequate, his actions are heroic and it is this incongruity between his theological convictions and his existential behavior that gives his character and fate its special poignancy.

Near the beginning of the epidemic he preaches a sermon in which he proclaims that it is a manifestation of divine justice. Later in the book, after he has become one of the most active fighters against the plague and a witness to the suffering and death of numerous innocents, Paneloux's simple vision of sin and punishment is shaken. He preaches a second sermon in which he advocates a blind, total acceptance of a God who seems, from the human vantage point, to be indifferent, arbitrary, even, perhaps, evil. And thus, driven to this extreme "either/or" position, Paneloux finally dies of the plague. Significantly, he is the only victim whose body is unmarked by the disease; he has been destroyed emotionally and spiritually because his religious vision was inadequate to the challenge and he could not live without that theological justification.

The most ambiguous character of all is Cottard. As a "criminal" he has lived in a constant state of fear and "exile." Unable to endure such separation he attempts to commit suicide near the beginning of the book. Once the plague sets in and all are subjected to that same sense of fear and solitude, however, Cottard "rejoins" humanity and flourishes; the plague is his natural element. But once it dissipates and he is again faced with isolation, Cottard goes berserk.

Thus, Camus describes the various human reactions to the plague—acceptance, defiance, detachment, solitary rejection, social commitment, criminality. The only "value" of the epidemic, Rieux admits, is "educational," but the price paid for the knowledge is much too high. Nevertheless, even in the midst of the ordeal, there are moments of supreme pleasure and meaningful human connection. Shortly before the plague's last onslaught that takes Tarrou's life, he and Rieux defy regulations and go for a short swim. For a few brief moments they are at one with the elements and in natural instinctive harmony with each other. But the interlude soon ends and both men return to the struggle, Tarrou to die, Rieux to chronicle its passing. And so, he finally concludes, the only "victory" won from the plague amounts to "knowledge and memories" and the conviction that men are, on the whole, admirable.

Keith Neilson

LES PLAIDEURS

Type of work: Drama
Author: Jean Baptiste Racine (1639-1699)
Type of plot: Satiric comedy
Time of plot: Seventeenth century
Locale: Normandy, France
First presented: 1668

Departing temporarily from the genre of tragedy, Racine at first planned Les Plaideurs *as an adaptation of Aristophanes' comedy* The Wasps, *to be presented by an Italian company visiting Paris. As it turned out, however, the playwright received collaboration from a group of his friends who dined together regularly; the result was a delightfully spontaneous and airy comedy ridiculing doctors and lawyers.*

Les Plaideurs is the only comedy of Racine. It was written largely by the inspiration of contemporary quarrels and a desire of the author to mock specific contemporaries. It was at first received poorly, then very well, after people heard that the king had laughed during its presentation at court. One tradition has it that Molière (an enemy of Racine) considered it "excellent," while another tradition, more probable, stated that Molière felt the play was "worthless." In any case, it has been remarkably successful since, and is often performed.

The play mocks limited social attitudes by exaggerating them, as is common in satire. Here the judgmental compulsion of Dandin, or the need of Chicanneau and La Comtesse to litigate is pushed to the point of absurdity. The exaggerated, clichéd thinking of these characters dominates the play. The relative sanity of Leandre and Isabelle is obliged to engage in the absurdities of their parents in order to assure their marriage. But it is notable that there is no real reconciliation, merely a successful adaptation and manipulation by the young couple. The two servants, Petit Jean and L'Intime, are, for the most part, merely bantied about by their masters' foolishness.

There is very little psychological depth to the characters. Leandre and Isabelle have, at least, two concerns—their love, and dealing with their parents. But Dandin's compulsive judging and the litigiousness of Chicanneau and La Comtesse are so cut off from complex motives as to seem self-generated, and therefore all the more ridiculous. La Comtesse, who has received a pension which forbids her further litigating, complains, "But to live without litigating, is that happiness?" This lack of depth creates a great "aesthetic distance." What might be seen as viciousness, were it connected to deeper motives, passes for mere foolishness.

As Henry Fielding says in his preface to *Joseph Andrews* (1742), satire derives from highlighting the one-sidedness of the victim's views of things. This play is perhaps a classic example of such a strategy because the three victims convert all experience into an instance of litigation with the same restless and absurd energy of the keystone cop. Mechanically, and delightfully, they pursue the mere physical object on a delightful and wild chase.

THE PLAIN DEALER

Type of work: Drama
Author: William Wycherley (1640?-1716)
Type of plot: Comedy of manners
Time of plot: Seventeenth century
Locale: London
First presented: c. 1674

Regarded in Wycherley's own time as his best play, The Plain Dealer *is a sardonic picture of life during the reign of Charles II, and moves in scene from booksellers' stalls to eating houses to private homes to Westminster Hall. All the characters except Manly and his page are presented as grasping, litigious, or belligerent types, or, like the two sailors, as mere simpletons. Manly is as set in his cynicism about mankind as any of Molière's or Marston's misanthropes.*

Wycherley's final play, *The Plain Dealer,* signaled a change in the mode of late-Restoration comedy. Unlike the sophisticated, witty comedies of Sir George Etherege and his own early mannered plays, *The Plain Dealer* is a sharp, mordant satire upon false wit. Wycherley's railing, bitter, misanthropic tone greatly influenced the exaggerated style of Crowne, Lee, Otway, and other lesser writers. By critics of the nineteenth century, most notably Macaulay, Wycherley was considered a libertine playwright whose indecent morality, judged by the conduct of Manly, rendered his drama repugnant for serious investigation. Among early twentieth century critics of Restoration comedy, Montague Summers offered a contrary point of view. Summers regarded *The Plain Dealer* as a moral satire; he also regarded Manly as the representative of Wycherley, but he noted how the hero's invective is directed at the prime evils of the age: hypocrisy, materialism, vice. The judgment of more recent scholars, who have carefully studied seventeenth century social conventions, has tended to reject Summers' view of the comedy as a moral satire, just as modern criticism has rejected the stuffy Victorian prejudices concerning the play's supposed immorality. Rather, most Wycherley scholars consider *The Plain Dealer* as a satire upon false wit (that is, foolish judgment); as a comedy of manners, the play demonstrates that naturalness, not artifice, is the proper mode of fashion.

For Wycherley, as for his contemporaries, the touchstone of wit is not mere cleverness, although spontaneity, freshness, and pungency are, to be sure, important signs of wit; rather, sound judgment is the practical test that separates a would-be from a true wit, a coxcomb from a gallant. To this convention, Wycherley insists upon the addition of naturalness—truth to reality—as a necessary part of wit. In *The Plain Dealer* Manly, the protagonist, is the major test for the author's theory of wit; but he is not, as some critics have asserted, either the mouthpiece for the author or the perfect model for his type of wit. Rather, until the conclusion of the play, Manly is deficient in judgment. He has mistaken the pretense of loving for real love, the affectation of friendship for truth. Olivia, his faithless lover, is quite correct in her cynical view of him: "he that distrusts most the world, trusts most to himself, and is but the more easily deceived, because he thinks he can't be deceived." Olivia puts her finger on the chief flaw in Manly—his vanity. Because he rebukes so heartily the evils of the world, he cannot believe that he himself can be guilty of the same evils. Yet Olivia is right when she says, "I knew he loved his own singular moroseness so well, as to dote upon any copy of it. . . ." By imitating the image of moroseness (sullenness) in Manly, Olivia and Vernish easily deceive him. His judgment is flawed because of vanity: that plain dealing—sincerity—makes a person whole, though all the rest of the world may lack integrity.

Yet in his satire on false wit, Wycherley makes the point clear that at least some people in the world possess integrity, in spite of the fact that they neglect to rail, as Manly does, against society. Fidelia is true to Manly, even though he mistreats her when she is disguised as a man. To be sure, she is a stock theatrical figure, quite wooden and lacking in human responses, except perhaps when she is threatened with Vernish's rape. A more convincing character is Freeman, a "complier with the age," who is nevertheless a friend to Manly, outspoken but not candid to the extent of injuring his own fortunes or humiliating fools. Although he cheats the Widow Blackacre out of £300 a year, he shows her some slight generosity, when he has power over her, in settling for money instead of marriage. For a widow with property, as she says, "Matrimony . . . is worse than excommunication, in depriving her of the benefit of the laws. . . ." Freeman is not perfect, as Manly wishes to be, and prefers to live with people, despite their faults, rather than condemn them as rascals. The chief model for tempered wit in the play is Eliza, a minor character so far as the action is concerned yet always an example of good judgment. Eliza is neither cozened by Olivia's fine speeches nor by her actions: she clearly judges, with wit, honesty, and amused detachment. A good test of her mettle is her conversation with Olivia concerning *The Country Wife,* Wycherley's third and most vigorous play, a cuckolding comedy. To Olivia, the play is a "hideous obscenity," although she remembers perfectly its ribald scenes. But to Eliza the play is amusing, not obscene; with admirable tact, she says that she can "think of a goat, a bull, or satyr, without any hurt." In another scene of the play, she expresses her contempt for the ill-tempered conventions of the age: " . . . railing now is so common, that 'tis no more malice, but the fashion"; Eliza's integrity is secure, so she responds to life naturally and rejects the artificial fashions that mark the failure of wit.

Other characters of the play, however, lack true wit and are satirized as fools, coxcombs, and mean-spirited materialists. The "petulant" Widow Blackacre belongs to the last group. She is by no means a fool, but because her whole energy is expended in litigation she is an object of censure. The subplot involving the widow, Freeman, and Major Oldfox, an old fop who imagines himself a poet, is coarse but not offensive. With sharp realism, Wycherley satirizes the creatures of the law courts, schemers and cheats. Yet his satire cuts mostly at the form instead of the substance of their corruption. Similarly, the author reduces to a single facile dimension the coxcombs who surround Olivia. Novel, as his name suggests, pretends to be a wit by copying the latest fashions of decorum; but he lacks originality. Lord Plausible, a "ceremonious," flattering coxcomb, employs the old-fashioned courtesies of the previous age; he too is unoriginal. As for Jerry, the widow's son, together with the sailors from Manly's ship and assorted minor characters, they are all blockheads too simple to imitate the manners of their betters or to understand the spirit of wit.

Manly, to be sure, understands most of the conventions governing true wit, although he exaggerates railing as necessary for plain dealing. Yet the coxcomb Novel disproves the need for railing when he says: ". . . railing is satire, you know; and roaring and making a noise, humor." Novel is wrong; so is Manly, whose misanthropy drives him to excess. But Manly is capable of reformation, unlike Novel; and Wycherley's point is precisely that the imperfect hero may improve himself by learning the truth about his nature. From Fidelia, Manly learns that not all women are treacherous; from Freeman he learns to be tolerant of the imperfections of others; from his own experiences he learns the most valuable lessons—that revenge is mean-spirited and that true wit must come from true judgment. By the end of the play, having recovered both wit and judgment, Manly is able to satirize his previous folly: "I will believe there are now in the world/Good-natured friends, who are not prostitutes,/And handsome women worth to be friends. . . . "

Leslie B. Mittleman

THE PLAYBOY OF THE WESTERN WORLD

Type of work: Drama
Author: John Millington Synge (1871-1909)
Type of plot: Realistic comedy
Time of plot: Early twentieth century
Locale: County Mayo, Ireland
First presented: 1907

In this symbolic play, Synge examines how a personality is shaped by other people's responses to it. Equally important to the plot is the incredibly rich and vigorous dialogue, which rivals any since Shakespeare's. Because it supposedly contained insults to "Irish womanhood," it caused "Playboy riots" when it was presented in Dublin.

The Playboy of the Western World, John Millington Synge's last completed work, is the author's greatest play, and in many ways his most difficult to interpret. The play may be viewed as a satire of Western myths and conventions, beginning with the age-old habit in the West of cheerfully, even eagerly, extending a welcome to criminals and fugitives seeking shelter. In the romantic sphere, the play uses a comic reversal of the traditional situation of man as the sexual aggressor, instead having Christy hotly pursued and competed for by Pegeen and her rivals. Greek myths are also satirized, begining with the obvious parallel between Christy and Oedipus as patricides. In the same vein, Christy becomes a mock-heroic counterpart of Odysseus as he wanders into the Mayo village seeking refuge, and eventually crowns his conquests there by winning a mule race.

On another level, *The Playboy of the Western World* is a deeply symbolic play; its meaning revolves around the emotional and moral growth of the hero through a series of three ritual "murders" of his father. The first "murder" is a spontaneous, an unself-conscious, almost accidental act; Christy's blow is a reflex action to his father's incessant taunting and ridiculing of the young man's physical and sexual prowess. It is crucial to examine the reactions of the Irish peasants to Christy's deed: steeped in mythical, pre-intellectual concepts, they view the patricide as a necessary and admirable act. Because the violence occurred far away and reaches them only by the report of an intriguing visitor, it exists for them only as a fantasy, not as a down-to-earth, bloody deed; the murder is like another folktale in which the hero gloriously kills all obstacles in his path. Thus they lionize Christy, who as a result blossoms from a snivelling, terrified boy to a confident braggart and ladies' man.

Unfortunately, Christy's new-found stature is based on a lie, as becomes known when Old Mahon appears in the village and humiliates his son, thus necessitating the second "murder." This second act of violence, however, is essentially different from the first; faced with a threat to his self-image,

reputation, and independence, Christy now makes a conscious—and therefore moral—decision to kill his father. The qualitative difference in the two
acts is immediately reflected in the villagers' reaction to this second "murder":
they are horrified, and drag the hero off to hang him; he has grown, through
this rational and very real action, past the comprehension of their primitive
unconsciousness, and must be punished. Christy's growth is completed and
his triumph as hero complete, however, only with the third "murder." This
time the act is purely verbal and symbolic, and consists of Christy's discovery that he can order his father to do his will; in future, their relationship
will be that of "a gallant captain with his heathen slave." Thus Christy at the
end of the play has transcended the primitive stage of physical murder; he has
asserted his power by throwing off the domination of a tyrannical father,
thus reaching the full status of hero.

THE PLOUGH AND THE STARS

Type of work: Drama
Author: Sean O'Casey (1884-1964)
Type of plot: Social criticism
Time of plot: 1916
Locale: Dublin, Ireland
First presented: 1926

Set during the famous Easter Rebellion of 1916, The Plough and the Stars *deals with the desperate situation of a group of tenement dwellers for whom the dream of national independence is overshadowed by the pains of poverty. The story reflects O'Casey's Marxist belief—probably nurtured by a bitter childhood and early manhood—that the Irish would have to deal with the poverty of their own people before they could ever hope to win independence, or else they would be faced with a class war.*

The Plough and the Stars is the last of Sean O'Casey's realistic plays about the Irish Civil War and, along with *Juno and the Paycock,* represents the high point of his artistic achievement. Although it may lack the depth of characterization present in *Juno and the Paycock,* it probably has a greater theatrical impact. Juxtaposing scenes of the most intense pain and violence against moments of earthy, vital humor, O'Casey succeeds in capturing and dramatizing both the folly and the heroism of this Irish national tragedy.

The play is set during the Easter Uprising of 1916, when extremists proclaimed an Irish Republic and seized the Dublin General Post Office. A short, bloody struggle ensued and ravaged most of the city for several days before the nationalists surrendered. *The Plough and the Stars* describes the impact of these events on the inhabitants of a single tenement dwelling which, because of O'Casey's careful selection of characters and conflicts, becomes a microcosm of Dublin at war.

The play's title points to many of its themes. On the obvious level it is the flag of the Citizen Army, a leftist labor movement which was one of the two groups sponsoring the uprising. Thus, O'Casey specifically identifies himself with the radical workers rather than with the ardent nationalists. But, on a more symbolic level, the flag suggests a conflict—the "plough" *versus* "the stars"; that is, the practical realities of poverty and human relationships versus the abstract ideal of pure nationalism. While O'Casey admired the courage and dedication of the rebels, he felt that their fanatical actions at best attacked only superficial evils and at worst were suicidal, unleashing forces that destroyed not only the insurrectionists, but large numbers of innocent people caught up in the resulting violence. The ways in which impersonal, abstract ideals can destroy human relationships, a major theme in O'Casey's previous plays, reaches its fullest statement in *The Plough and the Stars.*

This theme is illustrated in the play's first act in the dispute between newlyweds Jack and Nora Clitheroe. In spite of her social and cultural pretensions, Nora is the embodiment of domesticity, valuing only her husband, her home, and her family to be. She can understand neither Jack's devotion to a political cause nor his apparent taste for the military style; she fears only his injury or death and is willing to deceive him to keep him out of combat. For his part, Jack seems deeply, if sentimentally, in love with Nora, and at times he is tempted to accede to her desires, but his commitment is too strong. He and his comrades are caught up in the fervor of the times.

O'Casey makes us wonder, however, how much of that commitment is dedication, how much is ego, and, when the fighting becomes intense, how much is fear of being thought a coward. The outcome of the domestic conflict is predictable: Jack is killed in combat and Nora, too delicate to stand the pressure, goes insane.

But others are not so weak. If O'Casey's vision does not spare those who bring havoc on themselves and their loved ones, he also pays homage to those victims who are forced by circumstance to assume the burdens. Frequently, those who seems the least promising become, under pressure, the most heroic.

Fluther Good behaves like an amiable drunk during most of the play and is quick to loot liquor stores when given the opportunity. But, when Mollser Gogan dies and Nora has her breakdown, he braves bullets and arrest to bring aid and comfort. Bessie Burgess, the lone English partisan in the tenement, seems ill-tempered and bigoted in the early parts of the play, deriding Nora and fighting constantly with Mrs. Gogan, another querulous lady. Yet, in the last act, it is Bessie who ministers to the dying Mollser and the mad Nora, finally sacrificing her life trying to shield the girl from sniper fire. And it is her rival, Mrs. Gogan, who assumes the burdens after Bessie dies.

Bessie and Mrs. Gogan, like Juno in the earlier play, represent the strength of an Ireland torn to pieces by civil war. They do what they can—and must— to keep the continuity of life intact while the men, with their abstract notions of nationalism, heroism, and manhood, destroy the fabric of society.

While the fighting rages, young Mollser dies of tuberculosis because there is no one available to help her. Mollser is O'Casey's symbol for the real Irish situation: poverty and neglect are the real evils, and until they are dealt with, the question of nationalism is largely irrelevant. As long as the Jack Clitheroes and the Brennans can be stirred up to violence by the demagogic appeals of the "Voice," these problems will continue to be ignored. But, as long as Ireland is capable of producing people like Bessie Burgess, Mrs. Gogan, and Fluther Good, O'Casey suggests that there is hope.

THE PLUMED SERPENT

Type of work: Novel
Author: D. H. Lawrence (1885-1930)
Type of plot: Symbolic romance
Time of plot: Twentieth century
Locale: Mexico
First published: 1926

Colorful in setting and symbolic in theme, The Plumed Serpent *is Lawrence's plea for a restoration of the primitive values of potency and blood unity. The symbols of quest and discovery are the ancient gods of Mexico, Quetzalcoatl and Huitzilopochtli; these dark gods alone can revitalize modern man, for Christianity has failed completely.* The Plumed Serpent *describes a world of male domination, instinctive life, and sexual rebirth.*

When literature traduces life, it must be called to account. To deny this proposition is finally to negate the moral dimension of literature and to ignore its dynamic relationship with reality. To paraphrase the eminent American critic Lionel Trilling, literature does not always tell the truth, nor necessarily the best kind of truth. Before the Romantic movement, these statements were taken as self-evident. Classical and neoclassical aesthetic theory established truth as a criterion for judging the greatness of any work. Yet in the modern age, along with the apotheosis of art and the artist, the idea that art is above and beyond moral judgments has found general acceptance. The freedom of the artist to present any ethical view without the consequences of criticism is regarded as his inalienable right. As a result, modern criticism has been emasculated, reduced to mere interpretation and left powerless to evaluate the complex literature of its own time.

The impotence of criticism is never more apparent than when confronted with the great works of the early part of this century. Faced with the radical, antidemocratic visions of Ezra Pound, T. S. Eliot, W. B. Yeats, and D. H. Lawrence, for example, it could only admire their verbal skills and formal complexities, their daring innovations and the undoubted emotional power of their art. Yet at the basis of their thought and feeling resided a clear loathing for the great mass of mankind and an admiration of political authoritarianism. In the case of Pound these feelings led him to espouse Fascism, anti-Semitism and Mussolini's cause. After World War II, he was imprisoned as a traitor by the Allies. Yeats's association with Fascism was brief and comparatively innocent; he supported the Irish rightest, O'Duffy, and his blue shirts and then quickly withdrew his advocacy. Although Eliot never aligned himself with any party, his vision of the ideal political state, articulated in *The Idea of a Christian Society,* was that of a rigid theocracy.

Lawrence's belief in the necessity of the superman, which finds its fullest and most unnerving delineation in the characters of Don Ramón and General

Cipriano in *The Plumed Serpent,* is an expression of despair in the capacity of a democratic culture to afford man a true equality and nobility. If man is to avoid cataclysm, he must, Lawrence believed, subordinate himself in order to attain spiritual well-being as Kate Leslie does to her husband Cipriano, and to the god-man, Don Ramón, and his religion of pure blood. Lawrence's thought progressed from outrage against the capitalists, who had destroyed his own coal-miner father, as well as English communal life, to the embrace of a philosophy of blood superiority. Like Thomas Carlyle, he began as a champion of individual liberty and with a plea for spiritual rebirth, and ended in fear of the people's growing power and with a call for individual subordination to an irrational, totalitarian idea.

In *The Plumed Serpent* Kate Leslie's adventures in Mexico, her spiritual reawakening, her embrace of the ancient god Quetzalcoatl, and her commitment to Don Ramón's priesthood should probably be read more as a parable than as a theological prescription. Although Lawrence did spend time in both old and New Mexico and was fascinated by the rituals and beliefs of the Indians, he found in the reincarnation of Quetzalcoatl a convenient metaphor for his vituperative attack on modern politics and Christianity. Democracy, he felt—which certainly is not the politics of the Mexico of the novel—succeeds only in "leveling downward," bringing all men to the same grayness, thus destroying individuality. Similarly, he felt Christianity, which he reinterpreted in his brilliant novella, *The Man Who Died,* destroyed the passionate inner life by denying the sanctity of the body and celebrating death.

In contrast, Don Ramón's politics and religion both elevate the individual —at the expense of the majority—and celebrate the passionate, physical life. At the beginning of the novel Kate is presented as an enlightened liberal, the widow of an Irish revolutionary, who is alienated from her own sexual needs as well as ordinary life. Her revulsion at the bull fight typifies her response to all physical reality. When she meets Cipriano, however, she begins to sense her own emptiness and feels an irrational attraction to him. Then, drawn by the seductive rhythms of the Mexican countryside and intrigued by the prophecy of Quetzalcoatl's second coming, Kate refuses to return to the United States with her cousin Owen Rhys. This decision makes her vulnerable for the first time in her life: she is prepared for conversion.

Before Kate can be granted the "light," however, she must negate herself and become subordinate, first to Cipriano and then to Don Ramón. Just as the latter sets up a theocracy with the Mexican state in subjection—the Catholic Church no longer the official religion—in order to save the state, he requires that all his followers give up their individuality to gain their freedom. Kate must, in effect, prostrate herself before Cipriano and his maleness, acknowledging her dependence, her femaleness. When she finally does so, relinquishing her plans to return to Ireland, and admitting her insignificance, Kate affirms the new religion of blood consciousness and personal subordination.

Whatever caused Lawrence's bleak vision of the future, whatever led him to deprecate man's reason and to proclaim the need for an authoritarian Utopia ruled by a naturally superior elite does not excuse the inhumanity of *The Plumed Serpent*. Nor does the great power of his art grant him the license of prophecy and the accompanying immunity from criticism. If Lawrence remains a major artist who must be contended with, he is also one to be questioned and warned against.

David L. Kubal

PLUTUS

Type of work: Drama
Author: Aristophanes (c. 448-385 B.C.)
Type of plot: Satiric comedy
Time of plot: Fifth century B.C.
Locale: Athens
First presented: 388 B.C.

Plutus *is a moral fable based on a debate on the advantages of poverty* versus *the advantages of wealth; it is marked by delightfully irreverent humanizing of the gods and by pungent satire on ill-gotten wealth and ingratitude. The high point of the comedy is the scene of utter nonsense in the temple of Asclepius.*

Plutus is the last extant comedy by Aristophanes, written when he was around sixty. The play is a moral fable about money and its tremendous power in human life. The subject of wealth is often taken up by dramatists who have entered middle age or later. One thinks of Shakespeare's *Timon of Athens* and Molière's *The Miser.* However, *Plutus* thrusts satirical pins into the new Athens as it emerged from the debacle of the Peloponnesian War sixteen years earlier.

Here Aristophanes uses the conventions of Middle Comedy. The chorus is greatly reduced in its function from the way it was employed in Old Comedy, thus speeding the action to a more farcical pace. Another change is that political and personal satire no longer take priority as topics of comedy. Manners, ideas, and social tendencies gained precedence as humorous targets.

The idea that animates *Plutus* is this: wealth is the most powerful being in the world because it gives power of all kinds. But wealth is blindly bestowed on misers, rascals, and wastrels, while virtuous men are usually in poverty. Because it is indiscriminate, wealth is a poor, blind, sullen, beggarly thing, no different in aspect from poverty. Now if wealth were given according to a man's virtue and honesty, it would become the supreme god, honored by everyone.

Yet the best arguments in this comedy are advanced by Poverty in her debate with Chremylus. Wealth destroys one's physique, makes one vain, arrogant, and selfish, whereas need enables man to survive, for it forces him to work and produce useful goods, keeping him fit and active at the same time.

The end of the play is ironic. The virtuous are rewarded and the wicked are punished, but it is the virtuous who humiliate the sinners. We see the beginnings here of new pride in wealth and new corruption. *Plutus* pokes fun at the *nouveau riche,* ingratitude, servants, temple priests, and the gods themselves. But Aristophanes' imagination seems forced, subdued, tired, and his old freewheeling vitality has largely disappeared.

POEM OF THE CID

Type of work: **Poem**
Author: Unknown
Type of plot: Heroic epic
Time of plot: c. 1075
Locale: Fief of Bivar, to the north of Burgos, Spain
First transcribed: Twelfth century

This national epic of eleventh century Spain consists of 3,735 lines in three cantos which relate the major events of the life of Ruy Diaz, known as the Cid. The Cid is drawn as a typical Spanish warrior: proud, ruthless, and calculating at the same time that he is kind to his vassals and generous to a fault. Of all the epics about this national hero, this poem is the masterpiece, unique in its qualities of realism and poetic excellence.

Some forty years after the death of Rodrigo Diaz de Bivar, during a period of literary activity in Valencia and Castile, several epic poems were written about his deeds. They were written in the vernacular, in a spare, fast verse, and were meant to be sung or chanted in public places. Of these only "The Poem of the Cid" survives. It exists in a single manuscript copy made in 1307, and of this manuscript the first three pages have been lost. In Spanish the poem is embellished with assonance, large groups of lines all ending in the same vowel sound, an effect that is virtually impossible to render in English translation without twisting the sense. The rhythm is more easily reproduced, a short line with a pause in the middle that lends itself to the swing of oral delivery. The past tense is employed throughout, except when the poet wishes to bring forward an event or detail, in which case the historical present is used. Most of the characters in the poem are, like the Cid, known to be historical; historical events, though simplified, are accurately described.

The poem recounts the rise in the fortunes of the Cid from banishment to ultimate triumph in the royal marriages of his daughters. The Cid is depicted no less as a faultless vassal than as the unvanquished champion of Christendom, for he continues to serve and obey his king even after having been so basely treated as to dissolve the bond of fealty. Nothing more pointedly demonstrates his knightly worthiness than his victory over his enemies of Carrion, for he defeats them in the court of law as well as on the battlefield. That the Heirs of Carrion are highborn scoundrels, and their conqueror is of relatively low degree, makes the Cid still more sympathetic. Like Beowulf, Roland, and other epic heroes, he ornaments the order of which he is a part; unique among them, he is shown cozened and insulted by his sons-in-law, and humbly entreating the favor of an unworthy sovereign. His heroic character shows itself as much in patience and generosity as in courage and wisdom.

POINT COUNTER POINT

Type of work: Novel
Author: Aldous Huxley (1894-1963)
Type of plot: Social criticism
Time of plot: 1920's
Locale: England
First published: 1928

Point Counter Point *contains a novel within a novel; within the outer plot moves novelist Philip Quarles, who writes a novel whose fictional characters and events exactly parallel or counterpoint those in Huxley's story. The theme of each novel is the struggle of natural sexual desire and escapism from the bond of marriage.*

Point Counter Point can be seen as the culmination of Aldous Huxley's early works. In each of his previous novels, *Crome Yellow* (1921), *Antic Hay* (1923), and *Those Barren Leaves* (1925), Huxley had tried to develop a form through which he could present his satirical vision of, and philosophical ideas about, the intellectual, moral, and spiritual condition of upper middle-class English society shortly after World War I. Although each of these earlier books contains biting satire and provocative ideas, they are relatively static and formless. But, in *Point Counter Point,* Huxley hit upon the organizing principle which offered both the formal control and the flexibility he needed to realize his artistic intentions—a structural analogy between prose fiction and music.

This "musicalization of fiction" involves a counterpointing of various character types against each other in various "parallel, contrapuntal plots." Since Huxley was writing what he termed "novels of ideas" in these early works, he seldom presents well-rounded "realistic" characters. They are, rather, satirical embodiments of twentieth century "types" that Huxley wished to examine by showing what happens when their one-sided behavior is pushed to its extreme. To cite a few of the novel's many examples: Everard Webley, the fascistic apostle of violence, is murdered. John Bidlake, the painter, has "devoured" people and things all of his life; he is, in turn, devoured by the cancer growing in his stomach. Spandrell, a cynic who cannot accept his own nihilism, drives himself to increasingly "evil" experiences in order to "affirm" negatively, but succeeds only in destroying himself needlessly and pointlessly. Burlap, who sees himself as a grieving widower and religious leader, turns his "spirituality" into childish sensuality. And Quarles, Huxley's fictional alter-ego, is so much the intellectual that he only writes about the lives of others instead of living his own.

As an alternative to this gross one-sidedness, Huxley pleads for "balance" in life and "wholeness" in living. But his spokesman, Mark Rampion, a character modeled on D. H. Lawrence, is only a querulous voice (Lawrence called his fictional counterpart a "gasbag"). Since this society is incapable of utilizing positive values, there is no dramatic function for Rampion in the novel, aside from sardonic commentaries on the other characters.

Thus, Rampion's positive statements cannot offset the negative vision projected by Huxley's large cast of grotesque "perverts" (Rampion's term). What remains is a brilliant, vivid picture of an overly sophisticated, sex-obsessed, self-devouring society. In *Point Counter Point,* Aldous Huxley presented one of the definitive portraits of the age that provoked it.

POLYEUCTE

Type of work: Drama
Author: Pierre Corneille (1606-1684)
Type of plot: Religious tragedy
Time of plot: Third century
Locale: Mélitène, the capital of Armenia
First presented: c. 1643

Although The Cid *was traditionally considered Corneille's best work, some modern critics have argued for assigning that distinction to* Polyeucte. *Despite its somewhat improbable plot, climaxed by miraculous conversions, the play holds interest because of its treatment of the workings of grace in the human soul and its strong delineation of character and motivation.*

Pierre Corneille's *Polyeucte* is based on a pious legend which contains a kernel of historical fact—the execution of Polyeucte and Néarque, two Armenian soldiers of Rome's Twelfth "Thundering" Legion, for their devotion to Christianity, in 251 A.D. Corneille took only minor liberties with the legend, according to which Polyeuctus (Polyeucte in French) was a son-in-law of the Governor, Félix, who ordered his execution. The martyr was, according to the legend, reluctant to die because of his love for his pagan wife, the Governor's daughter, Pauline.

Corneille shocked many of his contemporaries by making this Christian legend into a "tragedy" or, as he later called it, a "Christian tragedy." Since *Polyeucte* was written, literary critics have argued whether the Christian doctrine of salvation is compatible with the Greek concept of tragedy. Perhaps it is not, but there is a sad irony that approaches tragedy in the situation of Félix at the end of the play. Although he has found eternal salvation, he must live the rest of his life on earth knowing that he had to execute Polyeucte and Pauline in order to find it.

The plot outline of *Polyeucte* resembles somewhat that of Sophocles' *Antigone.* Félix, like Creon, is torn between duty to the state, which requires him to execute his own child's spouse, and duty to the family, which forbids this. But the conflict in *Polyeucte* is not strictly that of family against state. Polyeucte's motive for defying his father-in-law, unlike Antigone's for defying hers, has nothing to do with the family; his duty is to the Christian God, who transcends everything. Polyeucte's love for Pauline, unlike Antigone's for Haemon, is not a comfort on the way to the grave, but the one source of discomfort on the way to Heaven. The climax—the sudden conversions of Pauline and Félix—is not the expected result of human nature; it is a dramatized miracle. By using Greek forms and devices, Corneille comes as close as possible to demonstrating on stage the Christian miracle of God's work in human hearts.

POOR PEOPLE

Type of work: Novel
Author: Fyodor Mikhailovich Dostoevski (1821-1881)
Type of plot: Impressionistic realism
Time of plot: First half of nineteenth century
Locale: St. Petersburg, Russia
First published: 1846

Poor People, Dostoevski's first published work, appeared serially in a literary periodical in 1846, and immediately established a thematic concern that was to run through all the author's later works: the misery of Russia's downtrodden masses. Written in epistolary form, the novel tells the story of a timid clerk's hopeless love for a poor girl who eventually marries a well-to-do landowner.

"Honor and glory to the young poet whose Muse loves people in garrets and basements and tells the inhabitants of gilded palaces: 'look, they are also men, they are also your brethren.'" With these words, the great critic Belinsky hailed the arrival of Dostoevski on the Russian literary scene. The epistolary novel *Poor People* is a remarkably perceptive account of the multifarious humiliations which torment "poor folk." In depicting the victimized and the eccentric, Dostoevski proved himself the equal of Dickens, by whom he was much influenced. His portrayal of life in "garrets and basements" is entirely devoid of sentimentality; both the dignity and the wretchedness of Makar and Barbara come to light simultaneously.

Makar's persistent generosity is what finally distinguishes him, while a poetic sensitivity to life ennobles Barbara. Both characters maintain these virtues in the face of impossible circumstances. To support Barbara, Makar must acept the chaos and stench of the three-to-a-room boarding house whose walls are "so greasy that your hand sticks when you lean against them." His increasing poverty turns the smallest economic reverse into disaster. The deterioration of his wardrobe is humiliating, yet it deepens his sympathy for those in similar straits. His aroused compassion for other victims induces him not only to give Goshkov twenty kopecks, but also to add sugar to the poor man's tea. As her response to Pokrovski's father shows, Barbara is also capable of great generosity. But more impressive are her lyrical descriptions of her childhood and her feeling for nature. Despite Makar's literary pretentions, Barbara is by far the superior "stylist," though she never boasts about her talent.

But Dostoevski's main characters are far from perfect human beings. Makar's love for Barbara is tainted by a desire to extract from her gratitude and praise. Barbara, in turn, reveals a shocking capacity for transforming Makar into her servant once she becomes engaged to the rich Bwikov. Both are too involved in private dream worlds and excessively preoccupied with their reputations. Yet these faults, suggests Dostoevski, must be seen partially as exaggerated attempts to maintain a modicum of dignity in an uncomprehending world. When one is absolutely vulnerable, certain defenses must be erected, or, as Makar explains, "Poor people are touchy—that's in the nature of things."

POOR WHITE

Type of work: Novel
Author: Sherwood Anderson (1876-1941)
Type of plot: Psychological realism
Time of plot: 1880-1900
Locale: Missouri and Ohio
First published: 1920

Poor White *is the story of one man's rise from origins of poverty and laziness to a career of creativity and self-realization. The novel is also significant as a study of the invasion of pioneer, rural America by industrialism. Anderson graphically describes not only the growth of America, but also the frustrations of individual men in conflict with an encroaching machine age.*

The intent of *Poor White* is, first of all, to describe the opening stages of industrialization in the great Ohio Valley; but this description, rather than being merely social or statistical, is set in profoundly human terms. That is, the birth and development of American industry are made specific and concrete through the individual lives of the people who invent the machines, who finance the enterprises, and who run the factories. Thus, *Poor White* is as much a historical novel as a novel dealing with the dramas of love and hate and individual psychology. Anderson catches a particular historical moment, and, almost in the manner of Tolstoy, explores individual reactions and contributions.

The two most significant human dramas are Hugh McVey's development on the one hand, and Clara Butterworth's relationship to him on the other. McVey, an inventor, and prototype of a creative personality—a genius of sorts—is shown by Anderson to have been influenced by the various regions of the United States. McVey is a product of "poor whites" dreaming near the banks of the Mississippi River and of discipline imposed on that dreaminess by a tough New England lady. If Anderson's attribution of innate characteristics to various regions of the country seems thin and stereotyped, Anderson does succeed in capturing the strengths and weaknesses of this individual and in exploring why this man in particular could play the historical role assigned to him in the novel.

The character of Clara Butterworth is mainly explored in terms of her sexual relationship with men, and this characterizaton lacks the force and focus of Hugh McVey's. Part of her vagueness may have resulted from Anderson's trying to describe her subjective confusion. Another reason may be that Anderson has made certain naturalist assumptions about her. Sexual urges that move her, and that drive the men around her, are heavily stressed by Anderson; and these urges, biologically irresistible, external and abstract, tend to rob her of her personality.

A final note should be added on the appearance of a socialist agitator near the end of the novel. The period Anderson describes is one in which the ideas of socialism, first introduced into this country, assumed vast popularity, especially in the farming regions of the midwest. Anderson suggests at the end of the novel that this agitator, and the ideas he supports, embody the next historical stage, the new society brought about by industrialization.

PORGY

Type of work: Novel
Author: DuBose Heyward (1885-1940)
Type of plot: Regional romance
Time of plot: Early twentieth century
Locale: Charleston, South Carolina
First published: 1925

Porgy is the love story of a crippled Negro beggar and the mistress of a brutal stevedore. Published in 1925 and dramatized in 1927 by the author and his wife, the novel became the basis for the famous folk-opera Porgy and Bess, *with lyrics by the author and Ira Gershwin and music by George Gershwin.*

DuBose Heyward is one of the best examples of an American one-book author. Although he wrote three books of poems, six novels, a short story, and three plays, he is remembered now only for his first novel, *Porgy,* and for the folk opera developed from it. The story of Porgy first caught the attention of George Gershwin in 1926, but it was not until 1935 that the opera *Porgy and Bess* reached the stage. Gershwin wrote the music, DuBose and Dorothy Heyward the libretto, and the Heywards and Ira Gershwin the lyrics of this first and most successful serious American folk opera, which achieved international fame through a four-year world tour climaxed by performances in Leningrad and Moscow in 1955.

Porgy tells of blacks living in a society dominated by whites; the blacks are presented as being elemental, emotional, amoral, and occasionally violent. Heyward develops in the reader a sympathy not only for the crippled Porgy, whose goat cart excites so much amusement among the whites, but also for Bess, who comes to live with him. Bess honestly tries to be true to Porgy, but she knows the weakness of her will and flesh when the brutal Crown touches her or when she has had liquor or dope. Porgy's brief happiness with Bess is doomed despite the efforts of both to hold on to it.

Heyward's portrayal of both character and scene contains the perceptive observation of detail found in the best local color fiction. Heyward may seem at times to romanticize his men and women, yet his style transforms the sordidness and bitterness of their lives into a sad, enduring beauty. Crippled Porgy, weak-willed Bess, and cruel Crown live on in one's mind long after the book has been closed.

THE PORTRAIT OF A LADY

Type of work: Novel
Author: Henry James (1843-1916)
Type of plot: Psychological realism
Time of plot: About 1875
Locale: England, France, Italy
First published: 1881

In this novel crowded with brilliantly subtle and penetrating character studies, James explores the ramifications of a naïve, young, high-minded American girl's first exposure and gradual acclimatization to the traditions and decadence of an older European culture. The reader follows step by step the mental processes of Isabel Archer as she gravitates away from the staunch and stuffy American, Caspar Goodwood, and her frail, intelligent, and devoted cousin Ralph Touchett, into a marriage with Gilbert Osmond, a worthless, tyrannical dilettante. The Portrait of a Lady *is an excellent example of the Jamesian technique of refracting life through the mind and temperament of an individual.*

The Portrait of a Lady first appeared serially in England and America (*Macmillan's Magazine,* Oct., 1880-Nov., 1881; *Atlantic,* Nov., 1880-Dec., 1881); it was published as a book in 1881. Usually regarded as the major achievement of James's early period of fiction writing, *The Portrait of a Lady* is one of the great novels of modern literature. In it James demonstrates that he has learned well from two European masters of the novel. Turgenev had taught him how to use a single character who shapes the work and is seen throughout in relationship to various other characters. From George Eliot he had learned the importance of tightening the structure of the novel and giving the story an architectural or organic form which develops logically from the given materials. He advances in *The Portrait of a Lady* beyond George Eliot in minimizing his own authorial comments and analysis and permitting his heroine to be seen through her own tardily awakening self-realization and also through the consciousness of the men and women who are closest to her. Thus his "portrait" of a lady is one which slowly grows stroke by stroke as touches are added which bring out both highlights and shadows, until Isabel Archer stands before us at the end a woman whose experiences have brought her excitement, joy, pain, and knowledge and have given her an enduring beauty and dignity.

Isabel is one of James's finest creations and one of the most memorable women in the history of the novel. A number of sources have been suggested for her. She may have been partly drawn from James's cousin Mary ("Minny") Temple, whom he was later to immortalize as Milly Theale in *The Wings of the Dove.* She has been compared to two of George Eliot's heroines, Dorothea Brooke in *Middlemarch* and Gwendolen Harleth in *Daniel Deronda;* to Diana Belfield in an early romantic tale by James entitled "Longstaff's Marriage";

to Bathsheba Everdene in Thomas Hardy's *Far from the Madding Crowd;* and even to Henry James himself, some of whose early experiences closely parallel those of Isabel. Yet, though James may have drawn from both real and fictional people in portraying Isabel Archer, she possesses her own identity; she grew from James's original "conception of a certain young woman affronting her destiny," as he later wrote in his Preface to the novel. He visualized her as "an intelligent but presumptuous girl" who would yet be "complex" and who would be offered a series of opportunities for free choice in the affronting of that destiny. Because of her presumption that she knew more than she did about herself and the world, Isabel was to make mistakes, including the tragic error of misjudging the nature of Gilbert Osmond. But her intelligence, though it was not sufficient to save her from suffering, would enable her to achieve a moral triumph in the end.

Of the four men in Isabel's life, three love her and one uses her innocence to gain for himself what he would not otherwise have had. She refuses marriage to Lord Warburton because, though he offers her a great fortune, a title, an entry into English society, and an agreeable and entertaining personality, she believes she can do better. She turns down Caspar Goodwood, who also offers wealth, because she finds him stiff and she is frightened by his aggressiveness. Her cousin, Ralph Touchett, does not propose because he does not wish her to be tied to a man who daily faces death. She does not even suspect the extent of his love and adoration until she is almost overwhelmed by learning it just as death takes him from her. She accepts Gilbert Osmond because she is deceived by his calculated charm and because she believes that he deserves what she can offer him: first, a fortune that will make it possible for him to live in idleness but surrounded by the objects of the "culture" she believes he represents; and second, a mother's love and care for his supposedly motherless daughter. Half of the novel is given over to Isabel's living with, adjusting to, and, finally, triumphing over the disastrous choice she has made.

In his Preface, James uses an architectural figure to describe *The Portrait of a Lady.* He says the "large building" of the novel "came to be a square and spacious house." Much of what occurs in the novel does so in or near a series of houses each of which relates significantly to Isabel or to other characters. The action begins at Gardencourt, the Tudor English country house of Daniel Touchett which Isabel finds more beautiful than anything she has ever seen. The charm of the house is enhanced by its age and its natural setting beside the Thames above London. It contrasts greatly with the "old house at Albany, a large, square, double house" belonging to her grandmother which Isabel in her childhood had found romantic and in which she had indulged in dreams stimulated by her reading. Mrs. Touchett's taking Isabel from the Albany house to Gardencourt is a first step in her plan to "introduce her to the world." When Isabel visits Lockleigh, Lord Warburton's home, she sees it from the gardens as resembling "a castle in a legend," though inside it has been modernized. She does not view it as a home for herself, or its titled owner as her husband, despite the many advantages he offers. The front of Gilbert Osmond's house in Florence is "imposing" but of "a somewhat uncommunicative character," a "mask." It symbolizes Osmond whose mask Isabel does not see through until she has married him. The last of the houses in *The Portrait of a Lady* is the Palazzo Roccanera, the Roman home of the Osmonds, which James first describes as "a kind of domestic fortress . . . which smelt of historic deeds, of crime and craft and violence." When Isabel later broods over it during her night-long meditation in Chapter 42, it is "the house of darkness, the house of dumbness, the house of suffocation."

We first see Isabel at Gardencourt on her visit with Mrs. Touchett, and it is here that she turns down the first of three proposals of marriage. It is fitting that also we should last see her here and by turns with each of the three men who have loved her. Asserting the independence on which she has so long prided herself, she has defied her imperious husband by going to England to see the dying Ralph, whose last words tell her that if she has been hated by Osmond she has been adored by her cousin. In a brief conversation with Lord Warburton after Ralph's death, Isabel turns down an invitation to visit him and his sisters at Lockleigh. Shortly afterward a scene six years earlier is reversed. Then she had sat on a rustic bench at Gardencourt and looked up from reading Caspar Goodwood's letter implying that he would come to England and propose to her—only to see and hear Warburton preparing to offer his own proposal. Now Caspar surprises her by appearing just after she has dismissed Warburton. There follows the one sexually passionate scene in the novel. In it Isabel has "an immense desire to appear to resist" the force of Caspar's argument that she should leave Osmond and turn to him. She pleads with streaming tears, "As you love me, as you pity me, leave me alone!" Defying her plea, Caspar kisses her:

> His kiss was like white lightning, a flash that spread, and spread again, and stayed; and it was extraordinarily as if, while she took it, she felt each thing in his hard manhood that had least pleased her, each aggressive fact of his face, his figure, his presence, justified of its intense identity and made one with this act of possession.

Caspar has possessed her for a moment only. "But when darkness returned she was free" and she flees into the house—and thence to Rome, as Caspar learns in the brief scene in London with Henrietta Stackpole which closes the novel.

James leaves the reader to conclude that Isabel's love for Pansy Osmond has principally determined her decision to continue enduring a marriage that she had freely—though so ignorantly and foolishly—chosen.

Henderson Kincheloe

A PORTRAIT OF THE ARTIST AS A YOUNG MAN

Type of work: Novel
Author: James Joyce (1882-1941)
Type of plot: Psychological realism
Time of plot: 1882-1903
Locale: Ireland
First published: 1916

This autobiographical novel follows the emotional and intellectual growth from childhood to young manhood of Stephen Dedalus, who is also the protagonist of the later, more complex Ulysses. *The development of artistic self-awareness necessitates young Stephen's rejection of the values of his upbringing, including blind patriotism and rigid Catholicism. The narration is in the stream-of-consciousness style which Joyce was instrumental in developing.*

A Portrait of the Artist as a Young Man by James Joyce is possibly the greatest example in the English language of the *bildüingsroman,* a novel tracing the growth and education of a young man, physically, mentally, and spiritually. Other examples of this genre range from Goethe's *The Sorrows of Young Werther* and Flaubert's *A Sentimental Education* to D. H. Lawrence's *Sons and Lovers.* Published in 1916, the work stands stylistically between the fusion of highly condensed naturalism and symbolism found in *Dubliners* (1914) and the elaborate mythological structure, interior monologues, and stream of consciousness of *Ulysses* (1922). In all three of these works there is a consistent concern for entrapment, isolation, rebellion from home, Church, and nation.

The novel is basically autobiographical, but in the final analysis the variants from, rather than the parallels with, Joyce's own life are of utmost artistic significance. The events of Stephen Dedalus' life are taken from the lives of Joyce, his brother Stanislaus, and his friend Byrne, covering the period between 1885 and 1902. The book begins with the earliest memories of his childhood, recounted in childlike language, and ends when Stephen is twenty-two with his decision to leave his native Dublin in search of artistic development to forge the conscience of his race. In the intervening years, like Joyce, Stephen attends the Jesuit Clongowes Wood School which he must leave because of family financial difficulties, attends a day school in Dublin, has his first sexual experience, his first religious crisis, and finally attends University College where he decides on his vocation as a writer. The dedication to pure art involves for Stephen, and Joyce, a rejection of the claims on him of duty to family, to the Catholic Church, and to Irish nationalism, either of the political type or of the literary type espoused by the writers of the Irish Renaissance. In his characterization of Stephen, however, Joyce eliminates much of himself: his sense of humor; his love of sport; his own graduation from the University before leaving Dublin; his desire to attend medical school in France; his deep concern for his mother's health; his affection for his father; and the life-long liaison he established with Nora Barnacle, who left Ireland with Joyce in 1904. The effect of these omissions is to make a narrower, more isolated character of Stephen than Joyce himself.

Portrait of the Artist as a Young Man is, on one level, an initiation story in which an innocent, idealistic youth with a sense of trust in his elders, slowly is brought to the recognition that this is a flawed, imperfect world, characterized by injustice and disharmony. Stephen finds this fact at home, at school, at church, in relationships with women and friends, and in the past and present history of his nation. Yet his pride prevents him from seeing any shortcomings in himself. In the second portion of the novel he becomes involved in the excesses of carnal lust; in the third portion, in the excesses of penitent piety, which also eventually disgust him. In the fourth section, in which he assumes the motto, *non servinum,* although he sees himself as a pagan worshiper of beauty, he becomes involved in excessive intellectual pride. In the final portion of the novel, Stephen develops his aesthetic theory of the epiphany—the sudden revelation of truth and beauty—through the artistic goals of "wholeness, harmony, and radiance." Thus his final flight from his real home—family, Church, nation—is still part of an almost adolescent rejection of the imperfections of this world and an attempt to replace it with the perfection of form, justice, and harmony of artistic creation.

Stephen Dedalus' very name is chosen to underline his character. His first name links him to Saint Stephen, the first martyr to Christianity and Stephen Dedalus sees himslf as a martyr, willing to give up all to the service of art. His last name, Dedalus, is famous from classical antiquity. It was Daedalus, the Athenian exile, who designed the great caste for King Minos of Crete and later designed the famous labyrinth in which the monstrous Minotaur was kept captive. Later, longing to return to his own land, but imprisoned in his labyrinth, Daedalus invented wings for himself and his son, Icarus, to fly from the labyrinth. Stephen, the artist, sees Dublin as the labyrinth from which he must fly in order to become the great artificer Daedalus was. It is important to remember, however, that Daedalus' son, Icarus, ignored his father's instructions on how to use the wings and because of pride and desire to exceed, flew too close to the sun, melting his wings. He plunged into the ocean and drowned. It is only later, in *Ulysses,* that Stephen recognizes himself as "lap-winged Icarus" rather than as Daedalus.

Joyce's technical skill is obvious in the series of interwoven recurrent symbols of the novel. The rose, for instance, which is associated with women, chivalric love, and creativity, appears throughout the novel. Water, also, is found in almost every chapter of the novel: it can be the water which drowns and brings death; it can also be the water which gives life, symbolic of renewal as in baptism and the final choice of escape by sea.

The central themes of *A Portrait of the Artist as a Young Man*—alienation, isolation, rejection, betrayal, the Fall, the search for the father—are developed with amazing virtuosity. This development is the second, following *Dubliners,* of the four major parts in Joyce's cyclical treatment of the life of man which moves, as the great medieval cyclical plays, from Fall to Redemption, from isolation and alienation to acceptance. The later development of Joyce's analysis of the human condition and of the relationship of art to life can be found in *Ulysses* and *Finnegan's Wake.* Joyce himself has emphasized the importance of the word "young" in the title of this work, and his conclusion, in the form of Stephen's diary which illustrates Stephen's own perceptions, words, and style, forces the reader to become more objective and detached in his judgment of Stephen. Knowing that all of Stephen's previous epiphanies have failed, the reader recognizes in these final pages, the human complexity of Stephen's important triumph in escaping from the nets of Ireland but realizes that his triumph is complicated by important losses and sacrifices.

Ann E. Reynolds

THE POSSESSED

Type of work: Novel
Author: Fyodor Mikhailovich Dostoevski (1821-1881)
Type of plot: Psychological realism
Time of plot: Mid-nineteenth century
Locale: Russia
First published: 1871-1872

The Possessed *is Dostoevski's answer to Turgenev's treatment of Russian nihilism in* Fathers and Sons. *Using a large number of characters representing all classes of Russian society, the author shows how an idle interest in nihilism brings on robbery, arson, and murder in a Russian community.*

Dostoevski was nearly fifty years old when the final version of *The Possessed* (also translated as *The Devils*) appeared. (His poverty had forced him to write the book first in serial form for a Moscow literary review.) Because the novel rages so wildly against liberalism and "atheistic" socialism, many readers decided that its once-progressive author had now become a confirmed reactionary. Dostoevski himself lent credibility to this notion by his public statements. In a famous letter to Alexander III, Dostoevski characterized *The Possessed* as a historical study of that perverse radicalism which results when the intelligentsia detaches itself from the Russian masses. In another letter he proclaimed that "He who loses his people and his nationality loses his faith in his country and in God. This is the theme of my novel."

Further, given the nature of Dostoevski's personal history, a movement towards thoroughgoing conservatism could seem almost predictable. An aristocrat by birth, Dostoevski involved himself deeply in the Petrashevski Circle, a St. Petersburg discussion group interested in utopian socialism. Part of this group formed a clandestine revolutionary cadre, and for his participation in the conspiracy, Dostoevski was arrested. There followed a mock execution, four years of imprisonment and another four years of enforced service as a private in the Siberian army. Although freed in 1858, Dostoevski remained under surveillance, and his right to publish was always in jeopardy. He thus had every inducement to prove to government censors his utter fidelity to the *ancien regime* and "safe" principles.

But in fact *The Possessed* is not a reactionary novel. Dostoevski does not defend the institutions of monarchy, aristocracy, or censorship. He upholds Russian orthodoxy in a way that suggests a theocratic challenge to the *status quo.* His exaltation of the peasantry affords no comfort for capitalism or imperialism. And while appearing to embrace Russian nationalism, he presents an image of small-town culture which, to say the least, does not inspire Russophilia. His portrait of the ruling class is as devastating as any essay on the subject by Marx or Engels. Thus, Dostoevski's critique of radical political ideas proceeds from a basis other than that of extremist conservatism. But what is that basis?

The answer is partially revealed in Shatov's statement that half-truth is uniquely despotic. *The Possessed* is at once a criticism of a variety of political and philosophical half-truths and a searching toward a principle of Wholeness, a truth which will reunite and compose man's fragmented psyche, his divided social and political order, and his shattered relationship with God. Dostoevski does not describe that truth, partly because *the* truth is too mysterious and grand to be expressed in human language. Rather, he merely points to it by showing the defects and incompleteness in positions which pretend to be the truth.

It is through the enigmatic character of Stavrogin that Dostoevski most fully carries out his quest for Wholeness. For Stavrogin has embraced and discarded all the philosophies which Dostoevski deems inadequate. As a result, Stavrogin is the embodiment of pure negativity and pure emptiness. He is also pure evil, more evil still than Pyotr, who at least has his absolute devotion to Stavrogin as a ruling principle in his life. From Stepan Verhovensky, Stavrogin learned skepticism and the tolerant principles of "higher liberalism." In St. Petersburg, he advances to utopian socialism and a more passionate faith in salvation-through-science. But the elitism and shallow rationalism of this faith cause Stavrogin to take up messianic Russian populism. Yet he is led even beyond this stage to an investigation of orthodox theology. Unable to commit himself to the Christian faith, he perpetrates the hideous crime he later confesses to Father Tihon.

At each step in his development, Stavrogin trains disciples who both propagate his teachings and carry them out to their logical extremes. Pyotr belongs partly to Nikolay's "socialist period," while Shatov embraces the populist creed and Kirillov elaborates the themes of the theological phase. In Pyotr, socialist criticism of traditional society has produced a monomaniacal fascination with the revolutionary destruction and violence by which the new order shall emerge. Modeling this character after the infamous Russian terrorist, Sergey Nechayev, Dostoevski suggests that Pyotr is the natural outcome of socialism's faith in the power of reason to establish absolute values. Shigolov's "rational" defense of a socialist tyranny shows how thoroughly rational structures rely on nonrational premises. For Pyotr, then, the absence of rational certainties means that all behavior is permissible and all social orders are equally valid. He thus chooses to fight for a society based on men's hunger for submission, their fear of death, their longing for a Messiah. Like Machiavelli, he decides that only by founding society on the most wretched aspects of human nature can anything really lasting and dependable be built. As his Messiah, Pyotr has chosen Stavrogin, whose awesome and arbitrary will could be the source of order in a new society.

Kirillov elevates Pyotr Verhovensky's fascination with strength of will into a theological principle. Kirillov is not content with man's limited transcendence of the determinisms of nature. He aspires to the total freedom of God. Paradoxically, this freedom can only be achieved through suicide, that act which overcomes the natural fear of death by which God holds man in thrall. Not until all men are prepared at every moment to commit suicide can humanity take full responsibility for its own destiny. The great drawback in Kirillov's view is that it causes him to suppress his feelings of love and relatedness to his fellow man. Shatov's nationalistic theology is an attempt to do justice to these feelings. Rebelling against Kirillov's isolated quest for godhood, Shatov wishes to achieve the same goal by submerging himself in the life of a "God-bearing people." Yet Shatov's creed remains abstract and sentimental until Marya returns, providing him with a real person to love.

The birth of Marya's child, together with Stepan Verhovensky's "discovery" of the Russian people, are the symbols by which Dostoevski reveals his own answer to Nikolay Stavrogin. The child is for Shatov an unimaginable act of grace. Significantly, Kirillov experiences a sudden serenity and a confirmation of his mystical insight that "everything is good." For Dostoevski, the source of this grace is God, who brings exquisite order to the most corrupted human situations. Shatov's rapturous love stands in utter contradiction to Stavrogin's empty indifference. In that the child's real father is Stavrogin, Shatov's love is all the more wondrous. Stavrogin's final inability to respond to Liza's love is the logical result of his long struggle to free himself of dependency on his family, his people, his church. He boasts that he does not need anyone; from that claim comes spiritual and moral death. All that Stavrogin has touched is, in the end, dead—even Shatov.

The magnificence of Dostoevski's artistry is nowhere more apparent than in the conclusion to *The Possessed*. For he does not finally embody his great theme—human Wholeness through human dependence—in a titanic character like Stavrogin or Kirillov, but in the all-too-human Stepan. This quixotic buffoon, whom we laugh at and pity, ultimately attains the dignity he seeks. But he himself is surprised by it all, for it comes in a way he least expected it: through an encounter with his people, reunion with Varvara, and the administration of the sacrament.

Leslie E. Gerber

THE POT OF GOLD

Type of work: Drama
Author: Titus Maccius Plautus (c. 254-184 B.C.)
Type of plot: Comedy
Time of plot: Second century B.C.
Locale: Athens
First presented: c. 195 B.C.

Although the figure of the miser is unusual in Roman comedy, Plautus had many models among the Greek comedies, particularly those of Menander. Like most of Plautus' comedies, The Pot of Gold *had considerable influence on European drama, and was the basis for seventeenth century versions by Ben Jonson, Molière, Thomas Shadwell, and Pieter Hooft.*

The Pot of Gold (Aulularia) is an excellent example of Plautus' dramaturgy at its best. The plot has two strands of action: Euclio's frantic attempts to keep his pot of gold safe from thieves, and Phaedria's offers of marriage on the very day she gives birth to Lyconides' illegitimate baby. Both lines of action are skillfully interwoven; the dramatic pace is swift and purposeful; and one scene arises from another with no digressions. This farce also exhibits Plautus' verbal exuberance to good effect—his punning, his comic alliteration, his idiomatic language, his metrical variety, and his keen sense of timing. Few playwrights knew how to handle a joke with such deftness, but merely reading them is tiresome, especially in translation. It is necessary to visualize the action taking place on a stage to get some idea of Plautus' ability.

Plautine drama was quite similar to our musical comedy. It used song and dance as part of the action; it required considerable theatrical experience; and it was based on adapted works. Plautus borrowed heavily from the Greek writers of the New Comedy, and it is often conjectured that *The Pot of Gold* was taken from a play by Menander, although it is impossible to determine which one. The miser has been a stock figure of farce almost from its inception.

Of Plautus' life little is known for certain. According to tradition he began writing his comedies after he lost a large sum in business and was forced to work in a flour mill. He wrote at least forty plays, some say over a hundred, but of these only twenty now exist. He was very popular and achieved wide fame. From his plays one can see that he knew theatrical technique inside and out, and he was attuned to his audiences in a way that only practical experience can give. From the name he took, Titus Maccius Plautus, one gathers that he played a clown, since *maccus* means clown and *plautus* means flatfoot.

The text of *The Pot of Gold* as we have it is not complete, since the conclusion is missing. However, on the basis of the two Arguments summarizing the plot—verses that preface the play and which were added by later Roman editors—one can reconstruct the ending. The translator, E. F. Watling, has composed an adequate and plausible finale on the information given in the Arguments. Plautus must have been about sixty when he wrote this play, because it was produced for the Megalensian games, which were first held in 194 B.C. The theme of money seems to fascinate playwrights as they grow older. One thinks of Aristophanes' *Plutus,* Shakespeare's *Timon of Athens,* and Molière's *L'Avare,* all of which were written in the authors' later years. The raciness of Plautus' earlier works is greatly subdued, although he could have introduced it easily considering Phaedria's unwed pregnancy.

The main interest of this play lies in the character of Euclio. Three generations of poverty, hard toil, and thrift have taken their toll on his personality. Euclio is so stingy that the neighbor's servants make jokes about it, and when he uncovers a pot of gold in his house, his only thought is to keep it from being stolen. The gold acts as a curse for him. It makes him suspicious of every kind word, of every good deed, of every person entering or leaving his house. He even suspects that the cooks are using a rooster to locate his gold. He acts like a madman in his apprehension, distractedly dashing in and out of his home. The gold is a burden that has cut him off from everyone. He does not realize that his daughter is pregnant, and learns of it only after she has given birth. Such a person invites the very thing he fears. Ironically, in trying to find the safest hiding place of all, he unwittingly gives himself away and the gold is stolen. But that only increases his frenzy. In the best scene in the play, where Lyconides tries to tell him he drunkenly made love to Phaedria, Euclio is so preoccupied with the theft that he thinks Lyconides is confessing to having taken the gold. And when he learns of Phaedria's pregnancy and birthing, it is a minor concern to him. Clearly, something dramatic must take place to induce a change of heart in him, and to make him realize that his daughter could use the gold as a dowry. What happened to transform Euclio is part of the missing conclusion. However, we do know that he gives the gold away, as a marriage gift to Phaedria, at the end.

The subplot by which Phaedria is at last married off to a man who loves her seems perfunctory, but it ties in nicely with Euclio's obsession. Megadorus is elderly, rich, innocent of Phaedria's condition, and willing to take her without a dowry. He sends his cooks to prepare the wedding feast at Euclio's, which prompts Euclio to remove the gold. And after it is stolen, Lyconides becomes the instrument by which it is returned, which establishes him as the successful suitor. Presumably Megadorus withdrew on learning that Phaedria was not a virgin. From the beginning of the play we know that Megadorus is simply the means of getting Lyconides to propose.

Like most Plautine comedies, this play had considerable influence on European drama. In the seventeenth century versions by Ben Jonson, Molière, Thomas Shadwell, and Hooft appeared. Fielding's *The Miser,* written in the eighteenth century, was also based in part on the Plautine comedy. But certainly the finest re-creation of Euclio was Molière's Harpagon in *L'Avare.*

James Weigel, Jr.

POWER

Type of work: Novel
Author: Lion Feuchtwanger (1884-1959)
Type of plot: Historical novel
Time of plot: Mid-eighteenth century
Locale: Germany
First published: 1925

In Power, *Feuchtwanger deals with the question of what makes a Jew, confronted with disdain, antipathy, and persecution, remain a Jew in spite of everything. The plot follows the gradual metamorphosis of a rank materialist who slowly comes to find inspiration in the teachings of Judaism, tenets which appeal to the sensitivity of his inner feelings.*

The focus of *Power* is the issue of anti-Semitism. The central thought which Feuchtwanger wishes to communicate is that no Jew can ever be safe, whether or not he trusts the political and social system, and whether or not he achieves power in that system. In the end, Feuchtwanger says, the Jew will be murdered—and there will only be other Jews to mourn his passing.

Feuchtwanger himself was an important literary figure in pre-World War II Germany who was forced to flee the Nazis; he was a friend of playwright Bertolt Brecht and was at the center of much of the significant literary activity of the Weimar Republic. The flavor of the cultural life of Weimar is evident in *Power*. The density of the prose, the brutality, the sensuality and perversion, the breakdown of values, minds, and political institutions, have all been taken by Feuchtwanger and transposed to eighteenth century Germany, where they become the perfect medium for tracing the development of anti-Semitism.

In the 1920's, when *Power* was first published, anti-Semitism had not yet reached genocidal proportions. There were a few groups, right wing nationalists for the most part, who denounced the Jews as the cause of Germany's defeat; but at the same time, there were still Jews in positions of prominence in German social, cultural, and political life. It is to Feuchtwanger's special credit that he had the historical and dramatic insight to understand the embryonic stirrings of homicidal racism in Europe and especially in Germany, and to develop this theme in a novel. Additionally, the use of a minority group as a scapegoat, and the casual indifference (or outright collaboration) of officialdom in the violence committed against it, are phenomena which retain their significance for the contemporary reader. *Power* is incredibly and horribly prophetic.

THE POWER AND THE GLORY

Type of work: Novel
Author: Graham Greene (1904-   )
Type of plot: Psychological realism
Time of plot: The 1930's
Locale: Mexico
First published: 1940

First published in the United States under the title, The Labyrinthine Ways, *this novel is a powerful psychological study of a lecherous, alcoholic Catholic priest fleeing political persecution in Mexico. Reflecting Greene's deep interest, as a convert, in Catholic idiom and doctrine,* The Power and the Glory *follows the process of redemption in a seemingly weak-willed, profligate man who nevertheless dies a Christlike death at the end.*

Although in all of Greene's fiction published between the late thirties and the late fifties, he is concerned with the moral and spiritual struggle of man caught between the Devil and God—indeed one might say Greene's setting is man's soul—he is also preoccupied with politics. Perhaps more than any of the so-called political writers of the thirties and forties, he handled topical matters: big business, revolution, war, international spy rings and diplomacy. One must take care not to think of these situations as mere "stages" on which his heroes work out their salvation or damnation. They are rather integral to the novels themselves, contributing significantly to the total meaning. They also point up Greene's continual awareness of actual events in culture and of their importance to his dramatization of contemporary man.

It is pertinent, for example, that the spiritual odyssey of Father Montez should take place in Mexico whose reactionary political and religious heritage is being assaulted by a radical ideology. The priest's temptation is not only of the flesh or of doubt in God's existence; he is also tempted by the honest humanitarianism of the lieutenant of police.

Specifically, the lieutenant attempts to persuade the priest that man does not have his sources in the supernatural but in the exclusively natural. Therefore, he goes on to argue, the Church, in its failure to mitigate the people's poverty in favor of ministering to their spiritual needs, has actually betrayed them.

It is a cogent argument—one which is frequently made by modern revolutionaries—and one which the priest can only respond to by dying. Still the priest's self-sacrifice remains a powerful political statement that man at times will assert his faith in all its irrationality against the State and its rationality.

THE POWER OF DARKNESS

Type of work: Drama
Author: Count Leo Tolstoy (1828-1910)
Type of plot: Domestic tragedy
Time of plot: Nineteenth century
Locale: Russia
First presented: 1886

In this play, the theme of sin and redemption is embodied in the traditional Russian conflict of father against son, the natural against the artificial life, and spiritual humility against worldly arrogance. As Nikita is led into adultery and murder almost unknowingly, the implication is that evil is a state into which everyone can fall if they once cease to be diligently on guard against it.

Count Leo Tolstoy came to playwriting relatively late in his career, after he had completed his prose masterpieces, *War and Peace* (1869) and *Anna Karenina* (1877), and at a time when his religious "conversion" prompted him to view his writing in moralistic, rather than artistic, terms. Hence, the works of this period are heavily didactic and lack much of the balance, scope, and humanity of this previous efforts. Nevertheless, *The Power of Darkness* is a potent realistic play, one of the most intense and moving dramas of the period, and perhaps the outstanding realistic play of the pre-Chekhovian Russian theater.

Although there was no direct influence, *The Power of Darkness* resembles the powerful naturalistic dramas which were, at that time, rejuvenating Western theater. As in a typical naturalistic play, *The Power of Darkness* shows a group of weak, ordinary people who, after committing petty crimes out of greed, sexual jealousy, and self-deception, find themselves caught up by forces they cannot understand or control, driven to newer, greater crimes, and ultimately destroyed by the momentum of the evil they so easily unloosed. Small sins automatically lead to bigger ones; lesser crimes require more extreme deeds to maintain concealment; casual observers or passive accomplices are drawn into active conspiracy, and so on. Each evil deed, the participants believe, will be the last one and lead them, finally, to "happiness." The opposite is the case; they bind themselves tighter and tighter in a "net" of their own making.

Tolstoy's chronicling of this disintegration is fascinating in its realistic accuracy. Even in the midst of their depravity, the characters retain a certain sympathy; they are trapped and drawn to their destruction almost unconsciously. The catalyst is Nikíta's mother, Matryóna, the one character who seems consciously and deliberately evil, and she is one of the most fascinating creations of the modern stage. She plays on the others like a musician on instruments and seems to enjoy intrigue for its own sake. And she is the consummate hypocrite, acting the role of pious matron, while engineering the diabolical schemes. For example, as Peter dies from the poison she supplied, Matryóna offers him religious consolation.

However, if the process of disintegration and self-destruction described in *The Power of Darkness* causes it to resemble the naturalistic plays, its resolution is quite different. To the naturalists, man was the helpless victim of biological and economic circumstances. Their plays and novels were intended to illustrate man's hopeless situation in the face of an impersonal "scientific" universe. Tolstoy's vision was quite the opposite. To him, the "power of darkness" was more than balanced by the "power of Light," and his play is, above all, not a story of damnation, but one of redemption.

The focus of redemption is on Nikíta. From the beginning of the play his sin is clearly the product of arrogance and sensuality, rather than any positive inclination to evil. When circumstances force him to the most vicious of the crimes, the murder of the baby, he is too weak to withstand the pressure of his mother, and commits the act in a half-conscious frenzy. Immediately he is overwhelmed by guilt and remorse. He hears the breaking bones, the cries of the dying child, and seems on the edge of madness—but he is not granted that escape. He prepares to commit suicide, but that, too, is denied him.

Nikíta's insight comes when, in the midst of his suicide attempt, he is accosted by Mítritch, a drunken laborer, who tells him a parable about the "devil's power," concluding with the statement that: "when you begin to be afraid of people, then the devil, with his cloven hoof, will snatch you up right away and stick you wherever he wants to."

Nikíta thus realizes that his descent into evil has been the result of this "fear" of the opinion of men and his own foolish desire for the transitory pleasures of the material world. Shorn of that fear he gains his resolve and goes to the wedding party to confess. He accepts all of the blame for the crimes, which is, in a spiritual sense, true: all the conspirators are responsible for all the crimes. But, in spite of the totality of his guilt, he is redeemed.

THE PRAIRIE

Type of work: Novel
Author: James Fenimore Cooper (1789-1851)
Type of plot: Historical romance
Time of plot: 1804
Locale: Western Plains of the United States
First published: 1827

This fifth and last volume of the Leatherstocking series closes the career of Cooper's famous frontiersman and scout, Natty Bumppo. Despite rather flat characterizations, stilted dialogue, and an overly coincidental plot, the story is acceptable, for it is action-filled and successfully captures the spirit of the old West.

The Prairie is the third title published in the Leatherstocking Tales. When the series of five tales was published together in 1850, *The Prairie* became the last. Since Cooper had never seen the Great Plains area in which the action of the tale occurs, he drew from descriptions and additional information in accounts by Lewis, Clark, and other explorers. Beyond this he used his imagination.

The Prairie is related in several ways to the two earlier Leatherstocking Tales. Two themes in *The Pioneers*—the wasting of America's natural resources and the vanishing of the American Indian as a race—continue in *The Prairie.* Leatherstocking in *The Pioneers* had condemned the wasteful cutting and burning of trees, the greater slaughter of passenger pigeons, and the seining of fish that were left to rot on the lake shore. In *The Prairie* the old trapper complains: "What the world of America is coming to, and where the machinations and inventions of its people are to have an end, tne Lord, He only knows. . . . How much has the beauty of the wilderness been deformed. . . ." The theme of the "vanishing American" had been touched on with the death of Chingachgook in *The Pioneers.* It became a leading theme in *The Last of the Mohicans* and it returns in *The Prairie* with the Pawnees and the Sioux warring as the Delawares and the Mingoes had fought in *The Last of the Mohicans,* making it easier for such white settlers as Ishmael Bush and his large family finally to take over what had been the Indians' ancient homeland.

Certain resemblances between characters and character relationships in *The Last of the Mohicans* and *The Prairie* may also be seen. The genteel Captain Duncan Uncas Middleton is a grandson of Duncan Heyward and Alice Munro, who represented gentility in *The Last of the Mohicans.* The love of the old trapper for his adopted son Hard-Heart parallels the feeling that Hawkeye had for young Uncas. The enmity of Hard-Heart and Mahtoree is as fierce as that of Uncas and Magua (but the good Indian kills the bad one in *The Prairie,* whereas the bad Indian killed the good one in *The Last of the Mohicans.*) The pedantic wordiness of Dr. Obed Battius surpasses in comic absurdity the talk and the psalm singing of David Gamut.

One may object to the complexity and many improbabilities of plot in *The Prairie,* to the old trapper's long-windedness, or to Dr. Battius' ridiculous vocabulary and views, but Ishmael Bush is one of Cooper's best-drawn characters, and the old trapper is both pathetic and noble as he approaches his death. The death scene itself so impressed the English novelist Thackeray that he imitated it with the death of Colonel Newcome in *The Newcomes* (1853-1855).

PRECIOUS BANE

Type of work: Novel
Author: Mary Webb (1881-1927)
Type of plot: Regional romance
Time of plot: Mid-nineteenth century
Locale: England
First published: 1924

Set in the English countryside, this novel is peopled with strangely fierce, tortured farmers who fight the harsh forces of nature to grind a living out of the land. A sort of evil spell lays on the Sarn family which even drives Gideon to commit murder; eventually this Bane is exorcised, and the harelipped heroine finds a loving husband.

The hero of Mary Webb's novel is Nature. Yet, it is a cruel force acting in a Darwinian universe that is only mollified when man acquiesces in its operation. Like a jealous owner, it brands him at his birth. The Sarn family is marked when Old Timothy, the grandfather, is struck by forked lightning. Prudence, the heroine, bears the scar, a disfiguring harelip. The main action of the novel is an account of Prue's and her brother's struggle with Nature to rise above the ordinary rhythms of life and gain the "precious bane."

By unlawfully assuming the Sarn land at his father's death, Gideon Sarn brings down Nature's curse. In his desire for money and status, he ignores his own passions; he rejects the love of Jancis Beguildy. Ultimately he pays for his avarice and his denial of his instincts by the loss of his soul and his life. He has dared to assert his superiority to Nature and in revenge it crushes him.

Initially he is abetted by Prudence. She binds herself to him under the promise that when their wealth is assured, he will pay for the removal of her disfigurement. Prudence, however, is saved from the curse by her realization of the corruption that wealth entails and her love for Kester Woodseaves, an enigmatic man of compassion and magnetic sexuality.

The final scene in which Woodseaves swoops down on his charger to save Prue from a mob which believes her to be a witch is primitive in its appeal, and the townspeople's dunking of Prue is a superstitious ritual designed to appease outraged Nature. The union of Kester and Prue itself is a ritual; it is one which signifies man's subordination to forces beyond him, unconscious forces that pull toward the rhythms of Nature and away from those of society.

PRIDE AND PREJUDICE

Type of work: Novel
Author: Jane Austen (1775-1817)
Type of plot: Comedy of manners
Time of plot: Early nineteenth century
Locale: Rural England
First published: 1813

In this masterpiece, Austen follows an empty-headed mother's scheming to find suitable husbands for her five daughters. With gentle irony, the author re-creates in meticulous, artistic detail the manners and morals of the country gentry in a small English village, focusing on the intelligent, irrepressible heroine Elizabeth. Both major and minor characters are superbly drawn; the plot is beautifully symmetrical; and the dazzling perfection of style shows Austen at her best.

In 1813, her thirty-eighth year, Jane Austen became a published novelist for the second time with *Pride and Prejudice.* She had begun this work in 1796, her twenty-first year, calling it *First Impressions.* It had so delighted her family that her father had tried, without success, to have it published. Eventually putting it aside, she returned to it probably at about the time that her first published novel, *Sense and Sensibility,* appeared in 1811. No longer extant, *First Impressions* must have been radically altered; for *Pride and Prejudice* is not an apprenticeship novel, but a mature work, which continues to be the author's most popular novel, perhaps because its readers share Darcy's admiration for the "liveliness" of Elizabeth Bennet's mind.

The original title, *First Impressions,* focuses upon the initial errors of judgment from which the story develops, whereas the title *Pride and Prejudice,* besides suggesting the kind of antithetical topic which delighted rationalistic eighteenth century readers, indicates the central conflict involving the kinds of pride and prejudice which bar the marriages of Elizabeth Bennet and Darcy and Jane Bennet and Bingley, but bring about the marriages of Charlotte Lucas and Collins and Lydia Bennet and Wickham.

As in all of Jane Austen's novels, individual conflicts are defined and resolved within a rigidly delimiting social context, in which human relationships are determined by wealth and rank. Thus the much admired opening sentence establishes the societal values which underlie the main conflict: "It is a truth universally acknowledged, that a single man in possession of a good fortune, must be in want of a wife." Mr. and Mrs. Bennet's opening dialog concerning the eligible Bingley explores this truth. Devoid of individuality, Mrs. Bennet is nevertheless well attuned to society's edicts and therefore regards Bingley only in the light of society's "truth." Mr. Bennet, an individualist to the point of eccentricity, represents neither personal conviction nor social conviction. He lightheartedly views with equal indifference both Bingley's right to his own reason for settling there and society's right to see him primarily as a potential husband. Having repudiated society, Mr. Bennet cannot take seriously either the claims of the individual or the social order.

As the central character, Elizabeth, her father's favorite child and her mother's least favorite, must come to terms with the conflicting values implicit in her parents' antithetical characters. She is like her father in her scorn of society's conventional judgments, but she champions the concept of individual merit independent of money and rank. She is, indeed, prejudiced against the prejudices of society. From this premise she attacks Darcy's pride, assuming that it derives from the causes that Charlotte Lucas identifies: " . . . with family, fortune, every thing in his favour . . . he has a *right* to be proud."

Flaunting her contempt for money, Elizabeth indignantly spurns as mere strategy to get a rich husband or any husband Charlotte's advice that Jane ought to make a calculated play for Bingley's affections. She loftily argues, while under the spell of Wickham's charm, that young people who are truly in love are unconcerned about each other's financial standing.

As a champion of the individual, Elizabeth prides herself on her discriminating judgment, boasting that she is a student of character. Significantly, it is Darcy who warns her against prejudiced conclusions, reminding her that her experience is quite limited. For Darcy is not simply the representative of a society which primarily values wealth and consequence—as Elizabeth initially views him—but he is also a citizen of a larger society than the village to which Elizabeth is confined by circumstance. Consequently, it is only when she begins to move into Darcy's world that she can judge with true discrimination both individual merit and the dictates of the society which she has rejected. Fundamentally honest, she revises her conclusions as new experiences warrant, in the case of Darcy and Wickham radically altering her opinion.

More significant than the obviously ironic reversals, however, is the growing revelation of Elizabeth's unconscious commitment to society. For example, her original condemnation of Darcy's pride coincides with the verdict of Meryton society. Moreover, she always shares society's regard for wealth. Even while denying the importance of Wickham's poverty, she countenances his pursuit of the ugly Miss King's fortune, discerning her own inconsistency only after she learns of his bad character. Most revealing, when Lydia Bennet runs off with Wickham, Elizabeth instinctively pronounces the judgment of society when she states that Wickham would never marry a woman without money.

Almost unconsciously Elizabeth acknowledges a connection between wealth and human values at the crucial moment when she first looks upon Pemberley, the Darcy estate:

> She had never seen a place for which nature had done more, or where natural beauty had been so little counteracted by an awkward taste. They

were all of them warm in their admiration; and at that moment she felt
that to be mistress of Pemberley might be something!

She is not entirely joking when she tells Jane that her love for Darcy began
when she first saw his beautiful estate.

Elizabeth's experiences, especially her discoveries of the well-ordered
Pemberley and Darcy's tactful generosity to Lydia and Wickham, lead her to
differentiate between Charlotte's theory that family and fortune bestow a
"right to be proud" and Darcy's position that the intelligent person does not
indulge in false pride. Darcy's pride is real, but it is regulated by responsibility. Unlike his aunt, Lady Catherine de Bourgh, who relishes the distinction of rank, he disapproves less of the Bennets' undistinguished family and
fortune than he does of the lack of propriety displayed by most of the family.
Thus Elizabeth scarcely overstates her case when, at the end, she assures her
father that Darcy has no improper pride.

Elizabeth begins by rejecting the values and restraints of society, as represented by such people as her mother, the Lucases, Miss Bingley, and Lady
Catherine, upholding instead the claims of the individual, represented only
by her whimsical father. By the end of the novel, the heart of her conflict
appears in the contrast between her father and Darcy. Loving her father, she
has tried to overlook his lack of decorum in conjugal matters. But she has
been forced to see that his freedom is really irresponsibility, the essential
cause of Jane's misery as well as Lydia's amorality. The implicit comparison
between Mr. Bennet's and Darcy's approach to matrimony points up their
different methods of dealing with society's restraints. Unrestrained by society,
having been captivated by the inferior Mrs. Bennet's youth and beauty, Mr.
Bennet consulted only his personal desires and made a disastrous marriage.
Darcy, in contrast, defies society only when he has made certain that Elizabeth
is a woman worthy of his love and lifetime devotion.

When Elizabeth confronts Lady Catherine, her words are declarative, not
of absolute defiance of society, but of the selective freedom which is her
compromise, and very similar to Darcy's: "I am only resolved to act in
that manner, which will, in my own opinion, constitute my happiness, without
reference to *you,* or to any person so wholly unconnected with me." Jane
Austen does not falsify the compromise. If Elizabeth dares with impunity to
defy the society of Rosings, Longbourne, and Meryton, she does so only because Darcy is exactly the man for her and, further, because she can anticipate "with delight . . . the time when they should be removed from
society so little pleasing to either, to all the comfort and elegance . . . at
Pemberley." Her marriage to Darcy is in a sense a triumph of the individual
over society; but, paradoxically, Elizabeth achieves her most genuine conquest of pride and prejudice only after she has accepted the full social
value of her judgment that "to be mistress of Pemberley might be something!"

Granting the full force of the snobbery, the exploitation, the inhumanity of all the evils which diminish the human spirit and which are inherent in a materialistic society, the novel clearly confirms the cynical "truth" of the opening sentence. Yet at the same time, without evading the degree of Elizabeth's capitulation to society, it affirms the vitality, the independent life which is possible at least to an Elizabeth Bennet. *Pride and Prejudice,* like its title, offers deceptively simple antitheses which yield up the complexity of life itself.

Catherine E. Moore

THE PRINCE AND THE PAUPER

Type of work: Novel
Author: Mark Twain (Samuel L. Clemens, 1835-1910)
Type of plot: Social criticism
Time of plot: Sixteenth century
Locale: England
First published: 1882

In this historical satire, Twain follows the twin adventures of the Prince of Wales and a street beggar, look-alikes who unwittingly trade identities. Besides the fascination of the storyline and the humor of many incidents, the novel is interesting in its scrutiny of the past from the point of view of modern morality, and for its satire of the foibles and injustices of the class system.

The Prince and the Pauper was Mark Twain's earliest attempt to join his recent fascination for the romantic past of Europe with his natural bent for satirizing the injustices and social conventions of his own age. He was to do the same later, with far better effect, in *A Connecticut Yankee in King Arthur's Court* (1889), and with less success in *Personal Recollections of Joan of Arc* (1896). It is generally agreed that *The Prince and the Pauper* is a story mainly for children—though if that is wholly true, it must also be said that it is a children's story very rewarding for adults.

Twain employs in this novel many of the themes and devices which he may have exercised to better effect in other works, but which are nonetheless used well here also. There are, for example, all the usual techniques he learned so expertly as a teller of tall tales—tongue-in-cheek irony, ridiculous understatement, and exaggeration, to name a few. Miles Hendon's separation from Edward gives Twain the opportunity for soliloquy, a favorite literary device used with great success in *Huckleberry Finn.* The exchange of identities—as in *Huckleberry Finn* and *Pudd'nhead Wilson*—is another common occurrence in Twain's works, as is his use of coincidence.

Twain was also able in *The Prince and the Pauper* to underscore some of the social follies and injustices of his own age without actually having to attack them directly in the novel. He did this by satirically treating the social and legal conventions of Tudor England, and then assuming his readers would recognize for themselves the parallels with their own times. Hence, religious intolerance is the target of "In Prison," a chapter in which two women, who have kindly befriended Edward and Miles, are mercilessly burned at the stake because they are Baptists. Tom Canty, as king, labors to change laws which are unduly harsh or blatantly unjust; and Edward himself learns of the unnecessary cruelty of prisons, as well as the nature of the kind of life poor people must endure as a result of their poverty.

However, Twain's major criticism of society, both Tudor and his own, is of its mistaking the outward appearances of men or their circumstances as a final gauge of their true worth. The novel suggests that, under different circumstances, any man *could* be a king—just as Tom Canty, given the opportunity, learns to be one. Tom and Edward are equally intelligent and virtuous young boys, but each is born to a different kind of "court." Chance and circumstances alone determine much of our outward behavior and appearance. For Twain, this was as true for his own times as he felt it had been for Tudor England.

THE PRINCE OF HOMBURG

Type of work: Drama
Author: Heinrich von Kleist (1777-1811)
Type of plot: Historical tragedy
Time of plot: 1675
Locale: Prussia
First presented: 1821

The Prince of Homburg, Kleist's last work, was not presented until ten years after the playwright's death in 1811. The play employs romantic, poetic imagery within a realistic framework, and contains rich characterizations which convey the Prussian virtues of discipline and obedience. It suffers, however, from an episodic plot, lacking in action and cluttered with secondary characters.

Kleist's last drama, *The Prince of Homburg,* was banned in his own time by censors who objected to seeing a Prussian officer show cowardice in the face of death. It was not published until 1821 and even in 1828, when it was produced in Berlin, the scene of Frederick's terror had to be altered. Modern critics, however, see in the work Kleist's most mature drama, a coming to terms with the demands of the state and its laws, while acknowledging the role of the individual and his spirit, including even the force of the irrational.

Kleist's earlier tragedies tended to the excessive, with extravagant emotions and a certain wild quality, notably in *Penthesilea.* With the defeat of Prussia by Napoleon, however, his work took a patriotic turn and though the censors saw in Frederick's character a slur on Prussian heroism, Kleist's drama is actually one of the finest embodiments of the Prussian ideal, created through the resolution of the initial conflict between the emotional power—moving as if in a dream—of the prince and the recognition of the validity of the law which governs the social community.

The two poles of the drama are Frederick, the Romantic, sleepwalking hero, who moves according to his own inner law, achieving success, but without taking his place in a structured society, and the Elector, who represents the demands of the state, yet tempers them with wisdom and a gentle humor. In Kleist's generally tragic view of the world, men are most often destroyed by the irreconcilable conflicts into which they are cast by an almost hostile fate. That Kleist here could avoid the potential tragedy and bring his hero to a recognition of his true role seems to be a personal as well as a dramatic development. Unfortunately, the drama failed and Kleist himself, in a mood of despair, ended his own life.

THE PRINCESS CASAMASSIMA

Type of work: Novel
Author: Henry James (1843-1916)
Type of plot: Social criticism
Time of plot: Late nineteenth century
Locale: London
First published: 1886

This novel takes up the later career of a character from an earlier work, Roderick Hudson, *which saw beautiful Christina Light married to the powerful Italian Prince Casamassima. The Princess, some ten years later, is now separated, and in* The Princess Casamassima *we follow her new life of social involvement with proletarian revolutionaries. James examines not only the motives of upper-class "reformers," but also the interaction between the world of princes and dukes and the world of bookbinders, dressmakers, and chemists.*

The Princess Casamassima is James's most concerted effort to catch the revolutionary atmosphere of the London during the 1870's and 1880's. In his Preface to the novel he speaks of his awareness of political forces brewing beneath the vast surface of society. He did not know these forces in any intimate detail, however, and the novel shows it. His portraits of lower-class characters are solid enough (Hyacinth Robinson, Miss Pynsent, Mr. Vetch) and even brilliant (Millicent Henning).

The trouble lies in the portrayal of the revolutionaries. Paul Muniment, who introduces Hyacinth into revolutionary work is vague at the center. The famous revolutionary leader Hoffendahl does not even appear on stage; his "potency" is merely a felt presence. Nevertheless, James's political fable has its finenesses. The drama of Hyacinth's gradual awareness of what revolutionary behavior amounts to is superbly done. The little bookbinder finds that he has been used by Muniment and the Princess, and at the same time he discovers that he has become deeply attached to those objects of art possessed by the class he has been working to overturn. In his youthful idealism, he has been working against all he now respects and wishes to preserve. The irony here is compounded by the case of the Princess herself. Under the influence of Muniment and her own idealism she comes to repudiate her wealth and position at the very time Hyacinth aspires to the finer things to which she has introduced him. In the Princess, James gives us a vivid picture of the upper-class revolutionary—a person in full-fledged rebellion from her class. In contrast to Lady Aurora Langrish whose enthusiasm for the revolution fades when she discovers she cannot catch Paul Muniment, the Princess' revolutionary sympathies are not so easily dissipated. There is something about her seriousness which is cold and inhuman. She is a good portrait of a revolutionary fanatic and reactionary. Needless to say, for James revolutionary politics was not a pleasing spectacle.

THE PRINCESS OF CLÈVES

Type of work: Novel
Author: Madame de La Fayette (1634-1693)
Type of plot: Sentimental romance
Time of plot: Sixteenth century
Locale: France
First published: 1678

Simple in outline but elegant in detail, The Princess of Clèves *had an important influence both on the* roman à clef *and on the later psychological novel. Its careful analyses of emotion, atmosphere of intrigue, conflict between duty and desire, and subjective portrayal of character make this romance a landmark in French literature.*

This novel, sometimes called the first modern novel, combines aspects of the chronicle and romance, as well as aspects of Racinian and Corneillian tragedy.

The background depicts, with the authenticity of a chronicle, the court of Henri II, although the values are those of the court of Louis XIV. Rather than supporting those values, however, the novel seems to implicitly criticize them. There is a marked discrepancy between the values of the court and those of the heroine. The Princess perceives the discrepancy between appearance and reality at court because "things are seldom what they seem." The novel depicts with lucidity and tedious repetition the intrigues, love quarrels, and petty disturbances that fill out the round of days at court. The seeming magnificence of the court is shown to be superficial, and, in addition, is devalued by the obvious burdensome routine of court life.

In the manner of the romance, the novel describes the ideal qualities of all the ladies and gentlemen. Each lady is the most beautiful; each lover is the most handsome. Their clothing, jewels, hair, eyes, and so on are all without equal. The analysis of the passions, however, is not ideal and serves in still another way to undercut the values of the court. The novel reveals the transitory quality of passion, and the ultimate awareness of this is one of the reasons that the Princess refuses the Duke's offer of marriage. All of the supposed "digressions" in the novel relating the multiple loves, shifts of affection, and duplicity of the King and others only serve to reinforce the view that passion is not of lasting value.

Like the tragedies of Racine, the novel depicts the overwhelming passion that comes upon one without any warning, a passion that completely absorbs one's being. Yet unlike the heroines of Racine's tragedies, and similar to the heroes of Corneille's tragedies, the Princess is able, through her will, to triumph over her passion.

The novel is thus part of a literary tradition (the chronicle and romance) and reflects values of the court while implicitly criticizing these values. But it is unique (in conjunction with the tragedies of Racine) in analyzing the passions, that is, the inner life of the individual. By undercutting the traditional social values, new emphasis is placed upon the need for the individual to construct values for himself, rather than accept those of the social body.

THE PRISONER OF ZENDA

Type of work: Novel
Author: Anthony Hope (Sir Anthony Hope Hawkins, 1863-1933)
Type of plot: Adventure romance
Time of plot: 1880's
Locale: "Ruritania"
First published: 1894

One of the most popular novels written on the subject of royal intrigues, The Prisoner of Zenda *brims with kings and pretenders to power, beautiful ladies, loyal subjects, and self-serving traitors. The excitement of the plot, replete with midnight duels, trysts, and daring rescues, makes for highly entertaining reading.*

Despite its severe brevity and occasional plot weaknesses, *The Prisoner of Zenda* is among the most enduring of adventure romances. In part the reasons for this are predictable: mystery, intrigue, suspense, and love are integrated neatly in the tale; there is plenty of adventure, much of it framed as a conflict between evident Good and Evil; lastly, there is a strong central character—Rudolf Rassendyll—to hold the book together. It is, then, a highly formulaic romance, hence a popular one, yet it is also much more than this: in its touches of ethical ambiguity and in its clever use of "disguise" (both thematically and dramatically), *The Prisoner of Zenda* takes up the complex matter of defining, then judging, man's moral nature.

Early branded a wastrel by his sister-in-law, Rassendyll in time proves his sincerity and honor. What he learns, simply, is value—a theme which Anthony Hope explores not only in his major character, but also socially in his excoriations of kings and gentry. What the reader learns, as the sister-in-law does not, is the difference between real and apparent nobility. We come to judge Rassendyll not by his complexion or his attitude of indifference, but by his courageous, constant actions. In the same way, his "kingliness" is evidenced not in borrowed robes and crowns, but in a quality of spirit which cannot be counterfeited.

Yet Rassendyll's character is also qualified throughout the novel. He is genuinely tempted by the throne and by Flavia's attendant charms. Too often he ignores the morality of his actions: once when he backstabs a guard; again when, madly vengeful, he destroys two of Black Michael's hirelings. With bold strokes Anthony Hope defines Rassendyll's identity through two character foils—the dissipated real king (significantly, a namesake and distant relative), and the brash knave, Rupert Hentzau. The former reinforces Rassendyll's worst qualities even as he illustrates, by contrast, the best. On the other hand, Hentzau appears at a glance to be thoroughly different from Rassendyll, yet Rudolf's fascination with Rupert's attractive evil clearly suggests an affinity between them. When Rassendyll spares his enemy, then later tries desperately to slay him, the psychological overtones are plain: regretfully, he has let escape the evil in himself.

The themes of moral ambiguity ("if it were a sin may it be forgiven me," says Rudolf at one point) and political chicanery in the novel fit well with the idea of individual honor. What is to be gained by acting honorably in a world without principle? This is a penetrating question, especially toward the end of the adventure when Rudolf and Flavia must elect honorable self-sacrifice or selfish love. Their choice of the former, it seems, points out the novel's answer: the world becomes a measure better and an individual a measure greater only as there are those ready to prefer honor over happiness.

THE PRIVATE LIFE OF THE MASTER RACE

Type of work: Drama
Author: Bertolt Brecht (1898-1956)
Type of plot: Social chronicle
Time of plot: 1933-1938
Locale: Germany
Partial presentation: 1938; first published: 1944

This exposé of the Nazi regime is composed of seventeen scenes or one-act plays taken from a longer work, The Fears and Miseries of the Third Reich. *These scenes form a pageant describing the first five years of Hitler's reign. They do not, however, form a play in the usual sense, for each character appears only once, and unity is achieved only by the historical sequence and by fragmentary narration.*

Perhaps Brecht's most important work, *The Private Life of the Master Race* marks a clean break from the Ibsen tradition. With seventeen locales over a seven-year period, the writer's demand on the propmen might seem absurd. Fortunately, props are unimportant to Brecht, as simple signs and bleak settings suffice; he depends on the talents of the actors to depict the tensions that existed between the responsibilities of morality and the expectations of a fascist state. Individuals are not the focus here, but society. Brecht asks a great deal from his audience or readers, who are assumed to be curious about the play's content, but not awed; it is a play to be viewed, not read.

The reader is moved from Breslau in 1933, through many scenes, and finally to Hamburg in 1938, all the while receiving information about the hidden atrocities of Hitler's Germany. The vocabulary recreates vividly such hideous Nazi practices as kidnaping women and "promising children" from occupied areas, and impregnating captive women with the semen of S. A. Nazi "ideal" men. From the Nazi Youth Movement-produced child informant, through scenarios of anti-Semitism, to the activity of the S. A., the reader with each new scene is bombarded by threatening illusions, especially the apparition of the Panzer. The Panzer, or armored personnel carrier, is loaded with various personality types in the guise of soldiers—"the pupils of the notorious Einstein, yet trained in the iron school of the Führer, and taught the truth about Aryan science." The Panzer symbolizes both merciless army strikes, and the constant oppression of Nazi S. A. activists.

In *The Private Life of the Master Race,* the reader confronts the perils of a controlled social attitude of optimism in the face of the realities of boredom and repression; Brecht offers an intelligent study of how intellectuals— doctors, judges, and scientists—could have allowed themselves to be "bossed by half-savages." Brecht dedicated this work to the "other Germany," not to the nostalgia of the Weimar Republic but into the future, the bright future of post-Nazi Germany.

PRIVATE LIVES

Type of work: Drama
Author: Noel Coward (1899-1973)
Type of plot: Comedy of manners
Time of plot: 1930
Locale: France
First presented: 1930

Private Lives, sophisticated high comedy at its best, is the story of misadventures created by an exchange of husbands and wives. Originally performed by Coward himself and Gertrude Lawrence, the play won immediate acclaim. There is little plot, but the brilliant dialogue and unconventional theme place the play among the best brittle farces of the modern stage.

That old combination of irresistible force and immovable object makes Coward's *Private Lives,* allegedly written in five days, one of his most popular and enduring plays. Elyot and Amanda (originally portrayed by Coward and Gertrude Lawrence) are the modern equivalent of the ever-dueling couples found in Restoration drama, and the constant battle between two such evenly matched foes makes the play sophisticated high comedy at its best. In the second act, usually considered the play's peak, the duo is alone on stage most of the time and head for their inevitable collision with all the finesse and flair of two tipsy diplomats who have designs on each other's territory. Neither can submit, for both must have the final word, and blasé as they are about most things, they fiercely maintain their independence. Ironically, considering its prickly partners, the play contains one of Coward's few effective love scenes.

Yet in this sparkling misadventure based on the then daring idea of an exchange of husbands and wives, it is not character, nor theme, nor plot (of which there is precious little) which sustains the play. Rather it is the brilliant dialogue and the atmosphere of magic playfulness which holds our attention. Coward creates a brittle farce and appeals to the audience's desire to vicariously identify with the casual superiority of his heroes. He gives us a smart and sassy world and does not permit us time to quibble over why we are so attracted. He makes us feel that anything two such charming, if selfish, people want must be acceptable; the morality and standards of life outside the play are absent from our minds. It is Coward's special talent that for a brief time he makes us use his ruler alone to take the measure of events.

THE PRIVATE PAPERS OF HENRY RYECROFT

Type of work: Novel
Author: George Gissing (1857-1903)
Type of plot: Reflective romance
Time of plot: Late nineteenth century
Locale: England
First published: 1903

This fictional biography is a series of episodes and sketches which give the views of Henry Ryecroft on the widest variety of subjects, from Xenophon to berries. The interest of the book lies in the minutely drawn character of Ryecroft—a thoughtful, literate man, a withdrawn humanist who is gentle and remote yet aware of his England.

Not really a novel at all, Gissing's long reflective essay is a prose poem, an elegiac celebration of true rest after enervating toil. The author, a persona for Gissing, mourns his past life of poverty, starvation, and loneliness but takes infinite consolation from the simple comforts of his cottage, savory meals, spring flowers, and good books. Walter Allen (*The English Novel,* 1954) finds Ryecroft "repellent" in his irresponsible rejection of life, but concedes that Gissing's cruel struggle to achieve literary success, in the hostile London of hack writer and journalist, explains Ryecroft's glorification of hermit-like peace.

Gissing's book is a philosophical meditation very much in the tradition of Thoreau's *Walden.* Unlike the American transcendentalist, Ryecroft does not go into isolation in order to return to the world a wiser man than he left it. His cottage in Devon is more comfortable than Thoreau's primitive cabin precisely because he plans to stay until the end. *Walden* celebrates withdrawal as a resting place in the journey of living and being; *The Private Papers of Henry Ryecroft* is stoical and resigned, and it is content to shore up associations and impressions that will prepare for death. It has a tragic dimension, whereas *Walden* is an idyl and a mental epic.

Ryecroft's stoicism gives him the courage to live without illusions. "Sympathetic understanding" strikes him as a largely illusory hope; his splendid isolation is far more satisfying: "The mind which renounces, once and for ever, a futile hope, has its compensation in ever-growing calm." Although still committed to the life of the mind and human values, Ryecroft is skeptical of democracy and contemptuous of science:

> I see it (science) restoring barbarism under a mask of civilization; I see it darkening men's minds and hardening their hearts; I see it bringing a time of vast conflicts, which will pale into significance "the thousand wars of old" . . . .

There are many today who would call Ryecroft's bias prophetic.

THE PROFESSOR

Type of work: Novel
Author: Charlotte Brontë (1816-1855)
Type of plot: Psychological romance
Time of plot: Nineteenth century
Locale: Belgium and England
First published: 1857

Although published posthumously, The Professor *was Charlotte Brontë's first completed novel. Its plot and characterizations foreshadow those in* Villette, *except that this novel is simpler and free of the atmosphere of mysticism and mystery which pervades the later work. The story of an English teacher who seeks his fortune in Europe, the book presents a touching love story and deals with the problems of Catholicism, marriage, and Continental culture.*

Charlotte Brontë's first novel, *The Professor,* if compared to her mature, well-structured works like *Jane Eyre, Shirley* and *Villette,* does fall short in many respects. It fails in balance, character motivation, dynamic moral testing of its hero, and an unskillful author intrusion.

Its length, neither that of a novel nor a short story, may account for some of these defects. In a full-length novel Brontë might have worked out better proportion in both the English and Belgian episodes, and had time to lengthen or shorten other episodes, such as Crimsworth's meetings with Mlle. Henri. Often the reader feels oppressed by prolonged set descriptions, such as the narrator's extensive delineation of his three students—Eulalie, Hortense, and Caroline—and the conference with M. Pelet and Mlle. Reuter. These might not seem so awkward and irrelevant had the work been longer and contained more characters. Often Brontë spends care on such scenes which have no great bearing on the plot at all. After she makes a close drawing of Edward Crimsworth and his wife, they practically drop from sight; only are they briefly reported on by Yorke Hunsden on his first visit to Brussels.

In fact, Crimsworth's two entirely different experiences in England and Belgium have little connection, united merely by the slender thread of Hunsden's friendship. Hunsden, without rational motivation and after months of silence, suddenly writes and appears at Crimsworth's door. The quite contrived introduction of M. Vandenhuten and his son (rescued earlier from drowning by Crimsworth) are used only as a means of Crimsworth's getting a job after his leaving M. Pelet's school. They function not at all before or afterward.

The hero himself meets with no impossible choices or tragedies. All is low-key, purposefully drawn so by Miss Brontë. Crimsworth, her narrator, retains a balanced, even interpretation of himself and others. But one wishes for a hero who would develop. One longs for dynamic situations, exciting dialogue.

Brontë attains the latter only in exchanges between Hunsden and Crimsworth; the former is her most striking achievement in *The Professor,* although she makes Zoraïde Reuter, the schoolmistress, a second fascinating
and well developed character. Unfortunately, hero Crimsworth and heroine
Mlle. Henri are quite lackluster.

It is customary for critics to read *The Professor* as a forerunner to the
later novels, a work in which Charlotte Brontë experiments with plot structure and character, both of which she skillfully handles in *Jane Eyre* and
Shirley. However, *The Professor* has story interest of its own and the novel
tells a great deal about the author's values from the many asides to the
reader. Brontë reveals her ideas of marriage, her intolerance toward the Belgian character, and her deep suspicion of Roman Catholicism. And much of
her personality is richly exhibited by the bold choice of a male first person
narrator.

THE PROFESSOR'S HOUSE

Type of work: Novel
Author: Willa Cather (1873-1947)
Type of plot: Psychological realism
Time of plot: A few years after World War I
Locale: Hamilton, a Midwestern university town
First published: 1925

Godfrey St. Peter, the main character of The Professor's House, *is one of the author's most sensitive and sympathetic creations, and it is the mirror of his nostalgic but discerning mind which reflects the tensions of shifting relationships in the St. Peter family. Cather skillfully uses flashbacks and indirect revelation of past events to throw light on a baffling and complicated personal problem.*

Critical estimates of *The Professor's House* always are forced to deal with Willa Cather's insertion of "Tom Outland's Story" into the middle of the novel. Cather once remarked that in writing this novel she was attempting to experiment with form by "inserting the *Nouvelle* into the *Roman*" and loosely arranging the novel's structure into the three-part form of a sonata. Nonetheless, many critics have argued that Outland's story is too much of a digression from that of Professor St. Peter, and that the lengthy inclusion seriously detracts from the novel's unity.

In many ways, however, Outland's story can be viewed as integral to that of the Professor. The Professor, in fact, recognizes a great deal of himself, especially when young, in Outland. Outland's enthusiasm for life rekindles in the Professor his own flagging interest in his work, as well as his zest for living. Idealistic, creative, intelligent, and altruistic—as well as sensitive and appreciative of the simpler values in life—both men are basically the same. Their characters are complementary, so that by knowing about the one, we gain a more complete understanding of the other. In one sense, Outland's "Story" is a metaphor for the Professor's: the kinds of fundamental values and meaning Outland discovers on the mesa are the same the Professor had experienced in finding the form for and eventually completing his work on the Spanish explorers.

Other characters in the novel lack the generous spirit for life which typify Outland and the Professor. Louie Marcellus comes the closest to such spirit, but like his wife, he is more concerned with spending money than discovering other values for living. The rest of the family are severely caught up in jealousies: Mrs. St. Peter of the Professor's friendship with Tom Outland, Kathleen and Scott of the wealth Rosamond inherited from Outland.

St. Peter feels great disappointment in his family's shortcomings, made all the more obvious by their contrast to his own and Outland's larger natures. He feels his family has stifled his better nature; without Tom Outland he has no one from whom he can draw a sense of delight of living. Having lost, momentarily, the will to live, he makes no effort to save himself from the leaking gas of the stove. He is doubly saved by Augusta, from both the gas and his sense of defeat in life, for he wakes with a new determination to survive even without the broad values in living which he had shared un-spoken with Tom Outland.

PROMETHEUS BOUND

Type of work: Drama
Author: Aeschylus (525-456 B.C.)
Type of plot: Classical tragedy
Time of plot: Remote antiquity
Locale: A barren cliff in Scythia
First presented: Date unknown

In this compelling drama, Aeschylus offers the spectacle of a demigod in conflict with his destiny and defiant in the face of severe punishment. The mood of the play is one of sharp irony and deep reflection, for the suffering of the legendary Fire-Bearer symbolizes man's inhumanity to man.

In several ways *Prometheus Bound* is something of a puzzle. We do not know the date of its production, although we can safely assume it came rather late in Aeschylus' career, possibly between 466 B.C. and 456 B.C., which was the year of his death. Nor do we know its exact order in the Aeschylean trilogy on Prometheus, because this is the only surviving play. But we know it was followed by *Prometheus Unbound.* Further, it is the one extant play by Aeschylus to deal directly with a metaphysical problem by means of supernatural characters. But even the questions it raises are unresolved. This drama is a mystery centering on a mystery.

The situation of the play is static: Prometheus is fastened to a Scythian crag for enabling mankind to live when Zeus intended to destroy this ephemeral creature. Once Hephaestus wedges and binds him down, Prometheus is immobile. Thereafter the theatrical movement lies in his visitors—the chorus of nymphs, Oceanus, Io, and Hermes. Essentially this is a drama of ideas, and those ideas probe the nature of the cosmos. We may forget that the characters are mainly extinct Greek gods. The issues that Aeschylus raises are still very much alive today.

The Greeks loved a contest, and *Prometheus Bound* is about a contest of wills. On the one side is Zeus, who is omnipotent in this world, while on the other is Prometheus, who has divine intelligence. Neither will give an inch, for each feels he is perfectly justified. Zeus rules by right of conquest, and Prometheus resists by right of moral superiority. On Zeus' side are Might and Force, the powers of compulsion and tyranny. But Prometheus has knowledge and prescience. The play consists of a strange debate between the two. Zeus in his inscrutability and majesty does not appear, but we see his agents enforcing his will.

The drama begins and ends with the exercise of Zeus' almighty power. That power is used simply to make Prometheus suffer. At first it binds him to a crag and finally it envelops him in a cataclysm. Zeus has a fearsome capacity to inflict pain, not merely on Prometheus but on Io as well. In both instances it seems due to disobedience. If Prometheus opposed Zeus by giving

man the fire and skills he needed to survive, Io resisted Zeus love. Because
of this Zeus exiled her from her home and changed her into a cow, while
jealous Hera forced her to flee from land to land, bitten by a gadfly. Thus
Prometheus shows rebellion on the divine plane (he being a Titan), while Io
rebels on the human level. The price of their rebellion is written in their
flesh, and both regard Zeus as their persecutor. Aeschylus certainly disliked
political tyranny, but it is a mistake to read this play merely as a parable of
man's inhumanity to man. The issues go far deeper.

Prometheus has omniscience and therefore knew what would come of his
revolt. He made a great personal sacrifice when he supported mankind out
of compassion. In a real sense he is a savior and a tremendous hero. His
knowledge does not keep him from suffering like man, nor does it make him
accept his pain calmly. He knows why he suffers but still defies his fate. He
feels that he is right and Zeus is wrong. Moreover, he claims that Zeus is not
the ultimate power, that Zeus is subservient to the Fates and the Furies.

Yet Prometheus holds the winning hand in this play and he knows it, for
he possesses a secret that Zeus needs to retain his power. No matter how much
suffering Zeus may caused him, one day Zeus will have to come begging.
That is his only consolation in torment. Every counsel to moderation or
humility is superficial and vain, for why should Prometheus give up the joy
of seeing Zeus humbled just to alleviate his own agony? This motivation
comes through clearly in the bitter dialogue with Hermes.

Thus Prometheus is not only self-righteous and vengeful, he is full of
arrogant pride. He chooses his pain; perhaps he even deserves it. No one
justifies Zeus, for he is beyond any notion of justice. But Prometheus exults
in justifying himself to any divinity who will listen. Yet we remember his
services to man and feel compassion for him. He is an authentic tragic hero,
arousing both pity and fear.

As a dramatic character Io represents the human condition. The daughter
of a god, she is shut out of her home by Zeus' command. Io is given a bestial
body and made to run over the face of the earth in pain, stung by the ghost
of many-eyed Argus (conscience). But in the distant future she and Zeus
will be reconciled.

We can only guess at the resolution of the Zeus-Prometheus conflict in
Prometheus Unbound by Aeschylus. Possibly Zeus gained in maturity after
centuries of rule and decided to release the Titan freely, after which
Prometheus gave him the secret. Just as man evolved through the gifts of
Prometheus into a civilized creature, perhaps Zeus changed and made his
reign one of wisdom and force. It is hard to believe that Prometheus would
alter unless such a change did come about in Zeus. But this is pure speculation.
The debate between Prometheus and Zeus remains open. Is Prometheus a
rebel because God is unjust? Or is it that he places himself above God, doing
what pleases him in the knowledge that he must suffer for it. Aeschylus never

solves this dilemma in the play—he merely shows it to us in the strongest dramatic terms. Tautly written, *Prometheus Bound* is profound precisely because it remains an enigma. In judging the debate we judge ourselves.

James Weigel, Jr.

PROMETHEUS UNBOUND

Type of work: Poem
Author: Percy Bysshe Shelley (1792-1822)
Type of plot: Lyric drama
Time of plot: Remote antiquity
Locale: Asia
First published: 1820

Valuable as a key to understanding Shelley's philosophy, Prometheus Unbound *uses the combined mediums of drama and poetry to expound the author's theory that universal love is the only solution to mankind's ills.*

Regardless of the difficulty in deciphering a concrete meaning from this "lyrical drama," one is nevertheless immediately struck by a considerable display of artistic ability in handling all the possible variations of the lyric form and verse patterns. (Bennett Weaver's *Prometheus Unbound*, 1957, deals with the many facets of this work in detail.) The work as a whole is unique in form and in tone, and it ignores blatantly Keats's famous admonition to Shelley: "load every rift of your subject with ore." Shelley fortunately clung to his own distinctive mode, however, letting himself project his style with such liquidity that he challenges music for comparison. Many of the songs in *Prometheus Unbound* are a remarkable lyrical flowering—nearly two dozen are in forms original with him. To a great extent these lyrical passages, providing melodic and variegated rhythms, account for Raymond D. Havens' remarks in "Shelley the Artist" that the entire work is "vital, rich, fresh, varied, alive." Newman Ivey White, whose biography of Shelley is the most accurate, complete, and judicious, goes even further in his laudatory comments, claiming that many of the passages in the work, if considered only as separate poems, would place Shelley among the greatest of English poets.

Numerous studies have been made of the various meanings of the drama; it is perhaps equally valuable to understand in what ways the poem may be considered a "remarkable lyrical flowering." From Prometheus' opening oration to the paean-like ending, the reader is carried along with the delicacy, vivacity, thunder, or choric effect of the lines. The spacelessness of the work is its virtue, and its muted, ethereal effect is lyrically matchless.

This work, worthy of the name "lyrical drama," illustrates supremely how Shelley has fashioned not only his individual lyric patterns but also the Pindaric ode, the "Fourteeners," the Spenserian stanza, couplets, and infinite variations of the Greek choral effects into a distinctively Shelleyan image. Every conceivable meter can be detected; the inversions, the intricately developed rhythm patterns are numerous. A "lyrical flowering" seems an appropriate phrase for the entire work, perhaps Shelley's greatest.

THE PROMISED LAND

Type of work: Novel
Author: Henrik Pontoppidan (1857-1943)
Type of plot: Social criticism
Time of plot: Late nineteenth century
Locale: Denmark
First published: 1891-1895

In The Promised Land, *Pontoppidan deals with the division between town and country dwellers in nineteenth century Denmark during a period of struggle between the People's Party—which sought an increased voice in public affairs for the peasant class—and the Conservative Party. Although excellent as a "problem novel," the work often lacks depth of characterization and tight plotting.*

Nobel Prize-winer Henrik Pontoppidan attempted in *The Promised Land* to illustrate the conflicts that overtake a human being who attempts to submerge his instincts to his intellectual beliefs. Emanuel Hansted is a complicated, tormented individual, divided between theory and instinct, duty and passion. He is not entirely sympathetic, but he is understandable and pitiable. A dreamer, he tries unsuccessfully to gain the confidence of the peasants, but, despite his efforts to make himself one with the soil and the peasant life, his urban background ultimately betrays his ambitions.

Pontoppidan writes with a deceptively aloof, almost cold, style, but his characters are warm-blooded and many-faceted human beings. Hansine, Emanuel's wife, speaks little, but it is clear that she feels deeply. He married her because she was a peasant, because he felt that she would help him to forget his past, but gradually she comes to realize that they are wrong for each other. With great artistry, the author subtly suggests her feelings, implying much with few words. Her sacrifice at the end of the book is both inevitable and touching.

Emanuel's past in Copenhagen is only revealed in pieces, through allusions in conversation. His former relationship with the attractive, sophisticated Ragnhild Tonnesen is disclosed bit by bit; the reader discovers the realities behind the appearances slowly. This technique requires great control on the part of the author, but it builds with relentless inevitability to the emotional crisis at the heart of the book. Politics and religion play an important part in the novel, but primarily it is a story of human beings.

Emanuel saw everything evil in the sophistication of his past life in the city, and made the mistake of seeing only good in the crude life of the peasants. He craved truth and justice, and saw a moral earnestness in the peasant faces which touched him deeply. So completely did he reject the city and its ways, including science and progress, that he refused to let a doctor see his son until it was too late to save the boy's life. There was a dormant power in the people, he believed, and he wanted to be the one to raise it.

But, as one of the other characters comments, he only sacrificed himself—
and his family—to his opinions. Niels, on the other hand, is his exact opposite,
a young upward-mobile peasant, writing for the local newspapers in his
spare time, ambitious, hopeful for the future. Everywhere, signs of change
are in the air, but Emanuel cannot understand where they are leading. His
vague dreams and misplaced ideals only lead him astray. His doubts and
struggles are vividly portrayed by the author in this important novel of the
birth of the modern age in Denmark.

PROSERPINE AND CERES

Type of work: Classical myth
Source: Unknown
Type of plot: Allegory of fertility and death
Time of plot: Remote antiquity
Locale: Mediterranean region
First transcribed: Unknown

One of the most popular of the Greek myths, the story of Proserpine and Ceres, *which offers a simple but moving explanation of the four seasons, has lived from age to age through numerous oral, poetic, and prose renditions. The imaginative appeal of the tale lies in its beautiful interpretation of grief.*

This fertility myth seems to have Mycenaean (pre-Homeric) origins, but the earliest and in many ways the most perfect version survives from the late seventh century B.C. in the Homeric Hymn to Demeter, that is, Ceres. Demeter (either "earth mother" or "grain mother") and her daughter Persephone (corrupted by the Romans into Proserpina) were originally two aspects of one mythic personality: the mother was associated with the harvest, the daughter with the sprouting grain. The Greeks, fearfully avoiding mention of the daughter's name, called her simply Kore, that is, (grain) maiden. This practice was usual with the powerful and mysterious chthonian (underworld) deities whom the Greeks wished not to risk offending.

The literary history of the myth is extensive, including two appearances in Ovid (*Metamorphoses* 5.341 ff. and *Fasti* 4.417 ff.), but there are only minor variations, such as where the rape occurred, who Triptolemus was, how many pomegranate seeds Proserpine ate, and how much of the year she remains with Hades. The above synopsis, which is a conflation of Ovid's accounts, differs from the Homeric Hymn in the Triptolemus episode. In the Hymn, Ceres' hosts, Celeus and Metanira, are not peasants but the rulers of Eleusis, near Athens. In her old age, Metanira has borne a child, Demopho(o)n, whom she gives to Ceres, disguised as Doso, to suckle. Triptolemus was one of Eleusis' youthful nobility, and was among the first to participate in Ceres' mysteries, or secret rites, in the temple built by Celeus. The hymn also has Proserpine spend one-third of the year with her husband below the earth; this reflects a tripartite seasonal year of spring, summer, winter. Despite mention in the Hymn that Proserpine emerges to the upperworld in the spring, reputable scholars argue that her four months' absence is associated with the summer-long storage of harvested grain in June (the grain was put in jars in the cool earth till planting in the winter). The traditional interpretation is that the fresh seed grain is planted in the winter and the maiden shoots emerge in the early spring.

The so-called Eleusinian mysteries most closely resembled what we might call a universal religion. Its objective was preparation for eternal peace through understanding the mystery of cyclic growth. Although great numbers of Greek-speaking persons were initiated into the mysteries, little authoritative information about them survives. Clement of Alexandria (fl. A.D., second century), a convert to Christianity, reveals that votaries dramatized the myth of Ceres and Proserpine, fasted, handled sacred objects, and partook of the sacramental porridge of water, flour, and mint which Ceres was offered at Eleusis. The so-called Lesser Mysteries were celebrated in Athens in the early spring; they consisted of prayers, purifications, and the like. The Greater Mysteries were performed in September/October; nine days of grand procession from Athens to Eleusis and back featured numerous rituals, at the height of which priests and priestesses were consecrated. Certainly the mysteries relied heavily on symbolic ritual and mythic reenactment. The nine days of the Greater Mysteries correspond to the nine days of Ceres' fasting as she searched for her daughter; the pomegranate with its many "bloody" seeds symbolizes fertility; Proserpine's marriage to Hades metaphorically explains the mystery of fertilization and growth within the earth. It is even theorized that the secret dramas included ritualistic sexuality, imitating the *hieros gamos* ("sacred union") of the underworld deities to bring fertility to the fields. (Such a ritual was common to a number of cults, and within the myth of Ceres herself is her union with her brother Jupiter, the sky god, which produced Proserpine.)

The basic structure of the myth is simple: peaceful innocence, sudden violence, misguided revenge, and finally reconciliation; within this dramatic structure the myth-makers have woven origins of the Eleusinian cult. (Ovid's insertion of the Arethusa myth is forced, since it is merely preparation for its lengthier telling immediately following in the *Metamorphoses*.) But there are also some excellent descriptive sequences: the gathering of flowers by Proserpine, the sudden dark violence of Hades, the awesome burning of Metanira's child in the fire. Finally, the characterizations of both in Ovid's versions and in the Hymn are classic: Proserpine as the innocent virgin, carefully protected; Demeter, the doting mother, the prototype of *mater dolorosa*; Hades, the lustful villain who brings havoc when he makes an unprecedented appearance in the upperworld; Jupiter, the supreme administrator and magistrate who must act to prevent the extinction of men (the gods' sacrificers) and who must strike a compromise between equally powerful forces. The resolution is no doubt necessary to explain why in other myths Proserpine seems quite at ease in her role as queen of the dead. (It is likely that this character is a further confusion of the witch goddess, Hecate, and a primitive earth goddess.) In fact, excepting her rape, she is virtually always found in the underworld, ruling with authority. There she appears in the various heroic *katabaseis*—descents by Orpheus, Aeneas, and others; there also is she the object of an attempted rape by Theseus and Pirithous.

The most significant modern adaptation of the myth is the musical drama *Persephone* (1934) by Igor Stravinsky and André Gide, in which the heroine willingly sacrifices herself to bring joy and youth to the gloomy realm below.

E. N. Genovese

PURPLE DUST

Type of work: Drama
Author: Sean O'Casey (1884-1964)
Type of plot: Satiric comedy
Time of plot: The present
Locale: Clune na Geera, Ireland
First presented: 1940

In this stylistically pleasing mixture of moving poetry and extravagant comedy, O'Casey portrays two stuffy Englishmen, Poges and Stoke, trying to adjust to the rigors of the bucolic life. The thrust of the comedy is to extol the hardy Irish and satirize men who blindly venerate the past without ever looking to the future.

Purple Dust may not be Sean O'Casey's greatest play, but it is probably his funniest. He begins with a potentially hilarious situation, the attempt by two stuffy Englishmen to "restore" an ancient, ramshackled Tudor mansion in the Irish countryside in the face of opposition from the local citizenry. To this beginning he adds a cast of broad, colorful, and sometimes poetic types, and, utilizing a thin but completely functional plot line, presents a sequence of zany scenes that would have fit nicely into a Marx Brothers movie.

But that is not to say that *Purple Dust* is without serious content. Eschewing the kind of abstract symbolism and forced rhetoric that damaged such earlier "idea" plays as *Within the Gates* (1933), *The Star Turns Red* (1940), and *Oak Leaves and Lavender* (1946), O'Casey mixes comedy with message so adroitly in *Purple Dust* that he is able to present some strident satire and provocative ideas without losing any humor or theatrical effectiveness.

Cyril Poges and Basil Stoke are two brilliant comedic and satiric creations. Poges is the self-made man, the blustery pragmatic tycoon who has bullied his way to the top and believes he can impose his will on any one and any thing. At the same time, he feels his lack of background and tries to compensate by consuming large amounts of "culture"; he fancies himself an instant expert on art, history, poetry, and literature because he has bought and paid for great quantities of it. Stoke, on the other hand, represents inherited wealth, position, and formal education. He considers himself a thinker and speaks in long, abstract, convoluted sentences that turn the simplest thing into a complex metaphysical problem. Their hilarious debate over the nature of a "primrose" would not be out of place in an "Absurd" play by Eugene Ionesco.

But, regardless of their differences, both men are embodiments of the British Capitalist. Their various pretensions and blind spots set them up as perfect dupes for the canny rural Irish workmen. The chief symbol of the play is, of course, the absurd Tudor house they mean to refurbish as a way of making a connection with the historical grandeur of the past (Tudor England restored in rural Ireland!) as well as finding pastoral simplicity in the present. They add any object to the house that seems vaguely historical, regardless of its authenticity or its appropriateness—a "Jacobean" table, "Cambodian" bowl (out of Woolworth's), a set of medieval armor, a "quattrocento" bureau—while at the same time denying themselves such "luxuries" as modern indoor plumbing and electricity on the grounds that they are historically inauthentic.

Their pseudo-culture soon turns to disaster—the bowls are smashed, the bureau is broken to pieces, and finally the house itself is submerged. Their dream of bucolic simplicity likewise turns into a nightmare; the animals keep them awake at night, a cow wanders into the house and they flee in terror from the "wild beast," and the gentle autumn rain grows into a flood that inundates them all.

But O'Casey is not attacking tradition as such—only a false, pretentious, and ignorant use of it. Opposed to the Old English Capitalists are the Young Irish Workers and two of them, Jack O'Killigain and Philip O'Dempsey, articulate O'Casey's positive vision of man, tradition, and Ireland. Poges' ignorance of history is contrasted with O'Dempsey's profound grasp of his heroic historical and cultural background. He divorces himself from most of his contemporaries and aligns himself with the Irish heroes of the past. These visions are put into action when, as the flood waters start pouring in on Poges and Stoke, O'Killigain and O'Dempsey spirit their women, Avril and Souhaun, off to a mountain sanctuary. The survivors of the new flood will be the young, the passionate, and the truly Irish.

THE PURPLE LAND

Type of work: Novel
Author: W. H. Hudson (1841-1922)
Type of plot: Adventure romance
Time of plot: Nineteenth century
Locale: Uruguay and Argentina
First published: 1885

Although not as masterful as Green Mansions, The Purple Land *displays the author's genius for writing sensuous and lyrical prose. Hudson's style is a happy combination of the botanist's keen exactitude of observation and the poet's imaginative coloration and interpretation of factual detail.*

Curiously, William Henry Hudson is not as famous for the two books (*The Purple Land* and *Far Away and Long Ago*) that he wrote about an area which he knew well (the pampas of Uruguay and Argentina), as for *Green Mansions,* a book written about an area that he did not know well (the Venezuelan jungle). Part of *The Purple Land's* true worth has thus escaped critics, who have not fully appreciated its worth as a socio-historical documentary about an interesting part of the world during the embryonic decades of its history. Hudson knew and loved the pampa well. He had the unusual experience of being a talented Anglo-Saxon bred in the pampa during wild times. His powers of observation and description were notable, and we are indebted to him for colorful vignettes of pampa life during the middle of the nineteenth century.

Many social types of Uruguay are clearly drawn in the pages of *The Purple Land.* The confusion of the times is also mirrored, when a wild, loosely knit society was taking control of the rolling, green pampa of Uruguay, a place blessed with deep top soil, green grass, and ample water. Armies of gaucho cavalry flying white pennants from their lance tips (the *Blancos,* or Whites) battled armies of gaucho cavalry flying red pennants from their lance tips (the *Colorados,* or Reds). They initiated the traditional struggle between these two political factions for dominance of the Republic of the Left Bank (*Banda Oriental,* or East Bank) of the Uruguay River. Richard Lamb's adventures are therefore more meaningful than they may seem at first glance, for through them we gain insights into the Uruguayan life of the times. Many rural types, customs, and above all the terrible political drawbacks of the times are depicted.

Lamb's apparently aimless travels are also typical of the life of the times, and Hudson enriches his narrative with many details of sociology and natural science. The interesting and adventurous phases of life on the rolling pampa, with its purple tints at twilight, are also given us. Therefore, even though Uruguayan literature has produced some of the best works from South America in the novel and poetry, this novel written by a foreigner occupies a position of merit in the letters of Uruguay.

QUALITY STREET

Type of work: Drama
Author: James M. Barrie (1860-1937)
Type of plot: Comedy of manners
Time of plot: Napoleonic wars
Locale: English provincial village
First presented: 1902

The action of this play is based on a potential love affair which is interrupted by a ten-year absence. When Valentine Brown returns from the Napoleonic wars, his ardor has quite cooled, and the mousey spinster Phoebe must win him back by posing as a lively young flirt, supposedly Phoebe's niece.

James Barrie's best plays are those in which he treads the thin line between "reality" and "fantasy" with the touches of fantasy adding a lively, imaginative dimension to the essentially realistic situations (except for *Peter Pan,* where touches of reality sharpen the meaning of the fantasy). *Quality Street* is a charming "realistic fantasy" about a prolonged love affair that finally succeeds against the obstacles of time, age, and human misunderstanding.

Even in 1902, the subject matter and attitudes present in the play would have seemed dated, had Barrie not taken the edge off of the play's realism with a number of adroit theatrical devices. His touch is light, sentimental, and gently ironic so that one is moved by the plight of the spinster sisters, but does not take them too seriously. By placing his story in an English provincial village during the Napoleonic wars and emphasizing period settings and costumes, Barrie further distances his action from the modern world and so justifies actions and speeches for his characters that would be excessive and trite in a modern context. But the appeal of the play can probably best be accounted for by the fact that in mood and feeling it is close to a fairy tale.

The specific fairy tale is "Cinderella." Phoebe Throssel is the girl kept from her Prince Charming, Valentine Brown, not by conniving stepsisters, but by her intended's perversity in enlisting in the army rather than proposing to her. Upon his return ten years later, it is age, exaggerated by Phoebe's spinsterly role as schoolmarm, that keeps them apart. The transformation is occasioned not by magical intervention, but by Phoebe's own frustration.

So she effects her change—into her own niece Livvy—and goes off to the ball. There, like her prototype, she charms everyone including the object of her affections, but must keep her true identity a secret. The "glass slipper" which reveals the heroine and resolves the hero to marry her is replaced by the more conventional device of a talkative maid. Valentine Brown is converted by his flirtation with Livvy to the idea that it is Phoebe he really wants because she is mature and ladylike. They will live, as in all fairy tales, happily ever after, with Phoebe getting her Prince Charming and Valentine getting both the ladylike Phoebe and the flirtatious "Livvy" in one woman.

Whether or not such a conclusion would be acceptable in the modern world—either Barrie's or our own—is very doubtful. But "Quality Street" is no more real than "Never Land," and, while not so obviously a "wish-fulfill-ment" play, *Quality Street* is as much a fairy tale for adults as *Peter Pan* is for youngsters.

THE QUEEN'S NECKLACE

Type of work: Novel
Author: Alexandre Dumas, *père* (1802-1870)
Type of plot: Historical romance
Time of plot: Eighteenth century
Locale: France
First published: 1848

Always a defender of the integrity of monarchy, Dumas here presents a lively picture of court intrigue and royal passion. As a mystery story, the novel does not contain a single loose thread or irrelevant detail; as historical fiction, it attempts to describe Marie Antoinette as a woman of extreme charm, intelligence, and honor.

The Queen's Necklace is a sequel to *Memoirs of a Physician* and is the second of the Marie-Antoinette series. It was written by Dumas in collaboration with Auguste Maquet. This is generally classed as the last of the most famous or great novels in which Maquet collaborated. The picturesque tragedy of the diamond necklace is narrated in Dumas' best style and is a very fine piece of work, usually considered to be a favorite with English and American readers because it moves steadily and uninterruptedly to its conclusion; there are fewer threads of plot to be followed than in some of Dumas' other novels.

In a brief introduction Dumas refers to the Revolution of 1848, just accomplished, and to his foretelling of it in 1832, in *Gaule et France*. The prologue is borrowed from La Harpe's *Prophétic de Cazotte*, but Dumas has instilled into it a great deal for spirit and life. The novel itself gives a thoroughly amusing and cleverly constructed picture of court intrigues and dissoluteness, and of the rumblings of the coming storm. It does, however, present Marie Antoinette as a sympathetic character of intelligence and charm amidst the decadence surrounding her. She is portrayed by Dumas as being victimized by her enemies, who try to cast doubts upon her honor. The queen shares with Count Cagliostro the distinction of being one of the most clearly defined characters in the novel and one who instigates most of the major action of the story—action that is lively and robust in the Dumas manner.

The novel first appeared as a serial in *La Presse* in 1849-1850 and was instrumental in helping Dumas out of some difficulties caused by a controversy surrounding the reissue of some of his earlier works in the Paris journals as new stories. The result of this controversy was a fine series of stories of which the most prominent was *The Queen's Necklace*.

QUENTIN DURWARD

Type of work: Novel
Author: Sir Walter Scott (1771-1832)
Type of plot: Historical romance
Time of plot: 1468
Locale: France and Flanders
First published: 1823

This historical adventure, the first of Scott's novels to have a foreign setting, tells the story of a young Scotsman who must go abroad to seek his fortune in the service of a foreign king. The character of the hero Quentin is idealized as a younger son who must rely on his wits and bravery to survive and better himself.

Quentin Durward appeared when Sir Walter Scott's career as a novelist was nearly a decade old. Although Scott was still signing his novels "By the Author of Waverley," his authorship was by no means unknown. The "Wizard of the North" touched the familiar formulas of his fiction with an undeniable magic. With *Waverley* (1814) he had invented the historical novel, a new genre. This fictional treatment of the last of the Stuart uprisings in 1745, manifesting genuine insight into events "Sixty Years Since," had been solidly founded upon his knowledge of Scotland, its history, and its people. The author had perceived in the Jacobite-Hanoverian conflict the clash of two cultures at the very moment when the former was passing away forever and the other was just coming into being. He had made figures from history a part of his fiction, through them creating the tensions in which his fictitious characters were caught. This first novel established the pattern and theme for the serious historical novel, not only Scott's "Waverley Novels," but those of later writers such as James Fenimore Cooper.

Abounding in wealth and fame, his energies given also to public service, business, an estate in Scotland, an active social life, and other kinds of writing, Scott worked too hard and wrote too fast—one novel a year, sometimes two. With his tenth novel, *Ivanhoe* (1820), he sagaciously determined that his English reading public, after so many Scottish novels, would welcome a foray into English history. *Ivanhoe* became the talk of London, and his career gained new impetus. However, by 1823, his publisher, conscious of a waning popularity, advised Scott to turn to other kinds of writing. But the author boldly moved into the foreign territory of fifteenth century France and once again created a literary sensation—the reception of his new novel in Paris rivaled that of *Ivanhoe* in London. After *Quentin Durward*, Scott was recognized as a great writer both at home and abroad.

Today, *Quentin Durward* stands as a milestone in Scott's career rather than as a significant novel. His own remarks on the work contain casual apologies for his license with historical facts; some critics charge him with the worse fault of allowing superficial knowledge to make of *Quentin Durward* a mere costume romance rather than a serious historical novel. Others rate it simply as a good tale of adventure.

Nonetheless, *Quentin Durward* provides a good example of the conflict at the heart of Scott's best historical novels—the thematic clash between the old order and the new. The order which is passing away is the age of chivalry with its feudal system and its chivalric code. The age which is coming into being takes its traits from the leader who, rather than the titular hero, is the central character of the novel—King Louis XI of France. Louis is the antithesis of the chivalric ideal. Honor is but a word to him; he studies the craft of dissimulation. His unceremonious manners express contempt rather than knightly humility. He exercises the virtues of generosity and courtesy only with ulterior motives. Crafty and false, committed to his own self-interest, he is a complete Machiavellian.

If Louis is the chief representative of the new age, no one is a genuine survival of the old, despite noblemen who cling to a narrow concept of honor or imitate medieval splendor. Although Louis' principal rival, Charles of Burgundy, is his direct opposite, he is an inadequate symbol of chivalry. When Quentin says that he can win more honor under Charles's banner than under those of the king, Le Balafré counters with a description more accurate: "The Duke of Burgundy is a hot-brained, impetuous, pudding-headed, iron-ribbed dare-all." The decay of chivalry is epitomized in the hopelessness of Quentin's search for a leader who would keep his honor bright, and is confirmed by his ultimate conclusion that none of these great leaders is any better than the other. During the dramatic episode at Charles's court, when the king, ironically, is prisoner of his own vassal, the court historian, Des Comines, reminds Louis—who knows better than anyone else—that strict interpretation of the feudal law is becoming outdated while opportunity and power drive men to compromise and alter the old codes of chivalry.

Quentin Durward himself is the standard-bearer of the old order. Desiring to follow a man who will never avoid a battle and will keep a generous state, with tournaments and feasting and dancing with ladies, he lives upon ideas of brave deeds and advancement.

However, Quentin's ideals are impossible from the start. His rootlessness is symptomatic of the dying culture he reveres. His only real ties are with the mercenary band of Scottish Archers. Their weather-beaten leader Lord Crawford, one of the last leaders of a brave band of Scottish lords and knights, as well as Quentin's kinsman, the hideously scarred, almost bestial Le Balafré, serve as evidence that the glorious past is irrevocably past.

Moreover, though Quentin is introduced as a simple and naïve youth, he is not a rare survival of perfect chivalry. Equipped only with a rude mountain chivalry, he has his fair share of shrewdness and cunning. Far more politic than his experienced kinsman Le Balafré, this simple youth counsels Isabelle on the ways of telling half-truths with a skill which would credit

Louis himself. Though it offends his dignity as a gentleman to accept money from a wealthy plebeian—ironically, King Louis in disguise—he immediately discerns that the simple maid of the little turret is far more attractive after she is revealed as Isabelle, Countess of Croye, a highborn heiress. Presented by the king with an unpleasant crisis—an order to be prepared to kill the noble Crèvecoeur from ambush—in which it would be "destruction in refusing, while his honor told him there would be disgrace in complying," Quentin chooses compliance.

Yet as an emblem of the future, Quentin is neither as contemptible as his wily king nor as foolish as his older comrades deem him. The venerable Lord Crawford defends him well when he argues: "Quentin Durward is as much a gentleman as the King, only as the Spaniard says, not so rich. He is as noble as myself, and I am chief of my name." Furthermore, the youthful squire successfully endures the perilous journey, the chivalric testing of a man, bravely and skillfully evading the snares of the wicked, from the literal traps in and around Louis' castle to the treacherous ambush planned by the king and the more horrible fate threatening him during the sack of Schonwaldt. Thus only partially valid is Crèvecoeur's ironic description of Quentin's trials as a pleasant journey full of heroic adventure and high hope. Crèvecoeur's capitulation at the end is more just: "But why should I grudge this youth his preferment? Since, after all, it is sense, firmness, and gallantry which have put him in possession of Wealth, Rank, and Beauty!"

In the characterization of both Quentin and Louis, Scott dramatizes the ambiguities which afflict a time of transition. Louis, lacking any real sense of moral obligations, nevertheless understands the interests of France and faithfully pursues them. Detested as too cautious and crafty, he nonetheless exhibits a coolness before the wrath of Charles that far outshines the brave deeds of arms which Quentin values. If Quentin too passively drifts into the service of Louis, he can summon courage enough to defy the king, and principle enough to support the king in adversity—even at the cost of telling a little falsehood and the risk of sacrificing his life.

Scott in this novel, as in others, vividly depicts the various ways in which men cope with a world of changing values, where as Crèvecoeur's speech jocularly implies, sense and firmness have replaced gallantry, and wealth and rank have toppled beauty in the scale of things. It is this view of reality which seems most characteristic of the author: he is, like Quentin, most certainly a Romantic, idealizing the glories of a legendary time; but he understands the practical demands of a present reality and the value of a Louis or of a shrewd and brave youth like Quentin Durward.

Catherine E. Moore

QUO VADIS?

Type of work: Novel
Author: Henryk Sienkiewicz (1846-1916)
Type of plot: Historical novel
Time of plot: c. A. D. 64
Locale: Rome
First published: 1895

Quo Vadis? is a work of tremendous tension and energy. No one has succeeded better than Sienkiewicz in portraying the broad panorama of Roman civilization in the last degenerate days of the Empire, and in presenting the early Christians as credible people.

The name *Quo Vadis?* means "Where are you going?" In the title of Henryk Sienkiewicz's novel, it alludes to a legend concerning Simon Peter who asked that question of a vision of Christ, and was told, "I go to Rome to be crucified again." The novel begins where the legend ends, with the story of Vinicius, a Roman who was touched by the mission which Peter then undertook in Rome.

Vinicius' story is a love story. His love begins as lust for the beautiful body of Lygia, a Germanic hostage. It is transformed, by his contact with Lygia and with those who share her Christian faith, into a deep love for Lygia, for her God, and for all mankind. This love leads him away from the lustful, gory world of the Roman aristocracy, in which he has lived all his life, into the hidden world of the Christians, with life in the catacombs, occasional memories of Christ in sermons by Simon Peter and Paul of Tarsus, and the constant threat of the arena. Both of these worlds are presented vividly.

The sympathies of Sienkiewicz, himself a devout Christian, plainly lie with the Christians. But *Quo Vadis?* gives a balanced picture of pagan Rome. True, Nero is present to preside over bloody spectacles and dinner parties lit by living torches, and, true, Sienkiewicz, for the sake of the plot, takes liberties with history by making Nero responsible for the fire that burned Rome. But, alongside Nero, there are truly noble Romans, like Aulus Plautius and Petronius, who despise the debauched emperor. Petronius finds comfort in philosophy and in the worship of Thanatos, the goddess of death, in whose honor he poisons himself when life can hold no good for him. His comfort is not as great as that of the Christians, with their hope of Heaven and their deep love for one another. The point is plain, but by no means overwhelming. The reader, like the first century Roman, has his choice.

THE RAINBOW

Type of work: Novel
Author: D. H. Lawrence (1885-1930)
Type of plot: Psychological realism
Time of plot: Nineteenth and early twentieth centuries
Locale: England
First published: 1915

Originally condemned as obscene, one entire edition of The Rainbow *was destroyed by court order. The novel chronicles the emotional and love lives of three generations of the Brangwens, an English farming family. Lawrence attempts to analyze the basis of sexual relationships in depth; he focuses in particular on Ursula Brangwen, a sensitive, fiery, rebellious young woman who escapes her claustrophobic environment by attending the university and becoming a teacher. Ursula's character is further developed in* Women in Love, *a sequel to this novel.*

When D. H. Lawrence was composing *The Rainbow,* he realized that the critics and the general reader would not accept the novel. During that time he wrote to Amy Lowell concerning the critical reception of a book of his short stories: "The critics really hate me. So they ought." It is a curious remark from any writer, but especially from one who was so intent upon working a moral change in his readers. Lawrence knew, however, that not only was his fiction "shocking"—and it was to become more so—in its treatment of sexuality, particularly that of women, but that he created character and experience that challenged the way the critics viewed the world. In his fiction, and it became fully apparent in *The Rainbow,* he dramatized experience as dynamic, shifting, and allusive. For him the world was neither stable, nor certain, nor finally rationally explicable; his vision undercut all the preconceptions of the Edwardian critics. So their "hatred" of Lawrence's fiction was actually a defense of themselves. The fact that *The Rainbow* appeared during the first years of World War I seems to have validated Lawrence's argument against those who saw civilization as stable, knowable, and controllable.

One question preoccupies Lawrence in this novel: is the self capable of expansion, of becoming an entity, of achieving freedom, especially in the modern age where the traditional supports of community, family, and religion have been weakened or eliminated? In Will and Anna Brangwen's generation, the first to enter the industrial world, the self does survive, if only at a minimum. If, unlike Tom and Lydia Brangwen, they fail to create the "Rainbow," an image of the fully realized self in passionate community, and if their love degenerates to lust, they at least endure. True freedom, however, is denied them.

For Ursula, their daughter and the novel's heroine, the question of freedom hardly pertains, at least at the beginning. It is simply a matter of her survival. Her vision of the "Rainbow" at the end must be taken as a promise of freedom—and for many readers an unconvincing one—rather than a fulfillment. Yet it is a perception she earns by surviving both the inner and the outer terrors created by the twentieth century.

Even though, then, *The Rainbow* is a psychological novel in which Lawrence is primarily concerned with states of feeling and being below the level of history, the social and political backgrounds are of utmost importance; indeed they are of central significance to an understanding of the question of self-realization. For if Lawrence explores the dialectic of the psyche, he does so in an understanding of the determining impact which history has on that psychological drama.

A novel of three generations, the time span of *The Rainbow* runs from 1840 to 1905. In the background yet always urging their attention on us are the major cultural changes of the age: the rapid expansion of industry; the diminuation of the arable land; the growth of society originally based on the hamlet and town to one centered in the city; the breakdown of the nuclear family and the spread of education. In short, Lawrence dramatizes the English revolution from a feudal to a democratic, capitalistic society. In the foreground of these radical changes are the relationships between Tom and Lydia, Will and Anna, and Ursula and Anton. And as the novel moves in time from the middle of the nineteenth to the beginning of the twentieth century and in space from Ilkeston, Beldover, and Nottingham to London and Paris, what becomes increasingly apparent is that both these relationships and the sanctity of the self are harder to sustain.

In the first generation Tom Brangwen and his wife, Lydia, are firmly rooted in the earth and their marriage, after an early crisis, flowers into a relationship of deep and lasting love under whose influence their daughter, Anna, also grows. Yet if their way of life moves according to the rhythms of nature, it is limited by its pure physicality and it is fated, moreover, to be overwhelmed by other rhythms, those created by the motion of the piston. In fact, Tom himself is drowned when a canal bursts and floods his farm. The symbolic significance of his death—the rural life killed off by the industrial—is emphasized by its appearance at the structural midpoint of the novel.

The second generation, Anna and Will, move from the farm at Ilkeston to the town Beldover, and finally to a major industrial city, Nottingham. Their escape from the limiting existence on the farm to the greater individual liberty of the town, however, exacts a great cost: their love and marriage, although bountiful, fails to fulfill them. Because of their insistence on the self, they cannot make the deep connection which Tom and Lydia achieved. They are sustained by the rich fecundity of their marriage, but are left without unity.

It is left to Ursula to carry out the quest which her parents abandoned: that search for the completely free self in unity. But the forces confronting her are even greater than those her parents faced. The new society, characterized by the machine, is not only hostile to the individual but it has successfully destroyed the community. Cut off as she is from the life of feeling, freed from the restraints imposed by the older society, Ursula wanders through London and Paris preyed on by all, especially by Anton Skrebensky who would swallow her if she allowed him. Yet she survives as an independent self, aided by the strength she has inherited from her grandmother. Still Ursula has not discovered the necessary relationship to the whole life of man. That she can only imagine in her final vision of the "Rainbow." It was precisely her vision, which was also D. H. Lawrence's, of man fully free, connected, and equal that challenged so effectively the world-view of the Edwardians and led to their "hatred" of him. Lawrence showed his critics that there was no hope for society based on what they themselves were.

David L. Kubal

RAINTREE COUNTY

Type of work: Novel
Author: Ross Lockridge, Jr. (1914-1948)
Type of plot: Regional chronicle
Time of plot: Nineteenth century
Locale: Raintree County, Indiana
First published: 1948

Although its central story deals with the events of a single day, Raintree County *encompasses almost half a century of American life and history through its use of a series of flashbacks. Panoramic in scope, the novel is filled with a spectrum of people, ranging from statesmen, soldiers, and shoddy politicians to prostitutes, gamblers and simple tillers of the soil.*

In *Raintree County* the author attempted to weave the history of a continent and nation into his tumultuous narrative of the story of a man and the women in his life. Crosscutting between July 4, 1892, and the preceding decades, the story is refracted from many different points of view: from that of the major protagonist, John Shawnessy, and that of his second wife, Esther, his daughter, Eva, his father, and others. Professor Jerusalem Stiles, a unique comic character, acts in the capacity of the classic Greek chorus, participating in and commenting upon the action.

The prose flows like a river, an image itself which reappears frequently in the book. The chapters do not end as much as catapult into each other. Always, the book, although long, seems to be rushing forward. The style is a strange and vital mixture of Thomas Wolfe and James Joyce, the novel an attempt to create an American epic. The author obviously relished language and enjoyed playing with words; his rich prose, narrowly avoiding lushness, is finely descriptive and evocative of the variety and size of the American landscape.

The characters hurl from scene to scene and decade to decade, meaning well but seemingly fated to compromised destinies. It is not enough for them to mean well. Life is full of missed opportunities. John Shawnessy possessed all of the traits and talents to be a great man, but frustrated by his own passionate personality, he had to learn to be satisfied with slowly ripening wisdom instead of fame or power.

The Civil War sprawls through the center of the book, the dramatic heart of Lockridge's epic. The Battle of Chickamauga is vividly portrayed from the viewpoint of John Shawnessy. Sharp ironic contrasts are shown between true patriotism and verbose, windfilled sentiments.

RALPH ROISTER DOISTER

Type of work: Drama
Author: Nicholas Udall (1505-1556)
Type of plot: Farce
Time of plot: Sixteenth century
Locale: England
First presented: c. 1553

Ralph Roister Doister, *the earliest English comedy, is a play in five acts written in rhymed doggerel. It was acted originally by English schoolboys, to whom the broad, earthy humor and slapstick scenes were especially well-suited. Udall based the play on Roman comedy models, although the character of Dame Christian is a unique English addition to the drama, a direct descendant of Chaucer's Wife of Bath.*

For the student of English drama the real significance of *Ralph Roister Doister* is its position as the first English comedy. Written by Udall, himself a schoolmaster, the play was probably first performed by his students. It is very much a literary reflection of the Renaissance and its "New Learning" in England, for on one level the play is a teaching device as an imitation of a classical pattern. In fact, since the study of Plautus and Terence was a part of the revival of classical studies during the Renaissance, some have seen *Ralph Roister Doister* as merely an adaptation of Plautus' *Miles Gloriosus.*

The play, however, is no mere translation from the Latin, but rather is a skillful combination of classical and native elements. Udall has carefully incorporated the classical rules of the Roman comedy into his dramatic structure. He follows, for example, the classical pattern of dividing the action into five acts, and further adds to its literary qualities by composing the entire play in rhymed couplets. By merging the recent classical influence with the older, native English drama of the morality plays and interludes, Udall makes this play an important stepping stone leading to the golden age of Elizabethan drama. In *Ralph Roister Doister,* not only does doggerel verse become smooth couplets and coarse language become witty conversation, but also the character types from the English and classical pattern merge. Merrygreeke, for example, shows similarities to both the flattering parasite of the classical tradition and the mischievous Vice of the native tradition. And further, within the classical framework, the setting is typically English.

The intricate plot of the play, too, is an important development in the English stage. As it unfolds, develops, and comes to a satisfactory conclusion it marks an important step in the movement of the English play from the medieval mysteries and moralities to the intricate unravelings of Shakespeare's *Twelfth Night.*

THE RAMAYANA

Type of work: Poem
Author: Valmiki (fl. fourth century B.C.)
Type of plot: Religious epic
Time of plot: Remote antiquity
Locale: India
First transcribed: c. 350 B.C.

Although relatively unknown to Western readers, the Ramayana *is extremely popular throughout India, where it holds great religious significance. To the Western reader the characters may appear to be human beings with supernatural powers, roughly equivalent to certain figures in Greek legend and myth, but to Hindus the characters of the* Ramayana *are gods. Rama is a reincarnation of the Hindu god Vishnu, and he and his wife Sita represent the ideal Man and Woman.*

The *Ramayana* is one of the two Hindu epics, the other being the earlier *Mahabharata.* Whereas the *Mahabharata* is genuinely a heroic (or "folk") epic deriving from an oral tradition, the *Ramayana* is more nearly like a literary epic, written in conscious imitation of the heroic-folk tradition. But whatever the original may have been, the *Ramayana* has been altered many times by subsequent rewriting and recension. In its extant versions, the *Ramayana* contains about 24,000 couplets (less than one-fourth the length of the *Mahabharata*) and is divided into seven books, as against the eighteen books of *Mahabharata.* In terms of conventional Western epic form, the Greek heroic-folk epic contains twenty-four books; the English literary epic contains twelve. Of the seven books of the *Ramayana,* the central story covers books two through six. Book I is introductory. Book VII appears to be a species of appendix. It is called *Uttara,* or "Supplemental," and provides both epilogue to and critique of the foregoing six books. It also provides instruction for the recital of the *Ramayana* by minstrels in much the same way that medieval *enseignements* coached jongleurs in their repertoire and their performance. Yet the *Ramayana,* like most Western epics and unlike the *Mahabharata,* has unity, which stems from concentration on one main story.

One of the major themes in the central narrative is the relationship between destiny and volition, with the consequent consideration of personal responsibility or the lack of it. The key questions ultimately revolve around the power of the gods, for the obligatory nature of human promises hinges upon belief in the divine prerogative of retribution. Hence, King Dasa-ratha rescinds his proposal that Rama should succeed him as regent in order to honor his prior promise of Queen Kaikeyi. So, too, Rama dutifully accepts Bharat as regent and goes into exile, in deference to the King's expressed wishes (really, the gods' demands). Just as Rama accepts his fate, so also his brother Lakshman and his wife Sita accept theirs. But while Lakshman simply does his duty and perseveres, Sita is subjected to the most stringent of tests. After being kidnaped by Ravan, she is called upon to prove her virtue. The trial being so debilitating, Sita is finally rescued by her Earth-mother. All of these claims upon human endurance require intervention by the gods. The message of the *Ramayana* thus seems to be that human volition is subservient to divine will. The corollary also appears to establish the social order as subject to the divine order.

Closely allied to the theme of free will versus fate is the theme of duty. One aspect of this theme of duty is Rama's behavior, often cited as a model for other men to emulate. Rama's submission to his father's decision, his acceptance of exile, and his fidelity to his promise to remain in exile all bespeak Rama's filial piety and deference to duty. This view of duty follows the pattern traditional for warriors, princes, and kings; as such, it is compatible with ideals presented in the *Mahabharata* as well as with Western ethical assumptions. The other, and more important, aspect of the theme of duty is less conventional as an issue proper to epic consideration, for it concerns not wars and the affairs of state, the usual epic grist, but human love and domestic matters. This aspect of duty, then, deals with Sita's story, which, all things considered, comprises the main plot line in the epic. Sita, like Rama, is held up as an exemplar of ideal behavior—for women. Her behavior is characterized by sweetness, tenderness, obedience, patient suffering, and, above all, faithfulness; her piety and self-sacrifice ultimately qualified her for relief from mortal travail by being resorbed into her Earth-mother. She endured all without complaint and thus became the model for the perfect woman, wife, and mother, her image of duty unalloyed.

The *Ramayana* also deals with typical Hindu motifs. There is, for example, the Brahman's curse which King Dasa-ratha remembered on his deathbed. Also, there is the asceticism, as exemplified in Valmiki's hermitage and in Rama's own abstemious life after leaving Valmiki's hermitage. In addition, this asceticism reflects another Hindu value; the emphasis on social order, which is manifested in the caste system. The orderly functioning of society, with all people acknowledging their proper places in it, is a high priority in the Hindu ethos. Furthermore, the concepts of truth and duty provide the definitive guidelines for action. Truth and duty go hand in hand to create twin obligations for Dasa-ratha and Bharat as well as Rama and Sita and every devout Hindu. And the didactic elements of the *Ramayana* reinforce these typical Hindu motifs. Most explicitly, the teachings of Valmiki convey the precepts. But the implicit message of the plot and of the human interaction conveys the ethical and moral substance even more clearly. Thus the Hindu ideals of faith and conduct are both taught and demonstrated in the *Ramayana*.

In addition to the Hindu motifs as well as the themes of duty and free will versus fate, the *Ramayana* also presents an interesting juxtaposition of the natural and the supernatural. The central narrative begins with the natural or "real-world" events: the political machinations at the court of King Dasa-ratha; the banishment of Rama, Sita, and Lakshman; and the death of King Dasa-ratha and the subsequent dilemma of Bharat when Rama refuses the throne. But the next half of the narrative deals with the supernatural: the intrusion of the demon-maiden; the intervention of Ravan; the alliance with the monkey people; the real and allegorical battle between the forces of good and the forces of evil; and the Earth-mother's absorption of Sita. This combination of natural and supernatural worlds synthesizes the ethical and spiritual concerns of Hinduism, incorporating the concepts of fatalism and duty. Through this synthesis, the *Ramayana* goes beyond the confines of a national cultural epic to become part of the sacred literature of Hinduism. As such, it joins company with the *Mahabharata,* the *Vedas,* the *Brahmanas,* the *Upanishads,* and the *Puranas.* The religious perspective has made the *Ramayana* one of the best-known and best-loved works in India.

Joanne G. Kashdan

THE RAPE OF LUCRECE

Type of work: Poem
Author: William Shakespeare (1564-1616)
Type of plot: Tragedy
Time of plot: 500 B.C.
Locale: Ancient Rome
First published: 1594

The story of Tarquin's violation of Lucrece, an ancient Roman legend, was a favorite with Elizabethan audiences, and a variety of poetic, prose, and dramatic versions existed upon which Shakespeare could have drawn for the source of his long poem. His version is marked by its powerful emotional impact and consistently beautiful poetry, superior to any other interpretations of the day.

The Rape of Lucrece was entered at the Stationers' Register on May 9, 1594. Like *Venus and Adonis,* which had been published the previous year, it was finely printed by Richard Field and dedicated to the Earl of Southampton. Both of these narrative poems had been written while the theaters were closed because of the plague, but these companion pieces are not the idle products of a dramatist during a period of forced inactivity. Rather, as the dedications and the care in publication indicate, they are efforts at a more serious, more respectable type of composition than playwriting.

Longer and graver in tone than *Venus and Adonis, The Rape of Lucrece* was extremely popular, going through many editions, and was frequently quoted by contemporaries. The stern Gabriel Harvey, a Cambridge fellow and friend of Spenser, enthusiastically approved of the poem and paired it with *Hamlet* for seriousness of intent. The poem may be the "graver labor" which Shakespeare had promised Southampton in the dedication to *Venus and Adonis.* Whether or not Shakespeare intended to pair the poems, *The Rape of Lucrece* does provide a moralistic contrast to the view of love and sexuality expressed in the earlier poem.

The genre of *The Rape of Lucrece* is complaint, a form popular in the later Middle Ages and the Renaissance and particularly in vogue in the late 1590's. Strictly speaking, the complaint is a monologue in which the speaker bewails his fate or the sad state of the world. Shakespeare, however, following the example of many contemporaries, took advantage of the possibilities for variety afforded by dialogue. The poem includes the long set speeches and significant digressions which had become associated with the complaint. The poetic style is the highly ornamented sort approved by sophisticated Elizabethan audiences.

The story of the poem is a familiar one. It appears in Gower's *Confessio Amantis,* Lydgate's *Fall of Princes,* and Chaucer's *Legend of Good Women,* although Shakespeare seems to have relied more specifically on Livy's *History of Rome* (I, Chapters 57-59) and Ovid's *Fasti* (II, 721-852). The rhyme royal stanza may have been suggested by its traditional use in serious narrative or, more immediately, by Daniel's use of it in his popular *Complaint of Rosamond*. Certainly *The Rape of Lucrece* shares with Daniel's poem the Elizabethan literary fascination with the distress of noble ladies.

Despite the potentially erotic subject matter, the poem is not at all sensual, except in the lushness of its imagery. Even the passion of the rape scene is attenuated by a grotesquely extended description of Lucrece's breasts. The long, idealized description of the heroine is a rhetorical tour de force, not sexual stimulation. The theme of heroic chastity is always paramount and we are never distracted by action. Indeed, the prose "argument" which precedes the poem describes a story with enormous possibilities for action and adventure, but Shakespeare, consistent with his higher purpose, chose to focus, reflectively and analytically, on the moral and psychological issues. Although the result is sometimes boring, there are occasional signs of Shakespeare's dramatic ability, especially in the exchanges before the rape.

The characters are static and stylized, bu the revelation of the characters is skillfully done. As Tarquin's lust wrestles with his conscience, he is portrayed in an agony of indecision. The main medium of his internal conflict is the conventional theme of the antagonism of passion and reason. This section is a compendium of reflections on and rationalizations for the destructive power of lust. Moreover, Tarquin thinks in terms of conventional images. However, the contrasts and antitheses, as he is tossed back and forth between commonplaces, effectively represent his inner struggle. When he gives in, it is more a tribute to the potency of lust than a delineation or indictment of his character. When Lucrece appeals to the very concerns which have bedeviled Tarquin, there is a dramatic poignancy which most of the rest of the poem lacks. After the rape, the change in Tarquin's conventional thoughts is striking: his recognition of guilt and shame is a narrative exemplum of Shakespeare's Sonnet 129.

Lucrece's complaint is also wholly conventional in substance, but once again contrast and antithesis give a vitality to her grief as she rationalizes her suicide as not the destruction of her soul but the only way to restore her honor. The imagistic alternations from day to night, clear to cloudy, reflect her anguish and the difficulty of her decision.

The whole structure of the poem suggests that the exploration and decoration of conventional themes concerning lust and honor are the main intent. The poem centers on the mental states and moral attitudes of the characters immediately before and after the crucial action. The rape is a premise for the reflections, the suicide a logical result. The set speeches are reinforced by free authorial moralizing. Significant digressions, like the long physical description of Lucrece and her extended apostrophe to Opportunity, further elaborate the main themes. The longest and most effective digression is Lucrece's contemplation of the Troy painting. The opportunities for finding correlatives are fully exploited. The city of Troy is apt because it has been brought to destruction by a rape and Paris is the perfect example of the selfishness of lust. Sinon, whose honest exterior belies his treachery, reminds Lucrece of the contrast between appearance and reality, nobility and baseness, which she had noted in Tarquin. The whole digression, which repeats by means of allusion, is ornamental rather than explanatory.

The severe paring of the plot further reveals Shakespeare's main concern. For example, Collatine, the offended husband, appears only briefly, suffers silently, and does not even personally initiate the revenge. He does not intrude on the crucial issues. In addition, the bloodthirstiness of Lucrece's plea for revenge is another sign that elucidation of character is unimportant compared to the beautiful expression of moral imperatives. The revenge itself is, mysteriously, instigated by Brutus (an action which makes more sense in Livy) and is carried out perfunctorily in a few closing lines, because it is secondary to the main, conventional themes of the poem.

Regardless of its moral earnestness and occasional tedium, *The Rape of Lucrece* is gorgeously ornamented with figures of speech, especially alliteration and assonance, and with figures of thought which please rather for brilliance of execution than depth of conception. *The Rape of Lucrece* is, like *Venus and Adonis,* a rhetorical showpiece.

Edward E. Foster

THE RAPE OF THE LOCK

Type of work: Poem
Author: Alexander Pope (1688-1744)
Type of plot: Mock-heroic epic
Time of plot: Early eighteenth century
Locale: London
First published: 1712

Generally considered the finest satirical poem in the English language, The Rape of the Lock *was written at the suggestion of a friend, John Caryll, ostensibly to heal a family row which resulted when Lord Petre playfully clipped a lock of Miss Arabella Fermor's hair. Pope's larger purpose in writing the poem, however, was to ridicule the social vanity of his day and the importance that was attached to affected manners.*

When Robert Lord Petre cut off a lock of Arabella Fermor's hair one fateful day early in the eighteenth century, he did not know that the deed would gain worldwide fame, attracting attention over several centuries. Nor did he perhaps foresee the ill feeling his act would create between the Petre and Fermor families. The story would probably have been soon lost among the trivia of family histories, had not John Caryll asked his good friend the poet Alexander Pope to write a little poem about the episode, one which would show the comic element of the family quarrel and thus help heal it.

What began as a trivial event in history, turns, under the masterly guidance of Pope's literary hand, into one of the most famous poems in the English language, and perhaps the most perfect example of burlesque we have. *The Rape of the Lock* was begun at Caryll's behest ("This verse, to Caryll, Muse! is due") in 1711; Pope spent about two weeks on it and produced a much shorter version than the one he wrote two years later; adding more additions in 1717, he then developed the final draft of the poem as it now stands.

The poem as we have it uses the essentially trivial story of the stolen lock of hair as a vehicle for making some thoroughly mature and sophisticated comments on society and man. Pope draws on his own classical background—he had translated the *Iliad* and the *Odyssey*—to combine epic literary conventions with his own keen, ironic sense of the values and societal structures shaping his age. The entire poem, divided into five Cantos, is written in heroic couplets. Pope makes the most of this popular eighteenth century verse form (rhymed iambic pentameter lines), filling each line with balance, antithesis, bathos, and puns.

The literary genre of "burlesque" typically takes trivial subjects and elevates them to seemingly great importance; the effect is comic, and Pope manages an unbroken sense of amusement as he relates "What dire offense from amorous causes springs,/ What mighty contests rise from trivial things."

From the opening lines of the poem, suggestions of the epic tradition are

clear. Pope knew well not only the *Iliad* and the *Odyssey,* but also Milton's
Paradise Lost. The narrator of *The Rape of the Lock* speaks like Homer,
raising the "epic question" early in the poem: "Say what strange motive,
goddess! could compel/ A well-bred lord t' assault a gentle belle?" Pope's
elaborate description of Belinda's toilet in Canto I furthers comparison with
the epic; it parodies the traditional epic passage describing warrior shields.
Belinda's makeup routine is compared to the putting on of armor: "From
each she nicely culls with curious toil,/ And decks the goddess with the
glittering spoil."

The effect of using epic conventions is humorous, but it also helps establish
a double set of values in the poem, making the world of Belinda and Sir
Plume at the same time trivial and significant. Epic conventions contribute
to this double sense in each Canto: (I) the epic dedication and invocation;
(II) the conference of protective gods; (III) the games and the banquet;
(IV) descent into the underworld; and (V) heroic encounters and apotheosis.
The overall result is that, although we have a basically silly situation, we have
characters such as Clarissa who utter the always sensible virtues of the eigh-
teenth century:

> Oh! if to dance all night, and dress all day,
> Charmed the smallpox, or chased old age away;
> Who would not scorn what housewife's cares produce,
> Or who would learn one earthly thing of use? . . .
>
> But since, alas, frail beauty must decay,
>
> And she who scorns a man, must die a maid;
> What then remains but well our power to use,
> And keep good humor still what'er we lose?

Clarissa in these lines from Canto V expresses the norm of Pope's satire:
the intelligent use of reason to control one's temperamental passions.

The heroic couplet merges perfectly with the epic devices in the poem, for
as a verse form the heroic couplet naturally seems to express "larger than life"
situations. It is therefore, profoundly to Pope's credit that he successfully
applies such a stanzaic pattern to a subject which is anything but larger than
life. The critic Maynard Mack has said that Pope "is a great poet because he
has the gift of turning history into symbol, the miscellany of experience into
meaning."

Pope, perhaps more than anyone else writing poetry in the eighteenth
century, demonstrates the flexibility of the heroic couplet. Shaped by his pen,
it contains pithy aphorisms, social commentary, challenging puns, and delightful bathos. (The last of these juxtaposes the serious with the small, as in
the line, "wrapped in a gown for sickness and for show"). But the key, if
there is a key, to the classic popularity of *The Rape of the Lock* is the use

of the heroic couplet to include—sometimes in great catalogued lists—those little, precise, and most revealing details about the age and the characters that peopled it. The opening lines of Canto III illustrate Pope's expert use of detail. The passage describes court life at Hampton Court, outside London, and is a shrewd comment on the superficiality of the people there:

> Hither the heroes and the nymphs resort,
> To taste awhile the pleasures of a court;
> In various talks th' instructive hours they passed,
> Who gave the ball, or paid the visit last;
> One speaks the glory of the British queen,
> And one describes a charming Indian screen;
> A third interprets motions, looks, and eyes;
> At every word a reputation dies.
> Snuff, or the fan, supply each pause of chat,
> With singing, laughing, ogling, and all that.

The poet's criticism of such life is clear by the swift juxtaposition of Hampton Court life with a less pretty reality in the following lines:

> Meanwhile, declining from the noon of day,
> The sun obliquely shoots his burning ray;
> The hungry judges soon the sentence sign,
> And wretches hang that jurymen may dine.

Though always its critic, Pope held a keen interest in the life of London's aristocracy. A Catholic by birth, he was not always in favor with the crown, but before the queen's death in 1714 he enjoyed meeting with a group of Tories which included Swift, Arbuthnot, Atterbury, and Parnell. Steele and Addison, England's first newspaper editors, courted him on behalf of the Whig party, but he refused to become its advocate.

Forbidden by law from living within several miles of London, he lived much of his adult life at Twickenham, a village on the Thames not too far from London but far enough. He transformed his dwelling there into an eighteenth century symbol, with gardening and landscaping; he included vineyards and the house had a temple and an obelisk to his mother's memory. During the 1720's he built his grotto, an underpass connecting his property under a dividing road; it was a conversation piece, with, according to one contemporary, bits of mirror on the walls which reflected "all objects of the river, hills, woods, and boats, forming a moving picture in their visible radiations." For Pope, 4-feet-6-inches tall and sick all his life, it was a symbol of the philosophic life and mind. Although he never married, his biographers tell us he felt a warm, if not always happy, affection for Martha and Teresa Blount, neighbors during his youth. Pope enjoyed great literary fame even during his lifetime, and near the end of his life, when he entered a room, whispers of "Mr. Pope, Mr. Pope," would buzz among the occupants.

Jean Marlowe

RASSELAS

Type of work: Novel
Author: Samuel Johnson (1709-1794)
Type of plot: Philosophical romance
Time of plot: Eighteenth century
Locale: Abyssinia and Cairo
First published: 1759

Although slow-moving and ponderous in style, The History of Rasselas, Prince of Abyssinia *was one of Johnson's most popular works during his lifetime, and is still widely read. The work attacks the superficial optimism that characterized the age in which Johnson lived. There is almost no narrative action, for the plot deals with the efforts of four people to find a workable philosophy to guide their lives.*

According to his own statement, Johnson wrote *Rasselas* in the evenings of one week in 1759 to defray the expenses of his mother's funeral. But one should not assume either that the tale was completely spontaneous or that its mood was entirely determined by the illness and death of his parent. Johnson had very likely been considering the subject for some time. His translation of Father Lobo's *A Voyage to Abyssinia* in 1735, his use of an Oriental setting in his early play *Irene* in 1737, and his employing the device of the Oriental apologue in several *Rambler* papers all pointed the way. Moreover, two *Rambler* papers (Nos. 204 and 205) suggested part of the theme of *Rasselas* in telling how Seged, Lord of Ethiopia, decided to be happy for ten days by an act of will and how this quest for pleasure was vain. Even closer in theme was Johnson's finest poem, *The Vanity of Human Wishes,* in 1749.

Though the mood of *Rasselas* may seem to be predominantly gloomy, involving if not cynicism at least a tragic view of life, it is possible to see in it some of the qualities of an ironic apologue or a Menippean satire. The manuscript title of the book, "The Choice of Life," is a key both to its plan and to its philosophy. Human nature being what it is, Johnson indicates, happiness can be only illusory, accidental, and ephemeral, existing more in hope than in reality, and always being in the end nothing to be compared with life's miseries. Thus those who seek for happiness through "a choice of life" are destined to end in failure. This kind of reading of the story may seem pessimistic enough. But there is another aspect of it that recognizes the kind of multifariousness in life that resists and defeats facile theories about existence like those of the young travelers in the novel. Here is plainly opportunity for some comedy or satire.

Johnson skillfully begins with the conventional notion that perfect bliss exists in an earthly paradise. Rasselas, an Abyssinian prince, his sister, and two companions escape from what they have come to regard as the boredom of the perfect life in the Happy Valley to set out on a search for true happiness in the outside world. They try all kinds of life: pleasure-loving society, solitude, the pastoral life, life of high and middle estates, public and private life. But though Rasselas holds that happiness is surely to be found, they find it nowhere. The simple life of the country dweller so praised by Rousseau and his followers is full of discontent. Men of wealth and power cannot be happy because they fear the loss of both. The hermit, unable to answer the question about the advantages of solitude, returns to civilization. The philosopher who preaches the philosophic systems of happiness succumbs to grief over the death of his daughter. Another philosopher who thinks one can achieve happiness by "living according to nature" cannot explain what this phrase means. The abduction of the maid Pekuah injects an element of plot so that Rasselas' sister, Nekayah, is able to learn that one "who has no one to love or to trust has little to hope." And Pekuah reports on her return that the female "happy valley" of the harem is boring because the women talk of nothing but the tediousness of life.

In the final chapter, all the travelers decide on an ideal vocation. But, says the narrator, "they well knew that none could be obtained." So they resolve to return to Abyssinia. Was it in defeat? Not necessarily. All had achieved a valuable education and had lost their insularity. Moreover, as one contemporary critic has suggested, instead of ending in rationalistic despair, they had learned to ask an important question: that is, What activity is most appropriate to man and can best satisfy him and fulfill his destiny? In short, like Voltaire's famous hero, they could be expected in some way eventually to cultivate their own gardens.

By accident, it should be noted here, Voltaire's *Candide* and *Rasselas* were published within two months of each other. Both attacked the fashionable optimism of their day: Leibnitz's "best of all possible worlds" and Pope's "Whatever is, is right." Candide begins in the best of all possible castles; Rasselas, in the Happy Valley. Each has a philosopher-friend—Pangloss and Imlac. Each sets out to explore the world, though for different reasons. Each is disillusioned. But here the resemblance ends. Voltaire's wit is brilliant, slashing, and destructive and is exerted on a tangible and vivid world. Johnson's is deliberate and speculative, balanced, measured, and wise. His world is fanciful. And, if like Sir Thomas More in his *Utopia,* Johnson chose a setting for his story in a non-Christian part of the world, he did so because he wished to deal with man on a purely naturalistic level and discuss basic issues without involving other considerations. In the process, he does not allow his deeply religious nature, so unlike Voltaire's skepticism, to go entirely unperceived. One does not forget, for example, that after Imlac's discussion of the nature of the soul, the Princess Nekayah is moved to insist that the choice of life is no longer so important as the choice of eternity.

To many readers *Rasselas* has long seemed to be chiefly a series of essays, narrative and digressive, like those in the *Rambler,* loosely strung together with a narrative thread that could be described more nearly as plan than plot.

Chapters like "A Dissertation on the Art of Flying," "A Dissertation on Poetry," "A Disquisition upon Greatness," and "The Dangerous Prevalence of Imagination" can be lifted out of their context to achieve all but complete independence as separate literary works. The characters are two-dimensional and the dialogue is far from lifelike. The style is in places so rhythmic and sonorous as to suggest poetry rather than prose. For these and other reasons, the right of the narrative to be called a novel has frequently been questioned.

So far as the structure of *Rasselas* is concerned, recent critics have been able to suggest illuminating patterns. One of the most useful suggestions is that the novel can be regarded as having three sections or movements of sixteen chapters each, ending with a kind of coda. The first concerns the Happy Valley and the theme of the "choice of life," centered upon the restless prince and his determination to find happiness outside. The second section, in which the travelers make their comprehensive survey of mankind, is focused on Rasselas' "experiments upon life" and the discovery that no one fits his theory and possesses happiness. The section ends with Imlac's famous apostrophe to the pyramids. In the third section, the travelers, now no longer mere observers, find themselves actually involved in life as the victims of others. The chief incidents here concern Pekuah's abduction and return, the encounter with the astronomer, the brief meeting with the disillusioned old man, and final visit to the Catacombs, and the abandonment of the quest. To some critics the coda, "A Conclusion in Which Nothing Is Concluded," is an aesthetic defect. But in all fairness, it can probably be regarded as such only by those who would require Johnson to append more of a moral tag than he plainly thought wise. The discoveries of the travelers concerning life and the fallacy of their quest can be considered to have positive rather than merely negative value and can be regarded as conclusion enough.

Lodwick Hartley

RAVENSHOE

Type of work: Novel
Author: Henry Kingsley (1830-1876)
Type of plot: Domestic romance
Time of plot: Early nineteenth century
Locale: England
First published: 1862

In Ravenshoe, *Kingsley attempts to cover several centuries in the history of an English family, but the novel actually focuses on one son, Charles. Lengthy and slow-paced, the work is encumbered by numerous asides; stripped of its digressions, however, the plot is a lively one in the Regency tradition.*

Appropriately, Henry Kingsley dedicated his second and best novel, *Ravenshoe,* to his older brother Charles; not only did the brothers hold each other in high esteem and affection, but their writing shared same common virtues and reflected similar interests and predilections. *Ravenshoe,* like *Westward Ho!,* is distinguished by typical Kingsley virtues: lively descriptions of noble, manly deeds; beautiful pictures of English sea and countryside; a good-humored joviality of tone; and an invigorating sense of the author's enthusiastic love of life. At the same time, Henry Kingsley's characteristic weaknesses are also evident in *Ravenshoe*; the plot is encumbered with too many incidents, the style is careless, the narrative flow is disrupted by too-frequent authorial intrusions, and the storyline is often melodramatic and implausible.

The most attractive feature of the novel is the characterization of Charles Ravenshoe. He hovers somewhere between obstinacy and determination, foolishness and whimsy, rebelliousness and independence; but in the end he always has the reader's affection and sympathy. The novel is essentially the story of the good-hearted, exuberant boy who must learn, through suffering and hardship, to accept the responsibilities of manhood. He needs to temper his boyish boisterousness with level-headed, adult patience and discipline; his animal energy and high spirits must eventually find constructive and worthy outlets. Kingsley shows us the external steps of this growth process in Charles, who at the close of the novel is a sober, dreamy, and even somewhat melancholy man, although he does not probe deeply into the hero's private thoughts, emotions, or motivations. In addition to Charles, *Ravenshoe* contains some memorable minor characters. The implacable enemies, Lady Ascot and Lady Hainault, are delightful comic creations; the villainous Jesuit, Father Mackworth, while he is a one-dimensional figure, nevertheless gains depth and life temporarily in scenes such as the moving description of Cuthbert's drowning. Lord Saltire, the atheist considered in his youth to be the devil incarnate, is an excellent example of the traditional type of the elderly and respectable reformed roué.

Ravenshoe is distinguished by its atmosphere of vitality and humor pervaded by a regretful sense of melancholy at the passing of the traditions of England's old rural houses. Although even the most avid admirers of Kingsley's fiction do not claim him as one of the great British novelists, they know the enjoyment that awaits readers of *Ravenshoe* in the form of spirited fun and excellent entertainment.

REBECCA

Type of work: Novel
Author: Daphne du Maurier (1907-   )
Type of plot: Mystery romance
Time of plot: 1930's
Locale: England
First published: 1938

Rebecca is an excellent example of a successful suspense novel. From the moment the drab and timid narrator marries Maxim de Winter, the reader senses something drastically wrong at Manderley, the fine house where Rebecca was formerly the mistress. Tension builds through a succession of hints leading to a startling disclosure.

For nearly four decades Daphne du Maurier has excited and terrified readers with some of the best suspense novels of the twentieth century. She is one of a small group of writers who have, by their artistic ingenuity, insight into character and situation, and technical virtuosity, elevated popular "formula" fiction into serious literature. And there is no better example of her skill and power than her early suspense masterpiece, *Rebecca*.

The basic structure of *Rebecca* is that of the modern "Gothic Romance," but Miss du Maurier has utilized and transformed the rigid formula of this popular genre to create a very original and personal fiction. The unnamed narrator, at least for the first two-thirds of the novel, is the typical heroine of a Gothic Romance. Although her character is not deep, her qualities and desires are carefully chosen to provoke maximum interest and sympathy. Two narrative questions animate the rather leisurely early chapters of the novel: can the heroine, an orphan with little training or worldly experience, adjust to the unfamiliar, demanding social role as mistress of Manderley? And can she win and keep the love of her passionately desired, but enigmatic, even sinister husband, Maxim de Winter? These two elements—Manderley, the isolated, beautiful, but ultimately threatening setting, and de Winter, the charming, handsome, but moody, mysterious "hero-villain"—are standard essentials in the genre.

After they set up residence at Manderley, these two questions become fused as the dominating, almost spectral presence of Maxim's first wife, Rebecca, becomes increasingly felt. This presence is made concrete by Mrs. Danvers, the efficient, sinister, intimidating housekeeper, who still "serves" her original mistress, and Jack Favell, Rebecca's crudely handsome, lascivious cousin. They, along with the gradual revelation that Rebecca's death was not accidental, give the novel that sense of growing threat and conspiracy that is *de rigueur* in the Gothic Romance.

Approximately two-thirds of the way through the book, however, Miss du Maurier adds a special twist to the story that takes it out of the Gothic

Romance category and establishes it as a unique suspense thriller. Maxim finally breaks down and confesses to the heroine that Rebecca was "vicious, damnable, rotten through and through," and that he murdered her when she tormented him about a "son and heir" that was not his. Thus, the focus shifts from the heroine's mysterious danger to her husband's legal fate. Instead of fearing for the physical safety of the narrator, the reader is placed in the ironic position of cheering for the criminal to escape detection and punishment. And the "villains," Mrs. Danvers and Jack Favell, become petty, pitiable creatures rather than serious conspirators..

Most importantly, the heroine is freed by this knowledge from Rebecca's "ghost." Knowing that Maxim loves and needs her, and faced with a threat that is real and specific, rather than undefined and pervasive, she can deal with her situation in a direct, forceful way as an emotionally whole, self-confident woman. Thus, the heroine grows from a pretty household decoration to the mistress of Manderley, from a girl to a woman, and from a child-bride to a mature lover and wife. It is, finally, Miss du Maurier's skill and sensitivity in describing her heroine's maturity in a manner that is psychologically believable and emotionally satisfying that qualifies *Rebecca* as a unique and serious work of art.

THE REBEL GENERATION

Type of work: Novel
Author: Johanna van Ammers-Küller (1884-1966)
Type of plot: Social chronicle
Time of plot: 1840-1923
Locale: Leyden, Holland
First published: 1925

In this sociological novel, Johanna van Ammers-Küller examines changes in middle-class Dutch culture through several generations of a single family. The novel follows changing ethical standards and mores, altered attitudes in parent-child relationships, and the struggle for women's equality.

The Rebel Generation, by Johanna van Ammers-Küller, was the first volume of one of the author's two trilogies dealing with Dutch family life in the nineteenth and twentieth centuries. Though not a success in its native country, this particular novel received world-wide attention and was a best-seller in several languages. What the reader sees in the novel is a series of portraits of strong-willed men and women who are related more by ideas and behavior than by the obvious familial connection. Ammers-Küller, though not a strictly feminist writer, has portrayed the struggle of women for equality in a way that blends in well with her overall picture of Dutch manners and morals of the era. She has perhaps not been listed with some of the great feminist writers of the early part of this century, however, for while she beautifully illustrates women's struggle for equality, she also shows how at least one generation of the Cornvelt family reversed the trend by their own desires.

One of the flaws of the book which strikes the modern reader is that the author has sacrificed imaginative writing for her "message." Plot, characterization, and even to some extent setting, are all subservient to the main theme of rebellion within three generations of one Dutch family. Her lack of subtlety will not bring her into the forefront of great writers of the twentieth century, and her faltering feminism will not allow her to be totally accepted as a champion of women's liberation either. What Ammers-Küller will be remembered for is her solid novel of Dutch middle-class life, something which has not been overdone and is little known outside The Netherlands.

THE RECRUITING OFFICER

Type of work: Drama
Author: George Farquhar (1678-1707)
Type of plot: Comedy of intrigue
Time of plot: Early eighteenth century
Locale: Shrewsbury, England
First presented: 1706

The prime attraction of this comedy is Sergeant Kite, one of the richest comic soldier figures in English drama, a descendant of Plautus' Miles Gloriosus and Ben Jonson's Captain Bobadil. Kite doubles as a fortune-teller and a pander for his master, Captain Plume. Farquhar increases the interest in his play by moving the action to Shrewsbury, a welcome change from the usual London setting.

Farquhar is one of those transitional figures in the history of literature, like Chaucer and Blake, who straddle different ages or ideologies. Their work seems either unerringly current, as was the case with Chaucer and Farquhar, or as in Blake's case, strangely remote. Farquhar was no prophetic genius like Blake, but he did have a touch of Chaucer's social imagination; just as Chaucer dramatized the emergence of pre-Renaissance individualism in his studies of medieval character, Farquhar achieved a happy balance between Restoration licentiousness and early eighteenth century sentiment. Had he lived (he died at twenty-nine), Farquhar possibly could have saved comedy from indulging its preference for feeling over wit—a trend that eventually defused comedy of its satirical power and resulted in the triumph of the sentimental comedy championed by Cibber and Steele.

Farquhar's characters, even rakes like Captain Plume, are brothers to Etherege's and Wycherley's rakes of the early Restoration comedy, but they do not sacrifice their feelings to a cold wit. They are also less devious and manipulative in seduction and deception than their Restoration models. Plume enjoys the selfish victories of the rake, but he also admits to a tormented conscience: "The world is all a cheat; only I take mine, which is undesigned, to be more excusable than theirs, which is hypocritical. I hurt nobody but myself, but they abuse all mankind."

The sentiment in Farquhar is expressed mainly in his sympathy for his characters. He develops them so that even minor characters are not merely caricatures or stereotypes. Morally, like Captain Plume, he has few illusions. "The world is all a cheat," and although Farquhar may make his sinners sympathetic, sinners they remain. Sergeant Kite is as immoral as he is alive, but his immorality cannot dehumanize him to the point where he becomes a ridiculed fop or fool, as would have been the case in the earlier comedy. Like Falstaff, the notorious "recruiter" of *Henry the Fourth, Part One,* Kite is a comic creation greater than the laughs he receives.

THE RED AND THE BLACK

Type of work: Novel
Author: Stendhal (Marie-Henri Beyle, 1783-1842)
Type of plot: Psychological realism
Time of plot: Early nineteenth century
Locale: France
First published: 1830

In this novel whose chief character is a villain, Stendhal analyzes the psychological undercurrents of Julien Sorel's personality, showing how struggle and temptation shaped his energetic but morbidly introspective nature. The novel is considered Stendhal's greatest work, equally for its portrait of Sorel and its satire of French society during the Bourbon restoration.

Stendhal's *The Red and the Black* is one of the most polished and refined artistic stones in the literary crown of European literature. While innovation and refinement are the binary supports of all literature, it is seldom that an author is able to combine these qualities in one work. Marie-Henri Beyle, better known by his *nom de plume* Stendhal, is just such an author, and *The Red and the Black* is just such a novel.

Stendhal took the French novel from the hands of romantic writers such as Chateaubriand and honed it into a rapier of social criticism and philosophical exposition. Although the French novel was the scion of other literary talents, Stendhal was its mentor. It is the content of Stendhal's novels that mark him as a harbinger, one who influenced a century of Continental literary *epigones*. He was the first French writer to battle with the social and philosophical implications inherent in the modern creed known as liberalism. Because liberalism was the prevailing philosophical buttress of the emergent French middle class, and because Stendhal sought to assess the social attitudes of that class, he must be considered as the first significant bourgeois novelist. *The Red and the Black* amalgamates the best of Stendhal's abilities as refiner and innovator.

Like each of Stendhal's novels, *The Red and the Black* is autobiographical. Published in 1830, the work reflects the author's ideas rather than the outer events of his life. Thus, to appreciate fully the novel, it is necessary to know the background of Stendhal's life and the broad social developments which determined the writer's complex and often contradictory *Weltanschauung*.

Stendhal was born into a provincial bourgeois family in Grenoble. His family background was a mixture of contradictions. The father was a middle-class businessman whose aggressive, pragmatic, Philistine habits the son professed to loathe. His mother's aristocratic family, however, attracted him. To Stendhal the family appeared to live a balanced, harmonious life with its social as well as cultural surroundings. It was a world of social hierarchy where all classes knew their place. Yet, despite his preference for the world of the provincial aristocrat, Stendhal followed a life which was markedly bourgeois in orientation and philosophy. He implicitly accepted the liberal ideas articulated in the French Revolution and became an avid supporter of Napoleon, the personification of French liberalism. Napoleon championed the notion of a French civil service staffed by men of talent rather than of high birth as had been the case in the pre-Napoleonic world. The writer launched his career with Napoleon's regime. He marched through Europe with Napoleon's armies and was present in the retreat from Moscow. Following Napoleon's defeat, Stendhal exiled himself to Milan, Italy. He returned to Paris in 1821 and compromised his values to the ultra-conservative political climate then existing in France. It was not a difficult compromise since the official values espoused in Paris were similar to those expressed by the maternal side of Stendhal's family. Stendhal's life in France between 1821 and 1830 was similar to that of the hero of *The Red and the Black,* Julien Sorel: he carried the social and intellectual baggage appropriate for survival in the intricate Parisian world.

Liberalism was the intellectual cloak of the French Revolution and Napoleon the child of the revolution. In Stendhal's France, the most important arrow in a liberal's quiver was his belief in self-determination. The liberal felt that man was basically reasonable and hence perfectible; he believed that man needed a society where talent could freely rise to its highest level of accomplishment and find expression in whatever political, economic, or intellectual manner deemed appropriate by the individual. This creed naturally appealed to those segments of French society which had been prevented by aristocratic privilege from assuming worthwhile positions in the French civil service. Stendhal aimed to make his mark in France by ascribing to this philosophy. Yet, however much he might have believed in French liberalism, or thought he believed in it, he was nonetheless troubled—aristocrat that he partly was—by the lack of parameters to this philosophy. Indeed, Julien's love affairs for Madame de Rênal, the wife of the provincial bourgeois mayor, and Mathilde de La Mole, the daughter of a French aristocrat, are symbolic of his own intellectual "affairs" with modern bourgeois liberalism and traditional aristocratic conservatism.

Was it possible to fuse such disparate social attitudes? Where were the limits on a person's right to individual self-determination? What were the social implications of such a philosophy? In an attempt to answer these questions, Stendhal wrote *The Red and the Black.* Julien Sorel was his litmus paper, recording the social concerns of Stendhal. Although Stendhal was a realist and recognized the inevitable triumph of the modern French bourgeoisie over the pre-modern aristocratic way of life, Stendhal's own confusion about his social values does not detract from the impact of his novel; in fact, it only enhances its historical value. For France, like Stendhal, was engrossed in precisely the identical dilemma and confusion of values. Like France, Stendhal knew that time was needed to assimilate contradictory social orientations.

Yet societies, like creative individuals such as Stendhal, are capable of amalgamating the most diverse elements into a cohesive unit. *The Red and the Black* represents just such a creative fusion.

John G. Tomlinson, Jr.

THE RED BADGE OF COURAGE

Type of work: Novel
Author: Stephen Crane (1871-1900)
Type of plot: Impressionistic realism
Time of plot: Civil War
Locale: A Civil War battlefield
First published: 1895

Marking a dramatic departure from the traditional treatment of war in fiction, this novel ignores powerful generals and historic victories and defeats in favor of probing the personal reactions of unknown foot soldiers fighting unknown enemies in skirmishes of indeterminate outcome. Henry Fleming is motivated not by courage or patriotism, but by cowardice, fear, and finally egoism, and events in the novel are all filtered subjectively through his consciousness.

The Red Badge of Courage, Stephen Crane's second novel (*Maggie: A Girl of the Streets* had appeared under a pseudonym in 1893) and his most famous work, has often been considered the first truly modern war novel. The war is the American Civil War and the battle is presumed to be the one fought at Chancellorsville, though neither the war nor the battle is named in the novel. Nor is there mention of Abraham Lincoln or the principal battle generals, Joseph Hooker (Union) and Robert E. Lee and "Stonewall" Jackson (Confederate). This is by design, since Crane was writing a different kind of war novel. He was not concerned with the causes of the war, the political and social implications of the prolonged and bloody conflict, the strategy and tactics of the commanding officers, or even the real outcome of the battle in which historically the combined losses were nearly thirty thousand men (including "Stonewall" Jackson, mistakenly shot in darkness by one of his own men).

From beginning to end the short novel focuses upon one Union Army volunteer. Though other characters enter the story and reappear intermittently, they are distinctly minor, and they are present primarily to show the relationship of Henry Fleming (usually called only "the youth") to one person, to a small group of soldiers, or to the complex war of which he is such an insignificant part.

Much of the story takes the reader into Henry's consciousness. We share his boyish dreams of glory, his excitement in anticipating battle action, his fear of showing fear, his cowardice and flight, his inner justification of what he has done, his wish for a wound to symbolize a courage he has not shown, the ironic gaining of his false "red badge," his secret knowledge of the badge's origin, his "earning" the badge as he later fights fiercely and instinctively, his joy in musing on his own bravery and valiant actions, his anger at an officer who fails to appreciate his soldiery, and his final feeling that "the great death" is, after all, not a thing to be feared so much. Now, he tells himself, he is a man. In centering the story within the consciousness of an inexperienced youth caught in a war situation whose meaning and complexities he cannot understand, Crane anticipates Ford Madox Ford, Ernest Hemingway, and other later novelists.

Crane has been called a realist, a naturalist, an impressionist, and a symbolist. He is all of these in *The Red Badge of Courage*. Though young Stephen Crane had never seen a battle when he wrote the novel, he had read about them; he had talked with veterans and had studied history under a Civil War general; and he had imagined what it would be like to be a frightened young man facing violent death amid the confusion, noise, and turmoil of a conflict which had no clear meaning to him. Intuitively he wrote so realistically that several early reviewers concluded that only an experienced soldier could have written the book. After Crane had later seen the Greeks and Turks fighting in 1897 (he was a journalist reporting the war), he told Joseph Conrad, "My picture of war was all right! I have found it as I imagined it."

Although naturalistic passages appear in the novel, Crane portrays in Henry Fleming not a helpless chip floating on the indifferent ocean of life but a youth sometimes impelled into action by society or by instinct yet also capable of consciously willed acts. Before the first skirmish Henry wishes he could escape from his regiment and considers his plight: " . . . there were iron laws of tradition and law on four sides. He was in a moving box." In the second skirmish he runs "like a rabbit." When a squirrel in the forest flees after Henry throws a pine cone at him, Henry justifies his own flight: "There was the law, he said. Nature had given him a sign." But he is not content to look upon himself as on the squirrel's level. He feels guilt over his cowardice. When he carries the flag in the later skirmishes, he is not a terrified chicken or rabbit or squirrel but a young man motivated by pride, by a sense of belonging to a group, and by a determination to show his courage to an officer who had scornfully called the soldiers in his group a lot of "mule drivers."

From the beginning, critics have both admired and complained about Crane's impressionistic writing and his use of imagery and symbols in *The Red Badge of Courage*. Edward Garnett in 1898 called Crane "the chief impressionist of our day" and praised his "wonderful fervour and freshness of style." Joseph Conrad (himself an impressionist) was struck by Crane's "genuine verbal felicity, welding analysis and description in a continuous fascination of individual style," and Conrad saw Henry as "the symbol of all untried men." By contrast, one American critic in 1898 described the novel as "a mere riot of words" and condemned "the violent straining after effect" and the "absurd similes." Though H. G. Wells liked the book as a whole, he commented on "those chromatic splashes that at times deafen and confuse in the *Red Badge,* those images that astonish rather than enlighten."

Yet judging by the continuing popularity of *The Red Badge of Courage,* most readers are not repelled by Crane's repeated use of color—"blue demon-

stration," "red eyes," "red animal—war," "red sun"—or by his use of images—
"dark shadows that moved like monsters," "The dragons were coming," guns
that "belched and howled like brass devils guarding a gate." Only in a few
passages does Crane indulge in "arty" writing—"The guns squatted in a row
like savage chiefs. They argued with abrupt violence"—or drop into the
pathetic fallacy—"The flag suddenly sank down as if dying. Its motion as it
fell was a gesture of despair." Usually the impressionistic phrasing is appropriate to the scene or to the emotional state of Henry Fleming at a particular
moment, as when, after he has fought he feels heroically, the sun shines "now
bright and gay in the blue, enameled sky."

A brilliant work of the imagination, *The Red Badge of Courage* will endure
as what Crane afterward wrote a friend he had intended it to be, "a psychological portrayal of fear."

Henderson Kincheloe

THE RED ROOM

Type of work: Novel
Author: August Strindberg (1849-1912)
Type of plot: Realistic satire
Time of plot: 1870's
Locale: Stockholm and X-köping, a provincial town in Sweden
First published: 1879

This biting satire of Swedish society, Strindberg's first published novel, follows the fortunes of a group of young intellectuals and artists struggling against poverty in Stockholm during the 1870's. Dedicated and honest, they are constantly tricked, victimized, and scorned by the insensitive bourgeois society in which they live. Strindberg also attacks government agencies, where large staffs do no work; newspapers that make or break reputations with no regard for factual accuracy; and a Parliament that endlessly debates inconsequential matters.

August Strindberg's status as a giant of the modern theater has greatly overshadowed the fact that he was also a prolific novelist. To most non-Scandinavians, Strindberg's fiction is remembered—if at all—as quasi-autobiographical adjuncts to such dramatic masterpieces as *The Father, Miss Julie, The Dance of Death, A Dream Play,* and *The Ghost Sonata.* But, to Scandinavian readers, Strindberg's reputation as a novelist almost equals his status as a playwright, and his first published novel, *The Red Room,* is frequently considered to be the first modern Swedish novel.

As in all of Strindberg's writings, there is a strong autobiographical flavor to *The Red Room.* The protagonist, Arvid Falk, in many ways resembles the young Strindberg and reflects his brief foray into journalism (1872-1874). Most of the characters who gather in the "red room" are modeled on artistic comrades acquired during those newspaper years. The financial manipulations and disasters, particularly the "Triton Insurance" affair, were suggested by Strindberg's own bankruptcy in the wake of the financial crisis of 1878.

But it is a mistake to read *The Red Room* as straight autobiography. Strindberg's tone throughout the novel is detached, ironic, and, although bitter at times, essentially comic. While Arvid Falk's experiences parallel many of Strindberg's own, the character is too naïve, foolish, and frivolous to be accepted as self-portraiture. The novel can be more easily understood as a skillful blending of comic *Bildüngsroman,* social satire, and "idea" novel.

Like all of Strindberg's novels, and, in a different way, his plays, *The Red Room* is basically a quest for identity. As the typical hero of a *Bildüngsroman,* or novel of education, initiation, and development, Arvid is personally bland and learns through the examples and advice of "mentors" who surround him. Each mentor represents a particular social role and/or philosophical viewpoint. At the same time, these figures are used by Strindberg as satirical targets, enabling him to vent his anger on any and all social abuses in view—

official indolence, creative exploitation, religious fakery, insurance swindle, feminine hypocrisy, journalistic distortion, parliamentary duplicity, and dishonest reformism. Thus, Strindberg is able to brilliantly combine his quest for identity theme with a satirical portrait of nineteenth century middle-class Swedish society.

Instead of equipping him to find psychological equilibrium and socially meaningful work, Arvid's search only confuses and demoralizes him. Each new mentor and every new learning experience only serve to further disillusion and depress him. His employers and business associates all exploit or disappoint him. His bohemian friends, who have committed their lives to art, all either starve, sell out, or commit suicide. Thus, Arvid's education brings him to the edge of madness and only the intervention of Borg, the cynical doctor, saves his sanity. In the end Arvid's only survival is in total conformity, suppression of all creative impulses, and escape into conventional marriage and esoteric scholarship.

Behind the personal psychology and social satire of *The Red Room,* Strindberg makes a number of philosophical speculations. Three attitudes toward life are offered: idealism, realism, and nihilism. Arvid is the idealist, first described as "a child; he still believed in everything, truth and fairy tales alike," and his is the one philosophy that is quickly and thoroughly discredited. Realism in this book means to accept the corruption of the system and attempt to turn it to personal advantage. The only characters in the novel who thrive are those realists—and they are also the most despicable.

Strindberg seems to side philosophically with the nihilists, Falander, the actor, and Olle Montanus, the sculptor. Both characters articulate their philosophies at length, but find them difficult to live with. Although externally successful, Falander is deeply disturbed by his painful vision and drowns his nihilism in absinthe. Montanus acts out the implications of the philosophy. Discouraged by his inability to make his contemporaries aware of the state of art and society in Sweden, as well as by his own limits as an artist—and the limitations of art itself—Olle commits suicide. Only Borg, whose cynicism is very close to nihilistic, but who emotionally detaches himself from the implications of his ideas, is able to survive both the corrupt materialism of his society and the metaphysical pointlessness of his existence.

Yet Strindberg does not rest easily with pessimism. There is too much energy and humor in his characterizations and too much lyrical beauty in his natural descriptions to support a completely bleak view. What remains is not a neat psychological, social, or philosophical statement, but a powerful and provocative vision of man in conflict with himself, his society, and his cosmos.

THE RED ROVER

Type of work: Novel
Author: James Fenimore Cooper (1789-1851)
Type of plot: Historical romance
Time of plot: Mid-eighteenth century
Locale: Newport, Rhode Island and the Atlantic Ocean
First published: 1827

Intended to repeat the success of The Pilot, *this novel of the sea offers excellent descriptions of life and work aboard a sailing ship. As is often the case in Cooper's fiction, the characters are types who undergo little or no development. The simple plot is plausible until the end, when improbable relationships among the characters unravel the mystery surrounding Henry Ark and the Red Rover.*

Though *The Red Rover* has never been as popular with readers as Cooper's two greatest sea romances, *The Pilot* (1824) and *The Two Admirals* (1842), it has its own sturdy merits as a suspenseful tale of intrigue and adventure. Superficially, the early scenes of the novel bring to mind the classic American sea novel, Melville's *Moby Dick* (1851). Harry Wilder, like Ishmael, is drawn mysteriously to a ship anchored in the harbor. Aboard the ship, Wilder encounters the notorious Red Rover, just as Ishmael meets the enigmatic Captain Ahab. And just as Ahab violates metaphysical laws in his pursuit of the White Whale, so the Red Rover is a law unto himself as he plunders merchant vessels in the period before the Revolutionary War. Beyond this point the similarities between the novels are less clearly marked than the contrasts. Melville's novel is composed on an epic scale, with a profound sense of tragic drama. *The Sea Rover,* quite the opposite, is an entertaining melodramatic romance, written without any pretentions to examine deeply the mysteries of man's place in the universe.

Nevertheless, the novel is interesting from points of view other than simply those of a sea adventure story. Considered from a psychological perspective, *The Sea Rover* reveals Cooper's contradictory ideas about the structure and philosophical ideas of the work. In *Studies in Classic American Literature* (1923), D. H. Lawrence suggests that Cooper's "white novels," among which the sea stories may be included, betray the novelist's confusion about the superiority of democracy. Cooper, according to Lawrence, believes that the American is bound to assert his superior claims over other peoples, even if these claims are undeserved. But this forceful assertion is a form of aggression. And Cooper, at least philosophically, is disturbed by aggressiveness. One side of him prefers gentle action, another violent force. Without pressing Lawrence's suggestion too far, it is certainly true that in *The Red Rover* Cooper is both repelled by and attracted to the brutality of the captain of the *Dolphin,* just as he is ambivalent about his feelings concerning Wilder. For Wilder is at the same time the gentle, chivalrous comrade of the women,

Gertrude Grayson and Mrs. Wyllys, and the tough-minded, rugged sailor-adventurer.

Cooper partially resolves the conflict between aggressive and gentle conduct through the mechanism of the Revolutionary War. The romantic rebel in the personage of the Red Rover emerges as the patriotic rebel, when the pirate reappears late in the book as a veteran and hero of the American Revolution. Now his violence has the sanction of patriotic duty. And Harry Wilder, formerly seaman, also changes roles. By the end of the novel he is Captain Henry de Lacy, gentleman. Thus, on a psychological level, Cooper justifies the intrepid, violent action of the story from the viewpoint of its satisfactory conclusion: both the Red Rover and Wilder are seen as American heroes who have advanced the cause of freedom.

REDBURN

Type of work: Novel
Author: Herman Melville (1819-1891)
Type of plot: Adventure romance
Time of plot: Mid-nineteenth century
Locale: New York, the Atlantic Ocean, and England
First published: 1849

In this authentic treatment of sailors and life on the sea, Melville presents events from the perspective of a common sailor who learned his trade the hard way. As a teenager, the author made a similar trip to that described in Redburn, *aboard a merchant vessel bound for Liverpool. The novel is also interesting in its foreshadowing of those philosophical concerns which were to lead to the writing of Melville's masterpiece,* Moby Dick.

The best way to read *Redburn* is as a prologue to *Moby Dick.* The story of the white whale is anticipated by the tragic themes of the earlier novel: its relentless depiction of misery and cruelty on board Captain Riga's ship, as well as in Liverpool port, develops a universal consciousness of human suffering, of the crushing effect of experience on innocence. F. O. Matthiessen called *Redburn* "the most moving of its author's books before *Moby Dick.*" Redburn is abused by the other sailors for openly showing his fright when a man with delerium tremens throws himself over the side; the isolation makes him dread lest he become "a sort of Ishmael." He does, of course, become just that (and seems strengthened by the transformation) in *Moby Dick,* which was published two years after *Redburn* appeared.

Not only is Redburn similar to Melville's narrator in *Moby Dick,* but the whole novel is strewn with anticipations of the great novel's themes and characterizations. The mad sailor Jackson foreshadows Ahab: "He was a Cain afloat; branded on his yellow brow with some inscrutable curse; and going about corrupting and searing every heart that beat near him." The friendship between Harry Bolton and Redburn is curiously similar to that between the cannibal Queequeg and Ishmael: Harry is the prodigal son of a genteel family and Queequeg a royal personage; Harry introduces Redburn to London, Queequeg introduces Ishmael to the *Pequod*; Harry is finally killed when he is crushed between a ship and a whale, while Queequeg dives into the heart of a whale to rescue Tashtego.

All these similarities indicate the direction of Melville's art. He was moving from a fiction of initiation and adventure to one of philosophical depth. The symbolic action of Redburn is a cruder version of the same superstructure that supports Melville's masterpiece.

THE REDSKINS

Type of work: Novel
Author: James Fenimore Cooper (1789-1851)
Type of plot: Historical romance
Time of plot: 1842
Locale: Upstate New York
First published: 1846

This final novel in the Littlepage series deals specifically with the anti-rent controversy and more generally with the conflict between a cultured, principled upper class and an uncultured middle class motivated solely by self-interest. In sympathizing with the landowning Littlepages as opposed to the grasping New-comes, Cooper uses caricature and satire to ridicule his villains and thus glorify his heroes.

As entertainment, *The Redskins* offers suspense, action, romance, and villainy. From a social and political perspective, however, this work depicts a period when the American people were becoming increasingly aware of their power and influence. The reader will discern Cooper's belief that Jacksonian democracy had degenerated into an ill-conceived, leveling movement which threatened the genteel American ethic in the pre-Civil War period. Hugh Littlepage—gentleman, world traveler, and landowner—represented the ideal America which Cooper wanted to preserve from the opportunistic and ma-terialistic self-interests of the middle class represented by Seneca Newcome.

The Redskins begins with an indirect approbation of the American leisure class and their values. The reader quickly learns that the Littlepage family had become wealthy in the course of two generations and were spending much of their leisure abroad. Their apartment in Paris and their recent return from faraway places set the tone for the Littlepages' adventurous spirit and cosmopolitan taste. At the same time, the news of trouble at Ravensnest serves as a means to depict Hugh and his Uncle Ro as representa-tive American landowners who willingly accept their responsibilities as paternal but benevolent superiors.

However, while Hugh and his Uncle Ro are members of the landed class, they can also identify with the lesser classes as illustrated by the disguises they adopt when they return to New York to investigate Ravensnest's troubles. Incognito as immigrant artisans, the two members of Cooper's "natural" aristocracy learn about the real feelings, ideals, and fears of such individuals as: the Reverend Mr. Warren and his daughter, Mary, and the true nature of the antirenter, Seneca Newcome, and his crass sister, Opportunity Newcome.

Cooper's message is clear. Jacksonian Democracy would work if America were a nation of Warrens who are basically honest, hardworking, and sen-sible. In reality, however, America also consisted of men like Newcome, who, under the guise of justice and reform, would tear down the American Republic and its noble principles and values. In *The Redskins,* these principles and values triumph at the ceremony where wise old Susquesus is reunited with the members of his tribe. Jaap, Susquesus's black companion, reveals the story behind the old prairie Indian's exile. This development illustrates Cooper's ideal values of benevolent paternalism and noble obligations as the anti-renter movement dissipates by the moral force of Jaap's tale—and the physical presence of Susquesus's braves.

THE RELAPSE

Type of work: Drama
Author: Sir John Vanbrugh (1664-1726)
Type of plot: Social satire
Time of plot: Seventeenth century
Locale: England
First presented: 1696

The Relapse, or, Virtue in Danger was written as a sequel to Colley Cibber's Love's Last Shift, and was intended to correct what Vanbrugh considered the false evaluation of human nature presented in the earlier play. Historically, The Relapse is important because it helped to break up the artificial formulas followed in comedies of manners.

Although the earthiness and witty cynicism of Vanbrugh's play provide a healthy correction to Colley Cibber's sentimental tendencies, Vanbrugh lacked Cibber's sense of dramatic form. He may have been more accurate than Cibber in depicting human nature, but he was less adept at fashioning a well-constructed play. This is particularly odd because Vanbrugh eventually became one of England's greatest architects, the builder of Blenheim Palace for the Duke of Marlborough and the designer of the Haymarket Theatre, which he managed for two years. He was well aware of the indifferent plotting of his play, however, because he apologized for it in the "Prologue" where he attributed the play's lack of "plot or wit" to the haste of its composition: "It was got, conceived, and born in six weeks space."

If Vanbrugh was weak in plot and dialogue, his characters were nevertheless compelling creations and very popular with actors. Even Colley Cibber, whose work was the object of Vanbrugh's satire, admitted that Vanbrugh's lines were easier to memorize than those of any other playwright. Vanbrugh gave actors a great deal to do in the sense that action in his plays is broad and suggestive; even if the language is not rich in wit, it often has a dramatically effective force. In the opening scene, Amanda fears that if Loveless goes to town, he will be unfaithful. She expresses this in a series of direct statements ending with a bathetic conclusion:

> I know the weak defence of nature
> I know you are a man—and I—a wife.

Vanbrugh is one of those writers of Restoration Comedy who fed the arguments of its moralistic enemies. His husbands *are* corrupt sensualists, and because of Vanbrugh's crude dramaturgy there is little to redeem them in their wit. When they seduce, they do so with their bodies, not a *bon mot.* Loveless actually carries Berinthia off stage. The humor is salacious and broad. Her response is to cry "I'm ravished"—in a soft voice. One can easily understand the enthusiasm of Vanbrugh's audiences, and one can also appreciate the opportunities for farcical acting that his plays provide.

REMEMBRANCE OF THINGS PAST

Type of work: Novel
Author: Marcel Proust (1871-1922)
Type of plot: Psychological realism
Time of plot: Late nineteenth, early twentieth centuries
Locale: France
First published: 1913-1927

The title of this seven-novel work reveals Proust's twofold concern of time lost and time recalled. The writing is distilled from memory, the structure determined entirely by moods and sensations evoked by time passing or seeming to pass, recurring or seeming to recur. For Proust the true realities of human experience are not contained in a reconstruction of remembered scenes and events, but in the capture of physical sensations and moods re-created in memory. Symphonic in design, the work unfolds without plot or crisis as the writer reveals the motifs of his experience from childhood to middle age, holds them for thematic effect, and drops them, only to return to them once more in the processes of recurrence and change.

In *Remembrance of Things Past (A la récherche du temps perdu),* Marcel Proust, together with Leo Tolstoy (*War and Peace*), Fyodor Dostoevski (*The Brothers Karamazov*), Thomas Mann (*Joseph and His Brothers*), and James Joyce (*Ulysses*) transformed the novel from a linear account of events into a multi-dimensional art. The breakthrough was not into Freudian psychology, or existentialism, or scientific determinism, but into a realization that all things are, or may be, interwoven, bound by time, yet freed from time, open to every associational context.

What is reality? Certainly there is the reality of the sensory experience; yet any moment of sensory experience may have numerous successive or even simultaneous realities as it is relived in memory in different contexts, and perhaps the most significant reality—or realities—of a given act or moment may come long after the moment when the event first took place in time. Percy Shelley, in *A Defence of Poetry,* said, "All things exist as they are perceived: at least in relation to the percipient." And things which may have seemed inconsequential at the moment of their occurrence may take on richly multi-faceted meanings in relation to other events, other memories, other moments. The initial act is not as significant, not as real, as the perceptions of it which may come in new contexts, Reality *is* a context, made up of moods, of recollections joined by chance or design, sets of associations that have grown over the years. This concept of the notion of reality, one that had been taking shape with increased momentum since the Romantic Movement, opened the way to "those mysteries . . . the presentiment of which is the quality in life and art which moves us most deeply."

The elusive yet pervasively important nature of reality applies not only to events, such as the taste of the *Madeleine* (or small cake), but also to the absence of events, for the failure of Marcel's mother to give him his accustomed goodnight kiss proved to be an occasion which memory would recall again and again in a variety of relationships. Thus reality can and inevitably for all of us does sometimes include, if not indeed center on, the nonbeing of an event. That nonexistence can be placed in time and in successive times as surely as events that did happen; moreover 'it"—that nothing where something might or should have been—may become a significant part of the contexts which, both in time and freed from time, constitute reality.

Such thematic variations and turns of thought have led some to identify Proust as a "dilettante." Perhaps, in its literal sense, the term is justified, for his mind must have delighted in what, to the reader, may be unexpected turns of thought. In this he is most closely to be associated with Thomas Mann, whose consideration of time in the first volume of *Joseph and His Brothers* leads us into labyrinthine but essential paths; or whose speculations about the God-man relationship in Volume Two, in the section headed "Abraham Discovers God," lead us down a dizzying path of whimsical yet serious thought. But the fact remains that Mann and Proust have opened doors of contemplation that modern man cannot afford to ignore if he would increase his understanding of himself, the world in which he lives, and the tenuous nature of reality and of time.

What Proust does with time and reality he also does with character. Although he is a contemporary of Freud, and although Freudian interpretation could be applied to some of his characters in part, his concept of character is much too complex for reduction to ego, id, and the subconscious. Character, like reality, is a changing total context, not static and not a thing in itself to be held off and examined at arm's length. Baron de Charlus is at once a study of character in disintegration and a caricature, reduced in the end to a pitiable specimen, scarcely human. But it is Marcel, the *persona* of the story, who is seen in most depth and frequently in tortured self-analysis. His character is seen in direct statements, in his comments about others and about situations, in what others say to him or the way they say it, even in descriptive passages which would at first glance not seem to relate to character at all. "Only the exhaustive can be truly interesting," Thomas Mann said in the preface to *The Magic Mountain.* Proust surely agreed. His detail is not of the catalog variety, however; it works cumulatively, developmentally, with the thematic progression of symphonic music.

But finally the totality of the work is "the remembrance of things past," or as the title of the seventh, the final volume, has it, "the past recaptured." To understand it in its full richness one must become and remain conscious of the author, isolated in his study, drawing upon his recollections, associating and reassociating moments, events, personalities (his own always central), both to recapture the past as it happened and to discover in it the transcendent reality which supersedes the time-bound moment of the initial occurrence.

The total work is a story, a succession of stories, and a study of the life process, which, as we come to understand it, must greatly enrich our own sense of ourselves and of the lives which we live.

Kenneth Oliver

REMEMBRANCE ROCK

Type of work: Novel
Author: Carl Sandburg (1878-1967)
Type of plot: Historical chronicle
Time of plot: 1607-1945
Locale: England and America
First published: 1948

Remembrance Rock, a first novel published when the author was seventy years old, is a sprawling ode to America—partly a saga, partly a chronicle, partly a collection of tales, fables, and folk themes. The work is divided into three sections, dealing with the settling of Plymouth, the American Revolution, and the Civil War, set between a prologue and an epilogue which take place in Washington during World War II. The style ranges from the grave, proud language of Bunyan and Defoe to boisterous American slang. Unity of theme is achieved by characters recurring in major episodes and by symbolic reappearances of a bronze plaque bearing an inscription of Roger Bacon's Four Stumbling Blocks to Truth.

Remembrance Rock is a long, complex, and occasionally rambling chronicle-romance that summarizes many of the poet's patriotic feelings about America. Sandburg devoted five years to writing the book, his only novel. With his accustomed diligence he researched the general social background of the Pilgrims, both in England and America; of the Revolutionary period from 1775-1777; and of the pre-Civil War era up to the death of Lincoln, roughly 1836-1865. But Sandburg's research was not intended to treat actual history, as he does in the Lincoln biographies; instead, he was concerned with the spiritual heritage of the people. To be sure, real historical figures and events crowd the pages of the novel; yet the major characters are clearly of heroic proportions—the creations of myth, not fact. To provide a "frame" for his narrative, Sandburg uses Justice Windom, a contemporary of the 1940's, as the mouthpiece for his own ideas. Thus, he examines four selective but crucial moments in the history of the nation to answer four significant questions: How did America come to be what it is now (in 1948)? When and where did it begin and develop? What is the "mysterious variable" that in moments seems to be a constant in the moral history of the people? And what is the "ever shifting and hazardous" principle that underlies the American Dream?

To answer these questions, Sandburg approaches American history as myth, symbol, and unified design. In each of the four narratives (really brief novels in themselves), he traces the lives of patriots who have inherited a 1607 medallion engraved with Roger Bacon's "Four Stumbling Blocks to Truth." Each Stumbling Block—or "Cause of Error"—corresponds to an adventure of the narrative; the moral lesson of the history parallels that of Bacon's warnings. For example, the Puritans in England oppose religious per-

secution, thereby avoiding the first error—"the influence of fragile or unworthy authority." In America, however, the Puritans practice their own
form of intolerance. They fall prey to the second error, "custom." Fortunately,
with the onset of the Revolutionary War, old customs are swept aside as the
patriots establish a more humanistic morality. During the Civil War, patriots
must overcome the third error, that of "the imperfection of undisciplined
senses." For the fourth historical period, Sandburg's own, the patriot Justice
Windom must avoid the error of "concealment of ignorance by ostentation of
seeming wisdom." In effect, the poet satirizes his own "ostentation" in creating
the bombastic rhetoric spoken by Windom. Thus, with gentle irony Sandburg
concludes his panoramic history: even he, the author-patriot, has a Stumbling
Block to overcome.

In addition to Roger Bacon's "Four Stumbling Blocks to Truth," Sandburg uses other unifying devices in the novel. The similarity of the names of
his protagonists—Windom, Windling, Wingate, Winshore, Winwold—serves
to remind the reader both of the continuity and variety that marks the American heritage. Windom (win-*doom,* the old word for *judgment*) is an appropriate name for the former Supreme Court Justice; just as Orton Wingate is a
"gate" to the future, Ordway Winshore provides a shore-mooring for freedom,
and Omri Winwold (*wold* as *forest*) helps to clear the wilderness and bring
civilization to mid-America. Sandburg's women characters are alike in their
patriotic devotion to the land; they, too, form a pattern of heroism. In each
section of the novel a woman treasures the Roger Bacon medallion. Typically,
the author develops his stories around the relationship between a young girl
(representing the future) and an older man (the past), or between the girl
and her fiancé or husband (the present). The characters, then, are treated
both realistically and symbolically, as protagonists in stories and as heroic
figures of a national myth. Because of the symbolic patterns of the novel, its
ideas cannot be appreciated fully from the perspective of a conventional
work of either fiction or chronicle. In spite of its sentimentality, repetitious-
ness, and grandiloquence, *Remembrance Rock* attempts to commemorate, in
a form approaching folk poetry, the very spirit of the nation.

RENÉE MAUPERIN

Type of work: Novel
Authors: Edmond (1822-1896) and Jules (1830-1870) de Goncourt
Type of plot: Domestic tragedy
Time of plot: Nineteenth century
Locale: France
First published: 1864

This "slice of life" novel, considered by many the Goncourt brothers' best work, is a detailed, naturalistic study of a nineteenth century middle-class French family. Perhaps nowhere in literature has the lingering death of a victim of any disease been as excruciatingly delineated as has the death of Renée, which consumes at least one fourth of the chapters in the novel.

Above all, the Goncourt brothers valued truth in literature; in all of their novels, they attempted to find the truth of the subject they chose. In *Renée Mauperin,* they analyzed with shrewdness and precision a particular segment of Parisian society. Viewing this world through the eyes of an intelligent and sensitive girl, they presented the shallowness and pettiness of many of the self-satisfied people who dominated it and who tried to dominate her. In particular, the book illustrates the various conditions of women in mid-nineteenth century France. First, there is the impetuous young Renée, who as a child cuts Denoisel's hair and smokes her father's cigarette, and who later struggles against the conventions imposed upon young women in the Paris of 1864. Then, there is Mme. Mauperin, with her passion for "symmetry" and her typical overvaluing of her son and undervaluing of her daughter. Mme. Davarande, the society matron, devoted to her position and religious only because she believes that God is *chic,* and Mme. Bourjot, an intelligent woman married to a shallow and petty fool, clearly are intended to represent two typical women of the period. In the society of the day, only a shallow person seems able to find contentment, the authors seem to suggest, particularly if the person is a woman.

Many of the other characters, notably Renée's doting and scholarly father, and the sophisticated and subtle Abbé Blampoix, are well-drawn. The Goncourt brothers were not known for character analysis, but they achieved in this novel a success with their characters above that in many of their other books. Renée's sudden admission of inadvertently causing her brother's death is skillfully and devastatingly handled; the moment reveals the complexities of Renée's character which up to that point had been only suggested. The novel is filled with witty conversations that bring the era to life. The authors knew the value and interest of precise details and skillfully integrated them into the book through conversations and descriptions, often using them to delineate character. Frequently, the conversations are used to suggest a comment on society, as when a room full of people talking is described as "voices . . . all mingled together in the Babel: it was like the chirping of so many birds in a cage." It is this cage which Renée wants to escape, but ultimately does escape only through her death.

The novelistic strength of the Goncourts lay in pure observation. Perhaps they were less broad in their accomplishments than the greatest nineteenth century novelists, but in their best books, such as *Renée Mauperin,* they combined a precise and vivid picture of the society they knew so well with both a sympathetic and touching story and shrewd observations on human nature.

RESURRECTION

Type of work: Novel
Author: Count Leo Tolstoy (1828-1910)
Type of plot: Social criticism
Time of plot: Late nineteenth century
Locale: Russia
First published: 1899

Resurrection *is a profound study of man's inhumanity on both a personal and an institutional level. Provoked into a deep self-examination by the unjust fate of his former lover, Prince Nekhlúdoff comes to understand the widespread hypocrisy and corruption of the "respectable" social institutions and learns, in his regeneration, that only Christian love and compassion can mitigate the evil that man has created for himself.*

The greatest strength of Tolstoy's novel *Resurrection* is in its penetrating exposure of an unjust social order, which is revealed through Nekhlúdoff's search for justice and spiritual atonement. A secondary focus is on the personal level in the effect of Nekhlúdoff's philosophical-political conversion, specifically in his relationship with Katúsha, without whom Nekhlúdoff's reawakening and self-sacrifice could not have occurred.

In his student days, Nekhlúdoff's social convictions were idealistic. He believed in perfectibility and rejected the principle of ownership of land by the elite. His idealism dimmed after he entered military life, however, and he quickly abandoned all thoughts of perfection. He sacrificed both his relationship with Katúsha and his own values to establish a public image that mirrored the standards of the aristocracy. It was not until his conscience was aroused at the trial of Katúsha ten years later that he questioned his life and, upon Katúsha's conviction, dedicated himself to her rescue and to his spiritual atonement.

Nekhlúdoff thus came to view man's nature as dualistic—animal and spiritual—and he struggled to negate the animal instincts which led him to sin. He realized that he could deceive others, but not himself, and he set about, guided by an inner sense of righteousness, to correct the wrong he had caused. The process of his resurrection is an interesting one.

When Nekhlúdoff entered the world of prisoners and peasants, he began to realize how great the injustice of society actually was. Innocent people incarcerated by error, political prisoners whose crime was in holding differing opinions, and a crew of stone masons imprisoned because of outdated visas were among those who flocked to Nekhlúdoff for help.

It soon became evident to Nekhlúdoff that social circumstance created criminals rather than the obverse: he rejected the concept of natural depravity based on individual or class characteristics. Nekhlúdoff further understood that the conditions which created powerlessness, poverty, hunger, sickness, and crime among the peasant classes were supported by the powerful in order to maintain the wealth of the privileged. Both government and science professed a desire to ameliorate these conditions, but actually refused to consider the root of the problem. The only real means of righting the situation, he found, was by returning the land to the people who worked it. Yet when Nekhlúdoff gave his land to the peasants, his wealthy friends and family grew concerned about his mental health, and the peasants eyed his offer with hostile suspicion. Nekhlúdoff's exploration of the causes of injustice led him to ask the haunting question of whether truth is at work in the process of law. It was obvious to him that the law did not contain truth by decree or by the process of the courts, although such a notion was popularly accepted. The fact was, Nekhlúdoff concluded, that the purpose of the law was to uphold class interests and that those who carried out the law and those to whom the law catered were equally criminal with those upon whom the judgment of the law fell. The basic fallacy of the legal system was the belief that people have the power to judge one another. Evil doers cannot judge evildoers, Nekhlúdoff contended. The processes of judgment and punishment were not only harmful, cruel, and immoral but also ineffective. Justice, he decided, was not served by social systems. That society and order exist at all, despite the acts of both lawful and lawless criminals, is simply because people still pity and love one another.

In the course of the novel, Nekhlúdoff's resurrection is paralleled by Katúsha's spiritual reawakening. At her first reunion with Nekhlúdoff after her conviction, she repressed her memories of youtn and the pain of Nekhlúdoff's betrayal to the point of oblivion. In addition, she had hardened herself to the necessities of survival as a prostitute. Nekhlúdoff realized that his sin against her was even greater than he had known, that Katúsha had died and another person called Máslova was all that was left. Although Nekhlúdoff assumed responsibility not only for Katúsha's freedom, but also for her spiritual renewal, his influence was only one of the factors which went into the emergence of the new Katúsha. Katúsha realized that Nekhlúdoff was again using her, but as he persisted in following her, old feelings for him reawakened. She then sacrificed her love in order to save him from degradation. Katúsha thus shouldered Nekhlúdoff's burden for the third time: first in suffering his betrayal and bearing his illegitimate child, then in allowing him to sacrifice for her, and finally in denying her love for him by releasing him from his pledge to marry her. Still, it is Nekhlúdof's resurrection which is the novel's primary concern.

The process of Nekhlúdoff's social reversal and spiritual regeneration is least convincing in his personal relationships. He shifts from victimizing Katúsha to rescuing her, first taking advantage of her for his physical gratification and then using her to achieve his spiritual atonement. He is still the overlord whose decision precludes dialogue. He professes to see himself, like

Jesus—not the master, but the servant—but he is indeed a masterful servant. He imposes upon Katúsha the heavy burden of his self-sacrifice—his offer to marry her—without speaking a word of care or love. Nekhlúdoff's primary concern, it seems, is for the good feelings he gets from humbling himself—a form of masochism. Nekhlúdoff proclaims that he is dedicated to following God's will in his own conscience as far as he is able to do so and that in fulfilling such a commitment he will find peace and security.

The final, or perhaps first, genuine step in Nekhlúdoff's resurrection is the revelation of the truth in the Gospel of Christianity. Accordingly, Nekhlúdoff recognizes that man's only duty is to fulfill these laws, but without the guidance of the state church, which Nekhlúdoff judges to be as corrupt as the other institutions in society. Priests, for example, swear in witnesses at court proceedings with an air of self-importance but do not question whether justice is done. Prisoners corralled into prison chapels ironically chant prayers for the powers which oppress them. Cynical, heretical priests lead their people farther into the darkness of superstition because "it is good for them." Nekhlúdoff's disgust for such hypocritical religion is as great as his disdain for his former life and all it represented, but it is his personal religious stance which propels him into a deep and revolutionary understanding of society and justice—an understanding of which Tolstoy himself would approve.

Mary Peace Finley

THE RETURN

Type of work: Novel
Author: Walter de la Mare (1873-1956)
Type of plot: Fantasy
Time of plot: Nineteenth century
Locale: England
First published: 1910

The Return *is a provocative fantasy in which the real and the supernatural are extremely blurred. Arthur Lawford contracts a bizarre illness that radically alters his appearance and deeply disturbs all of his loved ones and associates, before it leaves him in an equally mysterious manner.*

A painter may depict a ghost as an opaque white figure, or he may give it the transparent quality of steam emanating from a teakettle. Both ghosts may be frightening, but the latter is more eerie because it is less visible. De la Mare in depicting Arthur Lawford's ailment has given it the eeriness of a tea-kettle ghost. Because the cause of the ailment is unknown, it is more unsettling than a disease with a clear-cut origin. Carefully ambiguous about the cause, de la Mare leads the reader to wonder whether Lawford needs a physician to treat a physical disease, a psychiatrist to cure him of an emotional disorder, or an exorcist to rid him of a devil.

There are ample suggestions in the novel for a physical, emotional, or supernatural reason for the sudden change in Lawford's face. His "still and stony" expression might be the result of Bell's palsy, a facial paralysis which has a sudden onset, results in facial distortion, and rarely lasts more than a few weeks. Lawford's reference to his disorder as "lupus" indicates a possible rheumatoid degenerative disease with symptoms affecting the skin. However, Lawford's physician diagnoses the condition as a mild nervous disorder triggered by Lawford's weakness from influenza. His mood changes and erratic speech are characteristic of an emotional upset. Other details lend credence to the idea of supernatural possession. Herbert, a fanciful man who believes in ghosts, points out to Lawford his resemblance to the deceased Nicholas Sabathier. And Lawford, so unhappily wed that he sees little joy in life, is receptive to the idea of transmigration, the more so because he would like to escape through time to share life with Grisel.

By the time Lawford's face returns to normal, de la Mare has examined the complementary nature of life and death, body and soul, love and hate, reality and imagination, and other polarities. And the reader will have seen the reasons for the mysterious ailment, as well as the reasons for its cure, more clearly.

THE RETURN OF THE KING

Type of work: Novel
Author: J. R. R. Tolkien (1892-1973)
Type of plot: Epic romance
Time of plot: The Third Age in a remote legendary past
Locale: The Middle-Earth, chiefly Gondor, Mordor, and the Shire
First published: 1955

This volume concludes the Lord of the Rings *trilogy. In it the evil forces of Sauron are defeated at the Black Gate of Mordor, the Ring falls into the fires of Mount Doom, Aragorn is crowned king, and the Hobbits return to the Shire— where they must defeat evil once more before final peace is restored.*

J. R. R. Tolkien was a scholar of note in the field of medieval literature, the author of a seminal essay on *Beowulf.* That he should have turned his hand to the composition of an original romance, with considerable success, is not surprising; that the work should fail in the one particular in which it does fail, is. For in all its technical aspects *The Lord of the Rings* meets and exceeds the requirements of its form. But in the crucial quality of human sympathy, with all the great epic heroes from Beowulf to Dante to give example, it is signally wanting.

In setting out to write a believable fiction, Tolkien gave himself the advantage of a time setting in the distant, mythical past, and was thus able to work backward from effect to presumptive cause. This device is apparent to some degree in the narrative (for example, tales of dwarfs, elves, and Little People existing in the folklore of the Fourth Age are posed as evidence for the actual existence of these beings in the Third Age) but chiefly in the appendices dealing with languages. The Common Speech used by the Hobbits Tolkien records as deriving, as did the language of Rohan, from Adûnaic, the language of the Dunedain. In the note on translation the author explains that he has transcribed the Common Speech as English and the language of Rohan as Old English in order to show this relation: then, using the linguistic rules which in fact apply to the development of English, he "recreates" a fictional anterior language, Westron or Adûnaic. More interesting still, from a linguistic point of view, is the derivation of the Elvish Tongues. In this case, he actually invents a language, Sindarin or Grey-Elven; then, by applying an invented set of vowel and consonant shifts according to rules of correspondence, derives the language from which it supposedly developed, Quenya or High-elven.

In other appendices, Tolkien reconstructs the histories of the various peoples of the saga from their beginnings to the time of the War of the Rings. In still others he explicates the Rune alphabet (real) and the Tengwar Script (half-real, derived from the Insular Script of the early Middle Ages.) This combination of familiar and invented material all subjected to the same scholarly scrutiny has the effect of anchoring the whole airy fiction in the real Anglo-Saxon cultural subconscious. The very concrete geographical setting, the sharp characterizations of the various races, details of dress and gear, and consistency of times and dates cement the impression of authenticity. What is demanded of the reader is less a suspension of disbelief than a willingness to participate in the history of his kind.

But it is not, finally, the history of his kind. In a work so strewn with memorable characters, it is remarkable that there are so few human figures, and among those few only one, Éowyn of Rohan, truly comes alive. For the most part the nonhuman figures are far better realized than the human; indeed the wicked seem to have a life of their own. The foul vitality of the orcs fairly leaps out at one (one of the most memorable lines of the trilogy is the orc-sergeant's cheery "Where there's a whip there's a will, my slugs"), and Gollum is as sharp a characterization as ever graced a page. We never see Sauron in his proper self, yet he is the single most powerful figure in the work. His malice, cloaked in a beautifully developed and extended system of symbols, underlies and unifies the plot. The reader is never in doubt about what motivates him. In fact, the creation of this character is a masterstroke. On the one hand, he shows a genius for mischief that ferrets out the weakness of each race: the Hobbits' laziness, the Dwarfs's love of gain, the Elves' otherworldliness, and the pride of men. On the other hand he himself is so warped by the lust for power that he is disembodied, a craving void, yet beyond the One Ring he has no weakness. He cannot be corrupted, suborned, or made afraid. He cannot even die, unless the object of his craving be destroyed. Sauron and the get of Mordor which are his visible form are a monument to the many-faceted simplicity of evil.

The faces of good in the romance are multifarious, and the victory of the peoples of the West proceeds from a combination of their different virtues and talents: magic of the Elves, weapons of Dwarves, the chivalry of Rohan, the loyalty of the Stewards, persistence of Ents and of Hobbits, Gandalf's wisdom, and the nobility and daring of the Dunedain. Aragorn leads the armies of the light, and his coronation crowns their victory. Yet he is not a mere man, is never thrown utterly on his own resources; he relies on elven-lore, on the help of the shadow-men, on the palantiri and the heirlooms of Arnor, and on the promises of his heritage. For this reason his exploits, though they may rouse the blood, cannot speak to the heart. The real heroes of the work are of course the Hobbits, especially Frodo and Sam. They exhibit all those defects of character that are commonly, and fondly, recognized as distinguishing human kind: self-engrossment, sensuality, laziness, timorousness. But their heroism is also human in kind, stubbornness being its cornerstone and selfless courage its crown. Sam's efforts to cope with the external elements of the ordeal mirror Frodo's struggle to master himself and to fight off the effects of The Ring. But it is all writ small, because the vehicles of this gallantry are pint-sized. It is the peculiar defect of this otherwise admirably executed design that its best elements are cloaked in a shape that cannot quite be taken seriously.

Jan Kennedy Foster

THE RETURN OF THE NATIVE

Type of work: Novel
Author: Thomas Hardy (1840-1928)
Type of plot: Romantic tragedy
Time of plot: Mid-nineteenth century
Locale: Egdon Heath, in southern England
First published: 1878

In this novel Thomas Hardy creates two strong opposing forces: Egdon Heath, a somber tract of wasteland symbolic of an impersonal fate, and Eustacia Vye, a beautiful, romantic young woman representing the opposing human element. Her marriage to the idealistic Clym Yeobright is doomed both by the external forces of nature and the intense, differing needs of the two characters. Eustacia's death by drowning in the company of Wildeve, her lover, is the fitting symbolic end to her life.

Thomas Hardy was born in Dorset, England, on June 2, 1840. Although he attended several grammar schools and studied French at King's College, Hardy had little formal education. Later, however, he read extensively in the Bible, the classics, and recent scientific publications. From 1856 to 1874 he was an architect's apprentice and later an ecclesiastical architect. During this time he wrote poetry, which was not published until after he was a well-known novelist. His first novel, *Desperate Remedies,* was published in 1871. In 1872 he married Emma Gifford; after her death in 1912 he married Florence Dugdale. When storms of protest arose over the pessimism and the violation of strict Victorian sexual mores in *Tess of the D'Urbervilles* and *Jude the Obscure,* Hardy gave up the novel but continued to write poetry. He died on January 11, 1928, and his ashes were placed in the poets' corner at Westminster Abbey. Among his best works are *Far from the Madding Crowd* and *The Return of the Native.*

In *The Return of the Native,* there is a strong conflict between nature or fate, represented by Egdon Heath, and human nature, represented by the characters in the novel, especially Eustacia. The title of the first chapter, "A Face on Which Time Makes But Little Impression," establishes the heath's role as much more significant than merely a setting for the action. The word "face" suggests that the heath assumes anthropomorphic proportions and becomes, in essence, a major character in the novel; somber and dark, "The storm was its lover, and the wind its friend." And, while the characters struggle and become tired and disillusioned—or die—the heath remains indifferent and unchanged. The heath is a formidable foe; in fact, those who struggle against it—Eustacia, Wildeve, and Mrs. Yeobright—eventually die.

The heath, then, becomes a symbol of permanence. Other aspects of the setting become symbolic, and they also intensify the somber tone of the novel. Light and dark imagery is significant in that the dominance of dark imagery adds to the novel's pessimism. The bonfires on the heath provide small areas of light in the blackness of the night, yet the furze burns quickly and is soon extinguished, like the momentary happiness of Eustacia and Clym and the wild passion of Eustacia and Wildeve. The moon's eclipse on the night Clym proposes to Eustacia foreshadows the eclipse of their love. On the night of Eustacia's death, the violent storm echoes her violent emotions as she cries out against her fate.

Like his character Eustacia, Hardy often seems to blame fate for many of the catastrophes of life. Many critics believe that in this novel fate is completely dominant and that the characters are helpless victims of its malevolence. Such a view, however, seems inadequate. Admittedly, fate does play a significant role; for example, Eustacia accidentally meets Wildeve at the maypole dance. Mrs. Yeobright just happens to choose an extremely hot day to visit Clym, just happens to arrive when Wildeve is there, and just happens to be bitten by the adder when she collapses from fatigue. Eustacia does not receive Clym's letter because her grandfather believes she is asleep. However, much of the novel's tragedy can be traced to the characters' motivations, decisions, and actions.

Mrs. Yeobright may seem victimized by Eustacia's failure to open the door to her, but one must remember that Mrs. Yeobright never accepts Eustacia and attempts to turn Clym against her. She feels socially superior to Eustacia, distrusts her because she is a free spirit, calls her lazy and irresponsible, hints that she is behaving indiscreetly with Wildeve, and, in general, is jealous of her because she wants to keep Clym to herself. She refuses to attend Clym's wedding and treats Eustacia in a condescending manner as they speak together near the pool. Then, she harbors her grudge and keeps away from her son and his wife long enough for the gulf between them to widen greatly.

Clym, too, brings much of his trouble upon himself. He is flattered by Eustacia's attention and passion for him but never really sees her as an individual totally different from himself. Without regard for her hatred of the heath and her longing for the excitement of Paris, he assumes that she will be a vital part of his teaching mission. After their marriage, he ignores her and devotes his time to his studies, which, perhaps, helps to bring about the physical blindness that becomes symbolic of his blindness to reality. Martyring himself as a furze cutter, he intensifies Eustacia's hatred for the heath and fails to see that his physical fatigue and his degrading work deal a crushing blow to his marriage. Even his desire to teach is selfish and unrealistic; he tries to escape from life's conflicts into an abstraction of truth, and he desires to impose his views on others. The view of Clym at the end of the novel is ironic; as an itinerant preacher "less than thirty-three," he may suggest a Christ figure; yet in his self-righteousness he fails to find the meaning of love.

Eustacia, who blames fate for her tragedy, is the novel's most ambiguous character; even the author seems to have ambivalent feelings toward her.

She is an exciting, passionate "queen of the night" whose romanticism makes her long to "be loved to madness" by a man great enough to embody her dreams. Allowing her imagination to convince her that Clym can master this role, she marries him, hoping to manipulate him, as she had manipulated Wildeve, and thus get to Paris. After her marriage, however, her liaison with Wildeve is at first innocent; only after Clym banishes her from his house does she agree to accept Wildeve's offer to help her leave the heath. Yet in spite of her desperation, Eustacia refuses to be humbled. Realizing that a lack of money will cause her to lose her honor for a man who is "not great enough" to meet her desires, she drowns herself to avoid humiliation. It is more believable that she dies willingly rather than accidentally, because only in death does she seem to find peace.

Though Eustacia has lost in her battle with the heath, her struggle proves that she is a strong, defiant character who is defeated partly by forces beyond her control and partly by her own refusal to give up her dream. And, in spite of her selfishness and hauteur, her lively spirit gives life to the novel and makes her, in the end, its tragic but unforgettable heroine.

Janet Wester

THE REVENGE OF BUSSY D'AMBOIS

Type of work: Drama
Author: George Chapman (c. 1559-1634)
Type of plot: Tragedy of blood
Time of plot: Sixteenth century
Locale: Paris
First presented: c. 1610

The Revenge of Bussy d'Ambois *is a portrait of Chapman's ideal tragic hero. Clermont d'Ambois' stoic idealism gives him an interesting and compelling character, but unfortunately, one that does not lend itself to dramatization. The result is a superb character study, but a poor drama.*

The Revenge of Bussy d'Ambois, like Chapman's other tragedies, is a curious mixture of classical and Elizabethan patterns. In his use of sensationalism—the warning ghost, scenes of murder and torture, and the like—Chapman seems to be following the Elizabethan pattern of revenge tragedy, yet in his poetry—the epic similes, the long ethical and philosophical tirades, the grave and serious tone—he shows the effects of a strong classical influence. On the one hand Chapman shows a strong affinity to the revenge tragedy patterns of Kyd and Webster, while on the other he shows similarities to the style of Ben Jonson, whose tragedy, *Sejanus,* Chapman admired for its noble qualities, though it was a dramatic failure.

As in his other tragedies, Chapman's greatest weakness in *The Revenge of Bussy d'Ambois* is in plot construction. The play becomes a vehicle for thought rather than action, and though the poetry is sometimes profound, if difficult, it often inhibits the work as a stage play. However much we may be impressed with the expression of Chapman's stoic philosophy and with his concern for political conflicts between the individual and the state, we must be disappointed with his sense of theater. No doubt, it is partly Chapman's explicit didactic intent to make the play, as he says in the dedication, an "excitation to heroical life" that creates some of the theatrical shortcomings.

Though *The Revenge of Bussy d'Ambois* is a somewhat inferior sequel to *Bussy d'Ambois* dramatically, it is in other ways a more original work, for it is a type of protest against certain revenge tragedy conventions. Instead of a revenger after the type of Kyd's Hieronimo or Shakespeare's Hamlet, men full of passion or doubt, Chapman's Clermont is rather a stoic: a man fully in control of himself who will exact revenge according to his own rational pattern, not in the heat of passion or madness. Further, Clermont does not perish with his victim as a part of the revenge, but takes his own life following the death of his friend, the Duc du Guise. Though we may finally be disappointed by the play's lack of action, we can still be impressed by its thoughtfulness and high poetic style.

THE REVENGER'S TRAGEDY

Type of work: Drama
Author: Cyril Tourneur (c. 1575-1626)
Type of plot: Tragedy of blood
Time of plot: The Renaissance
Locale: A city in Italy
First presented: c. 1607

John Addington Symonds described The Revenger's Tragedy *as "an entangled web of lust, incest, fratricide, rape, adultery, mutual suspicion, hate, and bloodshed, through which runs, like a thread of glittering copper, the vengeance of a cynical plague-fretted spirit." This overdrawn plot is, however, somewhat redeemed by the splendor of the language.*

The intensity of the writing gives *The Revenger's Tragedy* its impact and places it in the canon of major British dramatic works. The fiery passions and the lacerating of the human spirit that sweep through the play leave the audience or reader exhausted; the bitterness of mood and inner violence are reflected in the external physical violence. Even Webster failed to match the hectic, biting irony, and savage, almost cannibalistic exposure of human emotions that dominate Tourneur's *The Revenger's Tragedy.* The amazing aspect of the drama is that the author maintained the level of intensity throughout the length of the play, without resorting to comic relief or passages of transition or dramatic contrast.

The unrelieved horror is almost unbearable to the audience. All of the characters are stained with evil. From the opening, in which Vendice holds in his hand the skull of his betrothed, declaring that he will have his vengeance, to the climax showing the duke dying in agony and Vendice boasting, after having murdered the Duke's family, that there were no enemies left, the plot constantly risks sensationalism and absurdity in its extreme situations. However, the sincerity of the writing and the power of the insights into certain aberrations of the human mind and spirit, rescue the play from these pitfalls. Technically, the play moves swiftly and with great dramatic skill, and the somber brilliance of its execution is never relaxed.

While much of the horror in the play was undoubtedly meant to be taken literally in its day, now the parade of murders and horrors assumes a symbolic quality, representing the darker side of man's nature. The tangle of incest, rape, suspicion, and violence seems to represent an effort on the part of the author to explore the boundaries of human corruption and the results of un-limited hatred. The melodramatic plot might almost be considered as merely an excuse for the unprecedented probings of mankind's capacity for cruelty. From this standpoint, as an exploration of abnormal psychology, *The Revenger's Tragedy* has perhaps never been equaled. In some respects, the play seems extremely modern, akin to the novels of Céline or to some of the dramatic and fictional works which have attempted, both symbolically and realistically, to dramatize and explain the atrocities of Hitler's dictatorship. However one approaches this unusual and powerful work, it is clear that the playwright transcended the limits of his genre and created a masterpiece.

THE REVOLT OF THE ANGELS

Type of work: Novel
Author: Anatole France (Jacques Anatole Thibault, 1844-1924)
Type of plot: Fantasy
Time of plot: Early twentieth century
Locale: France
First published: 1914

*Anatole France was a revolutionary who ridiculed the Church and the state in a
series of sharp, bitter novels. The Revolt of the Angels, one of the most abusive
satires of this century, is a fantasy about a revolt against Heaven that is aborted
when Satan intervenes out of the fear that he might, in turn, make himself into a
god. In this satire France attacks almost every established institution in the world,
sometimes to excess, but always with style and precision.*

Style is all with the satires of Anatole France, and *The Revolt of the
Angels* is no exception. The brilliance of the style is continually dazzling,
the crisp, ironic prose setting forth without comment the absurdities of the
plot. At the same time, the novel is rich with witty conversations and lengthy
and clever philosophical debates. The surface of the novel glitters, but beneath it lies the fundamentally serious nature of the work. Realities in the
world are but appearances, states one character in *The Revolt of the Angels,*
and Anatole France deliberately deceives the reader, confusing both reality
and appearance in this book. The realistic details so carefully described in the
narrative lend verisimilitude and plausibility to the essential fantasy of the
story.

The book is filled with delightful comic characters such as the absurd
detective Mignon and the doddering old librarian M. Sariette. The fallen
angel Théophile, who makes his living as a music teacher, and Arcade, the
would-be revolutionary archangel, are brilliant comic creations. But perhaps
Satan himself is the most original character in the book, when he appears at
the end and refuses to allow the angels to revolt because he is afraid that
they will win and set him up as a new God.

The Revolt of the Angels provides a perfect example of the comic inventiveness of Anatole France; the book is crowded with hilarious scenes such
as the old librarian begging the monkey to forgive him for suspecting that it
was raiding the library, or the incredible spectacle of a mortal man urging a
naked angel to cease rebelling against God and return to its duty in Heaven.
The entire comic-opera mystery of the disappearing and reappearing books is
a brilliant opening to the absurd plot. But the plot is only a vehicle for the
satirical intentions of the author. With impeccable logic, Anatole France proclaims the strangeness of the logical—a common theme in his novels. Deliberately, he turns cherished beliefs upside down, attacking the assumption
that men are essentially good or thinking creatures and, at the same time, de-

fending the much maligned Satan. Of all of the activities of mankind, France states, only art is of any value. The fact is that mortals judge their actions strictly by the pleasure or pain resulting, and moral values are entirely utilitarian. But whether or not the reader sympathizes with France's attack on Western civilization's sacred cows, he will enjoy the wit and grace of the writing and the brilliance of the comic passages.

REYNARD THE FOX

Type of work: Beast-epic
Author: Unknown
Type of plot: Satiric stories
Time of plot: Middle Ages
Locale: Europe
First transcribed: Eighth century (?)

Second in popularity only to the fables of Aesop is the old German tale of Reynard the Fox. *In it we see that cunning always conquers force, that one who lives by his wits will never suffer. We grudgingly admire the villainous hero even while hoping he will get his just punishment. In some explications Reynard represents the Church, Isengrim the baronial component, and Noble the monarchy.*

In strict literary terminology, *Reynard the Fox* is classified as a "beast epic." The underlying framework of this popular medieval literary form is a series of stories linked by the same characters—invariably, anthropomorphized animals (hence, *"beast* epic"). In *Reynard the Fox,* the character of Reynard provides the connective thread. The "epic" designation derives from the length of the series as well as from the use of typical epic devices such as the loose, rather episodic relationship among the stories. Accordingly, most versions of *Reynard the Fox* are lengthy, and the episodes are only vaguely related. In addition, the target of such beast epics is satire of the contemporary social and political scene. Indeed, *Reynard the Fox* satirizes human folly, the judicial system, and much else.

The origin of the form, however, is still subject to scholarly debate. Since *Reynard the Fox* is one of the most important examples of this genre, the debate, in this case, is quite significant. Some scholars maintain that the so-called beast epic derived from the oral folk tradition of storytelling, later being formalized in writing by medieval monastic scribes. Other scholars find precedents among classical Latin authors to explain the origin of the beast epic. Both schools of thought have defensible positions, and both take their stand on the same set of facts, since many versions of the *Reynard the Fox* stories are extant.

From the dispute some basic information emerges. First, Ovid's *Metamorphoses* contains stories similar to those in the *Reynard the Fox* series. Second, Aesop's *Fables* includes specific Reynard episodes. However, limited medieval access to such "classical" precedents renders the influence of these models moot. The earliest manifestations of *Reynard the Fox* are stories about the animosity between Reynard and his enemy, Isengrim, the wolf. These stories may be derived from popular origin in French, English, Dutch, Low German, and Latin folktales. They seem to have initiated in the Low Countries, Northern France, and Northeastern Germany, although precedence cannot now be definitely assigned. The earliest versions were predictably in verse, although the later redactions appeared in prose.

A rather short poetic rendering of *Reynard* stories was done in medieval Latin by an eighth century cleric, Paulus Diaconus (Paul the Deacon), from Charlemagne's court. Another medieval Latin version appeared about two hundred years later in *Ecbasis captivi,* attributed to a German monk in Toul. The basic "Isengrim" story—*Ysengrimus*—is attributed to Master Nivardus of Ghent, who wrote in Latin at about A.D. 1150, developing his stories from Aesopian fables.

The evolution of vernacular versions is still open to question; some scholars claim priority for France and others insist upon Germanic primacy. The issue has not been resolved, but there is no question that twelfth and thirteenth century Flanders, West Germany, and Northern France were fertile grounds for this literary form, especially for Reynard stories.

At approximately the same time that *Ysengrimus* was produced, there appeared in France a compilation called the *Roman de Renart,* from the hands of several authors (many, according to medieval custom, anonymous). This vernacular compilation dealt mostly but not exclusively with stories of the protagonist Reynard facing his antagonist Isengrim the wolf. The stories are usually arranged in chronological "branches" (to reflect the time when they were written), rather than in topical order; unfortunately, this arrangement tends to undermine the ideological impact of the stories. The didactic element was much stronger in the almost simultaneous (c. 1180) vernacular redaction of Heinrich der Glichesäre, surviving in an anonymous manuscript written c. 1240. Nevertheless, the most important Reynard series seems to be a Middle Dutch version (c. 1270) by Willem of Hulsterlo, minimizing Reynard's humanitarian acts (curing the sick lion and the like) while emphasizing his venality. Willem's version thus exposed Reynard rather than praised him, and it set the tone for many subsequent vernacular versions of the stories.

Reynard the Fox appeared in Latin, French, German, Flemish, Dutch, and English versions—testimony to its popularity. However, it is evident that questions about origins and the chronological order of various versions cannot be unequivocally answered with the information at hand. As is the case with much medieval history and literature, final answers must wait upon the discovery of further evidence, most likely from a presently unknown cache of medieval manuscripts—if such a cache exists.

In the meantime, it is still possible to evaluate the extant material on its own terms, because *Reynard the Fox* evolved as the archetype of the beast epic. The central focus of the series concentrates on a single significant episode—Reynard's healing of the sick lion, in most versions—and other stories are spin-offs from this episode, all involving moralistic messages. The cast of animals varies from story to story and from version to version: Fox, lion, and wolf are constants; badger, bear, stag, rooster, cat, hare, camel, bear, ant, and others appear occasionally. The didactic factor is, of course, another constant, and for the temper of the times, it is a remarkably pragmatic one.

Indeed, the Reynard series is a lesson in ethics and morality. None of the animals is a paragon of virtue. All are vulnerable or corruptible or both; not even King Lion is exempt. They live in a world which recognizes no moral codes and where survival depends upon wit and exploitation of others. Insengrim the wolf is doomed because he carries to extremes his penchant for besting everything and everybody. He is obsessed by the compulsion to surpass, a compulsion which blinds him to the necessary humanistic rituals required for survival. By contrast, Reynard is pliable, adaptable, and fundamentally amoral. He survives *because* he is flexible. Yet, in the process, he becomes venal, power-hungry, and oblivious to humanistic values. Significantly, Chaucer's "Nun's Priest's Tale" (in *The Canterbury Tales*) relates a Reynard story—the fox's attempt and failure to abduct the rooster Chanticleer—to demonstrate the weakness and the power of flattery. Reynard's tactics thus become an object lesson in compromised integrity. For Reynard is the ultimate opportunist, knowing no scruple but his own advancement at the expense of others. To be sure, Reynard is neither explicitly praised nor explicitly condemned in the context of medieval ethics or morality. Rather, he is held forth as an example—albeit, an implicit example of "what *not* to do." In this sense, the best didactic functions of the beast epic are upheld. For it is the didactic element in such words that constitutes their intended impact. Although scholarly disputes continue about the origins and the development of the beast epic, in the last analysis the more crucial point is the moral import of such stories. In this respect, *Reynard the Fox* succeeds extremely well.

Joanne G. Kashdan

RHADAMISTUS AND ZENOBIA

Type of work: Drama
Author: Prosper Jolyot de Crébillon (1674-1762)
Type of plot: Romantic tragedy
Time of plot: About A.D. 60
Locale: Artanissa, capital of Iberia
First presented: 1711

Although Rhadamistus and Zenobia *was quite popular on the eighteenth century stage, to a modern audience the play is impossibly complicated, excessively melodramatic, and verbally ponderous. Crébillon modeled the play on the tragedies of Seneca and wrote it in hopes of continuing the classical tradition of Corneille and Racine, but he lacked their scope and insight as well as the stylistic control of his contemporary, Voltaire.*

Eighteenth century French tragedy became weighted down with philosophical speculations and undramatic, polemical material. Even Voltaire's dramas were nearly unactable, despite his attempts to pour life into them with melodramatic horrors. Crébillon went even further than Voltaire in his attempts to startle and his efforts to fill his plays with stately speeches. Crébillon's tragedies were modeled after those of the Roman tragic writer Seneca, and like them specialized in horror; however, Seneca's tragedies were meant only to be read, while Crébillon's plays, such as *Rhadamistus and Zenobia,* were intended for the stage. Crébillon said that he aimed to move his audience to pity through terror, but his tragedies were more often merely sensational, depending less upon psychological analysis than upon violent and unnatural crimes. He attempted to carry on the tradition of classical tragedy in France after Corneille and Racine, but he replaced poetic grandeur with melodramatic violence, and distorted the tragedy with horrifying situations and inhuman passions.

Rhadamistus and Zenobia is considered Crébillon's finest play, although the plot is so complicated as to be almost incomprehensible. When it was first produced, it was greeted with tremendous respect and popularity. It was one of the most acted eighteenth century tragedies at the Comedie Francaise, and Zenobia was considered one of the choice tragic roles for eighteenth century French actresses. This play and a few of Crébillon's other most successful works were considered to possess a vigor and passion unsurpassed in French classical drama, but even his admirers admitted a want of culture and a lack of care in his style and verse, although isolated passages were well done.

The subject of *Rhadamistus and Zenobia* has close analogies with Racine's *Mithridate.* The heroine (disguised, of course) is loved by a whole family, who have been chiefly occupied with murdering her own family. There are swelling speeches and occasional inspiration, but the drama is melodramatic.

Crébillon does not reach the depths of the human spirit that he is aiming for; the result is that the play appeals mainly to the audience's curiosity or shocked sensibilities. In *Rhadamistus and Zenobia,* Crébillon kept within the conventional form of tragedy, but his plot became a chaotic swirl of mistaken identity, recognitions, and tangled family relations. The audiences of his day thrilled, however, to the suspenseful story and the violence and terror it stimulated.

In *Rhadamistus and Zenobia,* we can see how much Crébillon resembled Corneille, both in his defects and virtues as a dramatic poet. In his attempt to make his diction energetic, he gave way to excesses which became inflated and obscure, and, at times, absurd. He never possessed, even in this play, the polish of his enemy, Voltaire, although he achieved a rugged power beyond Voltaire. Crébillon did not fathom the heart of the human soul in this or any other of his plays, but he kept alive the classical tradition, and his genius for inventing tense and tragic situations (too often with far-fetched mistaken identities to help prolong the suspense) stimulated other writers. Voltaire himself used four of Crébillon's plots. By absolute standards, *Rhadamistus and Zenobia* is a bizarre historical curiosity rather than a masterpiece of tragic dramatic literature, but its importance in the development of French drama cannot be denied.

RICEYMAN STEPS

Type of work: Novel
Author: Arnold Bennett (1867-1931)
Type of plot: Social criticism
Time of plot: 1919
Locale: Riceyman Steps, a suburb of London
First published: 1923

In Riceyman Steps, a study of the disintegration of a miser, Henry Earlforward, Arnold Bennett narrows his scope, but demonstrates that incisive observation of English characteristics, manners, and mores which made him one of the best realistic novelists of his day. In this novel Bennett carefully balances the pathetic, the comic, and the bitterly ironic in a manner that makes it his most genuinely modern novel.

The last novel of Arnold Bennett to enjoy critical favor, *Riceyman Steps* (1923), is both a satirical comedy and a naturalistic study of the disintegration of character. Unlike Bennett's Staffordshire novels, the setting of this book is not provincial but urban London. Unlike the grandly conceived *Clayhanger* trilogy and *The Old Wives' Tale,* the novel is a miniature, limited in scope, with few characters, tightly unified in time and action. Yet within these limits, *Riceyman Steps* is a novel of unexpected power, and grim, astringent humor.

Henry Earlforward, the central character, is obsessively frugal. Through his miserliness, he paradoxically destroys his hopes for gain. His wife, Violet, dies of malnutrition; and he expires—symbolically—from the cancer that has slowly devoured his stomach. Nevertheless Henry is not the typical miser of romance. Compared to Molière's Harpagon, he is a man of character (however misguided), of determination, even of dignity.

Bennett was torn between two conflicting attitudes about his miser. Although he recognized in the man a compulsive weakness that would lead to tragedy, he also admired Earlforward's self-sacrificing resolve and will power that at times is insanely heroic. Bennett once stated that he could not quite make up his mind, because of his uncertainty about the miser, whether he should emphasize the story's comedy or its irony. The result of Bennett's vacillating purpose is that *Riceyman Steps* appears quite modern in temper. Both bitter and wildly funny, it adumbrates "black" humor, which appeared three decades later in fiction and drama. Moreover, as a realistic study in the forces of life (represented by Elsie) and death (Henry), the novel treats larger issues of survival on a symbolic level. Earlforward and Violet perish, victims of the old Edwardian ethic of gain. Elsie survives, indeed flourishes. She will take care of the shell-shocked Joe, nearly destroyed by the insanity of war, and create for both of them, for her generation, a more abundant and more generous life.

RICHARD THE SECOND

Type of work: Drama
Author: William Shakespeare (1564-1616)
Type of plot: Historical tragedy
Time of plot: Fourteenth century
Locale: England
First presented: c. 1595

Richard II *is profound both as a political vision and as a personal tragedy. Richard is an inept king—erratic, willful, arrogant, susceptible to flattery, blind to good advice—but a sensitive, deeply moving poet. The play demonstrates the inevitable results of his bad qualities (his dethroning by Bolingbroke), yet also reveals his growth as a human being.* Richard II *contains some of Shakespeare's most beautiful and moving verse.*

Part of Shakespeare's second tetralogy of historical plays (with *1-2 Henry the Fourth* and *Henry the Fifth*), *Richard the Second* is also his second experiment in the *de casibus* genre of tragedy—dealing with the fall of an incompetent but not unsympathetic king. It is also part of the "lyrical group" of plays written between 1593 and 1596, in which Shakespeare's gradual transformation from poet to playwright can be traced. The sources of the play include *The Chronicles of England, Scotland and Ireland* by Raphael Holinshed (second edition: 1587); the chronicles of Froissart, and Edward Hall; the *Mirror for Magistrates*; Samuel Daniels' poetical account, *The Civil Wars;* and an earlier play by an unknown author, *Thomas of Woodstock*. Nonetheless *Richard the Second* demonstrates Shakespeare's own inventiveness, especially in all the female roles.

Thematic interests in the play are associated, in one way or another, with the question of sovereignty. Bolingbroke's challenge to Richard brings into focus the divine right of kings, its historical basis, its social implications. Connected with this is the matter of a subject's duty of passive obedience, especially as seen in the character of Gaunt and of York. Richard's arbitrariness in the opening scenes suggest the dangers of irresponsible despotism; as we follow his thoughts and strange behavior through the play, contrasted with the caginess and certainty of Bolingbroke (whose thoughts are seen only as translated into effective action), he becomes a study of the complex qualities of the ideal ruler. In this last respect the play reflects the Renaissance fascination with defining optimum behavior in various social roles (for example, Machiavelli's *The Prince,* Ascham's *The Schoolmaster,* Elyot's *The Governour*). Yet Shakespeare's psychological realism does not reach a falsely definitive conclusion. This uncertainty creates a tragic aura around Richard which makes him a most attractive character. In many ways, the play is not so much a contest for power as a struggle within Richard himself to adjust to his situation.

In this first play where Shakespeare makes his central figure an introspective, imaginative, and eloquent man, it is not surprising that some of his finest lyrical passages abound. *Richard the Second* is the only play Shakespeare wrote entirely in verse, supported by a regal formality of design and manner, and a profuse and delicate metaphorical base. Intricately interwoven throughout the play are image-patterns centered around the eagle, the lion, the rose, the sun (which begins with Richard but moves to Bolingbroke), the State as theater, the earth as a neglected or well-tended garden, and the rise and fall of Fortune's buckets. The complicated imagery illustrates the subconscious workings of Shakespeare's imagination that will enrich the great tragedies to follow. As Henry Morley comments, the play is "full of passages that have floated out of their place in the drama to live in the minds of the people"—including Gaunt's great apostrophe to England (Act 2, scene 1), York's description of "our two cousins coming into London," Richard's prison soliloquy (5,4), and his monologues on divine right (3,2) and on the irony of kingship (3,2).

So poetic is Richard II, that critics speculate Shakespeare may have written the part for himself. As a lover of music, spectacle, domestic courtesy, and dignified luxury, Richard would be the ideal host to Castiglione's courtier. His whimsical personality is balanced, to great dramatic effect, by his self-awareness. Richard seems fascinated with the contradictory flow of his own emotions; and this very fascination is a large part of his tragic flaw. Similarly, Richard's sensitivity is combined with a flair for self-dramatization that reveals only too clearly his ineptitude as a strong ruler. He plays to the wrong audience, seeking the approval of his court rather than of the common people; he seems to shun the "vulgar crowd" in preference to the refined taste of a court that can appreciate his delicate character. The last three acts, emphasizing Richard's charm as a man, are obviously more central to the play's aesthetic than the first two, which reveal his weakness as a king. His sentimental vanity in the abdication scene is so effective that it was censored during Elizabeth's lifetime. The alternation of courage and despair in Richard's mind sets the rhythm of the play; Coleridge observes that "the play throughout is a history of the human mind." Richard's character is drawn with a skill equaled only by that of King Lear's.

When the king speaks of "the unstooping firmness of my upright soul" we understand that he is compensating verbally for his inability to act. Richard insists upon the sacramental nature of kingship, depending for his support on the formal, legal rituals associated with the throne; he is all ceremony and pathetically fatal pomp. Yet, from the outset, Richard contradicts even the logic of sovereign ceremony when he arbitrarily changes his decision, and banishes the two opponents in the joust. Bolingbroke is quick to note the king's weakness, and steps into the power vacuum it creates. For Bolingbroke is the consummate actor who can be all things to all men by seeming so.

He is impressed by the kingly power Richard wields: "Four lagging winters and four wanton springs/End in a word: such is the breath of kings." He likes what he sees and, in deciding to imitate it, surpasses Richard. Even when Bolingbroke is ceremonious, as he is when he bows his knee to Richard before the abdication, he is acting. And the difference is that he knows the most effective audience. Richard laments that he has seen Bolingbroke's courtship of the common people, "How he did seem to dive into their hearts." He recognizes the actor in Bolingbroke, and fears its power. It is not coincidental that York compares the commoners to the fickle theater audience. As in so many plays of Shakespeare—*Hamlet, Richard the Third, King Lear* —the theater itself becomes a central image; Richard's monologues are a stark contrast to Bolingbroke's speeches not only because they reveal internal states but also because they are narcissistically oriented. They reach inward, toward secrecy and communicative impotency; Bolingbroke speaks actively, reaching outward toward the audience he wishes to influence. His role can be compared usefully to that of Antony in *Julius Caesar,* Richard's to that of Brutus. The tension between the two styles of speaking, moreover, no doubt reflects the transformation in Shakespeare himself that will make the plays to follow much more strikingly dramatic than they are sheerly poetic. The Bolingbroke of *Henry the Fourth* is born in *Richard the Second,* his realistic, calculating, efficient, politically astute performance directly antithetical to Richard's impractical, mercurial, meditative, and inept behavior. Bolingbroke is an opportunist, favored by fortune. A man of action and of few words, Bolingbroke presents a clear alternative to Richard, when the two men appear together. If Richard is the actor as prima donna, Bolingbroke is the actor as director.

Kenneth John Atchity

RICHARD THE THIRD

Type of work: Drama
Author: William Shakespeare (1564-1616)
Type of plot: Historical chronicle
Time of plot: Fifteenth century
Locale: England
First presented: c. 1593

Richard III is one of the most fascinating villains in all literature. Despite his personal deformity, he exudes charm and wit, demonstrates a potent rhetorical power, and possesses a tactical ability that deceives and manipulates his adversaries with an ease that is as awesome as his ruthlessness is repugnant. In the end he is doomed by his own excessive ambition, but even in defeat his courage and style are impressive.

Richard the Third is the last of a series of four plays which began with the three parts of *Henry the Sixth*. These plays, though not strictly speaking a tetralogy, trace the bloody conflicts between the houses of Lancaster and York and interpret the events leading up to the establishment of the Tudor dynasty. Despite the painful experiences of Richard, the drama remains a history rather than a tragedy. Richard does not have the moral stature to be a tragic hero; a tragic hero may murder, but he does so in violation of his own nature; Richard, however, is quite at home when intriguing and slaughtering. Even as bloody a character as Macbeth implies an earlier Macbeth of nobler behavior. Richard is too intelligent and self-aware, too much in control of himself and those around him to raise any of the moral ambiguities or dilemmas which are necessary to tragedy. Nor does Richard come to any transcendent understanding of his actions.

Richard is, nevertheless, the dominating figure in the play and a fascinating character. All the other characters pale before him and the play becomes primarily a series of encounters between Richard and the opponents who surround him. Physically, Richard is a small man with a humpback. Many commentators have suggested that his behavior is a compensation for his physical deformity. But Richard is not a paranoid; everyone really does hate him. The deformity, which is a gross exaggeration of the historical reality, is more likely a physical representation of the grotesque shape of Richard's soul in a Renaissance world which took seriously such correspondences. In any case, it makes for good theater by representing Richard and his plots as all the more grotesque.

Richard is also the master rhetorician in a play in which Shakespeare shows for the first time the full power of his language. In Richard's speeches and in the staccato exchanges among characters, there appears the nervous energy that informs the more ambitious later plays. From his opening soliloquy, Richard fascinates us not only with his language but also with his intelligence and candor. Up until the very end, he is the stage manager of all that occurs. As a villain, he is unique in his total control and in the virtuosity of his performance. Even Iago pales before him, for Richard, in soliloquies and asides, explains to the audience exactly what he is going to do and then carries it off expeditiously.

In his opening speech it is immediately clear that Richard will preside if not eventually prevail. He reveals not only his self-confident awareness of his own physical limitations and intellectual superiority, but also a disarming perception of his own evil and isolation. His honest villainy is more total than Iago's both in the way that he is able to convince every character that he is his only friend and in the full step-by-step disclosure of his intentions to the audience. Since everyone is against him, he almost generates our sympathy against our will. Anyway, there is no one else in the play to turn to.

The plot is the relentless working out of Richard's schemes to his final destruction. His first confrontation, with Anne, the widow of Henry VI's son whom Richard had killed, is a model for Richard's abilities. The exchange begins with Anne heaping abuse on her husband's murderer and ends with Richard extracting from her a promise of marriage. Anne is overwhelmed more by the brilliance and audacity of Richard's rhetorical wit than by the logic of his arguments. Yet, the audience is left with the extreme improbability of the short time it takes Richard to be successful. The violation of probability, however, is as much a convention as Richard's speaking to the audience in soliloquy. It is one of the givens of the play. It is part of the definition of this villain that he could succeed in such a wildly improbable adventure. And repeatedly Richard is able to put those who hate him to his own uses in a perverse gratification of his ostensible desire for power and his submerged desire to be loved. Only his own mother is painfully able to see through to the total corruption of his heart.

For Richard, the path to kingship is clear: it is simply a matter of ingratiating himself to the right people and of murdering all of those who stand in his way. He contracts the murder of Clarence in the tower amid a good bit of gallows humor which appropriately sets the grim tone. Like a good Machiavellian, he both builds on past success and takes advantage of fortuitous circumstances. Thus, he uses the death of Clarence to cast suspicion on Elizabeth and her party and to get the support of Buckingham, and he seizes on the death of Edward IV to have the influential nobles imprisoned and killed. Richard is clearing the political scene and the stage of obstacles. Nothing happens except at Richard's instigation except for coincidences which he turns to his own advantage. He eliminates Hastings and choreographs his own reluctant acceptance of the throne by implying that Edward's sons are bastards. Then ruthlessly and relentlessly, he accomplishes the murder of the boys of his wife, Anne, the imprisonment of Clarence's son, and the discrediting of his daughter. He has efficiently removed all near claims to the throne by lies, innuendos, and direct, vigorous action.

So appealing is his virtuosity and so faithful is he in informing the audience of his plans, that we share apprehension as the tide of opposition swells under the leadership of Richmond. Shakespeare neatly figures the balance of power by setting up the opposing camps on opposite sides of the stage. The ominous appearances of the ghosts, to Richmond as well as Richard, portend that retribution is at hand. Although he is unnerved for the first time, Richard behaves with martial valor and struggles determinedly to the last. This last show of courage, amid all of the recognitions of evil, is the final complication of our complex admiration for a consummate villain.

Edward E. Foster

RIGHT YOU ARE—IF YOU THINK SO

Type of work: Drama
Author: Luigi Pirandello (1867-1936)
Type of plot: Expressionistic parable
Time of plot: Early twentieth century
Locale: A small Italian town, the capital of a province
First presented: 1917

In Right You Are—If You Think So. *Pirandello develops one of his favorite themes: the relativity of truth. Laudisi, who mocks the determination of the townspeople to pry out the secret of Signora Frola and the Ponzas and who several times vainly tries to stop them, serves as the author's spokesman and the explicator of his theme. Despite the philosophic nature of his theme, Pirandello's drama is eminently actable.*

This play is, perhaps, Pirandello's most extreme statement on the relativity of truth. He sets up a situation in which the truth, as we are accustomed to verify it, cannot be determined because of the inability to establish a single truth for all. An earthquake has destroyed the village from which the Ponza-Frola family came, dispersed or killed most of its inhabitants, and destroyed the official birth and death records. The author, however, further indicates that even were documents (factual evidence) to be found, they could in no way establish a single truth acceptable to all because they would be interpreted by "each in his own way," the title of another Pirandello play also dealing with the theme of the relativity of truth. This point, the theme of the play, is shown through the manner in which truth is perceived by various groups or characters within the play.

The first group consists of the townspeople (the Agazzi and their friends). To these people, truth is "specific and concrete." It represents what one can see and feel, a decidedly empirical approach to reality. They assume reality appears the same to all. It never occurs to them that they cannot find *the* truth because reality may appear differently to different people at different times. Thus, they vacillate from belief in Ponza's version of the truth to belief in Signora Frola's version, depending upon who is telling the tale.

For Ponza and Frola, truth is the illusion they have created in order to permit themselves to live. They have suffered a misfortune (exactly what it is, we never learn), but they have created "a" truth that permits them to overcome their individual sorrow and continue to live. Their truth is based upon love and consideration for each other. For this reason, Signora Ponza can state at the end of the play that she is "the daughter of Signora Frola . . . *and* the second wife of Signor Ponza." When the townspeople insist that she must be one *or* the other, she replies that she is "whom you believe me to be."

For Laudisi, truth is relative. He points out that we can never really know the truth about others because each one of us perceives reality according to his own point of view. We have a particular view of ourselves, but others perceive us differently. Which view is correct? Laudisi would suggest that all views are correct. Whereas the townspeople insist on a single reality that would be the same for all, the mocking laughter of Laudisi that closes each act of the play would seem to indicate that finding *the* truth is impossible.

By calling his play a parable, Pirandello seems to be saying to his audience that we must respect the truths of others. Attempting to force people to face "reality," that is, our version of the truth, is fraught with danger in that we may upset the delicate balance others have achieved in order to make their existence viable. In addition, he would suggest that our version of the truth is in no way more reliable or verifiable than anyone else's version.

THE RIME OF THE ANCIENT MARINER

Type of work: Poem
Author: Samuel Taylor Coleridge (1772-1834)
Type of plot: Ballad fantasy
Time of plot: Late medieval period
Locale: A voyage around the Horn into the Pacific and thence home
First published: 1798

Coleridge's intention in writing The Rime of the Ancient Mariner *was to make the supernatural seem real. To do so he carefully moves his reader from a realistic sea voyage, reinforced by concrete details from the everyday world, to a nightmarish otherworldly setting, where supernatural powers force the Ancient Mariner to undertake an allegorical quest for understanding and redemption.*

Critical opinion about *The Rime of the Ancient Mariner* runs the gamut from the sublime to the ridiculous; one commentator gives each line a gloss from the Bible, while another wonders why all the fuss is made about a bird. A modern critic (David Beres) finds in the poem a systematic description of an orally-fixated, homosexual personality; another (Elder Olson) declares that the poem does not have to mean anything, that it stands simply as a beautiful object. A beautiful object it undeniably is, for read aloud its stanzas fall on the ear like music. But to view the poem simply as a travelog is perverse. Coleridge's contemporaries, for all their bewilderment about it, never doubted its high import; Coleridge himself added the gloss to the fifth edition in order to make the allegory more accessible, so it seems reasonable to conclude that he did not intend it merely as a Gothic horror tale.

But what did he intend? Born the son of an Anglican minister, he turned to Unitarianism at Cambridge, but before writing *The Rime of the Ancient Mariner* he had returned to orthodox belief. But he had absorbed certain tenets of Neoplatonism. which clearly helped to shape *The Rime of the Ancient Mariner*; for example, Coleridge and other Romantics believed that men were united with all living things in having been divinely created. They thought that palpable reality was but a screen beyond which a higher reality existed. In addition, the notion that places and elements were inhabited by tutelary spirits had acquired a vogue in literary circles at least at that time. Elements of Protestantism and Neoplatonism, then, formed the philosophical impulses of the poem.

The physical circumstance and details that are their vehicle are equally easy to trace. At the time of composition Coleridge had never been to sea, but it is known that some years previously, perhaps in preparation for a voyage to North America where he and the poet Southey intended to set up a utopia, he had begun to read accounts of voyages around Cape Horn and to the hot climes of the Pacific. Navigational details of such voyages were familiar to everybody; the greater part of the descriptions of natural things, such as the green color of the polar ice and the sounds it makes, the phosphorescence clothing the "water-snakes," and the abrupt onset of night in the tropics, can be found almost verbatim in one or another chronicle or traveler's memoir of the time. The plot evolved strangely, from the smallest of seeds. A friend told the poet of a dream he had had of a skeleton craft worked by a ghostly crew. Coleridge decided to write a poem about this in collaboration with Wordsworth, in order to earn five pounds to pay for a walking tour. Wordsworth contributed a few lines and the suggestion that an albatross be the victim of the mariner's crime, before dropping out of the project, and Coleridge thereafter, in four months of sustained effort most uncharacteristic of him, completed the poem. It was and is the greatest of his poems, mysterious, ambiguous, and deliciously terrifying, defying pat interpretation.

Coleridge wanted to write a poem of which the virtue would "consist in the interesting of the affections by the dramatic truth of such emotions, as would naturally accompany [supernatural] situations, supposing them real." (Coleridge, quoted in *The Annotated Ancient Mariner* by Martin Gardner.) His first object, then, was to anchor the physical circumstances firmly in the known. To begin with, he employed the ballad form and strategic archaisms, as evocative and familiar as "Once Upon a Time." Then he set the tale upon the sea. No one in England can live farther from the sea than a hundred miles or so, and all Englishmen look on seafaring as their birthright. (At the same time, none would venture to point out the exact latitude or hour of the day when the sea ceases to be a mere element and becomes a force in itself.) In addition, the navigational details in the poem are flawlessly correct: the sun overhead at noon when the ship is on the Equator, the frightful cold and emptiness of the polar passage, the sudden glare of the sun when the ice-fog is left behind, the trade winds blowing northeasterly that carried the ship north to the line again. Other details too: the warping of the deck in the calm, the thin rotting sails at the end of the voyage, all help to anchor the story in quotidian reality. At what point, then, does the ship pass into the spirit-haunted world of guilt, retribution, and rebirth? At the point farthest from home, the passage around Cape Horn. It is here that the Albatross appears, that Christlike creature that "loved the man/who shot him with his bow." The act of shooting the albatross is so boldly stated, without any attempt at motivation or explanation, that it packs a tremendous emotional punch. Upon this act as on a pivot the entire plot turns; it is the reason for everything that follows. The reader is given notice that he is entering the realm of the supernatural. Yet it all happens so gradually that the sense of reality is preserved. The ship is becalmed in the tropics; what could be more ordinary?

The kind of suffering experienced by the mariner leaves no doubt about the Christian character of the allegory. The albatross is hung from his neck as a Christian wears a cross. He suffers the agonies of thirst, dryness being a universal symbol of spiritual drought, separation from the creative principle.

He is brought by the grace of God to understand his kinship to the monsters of the calm, and so to all living things ("Sure my kind saint took pity on me,/ and I blessed them *unaware*"). He is refreshed with rain, baptised anew when, by supernatural agency, the ship sinks in the home harbor. He is shriven of the guilt but not the memory of his crime, and like the Wandering Jew roams the world, telling his tale of death-in-life and rebirth in love.

Edward E. Foster

THE RING AND THE BOOK

Type of work: Poem
Author: Robert Browning (1812-1889)
Type of plot: Dramatic monologues
Time of plot: Seventeenth century
Locale: Italy
First published: 1868-1869

Based upon a murder trial in the city of Florence in 1698, The Ring and the Book *probes the inner motivations of the people involved in that old, sordid tale of passion and crime. A series of dramatic characterizations and episodes carries the reader to the magnificent conclusion. Pompilia and Caponsacchi are among Browning's most notable creations.*

Compared to Shakespeare's greatest plays when it first appeared, *The Ring and the Book* put the final stamp of unqualified distinction on its author and confirmed his equality with Tennyson, the other giant of Victorian poetry. The Shakespearean comparison was a tribute to Robert Browning's poetic range, his capacity to dig deep into the muck of experience only to raise up forms and people larger than life. Keats had thought Shakespeare divine because he could create both an Iago and an Imogen. Similarly, Browning was admired for the variety and complexity of his characters. In *Men and Women* (1855) he had revealed his gift for penetrating character analysis in such brilliant dramatic monologues as "Fra Lippo Lippi" and "Andreo del Sarto." The joyous realism of Lippi, his relish for portraying things "just as they are," contrasts sharply with the self-delusion of del Sarto, who betrays his talent and reputation for a worthless wife.

What Browning had accomplished with individual monologues (his characteristic poetic form), became the basis for a cosmic view of human evil in *The Ring and the Book.* For four years he worked on this ambitious project and published it at intervals in 1868-1869. It is a narrative poem consisting of many long monologues, each expressing a different view of the central action —Guido's murder of Pompilia and her parents. By reflecting each character in the thoughts of the other, Browning's monologues achieve dazzling effects in point of view and psychological revelation—despite the syntactical obscurity of much of the verse (Browning shares with the later Henry James that peculiar blend of impenetrable style with striking illumination). The monologue form enables each character to penetrate his own mind and speculate on the thoughts and feelings of the others with a depth denied the conventional drama. The effect is similar to what would happen if all the best soliloquies of a Shakespearean play were juxtaposed and still constituted a unified drama despite the absence of intervening dialogue and action. The analytical power of Browning's approach is reinforced by the variety of the characters themselves; they are so divergent in temperament and nature it is difficult to imagine them together in a conventional drama: ruthless, sensual, and manic-depressive Guido; saintly but dangerously immature Pompilia; the venal and pathetic parents, so petty in their thinking and so cruelly vulnerable because of it; worldly but impressionable Caponsacchi, the priest; and finally, the humanist Pope, who must judge Guido and does so with a mixture of compassion and contempt that captures perfectly the realism and tough-minded spiritualism of the Renaissance Church.

The blend of people, values, and emotions that informs this poem is anticipated by the opening part, in which the poet explains the title of his work. The "Book" is the Yellow Book, the old record of the story and trial that Browning found in a Florence book stall. The "Ring" is the result of mixing the raw gold of the Yellow Book with the alloy of his art; in other words, the "Ring" is the crafted result of the artist's sympathetic imagination—a power that penetrates the mysteries of experience with greater revelation than any other human effort. Browning's "Ring" is also a symbol of the poem's circular reflection: it is literally a house of mirrors, in which the reflections of several minds cross in the mind of the reader.

Browning's willingness to base a dramatic poem, full of what Matthew Arnold would have called "high seriousness," on a sordid story of crime and mayhem stems largely from his conviction that anything representative of life as it truly is, is worth facing. For Browning the only absolute evil is the rejection of life itself. Anything that affirms life is finally good, even if man's vileness is part of it. To recognize the existence of evil is not to condone it; Browning simply believed that an objective consideration of the vast range of evil in the world—from petty indifference to sadistic murder—only revealed in bolder terms the ultimate moral order of the universe.

Elizabeth Barrett, Browning's wife, took issue with his insistence on the relevance of the sordid and the ugly to a moral art. She wanted him to drop his "dramatis personae" and speak with his own voice. But he insisted that his objective dramatizations, his dramatic monologues, were the "best" he had to give the world. He was right. Browning had what André Gide described as an "eclectic soul." He could "put himself momentarily into someone else." Like Keats's "negative capability," Browning's ability to enter strange forms of consciousness enabled him to achieve states of perception beyond the mere self. What seemed an absence of identity, or even personal involvement on his part, became finally a means to a poetic understanding greater than that exemplified in the ardent subjectivism of his wife's poetry. Browning may have started off as an amoral dramatizer, but he ended as one of the major poet-teachers of his period.

It is the Pope, and his function in *The Ring and the Book,* that vindicated Browning's dramatic objectivism to his wife and all the other Victorians. The Pope is a spokesman for Browning's hard-won ethical vision; he represents a projection of Browning's own power to sermonize and idealize in the very act of demonstrating the venality and terrifying corruptibility of the human soul. Browning, finally, is not a tragic writer. There is too much of a sometimes naïve robustness in him; man's flaws do not define his fate. On the contrary, Browning saw in the very imperfection of life the seeds of God's power. William Clyde DeVane suggests Browning is closer to Milton than Shakespeare. Like the poet of *Paradise Lost,* Browning "justifies the ways of God to man." Man must strive to know all he can, as does the Pope in his soul-searching effort to comprehend the meaning of Guido's crime, but the Pope's limited understanding is God's design. Even as he passes judgment on Guido, the Pope realizes that his own moral vision is being tested and shaped: "All to the very end is trial in life." For the moderns this means anxiety and alienation. For Browning it merely marks off the arena.

Peter A. Brier

RIP VAN WINKLE

Type of work: Tale
Author: Washington Irving (1783-1859)
Type of plot: Regional romance
Time of plot: Eighteenth century
Locale: New York State
First published: 1819-1820

Even though "Rip Van Winkle" was originally based on a Germanic folk tale, it has become, since its first appearance in Irving's Sketch Book, *a basic American myth. The story of Rip's escape from his shrewish wife and his domestic responsibilities into the mountains with his dog and gun, and his subsequent return after all such entanglements are gone, has been a popular favorite since its publication.*

The Sketch Book made Irving the first American author to enjoy international fame. "Rip Van Winkle" is perhaps the best example in the collection of Irving's artistic movement away from the neoclassic cosmic interests of his earlier satirical writing toward a localized and sentimental romanticism. In a sense, Irving's romanticism is more superficial than that of the great American Romantics such as Emerson and Poe. Irving is concerned more with capturing, through vivid description, moods and emotions than with probing introspectively into metaphysical states. Even his later writing follows his early stylistic models, Addison and Goldsmith. Although he did not develop a style peculiarly his own, Irving nonetheless wrote with undeniable clarity, grace, and charm—making the "regional romance" a noteworthy and enjoyable American genre.

The author's introductory note calls Rip's adventure "A Posthumous Writing of Diedrich Knickerbocker," the imaginary historian Irving invented earlier for his *A History of New York by Diedrich Knickerbocker* (1809). The narrator's droll references to his own "scrupulous accuracy" and "precise truth," as well as the "confirmation" provided by Peter Vandervonk (a figure from the past parallel to the Dutchmen Rip meets in the mountains), add subtlety to the humorous claim of veracity. But the story clearly combines the literature of folk-fable with that of anti-feminism. Rip is depicted, almost heroically, as a kind of Socrates: "a simple good-natured man," a great rationalizer, always willing to help others (consequently henpecked, because unwilling to do his own work), ever found at the inn—"a kind of perpetual club of the sages." From this ironic-realistic basis the story leaps into myth, with the appearance of the strange little man carrying the keg, whose sullenness somehow enhances his mysterious character and the story's naïve credibility. When Rip awakens to present reality, himself now a fabulous figure from the past, he finds things much the same as before. Irving's satirical point is that political and social "revolutions" are superficial. Change is a myth.

THE RISE OF SILAS LAPHAM

Type of work: Novel
Author: William Dean Howells (1837-1920)
Type of plot: Domestic realism
Time of plot: Nineteenth century
Locale: New England
First published: 1885

In outline The Rise of Silas Lapham *reads like a typical naturalistic novel: a poor man struggles to success only to have it dissipate and collapse, leaving him broken and destitute. In actuality, however, the novel is inspired by Howells' moral vision of the universe. Lapham's failure is not due to impersonal forces, but to his own false values, and his financial ruin is no catastrophe, only a prelude to his moral regeneration.*

The reputation of William Dean Howells has suffered much from the charge of many modern critics that his scope was too limited to satisfy the requirements of complexity demanded by the sophisticated twentieth century reader. It is argued that his insights into man's social existence, for example, were based on tenets from a past age that are no longer viable in the face of present realities; the absence of certain intense passions and obsessions in the novels, as well as Howells' failure to explore in depth such areas as human sexuality and man's capacity for violence, are cited as evidence. Similarly, *The Rise of Silas Lapham*—the author's most popular work and in many ways his masterpiece—has been adversely judged by some on the grounds that its plot is too slender to support the weight of its own implications. To support such charges, however, is either to misunderstand the nature of Howells' moral vision of life, or to overlook its depth and breadth, its universality, its applicability to all times and places.

Howells believed in the interdependence of people upon one another; he viewed each person's life as inextricably caught up with the lives of others, thus creating the web of interrelationships which forms societies. Such a belief meant that for Howells, man's personal moral life and his life as a social being were fused; there was no such thing as a purely individual moral act, whether good or evil, since each personal act had its inevitable consequences in the interpersonal or social realm. This in turn led to the morally pragmatic stance that the proper course of action can often be chosen on the basis of which course will result in "the most good for the greatest number" of people. This utilitarian viewpoint is reflected in such concepts as "the economy of pain" principle, propounded by Howells through the character of David Sewell in the scene from *The Rise of Silas Lapham* in which Silas and his wife seek the minister's advice concerning the triangular love complication between their two daughters and Tom Corey. He tells them that in such a situation, for which no one is to blame, the best solution is the one that will cause suffering to the fewest number of people. In this case, therefore, Penelope would be wrong to sacrifice Tom to Irene, which would make all three persons suffer miserably; she should marry him herself, which would result in the great happiness of two people and the temporary hurt of only one.

Underlying this moral outlook were three basic assumptions: that all aspects of human life, including the social, are infused with moral purpose, thus making society an extremely precious commodity; that the preservation of society depended upon man's overcoming destructive passions with reason; and that the function of art is to reveal the superiority of the civilized and reasoning side of man's nature over the primitive and ignorant side. Howells' first assumption was shared by most people in his age, but it was his fervent espousal of the last proposition that placed him at the philosophical head of a group of writers whose aim it was to reveal the morality of life through the use of realism in their fiction. Yet Howells abhorred sermonizing, and attacked the didactic element in writing wherever he encountered it.

This seeming paradox is cleared up, however, when one examines more closely Howells' theory of literature. What he objected to was not the presence of moral purpose in a work, but rather any attempt by an author to force artificially his set of beliefs into a fictional structure without regard to the organic dictates of the work itself. When Howells was finally asked to summarize explicitly his theory of the moral purpose of literature, he began by identifying the three progressively worse stages of "immorality" often practiced in fiction. The first involves the obscuring of the reader's judgment through indulgence of his "gross appetite for the marvelous"; the second, the elevation of passion over principles; and the third (and most pernicious), the presentation of characters who commit serious sins, but are left unpunished by the penalties which follow such sins in the real world. The true function of the writer, Howells argued, is first to reject any absolute standard of morality, and then to portray lives of characters in honest and careful detail; as the characters meet each new situation in their everyday lives, as they are faced with decisions over what is right and what is wrong, they will respond as people do in life. Sometimes they will act in morally responsible ways, and will be rewarded, if not with worldly success, with inner peace; at other times they will commit wrong, and will suffer the inevitable consequences. Thus, Howells believed, all the author need do is describe reality truthfully, and the morality of life will come through the narrative naturally, as it does in life.

Howells carried out his theory to near-perfection in *The Rise of Silas Lapham*. This novel tells the story of a man who has been led astray from the true values in life by the corrupting influence of wealth. The action centers around Silas Lapham's fall into financial ruin, which turns out to be his salvation, his rise (hence the title) back into a morally healthy state. The plot is organic, reflecting the theme of the novel, and growing out of the main character's growth. The beginning and end are linked masterfully, while the midway point in the story—the dinner party given by the Coreys—serves to converge all the threads spun out so far, suspend them momentarily for our contemplation, and then direct them toward their climax and natural conclusion. In his interview with Bartley Hubbard at the opening of the novel, we see Silas in all the glory of his material success: he is proud of his rise from humble beginnings, of his newly-acquired social position, and of the new house he is just starting to build. The house becomes a symbol of Silas' fortunes; destined to be a magnificent mansion, it rises quickly until its construction is slowed down because of lack of funds. In the end it is burned to the ground. The destruction of the house represents Silas' rebirth, however, since his moral regeneration can only occur after he has been stripped of the false trappings of materialism. In his talk with David Sewell at the end, Silas' transformation is set in dramatic contrast to his initial appearance in the Bartley interview: he has grown humble and honest; bragging has been replaced by sincerity.

Lapham has been able to reach this new stage of awareness by progressing through a series of moral "tests," culminating in the legal, but morally dishonest deal urged upon him by Milton Rogers and the Englishmen; when he refuses to participate, both his financial ruin and his personal salvation are secured. He has painfully but steadily moved from the easiest stages of redemption—acts of unselfishness and generosity on a personal, one-to-one basis—through a wider area of commitment to people in large groups, and has finally reached the highest, most difficult to attain level of good action. This level involves an individual's commitment to the social body as a whole, to the welfare not of a personally known individual or group, but to all men as they comprise society.

Although Howells' efforts to uncover the underlying morality of all human action by focusing on the commonplace and familiar in his fiction reached a pinnacle in *The Rise of Silas Lapham,* he was not fully conscious of the nature of his achievement until a year after the novel's publication. It was in that year—1886—that he began reading Tolstoy. His exposure to the Russian novelist was like a religious experience for him; of its effects he wrote, "What I had instinctively known before, I now knew rationally." Following this illumination of his own motives and absorbing concerns as an artist, Howells was able to sum up the vision which inspired not only *The Rise of Silas Lapham,* but all his work: "Morality penetrates all things, it is the soul of all things."

Nancy G. Ballard

THE RIVALS

Type of work: Drama
Author: Richard Brinsley Sheridan (1751-1816)
Type of plot: Comedy of manners
Time of plot: Eighteenth century
Locale: Bath, an English watering place
First presented: 1775

One of the most popular of the English comedies of manners, The Rivals *is filled with great characterizations: Mrs. Malaprop, whose misuse of words gave the word* malapropism *to the language; Bob Acres, the bumptious but lovable country squire trying to behave like a gentleman; and romantic Lydia Languish with her head stuffed full of nonsense from current novels. The play is Sheridan's satire on the pretentiousness and sentimentality of his age—and ours.*

Together with that other masterpiece of late eighteenth century comedy, Goldsmith's *She Stoops to Conquer,* Sheridan's *The Rivals* represents a successful reclaiming of the essential spirit of English comedy. Too long subject to "the goddess of the woeful countenance—the sentimental muse" (as Sheridan addressed her in his prologue to *The Rivals*), English comedy had forgotten its boisterous heritage; a theater nurtured in the rich buffoonery of a Falstaff and the satirical malice of a Volpone had dissipated its energies in the moralizing and saccharin "genteel" comedies of Richard Cumberland (*The Brothers,* 1769, *The West Indian,* 1771). Although reluctant, and perhaps incapable, of returning to the cynicism of Restoration Comedy, Sheridan was anxious to rescue the healthy psychological realism traditional not only to English comedy but also, ever since Chaucer, to English literature itself. Sentiment was a French value. Despite Laurence Sterne and the imminent rise of Romanticism in European literature, Sheridan's insistence on steering a middle course between sentiment and wit, between morality and reality, puts him at the center of the English literary tradition.

At the heart of all pure comedy is the ridicule of affectation. We may not all be fools, but all of us are, at times, foolish. Sheridan exploited the irrepressible tendency in people to be foolish, regardless of their accomplishments in life. He did not resort to flat or stock "humours" characters, amusing only because they represent totally unrealistic or exaggerated foibles. His people are always human, and their foolishness often makes them more so.

Despite the "humours-like" effect of their names (Absolute, Languish, and Malaprop), these characters are all larger than the epithets. Captain Absolute may be "absolute" about refusing his father's choice in a wife, but he is forced into a profound relativity when he has to be two people at the same time. When Absolute is at last revealed as having masqueraded as Beverley, he is, in any case, no longer "absolute." Lydia Languish is ridiculed for "languishing" incessantly over sentimental novels, but she overcomes a

far greater kind of foolishness when she refuses, finally, to "languish" in
wounded pride for being duped by her Beverley. Mrs. Malaprop's name was
coined by Sheridan from the French "malapropos," that is, not to the purpose.
The word malapropism entered the language and defines a humorously misused word or phrase.

Sheridan, however, did not intend to reduce Mrs. Malaprop to this one
affectation: misused words. Her speaking "not to the purpose" is only symptomatic of a much deeper affectation; she *herself* is "not to the purpose":
She favors the wrong suitor, Acres, for Lydia; she presumes, incorrectly, that
the letters Sir Lucius O'Trigger has been writing are intended for her when
they are in fact directed to Lydia; and finally, at the end of the play, she
blames her own willful and deluded misconceptions on the opposite sex:
"O Sir Anthony!—Men are all barbarians." In short, she is "malapropos" in
more than diction; it is her human condition. But Sheridan is careful not to
pickle her in the brine of absolute ridicule. In her weakness lie the seeds of
her vitality; by refusing to adhere "to the purpose" of her age and limited
intellect, she achieves a touching transcendence which seems to turn the
heart of Sir Anthony at play's end. We must remember that Mrs. Malaprop's
line about "men" all being "barbarians" is only partially a misconceived
recognition, or what Aristotle described in his section on dramatic structure
in the *Poetics* as "anagnorisis." It is also a flirtatious response to Sir Anthony's
consoling compliment: "Come, Mrs. Malaprop, don't be cast down—you are
in your bloom yet."

Sheridan's fascination with the human led him to create a character that
many critics feel is at odds with his avowed purpose in writing the play,
which was essentially a broad attack on the sentimental in literature and life.
The character in question is Faulkland. On the surface, it is clear that Faulkland's excessive concern with the pitch and nuance of his feelings for Julia,
and hers for him, is so laden with anxiety that it is meant to be ridiculous.
As such, Sheridan must have intended Faulkland's misplaced sentiment in life
to complement Lydia Languish's misplaced sentiment in art. She models her
love-in-life after the sentimental romances she has read, and Faulkland constantly measures his relationship with Julia against an unrealistic idea of bliss
in an imperfect world. Lydia's sentimental values are blasted by the empirical
fact that the man she loves turns out not to be the penniless Ensign Beverley,
but the rich and titled Captain Absolute. What sentimental art had decreed
acceptable—the poor but dashing suitor—turns out to the very thing reality
withholds. The revenge of life on a superficial idea of art is "absolute." But in
Faulkand's case, the comic exposure is not as brilliant. As one critic puts it,
while Sheridan laughed at Faulkland, he also identified with his tortured
sensibility.

Anxiety is too serious a thing to dismiss categorically with laughter, particularly when it is fundamentally "existential" as is the case with Faulkland.

It may seem inappropriate to introduce so modern a term to describe this character's situation, but he does "fear and tremble" with the kind of doubt that a true awareness of reality implies. He may seem ridiculous in questioning his Julia's right to be healthy and happy in his absence, but his anxiety over the authenticity, as well as sincerity, of her love is the fate of his kind of mind.

Almost as if Sheridan sensed that Faulkland did not completely succeed as an attack on the sentimental, the playwright created another character in whom those anxieties are clearly absurd; namely, Acres. His cowardice is finally ridiculous because it is dehumanizing; he is less a person for falling prey to O'Trigger's theatrical overdramatizing of dueling. Faulkland's anxiety, although uncalled for, is finally metaphysical; Acres' is completely venial and selfish.

Sheridan wrote this play at the age of twenty-three. It is a work of youthful genius and together with *The School for Scandal* easily confirms his reputation as the outstanding dramatist of the eighteenth century. In his work the wit of Restoration comedy and the best of sentimental comedy—its gift for feeling characterization—come to full fruition. Between Congreve and Shaw, no writer of comic drama can vie with Richard Brinsley Sheridan for tightness of plotting, strength of characterization, or brilliance of dialogue.

Peter A. Brier

RIVER OF EARTH

Type of work: Novel
Author: James Still (1906-   )
Type of plot: Regional romance
Time of plot: Early twentieth century
Locale: Kentucky
First published: 1940

River of Earth *tells the story of a poor family's struggle to survive in rural
Kentucky in the first decades of the twentieth century. The force of the narrative
comes largely from the intensely poetic language of the narrator, the unnamed
"older boy" in the family. Through him we come to understand the author's theme:
life flows as a river flows and the cycle of life is never finished but goes on and on.*

Still's richly evocative style, particularly the sensuousness of his imagery,
brings to stirring life the full range of a young boy's introduction to experience. The anonymity of the boy narrator (we never learn his Christian
name) adds to the mythic dimension of his point of view. He recalls Wordsworth's persona in the early books of the poet's famous autobiography in
verse, *The Prelude*: raised by the "ministries of beauty and fear," like the
young Wordsworth, Brack's "boy" is initiated into the fullness of nature.

What distinguishes Still's novel from the Romantic nature myth is the
book's stark realism. Wordsworth's child fears strange spirits that haunt
dark coves; Still's narrator fears hunger. Nothing makes a greater impression
in this book than the many descriptions of hunger and its psychological and
moral implications. The primary urge is to get enough to eat, and it supplies
almost all of the motivation and action.

At the beginning of the novel Alpha announces to her husband: "We have
enough bran for three more pans of bread. If the children eat it by themselves, it might last a week. It won't last us all more than three meals. Your
kin will have to go today." With that kind of stark alternative, the story
takes on the epic dimensions of a struggle for elemental survival. Later, when
Brack brings home a table full of food, which he purchases on credit after
being taken on at the coal mine, the family reacts as if he had returned from
battle with an immense treasure: "We looked in wonder, not being able to
speak, knowing only that a great hunger stirred inside us, and that our tongues
were moistening our lips. The smell of meat and parched coffee hung in the
room."

In addition to its realism, the story is marked by compassionate humor.
Uncle Silas and his mysteriously clipped moustache together with Uncle Jolly,
the hopeless but lovable jailbird, balance the boy's tragic education with joy.

THE RIVET IN GRANDFATHER'S NECK

Type of work: Novel
Author: James Branch Cabell (1879-1958)
Type of plot: Social satire
Time of plot: 1896-1927
Locale: Litchfield, not to be found on the map of Virginia
First published: 1915

Subtitled "A Comedy of Limitations," The Rivet in Grandfather's Neck satirizes the American South and its adherence to the code of chivalry. The title is taken from a character in a fairy tale. Colonel Musgrave, the novel's protagonist, interprets the tale as an allegory about human limitations: everyone has a figurative rivet in his neck which signifies the action one cannot perform.

James Branch Cabell was a genteel Southern writer caught in the limbo between the crash of the old order following the Civil War and the rise of the Southern Literary Renaissance in the 1920's. A pragmatic realist, he was too hard-nosed to indulge in the luxury of romantic deception, and accordingly felt constrained to satirize fantasies and idealizations that delude individuals and mock reality. Cabell wrote social satire that wanted to be romance.

Here lies the conflict in *The Rivet in Grandfather's Neck.* Cabell's protagonist, Colonel Rudolph Musgrave, thinks of the rivet in the fairy tale as that which makes us what we are: it symbolizes the limitations of character. A Southern aristocrat conscious of his traditions and requisite obligations, Musgrave carries off self-sacrificing acts in the finest chivalric manner. However, the consequences are often tragic, comic, or absurd. Cabell relishes in deflating pretensions, and neatly lampoons not only the Colonel's idealistic acts, but also a wide range of pretensions, codes, and mannerisms characterizing the old South. Yet, Cabell also treats his material tenderly and fondly. He respects human dignity acting within human limitations, and is cautiously optimistic about man's potential. His style, moreover, is never heavy-handed. Suave, facile, and mannered—at times almost mandarin—style hovers over the novel constantly, bemusedly assessing and reevaluating the narrative experience. If some of the characters, particularly Colonel Musgrave, are ultimately unconvincing, it is because Cabell, cherishing what they are while parodying their limitations, burdens them too heavily with mannerisms.

Cabell's novel, which might seem to be a whimsical and elegant romance from aristocratic life, is also a pointed social satire. But much as the rivet in grandfather's neck led to happiness for the fairy-tale figurines, the novel offers comfort and dignity through adherence to the way we are.

ROAN STALLION

Type of work: Poem
Author: Robinson Jeffers (1887-1962)
Type of plot: Symbolic melodrama
Time of plot: 1920's
Locale: Carmel Coast, California
First published: 1925

Robinson Jeffers labeled his philosophy "inhumanism"—it is man who is the alien intruder in the world of nature—and the poem Roan Stallion *is probably his most powerful expression of that belief. The roan stallion, who embodies the power and beauty of nature, dwarfs the humans that surround him. Only the passionate California feels the beast's grandeur, but, caught up in her humanness, she destroys the animal, even while she worships it.*

From Jeffers' observation of a cabin about which nobody knew anything except that its owner had been killed by a horse, and from his knowledge of the story of a woman who, like California, had forded a swollen stream to bring presents to her daughter grew *Roan Stallion*. These elements combined in Jeffers' mind to produce what many critics agree is the most compact and unified of his long works.

The theme of the poem is characteristically that of man's tragic entrapment in his humanity and his institutions in spite of his consciousness of the greater power and purity of nature and the fredom gained from living by its inhuman priorities.

Certainly this is California's dilemma. Married to Johnny, the degenerate product of the old world and thus of the whole history of man's legal and moral structures, she, in both her name and her heritage, is suggestive of the potential vitality of the new. As such, she is conscious of, and intensely responsive to, the natural power of the stallion and the freedom inherent in living in relation to it, and she longs for it. Johnny, however, sees the stallion, and nature, as a commodity which will earn him money to buy wine.

The degree to which California is conscious of nature is implied in her vision of the Christ child surrounded by angels with the heads of animals. On the other hand, she is human, and this condition she cannot escape. Thus she is uwillingly loyal to all things human.

It is this conflict which leads to the quasi-tragic conclusion of the poem. Knowing that the stallion is God, and having worshiped him as such when she lays her head beneath his hooves, she, nonetheless, "moved by some obscure human fidelity" to man and his institutions, asserts the justice of the Old Testament and shoots the stallion, thereby killing God.

ROB ROY

Type of work: Novel
Author: Sir Walter Scott (1771-1832)
Type of plot: Historical romance
Time of plot: 1715
Locale: Northumberland and Glasgow
First published: 1818

Although opinion about Walter Scott's artistic stature has fluctuated, his historical importance is incontrovertible. He gave the novel a sense of historical solidity, showing man as a product of social, economic, and historical forces, and describing his characters with close attention to details of time, place, and manners. Rob Roy, one of his earliest and most popular Waverley novels, chronicles the complex adventure of Frank Osbaldistone as he attempts to deal with his devious cousin Rashleigh while helping "Rob Roy" Campbell, his charismatic outlaw friend.

One of the earlier of Walter Scott's Waverly novels, *Rob Roy* is fiction disguised as fact. According to a widespread custom of its time—a time when novels were considered sinful by many—it purports to be part of a letter from Frank Osbaldistone to a family friend. This device, not used by Scott in all of his novels, had become so common by 1818 that it probably fooled only the very gullible. (Indeed, later editions of *Rob Roy* carried a Preface which virtually acknowledged that the book was fictional.) But Scott uses the custom well in *Rob Roy*. Required to guess where and when the opening sequences occur, the reader gains satisfaction from guessing. Observations on the religious fervor of the Glasgow Presbyterians and on the dress and manner of the Highlanders sound better in a supposed letter to a friend than they would from the mouth of the omniscient author. Rob Roy's escape gains in suspense and color from being told by an eyewitness.

The narrator and principal character of *Rob Roy* is a man who has very little in common with Rob Roy. Frank Osbaldistone is English; Rob Roy is a Scot. Frank Osbaldistone is a Londoner; Rob Roy is a Highlander. Frank Osbaldistone is a Presbyterian; Rob Roy is a Roman Catholic. Frank Osbaldistone is a Whig; Rob Roy is a Jacobite. They are as far apart as they can be within the limits of Great Britain and Christendom. But the book could not have been entitled *Frank Osbaldistone*. It is about Frank, but, more importantly, it is about the adventure that leads him to Rob Roy and across the entire spectrum of geographic landscapes and of religious and political opinion that separate him from Rob Roy.

Frank's journey begins in London, where his father has raised him as a Whig and a Protestant—sentiments held by the older man because it is good business to hold them. It takes him to Osbaldistone Hall, where people are Roman Catholic and Jacobite for the sake of family honor. They willingly persuade the least honorable local gentleman, Inglewood, to betray his principles so he can become a magistrate. Frank's uncle, Sir Hildebrand, would betray his family or his faith in order to keep his horse. Hildebrand's son, Rashleigh, has no principles at all. Only Diana Vernon, Hildebrand's ward, with whom Frank falls in love despite political and religious differences, has any deep commitment. Her sincerity is, perhaps, one of the attractions she has for Frank.

The schemes of Rashleigh, who has taken Frank's place in his father's business, lead Frank into Scotland, where he discovers that Robert Campbell, formerly his traveling companion and benefactor, is Rob Roy, the Jacobite Highland outlaw. Rob Roy saves him from Rashleigh in a duel and foils Rashleigh's plot to embezzle money belonging to Frank's father. While these events are occurring, Frank sees a different world—that of the Highlanders— where the clan has the power of life and death, where people live in wooden huts, and where support for the exiled royal family is genuine, and not simply a matter of family honor.

Back in London at the time of the 1715 rebellion, Frank is able to understand the fierceness with which the Highlanders fight for the exiled king and the indifference with which the English Jacobites answer the call to arms. He is also able to view without shock the double treason of his cousin Rashleigh, who betrays both kings and both causes. The outcome of the rebellion makes Frank the heir to the estate of his uncle, Sir Hildebrand, and financially secure. Having lived among Jacobites, he is able to overcome his prejudices and to marry the woman he loves, Diana Vernon.

Many readers have probably opened *Rob Roy* expecting to read of clashes of claymores among the clans and of battles with the English soldiers. Some of these readers, no doubt, have been disappointed at the relative peacefulness of the book. There are some battles. But the most exciting part of the book, from an "adventure-story" viewpoint, does not occur during a battle. It is the sequence in which Rob Roy, by superior cunning, escapes the armed company which has taken him captive.

To those who can find excitement outside of battles and escapes, *Rob Roy* offers something exciting indeed. It offers two journeys through England and Scotland at the time of the agonizing change of dynasty from Stuart to Hanover. One of these journeys is across the countryside, and is made vivid by Scott's unusual talent for describing scenery in an interesting way. The other journey is into people's minds. Each of the major characters in *Rob Roy* has a different attitude toward the change of dynasty and a different reaction to the opportunity at hand to reverse it. The actual rebellion is not described in detail, but the reader knows what is going on because he knows what kinds of people are participating. Frank Osbaldistone's journey is also the reader's.

Charles Johnson Taggart